BS14

P9-CQM-525

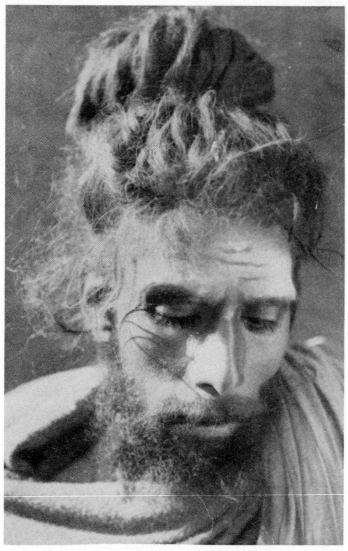

PLATE 1. STUDY OF A SADHU, DEEP IN CONTEMPLATION

He was seen near a Bombay temple. He had nothing but a blanket, an umbrella, and a beggar's bowl, and he spent hours in contemplation and on washing his long hair.

Occult and Supernatural Phenomena

D. H. Rawcliffe

DOVER PUBLICATIONS, INC.
NEW YORK

Copyright.
All rights reserved.

Published in Canada by General Publishing Company, Ltd., 30 Lesmill Road, Don Mills, Toronto, Ontario.
Published in the United Kingdom by Constable and Company, Ltd., 10 Orange Street, London WC 2.

This Dover edition is an unabridged and unaltered republication of the work originally published by Derricke Ridgway Publishing Company, Ltd., in 1952, under the title *The Psychology of the Occult.* It was reprinted by Dover in 1959 under the title *Illusions and Delusions of the Supernatural and the Occult.*

Standard Book Number: 486-20503-7
Library of Congress Catalog Card Number: 58-59697

Manufactured in the United States of America
Dover Publications, Inc.
180 Varick Street
New York, N.Y. 10014

CONTENTS

ILLUSTRATIONS

ACKNOWLEDGMENTS

I   *By permission of Mrs. F. E. Leaning, from the collection in the Society for Psychical Research.*

II   *By courtesy of the executors of Dr. A. von Schrenck-Notzing and Union Deutsche Verlagsgesellschaft.*

VI   *By courtesy of Mr. P. T. Plunkett and the " Illustrated London News."*

FOREWORD

by

JULIAN HUXLEY

M̲R. RAWCLIFFE has carried out a very useful task in assembling this extensive body of data on the Psychology of the Occult. He has drawn his net very wide, to include such phenomena as water-divining, fire-walking, and the Indian rope-trick, together with spiritualism, hypnotism, and psychical research in general.

His general attitude is—rightly—a highly critical one. In the first place, he draws attention to the numerous cases in which fraud has been proved or is obviously to be presumed on the evidence. In the second place, he reminds us of the importance of dissociation, autohypnosis, hallucination, and various phenomena of the subconscious ; these often provide strange and impressive experiences, which, however, are interpreted as of supernatural origin. His discussion of the role of hysteria and allied states in producing various kinds of " occult " or miraculous phenomena is particularly extensive.

Above all, it is important to be reminded of the widespread and dangerous tendency—very pronounced even in this scientific age—to seek for reassurance in the supernatural and the mysterious : the protean will to believe in occult powers. As illustrating this, I remember vividly an incident of some twenty-odd years ago. I was one of a team who were investigating various mediums on behalf of a newspaper. One medium was caught red-handed, masquerading as St. Theresa who was supposed to have been " materialised " while he was tied up in a chair. Yet one spiritualist present said that her faith was not shaken, and within a few weeks of his public exposure, the medium was again in action, and we had been accused by a spiritualist journal of having planted the evidence on the poor innocent . . .

Mr. Rawcliffe is very fair in acknowledging the genuineness of various extra-ordinary phenomena, such as the successes of water-diviners, or the ennobling effects of certain mystical experiences. But I must confess that I cannot follow him in stigmatizing studies on telepathy, clairvoyance. etc., as " occult research ", unfit to be admitted to our universities. Hypnotism was for long regarded as mere qackery, and if modern psychical research has some of its origins in superstition, it is also inspired by the desire for new knowledge.

To my way of thinking, one of the great needs of our time is to discover means for coping with the problems of quantity and value : after all, our most important experiences are qualititive, and when everything is reduced to mathematics. something essential has evaporated from reality. Until we can do this, we shall be in danger of what may be called the " nothing-but " fallacy—of assuming that the higher can be explained in terms of the lower from which it happens to have in part originated. Mr. Rawcliffe, I am sure, realizes this, but I would like to see the point made more explicitly. These mystical experiences may involve mechanisms such as infantile regression, hallucination, and so on ; but nonetheless can, when combined with certain kinds of conscious discipline, be "ennobling ", as Mr. Rawcliffe says —supernormal instead of subnormal or abnormal.

It may be that the methods of the exact sciences by themselves are insufficient in their field. What I would like to see is a full study of human possibilities, taking account of values.

I am quite prepared to find that certain techniques, such as those of Rajah Yoga involving withdrawal from sense-impressions, may reveal new properties of mind, or, to put it more scientifically, result in new modes of mental activity. After all, mental activity has been enormously intensified during evolution. And we simply do not yet know what is the basic relation between mental activity and physical brain activity. It is extremely important to try to find out whether under certain conditions mental activity may be detached from physical ; we can be sure that many possibilities of mind or mental activity are still unexplored.

However, this is for the future. Meanwhile, let me repeat that Mr. Rawcliffe has performed a valuable service with his critical analysis of a vast and difficult field. And his warnings against mystery-mongering and unreason deserve to be widely read and taken to heart.

ACKNOWLEDGMENTS

MY THANKS and gratitude are due first and foremost to my typist, Monica Hyde, who was burdened with the unenviable task of deciphering a virtually illegible manuscript. This she did with unflagging cheerfulness, efficiency and almost clairvoyant insight.

I desire also to convey my appreciation to the Society for Psychical Research for the unlimited use of its unique library and to the Society's secretary, Miss E. M. Horsell, for her unfailing courtesy and the readiness with which she supervised a flow of several hundred books through the post.

I further wish to pay tribute to the efficiency and dispatch with which the staff of the Cornwall County Library attended to my requests for books ; some of these were difficult to obtain, and it is fitting that acknowledgments should be publicly expressed to the librarians of the nation-wide system of lending libraries whose trained efficiency often means so much to those engaged in any form of literary research, I am indebted to ASLIB for much useful information. My thanks are also due to Dr. P. L. Brangwin, of Guy's Hospital, for reading through and checking the medical passages in Chapters 12 and 14 ; and to Dr. D. J. West for certain statistical data pertaining to Chapter 27, and for several lengthy and fruitful discussions on a wide range of subjects.

I am indebted to the publishers and authors concerned for permission to quote from the following : *The Mechanism of Thought, Imagery and Hallucination*, by J. Rosett (Columbia University Press, 1939) ; *Introduction to Abnormal Psychology*, by V. E. Fisher (The MacMillan Company, N.Y., 1937) ; *Adventures of the Mind by A. Castiglioni* (Alfred A. Knopf, 1947).

I am also greatly indebted to The American Folklore Society and the author for permission to quote from the paper " Lycanthropy as a Psychic Mechanism ", by N. Fodor, in the *Journal of American Folklore* (1945) ; and to the Society for Psychical Research (London) for permission to quote from the article " Were-Tigers of the Assam Hills" by C. P. Mills, in the Society's *Journal* (1922).

PREFACE

THE URGE TOWARDS MYSTICISM, the occult and the supernatural is fundamental in human nature ; to whatever degree of sophistication the individual may attain, he can seldom quite free himself from it. Today most people wonder, when faced with apparently well authenticated cases of the supernatural or " parapsychological " reported in the press, in books or in the vast literature of psychical research, whether there might not after all be " something in it." Reason may prevail, but a vague doubt may still persist. The mind searches for a natural explanation of the reported event, but not being able to find one dismisses it as just one of those mystifying things which have no explanation. It is to that numerous class of intelligent people who desire a rational explanation of the mysterious world of modern occultism that this book is primarily addressed.

The principal theme running through the present volume is the rôle played by various types of psychological anomaly in the creation and perpetuation of occult beliefs and practices. This is off the beaten track of medical psychology ; yet it is the author's hope that the present study, although written primarily for the interested layman, may prove to be of some value to psychology and anthropology in an important but much neglected field.

No attempt has been made to enter into the question of such groundless occult practices as astrology, palmistry or similar naïve forms of divination, except where they are incidental to the main theme. On the other hand crystal-gazing is included since this method of divination is connected with the interesting problem of visual hallucinations, and therefore represents one of those frequent instances in which an unusual psychological phenomenon is credited with a supernatural significance through ignorance of the true explanation.

Little mention is made of primitive superstitions, occult rituals or native magic except when they have a direct connection with abnormal psychology. On the other hand a considerable section has been devoted to those forms of occultism which are still practised in Africa and the Orient, and which still mystify the great majority of Europeans, e.g. the Indian rope-trick, lycanthropy, and certain practices of the oriental dervishes, yogis, fakirs and the Tibetan lamas.

Another class of occultism which has arisen as a result of ignorance concerning the more unusual functions of the human mind includes automatic writing, " mystical experiences," water-divining, faith healing and the occult in relation to hysteria, suggestion, hallucinations and hypnotism. These have been dealt with at length.

Finally, the entire range of psychical research has been surveyed from the spiritualistic " phenomena " of the séance-room to modern university research in telepathy, clairvoyance and psychokinesis.

It is over forty years since Podmore, Jastrow and Lloyd-Tuckett published their volumes dealing with the fallacies underlying psychical research, and since then no major work has appeared which can be regarded as their successor in this field. The present work may be regarded as an attempt to fill the vacuum. At no other time is such a work more needed than at the present when occultism, under the guise of scientific research, is invading the precincts of our most distinguished universities.

Lloyd-Tuckett's criticisms of contemporary experiments in telepathy in his *Evidence for the Supernatural*, excellent though they were, are no longer sufficiently up-to-date to meet the requirements of the present situation. Jastrow and Podmore failed to check or even to influence the popular beliefs in spiritualism and other brands of occultism which still hold so many otherwise intelligent people in thrall. Occult " research " today is assuming alarming proportions—a trend which started when the emphasis in psychical research shifted from the séance-room to the laboratory, from spirit communications and ectoplasm to the more methodical experiments in telepathy, clairvoyance and psychokinesis.

Only recently [1] Professor A. C. Hardy of Oxford University, a well-known zoologist, declared before the British Association for the Advancement of Science his belief that the existence of telepathy had been scientifically demonstrated. The professor informed the learned body of scientists that telepathy, or " the communication of one mind with another by means other than by the ordinary senses," might well alter our ideas on evolution if it were found to be a factor in moulding the patterns of behaviour among members of a species. Yet there is in fact no real scientific basis for belief in a metaphysical communion of minds, as the following pages will amply demonstrate.

It is when we come to instances where the facilities of national universities are put at the disposal of the occult " researcher " that one realises the extent to which occultism is pervading modern culture. Fellowships in psychical research have long been held in the American Universities of Harvard and Stanford. The College of the City of New York permits its psychology laboratory to be used for psychical experiments. Duke University has its own Parapsychology Laboratory. In England, Cambridge University possesses the Perrott Studentship in Psychical Research, while London University has officially espoused the cause of occult research by providing financial aid for experiments in metaphysical telepathy. The Continental Universities of Groningen, Bonn, Leyden and Utrecht have all given official sanction to psychical research within their precincts. It has been recently reported that a department of psychical research has been established in the University of Buenos Aires.

The spread of occult research to modern universities is in itself a serious matter. But when such research is blessed by the granting of academic degrees it cannot fail to arouse something like dismay. In recent years London University has granted a Ph.D. and a D.Sc. for a thesis on clairvoyance and for experiments in metaphysical telepathy respectively ; Cambridge has accepted a thesis on " paranormal cog-

---

[1] 1949.

10

nition " which gained its author an M.D.; Oxford has granted a well-known advocate of spiritualism a Ph.D. for a thesis (unpublished so far as the present author can verify) on the supernatural or " paranormal " powers of cognition possessed by certain mediums. Duke University was the first university to grant a Doctorate for research into the occult powers of the mind ; this honour was won by J. F. Thomas whose thesis, published under the title of *Beyond Normal Cognition*, dealt with his investigations among spiritualistic mediums and clairvoyants. The same University has since granted another Doctorate for research in telepathy, clairvoyance and psychokinesis.

The latest seat of learning to lend its support to occult research at the time of writing is the University of Melbourne, Australia. The Melbourne University Society for Psychical Research has for its president the Senior Lecturer in Logic and Scientific Method at the university—a paradox which excellently demonstrates the extraordinary appeal of modern occultism in its guise of scientific research.

Modern psychical researchers and parapsychologists prefer to ignore or explain away the fact that psychical research has its origins in magic, shamanism and superstition. In England and America the term " psychical research " was adopted at the turn of the century as a designation for investigations concerning the occult and certain psychological anomalies which had given rise to occult beliefs.

It is significant to note, however, that in Germany the term " scientific occultism " was adopted. The most important psychical research body termed itself The Society for Scientific Occultism, whilst the most advanced of the German psychical research publications went by the name of *Die Okkulte Welt*. By 1920, however, the more pretentious term " psychical research " had begun to make its appearance after the English and American style ; and following the publication of Oesterreich's *Grundbegriffe der Parapsychologie*[1] a new term, parapsychology, became increasingly used, to spread eventually to America.

Recognition of the fact that spiritualism, telepathy and allied subjects belonged to the sphere of the occult never extended to England and America. It remained confined

---
[1] *Die Okkulte Welt*, No. 25, 1921.

largely to Germany. That this was so is much to be regretted, for there can be no doubt that the more technical terminology which has come into use has been a very potent factor in gaining the sympathetic consideration of academic and scientific circles for whom the term " occultism " would otherwise be anathema.

It is time that the fallacies underlying psychical research were revealed in their entirety. It is an urgent necessity that the methodological and psychological bias lying behind all the published reports of experiments in telepathy, clairvoyance and psychokinesis should be exposed and their pseudo-scientific status clearly demonstrated. It is only through an understanding of the true nature of the factors involved that the insidious growth of modern occultism can be checked—whether it takes the form of crude supernaturalism or the application of pseudo-scientific methods to outworn superstitions refined and elaborated into speculative metaphysical theories. If the present volume contributes in only a small way to the repulse of the ever advancing tide of supernatural belief which present-day psychical research keeps in motion, it will have adequately fulfilled the purpose for which it was written.

Pelynt,   D. H. RAWCLIFFE
Cornwall.

DEDICATED

to the memory of Alcmaeon, Greek physician and disciple of Pythagoras, who, in the sixth century B.C., was the first to teach that the brain was the organ of the mind.

Chapter One

PSYCHICAL RESEARCH

BELIEF IN THE OCCULT is as old as mankind. To primitive man the forces of nature were the external manifestations of capricious and fearful spirits which had constantly to be placated and supplicated. As his mental development advanced the spirits became gods and a special caste, the priests, evolved, whose special function it was to intercede between the rulers of the elements and the ordinary man. With the arrival of the priest the magic and incantations of the medicine-man took on a more conventional and ceremonial form ; but always the basis of magic, and communication with the gods, depended on the vague but strong belief in the transcendental powers of human thought once certain conditions of ritual had been fulfilled.

Such natural tendencies towards belief in the occult which exist in the human mind always exert themselves most strongly when the powers of reason remain undeveloped. The individual, baffled by his own ignorance, tends to take the line of least resistance. Desiring some kind of knowledge concerning what he sees and hears he constructs his own logic of magical powers and mystical beings. Yet the reality of magic and the occult for man would have little substance were it not that the individual appears to see all around him proof of their existence. His own superstitions and expectations, leading him to illusory interpretations of natural events, generate the proof, thereby providing him still further stimulus to belief in the supernatural. From primitive occultism to modern experiments in telepathy this trend is discernible ; as Podmore excellently observed, " the existence of a belief is the most potent factor in the creation of its own evidence."[1]

It is a fact, invariably discounted by psychical researchers themselves, that psychical research, or parapsychology, has its genesis in the myths, the folklore, the magic and mysticism of pre-civilisation.   There is no large cultural chasm between the beliefs and superstitions pertaining to the Druidic circles of prehistoric Britain and the supernatural beliefs and " theories " perpetuated amongst the eminent respectability of the London Society for Psychical Research.   The difference between certain practices of medieval witchcraft and the experiments in " psychokinesis " carried out within university precincts in North Carolina is largely one of degree.

There is, in brief, an unbroken historical continuity observable between the superstitious occultism of former times and the more sophisticated occultism which flourishes at the present time under the euphemistic titles of psychical research, metapsychics and parapsychology.   The magic mirror wherein the olden-time necromancer claimed to be able to see the past, the present and the future, has its modern parallel in present-day psychical research concepts of clairvoyance.   The magic talisman which bestowed upon the wearer power over the forces of nature possesses a modern equivalence in the telekinetic " phenomena " of the spiritualistic séance and the " psychokinetic " experiments of Dr. Joseph Banks Rhine.

In the newer occultism of parapsychology technical-sounding names have replaced the age-old colloquialisms. Prophecy and divination of the future becomes " precognition ".   The warlock's art of descrying the past becomes " postcognition."   The soothsayer's reputed faculty of seeing events at a distance becomes " paranormal cognition " or clairvoyance.   The witch's ability to read the thoughts or influence the actions of other people at a distance becomes " telepathy."   With this change of nomenclature disappear also the old incantations, spells and farraginous ritual, leaving, the psychical researcher be-

[1] *Telepathic Hallucinations*, 1909.

PLATE II. "FACES IN THE DARK"

A vivid impression of a hypnagogic hallucination painted in water colours directly after full awakening   (*See Page* 125)

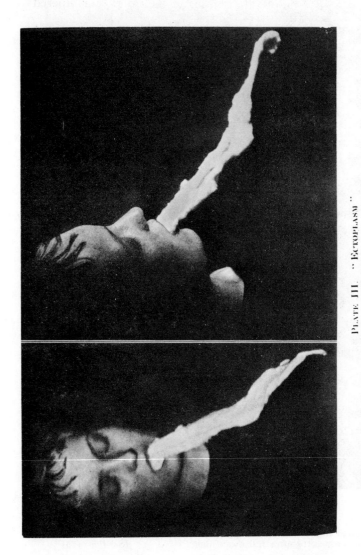

PLATE III. "ECTOPLASM"

"Teleplastic Emanation" issuing from the mouth of the famous Polish medium, Stanislawa P.
"Reproduced from "Gesammelte Aufsätze zur Parapsychologie""
(See Chapter 20)

lieves, the transcendental faculties of the mind unhampered by the superstitions of the past!

The sincerity of psychical researchers and parapsychologists is not to be denied. The vast majority of them have little to gain by a mere pretence. They believe that their methods of investigation are scientific and would seldom agree with Jastrow that in psychical research the term *scientific* implies intention and ambition rather than conformity to an exacting logical standard. Yet a perusal of the literature of psychical research completely reveals its occultist origin. As Julian Huxley has sardonically observed:

> The orthodox natural scientist who may venture into the field of psychical research is confronted with a literature portentous in bulk and elusive in quality. It ranges from the naïveté of ghost-stories and hauntings and the prattlings of the more childish forms of spiritualism, with their babble about ' Summerland,' to the elaboration of cross-correspondence tests and the statistical validation of telepathic results. It runs off at one side into folk-lore, at another into psychopathology.[1]

Anyone reading through the journals and proceedings of the various societies for psychical research cannot help being struck by the fantastic jumble of views presented in their pages. Here the ignorant and the naïve jostle shoulder to shoulder with the scientifically eminent. Levitation, " materialisations ", spirit-communications, ectoplasm, faith-healing, poltergeists, and oriental thaumaturgy form a weird and wonderful background to weighty pronouncements by world-famous savants—pronouncements clearly coloured, for the most part, by that irrational bias towards belief in an alluring world of the supernatural which is latent in all of us. Beneath the occult veneer, however, lies a dim underworld of psychological automatism, suggestion, hypnosis, hallucination, neurosis, hysteria, functional malady, sensory-hyperacuity, delusion, fraud, prestidigitation, and limitless credulity.

There is another side to psychical research, however, exemplified by the lengthy list of spiritualistic mediums who have been proved charlatans by indefatigable in-

---

[1] *Science and Psychical Research*, The Week-end Review, 6, 1932, p. 278.

vestigators. It was the London Society for Psychical Research who exposed the founder of Theosophy, Madame Blavatsky, as the blatant sensationalist and unscrupulous trickster she proved to be. And among the numerous publications of psychical research societies have appeared a not inconsiderable number of papers, articles and reviews by front rank medical psychologists concerning the various phenomena of abnormal psychology. Psychical research experiments in telepathy and clairvoyance have grown increasingly rigid and methodical and, while such experiments are still very unsatisfactory, the concomitant statistical methods of evaluation are of a high order, and may be said to have made a contribution of their own to the science of probability mathematics.

Despite all that can be laid to the credit of psychical researchers and parapsychologists, it is not really surprising that scientific opinion remains sceptical as to whether psychical research itself is to be considered a legitimate branch of study. Briefly the " field of study " in psychical research is the mysterious, the odd, the apparently miraculous—in fact anything at all that may be interpreted by the lay mind as due to the operation of occult or supernatural forces.

Can any serious study be the outcome of such a crosscurrent of subjective factors? The majority of psychologists would answer no. They point out that the *animus* of psychical research and parapsychology lies in the depths of the past, in myth and superstition, in magic, in the mysteries of ancient priestly cults ; above all in the inherent psychological tendencies of the human mind to attribute to the agency of unseen powers those phenomena which it does not understand. They conclude from this that the great majority of the problems of psychical research are raised by virtue of the peculiar bias or mental set of the psychical investigator, who, believing for various reasons in the possibility of mysterious occult forces in nature, seeks to find practical instances of it in order to justify his beliefs ; this approach generally tends to make him ignore or disrespect other approaches which possess the merit of coherence within the normal scientific scheme of things.

Acceptance of psychical research as a legitimate field of study, observe the psychologists, would only serve to perpetuate outmoded supernatural beliefs by giving them the stamp of semi-official sanction.

There is not the least doubt that the psychologists' view is a rational one ; for there is every reason to believe that *all* the problems of psychical research can be resolved in terms of modern psychology once the facts pertaining to those problems have been definitely elucidated. Owing to the peculiar mental bias prevailing in occult research, however, it often needs considerable acumen to arrive at the plain unvarnished facts which lie hidden in the shoals of tendentious reports presented for our perusal. The facts are so often reported so as to coincide with the ideas and preconceptions which have evolved in response to the psychical researcher's special bias. Fundamentally the psychical researcher's aim is not to serve the cause of science, but to satisfy a yearning curiosity which for him remains insatiable—insatiable for the reason that he can seldom reconcile his yearning for the supernatural with his desire to be rational ; neither can be satisfied. Hence the psychical researcher *selects* his evidence ; he is ever on the *qui vive* for facts and authoritative pronouncements which are favourable to his beliefs and theories.

Firm adherence to supernatural or paranormal " hypotheses " prevents the parapsychologist from investigating possibilities more in accord with principles of orthodox science. This bias is often accompanied by a tendency to regard as unenlightened sceptics all those who disagree with his own views. He will charge his opponents with being " unscientific " in their attitude towards his beliefs and theories—a charge which is absurd as it is naïve, since upon analysis even his most elaborate theories turn out to be nothing more than simple metaphysical speculations. Nevertheless as long as he believes in the possibility of transcendental mental powers the psychical researcher or parapsychologist will continue to carry out his " experiments," and he will continue to make the charge of narrow dogmatism against those who regard his claims with incredulity.

And yet, as Jastrow long ago pointed out, the incredulity of the psychologist towards psychical research springs, not from an *a priori* judgment that paranormal phenomena are impossible, but from an extensive knowledge of psychological causes of error. The psychologist realises that the paranormal phenomena reported by the psychical researcher are subsumed by obscure and complex psychological processes which tend to assume the pattern of the mould into which they are forced ; he correctly observes that these processes " will never be understood so long as the mould is cast according to a system of supernatural beliefs which the intellect has long outgrown." [1]

Reduced to its fundamentals psychical research is concerned, in the main, with the whole gamut of erroneous supernatural beliefs and occult practices which from time immemorial have been evoked by the various idiosyncracies and aberrations to which the human mind is liable. Hypnotism, hallucinations, automatism, hysterical syndromes, the more dramatic effects of suggestion and what may be described as the quirks and caprices of the subconscious mind—these have always been regarded as manifestations of the occult or otherwise attributed a supernatural significance. In the past insanity was regarded as evidence of diabolical influence or divine favour ; and although this belief has died out in civilised societies *there are still millions who believe in the supernatural significance of certain less severe types of psychological anomaly.*

To the superstitious or ignorant person a hallucinatory figure is a ghost, whereas to the psychologist it remains merely a visual hallucination. To the believer in "the psychic " certain odd coincidences of thought are interpeted as due to telepathy ; odd noises in the house are attributed to poltergeists ; automatic writing becomes the means of contact with dead persons ; hallucinatory images in a crystal are attributed to clairvoyance ; therapeutic suggestion becomes faith healing ; hysterical changes of personality represent the invasion of a person's mind by a " spirit-personality "; hypnotism is a manifestation of the supernatural powers of the mind ; ideomatic movements

---

[1] E.F.A., *Nature*, 1933, p. 802.

of a pendulum confer powers of divination ; dreams which possess a coincidental similitude to future events are prophetic or " precognitive ", and so on.

It would take several pages to make a comprehensive list of superstitions and occult beliefs which may have originated from, and been perpetuated by, the less common psychological vagaries of the human mind. Dreams, hallucinations, hysterical syndromes, psychological automatisms, hypnotism and the manifold phenomena of suggestion have always been surrounded by an aura of the supernatural, and for many people still remain indissolubly linked with occult conceptions. Such people are unable to see any distinction between a supernatural event and an unusual or obscure psychological phenomenon. For them prophecy, chairvoyance and " thought-transference " partake of the same general nature as hypnotism, hallucinations and automatic writing ; all are " psychic phenomena ", savouring of the " paranormal " powers of the human mind.

From the historical standpoint there is a fairly constant and observable relation between the reports of miracles or supernatural events and the beliefs and cultural patterns of the time. The beliefs and cultural patterns of the age largely dictate the form or type of supernatural event reported ; primitive magic, medieval witchcraft and modern psychical research are all examples of this tendency.

During the Victorian era the emphasis in psychical research, as well as in the occult in literature, was on apparitions, hauntings, poltergeists, dopplegangers, dreams, crystal gazing, " second sight ", death-bed visions and communication with the spirits of the dead.

Correspondingly, present-day psychical research reflects the modern scientific outlook, if not the scientific spirit, and the main focus of interest is now directed upon semi-scientific experiments in telepathy, clairvoyance, precognition and " psychokinesis ". These are modern versions of the ancient beliefs in the omnipotence of thought. To-day they are classified under the collective title of " psi-phenomena " by English and American parapsychologists.

" Psi-phenomena " are easily equated with simple magic. If one person can simultaneously influence another's mind at a distance, if certain persons can become cognizant of distant events or foresee the future without the intervention of the sensory faculties, if some individuals can influence the movement of tangible objects solely by an effort of the will, then we must accept the fact that Magic must take an important place amongst the psychological sciences! We should no longer be able to avoid the conclusion that we are all potential wielders of supernatural power. Unfortunately the experiments upon which the psychical researcher rests his claim to have established the existence of " psi-phenomena " are all, without exception, open to severe criticism, as a perusal of later chapters will amply demonstrate.

The standards of evidence must be drawn from the recognised sciences and, despite the claims to the contrary, this proviso is seldom, if ever, fulfilled in psychical research. In the few cases where the requirements of orthodox scientific methods have been unequivocally satisfied, the results of the experiments have almost invariably been negative. The psychical researcher appears to believe that the standards of the *psychological* sciences are sufficient to establish universal acceptance of new scientific principles. This is very far from being the case. In order to establish the existence of any *general* scientific principle, certain incontrovertible facts must first be proved. And the standard criteria must be those of the *exact* sciences; in no other way can the scientist be certain that the experiments have been properly controlled.

As scientific *facts* " psi-phenomena " possess no existence. Can it be said, however, that telepathy *et alia* have any scientific significance considered as hypotheses or as theories ? The answer again is no. Such theories, being metaphysical in design and scope, can *ipso facto* possess no scientific application whatsoever. Confined to the sphere of metaphysics or mysticism, they may be regarded as perfectly legitimate ; but they cannot be expected to take the place of proper scientific theory. Even if the parapsychologist were able to establish his claims regarding the existence of phenomena which contravene the accepted principles of modern science, it would be futile to explain such phenomena in terms of metaphysical theory.

Detailed analysis of the reports of psychical research experiments reveals that there is not even a *prima facie* case for the existence of " psi-phenomena ", judged from the scientific standpoint. The need for a theory to explain them therefore does not arise. In any event parapsychological experiments could, by their very nature, establish only one thing, *viz.* that there was a causal nexus involved which produced the results observed. It would, however, be absurd for any scientist to account for any such causal nexus by the expedient of falling back on metaphysical theories which derive directly from the primitive beliefs and superstitions of his ancestors. It is no wonder that the great majority of practical scientists regard psychical research with indifferent scepticism.

A reversion to occultist beliefs would seldom be accepted amongst intelligent people of to-day inless these were supported by a certain logic based on accepted ideas. The fundamental idea which upholds the entire structure of present day occult research is that of the Mind. The psychical researcher invariably speaks of the mind as a *ding an sich*—a thing in itself ; his basic axiom is that the mind is something which possesses a causal efficacy of its own. Indeed he expatiates upon this theme still further by attributing to the mind a causal efficacy only restrained from omnipotence by the shackles of the material body—a view which has a great many similarities to theological concepts of the soul.

" The mind " is a very vague and loosely defined concept. In everyday life the term has its uses. For example, we know well enough what a person is trying to convey when he tells us that his mind is confused, or that a certain friend of his has a brilliant mind, or that a neighbour's mind has become deranged. In each of these examples the word " brain " can easily be substituted without much, if any, loss of meaning. When philosophers take over, however, the term " mind " is used to cover an enormous variety of meanings—all of them metaphysical in concept and possessing no affinity to science or even to everyday life.

The issue has still been further confused by Freudian and allied schools of psychoanalysis who have attributed to the mind semi-mechanical attributes—a device which

works well anough within limits but which again has little
affinity with the philosophers' concepts or with its use in
everyday speech. To cap everything theologians and
mystics have added to the general confusion by their tendency
to equate the mind with the ancient idea of the soul. The
psychical researcher reaps the advantage of this confusion
by using any or all of these views on the nature of the mind
as it suits him, adding to them or subtracting from them
as he deems fit.

The great fallacy lying behind all such concepts lies in
the tendency to regard the mind as a thing in itself, something
which possesses a location in space and time. Modern
psychologists, apart from a minority of psychoanalytical
schools, recognise the naïvety of this idea. They recognise
" mind " to be a confusing term for the subjective aspect
of the *brain in action*. Mental processes, mental activity
and similar terms have largely replaced the word " mind "
in modern psychiatry. The mind as a specific entity does
not exist ; it is a convenient fiction. It possesses no *scientific* meaning and no amount of effort has yet produced a
precise scientific definition. As a basis for scientific theory,
as opposed to metaphysical speculation, it is quite useless—
unless it is first provided with an artificial set of mechanical
properties such as Freud gave to it. Even then such devices can, by their very nature, have only a limited function
and cannot possess any wide scientific significance.

The real mystery pertaining to mental activity is the
fact that the mechanism of the brain is accompanied by
the phenomenon of consciousness. The human brain is
not solely an intricate piece of machinery. Its multi-
tudinous actions and reactions are accompanied by a subjective awareness of pain, fear, pleasure, hunger, sense of
effort, drowsiness or excitement, together with a number
of other sensations which we call seeing, hearing, feeling,
tasting and smelling and which we experience when certain
stimuli reaching us from outside are " transmitted " to
the brain. In a word, the mechanism of the brain possesses
what no other mechanism possesses—the faculty of consciousness or subjective awareness.

The phenomenon of consciousness is an enigma which

modern science sees little hope of ever resolving—for how
can conscious thought ever hope to explain itself to itself?
Consciousness is the one great fundamental fact of our
existence beyond which we cannot explore ; any " explanation " of it would of necessity have to be made in terms yet
more fundamental ; and there are none available. Any
explanation of consciousness in terms other than that of
consciousness itself would be only a part explanation with
at most a limited pragmatic value. There are limits to
potential knowledge and the intrinsic nature of consciousness is one of them.

The majority of psychologists today believe that consciousness possesses little or no causal function of its own,
that it is merely a subsidiary accompaniment, a passive
epiphenomenon, of cerebral activity. This may or may not
prove to be correct. There is increasing evidence that a
specific area at the base of the brain is responsible for the
phenomenon of consciousness, an area which developed
early on in the history of animal evolution and which has
not greatly expanded since man emerged from the lower
forms of mammal life. This primitive part of the brain
possesses little or no bearing on the question of intelligence:
The degree of intelligence attained depends almost entirely
on the relative development of the cerebral cortex ; this
can be regarded as an extremely subtle and complex cal-
culating mechanism which synthesises and analyses the
myriad nervous impulses flowing into the brain from all
parts of the body.

Consciousness appears, at the very most, to be nothing
more than a biological device, a sensitiser, " amplifier "
or supercharger, which promotes smoother running or increased efficiency of the cerebral mechanism. The prevailing scientific view is that if consciousness is not a mere
passive epiphenomenon, then it must serve *some* biological
function. It will need far greater and far more reliable
evidence than psychical research has as yet provided,
before the scientist can ever consider replacing this well-
grounded belief with the notion that consciousness is an
aspect of the transcendental powers residing in the human
organism. As modern scientific knowledge advances, it

leaves less and less scope for speculation on possibilities concerning the transcendental powers of " the mind ".

One cannot be surprised at the metaphysical doctrines of psychical research. Almost every branch of science has at one time or another during the present century had its eminent metaphysical interpreters. It is only a little over three-hundred years ago that the English physician William Harvey exploded the prevailing belief of his day that " animal spirits " caused the blood to course through a man's body.

The theory of vitalism still lingers on among some of the older biologists, who believe that the phenomenon of life can only be explained in terms of teleology and " vital forces". It is only two decades since the physicist Sir James Jeans published (and later retracted) his belief that the cosmos was the creation of a divine mathematician. Vitalism, now discredited, was a remarkable modern development of the animistic beliefs of primitive man.

Animism is the belief that inanimate objects have minds or souls and that natural forces are due to the activity of various spirits. It is a relatively short cultural step from this primitive form of animism to the metaphysical (and metaphorical) intricacies of Bergson's theories concerning the *èlan vital*, in which the doctrine of vitalism reached its fullest expression.

To sum up : Psychical research represents a reversion towards occult beliefs which have had their origin in the earliest human cultures. Its claims to scientific status are confuted by the metaphysical, as opposed to the scientific, nature of its concepts and theories. These metaphysical concepts and theories are unmistakably derived from the supernatural beliefs and superstitions which have existed in various forms down through the ages to the present day. Even if the accuracy of parapsychological experiments were to be fully substantiated, the metaphysical theories and concepts upon which such experiments were based would not be scientifically established ; such experiments, if verified, could only prove that a causal nexus existed whose nature could not for the present be elucidated. *Parapsychological theories of transcendental mental faculties would still remain speculative essays in metaphysics, possessing no relation to scientific theory.* As such they possess no significance for the scientist, who recognises that the sole justification of any scientific theory lies in its usefulness as a basis for empirical deduction.

What cannot be avoided in psychical research "is the charge of a common weakness in logical argument, a prejudiced interpretation, a hospitality to extreme, unscientific hypotheses, an overlooking or too complacent dismissal of the sources of error, which give rise to the Psychical Research counterpart of what was and remains the ancient error of occultism."[1]

---

[1] Jastrow, J., *The Animus of Psychical Research*, The Case for and against Psychical Belief, p. 291, edited by C. Murchison, Clark University Press, Mass., 1927.

Chapter Two

THE SUBCONSCIOUS MIND

In GENERAL, when we think or apply ourselves to some task, we are more or less aware of what we are thinking or doing. Moreover, not only are we conscious of the objects of our immediate attention, but we may also be conscious of ourselves attending to the task in hand; we possess, that is, what no other species of the animal kingdom possesses, self-awareness. Nevertheless, the bulk of our actions and mental processes are carried out automatically and without conscious effort. As everyone is aware, there is no need to cease conversing the moment one starts to walk, run, or drive a car. One's hands, limbs and feet still continue to function with high efficiency even though one's conscious attention is being concentrated on the conversation. As many car-drivers know, it is possible to drive for miles deep in thought without much awareness of the passing scenery or the act of driving—the action of steering and gear-changing being looked after by that part of the mind with which consciousness is no longer fully associated, i.e. *subconsciously*.

The mind is so constructed that a part of it is able to deal subconsciously with those routine jobs requiring little or no originality; the most highly developed part—the part normally associated with consciousness—can thus be left to work without hindrence on tasks which require a higher degree of applied intelligence, or in coping with novel situations or ideas.

It is not often realised that nearly all mental activity is of the subconscious variety. From one point of view, of course, mental activity is synonymous with brain activity, the mind itself being merely the subjective or " personal " aspect of the brain in action. The brain is an incredibly intricate mechanism which rules over every phase of our thinking and actions. The *subjective* or *conscious* aspect of its activities, which we experience as imagination, ideas, thoughts, emotions, desires, memories, feeling and willing, is called " mental " for lack of a better term, for we remain in total ignorance as to how or why brain activity is accompanied by the subjective phenomenon of consciousness.

Only a small part of our cerebral activity is accompanied by consciousness. Such processes as the regulation of our breathing, heart-beats, digestion, the co-ordination of our movements, the maintenance of our balance and the smooth running of all the natural functions of our body, depend on unconscious activities of the brain. Such brain activities are not termed " mental " because they are totally automatic and do not depend to any degree upon conscious processes. Nevertheless we find that there are many brain processes which, although largely automatic, could never have been acquired in the first instance without the aid of consciousness. For example, when one ties a shoe lace automatically with the attention focussed on something else, we say, for convenience of expression, that the subconscious mind, not the unconscious brain, is directing the movements of the hands.

Subconscious mental functions may be regarded as half-way between the fully conscious aspects of brain activity and those of its activities which remain for ever unaccompanied by any spark of conscious illumination. As we grow older the range and complexity of our subconscious mental functions increases enormously ; they form the great bulk of our mental life and colour all our thoughts and actions, leaving only a relatively minor, but highly specialised, part of our minds associated with consciousness. These subconscious mental activities have given rise to the conception of the *subconscious mind*. This must not be confused, as it often is, with the theoretical concept of the *Unconscious*, originated by Freud, the use of which is mainly limited to the psychoanalytical schools of psychopathology.

The conscious aspect of mental activity is concerned only with what the individual is conscious of at any particular moment—a sensation of pain, a memory, an external object of interest, a feeling of sorrow, or perhaps a combination of any or even all of these things. The value of conscious thought, which is only an *accessory* (though extremely important) mental function, is to adjust the individual more efficiently to his immediate environment in relation to his past experience.

It is much to be regretted that the idea of the mind as a *thing* ever entered into psychology. For what we are really concerned about is *mental activity*—an active process, nothing static. One may talk about the brain as an object, for it is there to be seen ; but to say that the mind is merely the subjective counterpart of the brain is unwise, for the moment the brain ceases to be active, the mind can no longer be said to possess any existence. Nevertheless, in spite of the logical difficulty involved, the concept of the mind is so familiar to everyone that it is difficult to dispose of it altogether.

Most psychologists and psychiatrists today deny the existence of the mind, and they are undoubtedly correct in omitting from their work and writings a highly ambiguous term. However, it is not proposed here to omit such a familiar term, and in fact there is little need to do so provided that it is remembered that the term " mind " symbolises only the *subjective aspect of the brain in action*.

The " subconscious mind " may be regarded merely as a collective term for all mental activity which lies " below the level of consciousness ". Or, to put it another way, the subconscious mind denotes all that continuous mental activity which is either permanently or semi-permanently dissociated from the " main stream of consciousness ". Such terms as " mind " and its derivative " the subconscious mind " are not really scientific terms. The former derives originally from classical and neoplatonist metaphysical speculation, and these terms are therefore not amenable to an exact scientific definition. The above definitions, however, will be found quite adequate for the purpose of helping the general reader to attain a sufficient insight into those aspects of abnormal psychology with which the present work is largely concerned.

The bulk of our mental activity is of the subconscious variety. This may be said to be true of all the animal world in which the term " mind " is at all applicable. For example the present day monkey, unlike our own simian ancestors, is able to leap considerable distances from tree to tree ; one species, the gibbon, is reported to be able to leap as much as forty feet. Each leap requires a genuine subconscious estimation of distance, strength of branches, wind strength and direction, and the muscular effort required to cover the necessary distance.

All human actions require the aid of subconscious mental activity. The tennis player, for instance, who sends the ball swiftly over the net, does not consciously estimate the angle at which his racquet meets the ball or the positioning of his feet preparatory to making his stroke. These, and hundreds of other intricate calculations, are made subconsciously.

The mind—which has been pithily described as " brain plus consciousness "—may be regarded as an instrument designed for the most effective action under a maximum number of possible conditions. The great value of consciousness is that it helps to achieve maximum concentration upon what is immediately necessary. That highly specialised form of mental activity which is associated with consciousness, i.e. conscious thought, has behind it the less specialised but relatively vast mechanism of subconscious mentation. As a further illustration of this partnership, we may observe that if one had to concentrate consciously upon forming the letters of the words one is writing, creative thinking would be impossible. The subconscious mental process look after the task of forming the letters and words, leaving the conscious attention to that far more subtle business of supervising original idea-association which we call creative thinking.

As may be seen, all consciously directed mental or physical activity is backed by a continuous welter of subconscious mental activities of which the personal self is seldom aware, since conscious attention is usually directed towards objects, events or tasks outside of the self.

This subconsciously operating part of the mind never
ceases to function from the day one is born until death.   The
mind is continually registering sense impressions even when
we are not conscious of it.   For instance, it is only when the
clock on the mantelpiece stops ticking that we take notice of
it and realise that all the time we have been subconsciously
registering its ticking.

In sleep the activities of the subconscious mind lack that
purposiveness which conscious attention brings to it, as may
be seen from our dreams.   In the normal healthy individual
the subconscious mind only becomes fully coherently active
when it is called upon to support the conscious actions and
thinking necessary to the carrying on of the daily round ;
the individual gears it to his will, as it were, and it supports
him ably, carrying out the thousand and one automatic
activities which do not require conscious attention for their
function, thus enabling him to concentrate on any particular
matter which needs his undivided attention.

In cases of hysteria this co-ordination between the subconscious and conscious mental activities of the mind often
breaks down and (as will be seen later) this lack of co-ordination may produce some very odd results.

Despite the fact that the subconscious mental activity
usually fulfills its highest functions when geared to the needs
of the conscious attention, it may occasionally show, under
special circumstances, that it possesses *independent* powers,
not only of imagination and fantasy such as we see in our
dreams, but also of reasoning and intelligence equal—and
in some cases even superior—to that provided by fully conscious mental activity.

The fact that subconscious mental activity may in some
individuals possess powers of reasoning equal to those of
conscious thought might appear unlikely to those unaccustomed to the idea.   In dreams such powers of reasoning are
usually absent, but there are many cases on record in which
the dreamer has derived considerable benefit from this aspect
of his subconscious mental activities.   Robert Louis Stevenson, for example, stated that his dreams presented him with
some of the best plots for his stories.

Another famous example is that of Coleridge's imaginative poem *Kubla Khan*, which was remembered from an opium dream. This poem is an undoubted example of prolonged subconscious incubation. Mathematicians, too, have frequently observed that they have awakened with the solution to a difficult mathematical problem, the solution of which had defied their best efforts during their waking hours. A most striking and unusual instance of this was the experience of Professor W. A. Lamberton of Pennsylvania University. Professor Lamberton had for days been trying to solve a mathematical problem by algebraical methods without success. One morning as he opened his eyes he saw, outlined against the opposite wall, an hallucinatory outline of a diagrammatic figure which gave a *geometrical* solution to the problem ! During sleep his subconscious mind had worked out the solution to the problem in its own way and had succeeded in bringing it to his conscious attention by means of a hypnagogic hallucination.

Chapter Three

MENTAL DISSOCIATION

THE THEORY OF " mental dissociation ", or more simply,
" dissociation ", though largely obsolescent in modern
psychological literature, remains a convenient working
hypothesis in many respects, and still plays a major part in
some schools of psychopathology at the present day. It
also offers the layman, for whom the present work is largely
intended, an easily understood common denominator for a
variegated range of mental phenomena which include ordinary dreams, automatic-writing, mediumistic trance, and a
variety of hysterical and hypnotic phenomena. Dissociation may be said to cover the bulk of that fascinating and
extensive group of psychological anomalies whose manifestations have, throughout the ages, been universally
attributed to divine or infernal origin or to the supernatural
powers of gifted individuals.

Today most medical psychologists prefer, for purely
practical reasons, to interpret hysterical syndromes in terms
other than those of dissociation. Dissociation as a practical
theory has serious limitations ; nevertheless, if used in a
descriptive sense only, its retention proves both practicable
and useful, and it is mainly in this descriptive sense that the
term " dissociation " will be used from here on.

Dissociation denotes the existence of subsidiary mental
activity, activity which is operating more or less in independence of, or *dissociated from*, the main mental system which
constitutes the normal conscious personality.

Examples of dissociation are not difficult to find in everyday life. For example one has often had the experience of

32

reading a book and, in the middle of a page, starting to think about something else. While the conscious mind pursues its reveries, the eyes may continue to read the words line by line, even to the extent of several pages, before the individual realises that he has perused part of a page or chapter without being able to recall in the least what he has subconsciously been reading. While his conscious mind has been engaged in going down the aisles of thought, fancy free, part of his mind, below the level of consciousness as it were, has been diligently reading the printed pages ; the act of reading and the memory of what was read remain *dissociated* from the conscious mental activity of the reader, and as far as he was consciously aware he might just as well have not read that section of the book at all—although (as will be seen in another chapter) such dissociated memories may on occasion be recalled into consciousness in special circumstances, such as those afforded by deep hypnosis.

A similar example of mental dissociation, already quoted, is observable in the case of the professional piano player who is able to read and play a complicated piece of music while conversing intelligently at the same time. While his conscious mind is occupied with the conversation, another part of his mind is deciphering the notes and keeping his fingers moving across the keyboard.

In the above two examples, " dissociation " is seen to be a useful descriptive term, and this meaning of dissociation is the one mostly used by psychiatrists today. This must not be confused, however, with the full-fledged theory of mental dissociation evolved by the great French psychopathologist, Pierre Janet, to explain the various phenomena of patho- logical hysteria. Janet described hysteria as a *dissociation of the personality*, a theory which has been almost entirely superseded today. It was propounded on the assumption that the normal unity of the mind may, under certain circumstances and in certain individuals, become disorganised into two or more mental systems. The mind, according to this point of view, far from being a unity, is a battle-ground of conflicting instincts, habits, impulses, ideas—rational and irrational—sentiments and emotional reactions. Normally there is a sort of balance worked out in obedience to the demands of our environment, and this equilibrium between conflicting forces has given rise to the idea of the unity of the mind. There is a unity there, but in the sense that a global war possesses unity. More truly there is continuity ; and it is this continuity, together with our continuous memory of it, which gives rise to the sense of unity of consciousness.

From this standpoint the normal personality may be said to consist of an integration of various mental factors into a more or less homogeneous system. Under certain conditions of stress, however, these various aspects of the mind become integrated, not into one, but into two or more mental systems. A great deal of evidence was brought forward to support this view. A good example of such evidence is to be seen in the phenomenon of alternating personality, each personality often possessing characteristics highly antithetical to the other.

It is best, however, to forget Janet's dissociation theory of hysteria, while still bearing in mind that the term which he coined is now generally used simply as a descriptive label covering certain aspects of both the normal and the hysterical mind : it indicates a subsidiary stream of mental activity which is no longer fully integrated with the needs and activities of the conscious personality, but which takes on a certain independent activity of its own.

A different example of dissociation is provided by dreams. In sleep all conscious attention to the surrounding world is in abeyance ; consciousness and all the higher brain centres which are, in the waking state, responsible for judgment, discrimination, estimation of value and so on, are out of action. But the lower centres of the brain are still active in a rambling haphazard fashion, and between sleeping and waking—that is, with the gradual return of consciousness— we catch a glimpse of this somewhat chaotic activity which, on full awakening, is recollected as a dream. These rambling and often nonsensical dreams often appear of the most intense significance and coherence at the time : this is because the higher mental faculties responsible for judgment and logical appreciation are still asleep, while the more primitive and undiscerning faculties responsible for feelings of significance and emotion are still active.

The activity of the piano player whose conscious attention is directed upon his conversation has provided us with a good example of normal dissociation. In his case, the dissociated mental activity which directs his fingers on the keyboard is produced as the result of long practice until it has become an automatic process. However, in such phenomena as automatic writing, the dissociated mental activity becomes not automatic, as the name implies, but to a large degree spontaneously creative. Many cases are on record in which the subject reads a book or consciously performs some other mental task while his hand continues to write an imaginative story—generally childish in character —without the individual concerned being aware of what is being written until he reads it. Automatic writers who become tainted by the cult of spiritualism almost invariably produce scripts purporting to be written at the instigation of discarnate spirits.

The normal person maintains what may be called a standard equilibrium ; all the various intellectual and emotional factors are co-ordinated to a more or less standardised pattern, the intricate welter of subconscious mental activity being co-ordinated to the needs of the conscious personality, the whole forming a relatively homogeneous mental system.

In many types of hysteria we are presented with the phenomenon of subconscious mental activity which refuses to be integrated with the main mental system and which often retains a high degree of autonomy and complexity—amounting, in some instances, to complete secondary personalities. In automatic writing, often a sign of latent hysteria, evidence of secondary personalities is often manifest. In its extreme form the phenomenon of double or multiple personality is exhibited. " Possession " by a devil in biblical times, or by Satan in medieval times—a sure sign of witchcraft and punishable by burning alive—were often cases of multiple personality taking their form from the beliefs of the day.

An advanced stage of mental dissociation is reached in the phenomenon of sleep walking or *somnambulism*, also a sign of hysteria. The sleeper in such instances gets out of bed, frequently talks, and may perform quite complicated actions requiring intelligence comparable to that of his waking state

—all without his having the least idea of his activities when he wakes in the morning. During his nocturnal wanderings it is as if another personality had emerged, totally dissociated from his normal everyday personality in every way : his experiences in the somnambulic state form no part of his stream of memory ; the memory of his sleep-walking activities is there, but it normally remains buried beyond conscious recall. Hysterical somnambulism may reach serious proportions in extreme cases, coming on even while the patient is awake at the time.

Such limited forms of somnambulism shade off into a different category of dissociation in which the normal conscious personality is suppressed for long periods of time. Such mental states are known as *fugues* and may involve a complete forgetfulness of the patient's identity and his past. Such cases of " loss of memory " are fairly frequently reported in the newspapers. The patient is unable to recall his own name, his address or occupation. Otherwise his intellect often remains unimpaired, or, in a few instances, becomes *considerably superior to that of his normal self.*

In this category of mental dissociation may also be classed such anomalies as alternating or multiple personality ; the patient experiences alternating changes of personality, each often with its own watertight set of memories ; sometimes two, three or even more different personalities appear to emerge, often highly antagonistic to the other, even to the extent of enjoying reciprocal verbal recrimination !

Allied to these are the trance states of the spiritualistic medium. Here the normal consciousness is more or less in abeyance, and the dissociated mental elements take over control ; the only difference from automatic writing is that the medium speaks instead of writing. All these forms of dissociation have a hysterical origin, and up till comparatively recent times were explained either as " possession " by evil spirits or the devil himself, or alternatively by divine " inspiration ", whichever appeared the most likely interpretation.

Mental dissociation, however, can be induced artificially to extreme degrees, by the use of hypnotism or *hypnosis*. Hypnosis has been described as an artificial form of hysteria.

Up to a point this description is valid, for the hypnotic subject—like the hysterical patient—may undergo marked mental dissociation with an accompanying increase in suggestibility. Furthermore, most of the phenomena observable in hysteria have been induced under hypnosis at one time or another with specially sensitive subjects. According to the most reliable authorities, a deep state of hypnosis can only be induced in the case of those subjects who are naturally inclined to hysteria, although most people are hypnotisable to some extent. Certainly it is true to say that hysterical patients are by far the most easily hypnotised of any.

A subject who has been deeply hypnotised often reaches a state of suggestibility far beyond that attainable in any ordinary case of hysteria. In the case of hysterical subjects hypnotism may be regarded merely as a means of increasing the subject's already considerable tendency to mental dissociation. Suggestibility, which is the usual accompaniment of hysteria, also becomes greatly accentuated, sometimes to such an extent that the subject obeys every suggestion of the hypnotist like an automaton. In deep states of hypnosis, delusions can be induced on the largest scale at the operator's suggestion.

The occurrence of spontaneous visual hallucinations sometimes occurs in cases of severe hysteria, and accounts for many of the " visions " of saints and others—St. Paul and Joan of Arc changed the course of history through their experiences of visual and auditory hallucinations.

Genuine sensory hallucinations of all types may be said to involve dissociation—in the sense in which we have hitherto employed the term. While the main personality, with its continuity of consciousness and memory, remains more or less intact, autonomous mental activity below the level of consciousness is at work producing the fantasies which astonish, delight, worry, or terrify the conscious mind of the individual who sees or hears them. In abnormal psychology, or (as it is now generally called) psychopathology, the term " dissociation " covers a multitude of psychological anomalies which at first glance do not warrant this name.

In the case of dreaming, hallucinations, automatic actions,

or any other clear cut case where mental activity is evidently acting in independence of the conscious will or attention of the individual, dissociation of one kind or another is apparent. When it is used to describe situations in which memories, emotions, certain thoughts, or even physical sensations—as in the case of hysterical (functional) anaesthesia—are unable to enter the individual's field of consciousness, the existence of dissociated mental activity is not immediately obvious and is only to be inferred on theoretical grounds.

In hysterical *analgesia* or insensitiveness to pain, and hysterical *anaesthesia* where the patient loses all sense of feeling in the affected area, we have two very curious phenomena of dissociation. Without any observable physiological changes at all, a finger, a hand, an entire limb, becomes insensitive to pain or loses the sense of feeling altogether. The affected part may be burnt, or pricked with pins, but the painfully stimulated nerves do not succeed in transmitting their message into consciousness. There seems strong evidence that, in the case of functional anaesthesia, a part of the patient's mind is subconsciously aware when the affected area is being touched or not touched. Similarly in functional blindness and deafness, although the sights and sounds may not appear to enter the conscious mind of the patient, a simple trick will effectively demonstrate that the patient is *actively* repressing them and preventing them reaching the full light of consciousness.

In the case of functional analgesia—in the middle ages the mark of the devil and an infallible indication of witchcraft—the problem is less easily explained. Pain is no light thing to repress and it is often difficult to believe that the patient is " subconsciously " aware of the *pain*. Pain is not pain unless it enters consciousness. However, once we embark on the problem of consciousness, we find ourselves up to the neck in a mire of unproductive speculation. It may be noted in passing that a great deal of the confusion in psychology is due to the fact that the term " mental " remains largely undefined and hence open to a variety of interpretations.

In pathological dissociation we are presented with the existence of more or less *autonomous* mental activity acting independently of the main system of mental activity which constitutes the normal personality of the individual. The degree of autonomy varies. Sometimes it is fairly complete as in fugues, cases of multiple personality and hysterical somnambulism ; at other times it is only just appreciable, as in states of light trance. More important than the degree of autonomy, however, is the complexity of the mental process involved.

In hysterical chorea, or St. Vitus' dance, for example, the autonomous mental activity is comparatively simple. In hysterical hallucinations or in cases of automatic writing, on the other hand, the degree of complexity is far greater. In much automatic writing, too, the autonomous mental processes are extremely complex. Highly developed automatic writers have sometimes been able to engage in intelligent conversation while their hand writes good prose on a genuine creative level, without the conscious mind of the talker knowing anything of what is being written ; the dissociated part of the mind shows full evidence of a complete subsidiary personality. In fact automatic writing, as in some well known cases of fugues, may even manifest complete consistent personalities equal in all respects, and sometimes superior, to the normal personality of the individual.

The basis of all dissociative syndromes of a hysterical origin is traceable to repression in one form or another. Simple repressed impulses are common enough in everyday life, and we all possess numbers of unpleasant or undesirable memories which we keep repressed and successfully forget. These are simple types of repression. Where complexes are present, the repressed material is considerably more complicated ; for it consists of associations of emotionally coloured ideas and memories linked with some instinctive urge whose expression is undesired by the conscious personality. If complexes remain repressed the individual may remain hysterical, unbalanced and ill-adjusted to life.

Occasionally it happens that large groups of repressed ideas and emotions become so coherent and well-integrated that they come to constitute what is *potentially* the basis of a complete new personality. Sometimes these super complexes force their way into actual expression, ousting the normal personality altogether from its place in the stream of consciousness and taking complete possession of the conscious field for long periods of time ; in such instances there may result cases of alternating personality with accompanying amnesia, and fugues in which the two personalities may each possess their own stream of memory and remain oblivious to the mental life of the other, though both belong to the same individual. Such secondary personalities and other less complex mental systems are derived from fragments of the normal systems of thought, emotional tendencies, reactions and desires, which have been repressed owing to their incompatibility with the aims, beliefs, ideals and even illusions of the main personality ; they have for long periods been successfully repressed and hence dissociated.

Cases of alternating personality and fugues are relatively common in the history of psychopathology. Cases of genuine multiple personality, however, are rare. Up to the present, less than fifty cases of undoubted multiple personality have been reported in medical and psychological literature. [1] The patient may exhibit three or more different personalities, and one patient was even reported to have exhibited as many as seven ! In almost every one of these cases, however, the effects of the psychopathologist's own treatment or experiments have been mainly responsible for the emergence of subsidiary personalities other than the first one which was manifested. The hysteric is normally highly suggestible and in a great many instances hypnotism was resorted to during the investigation. We may safely conclude that such cases of multiple personality are generally due to suggestion, i.e. are artificially created hypnotic personalities. Today cases of multiple personality are virtually unknown, at least under modern civilised conditions.

Wherever there are mental processes imperfectly coordinated with others, mental conflicts, repressed impulses, moods, incongruities and inconsistencies of any kind, there is dissociation. We need not, then, be surprised to find vast amounts of it in everyone. There is no profound distinction between normal and abnormal dissociation, as, for example, between " doodling " absent-mindedly with pencil and paper, and automatic writing. Hysterical

---

[1] Sadler, *The Mind at Mischief.*

dissociation may be considered as an abnormal development of the normal mechanism of dissociation without which our minds would for ever be in a state of chronic indecision, incapable of initiating any decisive action.

Dissociative phenomena may be conveniently classified into two types : one type includes hallucinations, automatic writing, and such automatic movements as water-divining and the use of the planchette—with these the normal personal consciousness is retained. With the other type of phenomena, it is either clouded, as in the lighter stages of trance and in some hypnotic states, or else is totally in abeyance, as in fugues, deep hypnosis, dreams and somnambulism.

It may well be asked whether such phenomena as hallucinations or delirium, when the primary cause is traceable to organic disease, drugs, cerebral injury or insanity, are justifiably describable as manifestations of mental dissociation. The answer to this question is that the term " mental dissociation " is a relative one whose validity depends on the approach to the subject. If the approach is in terms of the disfunction of the *mind*, then there is no reason why mental dissociation should not be used to cover hallucinations and delirium, whether the cause is psychological or organic. However, if the emphasis is on a cerebral, physiological, bio-chemical or electro-encephalographical approach, then of course it would be totally unwarrantable to talk about " mental dissociation " in any of those contexts.

The patient, whether an hysteric or suffering from cerebral injury, who experiences a visual hallucination, has his conscious attention directed upon the visual scenes which apparently appear before his eyes. Whether we speak in terms of the brain or of the mind, it is quite evident that the hallucinations are brought about by a cerebral or mental activity working with a certain degree of independence of (i.e. dissociated from) the relatively homogeneous and co-ordinated activity which characterises and underlies the normal waking personality of the patient. It must be observed, however, that the label " dissociation " can only be *practically* applied when an individual noticeably experiences the effects of such autonomous or semi-autonomous activity.

Chapter Four

SUGGESTION

Another great factor in the perpetuation of occult and mystical beliefs and practices is that of *suggestion* ; this has its most dramatic expression in hypnotism, and in very primitive communities can so take hold of the mind of the individual that death has been known to occur solely through its agency.

Suggestion is a technical term which will be found to occur frequently throughout the present work. The word itself conveys a fair idea of its meaning but it must be recognised that " suggestion " is a very vague term and that a precise definition is not in fact forthcoming. The origin of the word in connection with psychology arose from its use by the Nancy school of psychotherapists to describe the docility and readiness to obey which was observed in hypnotised and hysterical subjects. Alongside of the readiness to obey there was observed a great readiness to believe in and accept ideas and information which the hypnotist or psychopathologist conveyed to the subject. Subjects with this tendency were classified as *suggestible*.

Suggestibility is seen at its most extreme in subjects who have been deeply hypnotised ; particularly if the subject is suffering from hysteria in the first instance. On the other hand suggestibility is not confined to hysterical patients : it plays an enormous part in the normal life of every individual. Janet has defined normal suggestion as " the induction of an impulse in place of reflective realisation ". [1] This definition is excellent so far as it goes, but it does not cover

---

[1] *Psychological Healing*, p. 246.

42

the *effects* of extreme suggestibility such as may be seen in many types of hysteria.

Although some of the extreme effects of suggestion still remain to be explained, we may agree with Janet that in regard to many of the lesser effects suggestion is simply the inculcation of ideas and beliefs in a person's mind without reference to his sense of logic ; appeals to reason, however, may naturally supplement the effects of irrational suggestion.

The more extreme types of suggestion depend for their effect upon the degree of personal *conviction* which the subject holds in regard to the idea suggested. In other words the effects of suggestion are easily weakened if the individual retains doubts as to the validity or correctness of the ideas presented to him, and it is part of the craft of the good suggestor to be able to lull the critical faculty of his subjects.

Unequivocal conviction is the essence of powerful suggestion. In fact the art of suggestion—and it is perhaps best considered as an art—lies in preparing the subject's mind so that ideas, statements, proposals and commands can be straightway accepted without reserve. Suggestion is a direct appeal to the irrational in human nature ; the successful agent must induce the acceptance of ideas which lack an adequate logical basis for their acceptance. Suggestion is therefore seen at its most effective with individuals who are unusually credulous, gullible, or easily influenced by others. It is evident from this that the effectiveness of suggestion depends mainly on the degree to which the subject's mind is deprived of its faculty for criticism—*both rational and irrational*. This is in fact the cardinal factor for its operation.

There are innumerable ways in which the mind may be disarmed of its critical faculties : fatigue, strong emotion, faulty reasoning, wishful-thinking, drugs, hypnosis, hysteria, enthusiasm, ignorance, prejudice—all these are capable of increasing the effect of suggestion. The working up of emotion is often a deliberate preliminary step in rendering the mind susceptible to suggestion, especially with crowds. A good example was seen in the Nazi rallies before the last war. Suggestion and emotion can of course be inculcated simultaneously, each reciprocally increasing the effect of the

other.   In many kinds of " faith-healing " the artificial
stimulation of the emotions is practised deliberately.   Anything, in fact, which will help the subject to become abnormally susceptible to the influence of ideas is an aid to the
effective operation of suggestion.

Suggestibility depends largely on nurture and hereditary
factors.   We all vary in the degree to which we are suggestible.   On the whole, well-educated people are relatively
unsuggestible.   Considerable stores of knowledge, a reasonable amount of well-founded rational beliefs, an ability to
sum up situations with fair rapidity, all help to provide a
stable and well-integrated mind.   On the other hand, young
children and primitive peoples are highly suggestible ;   so
to a less extent is the modern uneducated adult, particularly
in the mass ;   in such cases the mind lacks cohesion and
remains poorly integrated ;   it lacks the mutually supporting
interaction of its constituent elements which a sound education provides.

Among those many factors which help to make the subject's mind susceptible to the irrational influence of ideas,
is the personality of the agent from whom the suggestion
originates.   Roughly speaking, the agent's power of suggestion depends upon whatever conduces to render him impressive to the subject.   Under this very wide heading we may
include all those factors conducive to respect of authority,
such as an official position, age and experience, superior
talents, confident and authoritive manner, rank, wealth
and social position.   We must include also the subject's
beliefs concerning the agent's general reputation :   the agent
may be universally respected, may be considered frightening
or mysterious, ascetic or holy, or a person in touch with the
divine.   But for the operation of suggestion, more important
than all these considerations, is the personality of the agent
himself :   commanding presence, strong distinctive features,
a faculty of winning people's confidence, a pleasing voice,
an ability to " put it across ", powerful physique, a gift of
words, a flair for touching off emotions, a character which
possesses the power of gaining the respect, fear, reverence,
love or devotion or others.   Any of those diverse qualities
which may render a personality " magnetic " to others,

or which carry with them an atmosphere of prestige and authority, will in fact, contribute to the effective operation of suggestion.

Generally speaking, a group or body of people are more susceptible to the uncritical acceptance of ideas and beliefs than a single individual. All our moral codes, social conventions, and religious beliefs are examples of this form of suggestion. All such codes, conventions and beliefs to which we hold so strongly are purely arbitrary and are implanted in us during the uncritical period of our childhood —the period at which we are most susceptible to the influence of suggestion. Propagandists know full well the influence of suggestion on the mind of a child. Catholic and Communist alike know that the child can be induced to believe anything if it is reiterated often enough. The principle of constant reiteration as a means of effecting suggestion is seen in both trade advertising and in the nationalistic radio programmes of many countries.

While a body or a mass of people are able to induce uncritical acceptance of ideas in a single individual, far more dramatic examples of the power of suggestion may be effected by a single individual with an emotionally excited or expectant crowd, particularly if the crowd is composed of ignorant, uncultured persons. Ideas can sweep through excited crowds like wild-fire, no matter how fantastic the idea is. If the idea in question touches closely upon the crowd's beliefs, longings, or any other emotional spring, a state of mass hysteria may develop ; mass delusions, illusions and even hallucinations may occur. Under such conditions, if one man cried out that he saw an angel hovering in the sky with a flaming sword or brazen trumpet, there would be a dozen who subsequently believed they saw the same sight ; and right up to the present day instances of mass hallucination and illusion are still occasionally reported, mainly from Southern Europe.

Epidemics of hallucinations, ecstatic states, hysterical convulsions, confessions of witchcraft, voluntary flagellation, sweep spasmodically across the pages of history from earliest times. Strongest among these epidemics is the uncontrollable impulse to dance—sometimes intermittently for days on end until total exhaustion seizes the dancers. The legend of the Pied Piper of Hamelin probably originated in this way. One of the last major epidemics of hysterical dancing occurred towards the end of the nineteenth century in the great island of Madagascar. Scores of villages were involved over thousands of square miles.

Much that can be said to be true of mild suggestion cannot be said to apply equally to its more extreme manifestations. As already noted, there exists no adequate definition of any practical value which covers both types of suggestion. The effects of suggestion can be so extreme as to produce abnormal changes in the bodily functions and mental processes. With hysterical subjects who suffer from delusions, faulty memory, hallucinations, or secondary states of consciousness, the effect of suggestion can be almost limitless, especially if such patients are hypnotised.

The hypnotised hysteric has often been the subject of hypnotic experiments in the past, particularly in France at Nancy and the Salpétrière. Such experiments were not always directed at the rapid recovery of the patient, but they were often of extreme interest. Temperatures of the hand were reported as being raised or lowered, the pulse beat accelerated or retarded, functional paralysis of a limb, local anaesthesia, many kinds of hallucination, aphonia, deafness—these were some of the results reported as having been achieved by hypnotic suggestion directed at patients with advanced hysteria.

In hysteria and hypnosis we almost invariably find a great increase in suggestibility. It is common knowledge that in the fifteenth and sixteenth centuries tens of thousands of women were burnt at the stake for witchcraft. A great percentage of these women were subject to hysterical dissociation, and their delusions, hallucinations and secondary personalities took their form and colouring from the superstitions and beliefs of the age. Great numbers readily came to believe that they were really witches and in league with the devil. Their hallucinatory visions showed them evil spirits in abundance and even the devil himself, while their secondary personalities assumed the mental attributes of Satan or one of his legions—as they were then conceived—and gave utterance accordingly.

Such women suffered a terrible fate. The hardship of

their lives had produced the hysteria which in turn laid their minds ever more open to the pernicious beliefs of the day. Such syndromes of hysteria as hallucinations, local anaesthesia and multiple personality convinced the woman herself that she was a witch. Her fears were strengthened by the nature of the hallucinations or what others told her of her speech during her periods of clouded consciousness. From then on, her own mind contributed additional ideas to be absorbed by her stricken personality. Her own conviction that she was a witch and her terrifying sense of guilt, derived from the continual propaganda of the Catholic Church and the Inquisition often led her to confess openly her sinful relationship with the devil. Her fate was then sealed. So the vicious circle of suggestion and autosuggestion went on, destroying first the minds and finally the bodies of the wretched psychasthenic women, amidst an orgy of cruelty and spite on the part of the " normal " population.

Among the most remarkable effects found by experimental hypnotists was that of *post-hypnotic suggestion*. It was found that with highly suggestible subjects an order could be given during hypnosis which would be carried out after the subject had been awakened. The period between awakening and the performance of the command or " suggestion " varied from a few minutes to several days or weeks, or in some cases, even months! If amnesia supervened, either spontaneously or at the express command of the operator, the subject seldom realised why he carried out a particular irrational action at a particular time set by the operator.

Post-hypnotic suggestion has been much over-dramatised by those who performed such experiments. Their reports lacked perspective and their generalisations were too sweeping. From these reports, however, emerged a simple fact, namely that the effects of hypnotic suggestion could, in certain circumstances, affect the subsequent behaviour of the hypnotised subject to an unexpected degree.

Most people are today familiar with the term " autosuggestion ". It means " self-suggestion ", as opposed to hetero-suggestion or suggestion which comes from an outside source. The use of either of the terms has never been satisfactory, since all suggestion really contains " auto " and

" hetero " elements.   The distinction is in fact quite arbitrary but is often convenient to use.

We may perhaps sum up the situation as follows : where another person is clearly the active agent of suggestion, then we may be justified in referring to it as hetero-suggestion. Where, on the other hand, the subject's own mind is clearly the instigator, we may conveniently refer to it as auto-suggestion.   The difficulty arises with the border line cases, among which, perhaps, the bulk of all suggestion-phenomena may be included.   In the case of hypnotic suggestion the hypnotist is preponderantly the suggesting agent.   With the primitive tribesman or the hysteric who has come to believe, without real reason, than an enemy is poisoning him, and who begins to feel stomach pains, often of extreme intensity, the patient's own imagination is preponderantly the suggesting agent.   But in such cases as faith-healing, where the subject's conscious beliefs, ideas and emotions are generally as much a contributory factor to the operation of suggestion as the words or antics of the healer himself, the dichotomy is seen to be an unsatisfactory one.   The fact is that all auto-suggestion is ultimately dependent, however remotely, on extraneous factors of which direct hetero-suggestion may be one amongst others.

A very good example of auto-suggestion in everyday life is provided by those individuals who possess the faculty of waking up at whatever hour they decide upon before going to sleep.   The subconscious mind receives the suggestion, estimates correctly the passage of time—a thing which it often does very well—and consciousness returns at the stipulated hour.

Many functional disabilities with an hysterical background are brought on by autosuggestion.   A shock or accident resulting in a slight or temporary injury may become so greatly exaggerated in the mind of the patient that he becomes convinced he is suffering from a permanent injury. Latent hysteria may provide both the requisite state of suggestibility and the subconscious motivation which is generally traceable in such cases.   On the other hand auto-suggestion may also cure such disturbances, sometimes with dramatic suddenness, a factor which has been largely instrumental in perpetuating the belief in " miracle " cures.

Chapter Five

HYSTERIA

CHIEF amongst those abnormal psychological phenomena which have played such a large part in the creation and perpetuation of so many occult beliefs and practices are those due to pathological *hysteria*. The reason for this is that hysteria is accompanied by two important factors : increased suggestibility which, together with a naturally uncritical state of mind, makes the creation of delusions in the subject's mind a relatively easy matter ; and a whole host of accompanying psychological anomalies earlier noted, such as vivid and sudden alterations in personality, temporary loss of identity, paralysis, local analgesia or localised insensitivity to pain, automatic writing, involuntary speaking ("inspiration"), the onset of a variety of functional diseases (and often their sudden cure), somnambulism during which the individual carries out actions without being able to remember them subsequently, visual hallucinations or "visions", auditory hallucination—including the hearing of "voices", and occasionally hyperacuity of the senses; to these, anomalies, may be added a greatly heightened histrionic ability.

Some types of hysterical patients show the most amazing developments of the independent powers of the subconscious mind. Instead of co-ordinating itself usefully with the individuals' conscious requirements, it may become largely divorced from this, its main function, and start off on a separate course of activity on its own ; that form of subconscious mental activity which normally takes on an autonomous activity of its own in dreams is sometimes seen exaggerated to such an extent that it may become a very grave mental affliction.

In hysteria, too, the subconscious mind may show considerable powers of creative intelligence. It may show equal powers of cunning and craftiness, and not infrequently been known to perpetuate systematic and sustained deceptions upon the conscious mind of the patient concerned. This is also to be seen in the mediumistic trance and in much automatic writing. In these instances the medium or automatic writer generally comes to regard the " messages " produced by such means as emanating from spirits of the dead or even from God himself, and the style and contents of the trance utterances and automatic scripts do little to lessen the illusion. But in such cases it is not always wise to talk of the " subconscious mind " alone as being responsible. The problem is a great deal more complicated than that. So often there is a willingness in the subject to be deceived—a willingness which the latter successfully disguises from himself by an extreme form of wishful thinking. In such cases the distinction between autonomous activity of the subconscious mind and conscious mental activity is not always practicable.

It is an almost invariable rule that subconscious mental activity lacks the cohesion which consciousness provides. In certain circumstances, however, the adaptability and intelligence displayed by such mental activity debars us from making any hard and fast ruling on the subject. In fact, all such hard and fast boundaries between one set of psychological functions and another are to be avoided on principle. Such boundaries are no more than convenient divisions in the psychologist's system of working concepts, and must never be taken as indications marking actual fields of observation. Many an amateur psychologist, and not a few professionals, have blundered seriously by their failure to take this fact into account.

Pathological hysteria must not be confused with the commonly accepted notion of hysteria as an emotional attack of convulsive laughing or crying. This type of outbreak, often seen in women who have had a shock or been through a trying time, is only a minor form of hysteria, and in psychopathology the term " hysteria " is usually reserved for mental disorders of a deeper and more complex nature of which some indication has already been given.

A hard and fast definition of hysteria is not easily forthcoming : the term is generally used to connote conditions of mental instability and immoderate suggestibility, and is very frequently characterised by the phenomenon of dissociation in marked degree. It ranges in severity from mild neurotic tendencies to actual insanity. Most victims of hysteria are in a mental state approaching the juvenile which may largely account for the fact that nearly all hysterics are highly suggestible.

In abnormal psychology the two most important theories of hysteria have been those of Janet and Freud. There is a certain similarity between them. Briefly, Janet's view was that the disorder was due to lack of cohesion in the personality, and that in consequence certain ideas were " split off " or became dissociated from the main mental system which constitutes the conscious personality—the dissociated ideas bringing about independently the hysterical symptoms. Freud's theory, on the other hand, postulates the active repression of ideas, desires and memories and a refusal to allow them to enter consciousness because they conflict with the needs, aims and normal outlook of the individual. The result is that the repressed wishes and ideas emerge in some other disguised form.

Without going into the numerous antithetical aspects of the general theories of Freud and Janet, it must be observed that much of the difference can be explained as merely a difference in the terms used. Freud's repressed wishes and complexes, and Janet's dissociated ideas, both operate unconsciously and with an autonomy of their own to produce the same observable results.

Both their theories, if compared with the standards of other sciences, are vague and ill-defined. Nevertheless they have their uses, and it is perhaps on account of the vagueness of definition that many of the concepts used by the followers of these two psychopathologists may, in some respects, be used in conjunction. For example, it is not difficult to interpret Janet's *dissociation* theory of hysteria in terms of

Freudian *repression*, and *vice versa*, for the latter concept inevitably infers dissociation of some kind.

Hysteria, according to Janet, is the production of mental *dissociation*, and according to Freud is the product of unconscious mental conflict due to the *repression* of natural instincts. Today the psychiatrist makes considerable use of both these terms while largely ignoring the theoretical structures which subsume them. In abnormal psychology the tendency has been to fuse the Freudian and Janetian hypotheses into a relatively homogeneous practical working theory ; and this in turn has succeeded in reducing the somewhat artificial theories of both exponents to something more acceptable to the demands of common sense. The resultant composite theory of hysteria has been broadly generalised by Professor V. E. Fisher thus : " Let us rather say simply that hysteria is a result of mental conflicts within a personality which is not strongly enough integrated to withstand the strain imposed." [1] Such a broad generalisation as this has little practical value but it does serve to indicate the type of problem with which all cases of hysteria present us. Hysteria is fundamentally the result of the inability of the individual to cope with the strain imposed by his environment. It is so often a case of the spirit being willing but the *mind* being weak and it occurs frequently in people of high principles whose mental fibre is not up to the demands imposed upon it.

Hysteria occurs when there is continual conflict between the natural impulses and the demands of duty, loyalty, social conventions, and moral standards. The latter are constantly interfering with the full expression of our natural impulses, but in the average person a balance is successfully maintained between the two—our normal mechanism of repression providing enough give-and-take to avoid undue strain. In the neurotic individual, however, the conflict is, as it were, pushed underground, the patient may not even be aware of the conflict in existence. The result is that the more primitive impulses find expression in disguised forms, sometimes useful, as when " sublimation " occurs, and often retrograde, as in hysteria.

[1] *Introduction to Abnormal Psychology*, p. 235.

The occurrence of repression and dissociation is not ordinarily a sign of psychological disorder. Their extreme manifestations are, as in the case of the advanced hysteric, exceptional; in the average individual they are simply a normal part of his mental machinery. We see dissociation accurring every time we concentrate on one thing while automatically doing another, such as discussing a business project while going through the intricate motions of eating dinner. Repression, too, forms a part of the mind's normal protective mechanism. For when faced with two opposing sets of ideas, or two antithetical impulses, one is repressed so that the other may result in action; if we stopped to weigh the respective merits of each idea or impulse on rational grounds alone, we should be in a state of chronic indecision. But when the mechanisms of repression and dissociation work overtime, hysteria is liable to result.

Everyone is familiar with the simple act of repressing a momentary impulse. Such impulses usually take the form of a sudden idea which is linked to a strong emotional urge. It may be a sudden desire to slap Aunt Agatha's face or, in the case of a child, to pull Uncle Toby's nose. One's " better nature " usually comes to the fore in time and the impulse is repressed and soon forgotten. It may happen, however, that the conflict between one's " better nature " and one's more primitive impulses, desires, needs and emotions takes on a more permanent form. The frustrated young woman, for example, who feels obliged to remain at home to look after her ailing parents may honestly believe she does this out of love for them. Subconsciously, however, she hates the drudgery and loneliness and longs to get away, but she keeps these thoughts out of her mind—*repressed*. Associated with these repressed and emotional ideas there may be others, such as actual hate of her parents whom she deceives herself into believing she loves.

It is well known that ideas never enter the mind alone for any length of time. They are always associated with other ideas or with memories. All creative thinking is dependent upon the emergence of vivid trains of ideas and associated memories stored up from past experiences which well up into consciousness from the subconscious mind.

Often these ideas are strongly tinged with emotion ; the idea of red, for example, may bring into the mind the thought of Communism with its accompanying feelings of resentment, dislike and fear—or their opposites—depending on how the individual feels about the subject.

It is sometimes convenient to regard the subconscious mind as a hinterland of past experiences, memories, emotions, desires and ideas, all without cohesion, lacking all homogeneity until they enter the field of consciousness.   Their groupings and temporary co-ordinations are capable of limitless variety and are responsible for all our irrational ideas, impulses, actions, prejudices and enthusiams.   When we feel lazy and sleepy this "stirring and teeming wilderness" pursues a happy chaotic existence, occasionally entering our field of consciousness between sleeping and waking in the guise of dreams.

When associations of emotionally charged ideas are actively repressed from entering consciousness, as in the above example of the frustrated young woman, they may form an association which becomes endowed with some degree of autonomy of its own.   Such an association is commonly called a mental *complex*.

Everybody has minor complexes of one sort or another, but these are usually allowed some form of expression so far as this is practicable.   Such minor complexes may find expression in indirect ways, in sublimation, or else be so disguised that the individual takes no notice or is enabled to rationalise about them without any difficulty.   They are often to be seen colouring and giving shape to our dreams. Sometimes the repression is completely successful and the complex is only able to affect the general tone of our thoughts and actions in a mild way.

Occasionally, however, strong complexes ,and other products of subconscious mental strain and internal conflict, result in the teeming array of ideas, memories and emotions which hibernate in the subconscious mind, these form more or less integrated subsidiary mental systems, which continually strive to make themselves felt in the conscious mental life of the individual.   In hysteria they succeed only too well.   In very severe cases all the repressed emotionally charged ideas may so succeed in weakening the main mental system constituting the normal personality that they are able to emerge fully into the field of consciousness, entirely displacing the normal personality. This occurs, for example in hysterical fugues, better known by the popular term " loss of memory ". When this happens, a completely new personality may emerge, the old personality being totally repressed and with it all those memories with which the old personality was associated. The person concerned suddenly finds himself unable to recall who he is, where he lives or anything of his past life.

In some cases, where the individual has suffered some severe emotional shock, the memory of the incident may become repressed beyond conscious recall, only to emerge in the form of an intermittently recurring somnambulic pantomime, the patient involuntorily re-enacting the original scene which caused the distress.

Milder cases of hysteria may be brought about merely by an uncongenial life, this is a burden borne by many ordinary people of unimpressive personality and attainments, who find no outlet for their more grandiose ideas and desires.

Normally all our repressed wishes, subconscious needs and frustrated ambitions remain in the nebulous incoherent state of vague subconscious mental activity which only enters into our consciousness in the fantasies of our daytime reveries and our dreams. Most people who lead a practical existence keep a proper balance between the practical and the more imaginative sides of their mental life. The mediocre but highly imaginative person, however, who has had to repress the imaginative side of his nature through the exigencies of gaining a livelihood, may exhibit a tendency to a mild form of hysteria in which the repressed side of his nature finds expression in automatic writing or in slight trance states ; in the latter case he will be quite likely to capitalise his hysterical tendencies by becoming a spiritualistic medium. In automatic scripts and in the verbal utterances of the mediumistic trance, the hysterical individual is often able to give full but vicarious expression to the instinctive longings for admiration, love, wealth and authority which are rooted in his being.

Psychology can tell us little enough about such needs and longings. The psychologist has been able to do little more than roughly discern the patterns of interplay between, and the tensions arising from, the fundamental conflict between the primitive instincts of reproduction and self-preservation. Behind all activities of the mind lies the vast world of fears, longings, ideas, thoughts, instincts, memories and impressions which the psychoanalytical schools of psychotherapy collectively term the Unconscious. Although Freudian and similar theories may have a certain practical value in the treatment of hysteria, they cannot be said in any sense to explain it.

The manifestations of hysteria are endless owing to the capacity of the hysteric for imitation and his responsiveness to suggestion. For example, if a hysterical woman suddenly starts to scream out that she is burning in a hospital ward, her cries and gestures of terror may very easily rouse one or two patients with latent hysterical tendencies into the same state of hallucinatory frenzy, either at the same time or even hours afterwards. The mass outbursts of religious ecstacy in the middle ages was due to the same combination of imitation and suggestion. These " ecstatic " states sometimes brought with them queer " syndromes " : mass self-flagellation for example ; or odder still perhaps, dancing mania, a hysterical compulsion to dance until exhausted, virtually whole populations of towns and villages being involved on occasion. A famous outbreak of hysterical dancing started in 1347 in Aix-la Chappelle and spread for several weeks throughout the Netherlands.

Some of the more common of hysterical peculiarities are referred to by appropriate technical names : *chasmus hystericus* or hysterical yawning ; *acrophagia* or the habit of air swallowing by some hysterics ; *gelasmus* or hysterical laughter ; hysterical *acrokinesis* or extreme activity in swinging arms and legs ; hysterical *polypnea* or very rapid breathing which occasionally ends in a cataleptic trance—possibly due to the exhaustion of the carbon-dioxide in the blood ; hysterical *agitophasia* or talking with extreme rapidity ; hysterical *spasmodyspnea* which may result in stuttering, hysterical asthma, or *globus hysterics*—a " lump in the throat " which produces a sensation of choking ; hysterical *vaginismus* or spasmodic contractions of the vagina generally brought about by either revulsion from, or deprivation of, sexual intercourse ; hysterical *trichotillo-mania*, a condition in which the patient frenziedly tears the hair ; hysterical *chorea* or St. Vitus' Dance, which imitates organic chorea in the spasmodic twitching of the face, shoulder or arm muscles ; hysterical *narcolepsy*, in which the subject is afflicted with sudden and spontaneous short periods of deep sleep throughout the day ; *hystero-epilepsy* or the onset of violent convulsions in imitation of an epileptic fit, which often during the Middle Ages took a form known as demoniacal possession ; *catalepsy*, in which the patient loses consciousness and which is sometimes accompanied by a state of extreme rigidity or plastic resistance of the limbs ; hysterical *abrosia* or fasting, to be differentiated from hysterical *anorexia* in which the patient simply lacks an appetite ; hysterical *oniomania* in which the patient makes purchases indiscriminately and recklessly.

Another small group of hysterical syndromes are of considerable interest in that they show clearly the subconscious motives which lie behind them : for example, *astasia-abasia*, or functional inability to stand or walk despite the fact that the patient retains good muscular co-ordination while lying in bed. In *basophobia*, on the other hand, the hysterical fear of falling effectively prevents the patient from even making the attempt to stand or walk. If he does try, he falls. In hysterical *ananastasia*, the patient is unable to raise himself from a recumbent to a sitting position, while *acathisia* is the term used to denote the inability of a hysterical patient to *remain* in a sitting position. Such syndromes as these are clearly due to the subconscious desire to escape from the harsh realities of the world by sinking back into convenient invalidism. Such cases in former times were included under the vague term of " palsy ". They are often curable by suggestion, sometimes with drama-tic suddenness, a fact which has helped perpetuate the belief in miracle-cures.

In medieval times, to be " sick of the palsy " denoted any form of paralysis, whether it was due to organic or to

psychogenic causes, e.g. hysteria. Since the medical profession of the day knew virtually nothing of the aetiology
of disease this is not surprising. Only psychogenic paralysis
is directly curable by the use of suggestion or other psychological means. The commonest forms of hysterical paralysis
are hysterical *monoplegia* or functional paralysis of a single
group of muscles or a single limb ; hysterical *hemiplegia* or
functional paralysis of one side of the body only ; and
hysterical *paraplegia*, or functional paralysis of the lower
half of the body.

Functional paralysis does not conform to the well defined
areas marked by the distribution of the nerves as in organic
paralysis, but only to those areas which conform to the
patient's unenlightened ideas on the subject. A well known
form of hysterical *monoplegia* is writer's cramp, which is
almost always traceable to psychogenic causes. Clerks and
others who have a great deal of monotonous writing to do are
the most common sufferers.

Total psychogenic paralysis appears to have been reported seldom, if ever, in the psychological literature of
modern times. Its place has been taken by the cataleptic
trance. But in more remote centuries, total, or near total,
functional paralysis may have been quite a common hysterical syndrome, possibly owing to the opportinuties presented
for the imitation of organic paralytics, who did not possess
the same facilities as today for secluded care.

Superficially allied to functional paralysis are hysterical
anaesthesia or absense of cutaneous sensation, and hysterical
analgesia or absense of pain sensitivity. One or other of
these not infrequently accompanies hysterical paralysis in
the area affected. In the Middle Ages small localised areas
of hysterical analgesia on the body of a woman were regarded
as the Devil's brand. Many a poor hysteric was burnt alive
for possessing them, a fact which modern psychiatrists
would have difficulty in explaining as an " advantage
gained ". In more primitive times the effect of suggestion
upon hysterical persons often produced syndromes for which
the modern psychiatric theory of hysteria would prove an
inadequate explanation.

Such terms as *glove anaesthesia* and *stocking anaesthesia* and *hemianalgesia* were used by Janet to describe hysterical anaesthesia pertaining to the corresponding area of the hands feet and one side of the body respectively. Such effects do not conform to neurological patterns and are not produced by organic disorders ; they therefore reflect the patient's naïve ideas or else, in modern times, they may result from unintentional suggestions given by the psychopathologist during the course of his investigations.

In such phenomena as hysterical analgesia, we are faced with a psychological effect which is beyond the power of the conscious will of the patient to imitate. In one type of major hysteria, for example, the cornea—that highly sensitive transparent covering of the eye-ball—may be touched without the patient showing the least sign of pain. The same phenomena is often observed in catatonic schizophrenia.

In hysterical *hyperaesthesia* we have a subjective disorder which renders the patient subject to the illusions or hallucination of a great increase of sensory acuity. This is sometimes accompanied by a consequent concentration and fixity of attention which may result in the illusion becoming allied to fact. Hallucinations of tactile hyperaethesia can become so extreme as to produce what is called hysterical *haphalgesia*. The haphalgesia patient suffers torments from the pressure of his clothing or the weight of his bed-clothes.

Hysterical *topoalgia* is the term given to localised pain, often of great severity, where no organic cause can be traced and which is incompatable with the distribution of the sensory nerves. As will be seen in later chapters, suggested topoalgia is in large part accountable for many allegedly occult phenomena in the literature of stigmata, lycanthropy, faith healing and sorcery.

Other functional syndromes are hysterical *aphonia* or *mutism*, the hysteric being unable to utter sounds or to speak ; *copiopia*, or hysterical eye-strain ; hysterical *anopsia* or blindness ; hysterical *hemianopsia*, or the ability to see only one half of the visual field, which is generally due to involuntary suggestion by the psycopathologist during an examination.

In another class of hysteria may be mentioned the *fugue*, or temporary forgetfulness of personal identity and memory of the past, with a tendency to wander from home ; hysterical *amnesia* or temporary but complete inability to recall particular periods or events in the past, particularly after an accident or shock ; *multiple personality* or the apparent existence of two or more alternating personalities in the same person often with accompanying amnesia.

Analogous manifestations to multiple personality are seen in different and less developed forms in the *mediumistic trance* ; in *xenoglossia*—the uncontrollable utterance of unintelligible sounds under the influence of mystical or religious excitement, known euphemistically as " speaking in unknown tongues " ; [1] in *automatic writing* ; in *somnambulism* or sleep walking and *somniloquism* or talking in sleep ; in *demoniacal possession* of the Middle Ages ; in hysterical *inspiration* or automatic speech, usually on religious, mystical or moral themes ; and in hysterical *frenzy*, which is deliberately induced by many primitive sects, notably some dervish cults. All these dissociative phenomena may be followed by partial or total amnesia of the dissociative period.

Hysterical somnambulism deserves a brief note to itself. There are two recognised types. In *monoideic somnambulism* the same ritual or pantomime is carried out each time the somnambulic attack occurs ; in severe cases these attacks may take place spontaneously during the subject's waking hours. In *polyideic somnambulism*—the average sleep-walking performance—varied behaviour results. There follows almost invariably total amnesia in regard to the somnambulic attack. Many authorities state, however, that under hypnosis the actions during the attack can be recalled to the subject's mind.

Most of the pathological syndromes mentioned above are not confined to hysteria alone. They are also found in organic pathology and in the pathology of *psychosis* or insanity.

A broad term used to cover the various functional disorders of hysteria is *hysterical pathomimesis*, or the imitation of pathological symptoms in order to resolve tensions arising from subconscious mental conflict. Hysterical pathomimesis, however, must not be confused with deliberate conscious

---

[1] Acts. 2. 4-13.

malingering. *Adjustive illness* is another term used in psychiatry ; this term, however, is not confined to hysteria alone, but includes all psychoneurotic flights into illness whether real or feigned.

Under modern civilised conditions hysterical symptoms most often occur when the ordinary human sentiments and emotions, such as love, fear, hate, boredom, come into conflict with the dictates of conscience and the calls of duty or social behaviour and have to be repressed. Where the moral or social obligations necessitate complete repression of the natural instincts and the ideas associated with them, hysterical fatigue and exhaustion may result, particularly in the with the dictates of conscience and the calls of duty or social simpler, less complex, type of personality which unquestioningly accepts the contemporary social mores of the community.

The soldier, for example, who (for fear of being labelled a coward) refuses to face up to the possibility that he is becoming nervous and easily exhausted under battle conditions, simply pushes all such thoughts out of his head and carries on courageously doing his duty. The cause of his exhaustion is due to the conflict between his fear and his sense of duty ; his own contempt for cowardice helps him to ignore the conflict and keep it out of conscious awareness. But it is not to be repressed in this fashion with impunity. He becomes easily fatigued, irritable, and even brutal. Then something occurs which gives him a chance of getting out of the battle line altogether. A shell explodes near him. He believes himself hit. In his highly emotional and suggestible state a dramatic process of auto-suggestion may occur ; and when he finds himself unable to see for a few seconds he believes himself permanently blinded, and from then on it appears to him as if he has lost the use of his sight. The soldier is, naturally, withdrawn from combat as unfit, *which allows his repressed fear to have its way without in any way allowing him to feel that he has failed in his duty.* He is not aware of the subconscious motives underlying his functional anopsia nor of the subconscious mental conflict which produced it. When it is explained to him by the psychiatrist and he fully understands the reasons underlying his malady, the dissociative barrier eventually disappears, sometimes in only a few seconds ; he is then able to return to duty if this is demanded of him.

Functional disorders may often be simulated and it is the duty of the pasychiatrist to distinguish between the genuine hysterical patient and the one who is merely " swinging the lead ". In many borderline cases, however, the distinction is a very fine one.

When the hysterical patient suffers from a functional disability, it is reasonably certain that that very same disability has enabled him to avoid continuing to do something to which duty or other social pressure would otherwise have compelled him. It is often the single-minded person with a firm sense of duty who suffers from hysteria. The lazy person who knows he is lazy exerts himself but little to do what is expected of him, and is not likely to suffer from any subconscious mental conflict ; nor is the coward who admits his cowardice to himself, for the mental conflict will then take place in the full light of consciousness and will not remain repressed. Furthermore, by shirking or slacking, much severe mental strain is avoided. These individuals have no need for a device whereby nature removes the patient from an intrinsically hateful situation without causing him consciously to act contrary to his principles. The factory worker who injures his arm, and finds that it remains paralysed after all signs of physical injury have disappeared, is subconsciously providing himself with a reason for avoiding the work he hates without offending his ego or his conscience by any stigma of shirking.

A number of hysterical syndromes, spontaneous somnambulism for example, are in every way detrimental to the safety, health and comfort of the individual concerned, a fact which modern psychiatric theory is apt to ignore. In more naïve and credulous ages, when irrational belief largely dominated the mental life of an individual, the effect of suggestion upon hysterical persons produced harmful syndromes which were out of all proportion to any benefits gained and often led to complete mental derangement. Even in modern times, when psychiatric aid has not been forthcoming, hysteria may occasionally end in total insanity.

During the last century hysteria was the commonest of the neurotic ailments in Europe. From approximately the end of the century onwards, owing to changing social conditions, wider education, the disappearance of rigid beliefs and harsh discipline and many other factors, hysteria as a neurotic symptom appeared less and less often. The Great War, however, produced a great revival of hysterical cases among the troops of all nations. This fillip to the statistics of hysterical incidence was largely an artificial one, brought about by the abnormal strains and tensions of active warfare. During the second world war gross hysterical syndromes were considerably less prevalent, chiefly owing to the great advances in mass education and the broadening of the mind through such media as books, radio and the cinema. The tendency to other forms of psychoneurosis, on the other hand, was far greater.

The lessening of the incidence of hysteria by the influence of education was noted in the first world war. Both William Brown and MacDougall noted that the rank and file tended to hysteria while the officers, drawn almost entirely from the educated classes, tended to other forms of psychoneurosis.

In civilised countries today, cases of gross hysterical symptoms are comparatively rare. This. is due to the influence of liberal education in integrating the individual's mind and fortifying it against extremes of dissociation, and to the comparative freedom from religious, social and domestic compulsions and restraints which added to the strain and monotony of life in former years. In the East, however, gross hysterical conversion symptoms are still common. Yet it is in many ways to be regretted that this easily curable mental disorder is being superseded by other and more insidious types of mental neuroses such as schizophrenia. For whereas hysteria merely enables the patient to avoid the difficulties of his life by allowing him to drop his responsibilities without consciously trangressing his own moral code, the schizophrenic solves the same difficulty by withdrawing into an inner world of his own, supplanting the reality of the phenomenal universe for a reality of his own devising; it is not easy, it is often impossible, to bring him out of his world of fantasy.

The hysteric is naturally highly suggestible; and the wrong type of suggestion, whether deliberately given by another person, or operating through the beliefs of the patient himself, or through the beliefs, prejudices, traditions and superstitions of the age in which he lives, may easily aggravate the hysterical symptoms.   Today, all such harmful suggestive influences are but a shadow of their former selves.

Where there is naked superstition and gross prejudice, there exists also an unlimited capacity for *irrational belief*— a very potent factor in the operation of suggestion.   During the Middle Ages, and in fact until the latter half of the nineteenth century, the minds of the masses were steeped in prejudice and superstition, and these twin factors operated disastrously upon the susceptible mind of the hysteric, whose consequent reactions merely served to confirm the ignorant prejudices of those around him.

These days the great majority of the factors which contributed to the formation of extreme hysterical syndromes are absent.   Life, in the West at least, is lived on a far less arduous plane, and the minds of civilised men are seldom gripped by rigid fanatical beliefs and superstitions unlit by the rays of reason.   But in former times these factors resulted in hysterical syndromes of a severity virtually unknown since the relatively recent development of medical psychology.

The Western psychiatrist today may have to deal with hysteria, originating in subconscious mental conflict ; but it is a different brand of malady from that which has *its path deepened and broadened by the continual pressure of virulent and maleficent suggestion.*   In demoniacal possession we can see, from biblical times to the Middle Ages and after, a phenomenon of hysteria which resulted from the reciprocal play of popular superstition and the ready belief of the subject himself that demons existed and were capable of taking possession of a man's body.   Any such irrational and firmly held belief, inculcated since childhood, made the medieval man or woman subject to influences of suggestion on a scale unparalleled under modern conditions.

It is extremely doubtful whether, in such cases, modern psychiatric methods would have been very effective in curing the patient.   Yet there existed very effective methods of curing during medieval times which, be it noted, also depended on the operation of suggestion augmented through the patient's capacity for limitless belief. To the hysterical and hallucinated witch or to the foaming demon-possessed man, the ability of the priest or inanimate ikon to exorcise Satan and his minions was a cardinal fact of existence known since infancy. The astonishing results often achieved in exorcism were due to nothing more than the effect of powerful and readily assimilated counter-suggestion. It is of great interest to note that Janet himself, at the turn of the century, was not above resorting to a brand of medieval exorcism to cure a hysterical French peasant who suffered from hallucinations of demoniacal possession.

Chapter Six

HYPNOTISM

THERE IS a great deal of confused thinking among the general public in regard to the facts of hypnotism. To the uninformed hypnotism savours of " mysterious powers of the mind " with more than a hint of the supernatural. In actual fact, while our knowledge of hypnotism and suggestion is still incomplete, our understanding is more than sufficient to dispel any lingering belief in the operation of occult powers. Yet hypnotic suggestion has been used for thousands of years—and in many parts of the world today is still used—as a powerful adjunct to the thaumaturgist's and necromancer's repertoire ; and those who use hypnotism for these ends are seldom any freer from the delusion that the effects they produce are due to magic than their credulous and suggestible subjects.

Hypnotism was known to the priests of the ancient religions of the Near and Middle East, to the Egyptians, the Persian magi, and to many esoteric cults of India. Amongst the credulous and superstitious people of those days, for whom the gods, spirits and magic possessed the same degree of reality as the objects and forces of the material world, the effect of suggestion was infinitely more drastic than would be the case today in civilised communities. Their total acceptance of magic as a fundamental reality, combined with a simplicity and directness of outlook, enabled any form of suggestion to play havoc with the normal functioning of the mental and emotional faculties. Allied, too, with these factors was the emotion of fear aroused in the presence of the occult, engendering even more effective conditions for the induction of suggestion.

The whole problem of hypnotism is bound up with the problem of suggestion and the effects produced by suggestion. Hypnotism is, in fact, merely a particular method of inducing an increased state of suggestibility in the individual. The deeply hypnotised subject can be made to experience all kinds of delusions ; he can be compelled to carry out the most absurd and unreasonable actions ; he can be made to assume a totally different personality, to remember facts whose very existence he has long forgotten, to fall into a rigid cataleptic trance, or to become insensible to pain. If it is suggested to him that he is the Devil, then, owing to his heightened aptitude for dramatic impersonation and his freedom from inhibitions, the subject will act the part, leaving no doubt that he temporarily believes himself to be none other than the Devil himself.

It is not difficult to see how hypnotism can give rise to the most extreme occult beliefs. In former times the hypnotist was accepted as the possessor of magical powers without question, and this tradition is by no means extinct in Europe and the United States at the present day.

James Braid of Manchester first coined the term hypnotism in 1841. Before that date it was usually referred to as mesmerism or animal magnetism and was reputed to operate by means of vital fluids, magnetic currents or whatever else entered the hypnotist's head. It was Jan Baptista van Helmont, a seventeenth century Flemish physician, who first introduced the idea of a fluid called animal magnetism through the media of which the actions of other persons could be radically influenced. Over a century later Mesmer resuscitated the notion, claiming it as his own discovery. Mesmer brought the whole subject of hypnotism into disrepute by his wild claims and fraudulent practices. It was not until the latter half of the nineteenth century that serious investigation into hypnotism was revived, particularly under the leadership of two French psychopathologists, Hippolyte Bernheim at Nancy, and Jean Charcot at the Salpétrière Hospital. The Salpétrière School considered hypnosis to be a pathological state analogous to hysteria, while Bernheim and the Nancy school explained it in terms of suggestion. " War " was declared between the two schools with little quarter given. Bernheim triumphed and his

view is, in essence, the one generally accepted by contemporary psychology. But the fact remains that it is the hysterical patient who makes the best hypnotic subject—at least
under modern civilised conditions, so that Charcot's conclusions were by no means so wide of the mark as his opponents wished to believe.

In the sphere of medicine hypnosis has often been able
to play a very important part, particularly in the cure or
alleviation of disabilities of hysterical origin. Hysteria
has often resulted in functional mutism, blindness and
paralysis. Numbers of such cases have been directly cured
by hypnotic suggestion and there is no doubt that many of
the traditional stories of " miracles " of the blind being
made to see, the dumb to speak and the lame and halt to
walk had firm foundation in fact. The modern practice of
using hypnotic suggestion in the cure or alleviation of
psychogenic disabilities comes under the general heading
of psychotherapy, or, more specifically, hypnotherapy.

For information on the use of hypnosis in medicine the
reader is advised to turn to Chapter 12. The medical use of
hypnotic suggestion for curing patients of their psychogenic
ailments has serious drawbacks and for that reason has not
spread into general practice. But hypnotherapists have,
on occasion, produced the most amazing cures, and among
the less advanced communities of the world hypnotherapeutic
treatment ought certainly to be used far more than it is.
In modern psychotherapeutic clinics hypnosis, when used,
is generally employed in conjunction with other methods
of psychotherapy. Though the therapeutic effects of
hypnotic suggestion are often striking they are apt to be
ephemeral, since the basic nervous hypertensions which
produce the symptoms are not removed.

Today in civilised countries hypnotic suggestion is used
for two different purposes : as a therapeutic agent and as a
form of entertainment. Many authorities consider the
presentation of hypnotism on the stage as something undesirable, but there is no evidence that it has done any harm
and there is little reason why it should among modern
audiences. The ridiculous actions of the hypnotised person
on the stage can indeed be highly amusing, particularly
when the subject is an unsuspecting member of the audience,

and one dose of hypnosis will do no one any harm. One vaudeville hypnotist used to suggest to his subject—a member of the audience selected after a few elementary tests for susceptibility—that she was two years of age and just beginning to walk. The lack of inhibitions and the heightened histrionic powers often engendered by hypnosis guaranteed the success of this part of the show ; it was chiefly the expression on the adult's face during her imagined period of extreme infancy which amused the audience.

Hysteria may be regarded, for purposes of comparison, as a state of high suggestibility accompanied by a tendency towards mental dissociation. Many writers claim that the chief difference between hysteria and hypnosis in this respect lies in the fact that the effects or symptoms noted in hysteria are due to a pathological state of mind, while in hypnosis more or less the same effects are produced, artificially as it were, by a specific technique.

It is of importance to remember that in civilised communities, where fear, uncritical credulity or abject superstition are normally lacking in everyday life, the more striking effects of hypnosis are to be found mainly with individuals already subject to a considerable degree of hysteria. Under modern conditions, therefore, it often becomes problematical whether or not to regard deep hypnosis as an artificial *increase* in already existing hysterical tendencies. A number of writers have in fact taken this view. With normal subjects, however, the hypnotic state may be regarded merely as an increase—artificially induced—in the subject's natural suggestibility.

The problems of hysteria and suggestion cannot be divorced from those pertaining to hypnotism ; all three phenomena are inextricably bound up one with the other, and it is difficult to draw the dividing line between any of them.

A complete explanation of the psychology of hypnotism is not yet forthcoming. Nor is there likely to be one before psychologists have fully understood all the phenomena of suggestion. Once the latter have been successfully explained, it will almost certainly be found that the phenomenon of hypnotism is merely a special case of the general psychological problem of suggestion. There is considerable confusion of ideas on the subject of hypnotism amongst psychologists themselves. The reason for this is that many experiments in hypnotism have, until quite recently, been so conducted as to produce reactions from suggestible or hysterical patients which conformed to the experimenter's preconceived ideas on the subject.

HYPNOTISM AND ITS RELATION TO SLEEP

The term " hypnosis " (sleep) is a complete misnomer. Sleep can be induced by suggestion, likewise a drowsy, lethargic state. However, these states are not effects of " hypnotism " but of suggestion, and the " hypnotised " subject may remain thoroughly wide awake unless suggestions of sleep or drowsiness are directly given, or unless the subject—through his reading on the subject—consciously connects hypnotism with sleep and drowsiness ; in the latter case a process of autosuggestion occurs.

Numbers of laboratory experiments[1] have been carried out which prove conclusively that the hypnotic state itself is not allied to sleep. For example, subjects in a state of deep hypnosis give virtually the same patella reflex action or " knee-jerk " as in their normal state, whereas it is absent in sleep.[2]

Drowsiness and lethargy in hypnosis are due to the tendency of the hypnotised subject to fall into actual sleep. This in turn may be due to direct suggestion, expectation or autosuggestion, fatigue, or the relaxed position which the subject is generally expected to adopt at the beginning of a session. Genuine deep sleep can be induced by suggestion, and this must be clearly understood. But before sleeping subjects are able to carry on with the hypnotic experiment, they have first to be awakened. Generally the operator's voice is sufficient for this and the subject wakes, not to his normal state, but still susceptible to the operator's suggestions.

---

[1] See Hull, C. L., *Hynosis and Suggestibility*, N.Y. 1933.

[2] See Bass., M. J., *Differentiation of the Hypnotic Trance from Normal Sleep*, J. Exp. Psychol., 14, pp. 382-399, 1931.

While drowsiness, lethargy and sleep may be induced directly by suggestion, or accidentally owing to the state of relaxation adopted at the beginning of the session; the hypnotic state as such is to be rigidly distinguished from sleep as Bostroem first proved in 1925.[3] In extreme relaxation the knee jerk and other reflexes are noticeably diminished, but this is not in itself peculiar to states of relaxation induced by hypnosis. Hypnotism is, in fact, no more than *the induction of a state of abnormal suggestibility by certain well defined methods* technically known as *hypnogenic,* which will be described shortly.

Hypnotic phenomena can be induced only in people who are already suggestible by nature or who are in an unusually suggestible state of mind. Inducing an unusually suggestible state of mind is part of the hypnotisist's craft. If we wish to find the explanation of the *effects* obtained by the use of hypnotism, we must seek it in the psychology of suggestion—a great deal of which is still a closed book to us.

Most of the prominent psychopathologists who have regularly made use of hypnotism in the course of their professional duties possess only the most ambiguous ideas on the theory of the subject. Much of the difficulty appears to lie in the fact that, often enough, evidence of dissociation and trance states of consciousness have been induced, either unwittingly or through faulty suggestion on the part of the operator. Such results as these are due to the fact that very many of the hypnotist's subjects in the past have been hysterical, with consequent tendencies to dissociation which the hypnotist has unwittingly increased through the use of suggestion. The misinterpretation of these and similar observations, e.g. the tendency to drowsiness or sleep, has led to confusions in the literature of hypnotism without parallel in any other branch of modern psychology.

Generally when the operator wishes to hypnotise a subject he will first induce a drowsy lethargic state by a combined method of relaxation and suggestions of sleep—the *hypnogenic* method. If this is done successfully the subject is then considered hypnotised. Actually with numbers of subjects

---

[3] Boestroem, A., *Abderhalden's Handbuch der biologischen Arbeitsmethoden,* Abt. 6, Teil C, Heft 5, " Hypnose," p. 291.

there is no need to go through this first step at all in order to induce abnormal suggestibility. " Waking " suggestion can prove just as effective. One of the reasons why the hyp-nogenic method is so effective is because traditionally this is what the subject expects.

Many operators have referred to their ability to achieve effects similar to hypnosis by " Waking suggestion." This simply means that they have omitted the traditional first steps of suggesting drowsiness or sleep. The fact is that the moment the subject begins to feel drowsy at the *operator's suggestion* he has already become " hypnotised," i.e. rendered abnormally suggestible.

There are a variety of methods of inducing a state of hypnosis or abnormal suggestibility. It does not depend on any peculiar faculty of the operator. The majority of people can be trained as hypnotists if they wish to be, but the most successful are those whose personality naturally impresses others. " Will-power " has nothing to do with the ability to hypnotise successfully. First impressions, however, are important. The subject should believe in the ability of the operator to hypnotise him. If this belief is absent, the operator should try and inculcate it as a preliminary. Gen-erally nothing more than an efficient masterful " beside-manner " is required. Provided his technique is correct, a man with a relatively weak will should have no difficulty in hypnotising a man of dominant will power. It is in fact the shallow type of individual with an unstable and somewhat mercurial temperament who is more difficult than most to hypnotise.

A typical method of inducing hypnosis follows along these lines : The subject, *who must first agree to co-operate*, is placed in an armchair or couch and ordered to relax completely. The operator holds up a bright object upon which the subject has to fix his gaze (the " fascination method"). The operator talks firmly and convincingly to his subject, using a quiet and somewhat monotonous tone of voice, suggesting to him drowsiness, heaviness of the eyelids, obscurity of vision, heaviness of limbs, blankness of mind, fatigue and all the various appurtenances of sleep. The bright object will descend gradually until the lids of the eyes, unconsciously following its movement, are nearly closed. Sometimes the operator strokes the limbs of the subject. The monotonous flow of words reiterating the oncoming of sleep, the strain on the eyes, the relaxed position of the muscles—all tend to induce a heaviness in the eyelids and limbs and an increasing reluctance to move them, until the subject suddenly finds that he *cannot* move them (even when challenged) if the operator suggests to him that he is unable to do so. When this degree of suggestibility is reached, the operator is then able to put the subject's limbs into any position he wishes and give the command that the subject's limbs remain fixed in the position chosen. The subject can no longer move them. If the subject is now " awakened," by the simple expedient of telling him to wake up, he will usually be able to remember his experiences unless it is specifically suggested to him that he will remember nothing " on awakening," in which case it depends on the psychological constitution of the subject whether he will be able to recall his hypnotic experiences or not. In deeper states of hypnosis than the one just described, complete forgetfulness, or *amnesia*, can often be induced if desired.

The great value of the hypnogenic method of increasing suggestibility (hypnosis) is that a relaxed drowsy state robs the subject of mental energy, lulls his critical faculties and makes him disinclined to display initiative of his own. This is by no means the complete explanation, but the efficacy of drowsiness as an aid to increasing suggestibility is proved by the fact that some subjects who are otherwise refractory to psychological methods of inducing suggestibility are easily rendered suggestible by a moderate dose of such drugs as sodium amytal or evipan or thiopentone administered intravenously. Hypnotism, let it be repeated, is simply the induction of a state of abnormal suggestibility by hypnogenic methods. " Awakening from hypnosis " means nothing more than recovery from the suggestible state.

By no means all people are readily hypnotisable, although the majority of normal people can be hypnotised to a noticeable degree. In Europe and America it is estimated that between ten and twenty per cent of the normal population can be made to reach the deeper or " somnambulic " stages by expert hypnotists.   It may be noted in passing that when a patient is recalcitrant to hypnotherapeutic treatment the strain and monotony and fatigue of trying to induce hypnosis has been known to result in the operator being hypnotised instead ! Generally, it is the strong-minded person—those who can concentrate on a single idea without distraction— who are easiest to hypnotise. The butterfly-minded type of person, unless he be a hysteric, is not so easily subject to hypnosis. Again, those with no education, or a poor one, are generally more easily hypnotised than the well-educated ; the latter possess a better critical faculty and are not so susceptible to the influence of ideas emanating from others. Generally speaking, subjects in states of fatigue, or after a period of strain, are far more easily hypnotised than those who are fresh and alert. The insane can very seldom be hypnotised.

The term hypnosis is unfortunate. But it is difficult to avoid using it in view of its familiarity. Since it is to be retained, we will define it simply as a particular method whereby suggestibility is induced in a subject—the method which generally commences with relaxation accompanied by suggestions of drowsiness and sleep. In primitive societies the medicine-man dispenses with such methods. He can induce extreme states of suggestibility without them.

The hypnogenic method of inducing abnormal suggesti- bility is probably the most effective   in modern society. Unfortunately, a serious study of the effects of suggestion in primitive communities has yet to be undertaken ; but it is possible to state with certainty that among primitive communities the hypnogenic method of involving suggesti- bility, though practised amongst certain esoteric cults of the East, has no major advantages over " waking " suggestion. " Waking " suggestion, preceded by preliminaries designed to strike at the roots of the subject's emotions and beliefs, can operate powerfully in primitive societies, without the sub- ject's co-operation and even against his will—a feat which all European and American hypnotists find impossible in their own countries.

Yet the effects attained by use of hypnotic suggestion are often amazing. For example, hypnotic sleep can be so deep that major surgical operations have been carried out without the patient feeling the least pain. [1] Analgesia, or the inability to feel pain, can also be induced locally, in the thumb or the leg for example, at the suggestion of the operator while the patient remains fully conscious. The same phenomena is often observable in hysteria ; centuries ago hysterical analgesic patches were considered the work of the devil and the unfortunate person was usually burnt as a witch after gross tortures designed to obtain a " confession " of trafficking with the prince of darkness.

Suggestion in primitive society can be implanted with enormous effect. The combination of complete belief in magic and in the powers of the witchdoctor, the large element of fear, the accumulative effect of reciprocal suggestion always present among a crowd, the state of excitement and intense expectation—all operate to induce a state of extreme suggestibility. Stories of natives dying after being cursed by a witchdoctor—a phenomenon now called *thanatomania* by some anthropologists—are no product of the explorer's or missionary's imagination ; it is indeed a fact that an idea can so powerfully get a hold on the mind of primitive man that it can result in death within a few days. He believes that he will die and die he does—unless his friends manage to persuade the witchdoctor to " lift " the curse, whereupon he will immediately recover on having the news brought to his notice. Thanatomania (anthropological) serves to illustrate the enormous force of suggestion when conditions are favourable for it.

HYPNOTIC SOMNAMBULISM

The deepest stages of hypnosis (i.e. an advanced stage of suggestibility brought about by hypnogenic methods) is still generally referred to as the " somnambulic stage." The somnambulic stage is characterised by the ability of the operator to make the hypnotised subject carry out any series of actions he suggests, however incongruous or irrational. Suggested visual hallucinations will produce reactions which to the inexperienced eye appear as if the subject can actually see the objects or scenes suggested. Suggested auditory hallucinations produce like reactions, and the subject can even be made to carry on conversations with an invisible person.

It is extremely doubtful whether the modern civilised individual actually experiences hallucinatory sense impressions under hypnotic suggestion ; he is more likely to be acting a part, though all the time he may be under the delusion that he hears or sees the persons or objects suggested. It is probable, however, that numbers of hysterical subjects do experience hallucinations analogous to those experienced by crystal gazers.

Hypnotic somnambulism, in which the subject carries out a series of actions at the command of the operator, possesses an interesting parallel with a form of insanity known as *catatonic schizophrenia*. The catatonic schizophrenic frequently exhibits the phenonemon of " command automatism " in which the patient slavishly obeys every command given to him. There is no " rapport " observable in such cases. It is possible that in the case of the hysterical subject hypnotic somnambulism is related to the phenomenon of catatonic command automatism. In certain cases of catatonic schizophenia the patient may exhibit a state of catalepsy similar to that engendered in many hypnotised subjects. The schizophrenic may also be subject to sensory hallucinations. The conclusion to be drawn, albeit tentatively, is that the mental states of schizophrenics and certain hypnotised hysterics are not disimilar. If this is true, then hypnosis can effect deeper alterations in the psychology of the hysterical individual than is generally admitted. This conclusion should, however, be accepted with reserve until further information is forthcoming.

Hypnotic somnambulism is a term which possesses certain ambiguities. There are, in all likelihood, two types of hypnotic " somnambulism " : one, that to which normal but suggestible individuals may attain and in which the reactions of the hypnotised subject are not so very different from a subject who is putting on an act ; two, that to which the latent or overt hysteric often attains, in which natural tendencies to delusion or dissociation are intensified, producing what may be called a state of genuine trance. Borderline cases are, naturally, frequently found. In the first type the subject merely obeys the commands or suggestions of the operator ; and even when amnesia is suggested the consequent loss of memory frequently appears to be an apparent one only, resulting from the desire to obey the operator—i.e. the subject continues to maintain, perhaps deceiving himself, that he cannot remember while still retaining the ability to do so. On the other hand, the hysterical type of subject is often genuinely unable to recall the incidents occurring in his somnambulic state unless specifically ordered to do so by the operator. It is only in these latter cases that the term " somnambulism " can be applied with any justification. It is a fact that highly hysterical subjects may, when hypnotised, reach a state of consciousness nearly identical to that of the sleep-walker.

With both normal and hysterical individuals the procedure of attaining to the so-called somnambulic state is the same. The operator makes the subject relax and monotonously repeats all the appurtenances of sleep. The operator then orders him to open his eyes and carries out some minor experiments to test the state of suggestibility to which the subject has attained. If the required state of suggestibility has been induced, the subject is now capable of performing all the actions usual in his normal waking state and will answer questions readily ; but he remains virtually without a will of his own. He obeys the operator provided the latter does not try to make him say or do things which are genuinely abhorrent to him. If, for example, the subject is told to pour icy water over himself he would be likely to come out of the hypnotic trance or even to break into an outburst of hysterical weeping. But if the subject did not know what the container held and it was suggested to him that it was full of rose-petals, for example, there would be no difficulty in persuading him to drench himself !

Trance states of consciousness, such as those which are found in hypnotised subjects tending to hysteria and are characterised by genuine dissociation, have only too often in the past been regarded as a specific stage of deep hypnosis. This is not the case ; the hypnotic trance can be attributed to the effects of suggestion upon a   mind already possessing a tendency to trance states. The hypnogenic method of increasing a subject's suggestibility has no direct connection with the emergence of a state of trance. If the right technique is used, " waking " suggestion is often efficacious in inducing trance states in subjects who are prone to hysterical dissociation.

The pseudo-somnambulism of the non-hysterical subject is largely explained by the total lack of self-conscious and other inhibitive factors brought about by hypnosis. His histrionic powers are thereby increased far beyond what he is capable of in his normal state. The pathological hysteric often presents the same tendency, the main difference being that the hysterical patient has an underlying motive inspiring his performance, while the histrionic exhibition of the normal hypnotised subject is brought about by the effects of suggestion.

HYPNOTIC HALLUCINATIONS

Amongst practitioners of the occult the induction of delusions and even hallucinations, by suggestion, has played a great part. The ancient Egyptian magician's stock trick of turning staves into serpents and similar wonders are all attributable to delusions or visual hallucinations produced by the effects of suggestion. In more superstitious and credulous ages, as in primitive societies of today, extreme states of suggestibility were easily engendered, and there is little reason to doubt that under the twin influences of emotion and suggestion a state of hysteria was produced which may have resulted in actual sensory hallucinations. Even today the normal western individual who has been hypnotised can be made to believe that he sees persons, objects or events in limitless variety, however incongruous or fantastic.

It is extremely doubtful whether the normal European or American subject can be made to experience, at the suggestion of the hypnotist, a *genuine* sensory hallucination, i.e. an experience of the *actual sensation* of seeing or hearing persons and objects which are not present. Many such hypnotised subjects can undoubtedly be made to believe that they have experienced such sensations, and all "somnambulic" subjects can be made to act as if they *were* experiencing them ; the induction of such *pseudo-hallucinations* is a common hypnotic experiment. Whatever the answer to the problem may be, the fact remains that hypnotic[1] suggestion can produce, if not genuine sensory hallucinations, at least the pseudo-hallucinations as described above, and it is evident that the bearing of both on the psychology of occultism is of equal importance.

The power of suggestion can undoubtedly produce genuine sensory hallucinations in hysterics who are occasionally subject to them. Likewise, when intense psychological factors such as fear or hysterical frenzy are involved, all the evidence points to the fact that suggestion or intense expectation can result in the subject experiencing sensory hallucinations. Sensory illusions, it need not be emphasised, are easily induced by " waking " suggestion when the subject is under emotional stress. In primitive communities, however, there seems little doubt that powerful suggestion or expectation can result in genuine sensory hallucinations—or at least subjective optical and auditory illusions of sufficient intensity as to render the distinction of little practical significance.

POST-HYPNOTIC SUGGESTION

Some of the most interesting examples of suggested delusion and pseudo-hallucination are to be found in " post-hypnotic suggestion ". The subject, while in a state of hypnosis, is commanded to carry out some particular action after he has been " awakened ". The suggestion is forcefully conveyed to him that he will remember nothing of the command. He is then " awakened " and at the correct time proceeds to carry out the required action—without knowing why he does it. If, despite the suggested amnesia, he realises with his conscious mind that he has been ordered to do it he will be able to resist the impulse to obey ; otherwise he usually feels no need to resist and will make more or less rational excuses to account for his action, however odd it might appear to others present. For example, if the subject has been ordered to open the window on a very cold day exactly ten minutes after having apparently recovered from his suggestible state, he will excuse his action by saying,

" it's very close in here ; I'll open the window a minute", or something similar. He will account for his actions by a process of *rationalisation*, i.e. producing apparently logical reasons to justify irrational or impulsive actions.

Post-hypnotic *hallucinations*, either real or " pseudo", are of relatively rare occurrence. But among the ultra-suggestible primitive peoples of Africa or Asia this verdict is not likely to apply. " Delayed " suggestion was one of the tricks of the oriental magician. The old soothsayer who granted the wish of bereaved peasants by causing dead relatives to appear and even speak with them " at the mid-night hour " relied on this form of suggestion.

As an example of probable pseudo-hallucination or delusion of the post-hypnotic variety we may cite the amusing case of the practised hypnotic experimenter who hypnotised a very susceptible subject and told him that he would be swimming in a swimming-pool within seven minutes. Amnesia was suggested and the subject was immediately " awakened". Precisely at the time indicated the subject took a header on to the floor and started swimming vigorously, first side-stroke, then a breast-stroke, and finally kicking along the floor on his back, loudly calling to his friends by name.

There is often a struggle in the mind of the subject when the time arrives to carry out the delayed amnesic suggestion. Being to all intents and purposes, fully in command of all his faculties, he may begin to feel restless and uneasy and generally becomes aware of some compulsion to action for which he cannot account. Sometimes he feels he *wants* to do something and gets no peace of mind till the action has been carried out. On being rehypnotised, however, or often by verbal suggestion alone without hypnotic preliminaries, he can be made to recall the events which took place while he was hypnotised, and the impulse to carry out the action thereupon fades away.

Post-hypnotic (or delayed amnesic) suggestion may seem like something out of a fairy tale to those who are unac-quainted with the subject It might well be open to suspicion of fraud or mere histrionics, were it not that post-hypnotic amnesia is one of the two most thoroughly established phenomena pertaining to hypnotic suggestion.

All generalised descriptions of the various phenomena produced by hypnotic suggestion are at best only rough guides to what has commonly been observed. Exceptions to the rule are probably more numerous than the rules themselves, for *the reactions of hypnotised subjects vary enormously according to the ideas, theories and preconceptions, not only of the subjects themselves, but of the operators.* The latter may convey their ideas indirectly by unconscious suggestion : by their attitude, by leading questions, by the conditions of the experiments and so on. The subject is apt to react according to how he consciously or subconsciously interprets these.

The expression " to awake from hypnosis " is a very common one. Unless, however, the hypnotised subject has actually fallen asleep, or has been put into a state of sleep or drowsiness by the operator's suggestions, the expression may also be a very misleading one. Drowsiness and sleep are generally associated with the hypnotic state because the method of inducing the state of abnormal suggestibility is primarily a hypnogenic one. Once the requisite degree of suggestibility has been attained, however, the hypnotised subject can be roused from his drowsiness to a state of alertness, while still remaining amenable to the suggestions of the operator—i.e. while still " hypnotised".

It is commonly the practice of hypnotic operators to suggest sleep before returning the subject to his normal state. The command to " wake up " is then appropriate. But the subject can easily be brought out of his suggestible or " hypnotic " state without the use of this convention. In such instances the operator's command to " wake up " is then seen to be little more than a conventional signal which conveys to the subject that he is no longer susceptible to the operator's influence and is free to act normally.

In post-hypnotic suggestion—usually confined to hysterical subjects with a noticeable tendency to dissociation—the subject *remains* in a state of suggestibility. The command to " wake up " does not free the subject from his susceptibility to the operator's suggestions. He has the suggestion made to him explicitly or by implication, that he is to carry out a certain action at a certain time, that he is to forget that any suggestion has been made, and that he is otherwise to

carry on as usual (implied by the command to " wake up ").
In successful post-hypnotic experiments this is precisely what
the subject does.   Normally, the subject instinctively associates the command to " wake up " with the idea that he
is no longer susceptible to the suggestions of the operator.
In post-hypnotic experiments, however, the association of
ideas no longer operates because the subject is still aware
that the operator wants him to carry out certain actions.
On the command to " wake up " the suggested amnesia
intervenes ;   the subject is no longer able to recall the incidents which took place before the command to " wake up "
and his awareness of the operator's previous suggestions
likewise passes out of his consciousness.

HYPNOSIS AND THE SUBCONSCIOUS ESTIMATION OF TIME INTERVALS

In dealing with post-hypnotic suggestion we come across a
surprising thing :   the apparent ability of some hypnotised
subjects to estimate accurately the passage of time.   Numerous experiments have been conducted on the subconscious
faculty of time estimation.   For example, a hypnotised
hysterical subject may be commanded to carry out an action
seven days, three hours and fifteen minutes after being
awakened.   Such a time interval has been given in minutes,
or even *seconds*—616,500 to be precise.   The subject is
then given the suggestion that he will forget the command
and then is " awakened."   Astonishingly accurate successes
have been achieved by these methods though not nearly so
many as have been reported.   The subject subconsciously
estimates the time to elapse before executing the required
action, sometimes being only a minute or two over a period of
days.   Needless to say, unless a tendency to hysterical
dissociation is observable, the estimation of time intervals
should not be assumed to be " subconscious".
Time estimation may possibly be an atavistic function.
During Pavlov's experiments in conditioned reflexes the
repeated reactions of one of his dogs indicated that the
animal was able to distinguish without difficulty when a
metronome was beating at 100 beats to the minute and when

it was beating at only 96.   It has been established that bees are normally able to estimate time (and distance and angle) with surprising accuracy.

It was observed in the discussion of auto-suggestion that many people are able to wake up at a specified time in the early morning simply by " telling themselves " to wake up at the time required.   They awake often at the very minute stipulated.   Such an estimation of time is impossible to them in their waking state.   It would appear that the subconscious mind is able to use this faculty mainly when it is unhampered by the distractions forced upon it during full consciousness.

" Rapport " and Negative Hallucinations

A great deal is heard in popular literature of hypnotism concerning the phenomenon of " rapport." There is nothing peculiarly incomprehensible about this.   It is a fact that the hypnotised subject generally remains in touch with the operator only—is *en rapport* with him, as it was once termed. In extreme cases of " rapport " the subject appears to hear nothing at all except the commands of the hypnotist.   A pistol shot, or the shouted commands of bystanders, may have little or no effect on him ; but he will still react to and obey the barely audible whisper of the operator.   This state of affairs, however, is very easily countered by suggestion from the operator.   The fact that " rapport " can be so easily countered by suggestion shows that it is itself a product of suggestion.

This fact robs " rapport " of all the mystery which, a century ago, was attached to it by all who investigated the problem.   " Rapport " at that time was thought to be due to some mystical relationship between the mind of the operator and that of the hypnotised subject.   The early mesmerists dinned into their subjects, who felt for them an almost superstitious awe,   that it was their own peculiar " magnetick " powers which produced the mesmeric effects —effects which today we regard as due solely to suggestion. The patients, under this powerful form of suggestion, only reacted to the commands of those in whom they had been led to believe the "magnetism" resided. When all such theories as "animal magnetism" and "magnetic fluids" passed into limbo, the traditional belief in the special powers of hypnotic operators still persisted in certain psychotherapeutic institutes, thereby giving rise to the theory of "rapport" since the patients continued to take no notice of any command or suggestion unless it was given by the operator himself. "Rapport" may be still observed, unless contrary suggestion is given, because the subject is conscious that he is being hypnotised by one person—the operator. It is the operator who is going to hypnotise him, and no one else ; it is the subject's expectation of a special personal relationship between them which so often renders him suggestible to the operator's commands only.

In "rapport," elements of so-called "negative hallucination" enter into the picture. The term "negative hallucination" is common in the literature of hypnotism : a "negative hallucination" is said to occur when the subject no longer hears or sees certain persons or objects present around him. For example, if it is suggested to the subject that he can neither hear nor see a third person who is actually present in the room, and he is then told to sit upon the chair which that person is occupying, he will sit on that person's lap, apparently oblivious to his presence, neither seeing nor feeling him. He will claim that he is sitting on the chair and will even describe or invent in detail those parts of the chair which are obscured from view by the body of the other person as if he could actually see them. To account for this, it has often been supposed that the hypnotised subject hallucinates those parts of his immediate environment which are obscured by persons or objects which the operator has suggested are no longer there. This is extremely unlikely, though the subject may experience the delusion that he sees them. Nor is it in the least likely that in such circumstances the subject actually fails to see or hear such persons or objects when the operator suggests they are no longer present. He will either be acting a part or he may be suffering from a temporary delusion, but the negative sensory hallucination most certainly does not occur—if indeed such a thing is at all possible, which remains highly doubtful.

The term "negative hallucination," however, still has its

uses, although *negative delusion* would be far more appropriate. It is a curious fact that the literature of hypnotism possesses extraordinary few references to the subject of hypnotic delusions. Yet suggested delusions probably play a greater part in the phenomena of hypnotism than any other single factor—and they do nor appear to be always confined to the *subject* !

ABNORMAL EFFECTS PRODUCED BY HYPNOSIS

Reports of the extraordinary effects produced by hypnotic suggestion have reached absurd heights of exaggeration ; much of this, however, is due to the misinterpretation of results observed in hypnotic experiments. Suggestion *can* produce results which are not attainable by voluntary means in the normal state ; but it is not often realised that nearly every effect which has been obtained in the clinic through the use of hypnogenic methods of inducing suggestibility may also be obtained by methods of " waking " suggestion. It is mainly a question of technique.

Very commonly reported are experiments which purport to show that hyperaesthesia or extreme hyperacuity of the senses can be induced by hypnotic suggestion. Modern experiment has shown that there is little foundation in such claims. Minimal cues and slight involuntary articulations by the operator are frequently responsible for hypnotised subjects being apparently able to see or hear signs and sounds beyond their normal range. Increased ability to concentrate and *heightened powers of observation* are, indeed, often observed under the influence of hypnotic suggestion, and much of the " hyperaesthesia " reported can be attributed to such factors as these.

But the chief factor perpetuating the belief in hypnotic hyperaesthesia is the ease with which many subjects can be deluded that they have acquired hyperaesthetic powers under the influence of hypnosis. In the well-known experiments of Bergson and Robinet in 1887, a hypnotised boy was apparently able to read letters 3mm. in height in the corneal reflection of the operator's eye ;[1] but this is in fact a totally

---

[1] *Revue Philosophique*, November, 1888.

impossible feat (8mm. being the outside limit), and was undoubtedly due to slight involuntary articulation or other cues provided by the operator.

Until recent years virtually the whole of hypnotic experimentation has been carried out in an amateurish fashion. The reports of effects produced by hypnosis very seldom contain information concerning control-experiments, i.e. experiments to test the subject's reactions in his normal state which can be compared to his reactions when hypnotised. Without such control-experiments—particularly if the subject is a hysteric—it is impossible to tell whether the subject's reactions under the influence of hypnosis are in any way different from those of his normal state, or even whether the same reactions could not be produced by imitation or pretence.

Quite surprising effects have been produced by means of ordinary verbal suggestions from which all elements of hypnosis have been entirely absent. In fact only two phenomena peculiar to hypnotic suggestion are thoroughly established, viz. post-hypnotic amnesia and hypnotic analgesia. All the other effects reputedly brought about by hypnotic suggestion can, except in cases where hysterical dissociation is already present, be paralleled by " waking " suggestion.

For example, experiments carried out by Heilig and Hoff [1] have shown that the gastric secretions are easily affected by ordinary verbal suggestions of relish or disgust made before the subject starts to eat. Similarly, simple verbal suggestions of pleasant or unpleasant moods or emotions can alter the rate of secretions and the chemical content of the normal person's urine, though here the effect is noticeably greater when the subject's suggestibility has been increased by hypnogenic methods. [2]

Experiments carried out by Marx in hypnotic suggestion proved that the amount of urine secreted during the following hour can be artificially increased if the hypnotised subject is handed an empty glass and the suggestion is made to him

---

[1] *Beitrage zur Hypnotischen Beeinflussung der Magenfunction*, Medizinische Klinik, 21, pp. 162-3, 1925.

[2] *Deutsche Medizinische Wochenschrift*, 51, pp. 1615-6, 1925.

that he is drinking large quantities of water and enjoying it.[3] But with naturally suggestible subjects the same effects were achieved by non-hypnotic suggestion. It can be seen from this that the need for control-experiments is imperative if we are to be allowed to compare the subject's reactions when in his normal state and his reactions when hypnotised. Obviously they are bound to vary with each individual, and to a certain extent with each different operator.

A good illustration of the use of control-experiments is provided by Levine.[4] He successfully induced local analgesia by hypnotic suggestion and pricked the affected area with a needle. This normally painful stimulus failed to produce the usual alteration in electrical potential known as the psychogalvanic response. Waking suggestion, he found, could not prevent the psychogalvanic response from occurring. He then tried another experiment : he suggested *the hallucination* of being pricked with a needle ; this immediately produced a psychogalvanic response. Most operators in the past would have been content to publish this last effect as yet another spectacular example of hypnotic suggestion ! Levine, however, next proceeded to carry out control-experiments and found that precisely the same response occurred with non-hypnotic suggestion.

The conclusion to which the above-mentioned experiments lead us is that with subjects who are naturally suggestible the effects of waking suggestion are often far more striking than is generally recognised and that in general hypnotic experimenters have mistakenly regarded these effects as peculiar to hypnosis.

The question arises as to whether such psychological stimuli as suggestion can produce effects which are beyond the normal powers of the subject. The answer is that hypnotic suggestion is merely one of many psychological stimuli which can produce such effects ; it can produce effects which are beyond the normal control of the will, but

---

[3] *Untersuchungen uber den Wasserhaushalt.* II. *Mitteilung. Die Psychische Beeinflussung des Wasserhaushaltes*, Klinische Wochenschrift, 5, pp. 92-4, 1926.

[4] Levine, M., *Psychogalvanic Reaction to Painful, Stimuli in Hypnotic and Hysterical Anaesthesia*, Bulletin of the John Hopkin's Hospital, 1930, pp. 331-339.

usually only in individuals who are suggestible above the average or who tend to latent or actual hysteria. Suggested analgesia is one such effect, which finds a close parallel in hysterical analgesia. If the right subjects and the correct technique are used, suggestion may also increase a subject's physical strength or endurance. There is nothing surprising in this. Other psychological stimuli such as fear, or desire for reward or praise, can produce the same effects.

There is also the vexed question whether hypnosis facilitates the recall of events which have been forgotten by the subject. Can hypnosis, in fact, improve the memory? Modern investigation shows that with the normal person hypnosis has, if anything, a slightly deleterious effect on the memory. With hysterical subjects, on the other hand, especially cases of hysterical amnesia, the effect of hypnosis on the ability to recall past events is often very striking. Reports of hysterical subjects being able, through hypnotic suggestion, to recall memories of their foetal existence, or even of extreme infancy, can be rejected.

COLLECTIVE HYPNOSIS

There is still much discussion as to whether collective hypnotic suggestion is possible—whether one man can effectively use hypnotic suggestion on a large number of people simultaneously. Despite much that has been written to the contrary, this feat has been repeatedly performed by vaudeville hypnotists. One trick, used by a well known English vaudeville hypnotist, Casson, is for the audience to place their hands, with fingers interlocked, firmly down on the crown of their head, palms upwards. After a number of demonstrations of hypnotic suggestion on the stage, considerable numbers of the audience will be readily susceptible to any suggestion made by the hypnotist, so that when he announces that many of them will find it impossible to move their hands apart, a fair percentage of the audience—sometimes as many as a hundred or more—find themselves unable to do so until the hypnotist tells them to move them. There is no doubt at all that under favourable conditions collective suggestion can be extremely effective. In primitive peoples strong delusions, illusions, and possibly visual hallucinations, can be suggested *en masse*—the suggestion receiving extra force through the resulting contagion of ideas and emotions to which crowds of people are invariably subject.

The phrase " collective hypnotic suggestion " is, of course, only applicable in instances where the operator uses a hypnogenic technique in inducing an abnormal degree of suggestibility in his crowd of subjects. Usually " collective suggestion " is the more appropriate term. It is of great interest in this connection to note that in primitive communities genuine hypnogenic techniques are frequently the rule when the shaman or medicine man requires to exercise collective suggestion, monotonous chanting and the rythmic beating of the tom-toms taking the place of the less exacting methods of the western hypnotic operator.

It is perhaps a comment on the times that the British Broadcasting Corporation has banned hypnotism from the television screen. This followed a private test in 1946 in which Casson televised his ability as a hypnotist. Three of the audience of B.B.C. television engineers were soon in a deep hypnotic sleep. Two of them went into so deep a sleep that it required Casson in the flesh to awaken them. Effective hypnotic suggestion by television leaves us no reason to doubt that it could be done by means of a cinematograph film as well. Some psychotherapists have used gramophone records of their voices giving suggestions appertaining to sleep to patients suffering from insomnia. The success of this method depends on the patient having been given hypnotic suggestion a number of times previously by the operator in person.

FALLACIES CONCERNING HYPNOTISM

There is a widespread belief among the general public that to allow oneself to be hypnotised is to " surrender one's will " to another person. Within a very limited sense this is certainly true if one ignores the ambiguity of the terms involved ; for during the time that the subject is hypnotised his normal faculty of volition is largely in abeyance. Nevertheless this is only a very temporary affair, although with post-hypnotic suggestion it may be considered to have an extended influence.

In primitive society, however, suggestion can wreak havoc with the mind of the individual by working on fears and superstitions, inculcated since infancy. But there again hypnosis is not generally the means whereby the suggestion is implanted. To be hypnotised too frequently *may* result in harm, particularly in the case of hysterics, and to be hypnotised by unscrupulous persons is certainly a thing to be avoided on principle. But in any event the harm possible through hypnosis is extremely limited in civilised societies, and is confined almost entirely to people with a high degree of hysteria in their make up. While the average person has nothing to fear in allowing himself to be hypnotised, the effects on primitive and superstitious minds may be precisely the reverse, particularly if the hypnotist is malevolently or vindictively inclined.

Normally the hypnotised subject will not carry out actions which are contrary to his sense of what is criminal or immoral. This mechanism of self-protection under hypnosis has built up a belief that it is absolutely impossible to persuade naturally honest and normal persons to commit criminal offences at the instigation of the operator. While this is generally true, experiments have shown that by using certain specialised hypnotic techniques some subjects can undoubtedly be compelled to carry out criminal actions unwittingly.[1] It would be impossible, however, to make any normal subject carry them out unless he had first consented to experiments in hypnosis.

There is no truth in the belief that once the hypnotist has induced a deep hypnotic sleep the subject may never wake up. In primitive societies this might conceivably be possible although there is no direct evidence to affirm this. In modern society, however, such an occurence is out of the question ; if the operator does not awaken the subject, the latter will awaken himself after a few hours, though with

[1] Wells, W. R., *Experiments in the Hypnotic Production of Crime*, Journal of Psychology, 1941, 11, pp. 63-102.

Brenman, M., *Experiments in the Hypnotic Production of Anti-Social and Self-Injurious Behaviour*, Psychiatry, 1942, Vol. V, pp. 49-61.

deeply hysterical subjects the time taken to awake may last a day or longer if left to themselves ; a great deal depends on how tired the subject is at the time.

The cataplectic state, either rigid or " plastic " (when the operator can bend the limbs into any sort of fantastic position without much resistance and leave them there without moving), is easily achieved, even in comparatively light stages of hypnosis. In the deeper stages of hypnosis, cataplexy can become so rigid that some subjects of ordinary strength can support the outstretched body only by the head and ankles and can further support the weight of several stone on the abdomen without collapsing.

HYPNOTISM AND THE BRAIN

" Plastic " cataplexy can also be induced in such animals as crayfish, frogs and snakes by monotonous stroking of the back or belly. In some of Pavlov's experiments, this strange form of cataplexy was observed in dogs and was usually brought about by the monotony of repeated sensory stimuli and the general boredom resulting from the experiments. The dog would go into a kind of trance, standing perfectly erect and motionless, sometimes for hours at a time. There was no relaxation of the muscles as is found in true sleep, and if the legs were moved into a new position they would remain there. The dog's salivary glands could be made to excrete copious saliva when the appropriate sound or smell stimulus was applied, showing that at least a part of the dog's brain was in full operation. With chimpanzees hypnosis can be induced by " human " methods.

From such experiments Pavlov was led to formulate a theory of hypnosis and its relation to normal sleep. The *cortex* of the brain, often referred to as " the grey matter," is the outer layer of the brain, and is the part responsible for all our thinking, rationalisation, judgment, and discrimination. The subcortical centres of the brain look after all our automatic activities such as retaining our balance and co-ordinating our muscles. Sleep, according to Pavlov, involves almost complete " inhibition " of the activity of both the cortex and the subcortical centres. He believed that hypnosis involves the inhibition of the cortex only, leaving the automatic functions of the lower centres of the brain without the control normally provided by the cortex.

Pavlov's neurological explanation succeeds only in explaining certain very limited espects of hypnosis and his general theory that hypnosis is a partial sleep of the cerebral functions is no longer tenable. Yet judgment and discrimination were among the last faculties to emerge in the scale of biological evolution, and, as has been observed in mental and physical disease involving the brain, they are the first faculties to become impaired. It is possible that in many hypnotic effects we witness the partial obliteration of those acquirements of the brain which were the last to develop during the course of evolution.

If it were asked whether there was any one mental faculty through which the hypnotist mainly operated to bring about his effects, the answer would probably be that it was through the imagination. The effects of imagination upon mental and physical processes can be very great, as is well known, and the hypnotic operator appears to be able to make the mechanism of imagination work overtime.

Modern science has established beyond all cavil that imagination and all other psychological processes possess a physiological basis. A physiological explanation of suggestion, however, is still a very long way from being evolved. Great advances in our knowledge are required before we can even hope to resolve this problem. As a pointer, however, it may be noted that hypnotic suggestion can produce certain effects on the brain by psychological means which can normally be produced in healthy persons only by the use of drugs. General hypnotic anaesthesia is one example.

Since all psychological processes have a physiological, and hence physical, basis, we are not really dealing with two ultimately inseparable processes, *viz.* the physical and the psychological. All ultimately depends on changes in the electro-biochemistry of the brain and nervous system. Both morphine and hypnotic suggestion may disconnect the pain-perceiving element in the cerebrum without affecting the peripheral nerve centres, and we cannot doubt that we are faced with related physiological processes any more than we can doubt the relatedness of the processes involved in the production of visual hallucinations by drugs and those found in psychogenic insanity.

It is likely that susceptibility to suggestion is related to the facility with which a subject reacts to certain narcotics such as opium. Eastern peoples can be hypnotised with comparative facility and " it is a fact of experience that in comparison with the brains of Europeans, the brains of the people of Eastern Asia are far more sensitive to the distillation products of opium."[2] Such highly speculative topics, however, had best be left to future research.

[2] Hesse, E. *Narcotics and Drug Addiction*, p. 20. N.Y. 1946.

Chapter Seven

HALLUCINATIONS—VISIONS AND VOICES

T HE TERM " HALLUCINATION " was coined by the French psychiatrist Jean Esquirol in 1838. From time to time during the preceding centuries isolated attempts had been made to clarify the nature of hallucinations, but the views put forward were seldom accepted. As long ago as the seventh century Alexander of Tralles, a famous Byzantine physician, recognised the existence of hallucinations and proposed methods to cure them. Until comparatively modern times hallucinations have generally been credited with an occult significance. They have given rise to beliefs in magical or divine powers of the percipient, and have sometimes played a considerable role in altering the course of history—the hallucinatory voices and visions of Joan of Arc being one example. Today the cult of crystal gazing, or scrying, still draws great numbers of people to believe in the occult powers of certain individuals ; a correct understanding of the psychological basis of crystal and other types of " vision " would do a great deal to dispel such irrational beliefs. Many a tale of ghosts or apparitions would never have arisen if the true nature of such phenomena had first been appreciated.

Hallucinations mainly take two forms—auditory and visual. True hallucinations are genuine perceptual sensations, that is to say the individual concerned really experiences the sights and sounds which constitute the hallucination. Broadly speaking, the difference between normal vision and a visual hallucination lies in the fact that whereas normal visual perception is brought into existence by the stimulation of electromagnetic light rays impinging upon the retina of the eye, such stimulation is absent in the case of hallucinatory perception—the percipient experiences the sensation of seeing a figure, a scene or an object, without the normal stimuli provided by electromagnetic radiations. Similarly, in the case of auditory hallucinations, the percipient may clearly hear sounds and voices without the stimuli provided by the atmospheric vibrations which constitute sound waves. The visual or auditory percepts contained in the hallucination thus have no corresponding existence in the outside world. They are produced autopsychically, by the subject's own mental processes.

The difference between hallucinations and *illusions* should be clearly understood. Hallucinations may be defined as genuine perceptual sensations which arise when no stimulus is acting on the appropriate sense organ. An illusion on the other hand, may be defined as a misinterpretation of an actual sense-impression ; in the case of an optical illusion the percipient actually sees an object but mistakes its actual form, as when in the distance a cow is clearly seen which on closer approach is recognised to be nothing but a bush. There are, of course, all degrees of variation between an illusion and a pure hallucination.

In the case of a sane person hallucinations may or may not involve *delusion*, i.e. belief in the reality of the object perceived. Amongst the insane, as for example with schizophrenics (who frequently suffer from persistent hallucinations or *hallucinosis*), failure to recognise the figures or voices as unreal is the rule rather then tha exception. But even among the sane, as in the case of some who suffer from hysterical maladies, the more vivid and persistent the hallucinations the greater the tendency to believe in their reality.

Generally speaking, provided that the percipient has a reasonably rational outlook on life, he recognises a spontaneous hallucination as something which has no existence apart from his own mind. With some uneducated people or in primitive societies, however, the question of the reality or non-reality of hallucinatory visions and voices seldom arises ; they simply accept them at face value without further speculation. On the other hand, eminently sane

people who have occasionally experienced visual hallucinations have often taken the greatest pleasure and interest
in them while fully recognising their psychological origin.

Joan of Arc, a peasant girl, experienced hallucinatory
voices and visions of angels ; under their inspiration she was
led to the command of the French army which defeated
the English. Socrates, too, had his hallucinatory *daemon*
voice which warned and guided him. St. Paul's great hysterical crisis on the Damascus main road, in which he experienced the hallucination of seeing Jesus and hearing a voice
which succinctly expressed his own hitherto repressed and
emotionally supercharged doubts, is an excellent instance
of a hallucination. St. Paul's conversion to the new faith
was hammered home still further by the sudden functional
blindness which resulted from his hysterical attack and
of which he was eventually cured by a combination of
suggestion and resolution of mental strain—in accordance
with accepted psychiatric principles of today. It is possible
that Christ himself, in common with many other great
religious mystics, experienced visual and auditory hallucinations. This, however, is difficult to verify with any
certainty in view of the unreliability of many of the New
Testament texts.

The great majority of sensory hallucinations are found
among the insane and in certain affections of the brain.
In *delirium tremens* for example, which is due to chronic
alcoholic poisoning, hallucinations of rats, spiders, flames
or snakes occur with peculiar frequency ; these hallucinations are often of such a terrifying character that the patient
will scream with terror and struggle frenziedly in order to
escape from them. Epileptic seizures, too, are often accompanied by highly fanciful hallucinations which are occasionally beautiful or even noble in character.

Some of the most interesting of hallucinatory phenomena
are to be found in cases where the brain is affected by injury,
tumours, or surgical operations. In such instances hallucinations of vision, hearing, taste, or smell are not uncommon;
visual hallucinations appear in that side of the visual field
opposite to that in which the affected temporal lobe of the
brain is situated. Rosett describes how a lady who had
had a large tumour of the right temporal lobe experienced

many bizarre visual hallucinations which were always observed to the left. They usually consisted of people behaving very oddly, as, for example, a woman riding on horseback with a sheet of music propped in front of her and using her hands as though she played the piano on the horse's neck.[1]

As just noted, hallucinations of hearing and vision are common in several types of insanity.[2] Uncinate hallucinations—hallucinations of taste and smell—and tactile hallucinations, e.g. of crawling bugs or insects or of being pinched by " devils ", also occur. Auditory hallucinations are, however, by far the commonest. Many psychotics have chronic hallucinations of voices reviling them in the most obscene terms, mocking them or even urging them on to suicide. Other psychotics experience never-ending visions of devils, angels, the figures of their imagined persecutors, animals, or a whole phantasmagoria of the utmost complexity. Yet other patients may continuously experience awful tastes and smells (cacosmia) which make it nearly impossible to eat their food. Auditory hallucinations are sometimes in the very old during the phase prior to death ; not uncommonly they will hold prolonged conversations with their long departed husbands or wives and may be heard urging them to " speak more clearly ".

Among the sane, spontaneous visual hallucinations, though rare, appear to occur more often when the eyes are open and in the light. Less frequently reported are visual hallucinations when the eyes are shut or when darkness prevails. although more than one " ghost " or " apparition " has probably received its genesis as a self-luminous hallucinatory figure in the dark or one which appeared in a luminous mist.

Hallucinatory sounds or voices often appear to the percipient to come from outside of him, and even from certain well-defined locations in space. Others appear to hear the voices within their own heads or chests. Until comparatively modern days these voices were invariably attributed to devils, spirits, angels, God or the Devil, according to

---

[1] Rosett, J., *The Mechanism of Thought, Imagery and Hallucination*, p. 160, N.Y. 1939.

[2] " Insanity " is mainly a popular or legal term. " Psychosis " is its medical equivalent.

their general tone or content. Socrates' *daemon*, whose advice and monitions he valued so highly, was of the " internal " sort.

The vividness and clarity of genuine hallucinatory perceptions are more often than not equal to those of normal vision and audition. The painter Montana used to see the picture he was about to paint so vividly in front of him that he was obliged to request anyone standing between himself and the hallucinatory figure or scene to stand aside. Often enough a sane percipient only realises the hallucinatory nature of what he has " seen " after the experience has passed. This is not surprising since visual hallucinations are often projected with an amazing sense of perspective and reality equal to that experienced in normal vision.

Among the sane, spontaneous hallucinations may occur once in a lifetime and last only for a second or two, or they may occur more frequently when their genesis is of hysterical origin, and last for several minutes or even longer. Sometimes more than one of the senses is affected, as in those cases where the hysterical subject appears to see, and hold conversations with, his hallucinatory visitants, and even feel their touch. Amongst the insane, tri-sensory hallucinations are probably not uncommon, although this is difficult to assess since psychotic hallucinations are almost invariably intermixed with the patient's delusions.

It is sometimes claimed that hallucinations can be divided, superficially, into two types ; those which are totally fanciful and which bear little or no rational relation to the environment at the time—e.g. the schizophrenic who sees angels with blazing swords engaged in aerobatics ; and those less common hallucinations which fit into their physical background without much noticeable incongruity or anomaly. In point of fact, such " rational " hallucinations, often commented upon for the remarkable facility with which they are adapted to the immediate physical environment, are generally the product of delusion, dreamlike states, or sensory illusion. They are best evidenced with purported hallucinable hysterics who have been hypnotised ; if a figure of a friend or acquaintance is suggested by the operator to be in the room, the figure will apparently appear to the subject to be perfectly normally behaved, will sit down in the chair, flick cigarette ash into the ash tray and even cast a shadow on the walls ; there appears little or no incongruity of presentation.   Such " hallucinations " as these, however, seldom involve actual sense-imagery.

There has always in the past been great confusion on the subject of hypnotic and hysterical hallucinations, and it is still manifest in much of the contemporary literature of psychopathology.   A genuine sensory hallucination, properly so-called, invariably results from the disfunction of the cerebral mechanism pertaining to sensory perception. The perception-mechanism of the brain starts operating of its own accord, as it were, without the external stimulus of light waves, sound waves, etc., which are normally necessary for its operation.   Such disfunctions of the cerebral perception-mechanism are due to a number of different causes : amongst the more common are the effects produced by drugs, cerebral injury or disease, surgical operations on the brain, and different types of psychosis which result in deleterious changes in the cerebral functions.   Many of the hallucinations of the insane are attributable to delusions or sensory illusions, which may be so intense as to render the dichotomy of little significance for most practical purposes.

Normal healthy people may also experience an *occasional* sensory hallucination ; but the perception-mechanism of the brain is not easily disrupted, for it is too well geared to the incoming nervous impulses which arrive from the sensory nerve-terminals all over the body.   When otherwise healthy people experience genuine sensory hallucinations the cause, is usually found in some temporary toxaemia, extreme fatigue or prolonged fasting.   Intense emotion may sometimes result in genuine hallucinations through its effects on the brain, particularly the emotion of fear, although most reported cases of hallucinations brought about by this factor are generally attributable to vivid sensory illusions.

In hypnosis and hysteria genuine sensory hallucinations are a rarity.   With certain hysterics they do undoubtedly occur, but the great majority of hysterical hallucinations are the product of vivid sensory illusions, delusions, eidetic imagery and drowsy or dreamlike states of consciousness.

Hypnotic hallucinations, so called, are generally due to suggested delusion—i.e. the subject may *believe* he is seeing or hearing something when in fact he is not ; more frequent, perhaps, are those apparent hallucinations of the hypnotised subject which are due to miming or acting and which may or may not be accompanied by some degree of subjective delusion. With hysterics who are subject to occasional sensory hallucinations, however, it seems probable that hypnotic suggestion may induce actual hallucinatory sense-imagery.

Hysterical and hypnotic hallucinations are, in general, pseudo-hallucinations and should be rigidly distinguished from the genuine sensory hallucinations caused by the disfunction of the cerebral perception-mechanism. Nevertheless, there is no broad distinguishing line between the pseudo-hallucinations and the hallucination involving actual sense-imagery. There is to be observed a fine series of gradations often impossible to analyse since the degree of subjective delusion present is so difficult to assess. Elements of all three factors may be involved in what appears to be only a sensory hallucination, all finding a common meeting ground in the vagaries of memory, imagination, perception and the mechanisms which subsume them.

Many psychiatrists hold the view that genuine hallucinations under the influence of hypnotic suggestion never occur at all, that the subject merely speaks and acts the part indicated by the suggestions of the operator, with or without accompanying subjective delusions. That this is generally the case is certainly true, but as it is generally accepted that hysterical hallucinations occur in certain instances, there is no real reason to suppose that with certain hysterical subjects hallucinations may not be induced by suggestion, particularly if the emotions are strongly affected.

The view that genuine sensory hallucinations are brought about *only* when the physiological structure of the brain is affected by marked psychosis, drugs, toxic substances, cerebral lesions, surgical operations or delirium, is largely due to the failure to appreciate the real distinction between physiological and psychological functions. To say that hallucinations cannot be brought about through psychological causes alone is to ignore the fact that all psychological functions have a physiological basis. It is well-known that the effects of some psychological stimuli, e.g. fear, on the body's physiological functions can be extreme. The same physiological effects can often be brought about by the use of chemical drugs. Again, it is possible to induce a psychological state of extreme fear in a subject simply by the injection of a chemical drug! In fact, in view of the relationship between the physiological functions of the brain and that aspect of them which we term " psychological," there is no apparent reason why the same disfunction of the cerebral processes which is brought about by drugs or other physical causes and which leads to the emergence of hallucinations, may not also be brought about by disruptive psychogenic factors, e.g. hysteria or suggestion.

From the point of view of the study of occultism, delusory or *pseudo* hallucinations which are due to suggestion, hysteria or other psychogenic factors possess an importance and significance equal to the genuine sensory hallucination. Suggestion can result in the subject *believing* he has experienced a sensory hallucination when in fact he has not. Suggestion can furthermore make the subject act *as if he were* experiencing a sensory hallucination. Again, the border-line between dreams and hallucinations becomes tenuous where there is drowsiness or fatigue, and a dreamlike experience is often remembered forcibly as an hallucination; there are several examples in psychological literature where a dream figure or object was prolonged into what was apparently a vivid waking hallucination, lasting several seconds after the dreamer had opened his eyes.

Another form of pseudo-hallucination sometimes occurs when an inward reminiscence, which arises by virtue of some fresh idea-association, combines with an optical *after-image* to produce a hallucinatory effect of surprising vividness. Vivid optical or auditory illusions, the illusory nature of which is not suspected by the subject, may also be classified as pseudo-hallucinations for the purpose of the present chapter. The interesting phenomenon of eidetic imagery may conveniently be included under the same heading.

Hallucinations and pseudo-hallucinations possess a common characteristic in relation to occultism in that both types may produce the same superstitious reactions from the percipient. The superstitious Tunisian peasant who experiences a sensory hallucination of seeing his dead son will believe that he saw the boy's spirit. Likewise grief over his bereavement may well induce a momentary optical illusion under the right circumstances, probably with the same result. If he visits a local soothsayer who hypnotises him, the consequence will be the same whether genuine sensory hallucinations were induced or whether the soothsayer merely convinced him by suggestion that he *had* seen his son. In either case the report goes round the neighbourhood that the peasant in question has seen his son's spirit or ghost.

From the psychological standpoint it is obviously of great importance to know for certain whether sane individuals, in whatever part of the world, can be made to experience genuine sensory hallucinations through the operation of suggestion. From the standpoint of the investigator of occultism this question is not so important. In many instances circumstances render it impossible to establish whether the suggestion has resulted in a hallucination or a pseudo-hallucination. It is sufficient to note that the latter are fully as capable of providing a basis for the origin and perpetuation of occult ancedotes and superstitions as the former.

Oriental literature and African tales of the occult contain numerous references to soothsayers, witches and witch-doctors who have the power to summon or " conjure " the spirit of a dead man before the eyes of a bereaved relative. The basis of such tales need not always be attributed solely to common trickery, though the reputation of a spirit-conjuring shaman generally rests on his ability to deceive his clients ; the modern cult of spiritualism provides thousands of such examples, as will be seen in a later chapter. The possibility of suggested hallucination or pseudo-hallucination is one which cannot be ignored and there appears plenty of evidence that this was not uncommon in the ancient world. The ease with which hysterical subjects can be made to experience hallucinations or pseudo-hallucinations in this way lends added support to this idea.

The French physician Liébault gives an account of how,

under the influence of his suggestion, a hypnotised hysterical subject apparently experienced the hallucination of seeing his dead father. The subject sat still for a while ; after several minutes he arose and, with eyes fixed, turned towards the door of the room. Liébault and the other witnesses " saw him proffer his hand and deposit a kiss in the void."[1] Whether or not this was a case of genuine sensory hallucination or merely a pseudo-hallucination, the effect of similar exhibitions on the minds of simple and superstitious audiences needs no emphasis.

Hallucinations have undoubtedly played a large part in sustaining outmoded superstitious beliefs. Among hysterics and the insane, hallucinations often tend to reflect current beliefs and ideas of the age. Many hysterics during the middle ages and even later had hallucinatory visions of the devil himself ; in insane asylums today such cases are not uncommon. The beliefs in elves, brownies, fairies, sprites, gnomes, goblins, imps, leprechauns and other products of the childlike imagination of our ancestors doubtless received new impetus from time to time by individuals seeing small hallucinatory figures.

Here is a *modern* case of an intelligent educated lady who experienced such an hallucination. In this instance the woman had experienced occasional sensory hallucinations over a long period of time, some of which were highly fanciful in character : " One summer she was campling with her two children on a nearby mountain. They spent the night in the loft of a barn, sleeping on blankets spread on hay. She was uncomfortable and could not fall asleep. Suddenly there appeared before her diminitive human figures, about a foot tall, who were pointing at her children. Although she knew they were unreal, nevertheless she recongnised them as fairies and thought of waking up the children to show them the sight. She arose, leaning on her elbow, hesitated, and finally desisted from waking the children. The figures then disappeared."[2]

Amongst primitive peoples visual hallucinations often play a very important part in their rites and divination practices.

---

[1] *Du Sommeil et des Etats Analoques*, pp. 259 and 282.
[2] Rossett, J., *The Mechanism of Thought, Imagery and Hallucination*, p. 255, N.Y. 1939.

The art of scrying or crystal-gazing is frequently adapted for these purposes. The means to induce visual hallucinations or " visions " are many and varied. Mystics in the past have found that total sexual abstinence was conducive to hallucinations often of an ecstatic or *euphoric* character. Intense fasting, too, is still resorted to among religious cults all over the world as an aid in producing the desired visions. Both these methods are used in conjunction, as a rule, and have been employed by priests, ascetics, and medicine-men in most religions and mystical cults since time immemorial. Prolonged sexual repression may easily lead to a hysterical state of mind with its consequent tendencies to dissociation, particularly in cases where the repression is extreme to the extent of banishing completely all erotic thoughts and imagery. Extended fasting leads to light-headedness and eventually to delirium.

Amongst Asiatic and African cults sexual continence and severe fasting usually constitute the preparatory stage in the induction of hallucinatory visions ; they are interpreted as " purification " preparations which are carried out ostensibly to enable the medicine-man or shaman to approach the gods or spirits without fear. The actual induction of sensory hallucinations are often brought about by taking drugs or working the subject into a state of frenzy by orgiastic dancing, beating of drums and tom-toms, yelling and shriek-ing, castigation, or any or all of these.

The notorious whirling dervishes induce ecstatic visions —or, more correctly, euphoric hallucinations—by a peculiar form of " dancing " in which they spin at extreme speed like a top, finally falling exhausted or in a state of hystero-epilepsy. Other means of inducing hallucinations during the Middle-Ages were lengthy " vigils " without food. Partial strangulation which brings partial cerebral anaemia and eventual loss of consciousness is another method some-times used in primitive societies to induce hallucinations.

Fasting used to play an important part in many of the initiation ceremonies of the American Indians. At the end of the fasting period the young man began to experience hallucinations, and when he saw an animal in his visions it became his " medicine." In some tribes he was obliged to kill an animal similar to the one he saw and carry about with him a claw, feather, or some other part of it, which he must not lose on pain of forfeiting his " medicine."

It is significant to note that the word " shaman " is derived from the Sanscrit word meaning " ascetic." The relationship between sexual continence and the induction of ecstatic hallucinatory states has been appreciated for thousands of years. The visions produced by the aid of such means may take the form of erotic fantasies or else emerge in a variety of guises based on sexual symbolism. It is the sexual component which is partly responsible for the euphoria in many " ecstatic " states.

As J. L. Maddox has pointed out, the shaman or medicine-man is not always a paragon of virtue and sex morality ; he is sometimes the reverse. It is when he wishes to induce theoleptic fits that he practices continence. On his recovery from the theopneustic trance, his repressed emotions sometimes explode with abnormal violence. These emotions having been, as it were, diverted into a foreign channel, and meanwhile increased in force, when the reason for their repression no longer exists, break back into their normal course with intensified vehemence. Says an acute observer : ' I know no fact of pathology more striking and even terrifying than the way in which the phenomena of the ecstatic state may be plainly seen to bridge the gulf between the innocent fooleries of ordinary hypnotic patients, and the depraved and repulsive phenomena of nymphomania and satyriasis.'[1] By reason of the facility with which the ecstatic state passes into abnormal sexual emotion, it not frequently happens that after their return to normal consciousness the representatives of the gods are guilty of unspeakable dissoluteness.[2]

Anstie's observation, which Maddox quotes above, gains added weight and interest from the fact that he wrote it before Freud had formulated his *libido* theories of neurosis.

The use of drugs to produce hallucinations, either alone or in combination with other methods, is found among all peoples in all ages. The priests of ancient Mexico drank a delirium-inducing liquid called ololuiqui. Today in parts of Mexico the natives take peyotl (mescal) or the " snake

---

[1] Anstie, *Lectures on Disorders of the Nervous System,* The Lancet, 1873, p. 40.

[2] Maddox, J. L., *The Medicine Man,* p. 48.

plant." The Samoyeds of Siberia utilise poisonous toad-stools for the same purpose. One such toadstool known as fly-agaric, or scientifically as *amanita muscaria*, is bright red with white spots. Its intoxicating properties are retained nearly intact when passed out with the urine. The toadstool being rare, the Samoyed saves his urine to consume it later, or alternatively one of his friends will wait to catch the urine in a vessel and then drink it.[3] Several individuals may become intoxicated in turn by this means before the drug loses its potency.

In the Orient the plant *peganum harmala L.* is sometimes used in place of hashish. In human beings it results in a degree of euphoria and colourful hallucinations, but in dogs the effect is as if the animal experiences hallucinations of a frightening or terrifying nature.[4] Hashish, or Indian hemp, may also produce hallucinations in some individuals ; Persian dervishes are known to use it. One of the most effective hallucination-producing drugs is that used by the Indians of Columbia, Central America, which goes by the name of Yagé and which results in a state of strong delirium. The natives believe in its clairvoyant efficacy and often resort to it when wishing to trace thieves or lost articles.

All the world over we find varieties of deadly nightshade of which the leaves, roots of flowers are used to induce states of consciousness conducive to hallucinations. It was the deadly nightshade, dryly named *belladonna*—" fair lady "—by alchemists, which medieval witches used for inducing hallucinations. Such hallucinations frequently take on a sexual tone. Large doses of the drug are liable to result in irresponsible sexual behaviour, a fact which gave it a great reputation as an ingredient in medieval love potions. It is interesting to note, however, that atropine, the main activating substance in belladonna, produces a calming effect on habitual drunkards after a drunken sleep.[5]

The liquid *ololuiqui*, mentioned above, is produced from the seeds of *datura meteloides*, a plant which belongs to the same family as the deadly nightshade—the solanaceae. Ololuiqui was the fore-runner of the modern " truth drugs."

[3] Hesse, E., *Narcotics and Drug Addiction*, p. 107, N.Y., 1948.
[4] ibid., pp. 111-112.
[5] ibid., p. 104.

The beverage produces a pleasurable trance-like state and in this condition skilful questioning can elicit any information from the intoxicated person, a feature which is often found useful in native business transactions.

A large variety of modern drugs can be used to produce visual hallucinations. Although their significance in relation to occult beliefs and practices is nil, mention may be made of the drug *mescaline*. Until recently, this drug was obtained only from a spineless cactus which grows in north and central Mexico, known to the natives as peyotl. It has now been made synthetically in the U.S.A. The hallucinations resulting from mescaline may last for hours, and kaleidoscopic hallucinations in gorgeous colours are seen. The interweaving patterns of mosaics, landscapes, scenery and objects may present the subject with a jumbled, brilliant and ever changing tapestry whenever he closes his eyes. It is little wonder that the superstitious natives believed peyotl to be the gift of the gods and to be a means of achieving clairvoyant powers.

Vertigo and nausea generally precede or follow the hallucinations produced by mescaline, at least among western peoples. Despite this, there seems to be a growing tendency for this drug, which is not habit forming to become a vogue. The hallucinations have a similarity to those reported by people who have experienced hypnagogic hallucinations.

" Auras "

In the literature of spiritualism, theosophy and psychical research one may find frequent reference to " auras." Such auras may take a variety of forms, from circular haloes purportedly seen round the heads of individuals with a reputation for holiness of piety, to fulgent iridiscences of bright colours which " sensitives " are reported to see as emanating from other persons or animals or even inanimate objects, particularly magnets. Optical illusions, after-images, hysterical hallucination, delusions, suggestion, wishful-thinking, trickery and invention are the sole explanations of " aureole phenomena " in the case of sane individuals. Among psychotics, as might be expected, delusions and hallucinations of auras are not uncommon.

Experiments with hysterical subjects who claim to perceive auras quickly reveal their spurious character. Braid mentions one such subject, who whenever the idea was suggested, saw coruscating flames emanating from the poles of a magnet or wherever she imagined its influence to extend. Such cases were frequently reported in the psychological literature of the nineteeth century. Experiments showed, however, that the same " effects " were produced when non-metallic objects, disguised as magnets, were used.

Dr. W. G. Kilner of St. Thomas' Hospital, London, caused a good deal of speculation when he claimed to be able to see a semi-luminous aura surrounding the bodies of his patients, which showed marked colour changes according to the state of the patient's health. He used a specially made transparent dicyanin screen for the purpose. Other physicians tested the " Kilner screen " but did not observe anything unusual. One investigator writing in the British Medical Journal[1] made it clear that in most cases the illusion of the " human aura " could generally be attributed to after-image effects when seen with the naked eye, but that it was purely subjective when seen through the Kilner screen.

WARNING HALLUCINATIONS

There are instances reported from time to time of sane individuals who have experienced hallucinatory voices or visions which have warned them of approaching danger, forecast an illness, predicted an event, or directed a course of action. Bleuler has called these *teleological hallucinations*, a term which is somewhat unsatisfactory since it imparts a metaphysical flavour to what should be regarded as primarily the concern of medical psychology. A teleological hallucination is one which appears *prima facie* to serve some purpose or design. Such hallucinations do not require a theory of supernatural causes for their explanation, though spiritualists and others still argue to the contrary.

There are many ways in which tales of teleological hallucinations may arise. The great majority come under the general heading of the psychology of self-deception and wishful thinking, a subject which will be dealt with in another chapter. There are, however, many instances of hallucinations and dreams which were clearly related to subsequent events. Such, for example, is the *prodromal* hallucination or dream, in which premonition of unsuspected illness or disease is given to the subject ; he may, for example, be subconsciously aware of certain mild symptoms but unwilling for various reasons to recognise them for what they are—till a dream or an auditory hallucination brings his suppressed suspicions to his attention.

Prodromal symptoms, such as unusual lassitude, obscure pain or pruritus, might result, in the case of a hysterical patient, in an autoscopic hallucination of seeing himself ill in a hospital ward. Subsequently cancer or some other disease develops and the patient can then claim that he had warning of his disease " through a vision ", which he will doubtless attribute to occult or divine origin. Hallucinations showing a relative lying ill or dead were commonly reported in the nineteenth-century literature of psychical research and, in the few cases which were possibly authentic and veridical, may be attributed to previous impressions of the relative's state of health.

Coincidental hallucinations which purportedly occurred at the same time that a distant relative or friend died are open to a great number of suspicions. No case of such a coincidence has yet been reasonably proved.

Hallucinations, like dreams, may, naturally enough, suggest a course of action to the subject. He may ignore this factor and retrospectively believe that his dream or hallucination "prophesied" his subsequent actions. Again, circumstances of which the subject is aware, perhaps subconsciously, may rationally dictate a probable sequence of events ; a dream or hallucination occurs embodying one or more events in the sequence, and the subject may consequently believe that he experienced a forewarning by supernatural means.

Generally speaking, popular reports of teleological sensory hallucinations occurring in sane and healthy individuals must be accepted with the utmost reserve, although they may undoubtedly occur in certain types of hysteria, in incipient or borderline cases of psychosis, or in any proven case of intermittent hallucinosis whatever its cause. Genuine sensory hallucinations among the sane and healthy are a great rarity. On the other hand sensory illusions, dreams, pseudo-hallucinations and vagaries of memory may become so easily transmogrified into hallucinations by those who are looking for them !

Perhaps the least suspicious type of report is that in which the subject apparently experiences a sensory hallucination —generally a voice—warning him of immediate danger, such as a deep hole in his path at night or the proximity of an enemy or wild beast. Danger and fear, we know, can result in drastic physiological changes in the human organism. Therefore it is quite possible to believe that with some individuals a *subconscious* awareness of danger could result in an auditory or visual hallucination if the danger was extreme, and that by this device the individual in question could be made conscious of his peril. Another explanation, however, is that the sudden *consciousness* of danger evokes a surge of fear and a consequent hallucination or pseudo-hallucination, the actual sequence of the events being subsequently confused when later recalled to memory.

Subconscious ratiocination is a fact beyond dispute. Many a difficult problem is solved by merely " sleeping on it." There is some evidence to show that in individuals who have been subject to hysterical hallucinations subconscious ratiocination may dominate the form or content of the hallucinations, The hallucinatory voices of Joan of Arc, which advised her concerning her future course of action and estimated the course of events with fair accuracy, provide a historical example of this phenomenon ; so does the *daemon* voice of Socrates, who possessed marked tendencies to dissociation. The teleological character of many dreams, and also, we may suppose, of some hallucinations, may often be attributed to subconscious ratiocination in one form or another. Hallucinatory voices which give helpful advice appear to be related almost invariably to long-standing difficulties in the patient's life or to problems of adjustment. In borderline cases of psychosis such teleological hallucinations do not appear to be altogether uncommon.

In the literature of the Society for Psychical Research during the nineteenth century, reports appeared frequently of teleological and coincidental veridical hallucinations by sane and healthy individuals. It is a tribute to the increasingly critical standards of the Society's investigators that such reports are at present a rarity. Such tales are now confined mainly to the spiritualist journals, whose artful editors view wi'h scorn the celebrated principle of Occam.

COLLECTIVE HALLUCINATIONS

There is considerable evidence to show that among primitive peoples sensory hallucinations may be induced simply by the power of suggestion, particularly if the subject is under strong emotional stress, such as fear or intense anxiety. The mind may then become highly suggestible, and it is during such times that auto-suggestion, operating in the form of *expectancy*, may lead to the occurrence of hallucinations.

Expectancy, it is well known, is responsible for the majority of optical *illusions*. The individual who is waiting impatiently for a bus strains his eyes to read the distant number on the front as one approaches, and sees that it is No. 17—the one for which he is waiting. As it approaches, he sees that it is No. 24 and wonders why on earth he misread it so completely. This is a very common form of optical illusion.

Expectancy, however, which leads to a genuine visual hallucination is altogether a different matter. Extreme fright on hearing a noise might, in the case of a superstitious and simple minded person of a century ago, have resulted in a genuine visual hallucination of the very object which he imagined had caused the noise—perhaps a phantom apparition of some kind. Extreme fear may produce serious physiological reactions affecting the whole nervous system and circulation, and such physiological changes may produce effects on the brain analogous to delirium or insanity. Such extremes of emotion, however, were seldom present in all the best known cases collective hallucination during the past century.

Collective hallucination is a subject which has not been adequately studied. Literally scores of cases have been recorded and investigated by individuals well qualified to judge in other fields, yet medical psychology as a whole has contibuted little to the problem.

A century ago the mass of the world's population were far more credulous, superstitious and vulnerable to the effects of suggestion than they are today. Many generalisations and conclusions of psychologists and psychiatrists today are fully applicable only to a relatively small part of the world's resent population—that part confined to Europe, the Dominions, the United States and the upper and middle classes in the other countries of the world. Even in parts of Europe, in Sicily for example, the peasant mind is not very far removed from the minds of his peasant ancestors who lived centuries ago. When psychiatrists question whether in fact hallucinations can be induced by suggestion alone, it must not be forgotten that such viewpoints are based upon studies of the *relatively* non-suggestible inhabitants of civilised countries. Thanatomania (anthropological), or death due to suggestion alone, bears witness to the extreme effects on the mind of primitive man exerciseable by suggestion.

The individual in a crowd reverts more to the primitive than when he is alone. In a crowd the individual can become transformed into a savage as far as his thinking processes are concerned. Anyone who has ever heard the baying of the crowd at one of Hitler's rallies before the war, or even observed the reactions of a crowd at an American football game, can witness this for himself. The emotional hysteria which sweeps through a crowd, and the wildfire spread of absurd rumours which may become exaggerated out of all proportion within a few moments, are but two examples of the mutually reinforcing and reciprocal action of suggestion. Such forms of suggestion are seen at their most potent during times of religious fervour. It is not surprising therefore, to find that many tales of collective hallucinations occur in connection with churches or sacred statues and paintings.

One of the most frequent types of " miracle " reported is that of statues or painted portraits which have moved, even to the extent of stepping off the pedestal or out of their frames. Such stories have often been put down to mere fabrication or groundless superstition. But as Rosett has expressed it :

" The reports of mystics and of devotees about pictures and statues which moved and spoke like living persons and performed miracles are . . . not necessarily fraudulent. An understanding of the mechanism of attention and its relation to the state of falling asleep, and of the hallucinations associated with that state, offers a rational explanation of such reports." [1]

Where belief in miracles exists, evidence will always be forthcoming to confirm its existence. In the case of moving statues and paintings, the belief produces the hallucination and the hallucination confirms the belief. The same factors which operate for a single individual in the induction of hallucinations or pseudo-hallucinations may become even more effective in an excited or expectant crowd, and on occasion may result in mass hallucinations. This is not to say that any two people are capable of having precisely the same hallucination identical in every respect. But similar preconceptions and expectations can undoubtedly result in hallucinatory visions so alike that subsequent comparisons would not disclose any major discrepancy. Each individual's imagination necessarily makes its own particular contribution to the form and movement of each hallucination—for hallucinatory sensations of all types are the product of the individual's own mind. Accounts of comparatively dissimilar hallucinatory experiences often attain a spurious similarity by a process of harmonisation in subsequent recollection and conversation.

In 1919, at Limpias, Santander, in Spain, there occurred numerous cases of collective hallucination. Some of these were investigated by Professor A. Encinas of Santander University. Encinas approached Professor Jaensch in regard to these phenomena and together they came to the significant conclusion that the hallucinations had their basis in the vagaries of eidetic imagery.

The hallucinations in question were remarkable for their limited variety. They were concerned almost entirely with pictures of saints. The saints had moved and carried out various actions, including stepping out of their panels. Their eyes also were observed to move and certain of the pictures

[1] Rosett, J., *The Mechanism of Thought, Imagery and Hallucination*, pp. 211-212, N.Y. 1939.

appeared to drip blood. Naturally, when such reports spread, people for miles around flocked to the church where the " miracles " were taking place and stood gazing by the hour at the pictures. Jaensch writes that hundreds of sworn statements, including those of many educated and professional persons, bore witness to the reality of the hallucinations.

The hallucinatory " epidemic " lasted for many days. In such cases the scenes inside the church are of interest. The audience gazes at the pictures and from time to time someone will point a finger and cry out that the eyes are moving or that a drop of blood has appeared and is running down the saint's face. Others look eagerly and add their own exclamations and confirmations ; others fail to observe anything unusual.

Similar " miracles " occurred at Campocavallo in 1893, and at Rimini on five separate occasions between 1850 and 1905 ; here the eyes of the paintings were observed to move and to shed an occasional tear. In 1870 at Soriano, Calabria, occurred the celebrated miracles of the moving statue which appeared to move its hand and arm.

There is no doubt about these " miracles " being collective visual hallucinations of one type or another. Throughout history we hear of them—fiery crosses in the sky being a great favourite. Accounts by eyewitnesses who fail to observe anything out of the ordinary are of peculiar interest, for they see everyone around them straining their eyes and pointing excitedly towards nothing in particular with exclamations of wonder, frequently falling on their knees to give thanks for being vouchsafed such a " blessed sight."

While many of these individuals may experience a hallucination—probably eidetic in character—or compelling illusion, it is difficult to believe that all of them do ; most of them have probably persuaded themselves that they have seen the " miracles " ; with simple people this type of reaction is very common. Rather than admit they failed to see anything, they would imitate the lead given by those who did, and subsequently believe that they had in fact observed what they had originally only pretended to observe :

" Emotion is a great disturber of evidence. It confuses both the original observation and the memory of it. Certain details impress themselves vividly, while others, and the relations between them, are obscured. Memory will start with these characters, accentuate them, and thus a false colouring is given to the whole. Under very intense emotion memory may fail us altogether. The presence of a crowd often increases the bystander's disturbance. Emotion is heightened by being shared, excitement with its attendant confusion is intensi- fied, and chance words given an impetus to imagination. ' Did you see him skid ? ' says one, in a tone of perfect conviction, and others, who did not, promptly picture it, and at a later date cannot be con- vinced that they did not see it. In some cases a collective hallucina- tion is built up piecemeal in this way." [2]

In most instances of collective hallucination or illusion the main contributing factor must be sought in the emotional excitement at the time of its occurrence. There is a well- known case to illustrate this from the last century. The crew of a vessel were one evening frightened by what they took to be the ghost of a cook who had died some days previously.

" He was distinctly seen by all, walking on the water with a peculiar limp which had characterised him, one of his legs being shorter than the other. The cook, who had been recognised by so many, turned out to be a piece of wreck, rocked up and down by the waves." [3]

This example well illustrates the manner in which many stories of ghostly apparitions receive their genesis.

AUTOSCOPIC HALLUCINATIONS—DOPPELGANGERS AND " OUT-OF-THE BODY " EXPERIENCES

The tradition of the " human double " reaches back to the earliest days of the ancient Egyptians. In the Victorian era of romantic literature " doubles " or doppelgangers took on a variety of rôles, some of them of the guardian-angel type, others sinister and diabolical. In these stories the hero or

---

[2] Wolters, A. W. P., *The Evidence of our Senses*, p. 64.
[3] Parish, E., *Hallucinations and Illusions*, p. 311.

the villain came face to face with an exact replica of himself. This other " self " was often represented as his soul or his " destiny " and often appeared to him as a premonition of impending doom.

Another variation on the same theme is that of " out-of-the body " experiences, a frequent subject of psychical research. Authentic accounts of such experiences are comparatively numerous, and the authors of these accounts, amazed at a phenomenon altogether out of their ken, almost always present them with a mystical twist, often concluding that their souls have for a brief time left their bodies. In autoscopic hallucinations of this type the experient often has the vivid sensation of looking at his own body from a point exterior to it. Favourite times for such occurrences are at the crisis of a severe illness, during moments of extreme suffering—the subject's pain then appears to leave him—or while under an anaesthetic.

Reports frequently mention the subject's sensation of floating in the air over his own body ; a feeling of calm detachment usually accompanies these experiences. Patients claim to have witnessed their own surgical operations during such times. In very many cases the patient is reported as being, to all intents and purposes, in a state of total unconsciousness.

The average person, when confronted with stories of the " human double " and " out-of-the body " experiences will be inclined to strict disbelief and attribute the whole account to an over-stimulated imagination. Nothing could be further from the truth. Both these weird experiences find a common basis in the visual hallucination and analogous phenomena, though it must be admitted that the reason why such hallucinations take the form they do is not clear. Their impact on the imagination of ignorant or superstitious people, however, can well be imagined.

Until comparatively modern times almost any form of hallucination was attributed to the operation of occult powers, and today autoscopic hallucinations provide an excellent example of the type of phenomenon investigated by psychical research. Psychical researchers are attracted to such experiences by the occult significance which they believe they might possess ; the devotees of this pseudo-science have seldom been interested in hallucinations for their own sake but only for their supposed connection with the supernatural or " the paranormal." Such an attitude is reminiscent of the supernatural awe with which our not so remote ancestors regarded most forms of psychological anomoly.

Deprived of their halo of diablerie or enchantment, autoscopic hallucinations may be regarded more prosaically as psychological aberrations mainly due to delirium or hysteria. They may appear in the most irrelevant fashion. Jung, for example, reports a case of a lady, subject to hysterical dissociation, who had to have a splinter cut out of her finger. She may have drifted into an auto-hypnotic state for

" without any kind of bodily change she suddenly saw herself sitting by the side of a brook in a beautiful meadow, plucking flowers This condition lasted as long as the slight operation and then disappeared spontaneously." [1]

In such autoscopic hallucinations as the one just described the subject is fully conscious of himself as he is ; there is no loss of consciousness of self. He simply " sees " a facsimile of himself standing or sitting nearby. Usually these hallucinations are of short duration ; in other cases they appear to last a considerable length of time. Yet the time factor is difficult to estimate, for with some types of visual hallucinations—such as those induced by taking the drug mescaline for example—the time sense largely disappears and what appears to take an hour may in fact have lasted only a few minutes.

In the " out-of-the-body " type of autoscopic hallucination—an experience cultivated by some mystics and divines and referred to as *ekstasis* by Plotinus—consciousness of self assumes a peculiar form. Instead of the subject retaining awareness of himself as he normally exists, i.e. with his sense of self inseparable from his body and its sensations, he sees an hallucinatory image of himself and simultaneously experiences the vivid delusion that this hallucinatory image is in fact his real self ! The hallucin-

---

[1] Jung, C., *Collected Papers on Analytical Psychology*, p. 75.

ation and its accompanying subjective delusion appear to
be something like a dream in this respect, for in dreams it
is not an uncommon experience to see oneself as if from a
detached vantage point. The dream characteristics of
" out-of-the-body " hallucinations are further remarked
when it is recalled that most of them have been reported
as occurring while the subject was outwardly unconscious.
This again may be an error, and it is more than probable
that all such autoscopic hallucinations as these occur at
the moment of succumbing to unconsciousness or during
recovery from it ; no reliance whatsoever can be placed on
the subject's own estimation of the moment or duration
of his experience.

There are a number of theories purporting to account for
the peculiar nature of autoscopic hallucinations, but none
of them are fully satisfactory. They possess, without
doubt, more than one aetiology. Apart from hysteria
the main direct cause appears to be a shock of one sort
or another to the brain and nervous system.

It has been suggested that the characteristics of many
autoscopic hallucinations may be due to coenaesthetic
sensations. Apart from perceptions originating from the
five special senses, there are other bodily sensations which
reach the brain through the sympathetic nervous system,
viz. those sensations which, roughly speaking, indicate to
us our state of health and physical condition. The visceral,
muscular, glandular and nervous activities of our body
are registered in varying degree upon our consciousness by
sensations of physical well being, uneasiness, physical
alertness, tiredness, and all those other vague, often unde-
finable sensations, which have been termed *coenaesthetic*.
The sinking feeling in the pit of the stomach which the un-
practised orator experiences before he embarks on a public
speech is an excellent example of localised coenaesthesia.
It is well known that coenaesthetic impressions may give
rise to and direct the course of one's dreams ; the same
may be true in certain types of hallucinatory phenomena.

Cases have been reported, with no certainty of reliability
however, in which subjects see hallucinatory representations
of their own internal organs. Sometimes the patient concerned has perceived by means of the hallucinatory image,

the nature of the complaint he is suffering from—an adhesion, an internal ulcer, congestion of the bowel and other physiological ailments.

A case reported by Dr. Comar[1] is interesting in that the patient's hallucinatory image accurately represented foreign matter irritating and inflaming the transverse colon. The patient's hallucinations, which were of frequent occurrence, followed subsequent developments within the colon until recovery was complete. Naturally in such cases the questions to be resolved are whether the hallucinations in fact occurred at all; whether the patient's knowledge of the cause of the malady was gained by a highly discriminating faculty of the coenaesthetic sense presented to her consciousness via hallucinations; or whether the content of the hallucinations, if they occurred, was influenced by involuntary cues provided by the medical attendant.

To return to "out-of-the-body" autoscopic hallucinations, even the sanest individual may be tempted to find something savouring of mysticism in these experiences. One of their most extraordinary features is the way in which it sometimes appears to the subject as if his own "ego" has been transplanted to a location outside his body, from which vantage point he seems to see his body lying or moving below him. His "ego" often retains both the distance-senses of sight and hearing, though the latter is less commonly reported than the other.

Typical of such experiences is that of the tank officer whose vehicle was blown up by a mine and who was flung over a hedge into an adjoining field. He became suddenly conscious of floating in the air, from which point he saw his body lying injured, motionless and dishevelled below him. This hallucination may, as in very many other cases, have been a vivid dream. On the other hand, it may have been a hallucination experienced during the return to consciousness. The sensation of floating in the air was probably a direct result of his experience of being blown over the hedge—an episode, however, which he was subsequently unable to recollect. The vision of his wounded body may have been prompted by the realisation of what had happened

[1] *Revue Neurologique*, vol. 9, 1901, pp. 490-495.

to him, or it may have been brought about by his bodily
sensations during the process of recovering consciousness.

Under certain forms of shock, dreams may easily become
such vivid experiences as to combine many of the characteristics of a genuine waking hallucination. The difference
between dreams and hallucinations is largely one of degree :
whether or not they are brought about by the same mechanism, they are certainly closely related. Many cases have
been reported where a figure or an object in a dream has
been prolonged into a vivid waking hallucination lasting
several seconds after the dreamer has opened his eyes.

The vast majority of the hallucinations in which it seems
to the subject that he has actually left his own body are
found among psychotics. Only a small proportion of such
" extra-corporeal " hallucinations are autoscopic, however,
i.e. the visions which the subject experiences do not usually
include the illusion of seeing himself. This applies equally
to " extra-corporeal " experiences of the hysteric or psychasthenic. The autoscopic hallucination is merely an unusual
manifestation of " extra-corporeal " hallucinations and
delusions in general. Often the subject experiences the
hallucination of being drawn away from his body ; he leaves
it behind on the earth while he rapturously floats in starry
realms, listens to the music of the spheres, sees the spheres
themselves in beautiful colours, converses with spirits,
angels and even God himself.

Opposite types of hallucination may also occur, of course,
in which the patient descends into hell, is tormented by
imps and devils and meets the Devil in person. It is not
only among the insane that such types of hallucinations
occur. Hysterical individuals may also suffer the same
symptoms. The analogous visions which the brilliant
eighteenth century scientist and philosopher Emanuel
Swedenborg experienced in later life were due either to
hysteria or to incipient paranoia. Flournoy's Mlle. Smith
was a case in point.

Psychasthenic patients (i.e. patients suffering from certain
of a wide range of psychoneuroses not classifiable under
the heading of hysteria) often experience feelings of unreality,
loss of personality and delusions. Although hallucinations
do not generally occur in cases of ordinary psychasthenia,

delusions of the " double self " not infrequently do. " Feelings of unreality, depersonalization, and inadequacy always present rather conclusive evidence of a psychasthenic condition. Such a patient will usually describe his feelings somewhat as follows :

" There is a feeling of unreality about things ; although I recognize my customary surroundings, nevertheless there is a feeling of strangeness associated with them, they just don't appear naural. Often when I wake up or when I come in from the street my room appears strange ; I see my chair and bed, know they are mine, and yet it seems that I am seeing them for the first time. Also there frequently seems to be two of me instead of one ; I seem to be standing off looking at myself, watching and conjecturing about everything I do. At times I actually become embarrassed, so strongly do I feel that I am in the presence of a stranger who, however, is somehow a part of me. Finally, I an frequently distressed by a peculiar feeling that something about me is missing, that I have lost a part of myself, that I am incomplete." [2]

It is easy to imagine the form hallucinations might take if a psychasthenic patient suffering from sensations of depersonalisation were to become hallucinated as a result of a deterioration in his condition. A large proportion of his hallucinations would be of the autoscopic, " out-of-the-body " type.

Sensations of depersonalisation may become so extreme that the psychasthenic loses touch with reality. The term *acenesthesia* has been given to designate such states, the chief characteristic being that the patient feels that he has no material body. This symptom is sometimes found in certain types of paranoia.

The advocate of mysticism, occultism or spiritualism will prefer to reject the normal psychological explanation of autoscopic hallucinations in favour of his own primitive theories. He will point to the wealth of realistic detail pertaining to the hallucinatory scene in which the subject's own body was the central focus of attention. The patient who has had the experience of apparently witnessing an operation on his own body, for example, is not easily per-

[2] Fisher, V. E. *Introduction to Abnormal Psychology*, pp. 198-199.

suaded that it was of a hallucinatory character, that it was a vivid dream, or the product of delirium. He will simply assert that he saw himself lying on the operating table with eyes closed and that he watched the whole process of the operation, noting the actions and even the speech of the attendant doctors and nurses as if he had been floating ten or twenty feet above the scene. He may even feel that the psychologist's explanation is more improbable than his own, which, often enough, is that his " soul " left his body and observed the scene taking place at that time. In support of his belief he may claim that he, the observer, was no mere disembodied spirit but that he actually had another body—another self—which had shape and form but none of the actual characteristics of bone and flesh ; this he may call his astral body.

Many such stories concerning autoscopic hallucinations are, of course, mere fabrications ; others are products of memory delusions or delirium. In any event, supposing the hallucinatory experience to have occurred, the memory of the event is liable to gross distortion through wishful thinking, particularly if the subject possess inclinations towards spiritualism or theosophy.

A favourite theme of such autoscopic hallucinations centres on critical moments of an illness, e.g. pneumonia. The patient seems to be watching " himself " during the crisis. If the reality of the hallucinatory experience is granted, is it possible—the claim is often made—that the scene which the patient seems to observe could in fact corres-pond accurately with the scene which was actually occurring at the time ? This is unlikely, though the possibility cannot be rejected. Certainly a hallucinatory construction of the scene would not be correct in every detail. But in states of delirium and partial consciousness, coenaesthetic, kinaesthetic and sensory impressions might well be the means of linking the actual events to the events projected in the hallucination. Before the patient loses consciousness he has generally received at least a fleeting idea either of the position of his body or the circumstances which attend his loss of consciousness, whether the cause is due to illness, an accident or surgical operation. When delirium is present, or when unconsciousness is not so deep that all the higher cerebral centres are completely out of action, the senses of hearing, touch and smell are still capable of bringing their messages to the patient's brain ; the brain may then proceed to reconstruct its interpretation of them into visual and auditory form by means of an hallucination or vivid dream.

In the great majority of autoscopic hallucinations, however, the theory of simultaneous co-ordination between the actual scene and its hallucinatory reconstruction is unlikely. It is far more probable that the patient's experience can be attributed to a hallucination or a vivid dream which occurs afterwards, during the moments of recovery from consciousness.

Extreme cold and fatigue can bring about trance states of consciousness. Undoubtedly this is very often the explanation where the subject denies ever having lost consciousness, and yet appeared to have observed himself marching or toiling under conditions of great hardship. Many such cases may be regarded as unusual syndromes of acenesthesia or hysteria ; it is likely that most of the subjects who have actually experienced " out-of-the-body " hallucinations are psychasthenics or hysterics. Again, many such reported experiences are probably due to the delusions of incipient paranoia. There remain, however, a number of accounts of autoscopic and acenesthetic hallucinations by people of outstanding ability and integrity, which can only be explained by attributing them to temporary effects on the brain produced by such factors as fever, exhaustion, shock or drugs.

Delusions and hallucinations due to acenesthesia or hysteria have undoubtedly helped to perpetuate the myth of the " astral body." Such experiences inevitably gain in the telling and are passed on by spiritualists and others with added elaborations : thus the subject's " astral body " visits an old friend hundreds of miles away and is seen and recognised by him ; or a hallucinatory vision of a distant relative is taken to be a visitation by the relative's " astral-self ". Such tales represent, however, only a few drops in the great ocean of superstition and supernatural belief which have their roots in the vagaries of psychological anomaly.

HYPNAGOGIC HALLUCINATIONS—" FACES IN THE DARK."

The phenomenon of " faces in the dark " has never hit the headlines of occult literature. This is surprising in view of the extraordinary interest taken in other forms of hallucination and illusion. Perhaps it is because those who have experienced them have in the main been children, and, adults as is their way, have ascribed the experience to mere fancy and imagination. Faces, patterns, scenes and objects are seen when the eyes are closed and the mind is either dropping into sleep or recovering from it. They are not dreams, for the subject watches them while retaining possession of his critical faculties.

Hypnagogic hallucinations are comparatively rare phenomena. They are generally experienced during the half-way stage between full waking consciousness and sleep. It is sometimes convenient to refer to those hallucinations which occur before falling asleep as *hypnagogic*, and those which occur in the somnolent state immediately after awakening as *hypnapompic*. The term hypnagogic, however, is usually employed to cover both types.

Hypnagogic hallucinations are a type of hallucination possessing general features of their own which mark them off from the main body of normal waking hallucinations. There is, of course, no hard and fast dividing line between hypnagogic and other types of hallucination ; such a clear cut division is scarcely to be expected, and there are often instances where it is difficult to decide in which class to place them. In giving a brief description of such variegated phenomena as hypnagogic hallucinations, it is out of the question to cover every aspect of the matter. It is proposed, therefore, to give only a composite picture, although it must be recognised that such treatment possesses its limitations.

Hypnagogic hallucinations generally occur in the twilight state which is neither sleep nor full wakefulness. They may be roughly classified as something between a dream and an ordinary hallucination, except that they lack the variety and movement of the former. In a dream the dreamer himself appears to take part in the play of events, but in a hypnagogic hallucination this feature is absent. The percipient watches what is being presented to his consciousness with a keen yet curiously effortless interest, and generally remains comfortably aware of his real surroundings—a feature which is not noticeable in dreams and is often absent in other types of hallucination.   In all cases the percipient retains a sufficient degree of consciousness to be interested in the phenomenon.   Probably the nearest parallel would be the hallucinations induced in crystal gazing or " scrying."

Genuine hypnagogic hallucinations are found most frequently with children. Adults experience them with comparative rarity, although a few individuals claim to have had them over a period of years and even all their lives. The literature of the subject is, naturally, mainly derived from the experiences of adult observers. The hallucinations are generally intermittent and irregular in occurrence with long intervals between. It is probable that a considerable number of people have experienced them at least once or twice in their lives, although the majority have no remembered experience of this phenomenon at all.

The actual forms the imagery takes are, generally speaking, peculiar to this class of hallucination. They are often unnaturally clear and distinct, and many percipients see the scenes and objects presented to their vision as if diffused in a bright light or glow. Pictures, patterns, scenes and faces come and go, changing all the while, often too rapidly for proper attention by the intrigued observer. Some percipients only experience quickly evolving patterns and brightly coloured arabesques. Others see a continuous series of shifting scenes as if projected by magic-lantern slides. Yet others speak of views and panoramas as if seen from a rapidly moving trains. Often reported are bodiless faces shifting kaleidoscopically, occasionally beautiful, sometimes ordinary, frequently grotesque and even horrible, reminiscent of cathedral gargoyles. This latter feature causes us to wonder whether or not the traditional representations of demons and hob-goblins of former times derived their characteristics from hypnagogic hallucinations. Few percipients, even among children, mention having been frightened despite the ghoulish appearance of some of these hallucinatory faces.

Some percipients report that their hallucinations are

minute, the size of a small photograph or even of a stamp ; yet all detail appears abnormally clear. Most of the imagery is well, sometimes magnificently, coloured, though two or three cases of monochromatic hallucinations have been recorded.

Although the rapidly shifting pictures, patterns and scenes appear to be the most common forms of imagery, this is by no means always the case. There is no hard and fast rule as to what form a hypnagogic hallucination will take. Anything at all may, and often does, enter the hypnagogic field of vision and may remain for as long as a minute or two or even longer without shifting. One percipient, for example, reported a series of moving bricks, half gold and half black, floating evenly in the air in a bright glow.

The general concensus of opinion declares emphatically that attempts to influence the course of the imagery by exercise of the will are fruitless. Many have endeavoured to " create " what they wished to see, but without success. The effort to achieve this generally results in the disappearance of the visions, presumably because the attempted volitional control brings the percipient a stage nearer to full awakening ; it is an unfortunate fact that these fascinating and entertaining hallucinations are only too easily dispelled.

The great majority of hypnagogic percipients witness the hallucinatory phenomena while their eyes are closed. Some however, are reported as seeing them even after they have opened their eyes in the dark or half-light. Others again claim to have experienced them with eyes open in full daylight.

In regard to the psychological origins of the imagery displayed there is insufficient evidence to confirm any particular opinion. Most of the imagery is unrecognised and may be due to forgotten memories, composite memories, or pure imagination ; a number, on the other hand, are recognised as scenes with which the percipients had once been familiar. The only conclusion we can draw is the tentative but significant one that hypnagogic imagery seldom seems to depend upon recent events and happenings in the percipient's experience.

It is often claimed that the state of health of the percipient has little to do with the emergence of hypnagogic hallucinations in the case of adults. This is to be doubted. It is the author's opinion that hypnagogic hallucinations possess two different aetiologies. They are found most commonly among children at a range of ages corresponding to those during which the faculty of eidetic imagery is most noticeable. Like eidetic vision, hypnagogic hallucinations recur relatively seldom after twelve or fourteen years of age. Where cases of hypnagogic hallucination do occur after this age, particularly with adults, the hallucinatory imagery resembles that often produced by the drug mescaline and in sub-acute alcoholic delirium ; this indicates that the recurrence of the hallucinations later on in life is not simply a repetition of original spontaneous faculty but that some degree of toxaemia is responsible.

Some individuals, it is claimed, appear to be able to induce hypnagogic hallucinations, under favourable conditions, simply by closing their eyes and completely relaxing. It is doubtful whether such hallucinations can be termed hypnagogic ; they are probably due to the emergence of a light trance state, hysterical in origin.

A selection of water colour paintings of hypnagogic hallucinations, which on each occasion were painted as soon as practicable after the termination of the hallucinations, are preserved at the offices of the Society for Psychical Research.

Chapter Eight

SCRYING AND CRYSTAL GAZING

ALL THE WORLD OVER it has been discovered that steady gazing at clear, translucent or bright objects may, with some gifted individuals, result in the gazer seeing visions of varying interest and complexity. Until comparatively recent times such visions were invariably credited with an occult or religious significance. The crystal became the key to knowledge not only of the past and the future, and of distant events, but even of heaven and hell and their inhabitants. Dr. Dee, the famous Elizabethan savant, used magical divination by royal request to divine the most propitious day for Queen Elizabeth's coronation, and spent much of his time peering into his crystal in an effort to inveigle the archangels into discussing matters of philosophic import.

The occult tradition in connection with scrying has persisted down to the present day ; many a fortune teller makes his living among the great centres of western culture by gazing into a crystal and imparting information—for a sum— regarding the enquirer's future. Needless to say this class of " scryer " never sees anything in his crystal. He is a charlatan pure and simple.

Despite the claims of psychical research and spiritualism, there is not the least evidence of any supernatural powers accompanying the ability to scry ; nor is there any logical reason why there should be. Scrying, when genuine, is simply a convenient method, one of several, of inducing visual hallucinations in individuals who possess either a strong faculty for eidetic imagery or a natural tendency to

128

hallucination due to any one out of a number of possible causes.

Owing to the striking effects achieved by this method, scrying has, throughout the ages, been the most courted of all the methods of magical divination, and is the one which has aroused the curiosity of the mass of the people at all times. The term " to scry " comes from the English word to " descry " which means " to make out dimly", or " to succeed in discerning." Scrying is not confined to gazing into a crystal ball. The word covers the use of all types of objects employed for the purpose of inducing hallucinatory visions. Such objects are numerous and of considerable variety. Apart from the glass sphere beloved of quack soothsayers of modern fairgrounds, polished stones, concave mirrors, burnished metal and a host of other objects with polished or glistening surfaces, have been found effective.

The original crystals were, naturally, not composed of glass but of polished rock crystal. In Egypt a pool of ink or other dark coloured liquid, including blood, has been used for centuries. Tribes of the north-west frontier of India used the liver of an animal, although this must not be confused with the art of haruspication which involves observing the condition of the liver or entrails. Water too, has been and still is used among various primitive tribes from Africa to Siberia. In ancient Greece and during the middle ages a polished metal mirror was generally customary. In Arab countries the polished finger nail is still used.

In the past, hallucinations induced by scrying were inevitably attributed to the operation of occult powers. In primitive, semi-civilised and peasant communities today this belief is still held. At the beginning of the present century societies of psychical research, which included among their membership world famous savants, spent a great deal of time in finding out whether these beliefs held any truth. Efforts were made to establish the telepathic or clairvoyant nature of many of the hallucinatory visions. Such pseudo-scientific investigations produced no results worth serious attention. To the ignorant, the occurrence of " visions " in a crystal or other speculum is itself a super-

natural event. To such individuals it would appear quite
illogical to differentiate between the faculty of inducing
crystal visions and the faculty of being able to " see " into
past or future—they partake of the same magical nature !
To find such occult traditions forming the basis of sincere
attempts at scientific investigation demonstrates how
deeply the lure of the occult is engrained in human nature.

Despite such ill-judged attempts to put magic on a scientific basis, at least one psychologist of wide repute has used
scrying methods in the interests of medical psychology.
Dr. Morton Prince, whose work in this sphere bears witness
to unusual vision, used an electric light bulb as a speculum.
His patient was suffering from a hysterical disability and
was therefore readily hypnotisable. Interested to discover
whether a repeated hallucinatory scene was due to a forgotten memory or the product of imagination, Prince
hypnotised his patient and discovered that the scene represented an almost identical one which had been experienced
in real life years previously and of which the patient had
no conscious recollection.

In another experiment the content of the crystal hallucination was essentially the same as that of an experience
which the patient had undergone many years before when
ill with pneumonia. During this illness she had become
highly delirious, experiencing visual and auditory hallucinations. These she took to be real and acted accordingly.
In Prince's light-bulb crystal she saw herself as she would
have appeared to another person present during the period
of her delirium.[1] This particular episode is revealing in
that it shows clearly the hysterical genesis of a typical
autoscopic hallucination.

Morton Prince conducted two interesting series of investigations in which hallucinations and automatic writing were
combined. He made his hysterical subject give a simultaneous verbal description of a series of visual hallucinations ;
at the same time the subject's hand wrote automatically.
In a number of such tests subsequent comparison of the
automatic scripts with the parallel series of hallucinatory
scenes (described verbally and taken down) showed that the

---

[1] Prince, M., *An Experimental Study of Visions*, Brain, 1898 , pp. 528-546

latter formed a kind of picture series illustrating a story written automatically by the subject's hand. The subject, whose conscious attention was devoted to the task of describing the hallucinatory scenes which she was experiencing, did not seem to be aware of what her hand was writing. Moreover, the hallucinatory scenes appeared to possess no more significance than a random series of pictures until the automatic script revealed their coherent relationship.

These and other experiments serve to show that the hallucinations produced by scrying are not basically different from the general run of hallucinations or pseudo-hallucinations. While hysteria may often be held to account for the faculty of genuine scrying, in others it seems to be more nearly related to eidetic imagery. Eidetic imagery is allied to the imagery of memory and imagination. Many children who possess this image-forming capacity in high degree can gaze at a picture or scene and then project the resultant mental image upon a blank screen for a considerable length of time. In many cases the clarity and depth are so excellent that the image constitutes a genuine hallucination.

Jaensch, the standard authority on eidetic imagery, writes that with good eidetic subjects, if the objects gazed at are three-dimensional, the subsequent eidetic image will appear three dimensional on the screen. Of such highly developed eidetic images Jaensch reports that they may be

" as flexible and changeable as memory images, willingly and smoothly following every change in the flow of ideas. Their occurence, stability and disappearance hardly depend on sense-physiological or optical factors at all, but most decisively on psychological factors." [1]

As with hypnagogic hallucinations, the most frequent age at which eidetic imagery occurs is in childhood. In this connection it is probably not mere coincidence that in Arab countries young boys are traditionally regarded as the best scryers—using the polished thumbnail as a speculum. In these countries scrying has naturally a clairvoyant significance. The boy gazes at the thumb-nail until he sees pictures forming and is then asked whether he can see the whereabouts of a lost or stolen article, a missing relative, or

---

[1] Jaensch, E. R., *Eidetic Imagery*, pp. 28-29.

the features of a thief or murderer. By his descriptions it is hoped that the desired information will be forthcoming.

It is significant that after these boys have passed about their tenth or eleventh year their scrying faculty generally disappears ; the same thing is usually observed in connection with both hypnagogic hallucinations and eidetic imagery. The ability to scry, therefore, is probably more often related to the eidetic faculty than to hallucinations of hysteric origin. Occasionally, as with hypnagogic and eidetic subjects, the Arab scrying-boy may retain his faculty through life. Writers on the subject have hitherto largely overlooked the realationship between scrying and eidetic imagery.

One of the most successful scryers was a Miss Goodrich-Freer. In her hints on learning to scry, the method she advocates is remarkably similar in many respects to that adopted by Jaensch and others in their investigations of eidetic subjects :

The subject should gaze carefully at some simple object in the room in front of him, avoiding all objects likely to be actually reflected in the glass ball. He should then close his eyes and make an attempt to visualise mentally the object chosen. The next step is to see whether it is possible to project or " see " the object in the crystal. Miss Goodrich-Freer states that if one possesses a genuine gift of visualisation this projection ought to be achieved without much difficulty after a certain amount of practise. When success has been achieved with simple objects, the next step is to increase their complexity ; a person is next chosen for the object and finally a view or complex scene. After practise and a change over to a different technique the scryer may learn to achieve a state of mild mental dissociation and thereby produce autonomous imagery, without first having to gaze at an object, which will appear as novel hallucinatory images in the crystal and become activated on their own account.

Other scryers adopt different methods in learning. Some claim, for example, that all that is necessary is to visualise a well known face or scene and transfer this picture from " the mind's eye " to the crystal. Other scryers trace the genesis of their hallucinatory images to actual points of light or specks of dust—the so-called *points de repère*—on the crystal.

Morton Prince found that a crystal was not necessarily essential. " Merely fixing the attention with expectation of the development of the phenomenon is sufficient with susceptible subjects." He adds : " An examination of the content of visualisations thus produced shows that they are identical in structure and action with many of the hallucinations of the insane as well as with the spontaneous hallucinations of the sane." [2] According to the well-known psychologist, T. W. Mitchel, crystal gazing can also be experimentally induced by hypnotic suggestion. [3]

An excellent example of the rational adaptability of hallucinations to circumstances and suggestion is found in the use of a magnifying glass in scrying. Northcote Thomas mentions two occasions on which one of his subjects asked for a magnifying glass which enabled her to distinguish some small or blurred objects appearing in the glass sphere. [4] In this connection it has been reported that hypnotic hallucinations can sometimes be " doubled " by pressure on the eyeball. [5] This same phenomenon has also been observed in the hallucinations of a number of psychotics.

---

[2] Prince, M., *An Experimental Study of the Mechanism of Hallucinations*, Brit. Journ. Psychol., Med. Sect., II, 1922, p. 165.

[3] *Psychology and the Sciences*, p. 170.

[4] Thomas, N., *Thought Transference*, pp. 134 and 136.

[5] Parish, E., *Hallucinations and Illusions*, p. 201.

Chapter Nine

AUTOMATIC WRITING

It is now proposed to deal with a class of psychological anomalies which until relatively modern times have always been credited as evidence of a supernatural faculty and which have been among some of the chief factors contributing to the growth of the modern cult of spiritualism. These anomalies come under the general heading of psychological automatism, and manifest themselves in such activities as automatic writing, table-turning, operating the ouija-board, the planchette and the divining pendulum.

All these phenomena, of course, can easily be simulated, and indeed this may be taken as almost invariably the case when financial gain enters into the performances. There is no denying, however, that many professional mediums may originally have possessed a genuine automatic faculty; but the transition from genuine to spurious exhibitions is so easily made—and further has the advantage that it is always available—that no professional could resist the temptation. Nevertheless, genuine psychological automatism is not uncommon and can in fact be developed by the majority of people who are prepared to spare the time and patience. It is with the genuine brand of psychological automatism with which we are mainly concerned here.

Automatic writing implies the ability to write intelligibly without the direction of the conscious attention. The subject's attention may be occupied with reading or some other form of easy mental activity; alternatively he may simply relax while endeavouring to make his mind a blank.

134

" In these circumstances, the hand with the pencil may write not only voluminously, but often coherently and interestingly. What it writes would appear to be the product of some system of ideas which is denied full access to the normal main consciousness—more or less thoroughly dissociated, repressed, or buried." [1]

In the case of a few very versatile automatists, the writer may engage wholeheartedly in a conversation at the same time that his hand is writing good prose or even verse, its owner remaining oblivious to what is being written until he subsequently reads it.

The content and style of the writing almost always appears as if a different personality were the author, as if a part of the writer's mind possessed an autonomy of its own. Indeed a good many psychologists of the older schools hold precisely this view, maintaining with considerable wealth of argument that in such instances the repressed complexes of emotionally-toned ideas and desires which emerge have become dissociated from the main mental system and appear to have gained a coherence amounting to a subsidiary and autonomous *personality* with a will of its own.

Whether or not this is a suitable description of the state of affairs exhibited need not concern us at the moment. What is more important is that the hand of the practised automatic writer or *autonographist* can write without the writer being in the slightest degree *aware* of any effort of volition. It is little wonder that the general public have tended to attribute the authorship of such automatic writings to spirits, as in the past the automatic writings of witches and monks were believed to have been inspired by demons, angels, the devil or his opposite number, according to their content.

Among the simplest forms of autonography are those which involve the use of a pendulum or an ouija-board. The main difference between these two methods is that the former is confined to a single individual, whereas with the latter a considerable number of people can participate simultaneously.

Divination by means of a pendulum in the form of a suspended ring is found from Europe to China and has been

---

[1] Wells, Huxley and Wells, *Science of Life*, p. 1290.

common in all ages. One of the earliest references to the pendulum is that of the Byzantine historian Marcellinus. He records that in the time of the Emperor Valens a number of men were arrested and condemned to death for endeavouring to divine the name of the Emperor's successor. The method they used was to set the letters of the alphabet out in a circle, as in a modern ouija-board, and to suspend a ring over the centre of the circle. The ring, by the direction of its swing, indicated in turn various letters of the alphabet. This method, as used by these ancient Romans, appears to be a very slow one and is seldom resorted to now. In spiritualist circles, a similar method popular at one time was to suspend a pendulum or ring in any empty glass and ask the spirits questions. One tap on the side of the glass meant no, and two meant yes.

Some individuals, especially the adherents of the widespread cult of radiesthesia, claim to be able to divine practically anything by means of the pendulum. Their prognostications range from medical diagnosis to treasure hunting and criminal detection. The pendulum's direction of swing, range of arc, type of oscillation, either alone or in combination, are carefully " studied " for the purpose of divination. Radiesthesia is a new version of older occult beliefs. It is now regarded by its adherents as a science and possesses its peculiar terms and jargon and a variety of " scientific " theories all its own. Most radiesthetists believe, quite correctly, that their rods and pendulums register and amplify minute muscular movements in their hands and arms. They assert, however, that these muscular movements are reactions due to a variety of mysterious " waves," " radiations " and " fields " emanating from the object of divination.

Another school of radiesthetists maintains that all such divinations are due to the exercise of " psychic " forces and faculties such as telepathy, clairvoyance and prophecy. Most water-diviners who interest themselves in the theoretical aspect of their art cling to the " physical " theory of rays and emanations and so forth. Needless to say the naïvety of these theories precludes their being taken seriously, and they remain totally unsupported by modern physical science.

In cases where fraud can be discounted, the effects produced through pendulum-swinging, table-turning and the ouija-board depend on unconscious muscular movements. The instruments reflect with fair accuracy what are often called *ideomotor movements*, in this case of the hand and arm. Any-one can test the fact of ideomotor movements for himself by suspending a ring or any other weighted object on the end of a fine piece of string about ten inches long. It will be found impossible to keep the ring absolutely immobilised in this position. However hard one tries, there will always remain a slight movement due to involuntary movements of the hand. If the imagination is now directed towards visualising a to-and-fro movement of the ring and the attention remains concentrated on the expected movement, however still the hand is kept, the visualised movement soon becomes dis-cernible in the motion of the pendulum. If the motion thought of is lateral or circular, then similar movements of the pendulum will be forthcoming. The motion of the pen-dulum faithfully reflects the idea in the subject's mind—hence the term ideomotor. As will be seen in later chapters, small involuntary ideomotor movements are responsible for the " success " of many experiments in telepathy and clairvoyance. Muscle-reading is a performance which relies almost entirely on the cues provided by such movements.

In table-turning (-tilting or -tapping) two, three or more persons place their hands on a light table and the table moves in response to the unconscious ideomotor movements of the sitters. This being a spiritualist practice, the " spirits " are asked questions and the table "answers" by its movements, in the negative or the affirmative, or according to a code of signals evolved for the purpose. Sometimes a list of letters is run through verbally while the table gives a tap on the floor when the correct letter is reached. In this way messages are spelt out. This method would only succeed among groups of people continually associating together and possessing many ideas in common. The naïve assumption that it is the spirits who make the table move is due to the fact that the participants remain unaware of the ideas which sub-consciously activate their ideomotor movements.

" The table answers as if it was alive ; the emotions of the sub-conscious are faithfully translated by the kind of movements made by the inert object. This lifeless table seems to have a mind ; it hesitates, it shows irritation ; it affirms energetically ; or it sways solemnly. No one who has not witnessed such seances can imagine how well diverse sentiments can be expressed by the frequency or the forcefulness, the slow, hesitating, vigorous, or gentle movements. It is an actual language, sometimes eloquent and always interesting, and the simple-minded are easily led to conclude that some external intelligence is moving the table." [1]

One of the most interesting reports of investigations into table-tilting by spiritualist mediums comes, surprisingly enough, from the pen of Jung,[2] and though brief is well worth perusal. In it he points out that surprising results are obtained by mediums " reading " the thoughts of other persons purportedly by telepathy, whose hands are touching the table, simply by a variation of the muscle-reading technique in conjuction with carefully phrased questions and remarks.

Viollet records an interesting case of a woman with whom table-tapping became an obsession. This patient had voluntarily entered a mental home to be cured of her persistent delusions, and once there she was denied access to any form of table. She continued to converse with the spirits however :

"She had, above all things, retained her old typtological power ; the need to run to the table was always imperious, notwithstanding the facility of auditory converse with the spirits ; but as we opposed the use of the table, typtology was resorted to by means of the pencil striking letters on a book or on the bed ; we stopped that also.   Then the finger rapped ; finally the typtology became interior and purely mental. The letters were rapped out in her head in thought. This mental typtology became one of her chief means of communication with the spirits and particularly with God, the most assiduous of all her communicators." [3]

With the use of the ouija-board we come upon a method of autonography half way between the limited automatic movements available to the pendulum and the table on one hand and the free flow of automatic writing on the other.

[1] Richet, C., *Thirty Years of Psychical Research*, pp. 401-2.
[2] *Collected Papers on Analytical Psychology*, pp. 50-56.
[3] Viollet, M., *Spiritualism and Insanity*, p. 81.

The principle of the ouija—a term derived from the French *oui* and the German *ja*, both meaning " yes "—is a very simple one.   The letters of the alphabet are placed in a circle ; included in the circle of letters are a " yes " and a " no."   A form of indicator-apparatus commonly used in modern spiritualist circles comprises a small board on wheels upon which fingers of the participants rest.   One person or several may participate.   Very commonly used is an upturned wine glass on a polished table ;   the glass slides easily across the polished surface towards any letter which the spirits may feel inclined to choose.

The usual procedure is for one of the " sitters " to ask the spirits a question ;   the pointer or wine glass in reply will move to the " yes " or the " no ", or start to spell out some kind of a message.   With beginners the " messages " are almost invariably gibberish, but with continued practise the movements of the pointer become increasingly coherent and rapid, until a stage of true automatism is reached wherein the guiding movements of the hand and arm are directed by elements of the mind dissociated in some degree from the normal conscious personality of the individual ;   the conscious attention of the participants is directed solely to the task of reading the messages as they emerge.   Great speed and efficiency is frequently obtained by these automatic move-ments which spell out the messages, in some instances even warranting the services of a stenographer to take them down.

In contrast to the basically cumbersome methods of the ouija-board, the planchette represents a considerable advance. This instrument is a small heart-shaped board supported by a pencil at the apex—point inverted—and a small wheel at each of the two remaining corners.   The operator places one or more fingers lightly on it, avoiding any consciously directed movements.   As with the ouija-board the instrument may be operated either by a single person or by two.

True automatic writing may be obtained by use of the planchette.   The instrument glides easily over the paper leaving pencil marks wherever it travels.   With considerable practise two or even three persons may touch the instrument simultaneously and produce writing with a surprisingly degree of rapidity.   As with other forms of autonography, the automatic activity of the hand is generally attributed

to the influence of discarnate spirits of the " dear departed."
To the naïve and superstitious enthusiasts who indulge in
spiritistic autonography it is not the hands of the sitters
themselves which activate the tables, ouijas and planchettes ;
for them the placing of the hands on the chosen instrument
merely provides the " psychic " conditions most favourable
to the activity of spirits and the spirit forces.   Any suggestion
that the participants themselves produce the writing by a
process of psychological automatism is met with rigid and
determined disbelief.

AUTOMATIC WRITING

It is in automatic writing that we find the most interesting
phenomena.   And it is among some of the literary productions produced autonographically that many of the older
psychologists found the strongest evidence of dissociated
coherent personalities " lying buried in the depths of the
subconscious mind."   Parallel " evidence " is forthcoming
in some of the phenomena of hysteria, such as in fugues,
where the subject forgets who he is and takes on, perhaps
for months or even years, a totally new personality representing all those aspects of his nature which have always sought
expression but which have been hitherto firmly repressed.

There is nothing extraordinary about automatic phenomena.   The typist who concentrates all her attention on
reading the nearly illegible manuscript of an inconsiderate
author operates the keys of the typewriter automatically.
The pianist who plays a melody while talking to someone
else plays automatically.   By analogous means it is possible
to train the majority of people to write automatically while
their attention is engaged on something else at the time.

This has been proved by Dr. Anita Mühl, a trained psychiatrist.   Following the lead of Morton Prince and others,
Dr. Mühl studied the possibilities of autonography for
psychotherapeutic purposes.   She found that it was in fact
possible, given the right conditions, to train the majority of
normal well-balanced individuals to write automatically.[1]
With her patients she used autonography to delve into

---

[1] Mühl. A., *Automatic Writing*, Dresden, 1930.

their minds and resuscitate repressed memories and idea-
associations. It is worth recording that one of Dr. Mühl's
patients even wrote music autonographically. Others among
her patients autonographically produced bizarre, cryptic, and
sometimes beautifully coloured drawings, whose symbolic
content was resolved with the aid of subsequent automatic
writings and which together formed the basis of the analytical therapy.

The relationship between autonography and hypnotic
states of consciousness has been noted by Jung, MacDougall,
Morton Prince and Wm. Brown. All agree that automatic
writing can be readily induced by hypnotic or post-hypnotic
suggestion. Jung[2] and MacDougall[3] state that autonography proper is considerably more difficult to produce than
automatic table-turning or the automatic operation of ouija
and planchette. MacDougall writes that in many cases
" it is possible to obtain some retrospective account of the
thinking that governed the writing, if the subject is afterwards hypnotised."[4]

To train a person to produce autonography by post-
hypnotic suggestion is seldom the most practical method.
Morton Prince describes the method as follows. The
operator first hypnotises the subject

> " and during the trance state tells her she is to write something—a
> verse or anything one pleases—when awake. After being awakened,
> a pencil is put in her hand and she is given a book to read aloud, or
> told to count backwards, or do some mental problem. While her
> attention is occupied with this, the hand holding the pencil, if placed
> over a sheet of paper, will write what was desired. The subject
> herslf has absolutely no knowledge of what her hand writes."[5]

The hysterical character of many of Prince's subjects is
evinced by the fact that in several cases the hand of the
autonographist became, while writing, perfectly anaesthetic.[6]
With normal subjects such methods as post-hypnotic
suggestion would seldom succeed in producing genuine

---

[2] *Collected Papers on Analytical Psychology*, p. 57.
[3] *An Outline of Abnormal Psychology*, p. 257.
[4] op. cit.
[5] Prince, M., *A Contribution to the Study of Hysteria and Hypnosis*, Proc.,
S.P.R., 14, p. 96.
[6] ibid.

autonography. Although most fluent autonographists are undoubtedly hysterical, it is not possible to say this of all of them. In cases where the autonography appeared *spontaneously*, however, hysteria can safely be assumed to be the activating factor.

One of the most interesting contributions to the study of autonography is Morton Prince's *An Experimental Study of the Mechanism of Hallucinations.*[1] In this unique paper Prince describes his experiments with a subject who was able, while writing automatically, to give a simultaneous verbal description of a series of concurrent visual hallucinations. As she described her hallucinations her hand continued to write automatically. This subject could induce autonography at will and frequently experienced a series of hallucinatory (or pseudo-hallucinatory) scenes illustrating, as it were, what was being written. She appeared totally unconscious of what her hand was writing even though she apparently wrote slowly ; and during the experiments, in order that the subject should not see what she was writing, Dr. Prince covered her head with an opaque cloth. Prince took down a verbatim record of her descriptions of the hallucinatory scenes and this allowed him subsequently to compare them with the autonographic text.

The subject was originally a case of dual-personality who had been sent to Prince for treatment. The person evinced in the autonographic script went by the name of " Julia " and purported to be a Spanish peasant girl with high aspirations living in the thirteenth century. This " Julia " had been one of the subsidiary personalities which had emerged during the original dual-personality phase of her hysteria. With " Julia " purporting to be the author —and now calling herself " Juliana "—the subject's hand wrote (in the third person) romantic and picturesque fantasies in keeping with her rôle. The hallucinatory scenes were varied and there was to be seen, at first glance, little continuous relationship between them :

" The scenes shift as in a dream without apparent relation to one another.   The significant fact is that *the continuity will be found in*

[1] *Brit. J. of Psychol.*, med. sect., II, 1922, pp. 165-208.

the sub-consciously written script without which the varying hallucinations would not seem to be related to one another and could not be understood or interpreted as manifestations of one and the same theme." [2]

Prince remarks that the hallucinatory scenes were " much richer in detail than the description of the episode given in the script " and this can be seen from the following excerpt :

Automatic Script	*Simultaneous Hallucinatory Scene*
5. . . ." *I walk to early mass at the village church or mission.*	A road. At the end of the road a little *church.* A sort of white stucco mission church. Juliana's back is towards me. She is *walking down the road* barefooted *going to church.* The whole is as plain as a motion picture. I can see the grain waving in the adjoining fields. (I have the feeling as if she is lazy and does not want to go to church.)"
	[Shift]
6. " *At a village called in my time Medesa.*	A sort of square. I can see her Uncle Salvator. There is a tent propped up over a lot of vegetables exposed in the market place. A lot of foreign looking women are walking about. There is a crowd." [3]

Another set of experiments by Prince, equally interesting, reversed the process, so that his subject first of all induced the hallucinations with the aid of a crystal and was then given the command to write automatically ; with the result that instead of the autonography giving rise to accompanying hallucinations, the hallucinations in their turn dictated the style of the autonographic scripts.   Whether Prince's subject actually experienced genuine sensory hallucin-

---

[2] ibid., p. 175.
[3] Prince, ibid., p. 176.

ations is an open question ; it is equally likely that they were the product of suggested pseudo-hallucinosis.

Most beginners who wish to develop the art of autonography simply hold a pencil in one hand over a sheet of paper and purposely allow the attention to wander or else engage in conversation. The expectation of producing autonography has the effect of mild auto-suggestion, and after a considerable time the pencil will begin to make variegated movements beginning with upward strokes, zigzag lines, or even just a single line. The next step is the formation of single letters ; and then a series of letters, at first devoid of coherence. After further practise these will combine into words and sentences. In a number of instances autonographists have written and published long fantasies and even novels of undeniable merit. Such literary works invariably reflect the repressed longings and ideas of their authors, often in a complicated pattern of symbolism.

The Society for Psychical Research has published a large collection of extremely interesting autonographic scripts in its *Proceedings*. In the main, however, the Society has generally been more concerned with the occult aspects of these writings than with their psychology. There are partial exceptions, one of which is the interesting series of autonographic scripts by Dr. S. G. Soal. Dr. Soal found that he possessed a faculty for autonography which only proved effective when one particular person was guiding his hand in order to keep the lines straight and return his pencil to the correct position when he reached the end of a line. This dual autonographic partnership is unusual. Soal describes his method of inducing autonography as follows :

" By concentrating my mind on some trivial calculation, I have learnt how to create a mental state of internal distraction, and it is during the moments when my mind is thus occupied that the writing is produced. The moment my mind reverts to what my hand is supposed to be doing the writing stops as suddenly as it commenced. It is, however, impossible to maintain this mental attitude of complete abstraction for more than a few minutes at a time, but a fresh effort of rapid concentration made at the very moment when I feel my mind to be straying back will often enable the state to be renewed and the writing prolonged without noticeable interruption." [4]

According to Jung, the pencil in the initial stages may start to write in the air without touching the paper. Jung has also observed *strephographia* (mirror-writing) in connection with autonography. [5]

The idea at the back of the beginner's mind should be to allow the hand holding the pencil to move, as it were, by its own volition. When the hand takes over control while the conscious attention is directed elsewhere, we are presented with true automatic writing. With some subjects, however, the words are written down quite consciously but the autonographist fails to connect the words into sentences until he subsequently reads through what he has written. Others write down the words which seem to them to enter their minds from an external source. This interesting illusion, often a consequence of genuine dissociation, gives the subject the impression that he is taking down the words from dictation ; to those naïvely inclined to spiritualism, this type of autonography must appear as convincing proof of the truth of their beliefs.

It may be of advantage at this point to mention something of the phenomena of spontaneous strephographia. Mirror-writing is what its name implies—the letters, words and sentences being written in such a fashion that they look like the reflection of normal writing when held before a mirror. A number of individuals are able to write mirror-wise voluntarily, and spontaneous strephogragraphia is not altogether uncommon in the case of shifted sinistrals— naturally left-handed people who have been taught to write with their right hands.

In general strephographia is most often observed in cases of injury to the cerebral hemispheres, in mental defectives, in hypnosis and states of partial consciousness, in some types of hysteria, and occasionally in left-handed children. It is interesting to note that the majority of mirror-writers cannot read what they have written. Graphological hallucinations in crystal gazing are sometimes strephographical

---

[4] Proc. S. P. R., vol. 38, p. 332.
[5] *Collected Papers on Analytical Psychology*, pp. 57-58.

in character ; similarly the phenomenon of reversed word-order may also occur.

There is another class of writing—inverted writing and inverted mirror-writing; these, however, are rare.

Analogous to these graphological aberrations is " backward speech " which is very uncommon.   There are several types of this.   The sentences may follow logically enough but the words composing each sentences are spoken in reversed order.   Again, the words themselves may follow in logical order but they are pronounced backwards ; *cat* becomes *tac*, for example.   And there is a very rare disorder, *strephosymbolia*, when a book may have to be read upside down to be understood.

The above graphological anomalies, however, have little bearing on the main subject of autonography.   In the main, only mirror-writing has been conspicuously observed in autonography, although a few doubtful cases of the other types of anomaly have occasionally been reported.

The outlet afforded to repressed ideas and emotions provided by autonography frequently results in the content of autonographic scripts being completely alien to the accepted character of the writer.   An autonographist who is known as a somewhat fussy individual with mild manners may produce, in his automatic script, lurid stories of a sudden death or tales of heroic adventure written in the first person.

The literary achievements produced autonographically are sometimes remarkable, particularly in the case of those individuals with a good education and a wide range of miscellaneous knowledge.   In such a manner full length novels have been written and published, and polished poems have spontaneously emerged autonographically.   In most of these cases there is complete evidence that such literary productions are the result of prolonged subconscious incubation ; there seems little spontaneous about them except that the subject is not actually conscious of their existence at the back of his mind before they emerge autonographically.

In the *Proceedings* of the S.P.R. there are a good many examples of the remarkable manner in which the subconscious mind is able to assimilate experiences and items of knowledge and combine them in a synthesis virtually indistinguishable in form and quality from creative achievements of the conscious mind. It may appear odd that the subject remains unaware of the mental activity involved in such instances, but as we shall see later on in the case of Professor Flournoy's celebrated medium, the mind is occasionally able to create and memorise its creations subconsciously on a scale seldom attained by the conscious effort. Such cases are reminiscent of the sharpened powers of observation and histrionic ability often found in hypnotised subjects.

The pseudo-personalities brought into being by autonography are often hostile to the main personality of the subject. This is an espect of a number of analogous psychological anomalies, particularly among the auditory hallucinations of psychotics. Many psychotics experience inimical hallucinations—accusing, scolding or threatening voices, or menacing figures.

With nearly all fluent automatic writers, the writing purports to come from an individual personality distinct from that of the autonographer himself. In the case of spiritualists the pseudo-personality generally claims to be a discarnate spirit of the dead. In former days the verbal automatism or "involuntary speech" of certain hysterics took the guise of having been instigated by demons or the devil in person, thereby frequently condemning the unfortunate individual to death by stoning and in later periods to death at the stake. The phenomenon was attributed either to demoniacal possession or to witchcraft.

The cunning, patience, and elaborate inventiveness of many pseudo-personalities, as found in much autonography, often gives a strong impression to those who subsequently read the script that the writing emanates from a personal consciousness other than that of the automatist himself. The theory of *dual consciousness* is scarcely tenable, for upon analysis the term fails to reveal any definite meaning. Nor is it the least likely that in cases of genuine creative writing the process operates wholly without the concomitance of consciousness. Many people can acquire by practise the habit of writing letters or business memoranda while carrying on a conversation and without stopping the flow of the pen. They are subsequently able to recall both the context of what they have written and the conversation in which they engaged. Similarly some musicians are able to improvise on the piano while engaged in lively conversation. Experiments prove, however, that there is no intensity of concentration on either task and that if intensity of concentration is exerted on one, the subject fails entirely to carry out the other. It is the attention which is divided and there is a consequent loss of efficiency.

In some cases of autonography and trance mediumship, this process appears to be carried a stage further bringing with it a more or less marked degree of amnesia. In cruder forms of autonography and mediumistic trance, often marked by infantile characteristics, the process can be considered analogous to such activities as unconsciously talking to oneself. People who talk to themselves are often totally oblivious of the fact. Subsequent amnesia may be complete and the individual in question may remain convinced when challenged with the fact that he never uttered a word. The great common denominator of all forms of anomalous automatism is that the activity in question (whether mental or physical) is neither initiated nor sustained by the *normal* processes of volition ; this is the only generalisation which is not open to question. Until we understand more about the mechanism of conscious attention, a complete explanation of such phenomena as autonography, trance mediumship and hysterical dissociation remains unlikely.

Sometimes a " conversation " can be carried out between the subject and his hand. The subject simply asks questions verbally, generally addressed to a spirit purporting to " inspire " the writing, and the hand will write down answers in reply. An excellent example of this is provided by the autonographic scripts of Soal.[1]

Soal's interest in psychical research brought him into frequent contact with the cult of spiritualism. He was not unduly surprised to find, therefore, on discovering his own

---

[1] See *Proc. S.P.R.*, vol. 38.

faculty for autonography, that it reflected a typical spirit-ualist outlook. His autonographic scripts informed him that they were inspired by the spirit of a minor Victorian poet named Margaret Veley. Soal, naturally, was not able to take these claims at face value and recognised that the pseudo-personality manifested in his autonographic script was the product of his own subconscious mind. He was nevertheless prepared to believe in the possibility that the knowledge he evinced of the long-dead Margaret Veley might have been acquired by such means as telepathy or clairvoyance. His hand did everything in its power to persuade its sceptical owner that he was wrong in rejecting the spiritist explanation of the autonography. Soal asked questions and the hand replied.

A perusal of these scripts reveals the extent to which the autonographist's own dissociated mental processes can deliberately set out to deceive the conscious personality The resulting " conversations " have the appearance of being written by two entirely different people. The argu-ments, subterfuges and red-herrings produced by the pseudo-personality in urging the acceptance of its *bona fides* as the spirit of the dead poetess, though characteristically naïve, show a surprising ingenuity. Soal himself was able to recall next to nothing of Margaret Veley's life and poetry, with the result that the amount of factual corroboration produced by the pseudo-personality seemed to produce strong *prima facie* case for the theory of acquisition of knowledge by telepathy, chairvoyance or other super-natural means. There seems little doubt, however, that the knowledge exhibited was due to cryptomnesia.

That the subconscious mind ordinarily retains a host of memories beyond normal recall is a well known fact. In the phenomenon of *cryptomnesia* we witness a direct consequence of this ; a memory is recalled, but incompletely. Cryptomnesia is the spontaneous revival of former mem-ories, experiences, facts and items of knowledge, without the subject being able to recall in the least the circum-stances which originally attended them. Dissociation often exaggerates this tendency, which accounts for the appear-ance of many " clairvoyantly " acquired items of knowledge by trance mediums, autonographists, crystal gazers and the like. Because the individual concerned is unable to remember ever having acquired the piece of knowledge in question, he puts it down to the operation of his own " psychic powers "—preferring in these sophisticated times to avoid the term " magic ".

A number of cases are recorded wherein the " auto-nographic personality " writes with a handwriting approx-imating in style to that of another person ; with spirit-ualists the style imitated invariably purports to be that of someone who is dead. Autonographic handwriting often differs entirely from the normal handwriting of the subject. The writing usually conforms to the rôle played by the pseudo-personality. For example, if a child is the purported spirit-communicator, the writing will appear round and ill-formed ; this phenomenon is easily induced by suggestion with hypnotised subjects, but it is worth noting that such variations in style are not always so readily achieved in the normal waking state without considerable practise.

This faculty of altering the style of the hand-writing is sometimes combined with a cryptomnesic memory of a dead person's handwriting which is then unconsciously imitated in the autonographic scripts. Spiritualists take such instances as the culminating proof of the survival of the dead in a spirit world.

Allied to autonography is verbal automatism. Un-controllable verbal automatism is a common phenomenon among psychotics, although, unlike with hysteria, the process must be considered more nearly mechanical than intellectual. Hysterical verbal automatism may be regarded as a convenient bridge between autonography and the utterances of trance mediums. Such notorious pheno-mena known euphemistically as " speaking with tongues " and " preaching children ", various kinds of inspired " ec-stasy " and " diabolical possession ", frequently involve a degree of verbal automatism with subsequent amnesia.

In certain other cases of hysterical verbal automatism, the individual may be completely aware of what he is saying, yet remains powerless to prevent his mouth, tongue and larynx from operating ;[2] nor is he able to control the flow of ideas. There are few people who have not done a little " automatic speaking " on their own account. The dreamer who talks in his sleep, for example, may be surprised to learn that the psychological processes involved are not so very far removed from those pertaining to many cases of medieval demon-possession !

---

[2] Cutten, G. B., *Speaking with Tongues*, p. 192.

Chapter Ten

SOMNAMBULISM, FUGUES AND MULTIPLE PERSONALITY

THE LAST CHAPTER has given some idea of the range of expression which may be achieved by mental activity dissociated from the normal processes of volition. Such involuntary mental activity, however, may result in psychological anomalies more spectacular than autonography : almost any form of overt human expression may become involved.

It has already been noted that, apart from autonography proper, some hysterical subjects may paint pictures or even compose simple music autonographically. Some psychologists maintain that the subject here merely deludes himself and others that he does these things automatically. Very often this is clearly the case, but such an interpretation can not always hold good.

There exists nowhere a broad dividing line between such hysterical phenomena as extreme monoideic somnambulism, which is quite involuntary and amnesic, and such conscious activities as, for example, writing a letter or reckoning accounts. Between the two extremes we find a fine series of gradations which defy rigid and precise classification. If we start at the lower end of the series we eventually arrive at a point where it is impossible to say whether a subject is writing automatically or whether he is deluding himself that he is ; elements of both factors may be present and the distinction no longer possesses much significance. Immediately below this point in the series, we find cases where the evidence indicates genuine involuntary automatism as the predominating factor, and immediately above it elements of *conscious* deception are plainly discernible. Again, we can observe cases where wishful thinking, suggestion or an irrational impulse to imitation, is responsible for initiating an activity which, at first subject to volitional control, rapidly develops into an involuntary psychological automatism.

One example of this latter process is known as automatic dancing or dancing mania. This phenomenon, which was fairly common until the turn of the present century, is now a rarity. In the past there have been great epidemics of dancing mania in countries as far apart as Madagascar and Holland. This curious form of mass hysteria sometimes reached the proportions of a social menace. Music or percussion instruments set the feet dancing until most of the population of a village or town may be affected, so great is the contagion. The dancers dance in ecstasy until utterly exhausted. The performer's powers of endurance are often phenomenal.

Occasionally one comes across old psychiatric cases of hysterical individuals who danced while in a somnambulic trance. Some of these subjects who had scarcely danced a step previously reached impressive heights of choreographic expression. If these individuals capitalised their unusual faculty they were billed as " dream-dancers ".

It is a fact that the hysteric can frequently attain to greater facility, and even brilliance, of expression in writing, speaking and acting during his " automatic " phases than during his normal state of consciousness.

A perfect example of " automatic " behaviour is seen in monoideic somnambulism. With adults, ordinary sleep walking usually involves action without speech; with children, on the other hand, speaking more often occurs without any accompanying physical activity. In highly hysterical individuals somnambulism may involve both action and speech.

Clinical cases of hysterical monoideic somnambulism, however, are in a different category altogether, from that of the occasional sleep-walker or sleep-talker. Such somnambulism may manifest itself as a vivid re-enactment of some tragic or terrifying scene in which the patient has previously participated. Janet records many such cases. The patient will go through the same actions that he went through at the time of his original experience in a grotesque and pathetic pantomime. In extreme cases this hysterical pantomime may take place several times a day without any variation. In such cases it is a general characteristic that the patient cannot remember the *original* experience which he mimics so faithfully during the somnambulic state of consciousness. By psychotherapy, however, this memory can be restored to the patient and his somnambulic attacks then cease forthwith. During such attacks, which seldom last long, a limited personality is seen to have emerged quite different from that of the subject in his normal waking state.

In monoideic somnambulism the temporary personality manifested is naturally a very circumscribed one. In advanced cases of polyideic somnambulism, however, we witness the beginnings of a true secondary personality. The behaviour of such somnambules can be varied in the extreme, and they may even walk and talk as in normal life except that they are living through a kind of dream, oblivious to the events around them. When they are deeply hypnotised almost any form of " dream " can be suggested ; in such instances we witness true hypnotic somnambulism involving genuine dissociation or " trance ", Most instances of hypnotic " somnambulism " are attributable to imitative or mimetic responses to the operator's suggestion.

Cases of prolonged somnambulic states have occasionally been reported. Several of these have exhibited a wide range of intelligent activity. This type of somnambulism may be regarded as a rudimentary form of dual-personality. Other instances which exhibit many of the characteristics of somnambulism can only be termed partial-somnambulism, for the subject reacts intelligently when spoken to and answers questions asked by those around him. There is, in fact, a graduated series of somnambulic types, ranging from the patient who suffers from the repetitive pantomimes just described, to forms of partial-somnambulism in which the patient exhibits a complete new personality equal in many respects to the normal self so far as intelligence is concerned. This somnambulic personality, however, usually lacks all memory of the subject's normal waking life and remembers only those incidents and experiences which have occurred during previous somnambulic phases.

This selective continuity of memory is characteristic of nearly all such dissociated states of consciousness. The patient has virtually acquired two personalities, the normal one and the somnambulic one, and between the two there is a watertight compartment through which the memories pertaining to each personality cannot infiltrate. However all somnambules are easily hypnotised and once hypnotised the patient can generally be made to recall the experiences of his previous somnambulic phases.

It occurs sometimes that a partial-somnambulic personality emerges which lasts, not for just a few minutes or hours but for days. In such instances one can no longer speak of somnambulism, for this would be stretching an already overworked word too far. These are the cases, popular with authors and journalists, known colloquially as " loss of memory " and technically as *fugues*. One day a man may wake up unable to identify his surroundings, unable to recall his name, his address, his friends and relatives or his occupation. If he visits a psychiatrist, this hysterical syndrome can be cured without much trouble. Cases have fairly often occurred, however, which have lasted for months or even years.

These fugues are real changes of personality. All those elements of the personality which have hitherto been repressed suddenly take charge of the personal consciousness. They are very commonly the result of living a life bound by uncongenial duty or moral obligations such as are occasioned by family, work, and social considerations. Emotional stress or shock can bring about the same results. The subject detests his mode of living and longs to escape from it, but these ideas are sternly repressed and kept out of his conscious thoughts. Suddenly the repression fails, perhaps on account of some shock, and the repressed part of his personality emerges, bringing in its turn repression of all former memories and a consequent lacuna.

The patient now leads a life of relative freedom, no longer restrained by former duties or his conscience.

The fate of some of those who suffer from fugues is sometimes a very pleasant one. There is more than one case of a man building up a business and marrying again under such circumstances. The subject may also show surprising efficiency at jobs for which, so far as his normal self was concerned, he previously cared little. Other cases are not so fortunate, and a fugue often resulted in extreme hardship in days when the medical and public services were not so knowledgeable or extensive as they are today. In the less civilised parts of the world such as India, fugues, in common with other severe hysterical syndromes, are relatively frequent.

In the normal course of events, unless he visits a psychiatrist, the patient usually retains no memory of his fugue period when his normal personality spontaneously reasserts itself. He takes up the thread of his life at the point at which his fugue occurred.

The fugue is essentially an escape from an uncongenial environment. The escape motive is behind most types of hysterical ailment. The motive itself remains hidden from the patient's personal awareness so that he is no longer bothered by his conscience and considerations of duty. By forgetting his past he no longer feels bound to it.

There are several discernible variations of the hysterical fugue. *Alternating personality* is one such example. The patient may alternate every so often between his normal personality and his secondary one and back again. Where amnesia occurs, the secondary phases may be regarded either as minor fugues or major somnambulisms according to the dominant characteristics. Janet records the case of a French village girl who kept a small shop and who underwent at intervals a complete change of personality accompanied by amnesia. She generally sensed when these attacks were coming on, and if she was doing anything important at the time of the change she made a note of it on a piece of paper. By this means she was able, when the change occurred, to carry on with her work without being troubled by her loss of memory.

Loss of memory in such cases is, of course, a relative matter. Each of the patient's two personalities, the normal one and the secondary one, possesses its own stream of memory. In the fugal stage the patient will recall only those memories and experiences which occurred during previous fugal phases. The intervening periods remain blank. Similarly the memory pertaining to the normal personality will not include those experiences which took place during the fugal periods. The patient thus possesses two separate streams of memory, each in its own impermeable compartment. The same thing may occur in recurrent hypnosis. The operator, if not careful, may literally create a secondary amnesic personality in certain hysterical subjects who are hypnotised very frequently.

In a fair number of cases of alternating personality, amnesia may occur during the secondary phase of consciousness but there is no corresponding amnesia each time the subject recovers his normal personality, i.e. while in his normal state the subject's memory covers *both* phases and is continuous. The same thing may occur *vice versa*. The subject is then said to be *one-way amnesic*. The same phenomenon may occur in cases of multiple personality and in true hypnotic somnambulism.

The case of the French girl mentioned above is one of the most extraordinary in the history of pathological hysteria. Her normal personality was slovenly and cheerless and without much intelligence. During her fugal phases she exhibited a cheerful and lively disposition and felt full of energy and health. Her intelligence was correspondingly greater ; the change of personality was very similar to that often seen in psychasthenic patients who are given electric shock therapy. At first her fugal periods were short. Gradually they became more and more extensive until they eventually exceeded in duration her periods of " normality." Finally her periods of " normality " became the exception and the occasional short reversions to her old personality came to be looked upon as an unfortunate malady.

When, as often occurs in hysteria, the normal mechanism of repression works overtime, a great many emotionally-toned ideas and memories may become repressed to form an organised complex which cannot reach the threshold o personal awareness. It is such complexes which may lead to somnambulism, and to fugues and alternating or multiple personality, which may be regarded in some respects as extreme developments of polyideic somnambulism.

Some psychologists employ the sound method of accounting for such hysterical developments of mental life by comparing them with the normal processes of which they may be regarded as exaggerations. Lapses of memory are common enough in ordinary everyday existence, as also are changes of mood. Everyone is liable to aberrations in conduct at one time or another ; for example, a man in a temper does not exhibit the same type of reactions as when he is feeling pleased and happy. These normal lapses of memory and labile effects are of the same kind as those encountered, in more pronounced and sustained form, in multiple personality.

The hysterical syndrome of multiple personality is often confused in the public mind with the type of insanity now known as *schizophrenia* and formerly as *dementia praecox*. Schizophrenia, a term which derives from the ancient Greek, means literally, " split-mind." The confusion arises from the tendency of the layman to refer to cases of dual or multiple personality as "split personality" or "split mind." In actual fact, schizophrenia has little connection with hysterical changes of personality.

The first scientific account of a case of multiple personality was that of Mary Reynolds, published by the American psychologist Ellicott in 1815. In literature Robert Louis Stevenson holds pride of place for the use of the theme of alternating personality in his famous story of " Dr. Jekyll and Mr. Hyde," although Edgar Alan Poe was the first major literary figure to make use of the phenomenon.

The most celebrated case of multiple personality is the well-known Beauchamp case investigated by Morton Prince, [1] founder and editor of the American *Journal of Abnormal Psychology*. Prince's hysterical patient, known as Miss Beauchamp, exhibited four distinct and separate personalities, three of which possessed their own separate set of memories. Her original personality, B1, was studious, submissive, shy, religious and poor in health. Her other

---

[1] Prince, M., *The Dissociation of a Personality* : A *Biographical Study in Abnormal Psychology*, N.Y. 1906.

personality, B4, was self-assertive, wordly, irrascible and vain, intolerant of religion, and possessing abundant health and vitality. The two personalities were, in fact, the complementary sides of her character. Neither appeared to possess any memory of each other's mental life or experiences, although both could remember the events in Miss Beauchamp's life up to the first emotional crisis six years before. B4 heartily disliked all that B1 liked and often played spiteful tricks upon her during the former's periods of ascendence. B1 had different friends from B4. They communicated by writing notes and placing them where the other would find them. The changes of personality were frequent. The result was exactly as if two entirely antagonistic people inhabited the same body for alternate periods of time. Emotional crises over two love affairs had brought about the excessive repressions responsible for the personality changes.

This Jekyll-and-Hyde existence was further complicated by the emerge of a third personality who christened herself " Sally." Dr. Prince had previously been treating Miss Beauchamp by hypnotic suggestion, and Sally was a typical hypnotic trance personality, childish and irresponsible. Such regressive personalities may be observed in some types of hysterical somnambulism and in the artificial somnambulism produced by deep hypnosis. The secondary personalities of spiritualist mediums are often of the same order, only in their case the secondary personality focuses around the idea of a discarnate spirit, owing to the influence of spiritualistic ideas acting upon a suggestible (and often hysterical) mind.

In Miss Beauchamp's case there is no doubt that the emergence of " Sally " was a hypnotic phenomenon due to indirect suggestion by Dr. Prince. Her autobiographical writings exhibited her as a soul suppressed for most of its early life and finding at long last access to the joys of communication with the world of human beings ! B1 was aware of Sally's existence but B4 was not, until informed by Dr. Prince and by letters from B1.

Morton Prince, with the aid of repeated hypnotherapy, gradually synthesised the two antagonistic personalities of B1 and B4 into a well-balanced personality who commanded the memories of both of them. Sally fought this fusion tooth and nail, claiming that she felt she was being squeezed out of existence.   With the fusion, however, Miss Beauchamp no longer suffered from hysterical symptoms, and Sally, who latterly had been emerging spontaneously from time to time without hypnosis, died a natural death.

While fugues and simple dual or alternating personalities may be often regarded as spontaneous hysterical syndromes, multiple personalities are generally due to indirect suggestion on the part of the psychotherapist.   Often the psychotherapist has inadvertently brought about the emergence of yet further personalities by faulty hypnotic technique. Janet's subject, Leonie B., who developed two subsidary personalities with amnesia, is an excellent case in point.   But the record must surely be claimed for the case of multiple personality reported by Dr. R. M. Riggall in *The Lancet* in 1931. [1]   This subject, an unmarried woman of 37, was reported to have no less than *seven* distinct personalities !

This case presents unusual parallels with the Beauchamp case.   There were two major personalities, " Mabel " and " Miss Dignity," each complementary and antithetical. Mabel was religious, prudish and reserved, while Miss Dignity was spiteful, bold, totally lacking in modesty and bent on tormenting Mabel.   Dignity tore up Mabel's money, ripped her clothes, broke her ornaments and on one occasion inserted a broken wineglass in her vagina " to annoy Mabel." The glass had to be removed by Dr. Riggall.   There was a third personality who styled herself Biddy, whose status corresponded to the Sally of Morton Prince's case.   Biddy was a bright, cheerful, laughing, helpful personality.   There was total amnesia between each personality and they spent a considerable amount of time writing antagonistic letters to each other.   One letter from Dignity to Mabel advised suicide, saying that the letter enclosed a packet of poison. The handwritings of all were markedly different in style. Apart from these three personalities there were four others who made occasional appearances under hypnosis and which were undoubtedly due to indirect suggestion by the psychotherapist.

Although Dr. Riggall succeeded in fusing the persona-

---

[1] *The Lancet*, Oct. 17th., 1931, pp. 846-848.

lities by hypnotic treatment he failed to cure the underlying neurosis, the patient refusing to undergo further psycho-analytical treatment for this.

Dr. Riggall's explanation for the appearance of the secondary personality, self-styled " Dignity," is a sound one. Dignity, despite her name, represented the instinctive side of the patient's nature.   In the part played by Dignity, this instinctive side gained an outlet and was able to find satis-faction in the fulfilment of hitherto repressed anti-social urges.   Mabel represented the law-abiding civilised side of the patient's character and was hence the target of Dignity's anti-social instincts.   The emergence of Dignity was brought about by dramatising and personifying the repressed material.

This last conclusion is of particular interest, for we can see this process of personifying the repressed ideas and wishes in dramatic form in many hysterical syndromes ; in many examples of automatic writing, somnambulism, and in.var-ious trance states as exemplified by the spiritualistic medium. This is easily understood as far as it stands ; what is difficult to account for is the total amnesia between one personality and another.   This need not always be attributed to con-scious deception, as some psychologists are inclined to believe.   As noted elsewhere, marked phases of amnesia are found frequently among lonely people with tendency to hysteria, who have a habit of talking to themselves while day-dreaming or while " in a brown study."   Long mono-logues and even " conversations " may thus be held, but as soon as they are disturbed they "come to" with a start ; realising that they have been talking aloud, they feel an extremity of embarrassment if they suspect that they have been overheard.   Frequently they are able to recall only the last few words or sentences of what they were saying and cannot recollect the rest with any certainty unless they are able to think back and " hear " themselves talking.   It is to be noted, too, that many people who fall into habit of talking to themselves often visualise themselves in dramatic situations where they allow their emotions to guide their thoughts and imaginary actions on a level closed to them in actual life.

It should be emphasised that although some cases of multiple personality may give a *prima facie* impression that each personality possesses a continuous mental life co-conscious with that of the personality which is in the ascendant, such an impression is incorrect.   As a working hypothesis the concept of co-consciousness may be perfectly valid. Taken as an empirical fact, however, it becomes quite meaningless.   There is no *continuous* conscious existence for these personalities.

Chapter Eleven

THE SPIRITUALISTIC MEDIUM AND MEDIUMISTIC TRANCE

THE CULT OF SPIRITUALISM and the spiritualistic medium is a modern development of primitive shamanism. A noticeable difference between primitive shamanism and modern mediumship is that with the former the practitioners are generally men, while present-day western mediumship is generally practised by women. Modern spiritualism, unlike shamanism, differentiates between two types of medium, namely " physical " mediums and " mental " mediums.

The " physical " medium specialise; in the production of so-called " physical phenomena "—" psychic " lights, ectoplasm, visible spirit forms, movements of objects at a distance, levitation, spirit raps, bumps and knocks and a large number of other elementary conjuring tricks and illusions. These tricks naturally require varying shades of darkness for their performance and are claimed to be due to the activity of discarnate spirits.

The " mental " medium on the other hand purports to be solely the *mouthpiece* of the spirit world ; her utterances, while in a state of trance, are supposed to be inspired or directly controlled by the spirits of the dead—a feature which she shares in common with the " physical " medium. The " physical " medium is almost invariably a conscious fraud. But while the " mental " medium may also be fraudulent, she is often sincere in the sense that her trances may be genuine instances of dissociation, or allied states of consciousness, and that she believes in the supernatural significance of such trance states. Both types of mediumship arc as old as mankind, but it is comparatively recently that the shaman, in the person of the spiritualistic medium of western civilisation, has begun to specialise in the different branches of the trade.

The object of the present chapter is to investigate the psychology of the genuine "mental" medium, whose various states of trance still hold millions of otherwise reasonable people in a happy condition of superstitious awe, wonder and frequent emotional stress. A study of the mediumistic trance is not only interesting in itself but throws a good deal of light from an altogether new angle upon dissociated states of consciousness. It is therefore well worth while going in detail into this fascinating realm in which the spurious and the genuine reciprocally support and mutually benefit the other.

Amongst the well known psychologists who have investigated the mediumistic trance are Jung,[1] Flournoy and William Brown. Of these only Flournoy, one-time Professor of Psychology at Geneva University, can be said to have made a really extended study of the subject. Flournoy investigated at great length the trance states of the medium whom he made famous, Elise Müller, better known to the world as Hélène Smith. Jung's medium presented many affinities to that of Flournoy.

The majority of mediums may be said to be wittingly fraudulent i.e. they act a part with a view to monetary gain. On the other hand at the other end of the scale, there is the medium who believes completely in the spiritualistic *credo*, who does not conscously act a part during her trance, and who seldom resorts to conscious deception. This type of medium may be considered the exception. In between there exists a large class of professional and amateur mediums who possess a genuine enough faculty of attaining to dissociative and quasi-dissociative states of consciousness in varying degree and who improve upon them by artifice. Simulation of trance states is, of course, very easy, and it is this which renders investigation of the more intelligent spiritualistic mediums so difficult. Many a professional medium who once possessed a real trance faculty ends up by simulating article simply because she finds it easier.

---

[1] Jung, C. G., *Collected Papers on Analytical Psychology*, 1920, pp. 16-45.

Trance is a very loose term which embraces a number of widely differing psychological states ; these range in degree from the cataleptic coma of some " ecstatic " dervishes to the ordinary daytime reverie when one's thoughts are said to be " miles away ". In common with many other popular terms which have passed into psychology, no precise definition is available. The " somnambulic trance " of the sleep-walker, the " hypnotic trance " of the hypnotised subject, the "yoga-trance" of the auto-hypnotised Indian mystic, the " cataleptic trance " of extreme hysteria, the " ecstatic trance " of euphoric and hallucinated saints, shamans and visionaries—all possess one factor in common, namely a temporary forgetfulness or unawareness of the immediate physical environment. This is perhaps the chief hallmark of the trance. Unawareness of objects and people in the surrounding environment need not be total—it may he hazy or *anoetic*, on the periphery of consciousness.

In its fullest development, the trance is accompanied by extreme mental dissociation and automatism. At the other end of the scale there is a form of mild trance, engendered by wishful-thinking, self-deception or auto-suggestion, when the subject's peculiar actions and speech originate primarily in a neurotic desire for attention. Again, there is the fake trance, which among professional spiritualistic mediums is the commonest of all.

Nevertheless, " The capacity to pass into a trance-like state may be facilitated by practise and some mediums have developed this capacity very markedly."[2]

Subjects who are in a condition of abnormal suggestibility —for example, that engendered by hypnotic methods—are often referred to as being in a state of " trance ". The term is also applied to the periods of rapt contemplation which mystics are able to engender at will or which occur spontaneously. The techniques of attaining to a trance state are various, often involving an artificial over-stimulation of the emotions and senses, or unusual exercises in respiration. *Hypernoea*, or very rapid breathing, may even result in rigid cataleptic " trance ".

Drugs may also produce a kind of " trance " in which the

---

[2] Curran and Guttmann, *Psychological Medicine*, p. 193.

subject possesses little desire to exert his own will and speaks and acts in a sleepy daze, not fully conscious of what he is either saying or doing. Hysterical and psychasthenic individuals, and individuals with a tendency to minor forms of psychosis, may experience periods of trance-like states in which they are not fully conscious of their actions or speech. The term " trance " is also applied sometimes to individuals who experience periodic phases of stupor or extreme lethargy or even coma. Many mediums appear to sink into such states spontaneously at the commencement of their séances, though the great majority undoubtedly simulate these symptoms.

The term " trance " may be seen to be a vague unsatis-factory one. The concept to which the term gives expression originally arose in connection with the primitive belief, held since time immemorial, that a person who exhibits any of the various symptoms described above has had his soul drawn away from his body. The theme of the soul parting temporarily from the body is a common one in all climes and in all ages and is still prevalent in many parts of the world at the present day.

Many trance states of the spiritualistic medium are attributed to hysteria ; but others do not fall into this category. Between the two lies a large class which may best be described as mild forms of automatic speaking, partly due to hysterical tendencies, partly due to auto-hypnotic practices, partly due to suggestion. As with automatic writing, these mild trance states can be acquired. Like automatic writing, too, total amnesia can supervene, i.e. the subject is not able to recall anything written or spoken during trance. It is not often fully recognised that a great deal of automatic writing is produced in as much of a trance state as the verbal utterances of mediums.

So far as the spiritualistic medium is concerned, we can observe two distinct types of trance, apart from those which are simulated from base motives. The most interesting of these, and the least common, are those which involve an abnormal degree of mental dissociation or automatism. The second type, less easily definable, involves the acting-out of inward imaginative fantasies conditioned by tradition and suggestion. We will deal with this second type first.

We have already made some mention of day-time reveries and of people who are given to talking to themselves while temporarily oblivious of their immediate environment. This is precisely what is involved in the case of many mediums. The day-dreaming tendency has for them been developed into a definite neurosis, with escape from harsh reality as the driving factor. Many mediums have a history of lonely childhood behind them, and several, whose biographies are known, possessed in early childhood what is known in psychology as an *imaginary companion*, who took the place of the playmates they lacked. Normally only very sensitive children revert to an imaginary companion in their loneliness. With these they indulge in elaborate games and conversations and will often talk to their parents or guardians about their fantasy-playmate with every sign of conviction in its reality. Usually the imaginary companion fades out of the child's existence when the latter reaches the age of six or seven. With some children, however, the habit of talking to an imaginery person may persist into adult life. In some extreme cases the world of fantasy into which the adult falls becomes so intense that she or he gradually deteriorates into sustained delusions and eventually into schizophrenia.

The normal day-dream, even in the healthiest of individuals, can become abnormally intense if the habit persists. Day-dreams and autistic thinking are a form of outlet for frustrated or repressed wishes and instincts. By this means the individual is able to achieve a vicarious gratification of natural longings for love, authority, wealth, beauty, sex, or anything else which the human soul can desire. In schizophrenia the subject accepts the day-dream world of fantasy for reality, and the cure is generally a long and different process where it is not altogether an impossibility.

Erotic and sexual day-dreams are by far the commonest of all adult imaginative fantasies. Almost every normal adult has indulged in this form of fantasy at one period or another of his life. Erotic day-dreams may become such vivid experiences for sexually frustrated individuals, particularly women, that they engender a genuine trance state of consciousness to which psychiatrists have given the name *nympholepsy*.

Day-dreams may take any form, however, and one of the commonest of all involves long monologues or conversations between imaginary persons and the subject. Talking to oneself is very common with people who lack human companionship, and the process is usually an involuntary one. The individual's attention is directed away from the external environment, and focuses instead on the imaginative fantasy which the mind is spontaneously creating. The individual may not only address verbally the imaginary lover, inefficient cook, or hated enemy, but also gesticulate with his arms or stride furiously to and fro ; in extreme cases he may indulge in a complete pantomime, pleading, or caressing, or threatening, or laughing, or even going through all the motions of dying in order to gain the vicarious gratification of an imaginary funeral with all the trappings. In such extreme cases of day-dreaming the subject is invariably neurotic and over-sensitive by nature. If discovered in the midst of his conversational monologue or emotional pantomime, he or she will be filled with the acutest embarrassment. Usually, however, the unsuspected watcher gains only fleeting impressions of the emotional maelstrom occurring in the day-dreamer's mind ; a sudden fierce gesture or a few incoherent words or broken phrases are all that are observable.

The great emotional fervour or excitement which may accompany such day-dream fantasies often renders the individual completely absorbed in his imaginative world of people, scenes and events ; while the mood lasts, he is oblivious of the world of reality outside of him. For the moment the imagination supplies the reality. Occasional day-dreams do nobody harm. It is when they become prolonged out of all reason—even if the day-dream merely takes the form of a reverie—that the danger lies. Many a habitual reverie-addict has travelled down the path to schizophrenia. Often this path is a very pleasant one for the person concerned. Many a schizophrenic has lived in a world of perpetual joy and beauty ; unfortunately the reverse is the more likely.

Imaginary companions in childhood, the deep reverie, the unconscious verbal soliloquy, the emotional day-dream fantasy which is " acted-out "—all are examples of the way in which the individual will turn to an inner world of the imagination when he is cut off from the company of others either by force of circumstances or through the shortcomings, of his own personality. These examples throw an interesting light on the personalities and trances of many spiritualistic mediums. It is easy to understand how such quasi-trance states as the deep reverie, or such quirks of imagination as imaginary-companions, may become centred increasingly around spiritualistic ideas, once the subject's mind has been touched by them.

People given to intense day-dreaming and autistic thinking are generally attracted by what appeals to the imagination and the emotions—a function which spiritualism serves pre-eminently well. Again, the lonely, repressed or ill-adapted individual is normally far more susceptible to the influence of spiritualistic ideas than other people, and the day-dreamer belongs largely to these classes. *Once such day-dreamers become introduced to the ideas of spiritualism, it is only to be expected that many of them soon find their reveries, soliloquies, emotional fantasies and the rest, becoming more and more spiritualistic in content.* In such cases, the more they incline to complete acceptance of spiritualistic teachings, the less are they able to resist the wishful delusion that the spiritualistic fantasies of their day-dreams are evidence of clairvoyant powers or inspired by the spirits of the dead. From then on, it is but a short step to the beliefs and practices of the amateur, and eventually the professional, spiritualistic medium.

The practising medium soon acquires the knack of inducing her deep reverie at will, without delay and without self-consciousness. In this she is helped by the tradition of her profession and the sympathy and confidence of her sitters. If the medium's trance is of the reverie type, her verbal utterance may appear inconsequential, disconnected and dream-like. If it is an " acted-out " fantasy—one that is keenly felt by the medium herself—we may expect anything from emphatic *staccato* sentences or lyrical and fervent outpourings, to histrionics on the grand scale. With the

" imaginary-companion " type of medium, she may give the impression of conducting a telephone call which is being overheard at one end.

The intellectual level of all day-dreaming activity is naturally low, and it is therefore not surprising to find that the utterances of many trance mediums are characterised by a marked mental regression, which results in a form of speech more consonant with that of a child than an adult. On the other hand, as with some automatic writers, a small number of mediums have exhibited powers of imagination which are of a high creative standard.

Several mediums appear to have acquired the habit of describing their day-dream fantasies verbally while they are occurring. The majority of professional mediums who do this are undoubtedly putting on an act. This is not the case with all of them, however. Among those whom we may cite as probably authentic in this respect was the well-known medium Mrs. Willet (pseudonym), whose allegedly " paranormal " powers were for years the subject of investigation by the Society for Psychical Research. Mrs. Willet was in many ways a gifted and intelligent woman, and although much of her trance speech was childish in character, a great deal of it was quite the reverse. On one occasion she began a first person description of a scene in ancient Athens, which amounted to an imaginative reconstruction of an episode taken from Plato's *Symposium*. The medium joyously described the Hellenic scene of her imagination with an assurance which indicated that this particular reverie was one which had often recurred before, and that she temporarily imagined herself to be participating in it.

The day-dream type of trance, when genuine and not assumed, may be compared to the state which some people fall into when reading an absorbing novel. Such people may be spoken to or even shouted at several times before they realise they are being addressed. They are in a state of quasi-trance, with the printed words supplying the material for their imagination to work upon, instead of the imagination spontaneously bringing forth its own associations of ideas as in the case of the day-dreamer. In both cases the subject's attention is concentrated inward, upon a sequence of emotionally captivating or stimulating ideas.

With many mediums the trance appears to be similar to the hypnotic state. The medium lies down on a couch, relaxing completely with eyes closed, until a state of passivity is attained. In this state her speech often resembles that of the sleep talker. In many cases where the subsequent actions and speech of the medium resemble those witnessed in hypnotic " somnambulism ", it is evident that suggestion is the operative principle no less than in normal hypnosis. The main difference lies in the fact that normally in hypnosis suggestions are given direct by the operator, whereas in the case of the medium the suggestion derives from the state of expectancy not only on the part of the medium but also of her sitters. In a number of cases we may even assume the existence of a state of complete auto-hypnosis.

It is a fact that a great many mediums are hysterics or are strongly prone to hysteria. The hysterical medium is the true medium ; that is to say she may be subject to states of consciousness in which the normal processes of volition appear to break down, producing the phenomenon of genuine dissociation. Overt or latent tendencies to hysterical dissociation can, as is seen in hypnosis, be augmented or even brought about by means of suggestion, and it is in the highly expectant and suggestible atmosphere of the séance room that the medium's faculty of dissociation may manifest itself most strongly.

Once the habit of easily attaining a state of mental dissociation is achieved through constant repetition, the way is clear for the medium to give expression to a whole range of imaginative fantasies which would normally be unavailable to her. Hysterical dissociation may provide complete though vicarious outlet for the repressed tendencies, emotional complexes and latent memories which are themselves responsible for the medium's hysteria. These, and similar dissociative states of consciousness, may be regarded as the real " mediumistic trance ".

In most forms of mediumistic trance the medium may hear, feel, see and portray as facts, events which are the product of her own imagination, or which are due to aberrations of her own mental processes. With hysterical mediums, especially, such subjective delusions appear to be a dominant factor. Very frequently the medium may appear to be actually experiencing genuine hallucinatory sense-imagery, but this can be seldom be the case except with marked hysterics or incipient psychotics. In the mediumistic trance, as in hysterical *mimesis* and deep hypnosis, the boundary between reality and illusion often fails, so that the subject actually believes for the time in the reality of the world of fantasy provided by the imagination.

Where hysterical dissociation is present, the medium may. in rare cases, be subject to a form of verbal automatism, In such cases the trance state engendered can be compared to the state of consciousness observed in automatic writing. Hysterical verbal automatism, however, may become so extreme that the subject *cannot prevent* the tongue, lips and larynx from operating—the motor activity is quite involuntary. In such instances the subject may be able to hear and understand what he is saying but remains powerless to control his speech. A less extreme form of verbal automatism can be induced at will, much as the automatic writer induces autonography. Some hysterical mediums often give utterance to pure gibberish which they claim to be the language of the spirit world. This phenomenon presents an interesting parallel to xenoglossia, or " speaking with tongues ", known to religious mystics in all ages.

The interplay of hysterical tendencies, suggestion, autistic-thinking, subconscious motives, deliberate fraud, auto-hypnotisation, dissociation and automatism renders it virtually impossible to pin down the mediumistic trance and its various manifestations to any rigid scheme of psychological classification. Many mediums, too, are mentally unbalanced to a degree which verges on actual insanity, and only the most credulous among their changing clientèle of sitters can remain blind to the fact. Very many mediums show marked evidence of paranoia. One such case was that of the German medium, Mina Müller, who was investigated by Dr. Fünfgeld of the Frankfort University Psychiatry Clinic. [1]

Fünfgeld, though at first sympathetic to the medium's claims, found her reputed clairvoyant faculty to be without the least foundation. He found a marked tendency to

---

[1] Zeitschrift für die gesamte Neurologie und Psychiatrie, vol. cxix.

paranoia involving a strong desire to make her mark in the world, a total incapacity for self-criticism, an inability to accept the simplest rational argument when it tended to run counter to her fixed ideas, and above all a subjective delusion of the rightness of all that she said. She sustained this attitude despite the glaringly obvious fact that she resorted to conscious deception when the least opportunity occurred. It is difficult to classify a medium like Mina Müller as a moral fraud from the psychiatrist's standpoint ; although from the legal standpoint, with its practical emphasis on the individual's personal responsibility for his actions, the opposite view is perfectly tenable.

" SPIRIT PERSONALITIES "

We now enter upon the interesting question of " spirit personalities ". In common with all types of shamanism the world over, the *raison-d'etre* of the spiritualistic medium is her claimed ability to make contact with discarnate spirits. In less sophisticated forms of shamanism the spirits in question may be tutelary deities—vague anthropomorphic beings who control the forces of nature—or a host of good and evil spirits whose business it is to aid or persecute the human race. It is only in the most recent development of shamanism—the modern spiritualistic medium—that the focus of attention is exclusively directed to the task of contacting the spirits of dead persons.

There are various ways in which the medium may contact the spirits of the dead. Most mediums claim to possess a personal " guide " or " control ", readily available to them when they enter their trance. These guides and controls are generally the chief means of communicating with *other* inhabitants of the spirit-world. It is these spirits who are first " contacted " by the medium when she falls into her trance ; messages from other spirits are exchanged through them, or they bring other spirits directly into communication with the medium. These guides and controls often bear some high-sounding or exotic name, or claim to be the spirit of some long-dead legendary or famous person such as Hiawatha or Cleopatra. The spirits of ordinary deceased persons may also act as the medium's personal

" control ", although numbers of such " controls " are quite
fictitious in that their claims to a former earthly existence
are spurious.

The inhabitants of the spirit-world may send their messages
to the medium's sitters in several ways. The medium may
merely report what her guide or control " says " to her in
answer to the sitters' questions. She may act as the mouthpiece either of her own control, or of other spirits if " direct
communication " has been " established " with a sitter's
dead relative or friend ; in this latter case it is generally
assumed that the spirit in question has taken temporary
possession of the medium's body or at least of her vocal
apparatus. Of several variations on these two themes only
one need be mentioned here, and that is " direct voice "
communication. " Direct voice " mediums generally use
some mechanical apparatus, usually a trumpet, through
which they speak or whisper while attempting their impersonation of the deceased person. Such elementary
tricks of deception require no explanation other than that of
deliberate fraud.

Many of the spirit personalities evinced by the spiritualistic medium are readily explainable in terms of hysteria
or psychasthenic delusion. It is these which constitute a
most interesting subject of study from the standpoint both
of psychology and of the law, for they show the frequent
difficulty of assessing whether or not a medium can be held
morally or legally responsible for her mode of life. The
fact that a large class of mediums have become mediums
through a combination of psychological factors which are
largely beyond their control is not sufficiently recognised.
Nor, generally, is sufficient differentiation made between
those mediums who are deliberate money-seeking frauds and
those who believe strongly and sincerely in the spiritualistic
credo. The hysterical individual who converts her hysterical
syndromes into profitable and self-satisfying mediumship
must not be judged too harshly. The process is only too
often an inevitable one, once the hysteric has become introduced to the suggestible and often emotionally charged
atmosphere of the séance room.

With many hysterical mediums, the impersonations of
spirit guides and controls or dead persons bear a marked

relationship to similar phenomena seen in many hypnotised subjects, in automatic writing and—in the more extreme cases—in multiple or alternating personality.

Where dissociation is evidently at work, there is no need always to assume the existence of hysteria, latent or overt. Just as genuine automatic writing can be attained by most individuals with the time and patience, there is no need to doubt that an analogous form of automatic speaking—and this must be distinguished from hysterical verbal automatism—can also be acquired by practise ; dissociation, however, in the majority of such cases, is seldom likely to be so great as to involve the large degree of amnesia claimed by most mediums.

When marked hysterical tendencies are part of the medium's constitution, the speech and actions of the medium while in " trance " may take on a form analogous to the phenomenon of multiple personality, i.e. the medium may exhibit a true hysterical change of personality involving a high degree of dissociation with consequent amnesia. There are numerous parallels to be found between such secondary personalities as the " Sally " of Morton Prince's Beauchamp case (see pp. 158-160) and the controls or guides of many mediums. In such cases the personality of the spirit guide or control may be regarded simply as an aspect of the more general problem of hysterical multiple personality.

In regard to the Beauchamp case, if " Sally " had emerged during the auto-hypnotisation of the spiritualist séance instead of Dr. Prince's clinic, she would undoubtedly have taken on the guise of a discarnate spirit—probably as one of those child spirit-guides so often encountered in the literature of spiritualism. The case of " Sally " further provides a good instance of the way in which such secondary personalities play up to their audience, receiving ideas and suggestions from their interlocutors, modifying them and handing them back in confirmation of what the former have already presupposed.

This playing up to the audience at a spiritualist séance need not necessarily throw doubt upon the authenticity of the secondary personality, although it is often mistakenly construed by sceptics as evidence of conscious deception on behalf of the medium; doubtless this is generally the case, but it does not always follow. Dissociated secondary personalities are quite capable of achieving their own brand of duplicity, and this is often seen in the somnambulic personalities of deep hypnosis. In the case of " Sally " every effort was made to convince Dr. Prince of the authenticity of her claims to be an imprisoned soul struggling for years to attain her liberty—an act of creative artistry which played a large part in influencing Dr. Prince's conclusions. As was described in the chapter on autonography, a secondary personality claiming to be the spirit of a dead Victorian poetess, which manifested itself through Dr. S. G. Soal's automatic writing, made every attempt to deceive Dr. Soal himself into accepting her claims, and with a less informed autonographer might well have succeeded.

The hysterical tendencies of large numbers of mediums become increasingly evident, the more one studies the reports and resumés of their trance utterances. The secondary personalities (i.e. the " guides " and " controls ") exhibited by quite intelligent mediums very frequently show infantile characteristics, and in fact often claim to be the spirits of deceased children; the child-control " Feda " of the well-known medium Gladys Leonard is an excellent case in point.

The general low intelligence of mediumistic secondary personalities, in those cases where the medium is not practising deliberate fraud, finds numerous parallels in the secondary personalities of hysterical somnambulism, hypnosis and those evinced in a great deal of automatic writing. In view of this very widespread characteristic of mediumistic utterances during trance, it is all the more surprising to find that such mediums still find a great many sitters who believe completely in their transcendental powers. There is still no limit, it seems, to the naïve credulity of vast numbers of adults in modern society.

The predisposition to infantile regression seen in a great many mediums during trance is seldom, as is often thought, the direct product of the trance state. Rather it is the reverse. The predisposition is already present, and without it most mediums would not be able to relapse into a mental state where the imagination turns to naïve imitations of discarnate spirits; the medium would find other and worthier means of giving expression to suppressed wishes and latent memories.

All types of secondary personality of hysterical origin show themselves capable of assuming any rôle which is suggested to them or which suits the unconscious needs or conscious purposes of the individual concerned. In former times secondary personalities tended to take on rôles suggested to them by the traditions, beliefs and superstitions of the age. Thus we have secondary personalities who have claimed to be demons, the devil, or the mouthpiece of God and his angels. Such personalities tend to cohere round the frustrated desires of the individual, often in a sublimated form. As already noted somnambulic personalities in Biblical times and in the Middle Ages often took on the guise of evil spirits, and to be " possessed " by a devil or even ten devils was something to be taken seriously, since it often sent the poor unfortunate hysteric to death by stoning or at the stake.

In only relatively few cases does the mediumistic trance appear to involve an unequivocal degree of hysterical somnambulism. In its spontaneous form monoideic somnambulism could not be capitalised by any would-be medium to any advantage. The same may be said of true polyideic somnambulism, but there are states of consciousness which, if not truly somnambulic, possess many attributes of genuine somnambulism, and some mediums have probably acquired the faculty of inducing states almost at will. This faculty might appear spontaneously in cases where the original somnambulic tendency becomes susceptible to modification by suggestion or autosuggestion.

There is a close relationship between the hypnotic state and the state of mediumistic trance. Experiments have shown that it is possible to induce an involuntary mediumistic trance in a hysterical subject by post-hypnotic suggestion, and that under these circumstances the subject will claim to be controlled by a " spirit " whose utterances will be consonant with ideas previously suggested to him while under hypnosis.

The histrionic abilities of hypnotised subjects and those shown by many mediums also require mention. Most mediums lie down and relax as a preliminary to their séance, and there is little reason to doubt that in numbers of cases a process of auto-hypnotisation occurs, which, as in normal hypnotic procedures, may result in a spontaneous aptitude for impersonation and dramatic ability. In such instances the form of the impersonation is brought about, not by direct suggestion as in normal hypnosis, but by the medium's state of expectancy of communicating with the deceased.

To make broad generalisations on the mediumstic trance and its various manifestations is unwise. In only a relatively few cases does the trance emerge as a simple, easily analysed, phenomenon. Almost invariably a great number of factors are involved, subtly intermixed and often varying from séance to séance in their relationship to one another. The various manifestations of the mediumistic trance are, as will be seen shortly, not to be explained in terms of the psychology of the medium alone but also involve the reactions and attitudes of the sitters as well. With the genuine hysterical or psychasthenic medium the problem is even further complicated by the fact that the secondary personalities which emerge are themselves capable of influencing the course of trance development. Between the evolution of the trance state and the emergent secondary personalities there is often reciprocal influence and mutual interaction which makes accurate analysis virtually impossible. Only one such analysis has been attempted—that by Professor Flournoy at the turn of the century, and it is to this interesting case which we now turn.

THE CASE OF HÉLENE SMITH—HYSTERICAL MEDIUM

The case of Hélène Smith provides an excellent example of how hysterical tendencies can be capitalised by an intelligent woman through converting them into mediumistic channels. This remarkable medium was made the subject of a thorough psychological study by two Swiss psychologists ; first by Professor Flournoy and subsequently, until the medium's death, by Professor Deonna.

Hélène's trances were varied in the extreme. Sometimes they appeared little different from those of the majority of mediums, while at other times they appeared more allied to major manifestations of hysterical somnambulism. Like St. Theresa or Joan of Arc—probably the greatest " medium " of all time—Hélène talked to her spirits, heard them answer in reply and often saw them—or so it seemed to her. Whether or not she actually experienced genuine sensory hallucinations or whether they were the product of subjective delusion is difficult to say.

Today recurrent hysterical hallucinations are a rarity and are confined to the most extreme cases of hysteria or occur at moments when the hysteric is subjected to great emotional stress. Strong suggestion, expectation and emotion can all result in what we have, for the sake of brevity, called pseudo-hallucinations ; and as we have seen, pseudo-hallucinations can be just as powerful in their effects upon the minds and beliefs of the individual concerned as the true sensory hallucination. In the case of Hélène Smith there does seem quite a good deal of evidence for actual sense-imagery being present at times, particularly in the latter part of her history when she hovered on the borders of insanity.

Hélène, during the period of Flournoy's investigations, was a pleasant-natured and intelligent young woman. She worked in a big store and was conscientious and efficient. The only evidence of anything out of the ordinary in her character was, significantly, her advanced cryptomnesic faculty. For example, if asked for the location of a particular article, or for a date of any particular event, she could frequently recall the desired information spontaneously and without conscious effort, but without recollecting the circumstances under which she originally acquired the knowledge. This faculty of " hidden memory " stood her in good stead in her work and appeared somewhat uncanny to her superiors.

The facts of Hélène's somnambulic mediumship are so extraordinary as to warrant a lengthy description. There is only room, however, to indicate some of the salient points.

Those interested would be well advised to read the fascinating account of Flournoy's sympathetic study of the medium.[1]

The majority of genuine mediums confine themselves to one or two types of trance manifestation. Hélène Smith possessed four distinct types ; two of these, viz., automatic-writing and verbal automatism, were accompanied by a supression of the normal consciousness and were followed by amnesia. The third type of trance involved auditory hallucinations whose content she either wrote down or repeated aloud as from dictation. Dissociation in this last instances left her sufficient freedom of mind to allow her to observe the words she heard in a reflective and even critical manner. Her consciousness of her immediate environment was anoetic at these times, though not altogether obliterated.

The fourth and most complex type of manifestation was somnambulism with accompanying visual and auditory hallucinations. Hélène would often go through the most vivid and emotional enactment of a scene whose reality existed for herself alone. The effect on the witnesses of these highly dramatic exhibitions of her histrionic powers was one of enthralling fascination. Such extreme somnambulism was, however, the exception rather than the rule. For the most part she was able to take a detached view of her visions and voices up to a point, and remembered them without difficulty. Consciousness of present reality during these visions was marginal and vague, though seldom completely obliterated except in the extreme instances of histrionic somnambulism. When experiencing such hallucinations she no longer heard or saw what was going on in her immediate environment. Flournoy graphically describes the onset and disappearance of her visions, :

" For a few moments, for instance, the room, the light of the lamp, disappear from before her eyes ; the noise of the wheels in the street ceases to be heard ; she feels herself becoming inert and passive, while a feeling of bliss and ecstatic well-being permeates her entire

---

[1] *From India to the Planet Mars : a Study of a Case of Somnambulism with Glossalalia*, London, 1900.
See also further vol., *Nouvelles Observations sur un Cas de Somnambulisme avec Glossolalie*; and Prof. W. Deonna's *De la Planete Mars en Terre Sainte* ; *Art et Subconscience* ; *Un Medium peintre : Helene Smith.* Paris, 1932.

individuality in the presence of the spectacle which appears to her; then the vision, to her great regret, slowly fades from her view, the lamp and the furniture re-appear, the outside noises again make themselves heard . . . . " [2]

The central figure of her hallucinations was a benevolent spirit who styled himself Leopold. Leopold was her guide, mentor and protector, not only in her trance adventures in medieval India or forty-three million miles away on Mars, but also in ordinary everyday life. As previously mentioned Socrates had a similar protecting spirit or *daemon* whose voice he heard internally and which, to him, as with the hallucinatory angels of Joan of Arc and Hélène Smith's Leopold, was completely convincing evidence of the reality of a world of spiritual beings. Socrates' *daemon* certainly enabled him to face death calmly in the conviction that within a few minutes he would find himself in another and more interesting realm of existence. St. Joan went to torture and death rather than disbelieve in the reality of her guardian voices. Hélène never wavered in her belief that Leopold possessed a reality of his own.

Leopold is a magnificent example of the way in which repressed desires and tendencies may be personified and acted out in dramatic form. The illusion of Leopold's independence appears complete :

" He speaks for her (Helene) in a way she would have no idea of doing, he dictates to her poems of which she would be incapable. He replies to her oral or mental questions, converses with her, and discusses various questions. Like a wise friend, a rational mentor, and as one seeing things from a higher plane, he gives her advice, counsel, orders, even sometimes directly opposite to her wishes and against which she rebels. He consoles her, exhorts her, soothes, encourages, and reprimands her ; he undertakes against her the defence of persons she does not like, and pleads the cause of those who are antipathetic to her.   In a word, it would be impossible to imagine a being more independent or more different from Mlle. Smith herself, having a more personal character, an individuality more marked, or a more certain actual existence." [3]

There is no doubt that Leopold combined in his personality

[2] Flournoy, T., op. cit., pp. 52-53.
[3] Flournoy, T., op. cit., pp. 78-79.

a few facets of character and intelligence which were often of a higher grade than the medium herself normally possessed. Paradoxically, the general impression he gives is one of emotional immaturity, a combination often found in people called geniuses through their faculty of brilliant work achieved without a corresponding effort.

In the case of the spontaneous genius the formation, association and incubation of ideas is done at the unconscious level and the finished product emerges more or less complete into consciousness. Most writers and composers are familiar in some degree with this phenomenon—the pen just does not run fast enough to transcribe the flow of ideas on to paper. In Hélène Smith's case the unconscious incubation of ideas operated on a formidable scale. It reached the limit in the composition and retention of an entirely new language, used with permanent consistency, and ostensibly taught her by the omniscient Leopold. The term omniscient is appropriate, for the language he taught his protégé was that of the inhabitants of Mars !

Hélène's adventures and her description of Mars make extremely interesting reading. By automatic writing, verbal automatism, dictation from hallucinatory voices and descriptions of her visual hallucinations, a composite picture of the fauna, flora, topography, inhabitants and customs of Mars was built up. Her subconscious creation of the Martian scene was naïve and not beyond the powers of an imaginative school child. The construction of the Martian language also showed the same level of intelligence, being composed mainly of distorted European root-words, mostly French, with the most elementary grammar. But in view of the fact that Hélène spoke it with consistency and considerable fluency, Flournoy considered it a prodigious feat of subconscious memory. In his book Flournoy gives numerous examples of this form of *glossolalia* with accompanying translations. The volume also contains drawings by Hélène of the Martian scene copied during her hallucinatory experiences.

Hysterical mediums who are subject to abnormal states of dissociation are invariably convinced of the supernatural origin of their trance utterances. When the phenomenon of crytomnesia enters into the picture, such beliefs are easily

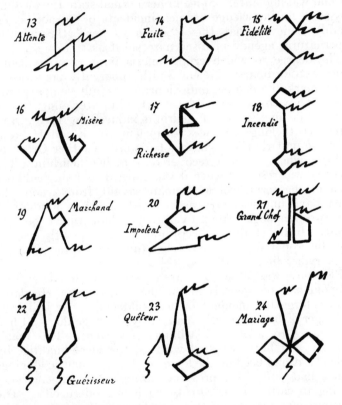

SAMPLES OF AN "ULTRA-MARTIAN" WRITTEN LANGUAGE COMPOSED DURING TRANCE BY THE REMARKABLE MEDIUM HELENE SMITH

(Reproduced from "Archives de Psychologie," Geneva, 1901.)

understood. Hysteria is largely the product of repression, and when in a state of trance such mediums may well be able to recall long-forgotten incidents and memories which have been repressed beyond conscious recall during their normal waking state. Since in her normal state the medium possesses no knowledge of such incidents or memories, she readily believes that they " came to her " through the supernatural agency of discarnate spirits.

The degree to which cryptomnesia may attain is sometimes extraordinary. Hélène Smith apparently possessed it to a remarkable degree, and Flournoy usefully compares her glossolalia with the case of a nearly illiterate young woman who, while in a state of delirium induced by fever, gave utterance to long sentences in ancient Greek and Hebrew. It was found that she knew not a word of either Greek or Hebrew when she had recovered from her delirium. The mystery was resolved when it was learned that she had once been in the service of a German savant from whom she must have unconsciously assimilated a certain amount of the two languages from overhearing him whilst he was engaged in his studies. Cryptomnesia is frequently responsible for apparent cases of " telepathy " or " clairvoyance " in everyday life.

Flournoy was able, by careful analysis, to show that Leopold had his genesis in the medium's past. He dated from a forgotten incident in her childhood. She had been in danger of being severely mauled by a savage dog and had been saved by a man of striking appearance. This man's memory had been invested with all the ideal qualities by Hélène ; it had become the focus of all her romantic longings which had suffered repression through the exigencies of having to earn a humdrum living in a modern city. The subconscious memory of this man became the central pivot of her repressed daydreams and fantasies. But as Flournoy has succinctly and intructively put it :

> " Without the spiritualism and the auto-hypnotization of the seances, Leopold could never have been truly developed into a personality, but would have continued to remain in the nebulous, incoherent state of vague subliminal reveries and of occasional automatic phenomena." [1]

---

[1] Flournoy, T., op. cit., pp. 92-93.

In 1929 Professor T. K. Oesterreich reported another remarkable case of hysterical glossolalia.[2] This case presents many parallels with that of Hélène Smith, except that in the case of the " Mädchen aus der Fremde " the dissociation was more complete and amounted to a semi-permanent fugue.   This girl's secondary personality took on the character of an oriental mystic.   She spoke a pseudo-tongue, which was her own invention created subconsciously by a technique similar to Flournoy's medium.   She imagined herself a priestess of a mysterious Buddhist cult.   This was eventually shown to have been derived from the vivid impression made on her by a statue of Buddha during the early days of her hysterical mental condition and its fusion with her naturally strong, though unorthodox, devotion towards Roman Catholicism.   There is not the least doubt that had the *Mädchen* been subjected to the influences of the séance room her secondary personality would have taken on the trappings of spiritualism instead of those of an imaginative form of Buddhism.

After Hélène Smith's death in 1930, Professor Deonna published a book[3] on the medium's latter years.   It shows a picture of Hélène, hurt and outraged by Flournoy's book explaining her spiritualistic visions and communications in orthodox psychological terms as products of her own subconscious mind, refusing further scientific investigation, and turning wholeheartedly to the development of her powers as a spiritualsitic medium.   Deonna describes how in Hélène's last years her secondary personality took on the guise of the reincarnation of Mary, the sister of Martha, and painted scenes from the New Testament at the guidance of heavenly spirits which surrounded her :   Mary's style was curious.   She painted here and there over the canvas without apparent cohesion until, quite surprisingly, the last few strokes rendered the picture virtually complete.   Deonna was not so sympathetic as Flournoy, or perhaps the medium's mental condition had declined with the years.   For although he drew comparison between Hélène and other inspired

---

[2] *Das Mädchen aus der Fremde. Ein Fall von Storung der Personlichkeit*,
     Stuttgart 1929.

[3] op. cit.

artists and mystics of the past, he emphasised a number of factors in her mental life indicative of insanity.

One is glad to note that Hélène was saved from the possibility of ending her life in a mental home by the devotion of one of her sitters, a rich American woman, who left her an annuity for life.

Despite the claims of the spiritualists and many adherents of psychical research, it can be amply demonstrated that the purported spirit personalities exhibited in the mediumistic trance display the same peculiarities as the secondary personalities witnessed in hypnosis, automatic writing or in certain hysterical phenomena. In a sentence, the " spirits ", " controls " and " guides " of the spiritualistic pantheon are nothing more than products of the medium's own mental processes. They are personifications or mirrored projections of the medium's own repressed impulses and wishes, moulded and conditioned by the ideas of spiritualism and the influences of the séance room. There is no need for the psychical researcher, however sincere he may be, to resuscitate the ancient theory of external possession to account for the phenomenon of the mediumistic trance. Such theories should remain what they are—either psychological problems or anthropological curiosities.

THE MEDIUMISTIC TRANCE AND THE QUESTION OF AMNESIA

Almost invariably, mediums claim that their trances are followed by virtually total amnesia—that they are subsequently unable to recall any of their utterances or actions which occurred during their trance. In the case of practising mediums who consciously and deliberately simulate the trance states—and that is almost certainly the majority —such claims may naturally be disregarded.

In regard to the other class of medium, any broad generalisation is out of the question, but it may be stated at once that *total* amnesia is unlikely to occur except where a high degree of genuine dissociation is exhibited, and which in the great majority of cases may be classified as a hysterical syndrome. Autosuggestion and auto-hypnotic practices *may* result in a high degree of amnesia, but the completeness of the amnesia must remain open to doubt except when hysteria is present. If genuine verbal automatism enters into the mediumistic utterances, we may provisionally assume, following the parallel of automatic writing, that subsequent amnesia does occur. True verbal automatism, however, is almost invariably a symptom of hysteria, and the parallel with *acquired* autonography cannot be followed too closely.

The question of amnesia is inevitably bound up with the question of whether the medium retains some degree of awareness of her environment at the time of her trance. If dissociation is complete, then the medium's normal awareness of her environment may be nil. If dissociation is only partial then she will retain a peripheral or anoetic awareness of her immediate environment and will be able to remember —*if she desires*—a good deal of what occurred during her trance.

The reasonable view to be taken concerning the great majority of genuine trance mediums is that they do retain some degree of awareness of their immediate environment and have the power to recollect a good deal of their utterances afterwards. It must be borne in mind, however, that there is every possible gradation between the full power of conscious recollection pertaining to the purely simulated trance and the total amnesia of extreme hysterical dissociation. The degree of amnesia, in fact, varies according to the psychological constitution of the medium and the type of trance manifested. This fact does not, however, prevent nearly all mediums from claiming total amnesia. Most mediums who make this claim are probably aware that this is not true. Others may delude themselves that it is true. In most cases, particularly with non-hysterical mediums, the medium remains largely conscious of what she is saying, though she may not voluntarily control the content or extent of her utterances once the trance state has been engendered.

With a considerable number of mediums a kind of pseudo-amnesia occurs. The cult of mediumship has its own traditions, and one of these is that amnesia follows the trance period. The young woman who finds herself drifting into mediumistic practices has, from her previous experiences of spiritualism, assimilated the traditions and preconceptions of the cult, and naturally takes the phenomenon for granted. The expectation of amnesia may not bring about a state of amnesia through a process of autosuggestion, but it may very easily lead to delusions of amnesia, i.e. a personal conviction that amnesia occurs. This delusion can become part and parcel of the autistic thinking — the vicarious gratification for deprivations and frustrations by wishful fantasies—in which the medium becomes increasingly merged.

As we have already seen in the case of the German medium Mina Müller investigated by Dr. Fünfgeld, mediums are typically unable to take a reasonable attitude towards their own mental processes, and there is nothing unexpected in the fact that many mediums who show no evidence of amnesia are able to delude themselves that total amnesia occurs ; nor is there reason to doubt that the delusion may be genuine and not simulated.

THE HISTRIONIC ABILITY OF MEDIUMS

Concerning the unusual acting ability displayed by the celebrated medium Hélène Smith, Professor Flournoy wrote :

" As regards the faculty of assimilating scanty sources of information, combining them, and reproducing them in a living dramatic form in the pantomime and the mimicry of somnambulism, there is nothing surprising to those who are acquainted—through examples drawn from hypnotic and automatist phenomena—with the fanciful creative abilities of the sub-conscious mind." [1]

Flournoy was writing about a medium who was exceptional in almost every respect compared to the general run of mediums. While it is true that some mediums have, in the past, exceeded the normal ability of untrained persons in acting, occasionally rising to considerable heights of inventive dramatic presentation, the efforts of most have been limited to those attainable by any ordinary person freed from the restraints and inhibitions pertaining to normal existence.

---

[1] *Nouvelles Observations sur un Cas de Somnambulisme avec Glossalalie*, Paris, 1901, p. 207 ; author's translation.

Most mediumistic displays, in fact, are banal in the extreme, and only fervent believers and simple-minded people could regard them as revelations from beyond the grave.

Flournoy's medium was a hysterical subject with a strong tendency to dissociation. She was, furthermore, normally a gifted and intelligent individual, before her personality became completely involved in her spiritualistic delusions to the point of incipient psychosis. In general, mediums who display an acting ability above average do so by virtue of long practice or because they possess a natural facility. The knowledge that they have the keen interest and sympathy of their easily gulled audiences or sitters lends them confidence. In the atmosphere of the séance room, they can " let themselves go " in a way which would be impossible for them before a crowd of sceptics.

These observations, however, apply mainly to simulated trances and those which are largely the product of self-delusion. With the hysterical class of medium, as with the hysterical type of automatic writer, although these observations undoubtedly play a considerable part, there is another and more important factor to consider. The dramatic ability evinced by certain types of hysteric is a well known phenomenon, and it is among the *hysterical* type of medium that we find outstanding examples of histrionic ability ; it is with these that we may how principally concern ourselves.

The hysterical medium—whose trances are so often the pragmatic expression of a hysterical disability—is ordinarily highly suggestible by nature. The rôle played by suggestion in the abnormal atmosphere of the séance room is a large one and may easily lead to psychological states of mind analogous to hypnosis. With the hysterical medium this tendency to hypnotic or semi-hypnotic mental states is facilitated by the traditional methods of entering the trance —the relaxed posture, the closing of the eyes and the expectant attitude of surrendering the mind to external influences. The autohypnotisation of the séance room is a process in which the sitters largely take the place of the hypnotic operator in the psychotherapeutic clinic. The *sitters'* conviction and expectation that the medium is about to enter a trance and make contact with the deceased exerts a powerful suggestive influence on the mind of the medium.

The result is often to produce a genuine state of mental dissociation in the case of mediums prone to this tendency, or else to produce a mental state, very similar to hypnosis, *in which the medium's mind is largely at the mercy of ideas and beliefs held by the sitters.*

One of the main features of deep hypnosis is that the hypnotised subject can be made to assume any rôle which the operator suggests. This is particularly easy in the case of hysterical subjects. Furthermore, whatever rôle is suggested, whether it be a famous historical personage or simply a small child, the subject appears temporarily to identify himself with the suggested personality.

In the séance room the medium often appears to identify herself with her spirit-guide or control, or with the purported spirit of a dead person. The spontaneous aptitude for dramatic impersonation in many hypnotised subjects finds a good parallel in the considerable skill which a number of mediums with known hysterical tendencies are able to impersonate dead persons during a trance. Dissociative states—as for example in extreme polydeic somnambulism— are frequently responsible for a heightened dramatic faculty, and in much of the autohypnotisation of the séance room the speech and actions of the medium may reasonably be considered the concomitants of genuine mental dissociation.

The parallel between the behaviour of hypnotic subjects and certain types of mediumistic trance has been noted by the psychologist, T. W. Mitchell :

"One of the most remarkable features of deep hypnosis is the unexpected aptitude for dramatic impersonation shown by the hypnotised person. The literature of hypnotism is strewn with descriptions of the astonishing representations of well-known people given by hypnotized subjects in response to suggestion from without, and are rendered possible by some release of power, or freedom from inhibition, peculiar to the hypnotic state, so the character of a (spirit) control may be merely a result of self-suggestion by the medium taking effect in a self-induced hypnosis. If it is suggested to a hypnotized person that he is Napoleon Buonaparte he will accept the suggestion and will act the part ; for the time being he appears to identify himself with Napoleon. So, if a medium goes into trance holding the conviction that he is controlled by the prophet Isaiah the trance personality will assume the title and play the part as well as he can. Some process of this kind would form the simplest explanation of the character of many of the ordinary controls of mediumistic trance, and it seems to me the most probable explanation of the imitation of the idiosyncrasies of dead friends seen in cases of 'direct control.' "[2]

Mitchell also concluded that consistent spirit-personalities which emerged in trance over a period of years were frequently analogous to those which emerged in cases of multiple personality. " Sally " in the Beauchamp case illustrates the similarity very well.

It is notable that the *permanent* spirit-personalities, such as those exemplified by the special spirit guides and controls which most mediums attach to their persons, seldom exhibit any remarkable dramatic power. Usually, as was the case with " Sally ", these guides and controls are infantile and pretentious. They may arise either spontaneously and in response to some inner conflict or need ; or as a product of suggestion preceding or during the initial trance states. In other words, the more permanent spirit-personalities of the hysterical or auto-hypnotic trance tend to exhibit those regressive characteristics often found in cases of multiple personality and hypnotic somnambulism.

The mediumistic trance generally tends to become increasingly a matter of habit as the years pass by. Certainly, as the medium comes to find life more congenial owing to the success of her calling, and with all the scope for expression that mediumship implies, the original hysterical tendencies will tend to disappear and any real dissociative trance state will become increasingly difficult to induce. With a few exceptions, therefore, it is hard to believe that the middle-aged professional medium of long experience is not fully conscious of resorting to deception when she " goes into a trance ". What may originally have started as genuine dissociative trance-state only too often becomes an easily simulated habit which provides an easy and interesting source of income.

It may happen, of course, that the practice of mediumship may increase the hysterical tendencies to a point where the

---

[2] Mitchell, T. W., in *Psychology and the Sciences*, pp. 172-173.

medium becomes subject to permanent delusions such as occurred with Hélène Smith. According to Viollet, this used to be of quite frequent occurrence at one time ; [3] nowadays, however, it seems to be rare.

THE MEDIUM AND INVOLUNTARY CUES

The problem of involuntary sensory cues in relation to occult practices and experiments will be discussed at length later.[4] It is therefore unnecessary to enter into the subject at any length in the present chapter. No emphasis is needed to show the relevance of sensory cues to the way in which mediums, fortune-tellers, clairvoyants and other occult practitioners may gain the necessary information to surprise, bewilder and delight their clients,

Mediums may gain informative cues from their sitters by a variety of means : by the sitters' own involuntary reactions to the questions and explanatory sounds, syllables, intonations and gestures of the medium ; by clues provided by the sitters' remarks, affirmations and denials ; by unconscious articulation, and the involuntary innervations of the throat muscles on the part of the sitters. The clever medium has far more chance of picking up apposite cues from her sitters than the laboratory experimenter in telepathy and clairvoyance. Most mediums *deliberately* employ the method of obtaining unwitting responses or involuntary reactions from their sitters in order to gain the vital clues they require. Dr. Fünfgeld's medium, Mina Müller, possessed a lively capacity for putting two and two together in this way. Fünfgeld termed the process *Kombinationsfähigkeit*. It was instructing to find that when such involuntary indications were counterfeited, Mina Müller still followed them even after she had learned that her secret had been discovered. This highly successful professional clairvoyant possessed little or no critical faculty and was in many ways remarkably unintelligent. Her critical faculty, however, was evidently superior to that of many of her sitters !

---

[3] *Spiritualism and Insanity*, 1910.
[4] Chapters 24 and 25.

PLATE IV. A MEDITATING SADHU

His posture indicates that he may originally have been trained in Yogic disciplines.

(*See Chapter 16*)

PLATE V. A FAKIR LYING ON A BED OF THORNS
(See Chapter 16)

Some hysterical mediums may well possess an unusually developed sense of sight and hearing. Hysterical " hyper-aesthesia " has often been reported in the literature, although this " hyperaesthesia " is due to nothing more than an increase in the normal powers of observation attributable to normal psychological causes. If a hysterical medium does happen to possess such abnormally acute powers of observation it greatly facilitates her task of picking up the small involuntary auditory and visual cues offered by her sitters. Whether this is indeed the case cannot be judged without prolonged investigation, but the possibility remains and might easily account for the successes of certain mediums.

With the deliberately fraudulent medium any means of obtaining information is employed. Her own personal know · ledge of the sitters is often far beyond that which the sitters believe and may be obtained in casual conversation with them or with their friends and acquaintances ; this may be quite easy since spiritualistic believers are often well-known to each other through their mutual interests. Private detectives have been used on more than one occasion. The gullibility of the sitters increases every time the medium demonstrates " supernatural " knowledge concerning themselves or their dead friends and relatives.

THE MORAL ASPECT OF MEDIUMSHIP

While it is certainly arguable that all mediumistic practices are morally reprehensible and harmful to the best interests of the community—a view taken by the law—it is doubtful whether the majority of mediums themselves can be regarded as morally fraudulent. That a great many mediums are consciously out to feather their nests by deliberately hoaxing the public is an undeniable fact. But for many practising mediums a number of mitigating circumstances must be taken into account. For most practising mediums undoubt-edly believe in the spiritualistic *credo*, at least to some extent. There are many who believe in it completely, and though these latter may resort to fraudulent practices, such is their lack of introspective critical faculty that they are easily able to reconcile the paradox in their own minds.

The individual prone to lying and invention who actually believes what he is saying is by no means a rarity ; most mediums exhibit this trait in varying degree. In its more extreme manifestation this continued lying may become pathological and is known as *mythomania*. A general characteristic of mythomania is that the individual concerned actually believes the improbable tales he relates, and therefore cannot be held morally responsible.

Many mediums live in a world where there is no marked frontier between imagination and reality. This trait is often found in people of unstable temperaments ; an excellent example being the French novelist Balzac. Being frequently unable to distinguish between the credible and the incredible, he could put all his heart into writing fantastic lies to his wealthy and titled lovers ; when writing or telling these lies, he felt the same intense emotions as if he had been telling the truth. From the social viewpoint he was a liar. From the psychological point of view he combined instability with over-imaginativeness. Yet he could still produce major works of the order of the *Comédie Humaine*. Many mediums exhibit the same characteristics. Socially and even legally, they may be open to condemnation as practising frauds. Fundamentally, they may deceive themselves as well as their public.

The charge of moral fraud is even less warrantable when the mediums—and there are very many of them—have come to believe completely in their own supernatural faculties. Particularly is this true of mediums with hysterical tendencies whose trances exhibit genuine dissociation ; it is even true of many mediums whose revelations of an unseen world are quite obviously invented on the spur of the moment—they may go away from the séance completely convinced that what they have been recounting was inspired by their clairvoyant powers.

Many a medium who started off as a deliberate fraud has become so enamoured of her role, and so steeped in it, that she has ended up by believing herself possessed of supernutural faculties. Even hysterical trance-mediums must have the common sense to maintain their infallibility as seeresses, and this can only be done by mixing a certain amount of chicanery along with the genuine dissociative

trances. If anyone should think that this must constitute
a blow to the medium's personal self-esteem, he would be
entirely mistaken. Most of us have known a relative or
acquaintance who habitually commits the grossest errors
of taste or judgment, and endeavours to cover these up
with outrageous falsehoods or " excuses ", while yet retaining
a strong conviction of his (or her) own intellectual and moral
superiority. To point this out to them would be folly, for
it would be met with frank disbelief !

Between the true trance states of the advanced hysterical
medium and the medium who is consciously acting, there
lies a large borderland which cannot be conveniently classified. In such intermediate types of " trance " the medium
may become so entangled, emotionally and intellectually,
in the impersonation she is playing, that she temporarily
identifies herself with the rôle. If sceptics are present in
the audience, her reaction is to defend herself and her reputation with all means at her command, and she is perfectly
willing to resort to any amount of deliberate fraud to prevent
exposure. It may be at moments like these that she realises
the truth about herself, and her delusions are stripped bare.
When her confidence returns again, and she is once more
subject only to the praise and gratitude of the faithful, her
delusions return in full force, and any amount of subsequent
argument and questioning will fail to shake her convictions.
Her belief in her spirit guide will be absolute.

The trance and pseudo-trance utterances of the medium
reflect not only the latent emotional tendencies of the medium
herself, but also the doctrines and ideas of her sitters, to
which she instinctively responds and in which her mind has
long been steeped. It is easy to understand how the medium,
once plunged into the ebb and flow of spiritualistic ideas and
beliefs, becomes enamoured of the idea of an omniscient
spirit-guide who is especially attached to her person, and
deludes herself into believing in its reality.

The fraudulent medium is not altogether morally reprehensible ; for her fraudulent practices are carried out against
a background of delusion, wishful thinking and sincere
belief in both her supernatural powers of cognition and in
the reality of the spirit whose mouthpiece she is. Hers is
a state of mind the more easily brought about because she

does not feel any need of self-criticism ; and this is due to the mental and moral environment supplied by those who believe in her, and, more important still, to the traditions of her calling. In primitive shamanism and in its offshoot, modern spiritualism, both the shaman and the medium play a rôle in keeping with ancient traditions, with which they completely identify themselves. This class of medium is very large, although there are probably greater numbers who can be classified as thorough-going rogues, cheerfully hoaxing their sitters for financial gain and regarding their clients as credulous fools.

No medium could convince her sitters of the authenticity of her trances without some calculated theatrical display. This is all part and parcel of the game, and the medium who wishes to capitalise her spontaneous or induced hysterical trances, which she believes to be manifestations of occult faculties, knows the advantages of a well-set stage. A full-staged trance with all the traditional trappings is a prime necessity to professional mediums, and the appurtenances of trance may be deliberately exaggerated until they become a fixed habit without which no form of trance becomes possible. This aspect of spiritualism may strike the unknow-ledgeable observer as proof that *all* mediums are conscious frauds. Yet such a deduction is false, since a fair percentage of mediums believe utterly in the spiritualistic firmament and in their power to contact it, while their trances may be genuine instances of mental dissociation or auto-hypnotisa-tion ; and their calling they often hold to be not only honour-able but a " light unto the world ".

Yet even these mediums fulfil the ancient traditions of shamanism by dramatisation and stage effects. The non-appearance of an expected trance must at times be covered up or their reputations would suffer. If they simulate the trance at these times, who can really blame them ? In any event, for those whose minds have long been exposed to the suggestion-laden influences of the séance room, the boundary between the simulated trance and genuine dissociation may often be very thin.

OTHER BOOKS
483 BLOOR STREET WEST
TORONTO, ONTARIO M5S 1Y2

TELEPHONE (416) 961-5227

12 / 2 / 74 197

(PN24) Dostoyevsky		
Crime & Punishment	1	95
(BS14) Rowcliffe	4	00
Occult & Supernatural		
Phenomena		

1 ☐
2 ☐
3 ☐
4 ☐

SUB TOTAL		
TOTAL	5	95

Rec'd by _____ LB

☐ CHEQUE   ☑ CASH

3459

A. TURLEY & CO., TORONTO, ONT. · 1-13156

Chapter Twelve

MENTAL HEALING

MIRACLE-CURES : THE PSYCHIATRIST AND THE MEDICINE MAN

THE TREATMENT OF DISEASE by mental means can be traced back to the very earliest days in man's history. The story of mental healing runs from the ancient magic of primitive medicine-men to modern methods of clinical psychotherapy. And oddly enough, the same principles operate in both; the main difference being that whereas the former understood nothing of the factors at work and attributed them to supernatural agencies, the psychotherapist understands something of the processes involved and is under no illusion in regard to their natural psychological basis. To the ordinary spectator, however, whether two thousand years ago or at the present day, psychotherapeutic methods of healing, utilising the principle of suggestion, savour of mysterious and supernatural powers. The human race as a whole has by no means escaped from its most primitive methods of thinking and turns towards tne supernatural instinctively whenever its ignorance bars the path to knowledge.

Today, in Europe and America, millions believe in the power of " psychic " healing. By the term " psychic " is meant the power of thought or the mind to exert an influence over natural conditions and to supersede the accepted laws of nature. Faith healing, homeopathy, miracle cures, psychic healing, " radiesthesia "— these are some of the terms which modern occult medicine has produced or inherited.

The great bulk of " psychic " cures may be put down to the effect of psychological suggestion in one or more of its multiple guises. Psychological suggestion, with or without the use of hypnotism, forms one of the principal working methods of that branch of psychiatry known as psychotherapy. Under this heading we can include the cure of pain in organic diseases and injuries, actual improvements in many organic diseases, and the restoration of the mental health to sufferers from neurasthenia and psychoneurosis. Psychotherapy might well be described as the art of the primitive medicine man brought up to date and placed on a rational basis.

Modern clinical methods in psychiatry during the last twenty-five years have tended to abandon the one-time dominant method of direct suggestion in therapeutic practice which reached its height in the schools of Liébault, Charcot —the "wizard of the Salpétrière", and Bernheim, Beaunis and Liégeois at Nancy. Instead, psychoanalytical practice and other methods of modern psychiatry prefer to effect their mental healing by getting the patient to assist in his own cure by enabling him to understand the causes which have brought about his nervous disorder. This latter aspect of psychotherapy, however, does not concern us a great deal here ; it has little bearing on mental healing outside the clinic.

Sudden, and to the lay mind miraculous, cures of physical[1] disabilities may occur when such disabilities are hysterical in origin. Such disorders are often called functional disorders, since they only affect the function of the organ concerned and can not be traced to any direct organic disease. The major functional disorders include partial or total blindness, paralysis, and mutism ; functional deafness, too, is not uncommon. Functional disorders are psychogenic in origin ; they are mainly due, that is, to mental causes. They are, furthermore, highly amenable in most cases to methods of mental cure, and often to methods of direct suggestion. Whether the suggestion therapy is applied in the calm

---

[1] The term " psychic " or " psychical " is a normal synonym for *psychological*. Amongst believers in the occult " psychic " and " psychical " are often used as euphemistic synonyms for *supernatural* or *transcendental*.

atmosphere of a modern clinic as part of hospital treatment, or by a thaumaturgic healer in the emotional atmosphere of a Christian Science church, dramatic cures are frequently effected. Writes Jolowicz :

" The chief domain of suggestive therapy is, from of old, hysterical phenomena ; and for our purposes we may approximately describe hysteria as abnormal physical re-action to psychic injuries. Since hysteria may psychogenically produce the aspect of almost every disease, it is in this domain that most of the ' miraculous cures ' have been attained—those for which all the quacks, magnetic healers and the like gain credit with an uncritical and credulous public." [2]

The same factors operate in the cure of functional disorders whether the therapist is a primitive witch doctor, an ancient Egyptian priest, a Christian Science healer, a rustic wart-charmer, a *soi-disant* radiesthetist, or an up-to-date clinical psychotherapist. The therapeutic *method* alone varies. We are in reality faced with two different but related aspects in dealing with the problem of mental healing and suggestion. one, the anthropological ; two, the psychotherapeutic. For we can not, in dealing with psychological healing outside the clinic, isolate the problem from tradition, belief and custom. Today we know that suggestion was responsible for many of the seemingly miraculous cures of the past. Yet all through the ages and right down to the present day occur stories of miraculous cures, of healing by faith, of extraordinary powers in certain individuals to cure the blind, the halt, and the lame.

The obscure junction where medicine and the occult meet presents a fascinating chapter in the history of the mental life of man. From prehistoric man until the present day the beliefs of a thousand generations in the occult powers of the medicine man have undergone little change. Are all these miracles explainable in terms of normal psychological principles ? The answer, regrettably, must be in the affirmative. And it may be added that few of the stories one hears are free of distortion, exaggeration or even downright falsification ; such is the natural reaction of the human mind when faced with the unknown. Reports of cures of incurable

---

[2] Jolowicz, E., *Suggestion Therapy* ; and Heyer, G., *Hypnosis and Hypnotherapy*, p. 29.

organic disease such as cancer, tabes dorsalis and similar affections invariably compel us to ask how the original diagnosis was arrived at in the first instance? For in all investigations of such cures, proof of competent diagnosis of the original disease has been inevitably lacking. This single point well illustrates the complexity of the task facing the ingenuous researcher into the case histories of " psychic " cures.

PSYCHOGENIC DISORDERS AND " PSYCHIC " CURES

To review the entire question of miracle cures and allied topics requires a brief knowledge of that branch of medical study now known as psychosomatic medicine. Roughly speaking, psychosomatic medicine concerns itself with physical disorders brought about by psychological causes and the question of psychological factors in disease generally.

There are, to begin with, a very considerable number of ailments and physical disorders which are due solely to a mental or emotional aetiology. In dealing with the problem of mental healing, the primary principle to bear in mind is that all physical disorders with a psychological origin— including those cases of organic disease and disability which are either aggravated or prolonged by psychological factors —may be cured or in some other way benefited by psychological methods of treatment alone. Cases of insanity, or *psychosis*, are generally not amenable to purely psychological methods of cure, although if a hysterical component is present they may be alleviated provided the patient's mental condition has not deteriorated too far.

It is worth while at this point to give a brief list of psychologically caused disorders which can be cured temporarily or permanently by psychotherapeutic methods involving the use of suggestion.

First of all there are those minor disorders generally associated with *neurasthenic* types of individual, in varying degrees of seriousness. These include feelings of extreme fatigue and complete lack of energy, aches and pains in all parts of the body—particularly in the back, digestive disorders, constipation, insomnia, headaches, blurred vision, menstrual disorders, general loss of appetite, etc. Along with these, but not so peculiarly symptoms of neurasthenia, may be included a number of skin diseases (e.g. eczema, acne, seborrhoeic dermatitis and psoriasis), and also some minor ailments due to an upset glandular system.

Other common disorders which may also have psychological origins are enuresis ("bed-wetting"), squinting, warts, peptic ulcers, and asthma.

The *major* functional diseases include complete or partial paralysis of body or limbs, blindness, loss of speech (aphasia), voice (aphonia), hearing, loss of the sense of feeling locally (local anaesthesia), *tics*, chorea, wasting and even atrophy, and convulsions. There is no need to point out that all these disorders may also have organic origins.

Functional disorders are not caused by any organic lesion or organic disease ; they are nearly always traceable to some form of subconscious mental conflict or inner nervous tension. A considerable number of these disorders are liable to sudden cure—the blind to see, the paralytic to walk, and the dumb to speak ! The skilled clinical psychotherapist has on occasion effected dramatic recoveries through suggestion therapy. With this functional type of disorder, we can, since they spring from mental causes, expect cures on " mental " lines ; and most of the more dramatic cures put down to " psychic healing " and " faith healing " have certainly been cures of functional, as opposed to organic, disease. But

" a general and satisfactory solution of the problem as to how psychological experiences and stresses can become converted into physical symptoms is no more possible than a general and satisfactory explanation of the relationship between mind and body." [1]

It is the cures of these functional disorders, the disorders due to morbid hysteria, which have largely built up the myth of miracle cures and miracle healers. We shall consider later the rôle of suggestion in aiding recovery and alleviating suffering in cases of *organic* disease. Here, too, the psychotherapist, the " psychic healer ", the " holy wells " and the primitive medicine man may exert considerable influence on the outcome of the disease.

---

[1] Curran and Guttmann, *Psychological Medicine*, p. 194.

The fact remains, however, that mental states do have strong effects on the body's functions which cannot be normally produced by conscious volition. An every day example, for the sake of illustration, is afforded by the uncomfortable phenomenon of blushing. A state of embarrassment or shame produces a flow of blood up the neck to the face which can seldom be checked or even initiated by conscious volition. By employing hypnotic suggestion more drastic effects can be brought about. In fact it is by the use of hypnotic suggestion that we are enabled to induce artificially all those symptoms which may be exhibited by hysterical individuals, including functional paralysis, deafness, blindness and mutism—the very cases in which the quack thaumaturgist and the psychotherapist alike produce their most dramatic cures.

What is truly surprising is the extent to which the action of the glands and secretions can be influenced by hypnotic therapeutics. Muscles which normally are completely beyond voluntary control can be often made to react to hypnotic suggestion. Constipation, milk secretion, menstruation and indigestion can all be excited or arrested by hypnotic suggestion in suggestible subjects. Pregnancy symptoms have been induced by the same method, and even the heart can be induced to alter its rate of beating. Janet even records the somewhat question-begging case of one highly suggestible subject whose constipation could be relieved at a single word of command ! According to Moll, the peristaltic action of the bowel is particularly easy to excite by suggestion, and there have been known a number of instances in which the effect of aperients has been checked by the same methods. Moll further states that menorrhagia can be induced by hypnotic suggestion in the case of certain persons. [2] There are several indications that even the vasomotor system may be seriously affected by hypnotic suggestion.

We see, then, the extent to which the human organism may be affected by suggestion. We now come to those very similar effects which may be brought about by hysteria and autosuggestion.

---

[2] Moll, A., *Hypnotism*, p. 114.

Some Effects of Hysteria on the Body's Functions

Hysterical disorders may affect the body's functions to an even greater extent than hypnotic suggestion. Hysteria, too, may take the form of imitating almost any disease with which the patient is acquainted, including some quite imaginary ones. It is frequently difficult to say, without a thorough inspection, whether the disease imitated is due to psychogenic factors or not, specially if the patient has had an opportunity in the past of acquiring considerable knowledge of the disease in question.

In severe cases of functional disorder the patient is generally unaware that the cause of his disability is psychological. He consciously desires the cure and alleviation of what appears to him to be a distressing, and sometimes totally incapacitating, physical disorder. Subconsciously he may be glad of his infirmity, but this knowledge remains buried, repressed into that part of his mind, " the sub-conscious ", which has instigated his disorder in the first place. Some very remarkable cases of psychosomatic disorders have been recorded in the last hundred years. Today, however, in Europe and America, such extreme disorders are becoming rarer owing to relatively easier conditions of living and the effects of education.

Here is an interesting example of hysteria resulting in paralysis of the lower part of the body accompanied by loss of the hair from the head :

" A girl aged 12, at the end of a term at school, suffered from hysterical paraplegia, and rapidly recovered under rest and massage, but six weeks afterwards the paralysis returned . . . . On the morning of the day after she was found with much of her hair out, or coming out. She went to bed with a good head of hair and lost most of it within a few hours. There was no febrile disturbance and nothing apparently wrong with the scalp." [1]

Functional paralysis has also been known to result in a degree of actual physical atrophy of the limb concerned. Fisher notes :

[1] Glynn, T. R., *Hysteria in Some of its Aspects* ;   Brit. Med. Journ., Nov. 8th., 1913.

" The paralysed limb may be blue and cold and have a clammy
' feel.' Atrophic changes sometimes occur, and even the fingernails
have been known to waste away. These atrophic changes have often
been attributed to disuse of the limb affected but the changes are
frequently too great to be accounted for in this manner, and besides
it has been demonstrated that the condition is amenable to psychological treatment in the same way that other hysterical symptoms
are." [2]

Hysterical *tics*, spasmodic twitches and jerkings of small
groups of muscles, demonstrate how deeply psychological
factors may affect those parts of the body outside normal
volitional control :

" The *hysteric tic* may involve apparently any muscle of the body,
even those belonging to the visceral organs. Thus we find tics not
only of the muscles of the face, eyes, mouth, hands, arms, neck, etc.,
but also of the respiratory and digestive musculature." [3]

Cases have been reported of hysterical pregnancies, in
which the patient undergoes all the symptoms of pregnancy
without any accompanying gestation. Janet describes the
case of a patient who had experienced a marked hysterical
contraction of her left leg which was cured by hypnotic
treatment without much difficulty.

" Eighteen months later, after some love episodes, she had a hysterical relapse. Menstruation was suppressed, her breasts swelled a
little, and the abdomen became rapidly and enormously distended ;
there were also severe pains in the belly and shaking movements of
the abdominal walls ; in a word, she presented almost all the symptoms of spurious pregnancy. The same suggestive treatment as
before relieved her of these troubles in a few weeks." [4]

Mary Tudor, daughter of Henry VIII and better known,
perhaps, as " Bloody Mary " through her cruel persecution
of the Protestant religion, presents a remarkable historial
case of hysterical pregnancy. It was brought on by the
desertion of her husband Phillip II of Spain and the consequent realisation that her longing for children could never
be fulfilled. It is an ironic fact that much of the bitterness

---

[2] Fisher, V. E., *Introduction to Abnormal Psychology*, p. 209, N.Y. 1932.
[3] Fisher, V. E., ibid., p. 211.
[4] Janet, P., *Psychological Healing*, p. 348.

and cruelties of her reign stemmed from her thwarted desire for a child.

The above paragraphs show clearly the potential effects of the mind over bodily functions. Glands and secretions, the vasomotor system, visceral organs, even the heart itself, may in some degree be affected, directly or indirectly, either by the consciously directed suggestion of a practised psychotherapist or by the unconscious autosuggestion of the subject himself. The scope offered here to the charlatan operating among credulous or suggestible people is obviously enormous.

MAJOR FUNCTIONAL DISORDERS

The greatest opportunities for the " psychic healer ", Christian Scientist or primitive fakir lie in the sphere of the major functional disorders, in which the senses and organs themselves may be unaffected organically yet remain unable to carry out their normal function of feeling, seeing, hearing or movement.

In Europe and America today, hysterical disorders are usually cured or at least alleviated in the vast majority of cases without undue difficulty. In former times, however, and even today in the less developed countries of the world where hardship and poverty are part of the daily round, particularly in the cities, functional blindness and paralysis are not infrequently found. In such conditions as these, ignorance and suggestibility and the sight of others stricken with like diseases lead to imitative hysterical syndromes. The imitative tendency in hysteria is a strong one, and the fact that diseased individuals are scarcely to be seen in the cities of western civilisation, being confined to hospitals, has contributed greatly to the reduction of functional maladies.

Nearly all cases of functional disease are the result of inner mental conflict—between the individual's instincts and his social duties and obligations. When the mental struggle becomes too violent, the sub-conscious mind seizes upon a compromise unlikely to arouse social censure, a compromise which at the same time circumvents the urge to give way to a shameful or socially undesirable surrender to primitive emotions. The first world war produced tens of thousands of such instances of what are now termed by some schools of psychiatry *conversion syndromes*. These are distinct from cases of conscious malingering and are easily distinguishable, though there are, naturally, border-line cases difficult to classify. Direct suggestion in such instances does not usually result in complete cures, but only in cures of a temporary nature. Amongst primitive peoples, however, direct suggestion may effect permanent cures owing to the greater suggestibility of the individual.

Autosuggestion, reacting on a temperament rendered suggestible by fear or other emotion, has very often resulted in the instantaneous occurrence of a functional disorder. Sir William Brown mentions a typical case of a soldier who became paralysed with fear when a shell burst near him. He became hysterically paralysed in his lower limbs through a process of autosuggestion inspired by his belief that he had in fact become permanently paralysed. He remained paralysed until treated by therapeutic suggestion. [1] It is evident that here we are faced with a situation analagous to that of hypnotic suggestion, the requisite degree of suggestibility being obtained by the man's strong desire, hitherto strictly controlled in the interests of duty, to get away from the battlefield.

The reality of functional afflictions cannot be denied when we are faced with cases of functional catalepsy, analgesia and blindness. A patient suffering from functional local analgesia appears not to feel the pin thrust into his arm. That a part of his mind is aware of the pin-thrust becomes evident, but the sensation of pain does not enter his consciousness.

The abolition of the sense of pain, as is well known, can be achieved in many individuals by means of hypnotic suggestion. In the same way hypnotic suggestion can *induce* states of functional blindness, paralysis, deafness, mutism and the whole range of functional disorders artificially. Functional maladies have been known, before the advent of modern methods of psychiatry, to last for many years. Even today long term functional disorders tend to remain permanent if neglected over a period of years. In past eras, before the medical profession had · realised their

[1] *Psychology and the Sciences*, p. 155.

nature, such conversion-syndromes frequently lasted until death. It is the dramatic cures of these long term functional diseases by suggestion which we witness in the stories of the New Testament and which have given rise to the belief in the supernatural powers of great healers from antiquity down to the present day.

THE CONDITIONS FOR MENTAL HEALING

" Faith healing " is not such a misnomer as it may appear. Faith, or belief in the powers of the healer, is a primary requisite for the full power of suggestion to take effect. The same applies to belief in the powers of holy wells, religious relics and the efficacy of prayers or talismans. All suggestion is ultimately dependent on the subject's belief in the possibility of the desired effect. And where conscious belief is lacking the subconscious mind may be able to supply this lack—in this way many a self-proclaimed sceptic has been " converted "—or belief may be artificially induced by hypnosis, or by the right kind of emotional stimulus such as may occur, for example, at religious revivalist meetings.

The importance of obtaining the right atmosphere in mass healing séances is fully appreciated by the professional thaumaturgic healers. Collective suggestion is stimulated by all imaginable arts. The hope of the patients to be cured becomes objectified into the belief that they will be cured, often to such an extent that patients with incurable organic disease depart believing that they have been healed and remain, for a time at any rate, convinced that their suffering has been totally banished. They may become oblivious to their pain, and, in certain cases when psychogenic factors play an important rôle in the development of their malady, the external symptoms may disappear, although the disease itself still continues its deadly work. The latter phenomenon is also to be observed in the clinic, often to a remarkable degree.

One of the greatest of the thaumaturgic healers was the German, Valentine Zeileis. He, like many others before him, used the old occult principle of " contact " between the patient and himself as conducive to obtaining the maximum

effect.   The belief in the benefits of contact with the healer
has existed throughout recorded history and is exemplified
in the traditional act of the " laying on of hands." Until
the days of Charles II the kings of England were reputed to
have the power to cure scrofula or the King's Evil by mere
contact with the sovereign, and frequently the scrofulous
swellings were reported to be alleviated.   Valentine Zeileis
supplemented the contact principle by the use of " magical "
apparatus whose effect was to increase the already suggestible
state of his credulous patients.   This is what Castiglioni has
to say concerning this famous wonder-healer.

"The first and most important point is the ' Contact ' between
the healer and the patient, by means of a magic wand touching the
body.   Such contact has all the characteristics of a magic practice,
and is performed to the accompaniment of highly suggestive phenomena.   The wand is connected with a high-powered current and,
according to Zeileis, becomes luminous upon contact with the diseased
organ.   Healing is brought about by this contact, repeated three or
four times at successive sittings.

" The second feature is the ' atmosphere,' the magic aspect of the
room, weirdly lighted by pieces of apparatus which throw off intermittent beams of light, with streaks of sparks which affect the skin ;
the thaumaturgic aspect of the healer, who appears in a priestly
costume and whose long white beard gives him a venerable appearance ;   the play of words that appear mysterious to the profane, who
know little or nothing of the helium lamp, or radium-bearing alloys,
and of ultra-violet rays ;   finally a complicated though apparently
simple set of preparations during the long wait of the patients,   the
suggestion exerted on them by the atmosphere, pervaded with conviction of the miraculous power of Zeileis, and, above all, the enormous prosperity that his abilities have brought to him, to his
collaborators, and to the whole district.

" The third and perhaps most decisive feature is the system of
receiving fifty or a hundred patients at a time, all half-naked, all
equally suffering and hoping, all equally ready to receive the miracle.
This feature gives rise to reciprocal and collective suggestion, manifested through phenomena that have been amply studied by specialists
in mass psychology.   There is no need to mention the numberless
examples given by history and experiments of the great importance
of collective suggestion : every single patient who claims to have been
cured, singing the praises and merits of the healer, immediately
arouses a wave of hope, a general will to be cured, and absolute faith
in the miraculous act." [1]

The same principle of building up the patient's expectation,
and the induction of the right frame of mind for the effect

---

[1] Castiglioni, A., *Adventures of the Mind*, p. 325.

PLATE VI.   A YOGI DEMONSTRATES A STRANGE BODILY CONTORTION

The *Hatha* Yogis are noted for their extreme acrobatic postures and
physical hardihood.

(*See Chapter* 16)

PLATE VII. A YOGI VERSION OF THE " LEVITATION " ACT

This illustration shows the Yogi poised in mid-air, his hand resting lightly on a draped stick.

(See Chapter 16)

of suggestion to operate, was followed by the organisers of the celebrated cures at Lourdes in its heyday. Here again, " atmosphere " is all important.

> " The patient is not allowed to dispense with preliminaries. He must not straightway touch the relic or drink the healing waters of the sacred spring. There is a probationary period, a propitiatory novena. There are long waits at the gateway of the temple during which the sufferer listens to sermons and repeats prayers. Above all, during these periods of probation, the sick hear a great deal about miraculous cures, and have an opportunity of looking at the number-less votive offerings. In a word, their entry into the temple is a slow one, and their minds are prepared by a special incubation." [2]

Not all the medical profession have despised the efficacy of the wonder cures. Professor Charcot, on occasion, sent patients to Lourdes on the grounds that, with some types of people, the effect of autosuggestion would be of more efficacy than any suggestion-therapy he might employ at the Salpêtrière. Castiglioni writes :

> " A greater contribution to these successes is made by the concur-rent influence of objects or actions which, because they are surrounded with the halo of supernatural power, are more apt to provoke the state of mind in which the healer's skill may be successful. This explains why a fortune-teller or a soothsayer who claims to have supernatural visions or an old peasant who enjoys the reputation of a wizard is able to obtain results that would be impossible for the most famous physician, possessing perfect scientific equipment."[3]

It is important, of course, not to be carried away by the successes of thaumaturgic healing. There are very many types of mental healing which are far more effectively carried out in modern psychiatric clinics. Nevertheless, the success of some of the thaumaturgists has often been little short of amazing. This success, let it be admitted, is due solely to the methods employed—methods which the psychiatrist very properly scorns to use.

It is well known that some individuals possess powers of mental healing of an order far superior to the majority of their fellows. It is this fact which has contributed a great deal to the occult myth. That there are differences of in-dividual ability in the art of psychological healing remains as true for the clinician as for the thaumaturgic healer. One thing can be stated with certainty. The moral qualities

[2] Janet, P., *Psychological Healing*, p. 47.

[3] Castiglioni, A., opcit, p. 313.

possessed by the healer affect the issue very little and only indirectly. Both saints and money-grabbing quacks have acquired the power to heal, the one as effectively as the other. The saint, however, may sometimes have the advantage in that he frequently evokes a feeling of awe due to the strongly ingrained religious beliefs and traditions of those around him ; if the miracles of the New Testament, the Koran, or the Bhagavad-Gita are in the back of the patient's mind or in the forefront of his consciousness, it will automatically lead to a state of increased suggestibility.

The ability to induce belief in the healer's own powers is a prime requisite in suggestion-therapy, be the healer a hospital psychiatrist or an oriental miracle worker. Some personalities have the remarkable quality which enables them to induce complete belief in their powers, despite failures and shortcomings which are often only too apparent to the critical eye. Saints and charlatans throughout the ages have been fully aware of this factor and have taken full advantage of it. The suggestibility of the sufferer is often increased when an element of personal devotion enters into his regard for the healer, a principle which the psychoanalytical schools, with their phenomenon of *transference*, have readily utilised.

Suggestion is sometimes held to contain three main variable factors : the source of the suggestion, the content of the suggestion, and the recipient of the suggestion. These three variables must be taken into account in every single instance of psychotherapeutic suggestion. The *source* of suggestion is the healer himself. His personality, his technique, his insight and his theoretical background inevitably varies considerably from those of his colleagues. The *content* of the suggestion consists of what is actually suggested to the patient, the manner in which it is said, the circumstances under which it is given, and the physical and emotional environment obtaining at the time. The *recipient* of the suggestion is the patient, with his incalculable characteristics, his potentialities and idiosyncrasies of reaction, his beliefs and preconceptions. Recognition of these three variables helps to explain why different psychologists publish different figures for the suggestibility of their patients, and why a psychotherapist succeeds in one case where another fails, though both use the same methods.

The psychotherapist, the medicine man and the thaumaturgic healer may frequently resort to the use of hypnotic suggestion for the cure of functional disorders and the relief of pain. Hysteria invariably renders the patient highly suggestible ; that is why functional maladies are often relatively easy to cure, for they themselves are symptoms of hysteria.

With patients who show little or no signs of overt or latent hysteria, hypnosis is generally the most effective means of increasing suggestibility. A patient who is already deeply hysteric does not always require hypnosis : suggestion can be given while he is merely in a relaxed state ; or alternatively a highly emotional state may provide the requisite susceptibility to suggestion, as in the séances of the thaumaturgists, Christian Scientists and others.

The power of suggestion is not necessarily effected by the depth of the hypnotic trance. Generally speaking, in modern clinical practice a drowsy state is all that is required, and in refractory patients this is sometimes brought about by the use of such drugs as evipan, thiopentone or sodium amytal. The primitive witch doctor induces the drowsy state by monotonous chanting, rhythmic beating of drums and tom-toms, and, like his civilised colleague, may also resort to the use of drugs. With most patients, however, the deeper the hypnosis the more effective suggestion becomes ; the more spectacular feats of hypnotic suggestion have generally been carried out while the subject is in a state of deep hypnosis.

Repeated hypnotisation may render the subject increasingly susceptible, and with some subjects a state of hypnosis may eventually be brought about by a single word of command given orally or even in writing. Such patients become highly suggestible and were apt, in the past, to fall into the rôle of somnambulic guinea-pigs for the experimental diversions of the hypnotist.

MENTAL HEALING

We now come to the question of the actual cures of disease and suffering by psychological means. During the first world war thousands of cases of " shellshock " were cured by therapeutic suggestion. The two great British authorities at that time were William Brown and William MacDougall. By their numerous contributions to the literature of the subject, the intelligent layman has been able to learn how cases of paralysis, blindness, aphonia, and a host of other incapacitating disabilities of psychogenic origin have been cured—sometimes in the space of a few minutes and with no more than a few carefully chosen words. " Rise, take up thy bed and walk " is not the product of a devoted enthusiast's imagination. It was the confident command of a suggestion-therapist who divined the nature of the paralytic's complaint and who took advantage of the sufferer's belief in his ability to heal. It was by the power of suggestion that the great Jewish mystic healed " issues of blood " or menorrhagia, made the dumb to speak and the blind to see. That he had numerous failures is not to be doubted ; these, understandably enough, were not recorded.

Suggestion is sometimes conveyed under queer guises. In the Middle Ages the main principle of any " physick " was its nasty taste or smell. The people of those times looked upon with suspicion any medicine that lacked these delectable qualities. Of the revolting brews concocted for the sick and ailing in those ignorant days many records bear witness. These frequently had the saving grace of producing seeming cures or bringing about expected results through the effects of suggestion.

Scatological " physicks " played an important part amongst the poor of medieval England. For example to hasten the onset of childbirth a common remedy was the quaffing of a mug of the husband's urine, while horse dung mixed with wine was considered efficacious in expelling the placenta or " afterbirth ", Such effects as these might naturally have produced through suggestion in a suggestible age were doubtless supplemented by the effects of the " physick " in its obvious rôle as an emetic or cathartic ; probably, therefore, they often achieved their object.

But although the actual medical properties of excrement

are in the main limited to its effect as an emetic, those of urine are considerable, so that one should not be too hasty in attributing any beneficial effects to suggestion only. To illustrate this point, it is not generally known that in many country districts of England today (and presumably in other countries also) the drinking of urine is still frequently practised as a recognised cure and preventive for severe boils and carbuncles. A cupful taken each morning for three successive days is usually deemed efficacious, but the " treatment " may be continued for a week if considered necessary. The salt, and the sulphates in combination with calcium and magnesium present in urine, are almost certainly responsible for any beneficial results achieved. The freedom with which the subject may still be discussed demonstrates an interesting absence of ethical tabu which may surprise many.

The older clinical cures of functional disease often seemed mysterious even to the psychotherapists themselves. Lys, for example, never understood the principles involved when he cured patients by first hypnotising another person who then, at the word of command, commenced to indulge in mimicry of the patient's symptoms in front of the latter.

Hypnotic suggestion, as has already been observed, frequently results in astonishing cures of psychogenic organic troubles. One of the earliest cases recorded in which the secretion of milk has been affected is that cited by Esdaile. His sister-in-law, when weaning a child, suffered from the accumulation of milk in her breasts which made them painful and swollen. He hypnotised her, and in half an hour she was free from pain. Next morning the breasts were soft and comfortable, and there was no further secretion of milk. Dr. Hessenstein, of East Prussia, has reported a case in which the secretion of milk entirely ceased owing to emotional causes, and was rapidly restored by suggestion. [1] In a remoter age this would be considered a typical example of supernatural healing, either by divine or infernal agency.

E. Ash, in his *Faith and Suggestion*, records the curious case of Dorothy Kerin who, after being bedridden for years apparently suffering from phthisis, had a visual and auditory hallucination of an angel who commanded her to get up and

---

[1] Macy, A., *Hypnotism Explained*, pp. 56-57.

walk.   The effect of this powerful suggestion springing from
her own subconscious mind effected an immediate cure of
what eventually turned out to be mainly a functional disability.   This rare type of cure has the strongest appeal for
miracle-mongers.   Many a religious movement has been
given birth by a less auspicious psychological anomaly.

When religious movements are based on purported miraculous healings, there is an invariable tendency to emotional
exaggeration and a complete loss of critical faculty among
the devotees.   Compare, for example, the " metaphysical
obstetrics " of the early days of the Christian Science movement, which resulted in much needless suffering and cost a
good many deluded women their lives.   Belief in the in-
efficacy of surgery and medical treatment and in the efficacy
of prayer has a long history.   Psychology has even given it
a name—*theopathia*.

The earlier excesses of Christian Science and similar
movements have today more or less disappeared, and
although there is still in the Christian Science movement a
great deal open to serious criticism there is another side to
be taken into account.   Like the spiritualistic churches,
it is undoubted that Christian Science has offered many
individuals a faith which is to some degree a measure of their
needs, and that its methods have frequently benefited the
health of many sufferers from minor psychogenic complaints
such as indigestion, headaches, insomnia *et alia*.   It provides
many lonely or " ill-adjusted " souls with an interest in life
which they would otherwise lack entirely.   The onlooker,
however, may well wonder and stare at some of their activities.   Here is an example of Christian Science autosuggestion in the form of a prayer which, although it may appear
merely amusing to most people, undoubtedly could be effective with certain temperaments :

> " Help us stoutly to affirm . . . that we have no Dyspepsia, that we
> never had Dyspepsia, that we never will have Dyspepsia, that there
> is no such thing, that there never has been any such thing, and that
> there never will be any such thing.   Amen."

Many of the cures effected by osteopathy in the past have
certainly been due to suggestion.   Suggestion is also a
principle factor in homeopathy.   Homeopathy is the purported treatment of disease by drugs, usually in minute

quantities, which in a healthy person would produce symptoms like those of the disease itself. It is an interesting relic of sympathetic magic.

The believer in miracles might justifiably claim that he is acquainted with scores of cases of purely organic disease diagnosed and confirmed by qualified physicians, which have been cured, or at least greatly relieved, by " psychic " healers, by prayer or by holy waters. The believer in miracles can, in fact, put up an excellent case for his belief along these lines. It is, however, in the occult interpretation of such cases that his error lies, due to his ignorance of the principles of psychotherapy. His misunderstanding of the real issues is not surprising, in view of the fact that the medical profession itself is, as a whole, quite surprisingly ignorant of the role played by psychological factors in organic disease and injury, and of the potentialities of psychotherapy.

The principle that diseases and bodily disorders generated primarily by psychological factors (psychosomatic disorders) are subject to cure by psychological methods of healing is easily understood.   Without repeating again the list of *purely functional* disorders, it may be as well to mention again certain of those maladies which may have, wholly or in part, a psychogenic origin and which may be cured or alleviated by psychotherapy. These include a number of *organic* troubles such as certain affections of the heart (e.g. pseudo-angina pectoris), kidneys, digestive system, menstruation and bowels ; climacteric disturbances and sea-sickness ; psychogenic bronchitis and asthma, psychogenic exopthalmic-goitre or Graves' Disease, and cerebral arteriosclerosis ; skin diseases such as eczma, psoriasis, acne and related afflictions.

Everyone is familiar with the village wart-charmer, who is generally regarded by the village folk as a purveyor of white-magic. Wart-charming provides a neat example of the effect of psychotherapeutic suggestion. Occasionally there crop up stories of individuals who claim to be able to cure warts on animals by similar means. It cannot be said dogmatically that such cures are impossible.

Two apparently well-authenticated cases of such cures of cattle and a horse are recorded in one of the Journals of the

S.P.R. [1] In each case the animals were badly afflicted with warts and were cured within a few weeks. Such tales, however, need further investigation before they are to be taken seriously. For whereas such cures in the case of human beings are simply explained as due to the effect of suggestion, it is scarcely likely that the same methods would succeed in producing any effect on livestock. In such instances it would be wise to assume that some form of internal or external medicament was applied.

A good many organic diseases of the body can be *indirectly* benefited by suggestion-therapy. Continental psychotherapists find that it often helps in cases of multiple sclerosis, tabes and pulmonary tuberculosis. Even if the organic disease can not be cured either by surgery or direct medical treatment, suggestion-therapy or other psychotherapeutic methods can relieve or even banish the pain or inconvenience, and can often retard the advance of chronic disease to a remarkable extent. In the case of pulmonary tuberculosis, for example, suggestion can contribute not a little to the cure by improving the general condition of the patient's appetite. [2]

Suggestion-therapy can mitigate *the effects* of incurable organic disease in several different ways : one, by the alleviation of pain ; two, by the removal of the overt symptoms or by inducing a compensative reaction ; three, by the relief of anxiety and other worries which have been draining the patient's reserve of strength. Such alleviations of disease are undoubtedly dangerous and may ultimately prove fatal if the suggestion treatment is carried out by thaumaturgic healers and their like ; for the patient is thus frequently deceived into believing that he has been *cured* of his disease and fails to obtain proper medical attention on that account. Hundreds of the tales concerning the alleged cure of incurable disease originate in this way. Perhaps the greatest factor in their origin is the relief or banishment of pain by suggestion. Even when the relief is only temporary and the disillusioned patient has become aware that his disease or injury is no better than before, the tale of his " cure " has already been

---

[1] Vol. 9, 1900, pp. 101-103.

[2] Jolowicz, E., *Suggestion Therapy* ; and Heyer, G., *Hypnosis and Hypnotherapy*, p. 29.

broadcast and believed by innumerable enthusiasts devoted to the cause of supernatural healing, and may even have found its way into the daily papers.

Every condition of disease and ill health presents symptoms which are psychological in origin. Mental factors exert a definite, and sometimes vital, influence on the course of disease or illness. Such psychological factors vary according to the patient's temperament. Therapeutic suggestion or other forms of psychotherapy can be used to aid in the cure of most diseases. The " will to live " and the " wish to die " attitudes of patients can profoundly influence the recovery during a serious illness or after a serious accident or operation. When the doctor's diagnosis is proved wrong by the unexpected death of a patient, it is not infrequently due to his lack of insight into the patient's mental state at the time.

The psychological condition of a sick or injured patient is of great importance in the progress or lack of progress towards recovery. Marked debility and loss of resistance to disease may be caused by purely psychological factors. Not only are such cases more susceptible to infection than others, but once the disease or infection has taken hold, it is often more serious in its consequences, recovery is retarded, and, in cases of the more exhausting illnesses and in injuries where shock is pronounced, the patient has not the energy to institute a recovery. Actually the situation is not as bad as it may appear, for in cases of serious illness subconscious mental conflicts and nervous strain generally disappear, since the factors which gave rise to them in the patient's everyday life have largely receded into the background. Nevertheless, there still remains great scope for aiding the patient to stimulate or revive those psychological factors which help in increasing his resistance to disease or shock.

In cases where debility and loss of resistance to disease or shock can be attributed to psychological causes, therapeutic suggestion, whether administered by a psychiatrist or by a " psychic " healer, can obviously be of great value.

If such treatment is given by a " psychic " healer it will often seem to the patient, in his ignorance, that the healer has had a *directly* beneficial (and supernatural) effect on the *disease itself*. He will fail to appreciate the true cause of his improvement in health. He only knows that his doctor has failed to give him any relief but that a so-called quack in a country village has made him feel fitter and stronger and a great deal more hopeful. His belief in the latter's occult power is confirmed and strengthened and this in turn makes subsequent suggestion more effective still. And so it goes on. Many individuals have their own " psychic " healer who alone is capable of giving them some of their " life-force ". With many old people of set convictions there can be no doubt that the so-called psychic healer has some advantages, not only over the medical practitioner but over the clinical psychiatrist as well. The *belief* in occultism is in itself a highly potent source of effective suggestion, with which the psychiatrist, on ethical grounds, prefers to dispense.

All physicians are aware of the importance of the patient's morale in serious illness or injury, yet relatively few are acquainted with the full rôle played by psychological factors in disease. However, it is becoming increasingly recognised that there is no organic disturbance which is not accompanied by psychological change, and that this in turn is liable to play an ever increasing rôle in the course of the illness, some-times ultimately effecting a *decisive* influence on the physio-logical processes involved. This is particularly true with patients of extreme natural sensitiveness ; psychiatrist and medicine man alike may contribute materially to the patient's well-being in such instances.

With nervous patients suggestion-therapy frequently has enormous advantages over other methods. The psycho-analyst knows only too well that by resolving the patient's subconscious psychological conflicts a reserve of potential energy is thereby released. Suggestion can, by a different method, render available a similar supply of energy which cannot fail to aid recovery in cases where debilitation and low resistance to disease occur. No one can tell with cer-tainty the extent to which disease generally is due to psycho-logical maladjustment. Groddeck has even put forward the extreme view that the subconscious mind could, under the right conditions, prevent the body from being affected by the majority of diseases to which mankind is prone.

All types of disease and injury are influenced by psycho-logical factors ; therapeutic suggestion can often use this knowledge to influence favourably the course of the cure. This is equally true, whether the sufferer receives the therapeutic suggestion at the hands of a clinical psychotherapist, through the thaumaturgic displays of a " miracle healer ", or through the effects of autosuggestion during a visit to Lourdes.   It is ignorance of the principles of psychotherapy and psychosomatic medicine which leads so often to beliefs in supernatural or " psychic " healing.   Unless, however, the suggestive treatment is continued, the beneficial results obtained are usually only temporary.

The temporary nature of many supposed miracle cures is a factor which the devotees of physic cults invariably ignore, if one may judge by the literature of the subject. In general, permanent improvements may be said to occur only when the patient retains a lasting belief in the efficacy of the psychic healing or in the powers of the healer ; and if this belief is supplemented at intervals by prayer or other methods of attaining concentration on the desired end, this may easily result in an autosuggestive situation analogous to repeated doses of suggestion-therapy.

Many of well-authenticated accounts of the beneficial effects of autosuggestion in the guise of prayer have been reported in the past.   Those for whom prayer has been the means of mitigating suffering can never doubt that the relief was brought about by means of a divine agency.   For such as these instructions in the principles of medical psychology would be pointless and many cases would be positively harmful.   They would gain little and lose much that is valuable in their lives.   The believer in divine intervention, in faith healing, or in the occult power of the " psychic healer" is, in any event, not likely, when presented with the rational facts of the matter, to change his beliefs, for they are too deep-set.

An interesting example of suggestion therapy is seen in so-called " telepathic healing ".   The patient arranges with the psychic healer for the latter to transmit his healing impulses " telepathically " at a certain hour each day.   The patient who places such confidence in the efficacy of his healer's thoughts generally suffers from mild mental disorders, neurasthenia or psychoneurosis, and, in consequence, from such maladies as recurrent headaches, backaches, depression, lack of energy and nervous exhaustion. Suggestion can often here be very effective.

With many elderly people, deep faith in a psychic healer often enables the latter to give relief where the professional physician or psychiatrist has failed. At the right hour the patient relaxes and opens his mind to the " healing thoughts " of his healer ; and, as knowledge of suggestion-therapy might lead us to expect, he finds that his depression lifts, his headache disappears and that for a time his mental and nervous balance is restored.

In such cases there is the great advantage that distance does not interfere with the curative process. Whether or not the healer bothers to think of his patient is obviously of little importance. It is doubtful whether he troubles his head about his devotee once the latter is out of his sight. The effect of the patient's own autosuggestion is sufficient. It is to be remembered, however, that such autosuggestion is likely to be ineffective without the patient's mind being rendered susceptible to suggestion by the healer in person during the first weeks of curative treatment, a point which Coué has repeatedly emphasised.

The same principle of suggestion hold good for " radiesthetic " treatment via the medium of pictures painted by the healer, in which the patient exposes himself to the " healing rays " of the painting.

Another method for securing results, sometimes used by the older schools of hypnotherapists, is for the latter to write down the curative suggestions on a piece of paper, sign it, and give the patient " the post-hypnotic suggestion that should, e.g., the pain or insomnia return he has only to read what has been written for the symptoms to disappear ". [1] This, of course, is merely a modernised version of the primitive witch-doctor's presentation of "healing" charms, and the medieval custom of healing through holy relics and amulets provided by the priest together with his blessing. Some modern clinics for the cure of dipsomania provide treatment which is analogous in principle.

---

[1] Cuddon, E., *Hypnosis : Its Meaning and Practice*, p. 123.

THE RELIEF OF PAIN 221

THE RELIEF OF PAIN

Therapeutic suggestion can play a supremely important
rôle in alleviating the patient's distress, by the relief or
mitigation of pain or injury. This is not difficult once
hypnosis has been induced ; even without hypnosis pain
can often be considerably relieved under the art of one skilled
in the use of suggestion, and in a few cases it may be altogether inhibited by such means.

The relief of pain through suggestion in such maladies as
sciatica, lumbago and neuralgia is a common experience.
Thous nds have testified to the ability of " psychic " healers
to alleviate their pains by simply touching or stroking the
affected part with their hands. In hospitals on the continent,
the terrible pains of pleurisy have been reported completely
banished by suggestion repeated at intervals. The banishment by suggestion of *pseudesthetic* sensations, often of extreme painfulness, in " phantom limbs " after amputation
has been repeatedly carried out, and many hospital authorities
are open to censure in that they do not attempt to employ
a psychotherapist even in the most severe cases of
pseudesthesia.

In the case of serious organic disease, suggestion can
do nothing to effect a cure if other methods are neglected.
Many physicians tend to look down upon psychotherapy
for this reason. But if it is recognised " that we are not
curing tabes when we attempt to suggestively influence
the lancinating pains and the gastric crisis, then scarcely
anything can be objected to such a therapeutic procedure."[1]
For many years hypnotism has been employed as a local
anaesthetic, as, for example, in the removal of boils or the
extraction of teeth. As in hysterical analgesia, local areas
may be rendered totally insensitive to pain by hypnotic
suggestion. More remarkable still are the carrying out
of major operations while the patient is in a hypnotic trance.
In this connection the name of James Esdaile stands pre-
eminent. In 1845 Esdaile was appointed superintendent
of a government hospital in India for the express purpose
of introducing " mesmerism ", as hypnotism was then called,
into regular hospital practice. This was before the intro-

---

[1] Jolowicz, E., op. cit.

THE MOST CELEBRATED CASE IN THE HISTORY OF HYPNOTISM

Showing the giant scrotal tumour, nearly 7 ft. in circumference and weighing 103 lbs., which Esdaile painlessly removed while the patient lay in hypnotic trance.

(Reproduced from "The Introduction of Mesmerism into the Hospitals of India," W. Kent & Co., 1856)

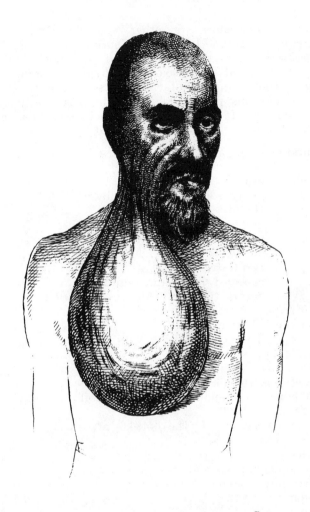

PAINLESS OPERATION BEFORE THE ADVENT OF CHLOROFORM.

Drawing of another great tumour removed by Dr. James Esdaile while the patient lay unconscious in hypnotic sleep.

(*Reproduced from "The Introduction of Mesmerism into the Public Hospitals of India," W. Kent & Co., 1856.*)

duction of chloroform or ether. Esdaile, dealing with the highly suggestible Indians, was spectacularly successful. He performed a total of 261 surgical operations while his patients remained unconscious in hypnotic trance. To illustrate the magnitude of Esdaile's success here is a list of his operations performed in the hospitals of Hooghly and Calcutta.[2] It is given in full since such an amazing document deserves to be perpetuated.

Amputation of thigh	... ...	2
,, leg ...	... ...	1
,, arm ...	... ...	2
,, breast ; one 7, another 10 lbs. weight	...	4
,, thumb	... ...	1
,, great toe	... ...	1
,, penis	... ...	3
,, one testis	... ...	3
,, two testes ...	... ...	2
,, enlarged clitoris and nymphae	... ...	1
,, Scrotal tumours of all sizes, from 10 lbs. to 103 lbs. weight	... ...	200
Cancer of cheek extirpated	... ...	1
,, of eyeball extirpated	... ...	1
,, of scrotum extirpated	... ...	2
Cartilaginous tumours on the ears removed	... ...	2
Cataracts operated on	... ...	3
End of bone in a compound fracture sawn off	... ...	1
End of thumb cut off	... ...	1
Great-toe nails cut out by the roots	... ...	5
Gum cut away	... ...	1
Heels flayed	... ...	3
Hypertrophy of penis removed ...	... ...	3
Hypertrophy of prepuce removed	... ...	1
Lithotomy	... ...	1
Lithotrity	... ...	1
Piles, suppurating, cut out	... ...	2
Prolapsus ani, the size of a child's head, reduced in the trance	... ...	1
Strangulated hernia reduced in the trance	... ...	3

---

[2] Esdaile, J., *The Introduction of Mesmerism into the Public Hospitals of India*, 1856, pp. 26-27.

Straightened contracted arms in the trance   3
Straightened contracted knees in the trance   3
Tumour in the groin removed (a fungoid undescended
    testis)   1
Tumour in the antrum maxillare removed   1
Tumour on leg removed...   1

Total   261

In 1842 John Elliotson, the inventor of the stethoscope, founded a hospital for the use of hypnosis in surgical operations. Despite this and despite Esdaile's success in establishing that major operations could be undertaken under anaesthesia induced by hypnotic suggestion, the general opprobium attached by the medical world of the day to the practice of mesmerism resulted in his work being mainly ignored—and this although it had been attested by a government commission. In all his 261 " mesmeric " surgical operations, ultimate mortality proved to be under 6 per cent of the cases—a very low figure for those days. Esdaile noticed, too, that the wounds made by the knife healed with less trouble. It seems curious and rather horrifying that surgeons of the day did not leap to welcome any idea which would help alleviate the terrible agonies of the operating theatre, where patients not infrequently died under the shock or had their minds deranged by the tortures of the saws and scalpels.

The following is Esdaile's own account of the amputation of a scrotal tumour nearly seven feet in circumference : [3]

" S., aged twenty-seven, came to the Native Hospital with an immense scrotal tumour as heavy as his whole body. He was mesmerised for the first time on October 10th., 1846, then on the 11th. and 13th., on which latter day he was ready for operation. The operation was performed on the 14th. The tumour was tied up in a sheet in which a rope was attached, and passed through a pulley in the rafter. The colis was dissected out, and the mattress then hauled down to the end of the bed ; his legs were held asunder, and the pulley put in motion to support the mass and develop its neck. It was transfixed with the longest two-edged knife, which was found to be too short, as I had to dig the haft in the mass to make the point appear below it and it was removed by two semi-circular incisions right and left. The flow of venous blood was prodigious, but soon

* ibid.

moderated under pressure of the hand; the vessels being picked up
as fast as possible.   The tumour, after half an hour, weighed 103
pounds, and was as heavy as the man's body.   During the whole
operation, I was not sensible of a quiver of the flesh.   The patient
made a good recovery."

Today the use of hypnotism as an anaesthetic in surgical
operations is rare.   Its use is generally confined to patients
who possess a weak heart or when a general anaesth··tic
or the suspense attendant upon an operation under a local
anaesthetic would be dangerous.   A number of dentists
in England and America have specialised in the hypnotic
technique in lieu of chemical anaesthetics for filling dental
cavities and extracting teeth.   In America the tendency
is for such dentists to avoid the term hypnotism and to use
instead the less question-begging term *psychosomatic sleep*.
Such dentists have to be able to assess whether each patient
is susceptible to hypnosis in the first place and they report
over ninety per cent success with those on whom they
try it out.   The British Dental Association, in contrast to
the American dental profession, is favourable in its attitude
towards the use of hypnotism in dentistry though without
specifically encouraging it.   Few dentists are trained in
hypnosis, and this factor prevents its employment becoming
more widespread.

Dentists who have continuously used hypnotic analgesia
are unanimous in their verdict that it is possible to stop
by suggestion the flow of saliva from the saliva glands in
the mouth.   With some patients they claim that the bleeding
can also be largely controlled.   The checking by suggestion
of bleeding from wounds appears to be practised by the
shamans of Lapland as a therapeutic measure and by the
fakirs of India in their thaumaturgic displays.   There is
considerable evidence that the natural processes pertaining
to the healing of wounds and broken bones can be considerably speeded up amongst primitive peoples by the use
of suggestion.   There is nothing very surprising in this.
It is no more than the psychotherapist does, for example,
in his treatment of tuberculosis by suggestion-therapy.
The process is an indirect one and is based on the fact that
the patient's mental state can affect the course of the
disease either for better or for worse.

Esdaile first called attention to the quick healing of wounds in operations performed under hypnotically induced analgesia,; and also to the quick healing of wounds self-inflicted by Arab pilgrims during ecstatic or autohypnotic states. Chemically induced analgesia produces a similar effect, shock and inflammation being considerably diminished under an anaesthetic in comparison to when the patient feels the knife and the pain of the operation. Clearly there is good ground for believing that suggestion could, in numbers of cases, generally benefit physical injuries, and when it is reported that a native has received such treatment at the hands of an African witch doctor there is no reason to disbelieve the story after making due allowance for the natural tendency to exaggeration.

Whether wounds can be healed in days in place of several weeks is open to question. However, in view of the effects upon the vasomotor system attainable through hypnotic suggestion and the known phenomenon of atrophy in functional paralysis, we cannot say dogmatically that a reverse process is not possible, that the mind may not be able to greatly speed up the natural curative processes. Reports of instantaneous healing of wounds and broken bones may be disregarded. No such case has ever been proved, and the sources of error and delusion are numerous.

Amongst those who go to " psychic " healers for relief from pain must be many who suffer from neurotic aches and pains with a psychological aetiology. Amongst hysterical individuals there are some who suffer from what is known as *topoalgia* ; the patient feels a localised pain in some part of his body for which no organic cause can be found or where the distribution of the sensory nerves renders an organic cause out of the question. Such pains are easily cured by suggestion, but unless the underlying mental conflict or source of nervous tension is discovered and dealt with, relief is likely to be only temporary.

The relief of pain by psychological methods can often be extended to cases in which the patient suffers from a painful and incurable disease. Fear and anxiety often make a great contribution to the degree of pain experienced, and suggestion can do much to diminish both. Many stories have at one time or another come into circulation concerning the powers of primitive medicine men and occult healers who, " at the touch of the hand ", banish the pain of the wounded or fevered traveller and give him the healing oblivion of deep sleep. To the uninitiated such stories are either disbelieved or regarded as proof of the transcendental power of the mind. There is no need to fall back on either explanation. That vague and unsatisfactory word " suggestion " is a term which embraces a number of things the psychiatrist does not understand, but the processes it refers to are recognisable by their effects ; and although some of these may be surprising, dramatic or even startling, there is nothing in them which gives the least support to the cult of supernaturalism.

The conquest of pain by suggestion is one of man's great lost opportunities. Had this comparatively simple knowledge been discovered and utilised by the medical profession from its earliest days, as well it might, mankind would have been spared mountains of suffering down through the ages. It is a tragedy that its full potentialities were realised only with the advent of chloroform.

SYMPTOMATIC CURES BY SUGGESTION

There are many diseases the course of which cannot be seriously checked by any known means. With some of these hypnotic suggestion can often be of inestimable service by removing the overt symptoms or by inducing a compensative action. The " psychic " healer, the Lourdes grotto and the primitive shaman have, in the past, received enormous *kudos* for these ostensibly miraculous " cures " of incurable disease. Not only do the witnesses of the cure vociferously acclaim it, generally with wild exaggerations, from the housetops, but the patient himself is frequently the loudest in his asseverations of miracles performed—even though he may subsequently lose the benefits of the " cure ", as he usually does unless the suggestive dose is repeated.

Symptomatic cures of astonishing effectiveness have been recorded in the clinic. For example Moll mentions the successful cessation of the staggering gait in locomotor ataxy by hypnotic suggestion.[1] Such an achievement by a " psychic " healer would be acclaimed as proof positive of his supernatural power to heal otherwise incurable maladies ; and many would believe him.

Another type of cure in which the " psychic " healer is able to claim resounding success, is in those cases where the overt *symptoms* of a disease have persisted as a psychological habit long after the organic cause has been banished.[2] Hypnotic suggestion is naturally effective in such instances.

Another method of achieving the miracle cure is to induce by suggestion, illusions or even hallucinations of well-being in the mind of the patient. Undoubtedly these form a very large number out of the total of purported " psychic " cures. An interesting and enlightening clinical example of such a " cure " is given by Rossette :

" As neither I nor any of my colleagues or associates had succeeded in curing postencephalitic Parkinsonian patients, and in a number of cases had failed even to alleviate their suffering, I availed myself of an opportunity to witness an alleged ' cure ' of such patients by suggestion, in a certain clinic. After the suggestion-treatment had been administered, I spoke to some of the patients. They were miserable victims of the dread disease, rigid, with abnormal involuntary movements. They had been receiving this treatment for months, some of them, for a year or more, and all of them, according to their own testimony, were cured ! Among them I was especially impressed by one. He was so rigid that he could hardly propel himself with the short, increasingly rapid, Parkinsonian gait. His right hand shook violently, his body swayed from side to side incessantly, his head moved continually up and down and from side to side, his mouth was open and saliva dribbled from it. His speech was of the classical explosive type, scanning and with abrupt pauses. And he, too, was cured ! I was as certain of the poor fellow's sincerity as I am that I have not seen many postencephalitic sufferers more pitiable." [3]

The above is an extreme example, and one inevitably wonders to what extent the hallucination of well-being alleviated the suffering of the patients. In less serious cases, there can be no doubt of the contribution to the happiness of the sufferer by such methods, for the alleviation of anxiety is always highly beneficial to the patient. As an illustration of this fact Drs. F. W. Freeman and J.

[1] Moll, A., *Hypnotism*, p. 211.
[2] Jolowicz and Heyer, op. cit., p. 218.
[3] Rosett, J., *The Mechanism of Thought, Imagery and Hallucination*, p. 214, N.Y. 1939.

Watts of George Washington University have performed prefrontal lobotomy—a surgical operation on the brain which frees the patient from fear and anxiety—on patients suffering from chronic disease accompanied by great physical pain. Although the course of the disease remains unaffected by the operation and the pain is not lessened, the patients, freed of anxiety and fear, find their suffering bearable, even to the point of making light of them. Patients who have had their worry and anxiety removed by methods of suggestion often experience the beneficent illusion that their disease is " getting better ". Not unexpectedly, if such suggestion is carried out by an occult or thaumaturgic healer the patient will credit their " improvement " to the latter's supernatural powers.

CONCLUSION

Belief in the occult or divine powers of " psychic " healers, holy wells, witches, Christian Science healers, charms or amulets is widespread. Such beliefs have arisen and been perpetuated through ignorance of the psychological principles involved. Mankind, universally prone to mysticism, has, in the realm of mental healing, an overflowing abundance of phenomena of an apparently miraculous nature. The psychological cure of a man functionally blind for years inevitably fills even the most intelligent but uninformed spectator with awe and a sense of uncertainty, particularly if the cure takes place in such an atmosphere as is generally attendant upon gatherings of a religious or esoteric nature.

Among primitive and suggestible peoples suggestion can effect the most dramatic recoveries. In modern civilised societies, however, education and other factors have largely mitigated the effects which were once attainable solely by the use of suggestion, and in modern psychiatric clinics the employment of suggestion therapy is on the wane; surer techniques of mental healing have gradually replaced the uncertainties inherent in hypnotism and other forms of direct suggestion, although direct suggestion still has an important rôle to play.

From earliest times the effects of suggestion and autosuggestion have provided the ignorant with a host of pheno mena which are easily attributed to the influence of trans cendental forces. And nowhere is this more true than in the sphere of psychotherapeutic healing. Therapeutic suggestion in its multiple guises forms the basis of belief in supernatural healing. The miracle healer, the primitive medicine man or shaman, the psychic healer, the supervisors and attendants at holy wells and springs, use the principle of suggestion to obtain their effects ; but this fact is almost invariably misapprehended by both healer and sufferer, both of whom attribute the observed results to the operation of supernatural powers. Suggestion can cure—temporarily and sometimes permanently—most physical diseases and disorders with a psychological origin ; the paralysed hysteric is known in modern times to have been cured instantaneously—a genuine miracle to many who known nothing of medical psychology.

In the case of psychosomatic cures (excellently typified by the village wart-charmer), the belief in the supernatural is sustained by the fact that few sufferers from psychogenic ailments realise that their malady is psychological in origin. Most people tend to believe that any physical ailment is primarily a symptom of physical disease or disorder. Hence, when such disorders are cured by psychological or " mental " methods of treatment, the cure is looked upon as an example of the mystical or supernatural power of " mind over matter." Such beliefs appeal to the irrational element in man's nature and have behind them the spurious sanction of thousands of years of similar beliefs.

In all types of disease, injury and ill-health there can be traced mental factors which exert a definite and often vital influence, for good or evil, upon the patient's condition. Sometimes the patient's physical disorders are purely psychological in origin and are directly amenable to cure by suggestion. In other types of disease, psychological factors play an important though secondary rôle, and here again psychotherapeutic suggestion may vitally influence the course of the disease. In the case of incurable diseases suggestion may give rise to illusions of healing by the banishment or alleviation of pain, the removal of overt symptoms, by inducing compensatory reactions or simply by inducing a fixed belief in the patient's mind that he is cured ! All these cures and alleviations of suffering—both real and illusory—are open to supernatural interpretation by ignorant or uninformed people.

Suggestion can also provide the sufferer with the temporary delusion or even hallucination that he is cured— and this is probably the greatest factor in the genesis of tales concerning supernatural healing. Suggestion can banish anxiety, worry and fear and replace it with cheerfulness and optimism thereby increasing the patient's reserves of energy and often bringing about remarkable improvements in a very short space of time. This again is often attributed to the supernatural powers of the healer.

Suggestion and autosuggestion have played a very important rôle in the history of miracle cures. Yet this is by no means the whole story. Charlatans and tricksters have added their full quota to the belief in supernatural healing, while self-deception and wishful thinking have perhaps made even larger contributions.

Tales of the instantaneous cure of broken bones and incurable disease are numerous and fresh examples arrive every month, particularly from the United States where every decade produces a new crop of religious cults with faith healing as the central theme ; in not one case has such a report been scientifically attested. In all such stories the first thing to suspect is the validity of the initial diagnosis. In instances where a person claims to have been cured of an incurable disease and no longer exhibits the symptoms pertaining to that disease, documentary evidence of the original diagnosis has never been forthcoming. And in cases where the original diagnosis has been verified as correct, the subsequent " cure " is generally found to be based on delusion or deliberate deception, unless the cure is a symptomatic one only. Proof of an instantaneous cure of an incurable disease or physical injury must necessarily be supported by irrefutable evidence of a competent diagnosis *before* the " cure ", together with a doctor's certificate stating that the patient no longer exhibits the disease or injury in question. It must, moreover, be established that the patient's recovery took place within a time limit which renders all possibility of a cure through the natural processes of healing out of the question.

Despite all these precautions faulty diagnoses are still made by general practitioners and nowhere is this more likely than in the case of psychogenic ailments. A broken arm or leg has often been known to have resulted in functional paralysis or topoalgic pains long after the bone has set. To all intents and purposes the patient remains incapacitated by his original injury, whereas in fact his continued invalidism is a hysterical syndrome. The doctor may fail to realise this and omit to call in a psychiatrist who would easily cure the patient. It may chance that the patient is treated by a " psychic " healer, visits Lourdes, or attends a Christian Scientist meeting and lo, the miracle is performed ; the " broken limb " that the doctor could not cure is healed at a touch or within the course of a few days. Such instances are admittedly rare, but it is this type of "cure" which lends a specious air of validity to the hundreds of other tales concerning the " psychic " healing of broken bones and incurable disease, which have little or no foundation beyond mere hearsay.

It is well known that hysterical maladies are often imitative and many a medical practitioner has had experiences of diagnosing a disease which has eventually proved to be merely a functional disorder. In the past, when the nature of functional disorders was not understood, the doctor was often helpless to effect a cure, whereas the quack thaumaturgic healer often succeeded in bringing about a cure by simple suggestion. In many parts of the world the same situation probably still arises from time to time, doubtless to the joyous elation of the faithful and the consternation of many of the medical profession.

Chapter Thirteen

MYSTICAL EXPERIENCE AND ECSTASY

A̲N̲ E̲N̲O̲R̲M̲O̲U̲S̲ A̲M̲O̲U̲N̲T̲ of literature has been written concerning so-called " mystical " experiences and states of ecstasy. Generally, these unusual phases of consciousness have possessed a religious significance to those who have experienced them, ranging from a belief in direct personal union with God, the Universe or " Reality ", to the crude howling exaltations of hystero-epilepsy induced among certain sects and individuals in primitive societies.

The psychologist is under no such illusions as to the real nature of mystical experience and ecstasy, and it may come as something of a shock to many people who have believed in the religious significance of such subjective states, to learn that they may be brought about by a variety of causes whose origin, judged by any criterion, is far removed from the divine.

The phenomena known as ecstasy and mystical experience are attributable to a number of different causes. Very frequently they possess a hysterical or pathological aetiology. They may also be induced by autophypnotic practises or by the use of certain drugs, amongst the most conspicuous of which is Indian hemp. The Indians of Mexico achieve analogous states of consciousness through *ololuiqui* intoxication. Ololuiqui is a derivative of a solanaceous plant allied to belladonna, or deadly-nightshade—the main component of witches' brews in the Middle Ages.

The use of Indian hemp as a narcotic is widespread.

Known as hashish in Arabic-speaking countries, *bhang* or *ganja* in India and *marijuana* in Mexico, hemp rivals opium in its ability to create an artificial world of escape from the realities of existence. As is well known, continued heavy use of both narcotics has often led to incurable insanity. Hemp has been used, as far as we can tell, for nearly 3,000 years; Herodotus mentions its use by the Scythians in the fifth century B.C. The drug is still something of a mystery, however, for its effects on human beings vary considerably, particularly in its psychological consequences. Its effects on the individual's mental faculties seems largely to depend on the psychological constitution of the subject. With certain individuals it may result in euphoric hallucinations, richly variegated sensory illusions or brilliant, easily remembered dreams. The frenzied ecstasies attained by certain dervish cults are undoubtedly connected with the eating of hashish. The dervishes themselves regard hashish as an aid to the induction of ecstatic visions of supernatural or mystical import.

The most interesting cases of ecstasy and mystical experience are those which are the product of hysteria or psychasthenia and which have no connection with the taking of drugs. These states of consciousness are often accompanied by a subjective sensation of *extreme euphoria*, or feeling of bliss, to a degree which is normally unattainable by the average individual whose mind is adapted to the exigencies of practical existence. It is this component of euphoria which so deeply impresses the mystic and which colours not only his thoughts and illusions at the time of his experiences, but also his memory of them afterwards.

With many ecstatics visual hallucinations are experienced which are called " visions." More frequent, perhaps, are auditory hallucinations, but hallucinations are by no means an invariable concomitant, and with some types of ecstasy are totally lacking.

Apart from true psychoses, ecstasy can usually be put down to hysteria or else to causes pathological in character where the physiological structure of the brain is affected : as, for example, in general paralysis of the insane, which is occasionally accompanied by extreme euphoria or *habromania*. *Habromania*, in combination with the delusions experienced by the syphilitic, may result in a state analogous to genuine "mystical experience".

It is the hall-mark of the mystic that he invests certain abnormal psychological states with an objectivity equal to or transcending the objectivity of his experience in the ordinary everyday world. This is the essence of all true mysticism. The mystic, knowing nothing of modern psychiatry, interprets his abnormal psychological experiences as a revelation of "ultimate reality", whereas in fact they are nothing more than extremes of mental and emotional complexes which are beyond the range of the average man.

For example, most people are acquainted with a feeling of happiness and optimism at times, in which the whole world is seen in a roseate glow; one feels that one is part of nature and that nature itself is transformed into something more vital, reflecting back, as it were, the joyousness within. Similarly, when one feels pessimistic and depressed, the whole environment appears bleak and without meaning, purposeless. In the ordinary way the human mental mechanism is fairly well adjusted to operate within the range of these two opposites, without being incapacitated for effective action in the daily round. In some types of insanity such feelings of extreme ecstasy render the patient incapable of attending even to the simplest of his needs. Such states may also be brought about by disease in which the brain becomes affected.

The true mystic, on the other hand, is often eminently sane. But whether through accident or design, he is on occasion able to achieve a state of ecstasy in which his normal faculty for optimism and happiness reaches abnormal heights. As with some types of insanity this may be simultaneously accompanied by delusions of depersonalisation (*acenesthesia*), identification with the cosmos, or omniscience (*sophomania*); it is nearly always accompanied by delusions of one sort of another. With one such delusion, also seen in the psychosis known as *somatopsychic paranoia*, the patient experiences the sensation of having no body. The mystic's ecstasy is sometimes accompanied by beatific hallucinations. Oblivion to the immediate environment frequently occurs, although, this depends largely on the type of experience involved and, concomitantly, on the causal factors involved in its manifestation.

Every single aspect of the so-called mystical experience is to be found in insane asylums or mental homes. When sane people experience these mental states, some degree of psychasthenia or hysterical dissociation is probably present. It is alike the error of the sane and the delusion of the insane, to suppose that these anomalous states of consciousness possess any more significance than other extreme types of mental experience.

The Indian cults of yoga attain to blissful and illusion-saturated states by special mental training, and have founded upon them impressive systems of metaphysical philosophy whose teaching becomes part of the individuals' outlook and is reflected in their ecstatic states. This type of ecstasy is probably the highest form attainable. Amongst all religions we find this pure and enobling type of psychological experience, which leaves the subject with a sense of joy and purpose and which may become the central pivot of his whole life.

But any and every object of longing or desire, no matter how grotesque, trivial, obscene or perverse, may also become the object of ecstasy ; the degree of euphoria attained may be the same whether the object of ecstasy is perverse or enobling. The true mystical experience may be considered to have been experienced when the euphoric state is allied to the highest mental and intellectual development, or with high religious themes. Such experiences may last, amongst the sane, from a few seconds to several hours ; they stand no comparison with the ecstasy of primitive peoples, whose low intellectual powers prevent their attaining to what may undoubtedly be the richest of all mental experiences, surpassing anything else known.

All types of mystic speak of the rapturous bliss of their experiences. To the religious mind, the ideas of bliss and Heaven, or bliss and God, possess a strong synonymity. The predominating sensation of euphoria, which leaves such an overwhelming impress on the mind of the subject both during and after his experience, often leaves him in no doubt that he has in fact had a direct personal experience of God himself.

Amongst primitive peoples ecstasy becomes simply the production of euphoric hallucinations by any means in their power ; the Rifái dervishes provide a good example. Beating drums, blowing on trumpets, frenzied dancing and chanting, convulsive movements, fasting, self-castigation, howling and shrieking, total sexual abstinence—all these are used separately or in conjunction to produce the desired effect.

The ecstatic experiences of many individuals have consisted of euphoric hallucinations in which scenes of brutal sadism and perverse sexual orgies predominate ; here may be most clearly seen the common relationship between euphoric experiences and sexual disturbances. In the Middle Ages some of the Saints had hallucinations which took this form—visions whose real nature was hidden from them by being represented to their consciousness under the guise of the wickedness and the tortures of the damned in hell, or a pre-view of the Day of Judgment. The medieval saint might take the view that his erotic hallucinations were but temptations of the devil ; but psychologically there is no difference between his experiences and those of the medieval witch who believed herself to be a friend of the devil and frankly enjoyed her hallucinatory walpurgis—where her partner in sin was often the devil himself.

Where sensory hallucinations occur, the ecstatic experience is usually on a simpler and more primitive level than in those euphoric states where there are no such hallucinations. In hysteria and mild psychosis, hallucinatory visions and voices are seldom accompanied by euphoria, and the subject therefore lacks that irresistible desire to repeat them which the true euphoric state induces in those who have once experienced it.

Many people still believe that great intuitive truths can be apprehended in these ecstatic states. This belief is merely part of the delusion involved in the state of ecstasy itself ; it is not surprising that ecstatic states have played a large part in all religions, for they give a degree of illusory corroboration to the universal religious teaching that man can have personal communion with the Godhead.

Unfortunately, most of the individuals who experience the mystical ecstatic state are to be found among the inhabitants of insane asylums, particularly among some types of schizophrenia. These individuals frequently experience feelings of overwhelming bliss which, as with the true mystic, is accompanied by an all-pervading sense of clearness of perception. Many saints and martyrs have undoubtedly presented schizoid characteristics. Oddly enough, psychotic ecstasy is not infrequently found to be associated with feelings of fear and suspicion.

This overwhelming delusion of clearness of perception, so characteristic of schizophrenic ecstasy, gives the mystical experience its deceptive appearance of genuine objectivity ; it is really an infantile regression, although nothing will ever convince the subject of the truth of this. Schizophrenics may also experience symbolic hallucinations which have for them a quality of the intensest significance, and this again is a fairly frequent characteristic of mystical experience. It is not surprising, therefore, that those who have experienced, are subject to, or can by some method induce, the so-called mystical experience in any of its various forms, are convinced of the objectivity of their experience ; their interpretation of it is simple and direct.

Yet, delusions of self-identification with God, convictions of omnipotence and omniscience, a sense of the uniqueness of their " revelations ", sensations of overwhelming grandeur —all these are familiar to the student of abnormal psychology in his studies of schizophrenia, paranoia, and manic-depressive psychosis. In the lives of many types of oriental mystic we can see how these characteristics of psychosis may be gradually induced in men of certain dispositions by the force of their beliefs. In catatonic schizophrenia we find a parallel to the immobile contemplator of the Orient who has withdrawn himself from the outside world. Hebephrenia sometimes includes a conviction of identification with the cosmos.

With some types of psychasthenic [1] patient sensations of unreality and depersonalisation are a common enough phenomenon. Such a patient has a constant feeling of unreality about things, and although he recognises his usual surround-

---

[1] Psychasthenia ; a mental disorder characterised by phobias, compulsions, obsessions, doubts, inadequacy, unreality, etc.

ings they seem strange to him as if seeing them for the first time.

Any or all of the above-mentioned variable factors of psychosis and psychasthenia may play a part in mystical "illumination"—the sense of clarity of perception, the feeling of intense significance, the delusion of the uniqueness of the experience, feelings of omniscience, depersonalisation, unreality, identifications with the Divine or the Cosmos, and above all the overwhelming euphoria which makes some of the insane the most blissfully happy people on earth. The true mystic, too, is often a supremely happy person, having his whole life lit up by the subjective beauty of his occasional euphoric states of consciousness.

Poets, artists and intellectuals down through the ages have known this vivifying experience. In an often quoted passage from a letter to a friend, Tennyson gives us his impression of his own mystical experience :

> " A kind of waking trance I have frequently had, quite from my boyhood, when I have been all alone. This has generally come upon me through repeating my own name two or three times to myself silently, till all at once, as it were out of the intensity of the consciousness of individuality, the individuality itself seemed to dissolve and fade away into boundless being ; and this is not a confused state but the clearest . . . surest . . . weirdest, utterly beyond words, where death was an almost laughable impossibility, the loss of personality (if so it were) seeming no extinction but the only true life."

In psychological terms this experience might be described as a temporary state of marked psychasthenia, characterised by subjective feelings of depersonalisation and delusions of omniscience with accompanying euphoria. Tennyson's account of his experience was undoubtedly conditioned by his reading of the literature of Indian mysticism and its specious offspring, Theosophy, in which he was known to be deeply interested.

Mystical experiences of all kinds have played an enormously important rôle in history. All the great founders of religions have been mystics. The strong delusory sense of revelation which the mystics experience at the time of the ecstasy often gives them a sense of historic mission ; the auditory and visual hallucinations of Joan of Arc provide an excellent case in point. The mystical visionary is usually ignored or laughed at by the world in general. Occasionally, by an accident of history, his delusions find themselves in curious harmony with the needs and trends of the times, and he becomes the leader of great national or religious uprisings.

" Mystical illumination " is a term often used in lieu of mystical experience, to denote a single event in the life of the individual which brings about a change in his whole outlook and beliefs. It often takes the form of a visual or auditory hallucination unaccompanied by any subjective sensation of euphoria.

The " vision " of St. Paul provides an excellent example of a hysterical hallucination with a religious theme ; the psychiatric term *conversion syndrome* takes on here a peculiar significance. As Saul, the liberally educated Jewish citizen of the Roman city of Tarsus, he had become a leader among the Pharisees, the strict, dogmatic and fanatical followers of the ancient Jewish Law. His rise as a young man to a position of respect and authority would naturally gratify a domineering and ambitious nature ; in consequence he sternly repressed the more humane side of his character and forgot the lessons of the wider culture of Rome. Doubts and scruples which would have interfered with his ambition he shut out from his consciousness, hiding them from himself and others by ever more brutal acts of fanaticism. The repressed ideas and desires of the gentler side of his nature lay dormant,. forbidden the cleansing scrutiny of conscious introspection. They formed a growing and increasingly powerful guilt-complex—repressed and emotionally super-charged—which was subsequently to become the basis for severe hysteria leading to hallucination, functional blindness, change of personality and a recurring hysterical affliction concerning whose precise nature we remain uncertain.

The subconscious conflict in Saul's mind suddenly burst for a brief moment into consciousness under the impact of a hysterical crisis. The auditory hallucination which accompanied it was the summation of his own repressed conscience, he heard the voice of the crucified Nazarene crying, " Saul, Saul, why do you persecute me ? " This was followed by functional blindness—the organs of sight being unaffected in any physiological sense, though the subject is unable to bring what he sees into consciousness and in consequence believes himself to be totally blind. Functional or hysterical blindness can always be cured by suggestion or by other psychological means such as the resolution of mental stress. In Paul's case both the resolution of mental stress and the healing suggestion were conveyed in the words of Ananias, and his sight was restored.

Saul, or Paul as he now called himself, was now a changed man. A hysterical change of personality, not uncommon in psychological literature, almost certainly occurred in Paul's case. The brutal, fanatical, intolerant side of his nature was replaced by the other gentler side which had long remained repressed. But he thereafter suffered from a grave " affliction ", of which he appears to have been ashamed. It was probably a hysterical disorder of some kind, either recurrent hystero-epileptoid crises, a chronic nervous tic, or hysterical stammering.

A further alternative—and one that would explain his reticence on the subject—is that he reverted for short periods to his original Saul personality which had, on the emergence of the nobler and gentler Paul, been more or less repressed ever since. Hysterical changes of this nature are often accompanied by subsequent amnesia. Such reversions to his former personality, even for brief periods of a few minutes, must have been exceptionally distressing both to Paul and to his friends, particularly those friends who were ignorant or uneducated, for they would attribute such reversions to " possession " by an evil spirit when they heard their leader inveighing against the followers of Jesus with all his old fury.

The phenomena known as mystical experience and mystical illumination are of great interest from the point of view of the psychologist. To the mystic, however, the psychiatric explanation of his experiences is anathema. Is there any possibility of truth in the claim that the mystic may, for an instant of time, make contact with the reality behind the appearance of the phenomenal world ? The answer, unfortunately, is no. Such a belief is merely one of the delusions of significance which go to make the higher mystical experience what it often is—the most beautiful and inspiring of all mental aberrations.

Chapter Fourteen

THE STIGMATA OF THE CRUCIFIXION

AT FREQUENT INTERVALS during the past seven hundred years stories have arisen concerning the miracle of the *stigmata*—the supernatural appearance of wounds or scars upon the hands and feet of certain devout saints and mystics similar to those inflicted on Christ during the crucifixion. In some instances it is recorded that the individual concerned showed the marks of the thorns, the scourging, or the gash originally inflicted by the Roman spear in the side of the Nazarene, and that blood flowed copiously from the wounds; or that the stigmata took the form of excrescences resembling nails—as was first reported of St. Francis of Assisi.

Many of these stigmata were self-inflicted or were the result of chicanery. Most of the stories, by the time they had been written down for the edification of posterity, were exaggerated beyond recognition. Nevertheless, certain well-authenticated cases of stigmatisation have come down to us, some of them relatively recent, which are, to say the least, something of an enigma. This phenomenon, which for hundreds of years has been considered by the devout as a sign of divine grace, is now thought by many to be an odd variant of those little understood disorders which may arise from psychological causes such as hysteria or autosuggestion. It is this aspect of the problem which will constitute the main focus of interst in the following pages.

The term stigmata (singular *stigma*), before it was applied by St. Paul to the wounds of the crucifixion, originally denoted the identification-marks inflicted on the criminals and slaves of the ancient world by branding with hot irons. Today the term has also a number of medical and biological connotations which, however, are of no concern here ; they have no connection with the subject of religious cruciform stigmata.

The first and most famous of the hysterics to experience the stigmata was St. Francis of Assisi in the year 1224. Once provided with an example of stigmatisation, the minds of later religious mystics and hysterics fastened on the phenomenon with avidity. From then on until today stigmatisation has made sporadic appearances amongst the ultra-devout and has been acclaimed a miracle by those who claimed to have experienced it and by most of those who heard of the event.

According to Dr. Imbert Gourbeyre,[1] approximately 340 cases of stigmata have been recorded after the time of St. Francis, the great majority being women. Many of these stigmata were accompanied by great pain ; in other cases simply the pain alone was experienced without any visible signs or marks appearing ; and a few of the stigmata were preceded or accompanied by a variety of visual and auditory hallucinations with pronounced religious themes determined according to the naïve beliefs of the day.

Several cases of prolonged stigmatisation have in comparatively recent times been made the subject of special observation. Louise Lateau, a Belgian peasant girl, first experienced the stigmatisation in 1868. Each Friday her stigmata exuded blood. The stigmata of Theresa Neumann of Konnersreuth also attracted a great deal of attention. She herself was born on a Good Friday, and during the twenty-eighth anniversary of that day, April 2nd 1926, marks of the stigmata appeared on the upper surfaces of her hands and feet. The same thing occurred on each subsequent Good Friday, accompanied by bleeding from the eyes. The latter phenomenon occurred whenever, according to her own account, she meditated deeply on the events of the Passion. The stigmata of a young Italian girl Gemma Galvani, who died at the age of twenty-five in 1903, also aroused great public interest. Deep wounds appeared on her hands, feet and side, and later lacerations appeared on her body in imitation of the scourging of Christ.

---

[1] *La Stigmatisation*, 1894.

Of these three modern examples of stigmatisation, however, only that of Louise Lateau remains a subject for speculation. Theresa Neumann, who also claimed to have lived for years without food, was a deliberate fraud aided and abetted by her father. Gemma Galvani's painful stigmata were, beyond the slightest shadow of doubt, the self-inflicted wounds of a major hysteric. Despite this, however, she possesses the proud honour of being the last of the stigmatists to be canonised; she was elected to the worthy freemasonry of the Saints seven months after the outbreak of the second world war.

The stigmata of Louise Lateau were subjected to strict medical observation by the Belgian Academy of Medicine. The bleeding from the forehead was examined under a powerful magnifying glass, and the conclusion was reached that the blood percolated through minute triangular abrasions of the skin which were scarcely visible to the naked eye. Drops of blood exuded visibly through the skin of the forehead to form beads like perspiration which coalesced and trickled down the face. The bleeding was found to occur even if the affected area was sealed off from external contact. In one experiment bleeding occurred from the girl's hand after the limb had been enclosed in a sealed-glass container overnight. Whether the minute abrasions in the skin were inflicted by methods known only to Louise herself (and there is little direct evidence of this), the question still remains as to how the haemorrhage started after being sealed off from all external contact. This might have been done by excoriation with the finger. On the other hand, it might possibly have been brought about by extreme emotional or other psychogenic factors following intense concentration on the crucifixion. The latter alternative is of great interest and is one to which we shall return later on in the present chapter.

Perhaps the best known, and certainly the most successful of contemporary stigmatists is an Italian Capuchin Monk, Padre Pio, who lives in a monastry near Foggia.

After ordination he developed tuberculosis and sometimes fell into trances while holding Mass. In 1918, during one such trance, he collapsed unconscious; stigmatic wounds were found on his hands, feet and side, such as might have been inflicted by a sharp instrument. The stigmata have continued to the present day ; the wounds, it is claimed, bleed constantly, saturating several handkerchiefs daily. Padre Pio still on occasion falls into prolonged hysterical trances while holding Mass.

At first the Vatican was sceptical, but after two years of investigation it pronounced the stigmata to be of miraculous origin. Padre Pio has collected over half a million pounds from the faithful, with which he has recently built a hospital containing five hundred beds. Inappropriately enough it is to be called the Fiorello La Guardia Hospital. It appears that we still live in the age of miracles.

The external appearances of stigmata have varied widely : some are like deep wounds which bleed freely, others festering sores or simply raw patches on the skin ; a few seem nothing more than wart-like growths ; yet others, like those of Louise Lateau, are reported as an effusion of blood from the hands or feet, side or brows, without any visible signs of a wound. Often the pains of the crucifixion have been experienced with no external symptoms or at most a reddening of the skin in the affected parts.

The numerous recorded cases of stigmatisation which have occurred during the past seven centuries were clearly not all brought about by the same means. The supernatural interpretation can be disregarded. Beliefs in supernatural stigmatisation can obviously be brought about in several ways : one, by self-inflicted wounds ; two, by deliberate faking, using blood or a red dye ; three, through accidental injury ; four, through localised skin eruptions, growths or lesions ; five, through psychosomatic factors ; and finally, in instances where the pains are apparently experienced without visible symptoms, through topoalgia (hysterical pains) or by conscious simulation. It has been suggested that many stigmatised subjects have suffered from haemophilia. This is unlikely, however, since haemophilia is mainly confined to males and the great majority of the stigmatised have been women.

It is evident from the above that the term *stigmata* is a misleading one, implying as it does a supernatural origin. Historically speaking, however, the term is useful because it accurately reflects the beliefs of a past age. In this historical sense, without indicating anything supernatural or psychologically abnormal, we may retain the use of the term here, whatever the true nature of the " phenomena ". For what concerns us is not only the various ways in which stigmatic lesions, pains and the rest may have been brought about, but also the ways in which the beliefs in supernatural stigmatisation have been perpetuated.

Historical cases of stigmata produced by fraud or deception are difficult, and sometimes impossible, to assess. These are, in any event, of little interest beyond the bare fact that a good many historical examples of stigmata undoubtedly originated in this way.

Many stigmata produced by self-mutilation were doubtless deliberate attempts to achieve a vainglorious and spurious reputation of saintliness with all its attendant satisfactions. On the other hand, self-mutilation by certain individuals after prolonged concentration of the crucifixion, perhaps following continuous ascetic devotions, may well have occurred during hysterical attacks followed by amnesia. It is probably not a coincidence that many of those who " received the stigmata " were subject to epileptiform attacks, and one conclusion to be drawn from the evidence at our disposal is that the great majority of such attacks were hystero-epileptic rather than due to recurrent epilepsy. Purposive self-mutilation during hystero-epileptic attacks followed by amnesia would strike no psychologist as surprising. It is perhaps worth noting that self-mutilation with knives is a prominent feature of the artificially induced hystero-epileptoid attacks of certain Moslem Dervish cults in the Near and Middle East.

Hysterical or deliberate self-mutilation is certainly the explanation of most recorded cases of stigmatisation. Certain modern instances of stigmatisation, e.g. those of Gemma Galvani, show clearly that the extent, location and form of the lesions are largely determined by conceptions which the subject held before the stigmata appeared.

Stigmatisation has very often followed hysterical or somnambulic re-enactments of the events surrounding the Crucifixion. The scourging, the carrying of the cross, the crowning with thorns, the crucifixion, the wounding with the spear, and even the drinking from the sponge,

have been included in these horrifying pantomimes with
all the agony of one who is actually experiencing the events
enacted. It cannot be denied that such mystics suffered
greatly during their repeated hysterical and often convulsive
attacks, which sometimes lasted for hours : often the attacks
involved self-flagellation (the scourging) and postures requiring great endurance to maintain ; self-inflicted wounds
similar to those of the crucifixion are only to be expected
in many such performances.

Many of the mystics often felt in their sufferings a hysterical ecstasy which has a parallel in the common psychological
aberration of masochism ; the self-imposed sufferings of
many mystics and religious ascetics had undoubtedly a
sexual aetiology.

One excellent example of self-inflicted stigmatic lesions
has come down to us from the contemporary biography of
the nun Lukardis of Aberweimar. [1] Lukardis had long
desired the stigmata and eventually achieved it by persistently stubbing her palms with the tips of her fingers and by
chafing the upper part of the feet with her big toes. This
practice was in all probability a nervous habit brought on
by her intense desire for the stigmata. It was seen that
she continued the practice after the wounds had appeared.
Yet this did not prevent herself and others from regarding
her stigmata as supernatural manifestations. Like Louise
Lateau, her stigmata bled every Friday (presumably through
further stubbings and chafings), a fact which certainly casts
a good deal of suspicion upon the origin of the Belgian girl's
stigmata, and indeed upon all stigmata which manifest
themselves in periodic bleeding.

Accidental injury to the hands or feet, during moments
of mass religious frenzy, might have well given rise to beliefs
that the wounded person had been the recipient of divine
stigmatisation. In the Middle Ages such a scene can easily
be imagined. The wounded man raises his bleeding hands
in fright or pain and those nearest him, in the excitement of
the moment and ever on the watch for " signs " and miracles,
cry out ecstatically that they have been vouchsafed the
blessed sight of the stigmata. The cry spreads like lightning,

---

[1] See Herbert Thurston, S. J., *The Phenomena of Stigmatization*, Proc.
S.P.R., 32, 1922, pp. 185-187.

and yet another case of stigmatisation is recorded in the
ecclesiastical archives.

There is no doubt that injuries to the hands, in the case
of religious hysterics of the Middle Ages, could give rise to
subsequent delusions of stigmatisation, even though the
individual concerned was under no illusion at the time the
injury was received. Yet again with hysterical individuals,
a deliberate infliction of wounds on the hands and feet could
easily develop a delusion that the wounds were in tact conferred supernaturally. Delusion has played a very large part
in the production of historical cases of stigmatisation. To
reason otherwise would be to gainsay human nature. From
what we know of the Middle Ages and later periods it is
even probable that enterprising monastics inflicted by force
the marks of the stigmata on unwilling victims. For it was
always accounted a thing of great credit and glory to the
abbeys and monasteries of those days, that signs of divine
favour should visit any one of the inmates; and this is
scarcely surprising, since such miracles increased their fame
and filled their coffers from the pockets of innumerable
pilgrims.

Delusions of supernatural stigmatisation in earlier centuries
are attributable to a variety of factors, among them certain
localised skin disorders. Ulcers, carbuncles, warts, excoriations and some forms of dermatitis appearing in more
or less symmetrical form on both hands, either by chance
or from various other causes, are all possible sources of
delusory belief in stigmatisation. In this connection it is
of interest to remember that the stigmata of St. Francis
took the form of fleshy excrescences which were subsequently reported as resembling the nails wherewith Christ had
been crucified.

Localised and symmetrical affections of the skin could
have been brought about in several ways. Chance coincidence is obviously one. Infection of the hands by scratching,
in the case of those mystics who longed for the divine grace
of stigmatisation, is another. Diseases peculiar to the
hands and feet can also be considered, such as *cheiropompholyx* (in which blisters filled with fluid suddenly appear).

One possible explanation of stigmatic lesions has been
suggested to the author by Mr. Joseph Northcott of Pelynt,

Cornwall. He himself frequently suffered from painful chaps in the palms of his hands from working on the farm—work to which he has been regularly accustomed. These chaps, or coarsening and splitting of the skin, sometimes healed and broke out again several times in the course of a winter, although they occasionally lasted for months. They were generally deep and accompanied by a small suppuration, and tended to inflammation if neglected. The nuns and monks of the monasteries were often compelled to carry out hard manual labour, and if some of them developed severe inflamed chaps in the palms which " miraculously " refused to heal, or which healed and broke out again periodically, they might easily come to regard them as manifestations of divine stigmatisation.

Po sibly the most likely source of stigmatic delusions are neurotic excoriations, caused perhaps by some minor irritation or local skin disorder but prolonged and exacerbated by a nervous habit of scratching. It is significant that such excoriations occur most often with hysterical individuals, for symptoms usually associated with hysteria have often accompanied delusions of stigmata.

The most common form of neurotic excoriation is *dermatitis artefacta* or lesions of the skin self-inflicted by scratching. The hysterical or neurotic individual may inflict such lesions for a variety of motives, sometimes consciously, and often, in the case of hysterics, involuntarily. He may be activated by a desire for sympathy or attention, or for an invalidism which would enable him to be moved from uncongenial work or to escape from an environment to which he (or she) is ill-adjusted. These excoriations, in fact, are typical hysterical syndromes. They may become so extreme as to cause the loss of a limb through excessive ulceration. It is worth observing that with many such cases, even when the psychiatrist has conclusively demonstrated to the patient that his excoriations are self-inflicted, it is often impossible to obtain a confession.

There are sound psychological reasons for believing that in the past many religious hysterics who regularly practised, as part of their devotions, prolonged contemplation of the events surrounding the Crucifixion, produced their stigmata by neurotic excoriation. Such mystics frequently entered a state of trance by virtue of the very intensity of their meditation—meditation which often took upon itself a virtually pathological character. Neurotic scratching can be carried out without the conscious awareness of the individual concerned. The scratching may even occur during sleep, particularly where the cause of the scratching is a subjective sensation of localised irritation or itching (*neurodermatitis*). Probably most people have felt the uncomfortable sensation of itching when the conversation turns on to such lowly subjects as fleas. Such itching is almost entirely imaginary and in hysterical individuals may result in an involuntary habit of constant scratching leading to severe excoriation.

It is by no means improbable that certain hysterical mystics who contemplated the crucifixion felt the intense itching or irritation of neuro-dermatitis in the hands and feet—whether the underlying cause of the irritation was a subconscious desire for the miracle of the stigmata or a subconscious fear aroused by the contemplation of a realistically painted image of the crucified Christ.

Historical records leave little doubt that some cases of stigmatisation have been nothing more than a transient hallucination or delusion, whose authenticity depends solely on the word of those who claim to have experienced it. Other cases of hallucination, however, are of great interest, particularly where the subject has experienced intense pain in the hands and feet without visible lesions.

Some mystics experienced similar pains in the side of the body corresponding to the gash inflicted by the Roman spear in the side of Christ. While some of these may have been instances of deliberate simulation, others were certainly cases of hysterical topoalgia. Topoalgia pains are localised hallucinatory pains, sometimes of great intensity, which have no organic reason for their existence and where the nerve distribution excludes the possibility of a physiological cause. In a superstitious age a supernatural interpretation of such pains is only to be expected. In many cases the pains came suddenly during moments of rapt contemplation or hysterical frenzy.

According to the Rev. Herbert Thurston,[1] intense pain

---

[1] *The Phenomena of Stigmatization*, Proc. S.P.R., 32, 1922, p. 195.

was in many instances felt for months, and sometimes for
years, before the appearance of the stigmatic lesions.   If
this was the case, it seems probable that hysterical topoalgia
first gave rise to the delusion of stigmatisation and that
subsequent excoriation or mutilation produced the physical
symptoms—a sequel doubtless rendered expedient by the
disbelief and ridicule which the topoalgic sufferer must have
often faced.

Topoalgic pains in the hands, feet, the side and even the
brows (in reference to the crown of thorns), may be reckoned
as the true stigmata, i.e. stigmata which, although not
conferred by supernatural means, are the product of solely
psychogenic factors.   Psychogenic stigmata can be conveniently divided into two classes : first, topoalgic pains corresponding to the wounds of the crucifixion ; second, visible
physical symptoms with a similar correspondence which have
a purely psychological aetiology—these latter we may call
psychosomatic stigmata.   Have genuine psychosomatic stigmata ever occurred ?   Can mental factors alone produce
external lesions and the like in specific locations on the body ?
Can certain forms of hysteria, suggestion or autosuggestion
affect the body's tissues, directly or indirectly, to produce
the phenomenon known since the thirteenth century as
stigmatisation ?   These are the questions to which, as yet,
no *certain* answer is forthcoming.

All that can be said is that although little convincing
proof of psychosomatic stigmatisation has come to light,
certain psychiatric evidence favours such a possibility.
Briefly, what we must consider is the possible occurrence
of localised organic changes in specific areas of the human
body brought about directly by psychological processes.
Such changes may occur in certain nervous or hysterical
individuals but not, as far as the psychiatrist is aware, of
sufficient intensity to account for the more dramatic manifestations of stigmatisation.

THE EVIDENCE FOR PSYCHOSOMATIC STIGMATA

Occasionally one comes across clinical cases very reminiscent of the reputed phenomenon of stigmatisation. R. L. Moody describes such a case. [1] His patient, who had been brutally beaten by one of her parents in her youth, was subjected to analytical treatment. During analysis the events of her past returned vividly to her mind and this resulted in the emergence of urticareal weals on those parts of her body upon which her injuries had originally been inflicted. This is an unusual case. While it is well known that urticareal eruptions may be produced by emotional factors, the specific localisation of such eruptions is relatively rare.

Moody's case and a few similar ones establish with a fair degree of certainty that *certain physiological changes can be produced in specific locations on the body which are predetermined by mental factors alone.* This fact is obviously of great interest in relation to the phenomenon of stigmatisation. It appears to render possible the localisation of certain psychogenic disorders and eruptions whose distribution depends on the direct influence of unconscious mental processes.

Atopic (allergic) dermatitis, warts, cheiropompholyx, urticaria, seborrhoeic dermatitis, all may have a psychogenic aetiology. Small localised rashes on the hands may have been the explanation of a number of historical cases of stigmata, though this in itself is of little importance unless they led to a degree of suppuration or ulceration which could be interpreted by the superstitious mind as evidence of stigmatisation.

What we wish to seek is evidence that mental factors alone can produce changes in the vasomotor system such as to cause capillary haemorrhage (ecchymosis), or at least subcutaneous congestion of the capillaries (erythema) leading to severe inflammation. If localised erythema can be brought about by psychosomatic processes, then it is quite possible that localised ecchymosis and even chronic ulceration might similarly occur. Part of the process of ordinary inflammation is *diapedesis,* or the in-

---

[1] *The Lancet,* 1948, 1, p. 964.

filtration of white blood corpuscles (leucocytes) through the capillary walls. With certain subjects it appears possible that red corpuscles might also infiltrate through the capillary walls, without rupturing the capillaries, to produce a suffusion of blood under the skin. This may well be the explanation of certain very rare clinical cases of " sweating of blood " (*haemetidrosis*), where the blood apparently percolates through the skin via the sweat ducts ; numbers of such cases in the past are doubtless attributable to a disorder known as *chromidrosis*, or the excretion of abnormally coloured perspiration ; it has also been suggested that chromidrosis might explain certain cases of stigmatisation. Subcutaneous capillary haemorrhage, if extreme, could certainly lead to raw open patches on the skin and subsequently to chronic ulceration. This very fact, however, leads us to suspect that all reported cases of stigmata in which the haemorrhage was *copious* were inflicted by external means of injury or were the product of chicanery or delusion. Proven cases of chicanery are certainly not lacking.

There is considerable evidence that the vasomotor system (the mechanism which controls the normal dilation and constriction of the blood vessels) can be affected by hypnotic suggestion. The autonomic nervous system—that part of the nervous system which regulates many of the internal organs which are not subject to volitional control—can also be affected by the same means. But the use of suggestion to produce changes in the vasomotor and autonomic nervous systems is an indirect process affected mainly by the operator's control of the imagination and hence the emotions. The unresolved question concerning stigmatisation is whether or not the vasomotor system can be sufficiently controlled by subconscious mental processes as to be able to produce localised changes in the capillaries—changes which would result in capillary congestion or even haemorrhage.

Moody's test-case [2], witnessed by a medical colleague, involved actual bleeding, apparently through the action of psychosomatic factors alone. Red streaks appeared across the back of the patient's hands after dramatically reliving an accident in which she had been struck across the hands

[2] ibid.

with a whip. The right hand was then encased in lint and plaster. Bloodstains were revealed on the lint dressing when the plaster was removed the following morning and the weals showed small eruptions of the outer layer of the skin (*epidermis*).

This case presents a number of parallels with the investigations conducted by the Belgian Academy of Medicine concerning the stigmatic bleeding of Louise Lateau. In both cases bleeding occurred after the affected area had been effectively protected against possible excoriation on the part of the hysteric. Yet such cases do not, unfortunately, provide conclusive evidence for localised psychosomatic bleeding ; for there is always the possibility that the hysteric has managed to outwit the doctor or psychiatrist when unobserved for any length of time.

Moody's observations are of the greatest significance if confirmation is forthcoming. They would indeed indicate that bleeding may be induced by psychosomatic processes, including suggestion. In this connection we may turn to the experiments conducted by some of the French psychotherapists of the latter half of the nineteenth century. The hysterical subjects with whom they experimented had been reduced to a state of ultra-suggestibility by the frequent recurrence of hypnosis ; today few psychiatrists would care to put their own experimental interests before the wellbeing of their patient in this way.

A number of these experimenters claimed to have induced bleeding by hypnotic suggestion :

" I may further mention the experiments of Bourru, Burot, and Berjon, who induced bleeding by suggestion in the same subject as Mabille, Ramadier and Jules Voisin. Puységur had witnessed the same thing. Bleeding of the nose appeared at command in the above-mentioned subject, and later on bleeding from the skin at a time decided on beforehand."[3]

Modern psychotherapists generally reject the evidence of these experiments as being insufficiently well-controlled, nevertheless there is always the possibility that their findings may one day be confirmed.

Of lesser moment, but of considerable importance if verification is forthcoming, are those experiments in which localised disturbances of the lymphatic mechanism are

[3] Moll, A., *Hypnotism*, p. 114.

reported to have been brought about by suggestion. Lymph is a watery colourless fluid which is derived from the blood through the walls of the capillaries. The aim of the experiments in question was to produce blisters by hypnotic suggestion. Kraft-Ebbing, Foucachon, Forel and Delboeuf all reported the raising of blisters by hypnotic suggestion. Stories have also been recorded, though they lack full medical confirmation, where the subject has turned on a cold tap in very cold weather and the stinging sensation due to the icy stream onto his hand caused the painful illusion of being scalded. Swellings and even blisters are reported to have resulted.

Dr. J. A. Hadfield gives an interesting account of some comparatively modern experiments of his own in the suppression of inflammation and the raising of blisters by hypnotic suggestion. The subject was first hypnotised. His arm was then touched with the red-hot end of a steel pencil-case after the suggestion had been given that he should feel no pain.

" There was no pain either when the skin was touched or afterwards. But the remarkable thing was that in these burns there was *no hyperaemia* around. Round each of the two spots, which themselves presented the ordinary appearance of blisters, there was a thin red line and nothing more. These blisters healed very rapidly and never gave any sign of inflammation or pain."[4]

With the same subject a blister-raising experiment was tried. The subject, a leading seaman suffering from combat hysteria, or " shell shock ", was first hypnotised. Hadfield touched his arm with his finger while telling him that his arm was being touched with a red-hot iron, and that a blister would form. The patient winced as though badly hurt. Within nine hours a blister had formed.

" There was a white patch of dead skin in the centre, underneath which was a slight amount of fluid and hyperaemia (congestion) around, . . . the blister increased in size, and by the next day there was a large quantity of fluid, giving the exact appearance of a blister by heat."[5]

Hadfield successfully repeated the experiment with the same subject.

---

[4] Hadfield, J. A., *The Lancet*, 1917, ii, p. 678.
[5] loc. cit.

It has always been difficult to ensure maximum control during such experiments. The possibility of trickery by the subject must always be considered, and generally speaking, the medical profession are inclined to be sceptical. But some form of initial stimulus slightly damaging to the tissues, such as heavy pressure or rubbing, might well be a prerequisite for the appearance of psychogenic stigmata, both in the case of the religious hysteric and in the psychotherapeutic clinic.

Though localised disturbances in the lymphatic mechanism may possibly be produced by suggestion, this does not indicate that capillary haemorrhage can likewise be induced. For although lymph issues through the walls of the capillaries, a very great pressure would be necessary to force the blood through the healthy tissues ; the blood's far more rapid rate of congealing would certainly limit any capillary exudation. The problem therefore still amounts to whether or not localised psychosomatic lesions of the skin are possible, and at our present stage of knowledge this appears unlikely unless, as just noted, certain damage to the skin has already been inflicted.

The next question to consider is whether or not psychosomatic processes can initiate or retard a haemorrhage once the skin has been broken by a cut, wound or other lesions.

We have already mentioned the influence which psychological factors may play in aggravating or mitigating the consequences of physical injuries. Particularly relevant to the problem of the stigmatisation are the many recorded instances where bleeding from wounds or surgical operations has been partially or completely arrested by suggestion.

Janet records an excellent experiment in which he established that a restriction of bleeding can be brought about by a change in a patient's mental state. His patient suffered from functional paralysis accompanied by anaesthesia and a retarded circulation. The patient was cured by suggestion and

" simultaneously with the return of sensibility, a number of other movements could be detected. The circulation was restored, so that the skin lost its pallor. Whereas previously a prick did not bleed, now when the skin was pricked with a pin a droplet of blood would appear, and the skin would redden in the neighbourhood of the prick."[1]

This and other experiments give some credence to the view that psychosomatic affections of the vasomotor system, in particular the arresting and excitation of capillary haemorrhage, may sometimes be a contributory cause of stigmatic bleeding. In any event, it seems possible that intermittent haemorrhage may be produced by psychogenic factors, in the case of certain hysterical individuals with chronic lesions on the hands or feet. This would certainly conform to the traditional conception of stigmatisation and also explain a number of the more modern instances of the phenomenon ; the question of the actual origin of the lesions is relatively unimportant. The drawback about such an explanation of intermittent stigmatic bleeding is that there is nothing to prevent the self-proclaimed receptor of the stigmata from causing a recurring haemorrhage by excoriation of the affected area—longstanding lesions often become relatively insensitive to pain—and this seems to be the most likely explanation in the vast majority of cases of purported stigmatisation.

Instances of the psychosomatic arrest of bleeding are numerous, although some of the more dramatic claims are open to other interpretations. Moll mentions that menorrhagia may be induced or arrested by suggestion.[2] Esdaile and others reported that operations under hypnotic analgesia sometimes resulted in a diminution of haemorrhage but that when the patient was awakened the bleeding increased to the normal degree. Professor C. G. Seligman records that he himself has witnessed the rapid cessation of bleeding from self-inflicted wounds by the Aisawa dervishes.[3] Similarly, the speciality of the Lapp shamans is reputed to be the cessation of bleeding from wounds by suggestion.

There remains little doubt that the mitigation or even suppression of inflammation may be brought about psychogenically. Professor Delboeuf's experiments at the end

---

[1] Janet, P., *Psychological Healing*, vol. II, p. 793, 1925.
[2] *Hypnotism*, p. 114.
[3] " Ritual and Medicine," in *Enquiry into the Unknown*, p. 57.

of the last century are of considerable interest in this connection. He made symmetrical burns on each arm of two hysterical patients. He suggested to these patients, while under hypnosis, that the burns on their left arms would heal more rapidly than those on their right. In his report he states that the effect of the suggestion was very marked, the left-arm burns healing more rapidly than the others and with less inflammation. Such experiments as these are difficult to repeat these days. Ultra-hysterical subjects are difficult to come by, and the modern psychiatrist who found one would scarcely be likely to make a guinea-pig of his patient.

The effects obtained by the continental psychotherapists of the nineteenth century were the result of experiments on uneducated and highly suggestible hysterics rendered increasingly sensitive to suggestion by calculated repetition of hypnosis. Ultra-suggestibility is now, with rare exceptions, only to be found in primitive societies; and until experiments are carried out upon some of the world's " backward " races we shall probably not find out the degree to which suggestion and hysteria can effect human physiology.

Such modifications of the vasomotor system as are involved in the psychogenic arrest of haemorrhage and mitigation of inflammation (and possibly the raising of blisters) are very little understood. That a degree of control is at all possible by psychological means is still a disputed topic in medical and psychiatric circles. But it is well known that in many hysterical disorders bodily functions normally dependent upon the autonomic nervous system have often been profoundly stimulated or retarded. Hypnotic suggestion, like hysteria, may result in the increase or decrease of glandular functions and secretions, often to a remarkable degree. It cannot therefore be stated categorically that localised and symmetrical psychosomatic erythemata, ecchymoses and even lesions are impossible, even though they remain unlikely. In any event it would always be impossible to discover whether a lesion resulting from a psychosomatic ecchymosis had not been initiated by physical injury. No case at all can be made out for the *sudden* emergence of psychosomatic lesions through suggestion or hysteria.

If psychogenic modifications of the vasomotor system are at all possible, it does make more credible the theory that sporadic bleeding from open wounds or ulcerated areas can be brought about by changes in the stigmatist's mental state. Nevertheless, after surveying the numerous cases of stigmatisation of which a reliable record exists, one gains the impression that the psychosomatic explanation of the stigmata is something of a red herring. In the opinion of the present writer, religious stigmatisation is principally a hysterical phenomenon manifesting itself in self-mutilation, delusion and in topoalgia or localised neurotic pain. There is not the least doubt that genuine suffering was experienced by a number of stigmatised mystics who, after intense meditation upon the events surrounding the Passion and the Crucifixion, felt their hands and feet burning and aching in response to their topoalgic hallucination. Topoalgic stigmata are the true stigmata. Such a phenomenon could only be interpreted in the way it was, even by the most high minded and intelligent of the Saints—as a sign of divine grace supernaturally bestowed by God. No other explanation was open to them.

Religious stigmatisation is mainly a hysterical syndrome from the psychiatric point of view, and the stigmata follow the usual trends observable in hysterical disorders. The syndrome often takes a form which the subject can turn to good account, and it has been of inestimable value from the religious point of view, especially during the miracle-conscious Middle Ages.

Chapter Fifteen

LYCANTHROPY

FROM TIME TO TIME explorers, missionaries and empire administrators publish accounts of weird happenings that have come within the ken of their experience. Such stories of the occult, offered in a half-apologetic manner, usually include the observation that those who have spent their lives among primitive or savage peoples no longer scoff at tales of " the queer side of things ". Amongst the most persistent of such tales are those of *lycanthropy*— the reputed ability of certain individuals to take on the external form of a wild animal or to " enter into " the body of one and so direct its movements.

Lycanthropical legends have their origin in the dawn of history and have continued down to the present day ; it is only in the last fifty years or so that wide-spread belief in were-wolves has died out in Europe. All primitive and peasant societies have their lycanthropical beliefs. It is not surprising, therefore, that educated and intelligent people should occasionally become infected with the same brand of superstition after living for years among such communities. The lycanthropical tale often follows a peculiar pattern which has been in evidence as long as such beliefs have existed : An animal is killed or wounded by hunters and a man is found dead or wounded in his hut with marks of injury similar to those found on the beast itself.

Some of the published accounts are so circumstantial and detailed that if we accepted the author's integrity or trusted his judgment the validity of an occult lycanthropical interpretation could not be doubted. Travellers' tales, however, have a well-deserved reputation for exaggeration and convenient distortion : even today intelligent white men report such happenings with a lack of scepticism which shows how far they have unconsciously imbibed ideas of native magic and superstition. Yet travellers' tales of lycanthropy often have a basis in some kind of fact and it is this aspect of the problem which will be discussed in the ensuing pages.

The belief in lycanthropy very probably had its origins in primitive magic, but the *perpetuation* of such beliefs into comparatively modern times in Europe must rest on other grounds. And in point of fact we are often faced with psychological anomalies in regard to which both the superstitious savage and the average educated European are almost equally ignorant.

Belief in lycanthropy is well-nigh universal in primitive societies. In West Africa and Northern Burma it has attained such proportions that the native judicial system makes provision for it as for any other misdemeanour by which life or property is destroyed or injured. Here is an amusing example of the extent to which the native mind may confuse the real and unreal :

"In the more remote district where the hippo had destroyed the cabbage patch, the irate owner also took the matter to court and was awarded £2 for malicious damage to his property ; not, of course, against the hippo, but against a fellow villager, an enemy of his and a member of a very secret society whose initiates were believed to possess dual souls. The defendant in this case admitted that the particular hippo that had caused the damage was his own animal soul, but he pleaded that the damage was not malicious—he had not incited the hippo to commit the act. Indeed, he said, he had strictly warned it not to damage people's gardens in case it got shot—for when the animal dies the man dies also. The court, however, found that the damage was malicious, for the defendant had gone around boasting that his animal soul had done it ; and ' because '—I quote from the judgment—' those who have hippopotamuses as their bush souls must know how to control them.' "[1]

---

[1] Jones, G., " Stories of West African Juju," *The Listener*, August 21st, 1947.

In Africa such beliefs have been turned to hideous advantage by secret societies : calling themselves the leopard-men, the hyena-men or the crocodile-men, they deliberately foster belief in their lycanthropical powers by dressing in the skin of the wild animal, leaving tracks in the ground pertaining to the animal-fetish of the secret society in question, and leaving their victims torn and lacerated in imitation of a wild beast. Such practices for the most part serve merely to gratify a ghastly cruelty, inspired and directed by the local ju-ju-man or witch doctor. The unfortunate victims frequently have their entrails torn out while they still live.

Such secret societies were often cannibalistic—they practiced devouring parts of the human anatomy such as the heart, eyes and liver and the more tender parts of the flesh. The trails leading away from the scene of the crime would be those of a hyena or leopard or crocodile, but after some distance the tracks of human feet would supplant them to leave no doubt that it was the leopard-men or hyena-men who had been at work. The terror created by such methods in the minds of the primitive blacks can well be imagined. Furthermore, if one of the lycanthropists was shot or wounded, it is easy to see how stories of lycanthropical metamorphosis might spread. A state of extreme emotional tension and high suggestibility and expectation would be aroused among the local population, in which delusions and even visual hallucinations might occur, giving further impetus to the myth of actual lycanthropical transformations.

N. Fodor, a psychoanalyst, mentions a case where a white man experienced such a delusion or hallucination while watching an orgiastic jackal dance. Fodor gives an interesting psychoanalytical interpretation of the events :

" I have in my records a first hand account regarding lycanthropy. This account is dated March 23rd, 1933 and it comes from a Dr. Gerald Kirkland, then a 37-year-old medical practitioner at Trellwis, Glamorganshire, England and formerly Government Medical Officer in Southern Rhodesia. Dr. Kirkland had seen a native jackal dance and *could almost swear to it that two natives actually transformed themselves into jackals*.[2] His account, first sent to me in a letter, was printed two years later; it is not only vivid and detailed, but exposes the psychological motive behind the lycanthropic ceremonial he witnessed. The motive is clearly orgiastic. Desiring to be as potent as only dogs can be, the African natives succeeded after eating ' high ' meat and drinking large quantities of liquor, in playing the part of jackals with an uncanny realism. By the time the orgy reached its climax Dr. Kirkland was so overwrought that he may have easily entered into the psychic atmosphere of the group. The fact that he was unobserved (if he was) would not exempt him from such contagion.

" The phenomena he describes represent an evolutionary regression, an escape from the human onto the animal level. Eating ill-smelling meat and heavy drinking was apparently part of the self-persuasion necessary for the lycanthropic climax. Besides the purely sexual and sadistic motives, the cannibalistic and the necrophilic instinct may be divined behind the escape, because on the animal level no guilt is attached to satisfying them. The gateway to the outpour of the primitive unconscious was the Nanga or witch doctor in trance who acted collectively for the group and whose normal office as witch doctor invested the ceremonial with the stamp of legitimacy."[3]

It is well known that the monotonous beating of drums can produce a hypnotic effect, and this probably occurred in the instance quoted above. A hypnotist could, of course, very easily induce a hallucination or delusion of lycanthropical metamorphosis in a suggestible individual who had been deeply hypnotised.

We now come to those actual psychological aberrations known as *lycanthropy* and *zoanthropy* respectively. The terms are often confused : lycanthropy is generally reserved for certain delusions, beliefs or practices which are not in themselves characteristic of insanity. Zoanthropy, on the other hand, is the term applied to a form of psychotic paranoia. Both forms of aberration are often accompanied by such degeneracies as cannibalism, necrophilia (sexual assaults on corpses), sadism, zoerasty (sexual relations with animals), a craving for raw flesh, and hemothymia (pathological excitement at the sight of blood). While the delusions of zoanthropy are easily explained as the product of mental derangements, lycanthropy often manifests itself as a form of hysteria, and

---

[2] Author's italics.
[3] Fodor, N., *Lycanthropy as a Psychic Mechanism* ; Journal of American Folklore, Dec. 1945, p. 310.

there is little doubt that hysterical lycanthropy was largely responsible for the perpetuation of the were-wolf myth in Europe until after the turn of the century. Witch-craft, too, had many lycanthropical associations.

In the Malayan States lycanthropy is often associated with the phenomenon of *latah*. *Latah* is characterised by high suggestibility ; it is a hysterical affliction similar to the " jumping-disease " observed at one time among the woodmen of New England, U.S.A., in which the afflicted individual makes violent movements and rapid ejacul-ations in imitation of the actions and words of other people. [1]

According to the well-known anthropologist, J. H. Hutton, it is considered a source of amusement to hypnotise a lad subject to *latah* and suggest to him that he is a civet cat, whereupon he runs around on all fours and endeavours to devour live chickens. Hysterical lycanthropy, where it still occurs, may obviously be a source of danger ; but, being born mainly of suggestion and imitation, it is not likely to occur where the local population is not given to lycanthropical beliefs.

In many parts of Europe mental derangement was often taken to be a sign of the were-wolf—perhaps on account of the animal-like groans and ululations to which some psychotics give utterance. Certain unusual distinguishing marks were also regarded as peculiar to were-wolves : in Germany and Denmark, for example, eyebrows which met across the forehead were a sign of being a were-wolf, while in Greece the same characteristic denoted a *brukolak* or vampire. The belief in vampirism is merely a more ghoulish variant of the more typical lycanthropic beliefs.

In the type of insanity known as zoanthropical paranoia the subject suffers the delusion that he is an animal, some-times harmless but often very much the reverse. Paranoia connotes systematised delusions without serious impair-ment of the mental functions, and the cunning of certain types of paranoiac is well known. If the delusion takes the guise of a were-wolf or tiger and the subject takes to the woods or bush, he may constitute a serious menace to anyone passing in the vacinity. Victims of attack by

---

[1] *Webster's International Dictionary*, 2nd edition.

zoanthropical paranoiacs have been mauled and torn and partly devoured as if by a wild beast.   Some zoanthropical psychotics have been known to dress themselves in the skin of the beast they imagine themselves to be and to prowl around at night looking for victims.   In some famous European cases of the past whole neighbourhoods have been terrorised by such paranoiacs for long periods.

Many zoanthropic paranoiacs probably arrived at their degraded state through the continued use of the drug belladonna, much used in medieval times as a witch's salve and as an aphrodisiac.   Consistent use of solanaceous drugs often leads to insanity characterised by zoanthropical delusions and hallucinations including the sensation of having grown hair or feathers.   Zoanthropical psychosis due to belladonna was probably confined to women who either fancied themselves as witches, or who were the dupes of witches who dispensed belladonna brews for love-philtres and abortions.   It is of interest to note that certain depraved lycanthropical practices have been traditionally associated with pregnant women.

In contrast to violent lycanthropical practices just described are the gentler "tiger-men" of Assam and the northern reaches of the Chindwin in Burma.   This region of the world is the lycanthropologist's paradise, for here, if anywhere, the tiger-men exhibit almost all gradations which pertain to their calling.   Here, too, are authentic cases of tiger-men dying when their animal-familiars are killed.

Many individuals of the tribes in this area show symptoms of latent hysteria such as high suggestibility, catalepsy and hystero-epilepsy.   Herbert Tichy, a young Austrian geologist and explorer, recounts that there is a village near the Burma-Assam border known as Tomati, which can only be reached by flat-bottomed boats.   The inhabitants of this area are held in considerable respect by neighbouring villages for they are credited with a great variety of supernatural powers including an undoubted faculty as hypnotists. [2]

The tiger-men of this area are as far as could be imagined from the popular idea of a tiger-man.   Instead of mur-

---

[2] *Tibetan Adventure*, 1938.

derous savage sadists or schizophrenic paranoiacs, we find a very different picture. The West African leopard-man is a ferocious and sadistic individual whose main aim is to indulge his penchant for fiendish cruelty among his own people. He flourishes in the dreaded secret societies. The Assam tiger-men, on the contrary, often become tiger-men without having any *conscious* choice in the matter, and are sometimes unwilling. A native will perhaps announce one morning that he has become a tiger-man, with the result that from that day on he believes his soul capable of entering into the body of a particular tiger.

Without going into the many psychological factors which contribute to such sudden beliefs, we can say that from the time his belief is firmly fixed, the native's mind becomes open to further suggestive influences. His conviction may result from a minor hysterical crisis or be the result of a vivid dream. Since birth his mind has been steeped in lycanthropical beliefs. Unconsciously, perhaps, he has yearned for the added prestige accruing to those chosen by the gods to have tigers as their familiars.

The sudden conviction may be regarded as a typical compensation reaction often found in cases of hysteria. Usually, however, the privilege is deliberately sought for a multitude of reasons—such as the hope that it may prove efficacious in achieving revenge or in guarding the crops. The Tamans of Burma believe they can achieve their wish by rolling in the earth where a tiger has micturated. In West Africa the intimate relation between man and animal is brought about by a blood-bond ceremony.

Amongst many primitive peoples of the world is found the belief in the transmigration of souls after death into the bodies of animals. It is not a far cry from this conception to the idea of the soul taking temporary possession of the body of an animal during the individual's life-time, which is the universal claim of the Burma-Assam lycanthropists. Sometimes, we are told, the soul of the tiger-man is away in the body of a tiger for as long as three days ; during that time the man may appear, in extreme cases, waxen-coloured and scarcely breathing. Even those with less tendency to naivety than the ignorant and superstitious natives of those regions might well say that his soul had left his body.

In point of fact the tiger-man is suffering from hystero-catalepsy or else has induced a cataleptic trance by some process of autohypnosis. When the man awakes from his trance he believes that he has in fact been sharing the body of a tiger. He will give graphic descriptions of his adventures, how he hunted, mated, or killed and devoured his prey. Sometimes he reports that he, i.e. the tiger, has killed a man. Tichy tells the story of such a case and quotes the tiger-man as saying that he did not want to kill the man " but the tiger was too strong ".

There is a were-wolf tradition in Europe that during the cataleptic trance the limbs of the subject twitch and move as his wolf-familiar commits his depredations amongst the cattle. Hutton points out that this form of lycanthropy is identical with that in Assam and records that the body of the tiger-man may feel exhausted and aches as after violent exercise.

The more one investigates the type of lycanthropy under discussion, the clearer it becomes that we are dealing not with a single phenomenon but with a variety of hysterical manifestations centreing on lycanthropical ideas. In some forms of hysteria hallucinations may occur and it is quite possible that some lycanthropists hallucinate those experiences which they subsequently relate.

Catalepsy is a condition often associated with hysteria. In this condition the vital functions have sometimes been reduced to a limit only just sufficient to maintain the continuance of life. There need not be total insensibility but there often is. Sometimes the patient utters wild exclamations or even sings. Although unconscious to outside events his mind may be in full activity pursuing its own trance fantasies. In the less extreme state of catalepsy, muscular rigidity is absent and the patient retains a considerable degree of consciousness such as we find in some European and American trance mediums. In such cases the tendency to mental dissociation is incomplete.

The trance of the Assam-Burma men is comparable to some types of mediumistic trance. But instead of experiencing delusions or hallucinations concerning " controls ", " guides " and other inhabitants of the spiritualistic firmament, the native lycanthropist is concerned with the adventures of his trance-life as a tiger. If Professor Flournoy's famous medium, Hélène Smith, had been subjected to lycanthropic instead of romantic and spiritualistic ideas, her Martian tongue might well have become the growl of a tiger or the cackle of a hyena !

Finally we come to the most interesting of all lycanthropic phenomena—the death of the lycanthropist following the killing of his animal-familiar. Contrary to general belief, this is not altogether a myth. The effects of suggestion can by very great on a primitive and credulous mind subject to, hysteria ; and, as we have seen, the lycanthropic trance is primarily a hysterical disorder.

The belief that when a man's animal-familiar dies he also dies is found wherever lycanthropical beliefs exist—in Africa, in Asia, and in Europe where the were-wolf flourished. For example, a wolf or a tiger is shot through the head, and in the morning it is reported that a man, well known as having the power to transform himself into a beast, is found dead in his hut, with an identical wound in his head. In cases where lycanthropists and zoanthropics wear animal skins with the head of an animal still attached and worn above the wearer's own, like Sigmund the Volsung or the old Scandinavian berserkers, it is easy to see how such stories arose.

But another way in which the myth may partly have been perpetuated is by the self-infliction of wounds after the man had learned of the death of the particular animal with which he felt himself deeply associated—particularly in the case of lycanthropists subject to hystero-epileptoid attacks.

In Assam and Northern Burma the tiger-man usually comes to identify himself with a particular tiger in the vicinity. We may take it for granted that the delusion of identification often becomes a very vivid one in the subject's normal waking state ; its vividness and reality is inextricably bound up with the mental attitude of the tribe towards such things. His belief that the death of his tiger must be followed by his own is part and parcel of his mental background, fixed ineradicably in his mind by centuries of tribal superstition. His belief fosters the form that his delusions and hallucinations take. The identification-delusion may even become the dominating feature of his life ; with the result that when he learns of his animal-familiar's death the belief that he will not outlive it acts with all the force of a powerful suggestion, he loses the will to live, and death results.

The fact that death or illness does not follow until the tiger-man has learned of the death of his supposed familiar is confirmed from several reliable sources. Here is an account by C. P. Mills taken from an article entitled " The Were-Tigers of the Assam Hills " : [1]

" It should be understood that the wound on the human body does not appear simultaneously with that inflicted on the animal, but some days later, when the man has learnt of the condition of his leopard or tiger. This point is illustrated by an incident which occurred in March, 1919, and of which I heard immediately afterwards.

" While Mr. Hutton was in camp at a village called Melomi, one of his Angami interpreters while wandering round with a gun met a large tiger. He fired and wounded the animal, hitting it rather far back. The beast got away, however. It was said, more in jest than in earnest that the tiger was really a man-tiger. This came to the ears of Saiyi of Zumethi, a subordinate in the Civil Works Department, but a tiger-man withal. He announced to his friends that his tiger had been wounded, and took to his bed. Three days later he was met by Nihu, head interpreter of Kohima, being carried into Kohima on a stretcher for treatment in the Government hospital. Nihu, who is a most intelligent and entirely reliable man, told me that he questioned and examined Saiyi, who said that he was suffering terrible pains in the abdomen owing to the wound inflicted on his tiger, and showed an inflamed swelling on either side of the stomach, corresponding, of course, to the entrance and exit holes of the bullet which had hit the tiger. He eventually died in Kohima hospital."

The case just cited is interesting for several reasons. It provides confirmatory evidence that modifications of the vasomotor system can be induced by suggestion ; a possibility

---

[1] Journ. S.P.R., XX, 1922, p. 387. See also Roth, W.E., North Queensland Ethnography, Bulletin No. 5, p. 30.

by which many seek to account for the phenomenon of religious stigmatisation. Such an explanation of stories where a lycanthropist is reported to have manifested the same wounds as those inflicted on his animal-familiar is one which would account for a great deal not understood hitherto. But even if autosuggestion and hysteria cannot produce psychosomatic lesions or swellings, they quite certainly *can* induce hallucinatory sensations of extreme pain (topoalgia). The appearance of topoalgic pain in hysterical disorders is not uncommon. We may suspect that where lycanthropical delusions have a hysterical basis, the wounding or killing of an animal-familiar would not infrequently result in topoalgic pains in those parts of the body corresponding to the positions of the wounds.

The lycanthropist's beliefs are in themselves a powerful suggestive influence. Where hysteria is present or latent, suggestibility is thereby greatly increased. Death by suggestion is known to have been a weapon of primitive witch-doctors up to the present day, particularly among the Australian aboriginees and, until the last century, among the Maoris of New Zealand. When the suggestion becomes firmly embedded in the mind of a superstitious native that he will die, die he may. Death may take from a few days to a few weeks or longer, but cases have been reliably reported where it has resulted within twenty-four hours.

W. E. Roth, an anthropologist, has termed this fatal form of autosuggestion *thanatomania*, (not to be confused with *thanatomania* meaning a neurotic obsession for attending funerals and the like). Thanatomania undoubtedly provides a possible explanation of those tales in which the death of the animal-familiar is followed by the death of the lycanthropist himself. In this respect at least the ancient were-wolf and tiger-man legends may not have strayed very far from the truth.

Chapter Sixteen

THE ORIENTAL THAUMATURGISTS

DERVISHES AND FAKIRS

FROM THE EAST tales still arrive of burials alive, self-torture and trials of endurance—ordeals which are reported to result in no permanent harm to the individuals concerned. The Moslem *dervish*, the Siberian *shaman*, the Hindu *fakir*, the Indian *yogi*, the Tibetan *lama*—all, in their different fashion, continue to excite the wonder of a naturally agnostic West. Despite many trustworthy eye-witness accounts and good photographic evidence, there is still considerable scepticism concerning many of the feats of these oriental thaumaturgists which it not always justified.

Dervish is a Persian word signifying " beggar ". Usually it denotes a religious mendicant. The dervishes have many sects and orders within the Moslem religion. In Arabic-speaking countries, however, outside of Persia and Turkey, they are known as *faqirs*. The term *fakir* has also come to be applied to Hindu religious mendicants in India.

Although dervishes and fakirs originated in strict religious and monastic orders—much the same as European orders in the Middle Ages—discipline often broke down and mendicancy became a cloak for extortion and for the pretence of occult powers. It is principally this type of " holy-man " who gives wonder-working displays based on conjuring and trickery.

The itinerant fakir is frequently a clever trickster living on his wits. Apart from feats of prestidigitation, some of them undoubtedly excel in the art of inducing delusions and hallucinations by their skill in the use of hypnotism and suggestion. Their reputation as magicians is usually turned to good advantage through the sale of love-philtres and quack medicines.

Other itinerant fakirs and dervishes are genuine in their claims and beliefs, and some undoubtedly warrant the title of " holy-man " traditionally given to them. Extremists are to be found in all types of religion, however, and there are many sects in the East which practise extreme asceticism, self-mutilation, and endure the most agonising tortures, to earn a place in paradise. Some of them endure their pain by practised effort of the will. Others achieve a state of contemplative dissociation and are oblivious to the outside world. Yet others appear to achieve conditions analogous to schizophrenia and involutional melancholia, and perhaps have actually reached those psychotic states. In catatonic schizophrenia, for example, we observe a parallel to the immobile contemplative of the orient who has forgotten the existence of the world around him. Others of these mystics are probably liable to either functional or hysterical analgesia in which sensitivity to pain disappears.

Amongst these less extreme ascetics are those fakirs who preserve their mental balance while at the same time practising painful self-castigation in a minor way. These may be seen in India, sitting or reclining on a bed of blunted nails, reading out their prayers. The nails are not sharp enough to penetrate the skin but sharp enough to cause severe pain to anyone who is unaccustomed to the practice. Most of these fakirs, however, wear a thick, twisted loin-cloth to help mitigate their discomfort.

Amongst the Moslem dervish sects, two in particular have gained for themselves great notoriety outside Moslem countries. These are the " whirling dervishes ", the *Mawlawis*, who whirl themselves round and round until they reach a state of hysterical trance ; and the " howling dervishes ", the Rifa'is, who induce in themselves a state of frenzied ecstasy.

The phenomenon of *ecstasy* is to be found in many parts of the world and is cultivated by shamans and medicine-men from the Arctic to Australasia. The well-known Dionysiac frenzy, cultivated by the devotees of the cult of the god Dionysus in ancient Thrace, provides what is probably the earliest recorded version of ecstasy similar to that of the dervishes. There is little doubt that the Dionysiac frenzy and similar forms of " ecstasy " were hystero-epileptoid in character. Such ecstatic states manifest themselves in rigidity of the body, contortions, tremors, frothing at the mouth and are often accompanied by visual and auditory hallucinations and extreme euphoria. The hallucinations and the euphoria provide the component of visions and exaltation, which in Thrace used to take the form of mystical union with the god and which in later times was followed by wild sexual orgies. The soul of the ecstatic was supposed to leave the worshipper's body and hold communion with distant gods and daemons.

This form of ecstasy must not be confused with the ecstasy of the contemplative mystics and with that claimed by the adherents to yoga practices. In both types of ecstasy, however, the intense feelings of elation, bliss and exaltation are primarily pathological or hysterical in character ; apart from hysterics and mystics they are found most commonly in some types of schizophrenia, and occasionally in general paralysis of the insane which is brought about by syphilis.

Amongst the dervishes ecstasy is sometimes accompanied by functional analgesia, though not (as some have surmised) by psychosomatic modifications of the bodily tissues to injury. In this state, which they consider to be a sign of divine afflatus, they gash themselves with knives, handle red-hot irons, devour snakes, eat glass and purportedly devour live coals.

It must be admitted that Rifa'i practices have not been thoroughly investigated. While most observers agree that the gashes they inflict on themselves during their state of hysterical ecstasy stop bleeding in a remarkably short time and that the same psychosomatic factors may well result in the suppression of blisters caused by handling red-hot irons, it is not certain to what extent trickery and legerdemain may be held to account for some of their feats. The feat of swallowing live coals, one imagines, is merely the result of prestidigitation. Nevertheless, it is curious to note that a number of Russian and English authors have noted almost identical feats amongst the Siberian shamans. In some parts of Siberia the shaman induces a state of ecstasy identical

with that of the Rifa'i dervishes. In other parts the " ec=
stasy " becomes anything but ecstatic and is more reminiscent
of demoniacal hysteria or the " possession " of the Middle
Ages.

Oriental practices involving self-mutilation during hysterical states of consciousness find a parallel in the hysterical
flagellantism of medieval Europe, in which monks, nuns and
many others whipped themselves till the blood flowed " for
the greater glory of God ". Mass hysterical flagellantism
often reached extraordinary proportions and many who
practised it told of the " divine " ecstasy which accompanied
the pain.

A sub-sect of the Rifa'is, the Sa'dis, used to practise the
Doseh, in which the head of the order rode his chariot over
the bodies of his dervishes in Cairo without causing them
injury. Such feats can be attained by training and practise.
On account of this and other similar practices, however,
they claimed immunity to injury and miraculous healing
powers. V. G. Rele mentions a similar feat in one of his
books on yoga : [1] " Some youths perform the daring feat
of allowing a loaded cart to pass over their chests without
suffering any injury or having their ribs broken ". Rele
accounts for this ability by accrediting it to *pranayama*, the
yogic practice of breath-control achieved by ardous respiratory exercises often accompanied by gymnastic and even
acrobatic bodily postures. The lungs and relevant muscles
thus strengthened would give the support which the chest
and ribs required to withstand the weight of the loaded cart.

Some of the practices of the Rifa'is are even more extreme
than those just mentioned. Hysterical analgesia, or insensitiveness to pain, is not altogether an uncommon phenomenon. Similarly, profound analgesia can often be induced
by hypnotic suggestion, or spontaneously through many of
the rites and ceremonies of primitive peoples by psychological processes analogous to hysteria or autohypnosis.' This
appears to have reached a practised art among certain of the
Rifa'i. Professor Seligman writes in this connection :

---

[1] *The Mysterious Kundalini*, p. 9.

" Apart from the ceremonies of some North American Indians (now extinct), designed as tests of endurance so that anaesthesia was scarcely desired, the most astounding examples of what in Europe would be called self-torture, is provided by Indian members of the Rifa'i sect of Dervishes.   In 1931 Dr. Hunt exhibited at the Royal Anthropological Institute photographs and cinema films of men thrusting long iron skewers through the neck between the gullet and the backbone, of dislocation of the eyeball outwards—it might almost be said on to the cheek—and of the hammering of a very heavy ball-headed metal spike into the top of the skull, the spike in some instances being fixed so firmly that it was difficult to withdraw.   In all these cases there was preliminary ecstatic dancing at the tomb of the holy man, the founder of their sect in India, after days of fasting and spiritual preparation ; even then the subject would sometimes refuse an exhibition on the ground that at that time he did not feel capable of it." [1]

While functional analgesia may be the explanation of such feats, this does not explain the observed acceleration of the healing processes.   It is possible that the same psychological processes which induce the functional analgesia may result in indirect psychosomatic reactions conducive to the relatively rapid healing of the wounds.

While many of the dervishes' performances are attributable to abnormal psychological factors, it is well known that they are often addicted to the smoking or eating of hashish. Many of their ecstatic frenzies are certainly aided by taking hashish before the performance, and it may well prove that the consumption of hashish nearly always precedes certain dervish rituals.   Hashish may also help to mitigate haemorrhage from newly inflicted wounds ; it possesses, moreover, certain anaesthetic properties.   So does opium, owing to its morphine content, and many dervish practices may make use of this drug as well.

Other dervishes and fakirs who practise thrusting metal skewers through their flesh lack the benefits brought about by hysteria or autohypnotic states.   Paul Heuzé has probably investigated this problem more thoroughly than anyone else.   In his book *Fakirs, Fumistes et Cie*, he discusses the claims of itinerant fakirs and points out that such feats as sticking metal spikes through the flesh is simply an

---

[1] Seligman, C. G., Ritual and Medicine, *Enquiry into the Unknown*, p. 57.

acquired trick, not unbearably painful, which can be learnt by anyone of quite average patience and fortitude. Heuzé himself performed the trick of sticking hat-pins through his own flesh.

On December 11th 1928, the celebrated " duel " took place between Paul Heuzé and Tahra Bey, the Egyptian fakir, at the former's instigation. Tahra Bey, before a huge audience in the Cirque de Paris, thrust long needles through his cheeks and chest muscles, plunged a thin stiletto into his neck, lay down supported only by two steel blades at his neck and ankles, and finally stripped himself and reclined on a bed of nails. He showed little evidence of bleeding. He then invited Heuzé to repeat the performance. Heuzé contented himself by thrusting a needle through his cheek and explained to the audience that Tahra Bey's doughtier deeds were simply a question of practise and training. The crowd howled for him to justify his remarks by lying down on the bed of nails. Meanwhile, a French conjuror, who called himself ' Karma ', and who had entered the contest virtually at the last minute, entered the arena and repeated Tahra Bey's act with the steel blades and the bed of nails, and declared there was nothing mysterious about the trick.

The committee of doctors and scientists present declared their opinion that the fakir had shown considerable courage but had demonstrated nothing beyond the limits of normal experience.

Yoga

Tahra Bey's claims to occult powers were mere showmanship and his tours of Europe and America were spectacularly successful. He was, of course, no fakir, in any proper sense of the word, yet it is not to be doubted that he had, as he claimed, mastered a number of Yoga practices including unusual voluntary control of certain physiological functions of the body ; to what extent, however, is difficult to decide, since any ability he had in this direction was certainly augmented by many of the devices of the conjuror.

Contrary to popular belief, the practice of yoga is not

supposed to confer occult powers on the individual concerned·
K. T. Behanan, an American East-Indian who investigated
yoga with the aid of a grant from an American University,
and whose thesis on the subject gained him a doctor's
degree,[1] describes the yogis as sound, sensible men with
poise and insight, radiating a quiet power, with a capacity
for enjoyment and humour.   Yoga is, in fact, one of the six
classical systems of philosophy stemming from the Upanishadic teachings of ancient India.   It practises a psychological, moral and physical system of training designed to
emancipate the individual from the needs, wants and desires
which are the lot of the average man, and to develop
certain unusual states of consciousness.

The word *yoga* means literally " to yoke " (i.e. the individual soul, or *Atman*, with the world soul, or *Brahman*).
The yogi neophyte undertakes a long series of graduated
mental, physical and respiratory exercises designed on the
assumption that by such means the mind can be made to
function at far higher than the normal levels ; the attainment
of spiritual purity and supreme mystical experience is the
ultimate aim.

There are probably about a dozen types of yoga practices
and beliefs, the best known of which are Rajah Yoga, Hatha
Yoga and Bhakti Yoga, which lay the chief emphasis respectively on the principles of the Will, Courage and Love.   It is
the Hatha Yogis who have attracted the attention of the
sensation-hungry West through their extreme physical contortions and strange acrobatic postures.

Rajah Yoga is the most universally respected owing to the
depth of its philosophy and the obvious soundness of many
of its practices.   Its philosophy stems from the oldest of
all Indian philosophical systems—that known as *Sankhya*—
and has evolved a brand of religious metaphysics greatly
superior in some ways to that of any other of the world's
great religions.

There is widespread belief in the occult powers of the yogi.
This belief is unfounded, as a study of the genuine literature
of the subject will show.   Telepathy, levitations, the lifting
of massive objects, and the ability to move long distances

---

[1] Behanan, K. T., *Yoga : A Scientific Evaluation.*

in a few seconds and other occult powers (the *siddhis*) are mentioned in the yoga manuals only to warn the student of their dangers and to direct him to avoid them at all cost.

Behanan [2], who himself undertook a part of the yogic training in India, disparages any notion that the yogis have occult powers or that the yogis themselves take them very seriously. It is the fakir, sometimes an ex-yoga student who has failed to complete the ardous training, who claims occult and magical powers. The true yogi is not interested in such questions. His manuals tell him to regard any occult manifestations in himself as an obstacle which will prevent him attaining the mystical *kaivalya*—final and complete liberation from the bonds of the flesh. That a considerable number of yogis have " fallen by the wayside " through the discovery of hypnotic powers is clear. The older yoga manuals would naturally classify hypnotism as a supernatural manifestation.

The aim of all yoga training is to achieve a fusion of the individual soul with Reality or World-Soul. In Rajah Yoga this is carried out by a long and difficult process of training. Several stages are involved : (1) Difficult and sometimes semi-acrobatic meditative postures (*asanas*) are adopted. (2) A complicated breathing exercise, often varied, is performed. (3) The trainee, having mastered these then learns the specialised mental exercises. These comprise :

(a) *Pratyahara* or sense-withdrawal ; the yoga learns to restrain the flow of external sense-impressions to his mind.

(b) *Dharana* or concentration ; not the western equivalent of concentration. The final phase in this state is rendering the mind a blank. Thought has ceased and " one-pointed " contemplation of an object is at last impossible.

(c) *Dhyana* or contemplation ; the yogi begins to " perceive " new and subtle aspects of the objects of his contemplation.

(d) *Samadhi* or trance ; the desire of all yogis is to reach this stage. Many fail. There are five stages of this trance according to the manuals and the final stage is that of *Kaivalya* or total liberation.

[2] op. cit.

The above is, very briefly, the rough gist of Rajah Yoga practice. In the final stages of *Samadhi* the yogi claims that perception becomes " super-conscious ", transcending space and time ; a stage of bliss is reached and eventually surpassed as the Truth dawns and his real-self merges with the Ultimate Reality.

The Yoga trance, like the trances of many mystics, is undoubtedly a source of great happiness and inspiration. Its psychiatric interpretation, however, sheds a ray of disillusion over the whole subject. The trance is almost certainly in most instances the product of autohypnosis. In a few cases a technique of very rapid breathing may result in a cataleptic trance through the exhaustion of the CO_2 content in the blood (as sometimes occurs in hysteria). Otherwise no particular importance can be attached to the acrobatic postures and special breathing techniques in the induction of the trance ; they teach the yogi control of the will and the body and no more.

Nor is the claim that yoga practices heighten the mental powers to be considered seriously ; Behanan, who was sympathetic towards the practice of yoga, came to the conclusion that the onslaught of trance brings about a *retardation* of the mental functions. According to the same authority the rate of breathing during trance does not differ greatly from the normal.

" Hypnosis ", writes Behanan, " comprises various stages ranging from mild drowsiness to deep trance. Yoga, likewise, has its gradations of experience." Behanan also points out the similarity of hypnosis and the yoga trance :

> " There is one feature which is strikingly common to both hypnosis and yoga. It is well known that hypnosis can be induced by staring steadily at an object or by thinking exclusively of one idea. This monoideism has its parallel in yoga during the meditative period when the yogin aims to eliminate from the mind everything but the thought of the minute object of concentration."[1]

It is through a process of autohypnotisation and autosuggestion that the yogi attains his euphoric trance. The euphoria and delusions of significance which it brings are

---

[1] *Yoga, A Scientific Evaluation*, p. 236.

remembered by the yogi as a blissful though transitory experience which makes him long to repeat it. [2]

The myth that certain yogis can levitate their bodies into the air by magical means is prevalent in the East. Itinerant fakirs (often styling themselves *yogin*) still perpetuate this belief by using a simple trick which was first introduced to Europe by the oriental magician Ling Lau Lauro in 1826. In it a man sat cross-legged suspended several feet in the air. The fingers of his outstretched arm rested lightly upon a bamboo rod. The effect was impressive. The secret of the trick was that inside the bamboo ran an iron bar bent at right angles at the top. Attached to this was a metal bracket to support the magician's body. The metal support and the horizontal iron stay were covered by the clothes and the sleeves of the magician.

In this trick the actual preparations are always carefully screened, since often (when no other method is readily available) a deep hole has to be dug to hold the base of the bamboo-covered iron rod. The famous French conjuror Robert-Houdin improved on this trick and first demonstrated his own version of it on the stage in 1849. In June 1936 the Illustrated London News published photographs taken in India of a fakir carrying out the levitation act. Needless to say a fold of cloth draped the outstretched arm.

Some of the yogis more extreme claims—e.g. to be able to control functions of the body normally controlled by the autonomic nervous system—are unlikely from the medical standpoint, and are probably mere exaggerations due to the air of mystery which has traditionally surrounded the cult of yoga. Some yoga tenets, however, bear an astonishing resemblance to those advocated by a number of European and American psychiatrists. Here are two paragraphs by Sir William Brown which might well have come from a yoga manual translated into a modern idiom.

" You can gain power over involuntary muscles, stomach, heart, or whatever it may be. I believe that we can get more and more power, through our sympathetic nervous system, over the different parts of our body, if in earnest about it, and if we carry out a certain

[2] See chapter 13.

amount of self-training.   You can only convince yourself of this by doing it for yourself.

" This is not hypnotism, but a genuine development and increase of the power of the will over the body.   One can influence one's own digestion, heart-beat, the processes of elimination, and the general functions of almost every part of the body by resolution and calm determination.   The important thing is to avoid spasmodic effort, to get muscular and mental relaxation ; to imagine success with calm certainty, and then to affirm it with conviction."[3]

Behanan describes how the Rajah yogis learn to open and close the anal sphincters at will, and by exercising the muscles of the belly are able to draw water in and out for the purpose of colonic lavage.   Cleansing of the bladder by similar means is also practised.   The more extreme claims of some of the yogis is a disputed matter.   They claim to be able to di-synchronise their pulse and even to stop the pulse-beat altogether.   Rele gives an account of a Hatha yogi named Deshbandhu who demonstrated the feat of di-synchronisation of the pulse and who later demonstrated the partial stopping of the heart-beats under an X-ray screen :

" His heart was first examined under normal conditions and the point of its apex-beat was marked on the screen.   He was then asked to breathe deep in and out, and again the apex-beat was marked on the screen.   We found that, after each complete inspiration his apex-beat was about half an inch internal to its normal position.   Then he was asked to stop the beating of the heart.   His heart, thereupon, contracted and became smaller and smaller in size until it reached a minimum limit when its apex was about two-thirds of an inch internal to its normal position.   The apex-beat of the heart became inaudible, though the rhythmic contraction of the heart-muscle still persisted.   A graphical representation of his pulse and heart corroborated the facts mentioned above.   The cardiogram showed that the heart-muscle was rhythmically con-tracting sixty times a minute though its beating was inaudible."[4]

Unfortunately a full description is lacking and we cannot say whether Deshbandhu induced a momentarily cataleptic state or not or how accurate Rele's account is.

---

[3] *Mind, Medicine and Metaphysics*, p. 33.
[4] Rele, V. G., op. cit.

Burial Alive

In extreme catalepsy, as is well known, the vital functions may be reduced to a minimum consonant with the maintenance of life. Certain yogis and *sadhus* (ascetics) claim to be able to induce this cataleptic state at will for the purpose of immuring themselves in a coffin underground.

Tahra Bey regularly demonstrated the feat of being buried in a coffin underground, and the redoubtable Frenchman Heuzé repeated the feat, remaining immured for an hour ; he declared afterwards that there was nothing mysterious about it and that no state of trance was necessary.

Tahra Bey, on the other hand, stated that a trance *was* necessary, and that he induced it by " reducing the heartbeats to a minimum ", pressing on certain nerve-centres on the head and neck, throwing back the head and retracting the tongue back into the throat. The cutting of the air supply in this way, he explained, resulted in a cataleptic trance so extreme as to constitute a state of suspended animation. All breathing, he claimed, ceased. It was his custom to stuff his nose and ears with cotton ; and it was observed that his body was dry upon emergence. This fact convinced many of the truth of his claims.

There is, however, no need to take seriously Tahra Bey's claim to be able to engender a state of suspended animation analagous to the state of hibernation or aestivation of certain animals in latitudes subject to prolonged cold or drought.

It is true that cataleptic states can become so extreme that breathing is scarcely perceptible. Sometimes the resemblance of such states to death is very deceptive, and cases have been known in which individuals have been placed in their coffin only to " come to life " in time to save themselves from death by suffocation in the actual grave. But whether such extreme states can be induced voluntarily without the aid of drugs is unlikely.

Some confirmation for the theory that some human beings can exist for a considerable length of time without any oxygen other than that retained by the lungs is supplied by the anthropologist Gorer.[1] He writes that near St. Louis,

[1] Gorer, Africa Dances, p. 47 ; 1949.

French West Africa, certain fishermen or *mol* claim to be able to stay under water " almost indefinitely ". He states that he actually witnessed one of these men dive into clear water where he remained at the bottom for three quarters of an hour. The man stayed continuously in view and " had no apparatus of any kind ". This gift, it is stated, is confined to a few families, and is developed by training.

The " official " world record for breath-holding is 15 min. 13 sec. This was rendered possible by forced breathing and the inhalation of oxygen before the commencement. Without such aids the breath cannot be held for more than a few minutes at most. Gorer's account is presumably inaccurate, and in any event the breath-holding feat he describes is very different from the state of suspended animation claimed by certain fakirs, sadhus, and self-styled yogis.

The claim that the respiration may be stopped for a period of days can be rejected out of hand. Even if it were possible for a human being to enter a prolonged and extreme state of catalepsy analagous to hibernation, *some* breathing would have to occur, however slight.

A state of true hibernation has actually been induced *artificially* in monkeys—man's nearest relative on the evolutionary scale—which never hibernate in their natural state. The monkeys were first anaesthetised and then placed in a cold chamber. When the temperature had fallen gradually to about 25 degrees centigrade the anaesthetic was no longer necessary—the animals remained immobile and insensible to pain, and scarcely breathing. Such methods as these, however, scarcely apply to the oriental fakir.

There is, in fact, no need to postulate either an extreme cataleptic state or any great reduction in the rate of breathing to account for such feats as " burial alive ", as Prof. J. B. S. Haldane demonstrated many years ago. Nor is there any need to attribute such feats to trickery, as the following account by Dr. R. J. Vakil bears witness.[2]

Dr. Vakil records how on February 15th, 1950, at five p.m. an emaciated middle-aged sadhu called Shri Ramdasji

---

[1] Haldane and Priestly, *Respiration*, p. 181.
[2] Vakil, R. J., *Remarkable Feat of Endurance by a Yogi Priest*, Lancet, 1950, ii, p. 871.

entered a subterranean concrete cubicle near Bombay
before a large crowd. The cubicle measured approximately
$5\frac{1}{2}$ft. by $4\frac{1}{2}$ft. by 8ft., with a total air capacity of some 216
cubic feet. All six walls of the cubicle were studded with
nails, most of them old and rusty.

After Shri Ramdasji had sat down in the cubicle, a concrete lid was sealed down over him with cement, rendering
it perfectly air-tight.

Fifty-six hours later a hole was bored in the lid of the
cubicle and 1,400 gallons of water were poured in by means
of a fire-hose. The hole was then sealed up. Approximately six and a half hours later the concrete lid of the
cubicle was removed ; the sadhu was taken out of the water
in which he was almost completely immersed. Dr. Vakil
subjected him to a clinical examination on the spot. He was
semi-conscious ; his pulse was weak, though regular ; his
respiration was also regular, but was rather slow at eight to
ten a minute.

The application of smelling salts soon revived him and he
" opened his eyes and took heed of his surroundings ".
Apart from some scratches and cuts he appeared little the
worse for having spent sixty-two hours under such gruelling
conditions.

The followers and disciples of the sadhu claimed that he
had remained in a state of suspended animation and meditation throughout the ordeal. The way in which Dr. Vakil
refers to the " dry stage " and the " wet stage " as *bana
samadhi* and *jala samadhi* respectively, makes one suppose
that they are traditional. *Samahi*, of course, is a yoga
term designating a blissful trance state.

But, as Dr. Vakil points out, there is no need to attach
any mystery to this feat. The yogic feat of immurement
clearly depends on the size of the " coffin " and the rate of
oxygen consumption. The relevant experiments were carried out many years ago by Prof. Haldane, who calculated
that an oxygen consumption of about half a cubic foot per
hour, or two and a half cubic feet of air, would be the minimum allowance if a man lay perfectly still. According to
these figures Shri Ramdasji could have remained in his
cubicle of 216 feet for around 85 hours had not water been
inserted during the latter stages of his immuration.

It is impossible to say whether Shri Ramdasji induced a state of trance while in his subterranean cubicle, or whether he exercised a high degree of fortitude. He may possibly have taken some kind of narcotic drug into the cubicle with him. Any trance state would undeniably serve to mitigate the severe physical discomfort and mental strain of such prolonged immuration. It would further have the advantage of enabling the sadhu to keep perfectly still and so reduce oxygen consumption to a minimum.

But in Shri Ramdasji's case it was not very likely that he went into a deep trance after the water was poured into the cubicle, for the danger of drowning was a very real one. Nor is it really likely that he *required* a trance state to help him through the previous 56-hour ordeal. Many a sadhu has remained immobile for months and even years under conditions just as gruelling. The phenomenal powers of endurance of the oriental religious ascetic has been demonstrated times without number.

Tahra Bey's method of inducing the " yoga sleep " can be taken with a grain of salt. A more typical—and more credible—yogic method is by making an intense effort of abstraction from all impressions of the external world, slowing down the respiration to an absolute minimum (an ability purportedly engendered by years of specialisation in scientific breath-control), fixing the eyes upon the tip of the nose, and the consequent induction of a state of extreme auto-hypnosis.

It is impossible to state the maximum duration of any " yogic sleep " engendered by this method. But it is to be remembered that " burial alive " and similar feats are not consonant with genuine yogic practice, and claims to have achieved such feats by inducing a " yogic sleep " are therefore suspect from the beginning.

Tradition has it that some yogis have remained buried for periods of months. This claim cannot be taken seriously, even if a state of artificial hibernation were attained by the use of drugs or any other conceivable method. The functions of the human body cannot be made to imitate such animals as the field-mouse which may lie for as long as six months, scarcely breathing; (the rate of breathing of some hiberna-

ting mammals—the hamster, for example—may be reduced
to as little as one per cent of normal).

It might, of course, be possible for a person in an extreme
and prolonged cataleptic trance to remain immured for a
period of a fortnight in a big roomy " coffin ". But there
is no evidence that such prolonged trance states can be
induced voluntarily. Trickery must always be suspected.

The professional magician Ottaker Fischer records that
in several cases of " burial alive " it was found that the
fakirs were buried near hollow trees, from which tunnels
had been excavated to the burial place.[1]

THE LAMAS OF TIBET

There is one other oriental religious sect which has had a
strong hold upon the imaginations of those given over to
the literature of mysticism and the occult—the lamas of
Tibet. There are several reasons for this interest. In the
first place relatively few white men have visited this land.
Secondly Tibetans are the most religion-conscious people
in the world, venerating a supreme semi-divine ruler-priest—
the Dalai Lama. The setting of Lamaism is the " roof of
the world ", the high plateau of mountainous Tibet. The
centre of religious activity, and the residence of the Dalai
Lama, is the fabled holy city of Lhasa, which, is, in fact,
the " Mecca " of the Buddhist religion. Each year numbers
of pilgrims from all over Asia crawl in the snow, often half
naked, around sacred Mount Kailas which rises 20,000ft.
above sea-level.

Lamaism is actually a modified form of Buddhism. The
tendency in this religion towards magic and divination is
strong and it is not surprising that it has given rise to so
many esoteric pseudo-religious cults in America and Europe.
Its somewhat crude mysticism arose in response to the
superstitious and primitive ideas of the hardy Tibetan peasant folk. The magical and divinatory practices of the
priests, the total number of which is estimated at over a
quarter of the male population, are generally primitive in
comparison to those of the other great oriental religions.

[1] Fischer, O., *Illustrated Magic*, p. 190.

Among certain of the Lama sects, however, are those who practise extreme asceticism and others who pass their lives in teaching and contemplation. Some of their practices have aroused the curiosity and wonder of the West. Photographs have come back to Europe showing Tibetan priests or neophytes standing stark naked in the snows of Mount Kailas as a test of endurance or as an act of worship. These lamas may stand in the bitter cold for a period of twelve hours and sometimes for as long as twenty-four without apparently suffering; it is even recorded that the perspiration is sometimes visible on their bodies.

According to Tibetan lore the ability to withstand the cold during such vigils is due to a mystical force called *tumo* which, by warming the semen, liberates its energy until it courses through the body via innumerable minute channels called *tsas*. The term *tumo* itself denotes warmth or heat, though not in the ordinary sense of the words.

Neophytes who wish to be initiated into the mysteries of *tumo* must first undergo a long period of probation, the probable aim of which is to test the robustness of each candidate and weed out those physically unsuitable. Those finally selected for training then undergo long hours of practising certain mental disciplines, physical postures, and breathing exercises, in the bitter cold—clad only in a cotton garment or completely naked.

Those who pass the final test gain the coveted title of *respas*. For this test a frosty moonlight night is chosen, often with a hard wind blowing. The candidates sit naked on the ground, near a lake or river. Small cotton sheets are then dipped into the icy water which are then placed round them. The candidates are expected to dry the sheets by the heat of their bodies; in former times they were expected to dry at least three sheets in this way.

Having passed this test they renounce, in theory at least, all wool or fur clothing, and the comfort of a fire. Some of the more ascetic will spend whole winters in caves among the snow-covered mountains, clad only in a single cotton short, keeping warm, they claim, by nothing more than the mysterious force of *tumo*.

The explanation of such feats, however, can be attributed

to a combination of factors : the gradual acclimatisation to cold through long practice ; the naturally high resistance to cold of those selected for training ; and the dry climate. During the long motionless vigils in the snow an undoubted trance-state is engendered in which intense autosuggestion plays a leading role ; the special breathing exercises, performed automatically after long practice, may also have a cold-resistant function. The character of such trance-states, and the method of evoking them, are similar to those of yoga.

Control of the body-temperature is also reputed to be yogic practice. Some yogis, by a certain technique of breathing and by fixing their thoughts on cool scenes, such as mountain streams or snow-capped peaks, claim to be able to keep cool even in the hottest weather if they so desire. The lama priest or neophyte, on the other hand, reverses the process ; he first induces an autohypnotic state and fixes his imagination on objects associated with great heat—fires, or the hot sun in a secluded valley. The imagination, in hypnotic or hysterical states of consciousness, may have all the effect of suggestion forcefully uttered by a hypnotist.

Psychosomatic control of body temperature is virtually unexplored territory. However, among a series of interesting experiments, J. A. Hadfield of London University described how he produced changes in the temperature of a patient's arm by waking suggestion. Dr. Hadfield first had his patient taken for a five mile walk and on his return the skin temperature of his arms was found to be 95°F. Suggestion was then given that the right arm was to get cold ; Hadfield reported that within half an hour the skin temperature of the right arm fell to 68°F. which was the precise temperature of the room. On reversing the suggestion the surface temperature of the palm rose again to 94°F which is near the normal blood temperature of the human body. The patient was naturally suggestible and had frequently been hypnotised by Hadfield ; but in the above experiment it is reported that the patient had not been hypnotized and was in the waking state throughout.[2]

---

[2] Hadfield, J. A., *The Influence of Suggestion on Body Temperature*, The Lancet, July, 1920, p. 68.

Few similar experiments appear to have been reported. However, A. Macey records how he once induced, by *hypnotic* suggestion, a state of perspiration in a subject in circumstances possessing many parallels to the vigils of the Tibetan lamas : " During one winter at Berlin in an internment camp, when thick snow lay on the ground and the army hut was altogether unheated, the writer suggested to a subject that he was at home in England during August, lying in a garden hammock, with the hot August sun blazing so fiercely upon him that he was in a bath of perspiration. In accordance with this suggestion the subject burst forth in a violent state of perspiration." [1]

If suggestion can influence the physiological heat-processes of the body normally controlled by the automatic and vaso-motor systems, what is the process actually involved ?

The great heat regulator is the skin, which controls the loss of heat through the vasomotor system and the nervous mechanism of perspiration. Food temporarily increases the rate of heat production, particularly if sugar is present, by an increase in the body's metabolism. It is possible that suggestion may indirectly affect the rate of metabolism, enabling the fats and sugar to be consumed more rapidly than normal and thus enabling the body to produce more heat in a given time. Such an increase normally takes place when the heart action is accelerated by strong emotion. It also occurs to a certain extent during periods of intense mental concentration. Some such process may occur in the case of the *respas* who stand motionless in trance in the snow for hours at a time.

The state of trance almost certainly engenders the delusion of warmth, and would at the same time render the *respas* oblivious to the increasingly unpleasant effects of cold upon his system during the latter stages of his vigil.

---

[1] Macey, A., *Hypnotism Explained*, p. 56.

Chapter Seventeen

FIRE WALKING

FIRE-WALKING is a practice dating from great antiquity. Originally fire-walking ceremonies often formed part of the primitive spring festivals designed to ensure a plentiful harvest. Today these rites are still practised in many parts of the world but they are a great deal less common than they were half a century ago when reports of such performances were comparatively frequent. Modern fire-walking ceremonies are performed for a variety of purposes, but some have degenerated into mere exhibitions with no further object in view than to impress the bystanders with the walker's apparent immunity. Details of the ritual vary considerably in different countries, especially in regard to the preliminary rites and preparations. The main essential, however, is invariably the same : the walkers stride barefooted, at a rapid pace, over intensely hot embers or heated stones.

The ceremonies are impressive to observe, particularly if considerable numbers of people are engaged in passing over the glowing embers. But as to the details reports vary a great deal since most observers have apparently come away with the probability of occult powers strong in their minds. This has tended naturally to colour their reports, some of which are exaggerated out of all proportion. Some observers appear to have been exceptionally credulous about the performers' claims, even to the extent of accepting the latter's highly mystical interpretations of the cause of their immunity to burning. In point of fact, the fire-walk can be performed by almost anyone and many Europeans have followed successfully in the wake of oriental fire-walkers with little or no injury. The priest or fakir generally explains this by claiming that he himself has extended his own immunity to those that follow.

In general, the fire-walk is confined to walking over glowing embers. Virgil, Strabo and Pliny give accounts of such ember-walks in Cappadocia two thousand years ago. Until well into the nineteenth century ember-walks took place as far west as Bulgaria. In the past, ember-walking was common in China and Japan, and it is still practised in many parts of India and Malaya today. Wherever there are emigrant Hindu communities the ember-walk is still occasionally practised. Such a rite occurred in 1927 in Pietermaritzburg, South Africa, and was performed by Hindu settlers in fulfilment of a vow. A number of Dervish sects in North Africa include the ember-walk among their repertoire of pain-defying practices, often thrusting skewers through their muscles before and during the event. Some Hindu ceremonies also include this latter spectacle.

The ember-walk is particularly impressive if it takes place at night when (to the uninitiated) the glow from the embers makes it seem impossible for a human being to pass over unscathed. More impressive still, however, are the stone-walks in which the fire-walkers walk over stones heated to an extraordinary degree ; some descriptions make it clear that the stones and small boulders glow red with the heat. In both ember and stone walking the heat arising from the embers or stones frequently makes it impossible for the spectators to approach the side of the fire-trench for more than a few seconds at a time. Some reports even speak of articles of clothing worn by the walker smouldering or catching fire.

Stone walking is indeed a feat to be wondered at, and it is doubtful whether any European has succeeded in actually walking the stones. The intense heat given out by the stones puts it on a level altogether different from the ember-walk. One of the conjectures brought forward to account for the stone-walk was the induction of a " spheroidal state ". It is well known, for example, that a hand may be dipped for a brief moment in molten lead without resultant harm, provided that the temperature is greatly above the metal's melting point. This effect is aided considerably if the hand is first damped by a wet cloth. A cushion of vapour is thus formed between the molten metal and the skin. As a result of experiments carried out before the war, however, the spheroidal theory may be considered superfluous.

Other theories purporting to account for the fire-walk included the idea that the fire-walker induces an autohypnotic state with accompanying analgesia and a psychosomatic modification of the tissues to injury by burning. This theory is not to be rejected as altogether fanciful. Some such principle may be involved, in a minor way. It is not likely, however, that it constitutes a major factor in the walker's immunity, though it is given countenance by some of the initial rites and tabus which act as a prelude. These include fasting, sexual abstinence, prayers, monotonous chanting, exhortations, frenzied rhythmic dancing and a variety of activities calculated to purify the walkers before their ordeal. The combined effect of many of these initial purification rites must often produce in the walker a highly suggestible trance-like state. There is, however, little indication that the primary function of such preliminaries is anything more than to bring about the expulsion of the walkers' natural fear, and this is probably aided by the use of such drugs as hashish when occasion demands.

Absence of fear is a vital point in all types of fire-walk. It is necessary to keep one's wits ; for poise, correct pacing, and timing are all important. It is for this reason that alcoholic liquors are never taken beforehand. Fear, by undermining confidence, spoils the walker's judgment. The initial rites therefore play a big rôle in bolstering up confidence.

There is scarcely an eye-witness account of the fire-walk in which inaccuracies are not evident. The tendency is one of exaggeration ; wishful thinking, a penchant for the mysterious, and lack of reporting experience are all largely instrumental in accounting for the discrepancies of so many accounts. Such reports tend to accentuate the mystery and the marvel of the performances, particularly those which date from the last century. A tradition of occultism surrounds the fire-walk which is totally unwarrantable by the facts. As a result, the genuineness of the phenomenon is frequently called in question even today.

The fire-walk usually takes place along the length of a wide trench filled with red-hot embers. The depth of the embers varies very considerably from a few inches to around four feet. In Fiji, the traditional home of the stone-walk, and in other Pacific islands, large stones are cast into the trench among the burning wood so that as the latter becomes incinerated only the stones are left, interspersed with whitely glowing embers. The heat given out by such furnaces is so intense that raking the embers and clearing the stones is carried out with long poles.

The trenches may vary from between fifteen to thirty or forty feet in length. The walkers stride quickly from one end to the other—at most they are in contact with the fire only a few seconds. In the ember-walk the feet generally sink into the ashes several inches and a steady, even stride is necessary to avoid sinking too deep. The feet are actually in contact with the embers less than half a second during each step; this is the secret of the fire-walk; and provided the feet are completely dry and free from perspiration, so that no burning ashes adhere to them during the time each foot is in the air, the risks of burning are relatively small.

In regard to the stone-walk, with its far greater surface heat, the thick calloused soles of the average Fijian or Kanaka undoubtedly play a major part in the immunity to burns. Probably a special heel-and-toe technique has been acquired as well, so that the time during which any one part of the foot is in contact with the stones is thereby halved for each stride the walker makes.

A great deal of the mystery of the fire-walk was cleared up in 1935 by an experiment conducted in England under the auspices of the University of London Council for Psychical Investigation and a further experiment by the same body in 1937.[1] These probably represent the best reports

---

[1] Price, H., *A Report on Two Experimental Fire-walks*, University of London Council for Psychical Investigation, Bulletin II, 1936; Brown, G. B., *Three Experimental Fire-walks*, Bulletin IV, 1938.

on the subject that are available and they have the solid advantage that the texts are supported by twenty-one excellent photographic plates. There is also appended a bibliography on fire-walking.

The first of the 1935 tests, which was witnessed by William MacDougall amongst others, proved beyond all doubt that the fire-walk was a genuine phenomenon. An Indian, Kuda Bux, walked quickly along a twenty foot trench of glowing embers, several inches deep, four times. His feet were medically examined before and after the walks; there was no sign of blistering. With great courage Digby Moynagh, Editor of the *St. Bartholomew's Hospital Journal*, walked half the distance before jumping out. Blisters subsequently formed on his feet. At the second of the 1935 tests the surface temperatures were found to be 430°C. (806°F.) and the interior temperature 1,400°C. (2,552°F.). Price reports that the heat made it impossible to remain near the fire trench for long. At these tests the scientific and medical world were well represented, reports subsequently appearing in *Nature*[1] and in *The Lancet*[2].

During the 1937 tests a Moslem Indian from Cawnpore, Ahmed Hussain, was the fire-walker. He claimed to be able to convey his immunity to others and it was arranged for three volunteers, all Englishmen, to follow him across, which they did. Two other volunteers then walked across alone. All showed traces of slight burns. In the next experiment Hussain took six steps to cross twenty feet and was badly burned; the surface temperature was formidable, being 740°C. A Mr. Adcock, one of the volunteers of the previous experiment, crossed the trench after him, taking four steps, showing only slight signs of burning. Adcock's performance, in point of fact, was superior to that of Kuda Bux, for he walked on a fire whose surface temperature was *nearly twice* as great, thus disposing of the idea that any mysterious agencies are involved. Among the conclusions reached in Dr. Brown's report were these:

(1) " The fire-walk is in no sense a trick : the walk is performed in the normal manner with bare and chemically unprepared feet.

[1] Sept. 21st., and Sept. 28th., 1935.
[2] Sept. 28th., 1935.

(2) Owing to the fact that the surface of the fire is a very unstable one and the feet may sink in several inches, it is impossible to walk so that a constantly changing portion of the foot is in contact with the hot embers (this would be possible on a firm plane surface) and skill of this kind is not a factor necessary for success. Nevertheless, steadiness in walking is an advantage in order to avoid remaining with the weight on one foot for too long an interval.

(3) Moisture on the feet is a disadvantage since it may cause hot particles to adhere to the skin and thus produce blisters.

(4) The ' spheroidal state ', i.e., the sudden formation of an insulating cushion of vapour between the foot and the hot embers, does not occur.

(5) No abnormal degree of callosity of the feet is required.

(6) Fasting or other initial preparation is not necessary.

(7) No evidence was shown that immunity from burning can be ' conveyed ' to other persons.

(8) The fall in the temperature of the surface of the soles of the feet during the experiment was possibly due to a number of steps being taken on the grass after leaving the fire, before the place of examination was reached.

(9) Immunity is not due to contact with layers of relatively cold ash in which combustion has ceased, since in experiments with Kuda Bux, the ash was removed ; and in any case, the feet sink in sufficiently far to be in contact with the burning embers and small flames below the surface."[3]

Dr. Brown also points out[4] that in tropical countries the calloused feet of the native would probably give fire-walkers greater immunity than people used to wearing shoes. Both Bux and Hussain and the European volunteers were accustomed to wearing shoes, and one can only conclude that what is possible in the case of Europeans must of necessity be far easier in the case of the habitually barefooted inhabitants of India or the South Seas.

[3] Brown, G. B., *University of London Council for Psychical Investigation,* Bulletin IV, p. 6.
[4] ibid.   p. 8.

Chapter Eighteen

THE INDIAN ROPE-TRICK

T HE TRADITIONAL FEAT of the Indian rope trick has come down to us through the centuries. It is reputed to be the culminating achievement of the oriental magician's art. At one time it was apparently demonstrated fairly often ; today, however, despite numerous " eye witness " accounts, it has grown into something of a legend, and most people now wonder whether it ever had any basis in fact.

In the ancient world of Rome, Persia and the civilisations of the North African littoral, the oriental magi used to ply their skill to the astonishment of kings and princes and their courts. Many of their tricks varied little from those of modern conjurors. But they made much use of hypnotism and suggestion, and it was in the art of inducing hallucinations and delusions among their superstitious, awed and credulous spectators that the reputation of the oriental magi mainly rested. The Indian rope trick has all the appearance of being in this category ; and today, the modern descendant of the ancient magi, the itinerant fakir, still on occasion hallucinates the gullible and suggestible audiences of the Orient.

This is what a well known American psychologist, Professor V. E. Fisher, has to say in this connection :

" There is perhaps no phenomenon in the entire field of psychology which is more interesting than hypnosis, but which at the same time has received less experimental study. Yet as far back as we have written history we find evidence of suggestion and hypnosis playing an important part in man's life and activities. The ancient

297

medicine man cured the sufferer by means of incantations and phantastic ceremonies. The East Indian fakirs mystify their onlookers by arousing, or inducing, in them a high degree of suggestibility and then causing them to hallucinate a boy climbing hand over hand up a rope and finally disappearing into the sky."[5]

There are many modern accounts of the Indian rope trick. Some of them are so ingenious that it becomes plain the writer merely wishes to incorporate his own special theory on the subject in literary form. Others are so ingenuous that plausibility is totally lacking. Accounts have been printed where numbers of Europeans claim to have simultaneously witnessed the feat and taken photographs of it, only to find that the plates showed nothing when developed. Such accounts, while possibly true, must be viewed with suspicion. Most of them, at any rate, can be taken with a grain of salt. Educated white people are not usually subject to hypnotic or suggested hallucinations without preliminary experience of hypnosis, and under special conditions. Mass hallucinations and delusions invariably take place in an atmosphere of intense expectation under high emotional strain and are not altogether an uncommon phenomenon in the history of religion. The reports give no indication that the Europeans concerned were anything but highly sceptical at the time.

Probably one of the first such accounts was published by Lord Frederic Hamilton in " Here, There and Everywhere ". Colonel Barnard, Hamilton relates, when Chief of Police in Calcutta, had been invited with a subordinate officer to witness the rope-trick. They took a camera with them and in due course saw the rope thrown into the air and a boy climbing up it with a man after him. Both boy and man vanished, but the latter soon returned with a blood-stained sword in his hand. The camera, doubtless to the Colonel's surprise, revealed none of the events witnessed.

In 1934 one of the big London weekly periodicals published a series of eight photographs taken in the grounds of an official Residency in which the *final* pictures depicted the rope lying on the ground and the small boy scuttling

Fisher, V. E., *Introduction to Abnormal Psychology*, N.Y., 1932.

towards some adjacent bushes. The Resident had been shown the rope-trick by a wandering fakir and had persuaded him to repeat the performance a few days afterwards, ostensibly to have it demonstrated in front of a number of independent European witnesses. When the fakir repeated the feat for the second time the Resident had concealed someone with a camera behind a corner of the Residency building, with the result just described.

These and other similar accounts, as might well be expected, lack full details. In point of fact, only one well versed in the psychology of hypnotism and suggestion would be competent to present a proper detailed report. It remains, therefore, despite claims to the contrary, an open question whether any European has " witnessed " the Indian rope-trick—i.e. has unwittingly experienced a visual hallucination at the instigation of an oriental fakir or magician skilled in the use of suggestion.

In 1875 Lord Northbrook, Viceroy of India, offered the sum of £10,000 to anyone who would demonstrate the Indian Rope Trick. Though the offer was widely advertised, no claimant came forward.

It is surprising that the Indian rope trick has never been taken up by vaudeville hypnotists on the European and American stage. Any experienced hypnotist operating with a suggestible subject may induce visual or auditory hallucinations or delusions in almost limitless variety. The rope trick would not be any more difficult to suggest to a hypnotised subject than any other variety of hallucination. In such performances, of course, the subject is always willing to be hypnotised in the first instance.

We can assume that there were, in former times, two techniques for inducing hallucinations or pseudo-hallucinations by the professional magicians. The hypnotic technique would be more convenient for situations where the magus or fakir was summoned to private audience with reigning princes or members of the nobility with, perhaps, a few of their favourites. This was of frequent occurrence when any famous magician visited a city or the abode of a princely court. In fact, for any situation devised by the magus where just a few people were present as spectators, he was in a position to make full use of his powers as a hypnotist.

A different technique, we may conjecture, was used for large crowds of ignorant peasant folk. Such is the suggestibility of an ignorant excited crowd that they can be induced to believe in almost anything, however improbable. Instances of collective visual hallucinations and delusions have been known to occur from time to time through the cumulative effect of mass reciprocal suggestion, as for example in the hallucinatory phenomena of moving statues and paintings or the apparition of fiery crosses in the sky, during times of religious excitement. In such instances only a proportion of the crowd experiences any sort of hallucination, but such is the contagion of their excited cries and gesticulations that the others will stare and repeat their antics ; and although these others see nothing they will depart convinced that they have witnessed a miracle or a feat of magic.

The nature of the Indian rope trick becomes apparent when it is remembered that the boy is reported as disappearing into thin air after climbing up the rope in full view of the audience. It seems scarcely possible that such a feat could be accomplished by mere prestidigitation unless elaborate apparatus was in use. The fact that European and American trick-magicians have been totally unable to perform the feat in the *open* is significant, for (contrary to popular belief) western conjuring is vastly superior to that of the orient. The reputation of the latter rests on the effects they achieve through the use of suggestion, and their success in this is mainly due to the relative gullibility and suggestibility of their audiences. European and American conjurors have only simulated the illusion of the rope-trick on the stage with the aid of comparatively cumbersome apparatus, using mirrors, or else light-absorbing material for the boy's clothes and stage back-cloth, and special lighting.

Some accounts of the rope-trick describe a boy climbing up a " rope " consisting of cleverly jointed and threaded bones or bamboo rods. Others describe a monkey dressed in turban and *dhoti* clambering up a stiff rope. Nevertheless, despite these dubious imitations, it is safe to say that the traditional rope-trick has never been performed in actual fact. It has never been anything other than one of the stock hallucinations suggested by the itinerant oriental magus or fakir to the credulous and highly suggestible audiences of the East.

Chapter Nineteen

PRIMITIVE SHAMANISM AND MODERN SPIRITUALISM

SHAMANISM

SHAMANISM IS A generic term covering many primitive cults which involve a belief in spirits and in the power of certain individuals to influence them or communicate with them.

The term derives from *shaman*, a Siberian medicine-man or " mystery-man ", who is noted for his mediumistic practices. Nowadays anthropologists use the word "shaman" to designate almost any class of tribal magician whose magic is in any way attributed to practices designed to control, placate or otherwise influence discarnate spirits.

Modern spiritualism is a direct off-shoot of primitive shamanism.

Unlike the modern medium the shaman is usually one of the most prominent figures in the life of the community, and he also fulfils the function of healer. He contacts not only the spirits of the dead, but the spirits of nature, and various demons and gods as well.

The modern seance-cabinet is directly derived from the North American Indian conjuring lodge. Such " seance-cabinets " are found all over the world ; typical of these is the *pano* hut of the Semang mediums of Malaya.

Shamanistic mediums are known by scores of different names : the Semang medium is called a *Halak* ; the Eskimoes have their *Angakok* ; in parts of Australia the shaman

is known as the *Gomerah* or *Boyla* ; ' in South America the
Piai ; in Korea the *Pan-Su* ; in Borneo the *Manang* ; in
Southern India the *Kurumba* ; in Burma the *Myihtoi*, and
better known the *Thumoni*. The spirits they call upon also
have their own particular names.

The importation of Red Indian shamanistic practices
into American society during the nineteenth century had a
very important effect. For it brought a great resurgence
of superstitious beliefs and practices which had largely
disappeared since the decline of witchcraft in European
cultures.

This is not to say that there has ever been any strong
connection between witchcraft and modern mediumship ;
the great European cult of witchcraft, with its pronounced
sexual emphasis, secret meetings, blasphemous rituals and
covert defiance of Church and State, has died out almost
completely. But the fact remains that the waning belief
in spirits and the supernatural received new impetus from
the modern cult of mediumship.

Witchcraft still . flourishes in primitive societies. With
many types of primitive shaman (though by no means with
all) the medicine-man combines the attributes of witchcraft
and mediumship. The voodoo-men and obeah-men of the
West Indies provide a good example of this. Their speciality
used to be the administration of deadly poisons to ensure
that their curses worked properly. But the voodoo-man's
biggest claim to fame lay in his purported ability to bring
the dead to life. He achieved this useful little trick by
means of hypnotic suggestion ; first he would induce a
cataleptic trance in his victim, and after burial he would
" restore " them to automaton lives as slaves.

The cults of voodoo, obeah and myalism spread to the
West Indies from Africa. Their West African counterpart
is *ju-ju*, which may mean anything from an amulet, charm,
magic, or curse, to the spirits or gods supposedly connected
with them.

The African witchdoctor does not conform to a single
pattern, however. The Zulu *Ganga* is more of a medium in
the western sense than the ju-ju man. He is an adept at
acquiring information from the *amadhlozi*—the spirits of
the dead.

Tales of the supernatural powers of African medicine-men are still reported by gullible white people. One of the most persistent is that of the reputed power of certain witch-doctors to cure snake-bites in a few minutes, or even seconds, by means of charms and incantations. It is probable that many such stories can be explained by the use of hypnotic suggestion; by inducing a trance-state or an analgesic condition the patient would be spared much of the debilitating exhaustion normally produced by the pain and wracking spasms; and if he survived he would naturally attribute his recovery to the witch-doctor's magic.

Many Europeans have borne witness to the apparent ability of witch-doctors and shamans to bring badly needed rain. "Rain-making" rituals are found the world over. The secret of successful rain-making is in waiting for the first indications of rain before conducting the ceremony. General Smuts gained quite a reputation in this way. He often timed his arrival in drought-striken areas just as the drought broke. But unlike the witch-doctor he was able to consult the Meteorological Office beforehand.

The African medicine-man often makes good use of messages exchanged by native drummers. To many people the "bush-telegraph" beaten out by African drums still constitutes an unsolved mystery with a flavour of the super-natual. The explanation, however, is a prosaic one. Messages can, indeed, be sent hundreds of miles in a short time by relays of drummers. But the usual range of each drum extends only about ten to fifteen miles; and most drummers can only send a limited number of stereotyped messages, rather like those printed on prisoner-of-war postcards during the war.

In many primitive communities a medicine man's curse can produce grave consequences through the operation of maleficient suggestion. The Australian aboriginee is particularly susceptible to the influence of the tribal witch-doctors, and many reliable accounts bear witness to the fact that powerful suggestion in the form of malevolent incantation or a curse, may cause the victim to fall into a coma which ultimately ends in death. The anthropologist

W. E. Roth termed this lethal form of suggestion *thanatomania*.

There is nothing supernatural about this weird phenomenon. All doctors know that a seriously ill person's "will to live" or his resignation to death is often the deciding factor as to whether he lives or dies. The same psychological factors are involved in thanatomania, only in a much more extreme form.

SPIRITUALISM

The primitive shaman, unlike his modern western counterpart, employs any trick which will add to his supernatural reputation. Modern mediums play for safety by confining themselves to a much narrower range of " phenomena "—mostly simple conjuring tricks.

The credulity of a primitive audience occasions no surprise. What *is* surprising, however, are the equally credulous reactions of great numbers of people in western society to the arts of shamanism exhibited in the séance room.

Perhaps the most enlightening book on spiritualism is *The Road to Endor*. Its author practised mediumship for the diversion of himself and others at a prisoner-of-war camp during the first world war. His prolonged and elaborate hoax was brilliantly successful. In his preface he writes

" We do know that, in the face of the most elaborate and persistent efforts to detect fraud, it is possible to convert intelligent, scientific and otherwise highly educated men to spiritualism, by means of the arts and methods employed by mediums in general." [1]

All " physical " mediums use conjuring and trickery ; " most of these have already been unmasked as frauds, and we are tempted to expect that the same will happen with the rest as well." [2]

The counterpart of the medium is the ready believer, as Culpin once observed.[3] Mediums, knowing the illimitable credulity of their clients, snap their fingers in the face of

[1] Jones, E. H., *The Road to Endor*, p. ix.
[2] Sigmund Freud, *New Introductory Lectures on Psychoanalysis*, p. 50.
[3] Culpin, M., *Spiritualism and the New Psychology*, p. 158.

exposure. They are soon able to restore confidence in themselves, for they know that the true believer can never resist the temptation to seize upon the flimsiest evidence of the supernatural. It is the subtle co-operation of fraud and self-deception which keeps the cult of spiritualism so vigorously alive.

It is a fact that the convinced spiritualist and the impartial observer will usually write totally differing accounts of the same seance. This is not surprising for it is well known that any short-lived incident reported in detail by untrained (and unbiased) observers will include false additions, and the omission by each observer of about half the essential points.

Experiments carried out in 1931 by Th. Besterman under the auspices of the Society for Psychical Research[4] emphasise quite clearly the unreliability of witnesses' reports of what had occurred during a simple fake séance, even after the sitters had been warned to observe accurately with a view to subsequently answering a questionnaire.

When the observer is under emotional strain, his powers of observation become correspondingly reduced. In such circumstances self-deception " is so potent a factor that descriptions by a believer in psychical phenomena and by an unbeliever of the same events are often hardly identifiable as referring to the same affair." [5]

It is little wonder that thousands of people claim to have repeatedly witnessed such phenomena as levitations, elongation of the body, and the " materialisation " of dead friends and relatives. One of the most striking examples of the spiritualist's capacity for self-deception occurred during the trial of the French photographer Buguet. Buguet admitted that he faked his photographs, used a draped doll or lay figure for his purpose. Yet witness after witness testified that Buguet had given them photographs of their dead loved ones, refusing even to accept the photographer's explanation of how he made them.

Self-deception in regard to the occult is not confined to

---

[4] Besterman, T., *The Psychology of Testimony in relation to Paraphysical Phenomena*, Proc.S.P.R., xl, 1932.

[5] Schiller, F. C. S., *Psychology and Psychical Research*, The Monist, xl, 1930, p. 446.

mediums and spiritualists; even the most intelligent of psychical researchers have their own brand. A good example is provided by the well-known " cross correspondence tests," in which stupendous ingenuity and perseverance were displayed by a group of psychical researchers who strove for years to find some factual correspondence between a dead scholar's purported communications and the writings of ancient classical authors. The difficulty in doing this was attributed to the subtlety of the dead scholar.

Psychical researchers have always indulged in wishful interpretation of mediumistic utterances. The object of this pastime is to try and squeeze out evidence of paranormal powers from the medium's utterances, however allusive. Ambiguous, and usually pointless, utterances of the medium are carefully noted down; and then a search is made to find " veridical " events which would make sense of the utterances. " Solutions " are eventually unearthed which usually possess considerab'e textual incongruity and which are applicable only within the widest limits of relevance. The resultant " report " is presented for public perusal with a convincing air of restraint and impartiality, which, however, is quite spurious. This process reached the height of absurdity in the psychical researcher's investigations of " proxy sittings."

The level of intelligence displayed by spirits of the Great Beyond is depressingly low; the sort of life they lead would furnish any reasonable person with a good argument against suicide. Yet there is scarcely any limit to the lengths to which some spiritualists will go in trying to establish proof of their reality.

A classical example of this was provided by a certain Dr. Watters in 1933. He published an account* in which he claimed to have photographed the " immaterial bodies " of certain animals at the moment of death. This epoch-making feat was carried out by means of a Wilson Cloud Chamber ! Unfortunately, Dr. Watter's photographs were a little blurred. Three years later a Mr. Hopper tried to repeat the experiment. He failed to detect any " immaterial body ".

Bulletin of the Bernard Johnston Foundation for Psychological Research, October, 1933.

For people of unbalanced minds spiritualism undoubtedly presents a real danger. Fixed delusions, and even insanity, may be the final result. J. D. Quackenbos, writing in 1908 mentions three women " who sought the objects of their erotomania in extra-planetary life, and solemnly declared they were having love relations with discarnate spirits". [7] It is perhaps fortunate that no one has as yet tried to commercialise this attractive idea.

Cases have been known where mentally unbalanced people have become so obsessed by spiritualistic ideas that they have killed themselves in order to join their lost loved ones in the spirit-world. [8]

The dividing line between sanity and insanity in mediums is often a thin one. The final phases of Hélène Smith's life provide a good example of this. Many mediums suffer from fixed delusions and obsessions. Several have become obsessed with the idea that God addresses himself directly to them through their table-tilting and automatic-writing. Others have the delusion that they are bodily transported through space by discarnate spirits, to the planets or even Heaven itself.

On the other hand, for many people spiritualism is an undeniable blessing. The shamanistic performances of the séance room should not be confused with genuine religious or Christian spiritualism. Religious spiritualism, for many, transforms the facts of death and suffering into something which does not hurt quite so much. [9] It often helps the individual to adjust himself to the problems of life, compensates for frustrations, and provides a seemingly logical justification to existence.

---

[7] *Hypnotic Therapeutics*, p. 202.
[8] See Viollet, M., *Spiritualism and Insanity*.
[9] Lawton, G., *The Drama of Life after Death*, p. 347.

Chapter Twenty

THE "PHYSICAL PHENOMENA" OF THE SÉANCE ROOM

A STUDY of the "physical phenomena" of spiritualism " produces the uncomfortable feeling of walking on a swamp, in which healthy commonsense is liable to sink", wrote Professor B. Bavink in his *Anatomy of Modern Science.* This observation is an apt one. Unless the student of spiritualistic phenomena has a working knowledge of the psychology of deception and delusion, and has first read the literature exposing the fraud and trickery to be found in the séance room, he had better keep away from spiritualism altogether, else he stands in danger of drifting imperceptibly into belief in a cult which has little to recommend it. This has been the unfortunate experience of many intelligent and gifted people in the past.

The best example ot the degree to which a brilliant intellect may sink into the spiritualistic swamp is provided by the well-known physicist Sir William Crookes, who claimed to have strolled arm in arm with a materialised spirit who called herself Katie. Such a degree of credulity appears almost impossible. Yet many fine minds have been bitten by the spiritualist bug and they have left an impressive array of arguments and testimony which is only too apt to trap the unwary into similar beliefs. As a subject of psychological study spiritualism offers many interests, but it cannot be sufficiently emphasised that the " physical phenomena " of the séance room have been exposed as mere trickery times without number. Most of the leading "physical" mediums have been repeatedly detected in fraud and exposed as little more than clever tricksters, including the notorious Eusapia Palladino, who for years puzzled many learned savants in Europe and America.

The first thing that may strike the impartial investigator is that fraudulent or not, precisely that type of happening occurs at these " physical " séances which one would fully expect to happen were trickery the basis of the phenomena observed. On scores of occasions intelligent investigators have testified unequivocally to their absolute conviction that such and such " psychic " phenomenon took place which were afterwards proved to have been produced by tricks or mechanical means. In recent years, however, since the introduction of the infra-red telescope, which enables the viewer to see all that goes on in a completely dark room, no medium has been able to demonstrate her " psychic " ability to the scientifically equipped investigator.

There are many arguments put forward by psychical researchers for the scientific thoroughness of their investigations, and such arguments are patently naïve. Scientific methods of investigation are based on universally accepted principles, and these are very different from those adopted, until quite recently, by psychical researchers in their investigations of " physical " mediums. There is no need to go into these claims in any detail. For the fact remains that after sixty years of investigation psychical research still has not decided whether the claims of the " physical " mediums have any basis in actuality. If genuine scientific methods had been employed all through this period, the issue would never have remained in doubt.

The medium, in order to protect herself against exposure, is forced to maintain the worst possible conditions for the control and observation of the events which take place during the séance. If the sitters refuse to comply with these restrictions, then either no " phenomena " occur or the séance is terminated. Under such conditions no scientific observation is possible. All that such investigations amount to is pitting one's wits against those of the medium, with the disadvantage that one must pretend to conform with her innumerable regulations which are specifically designed to make observation difficult. And with the failure to outwit the medium the illogical verdict is only too often reached that her claims to supernatural powers must be true.

All the leading mediums who have been seriously investigated have been exposed as frauds at one time or another. Nevertheless it is still argued that proof of fraud is not necessarily disproof of supernatural faculty. The psychical researcher often expects us to believe that, although the medium is detected on numerous occasions practising conjuring tricks, supernatural powers may have been displayed on those occasions when the investigators failed to see how the " phenomena " were brought about. The tendentiousness of such an argument is clear ; Moll, Jastrow, Podmore, Dessoir and Gulat-Wellenburg have all pointed this out, and all possessed a wide knowledge of the literature and practice of spiritualism.

Perhaps not so surprising is the rejection of the spiritualistic interpretation of the physical phenomena of the séance room by the most intelligent psychical researchers. While the medium maintains that it is by the help of her " spirit-control " that she produces the " phenomena ", the psychical researcher often holds that the spiritualistic content of the medium's utterances is due to unconscious automatism, and that the supernatural powers purportedly exhibited are due to the medium's own " paranormal " or " psychic " faculties. In point of fact, both the spiritistic utterances and the accompanying " phenomena " are quite easily explained by the simple hypothesis of conscious deception. There is good reason to believe that many mediums do induce a state of psychological automatism, but this is by no means certain in the case of any professional "physical" medium.

The tricks used by mediums to produce the phenomena of " materialisation " have been described too often to warrant further repetition here. " Ectoplasm ", " teleplastic materialisations " and " ideoplastic pseudopods " are some of the terms used by Richet, Schrenck-Notzing and Geley to describe such manifestations. But these spirit-substances, which photographs reveal as white doughy streams issuing from the mouth (sometimes regurgitated cheese-cloth), the nose and even the genitals of female mediums, are no longer fashionable subjects of investigation in the more serious psychical research circles. One enterprising medium even hid her " ectoplasm " in a hollow comb which searches previous to the séances for a long time failed to reveal.

As an example of the ridiculous lengths to which investigators of the psychic prostitute their intellects, here is an extract by Dr. Schrenck-Notzing, who in many ways was a highly gifted and intelligent psychologist :

> " With regard to the pieces of paper found in Paris and London, we have no occasion to doubt that even paper-like substances can be materialised (by the medium), as can substances of the nature of gauze veiling and cotton, including the morphological structure of the weft, folds sewn in, etc.

> " Just as traces have repeatedly been left of the pure, organic-teleplastic substance, so may similar fragments of the materialised products, textile or cellular, have been left behind."[1]

The production of spirit-forms provides an amazing example of the scope and completeness of self-deception which may occur when the individual is under emotional stress. Men as well as women have been known to recognize a dead father, mother, sister or cousin in the figure of a thinly disguised medium who, her head wrapped in a white scarf or veil, is seen moving around in the gloom of the séance room. Many descriptions have come from competent observers who have looked on aghast at the success of the most flagrant deceptions : before their eyes stands the patently disguised figure of the medium, and with each insignificant change of apparel a bereaved mother or daughter or wife cries out a heart-rending greeting to one long since dead and buried. The illusion, brought about by frustrated longing and the overwhelming will to believe, is complete. One is inevitably reminded of the collective hallucinations that have occasionally occurred at moments of religious fervour.

One form of spirit-evoking magic was the " ectoplasm box ". In 1937 the New York *World Telegram* published a series of articles on Harlem *voodoo*, amongst which was a description of an " ectoplasm box ", manufactured by a small

---

[1] Schrenck-Notzing, *Proc.* S.P.R., 1923, p. 669.

factory in Chicago, costing about fifteen dollars, by means of which a smoky shape, roughly resembling a hooded man, floats upwards.

In 1930 Dr. E. Osty created a sensation by his investigations of the well-known spiritualist-medium Rudi Schneider. Rudi, and his brother Willi, had been repeatedly and comprehensively exposed as fraudulent tricksters, yet such is the faith of those imbued with a penchant for the mysterious that both spiritualists and psychical researchers alike continued to believe in the possibility of their supernatural powers. " Ectoplasm " and other " teleplastic manifestations " were their main specialities. These, however, were investigated by Professor Przibram of the University of Vienna and found to be nothing more than deceptions.

Until 1930 the Schneider brothers had produced no " phenomena " that had not been covered by their exposures. But the experiments of Osty and his son opened up a new sphere of mediumistic phenomena. Not since the day of Palladino had the " physical phenomena " of the spiritualists attracted so much attention amongst susceptible scientists and equally sceptical psychologists. For Osty reported that Rudi Schneider was able to interrupt an infra-red beam " supernormally " under conditions which made fraud impossible !

In a series of 77 sittings Dr. Osty, the Director of the French equivalent of the Society for Psychical Research — the *Institute Métapsychique International,* used infra-red beams. galvanometers, chronometers, a quartz lens and ultra-violet light in an effort to provide convincing evidence of Rudi's " psychic " emanations. There is no doubt whatever that this was Osty's main concern. Most of his life had been spent in psychical research. It was his all-absorbing interest. A perusal of his writings clearly indicates that his approach to the subject was not dictated by an unbiased desire for knowledge but by a frank hope of finding conclusive evidence of supernatural faculty. Any such evidence coming from such a source is highly suspect, and it is difficult to believe that he avoided the fault, common to all psychical researchers, of emphasising the points favourable to his preconceived ideas and omitting or minimising those which were unfavourable.

The suspicion surrounding the experiments of Osty and his son was not mitigated by the results reported by Besterman and Gatty of the Society for Psychical Research, who investigated Schneider with infra-red apparatus four years later in 1934. None of the effects reported by Osty was observed. The usual excuse put forward for all such failures is that the medium's powers were on the wane. In one sense this is generally true for with increasingly efficient means of investigation the medium finds it increasingly difficult to produce his " phenomena ", for very obvious reasons.

Osty's experiments with Rudi Schneider took place in the dark. Apart from the usual hand and foot controls luminous patches were placed on the medium's person which would indicate his movements. This is scarcely an auspicious beginning for an allegedly scientific investigation, for such conditions of control present little difficulty to an experienced conjuror.

When in trance Schneider's rate of breathing averaged over 200 respirations a minute as compared with the normal of fifteen. At times the rate of breathing rose to nearly three hundred. Osty assumed that such sustained hypernoea was impossible for the normal individual and adduced it as evidence of the supernormality of the medium's trance state. In point of fact Besterman and Gatty showed that it could be imitated without difficulty. This is something which Osty could easily have verified for himself. That he neglected to do so is a good indication of his approach to the investigations.

However, the crux of the Osty experiments lies in Schneider's reported ability to interrupt an infra-red beam. The beam was only *partially* interrupted, not wholly, as would have been the case if a thick solid object were interposed. Furthermore the interruption varied rhythmically in time with Schneider's rapid breathing. More curious still, the flashlight photographs revealed no discernible cause of the interruptions. Osty explained this by saying that an " invisible substance " was responsible !

Osty's report was, superficially, an impressive one.   Professor Julian Huxley wrote :

" The experiments, of which a full record is given in the *Revue Metapsychique* for 1932 seem conclusive. . . . Taking them at their face value, they would seem to prove that under certain conditions certain human beings are capable of giving out an emanation of a type which is new to science."[1]

Since that date, however, various discrepancies have come to light which throw the whole of Osty's experiments into doubt.   Harry Price made a prolonged investigation of Rudi Schneider and proved conclusively that the medium resorted to trickery when he believed himself to be unobserved.[2]

In matters pertaining to the psychic Osty has too often shown in the past, despite some intellectual ability, evidence of an amateurish and uncritical approach to his subject—a tendency to which most psychical researchers are prone. This, taken together with Rudi Schneider's record of detected fraud and his subsequent failure under stricter experimental conditions, makes it difficult to arrive at any other conclusion than that the medium achieved his novel success through his long experience in the art of deception and prestidigitation.

Turning from Osty's experiments with Rudi Schneider, which represent something out of the usual in the way of mediumistic investigations, there arises the problem of how the ordinary " physical " medium manages to deceive his (or her) audiences.

Contrary to general belief, conjuring is not primarily a question of tricky manipulation and concealed devices. These two factors are completely subordinate to the difficult art of artlessly misdirecting the observer's attention at critical moments.   The first task of the " physical " medium, like the conjuror, is to misdirect the attention of her sitters or investigators.   But, unlike the conjuror, she must also be on constant watch for those inevitable moments of non-attention during the course of the séance in order to take advantage of them when they occur.

---

[1] *The Week-End Review*, 6, 1932, p. 303.
[2] See Price, H., *Rudi Schneider : a Scientific Examination of his Mediumship with Rudi Schneider*, Bulletin of the Nat. Lab. of Psychical Research, 1933.

The clever medium combines the dexterity and psychology of both the conjuror and the pickpocket. Both for the conjuror and for the medium sleight-of-hand consists mainly in the correct use and swift application of certain psychological principles. This is fundamental to most types of conjuring trick, and in relation to this fact manual dexterity becomes entirely secondary, and with a great many tricks is even unnecessary. The medium and conjuror, by their different types of " patter ", keep the attention of their observers directed away from the real points of importance. Their whole act consists in making the observer draw inferences which would be perfectly valid under normal conditions but completely misleading under those in question.

The medium's life in relation to her " sitters " consists of speaking and acting in consonance with the part she is called upon to play at her séances. The conjuror, on the other hand, only has to act his part when on the stage. The medium has the advantage in that she is able to build up the expectations and play on the interests and emotions of her clients between each séance. She does her best to mould their beliefs and mental outlook so that, unknown to her sitters (or investigators), their attention loses its critical edge and they become ever more susceptible to the constant flow of misleading ideas and suggestions.

Like the conjuror the medium directs the attention to what she does *not* do ; what she pretends to do she may refrain from actually doing ; and what she actually does she does at a moment when her own attention is ostensibly directed elsewhere. If, for example, a conjuror wishes to distract the audience's attention for a second from what his right hand is doing he may give a couple of taps with a wooden hammer with his left hand, on the supposed pretext of testing the solidity of the particular object with which he proposes to demonstrate his sleight-of-hand. For that one second all eyes in the auditorium instinctively switch to the tapping hammer. That second is usually sufficient for the conjuror's purpose. And it is all done with the most natural air in the world.

The medium whose object it is to produce " physical phenomena " has to misdirect her sitters' attention from those manœuvres designed to free a hand or foot from the control of her investigators ; by her talk, by her exclamations of alarm, surprise, pain, annoyance, bad-temper or amusement, by various pretexts of discomfort or grumbling at the way she is being controlled, by false movements, and by her own pretended observations of " phenomena " which have not occurred.   If all this fails she may resort to direct orders from her familiar-spirit, who usually compéres the séance, which, of course, have to be obeyed.   If she wishes to practise substitution of her feet she will make guilt-laden movements of her hands.   In fact, her devices, like those of the conjuror, are limitless.

> " Her greatest accomplishment of all is this, that she knows where everyone is putting his attention.   If you should look at the critical place, nothing would happen there.   But she is a consummate mistress of all the arts of how to direct your attention from the critical place.   If she wants to do something with her hands, she bids you be careful that you have a good control of the feet.   If she wants to slip her foot on yours so as to get the heel where the toe has been and put the toe on the other foot, she will make mystic passes in the air in front of your eyes, and at each stroke of her hand, slip goes the foot—a slight motion which is virtually certain that you will not notice.   A jerk in one place covers a lesser jerk in another. She is a supreme eluder."[1]

If the light is sufficiently bright for the medium's sitters to see, then she will make more use of her table, her skirts, and her cabinet curtains as screens.   If that proves insufficient then she will move her body or even those of her controllers into the position most advantageous for that purpose. Her sitters are forbidden in any event to look under the table—for distrustful humans soon alienate the sensitive spirits !

Since the crux of the medium's performance depends upon getting a hand or foot free without being observed, what are the means usually adopted ?   Here, to begin with, is a description by the conjuror Houdini of one of the methods employed :

> " The medium's shoes are especially made for her in such a way that by a certain pressure on the sole it is possible to withdraw the

---

[1] Jastrow, J., *The Psychology of Conviction*, p. 119.

greater portion of the shoe, with the foot, from a false front. This front is made of metal and padded. When the medium asks the committee to place their feet on hers she makes sure that they do not overreach the portion she can withdraw from. In the full glare of the light the investigator thinks he feels the medium's foot securely held under his own and as he cannot see under the table the medium has the full use of her foot to produce manifestations."[2]

Many mediums who practise " levitating " tables wear soft leather boots or shoes with wide thin flanges on the soles to enable them to get a good purchase on the table leg. Some use devices such as a small hook fastened to a tape which runs over the shoulder under the outer clothing and made fast to a belt at the medium's back. Amongst those mediums who are accustomed to naïve clientèle any type of device may be employed. To those mediums, however, who have made a speciality of being investigated by scientists or semi-learned societies such devices are a good deal less common. Here the prime necessity is to insure the release of a hand or foot or both from the control of one of the controllers who sit on either side of her. This is not nearly so difficult as it may appear. In fact, in the obscurity of the average séance room and with obedient sitters, even the most experienced can release a hand or foot without being detected by the two controllers.

The simplest means of releasing a foot is for the medium to have shoes with stout toe-caps ; she simply withdraws the foot from the shoe while the controller's own foot is pressing firmly down on the toe-cap. While this is happening the medium may tell her controllers to grasp her wrists as tightly as they wish. This distracts the attention and during the brief diversion thus caused the foot is quietly slipped out of the shoe.

If the substitution of one foot for two is practiced then the medium generally pretends that she has a corn, or on some similar pretext refuses to have her controller's shoes pressing on top of her own. Instead she insists that at least one of her shoes shall be pressing down on one of her control-

---

[2] Houdini, H., *A Magician Among the Spirits*. The Case for and against Psychical Belief, p. 324, edited by C. Murchison, Clark University Press, Mass., 1927.

lers', on the assumption that if she lifted her foot off then the latter would be able to detect the sudden cease of pressure.

Having arranged matters thus far the medium puts on an act which may vary from small restless movements of her whole body to a realistic imitation of a nervous hysterical attack. Her continual restlessness and little shiftings of her feet soon provide an opportunity of placing the heel of her left shoe on the same part of her controller's shoe where her right toe had been pressing a half second before. Thus with one foot doing service for two, both controllers still believe that each of the medium's feet are where they ought to be. In actual fact the medium has one foot free with which to produce " phenomena ".

The same procedure is used for making one hand do service for two. If her right wrist is grasped by the controller on her right then she insists that her hand be " controlled " only by the pressure of *her* fingers on the hand of the other controller. In the dark it is not difficult for the medium to substitute one hand for two—leaving her dupes to believe that they still control both.

The limitations of such substitution tricks are that the " phenomena " brought about by such means usually occur only within a radius of a few feet of the medium. Yet in the following chapter we shall see that such methods may achieve results apparently out of all proportion to the means employed. We now turn to the cleverest of all " physical " mediums, Eusapia Palladino, whose career is regarded by many psychical researchers and spiritualists as the test case for the existence of supernormal faculties in the " physical " medium.

Chapter Twenty-one

EUSAPIA PALLADINO

THE " physical phenomena " of the spiritualist séance-room still attract the serious attention of many intelligent people. In an age of scientific enlightenment this may appear surprising, the more so since the " phenomena " of the spiritualists would, if accepted, hurl to the winds the most cherished principles of modern physics and biology. The one person who might have been able to lay claim to the perpetuation of shamanism as a serious field of study in modern civilised countries was a Neapolitan medium who answered to the mellifluous name of Eusapia Palladino.

Palladino is still an enigma to many. To most psychical researchers her case presents cogent evidence that human beings can wield supernatural powers—can move objects at will without physical means and can create substance by the power of thought.

The present day reputation of Palladino in psychical research circles rests mainly on a series of eleven séances held at Naples in 1908. The investigators, Messrs. Feilding, Baggally and Carrington, produced a lengthy verbatim record of the séances which, taken alone, present a strong *prima facie* case for the supernatural powers of Palladino, although Podmore effectively criticised it on a number of grounds. It is time, however, that the Palladino myth was finally exploded, and with it one of the main bases for belief in the supernormal phenomena of the séance room. It is with this object in mind that the present chapter is undertaken. However strong a case may be made out for the genuineness of the 1908 séances, they take on a different aspect when

320

PLATE VIII. How the Diving Rod is Held (I)

The author demonstrating one of the several methods used by diviners of subterranean water and minerals.

(See Chapter 22)

PLATE IX. How the Divining Rod is Held (II)

The same method as in the previous illustration, from a different angle.

viewed against the background of detected deception and
fraud which littered Palladino's career. Here then is the
story of Palladino as the clever charlatan she really was.

. . . . . .

Unlettered, of obscure origin, and bred in the slums of
Naples, Eusapia Palladino was for years the object of investigation by some of the most eminent scientists and
savants of Europe and America. Born in the year 1854,
her eruption into the scientific world began with a letter in
1888 from Professor Chiaia of Naples to Professor Lombroso,
famous criminologist and psychiatrist. By 1891 Lombroso
had become convinced of her supernatural powers and within
four years Palladino had converted many notable men of
science in Italy, Russia and France to the same belief.

Early in life Palladino married a travelling conjuror,
whence she doubtless picked up the knowledge, common to
all conjurors, that conjuring is mainly a question of distracting the attention and misleading the expectation of the
audience. By temperament Palladino was ideally suited for
this. Possessing a strong personality and a gift for talking,
she soon learned that the art of lulling suspicion lay in making
friends and keeping the respect of her investigators ; they,
for the most part, were psychologically predisposed to accept
her claims to supernatural powers though they rejected her
spiritualistic interpretation of them.

Her " phenomena " in the main purported to consist of
movements and levitations of a light table and other smaller
objects without the intervention of any physical means.
Other " phenomena " were the appearance of spirit hands
and forms, spirit raps, knocks and thumps—on articles of
furniture or on the persons of her sitters, movements of
curtains, and breezes issuing from her forehead. The master
of ceremonies was an elusive spirit she called " John King ".

Palladino's success lay in the simplicity of her performances
and a sound knowledge of the psychology of her " open-
minded " investigators. It was only when she came into
contact with a harder-headed type of investigator, who
assumed from the start that it was fraud throughout and
acted on that assumption, that she finally came to grief.

The first serious investigation of Palladino took place in 1893 in Milan, under the auspices of some famous Italian scientists including Schiaparelli and Lombroso; they pronounced in favour of her genuineness. How far these Italian savants were prepared to go to find out the physiological principles involved in producing supernatural phenomena, is exemplified by the reports of their clinical examinations. Lombroso, Morrelli and others hit upon the theory that Palladino's phenomena were due to a redirection of fundamental sex energy. They reported that her menstrual secretions increased at the commencement of her trances, that she had a particular zone of hyperaesthesia, especially in her ovaries, and that when " phenomena " were about to occur it was sometimes accompanied by voluptuous erotic sensations followed by genuine orgasm. How far such reports are to be relied on is problematical. It is difficult to imagine under what conditions they were verified.

In the following year, in 1894, Palladino repeated her success with Professor Richet, the famous French physiologist, at Paris. Myers, Ochorowicz and Sir Oliver Lodge also attended. An incident mentioned by Grasset in his *Occultisme* serves to throw considerable light on that element of her character which enabled her to carry on undisturbed by temporary setbacks. She had begun to produce some spirit-raps with the aid of her familiar spirit, " John King ". Ochorowicz observed that the medium was producing them by striking her shoe against the table. When Ochorowicz pointed this out she drew back a little, denied it, and then added;

" It is strange, all the same; something is pushing my foot towards the table. Sentite! Sentite!" *Nevertheless* " she was so sure of the phenomenon," *Ochorowicz continues*, " that she insisted on my tying her foot to one of mine by means of a cord. And when I did so, I felt that she drew the cord by turning her foot round; she turned it in such a manner as to be able to strike the table with her heel. It was evident to everyone except to herself."

It is amazing that after such exhibitions the investigators did not wash their hands of Palladino. This was by no means the first time that she had been detected practising her tricks. The explanation lies in the fact that the investigators held the theory, from which Palladino was not averse, that the production of spurious phenomena in no way invalidated her claim to be able to produce the genuine supernatural article. That this argument is quite specious will be shown further on, but it still predominates in the arguments of the " believers ".

In point of fact Palladino's investigators were not really investigating her " phenomena " at all. What they were all hoping to do was to prove her " phenomena " authentic. Their " will to believe " was continually in conflict with their " will to know ". Richet, Myers and Lodge all believed in the unseen spirit world and died steadfast in their belief. This battle between the unconscious primitive tendency towards mysticism and the consciously felt desire for knowledge is the breeding ground of psychical researchers. To the average psychical researcher Palladino's career provides serious food for thought on issues affecting the whole of science and philosophy ; to the average psychologist that same career provides an object lesson in the vagaries and paradoxes of deception.

Richet provides an excellent example of a great scientist succumbing to the insidious yearning for mysticism. He himself had commented upon the suspiciousness of the Palladino séances of 1893 and had quite accurately observed that " to the extent to which the conditions were made rigid, the phenomena decreased ". Yet before long his will to believe had again assumed the dominant position in his mind. His story has been repeated over and over again in the annals of psychical research.

The objective investigator in psychical research is rare.
" There are, it is true, cases of originally credulous persons going to séances with the firm intention of forming an objective opinion and being convinced. This, however, does not invalidate the fact that in cases of this kind the desire to be convinced and expectation quickly overcame incredulity, because such incredulity was flaunted with the aim of concealing a profound repressed need for faith."[1]

The séances in Italy and Paris took place for the most part in complete or semi-darkness and Palladino had little

---

[1] Castiglioni, A., Adventures of the Mind, pp. 307-8.

difficulty in imposing her tricks upon her learned investigators. The precise nature of these tricks was fully ascertained
at the Cambridge séances of 1895 held under the aegis of
Myers; they were precisely those which had been predicted
by Dr. R. Hodgson two years previously. By deliberately
faking loose conditions of control Palladino was deceived
into taking chances which she would otherwise not have done,
and in the Journal of the S.P.R. the investigators published
their conclusion that Palladino habitually contrived to get
her hand or foot free and that the bulk of her " phenomena "
were to be explained in this way. Thus Myers wrote : " I
cannot doubt that we observed much conscious and deliberate
fraud, of a kind which must have needed long practise to
bring it to its present level of skill ".

Myers and the S.P.R. refused to have anything further to
do with Eusapia for the next three years. But in 1898
further séances were held at the instigation of Professor
Richet with the result that Richet, Myers and Lodge re-
affimed their belief in the supernatural powers of the medium.
Palladino's heyday had begun. For the next ten years she
was an international celebrity. A considerable number of
the most eminent scientists of the Victorian era were converted wholeheartedly to the new scientific study of supernaturalism. The belief in magic had gained a new lease of
life though it was dignified by other names with Greek
prefixes and suffixes.

Between 1905 and 1907 the voice of Palladino was heard
calling upon her familiar spirit, the elusive " John King ",
to help her lift the table with his psychic power at séance
after séance, held either under the auspices of the Institut
Général Psychologique de Paris or before committees of
distinguished professors at Naples and Turin. The Italians
reported her performances as impressive but had to admit
that in each case when really conclusive tests were arranged,
the safeguards protecting their test devices were either
damaged or else the " phenomena " ceased. Sealing tapes
were torn away, the lid of a cardboard box was forced off
and a cloth covering was ripped, demonstrating Palladino's
determination to get at the devices they were intended to

 October and November, 1895.

protect. " John King ", Palladino asserted, was responsible for these outrages.

Yet despite these setbacks Palladino's investigators did not give up hope of finding some really conclusive genuine phenomena if it was at all possible. The French investigators at this period, the most distinguished of whom were the Curies, excelled themselves at this game and devoted forty-three long séances to this end. The resultant report provides a good example of the ludicrous lengths to which the scientific mind is prepared to go when under the influence of super-natural beliefs. Here is what Podmore wrote in 1910:

> " The Committee then turned their attention to Eusapia's person. They tested her memory, her reasoning powers, her keenness of sight, and her visual and auditory reactions generally ; they measured her rate of respiration and tested her hyperaesthesia ; they employed the dynamometer, the sphygmograph, the pneumograph, and Hallion and Comte's plethismographic tube ; they took her temperature ; they made uroscopic analyses ; they applied thermoscopes and galvanometers ; they made a chemical analysis of the air in the seance-room, and M. Curie took some trouble to draw off the air behind the curtain to see whether it was ionised. And after all these labours, the results of which are to be seen in many pages of curves and tables, they found that Eusapia is just like everybody else."[5]

The French investigators gave Palladino every chance to carry out conclusive tests of her supernatural " tele-kinetic " powers, yet despite demonstrations of real skill she failed—but only just. A little less watchfulness on behalf of some members of the committee and she might well have succeeded. In their report the Committee ob-serve that there was no doubt that Palladino used trickery, for she had been detected using a hair to move light and delicately balanced instruments. Yet despite this the Committee's report was still sympathetic to her claims on the grounds that certain movements of objects were puzzling, and it even went so far as to offer an excuse for her fraud, on grounds of old age and the profit motive. The will to believe still predominated.

So far Palladino had more than managed to hold her own. Her supporters minimised or forgot her setbacks and mag-

---

[5] Podmore, F., *The Newer Spiritualism*, pp. 107-108.

nified her successes. For many years the Neapolitan had
had some of Europe's most notable savants sitting in circles
and holding hands amongst a jumble of scientific equipment
in ever changing conditions of lighting, strictly dictated
by herself or by her " spirit-control ", and which averaged
a deep twilight gloom. And in 1908 she conducted the
series of séances which led to the Feilding-Baggally-Carrington report and which may be regarded as the high-
spot of her career.

It had occurred to many investigators that the only
way of testing Palladino's claims was to have her levitating table and her cabinet insulated from all possible *legerdemain*. Whenever this was done, all " phenomena "
ceased or Palladino refused, under a variety of pretexts,
to carry on with the séance. This is where so many of the
investigators allowed themselves to be deceived, for by
giving way on this point they allowed Palladino to control
the conditions of the tests. The investigators even appeared afraid that Palladino would walk out in a huff if
the controls became too effective. It is evident that they
subordinated their reason to the combined effect of the
medium's personality, her claims to supernatural powers,
and their own desire to believe in her claims which they
regarded as theoretically possible ; most scientists decry
the possibility of magic and point out that wherever
ignorance exists, belief in the supernatural flourishes alongside of it.

Palladino's performances were in themselves suspect
by virtue of their limitations. That they were due to
conjuring could well have been deduced by anyone whose
mind had not been subjected to the insidious propaganda
of supernaturalism. Her phenomena were usually limited
to within a radius of three to four feet of her person. Looking under the table was usually forbidden. Her sitters
had to hold hands or place them on the table to prevent
any trickery. Isolated observers standing nearby were
not permitted. Her feet must rest on those of her controllers and not vice versa. The hands of her controllers might
not grasp her wrists but only maintain contact by pressure.
The light varied from total darkness to a crepuscular gloom.
Often the sitters had to talk amongst themselves, rendering

concentrated observation impossible. The table, her long skirt, and the cabinet curtains served as effective screens. Above all there was the continual movements of her hands and feet, over which proper control was seldom allowed— all these factors were understandable on the simple hypothesis of conjuring.

Palladino varied and relaxed one or more of these restrictions from time to time, but always at her own dictation or with her previous consent. In general they remained the standard practice of her séances and by insisting on their observance she retained control of the investigating conditions. In Europe her investigators were gentlemen and adhered to a strict code of etiquette. Any behaviour which savoured of snooping and spying was anathema to them. Such honourable behaviour was Palladino's greatest shield, and when she went to America she probably expected the same treatment. This was her chief undoing ; for the Americans, though not a whit less courteous than their European confréres, did not mind employing the method of setting a thief to catch a thief.

The main fallacy which animated the investigators of Palladino was the idea that exhibitions of fraud need not exclude the occurrence of genuine phenomena. This argument would be perfectly valid, if it were certain that such a thing as a supernatural force existed. But as Palladino's own case is upheld as the most cogent evidence for its existence, and as all other such evidence is affected by even more suspicion than surrounds the artful Neapolitan's, the argument is clearly absurd. So strong, however, is the urge towards the supernatural once the individual feels its pull, that such logical considerations would probably not have weighed very seriously with Palladino's investigators.

We now come to the Feilding-Baggally-Carrington report, the subject of which was the series of eleven séances held in Naples in the year 1908. Like the Cambridge series, where Palladino was exposed as an imposter. these séances were investigated by representatives of the Society for Psychical Research.

There is a belief in psychical research circles that the 1908 investigations of Palladino reached a high standard of efficiency. In point of fact they were extremely limited in their scope. The gentlemen concerned being afraid to give offence to the medium, Palladino retained control of the investigating conditions throughout; for Palladino's assumed sensitiveness was one of her greatest weapons. Believing as they did in the possibility of her supernatural powers, they were bound also to believe in the possibility that she spoke the truth when she stated the innumerable conditions which attached to their manifestation—conditions, be it noted, which invariably hampered the investigators and always offered her an excuse for avoiding effective controls or, if necessary, for discontinuing the séance. When these methods were ineffective she could always fall back on the " sensitive " nature of her own self or that of her guiding spirit, Signor John King.

Under such conditions no investigation can be carried out in the proper sense of the word, and it is not surprising that we find the investigators did not attempt to impose a conclusive test on Palladino. Yet again, they allowed the Neapolitan so to impose on them that they could not utilise any foolproof precautions against fraud for any length of time. One need hardly point out that if such precautions had been taken the séances would have ended forthwith; Feilding, Baggally and Carrington had to avoid such a contingency at all costs if they wished them to continue.

Under such conditions Palladino was in her element: her inquisitors believed in the possibility of supernatural powers; they were apprehensive that she would walk out on them; and they were such real gentlemen—no underhand tricks that some other investigators had tried; moreover they actually respected her wishes and fads as if they were sincere.

To pretend that the Feilding-Baggally-Carrington report constitutes anything in the nature of a scientific document is ludicrous. For example, considerable importance was attached to the fact that before one particular séance Palladino was searched for trick-devices. The search was carried out by two ladies, " Signora X " and " Miss Y." We are told that " Madame Palladino first took off a black serge bodice and skirt of the same material and colour. She then slipped over her head a white knitted cotton stay-cover. She also drew off her neck a white linen scarf a little over a foot in length and about four inches wide. Next came a long dark blue petticoat and white embroidery round the bottom. After that she took off a short white flannel one, and a pair of pink and brown stays. She then removed a long shift of coarse white linen and stood in what one might call a pair of grey, woolly, divided combinations, that is to say, body and drawers, a pair of white stockings, black elastic garters under her knees, and a pair of brownish coloured boots, with heels, *which were only buttoned by the top button"* (author's italics).[1]

As a resumé of the type of underclothing worn by the Italian middle-classes in the early twentieth century this document may possibly represent an interesting contribution towards the social sciences. As an example of how to search mediums it fails to carry conviction. Schrenck-Notzing might have given the gentlefolk of the S.P.R. a lesson in searching mediums for he did not hesitate to carry out anal and vaginal examinations if he thought it necessary. In any event to search a good conjuror is not so simple as it may appear. The searchers, misled by the apparent frankness of the medium, are seldom on the look-out for sleight of hand.

The argument put forward that Baggally and Carrington were excellent amateur conjurors and could easily have detected fraud were it practised, is of little significance. S. J. Davey, for example, who did so much to demonstrate how " spirit " slate-writing was achieved and who was himself a really expert amateur conjuror, had previously recorded his conviction that " the idea of trickery or jugglery in slate-writing is out of the question." According to Professor Jastrow even the professional conjuror is easily deceived in the gloom of the séance room " if he have no experience in the special kind of sleight of hand required for the trick." He cites the admission of the professional conjuror, Harry Kellar, " who at first declared himself unable to explain slate-writing as a trick, but now can

---

[1] Feilding, Baggally and Carrington, *Report on Sittings with Eusapia Palladino*, Proc. S.P.R., XXIII, 1909, p. 505.

repeat the process in a variety of ways, and with far greater skill than is shown by mediums."[1]

According to Mulholland about eighty per cent. of the success of a conjuror's performance depends upon the utilisation of psychology, ten per cent. upon skilled manipulation and the remaining ten per cent upon the use of equipment.[2]

In the Naples séances the subjective bias of Palladino's investigators is apparent from the start and there can be no doubt this was Palladino's greatest asset. Feilding virtually admits the subjective character of his impressions at these séances. He writes :

" Re-reading the shorthand report after this lapse of time, and studying it critically, I can appreciate what an absolutely different impression it must make on the mind of anyone not present, . . . "[3]

Such was the mental set of the investigators that we are asked to believe that when a hand was observed in the gloom by Feilding, Carrington and the stenographer, which untied a bell on Palladino's head, rang it, and threw it on the table, it was not a human hand at all but one constructed of " ectoplasm "! The stenographer showed less enthusiasm for the suggestion ; he thought it was either the medium's hand or that of one of the investigators.

Four times in all was Palladino detected in practising substitution of hands. Podmore suspected Baggally more than the others of faulty control of the medium's hands and feet and makes out a good case to substantiate this ; in his thirty page criticism of the Feilding-Baggally-Carrington report[4] he concludes : " No other record of the physical phenomena of spiritualism, it may be said, is of any value beside it. And yet the record, as we have seen, is at critical moments incomplete and at almost every point leaves obvious loopholes for trickery." Only the most prejudiced or those afflicted by the insidious " will to believe " could arrive at any other conclusion. Those interested in a

---

[1] *Fact and Fable in Psychology*, N.Y. 1901.
[2] *Ency. Brit.*, 1947.
[3] *Proc.* S.P.R. XXIII, 1909, p. 374.
[4] Podmore, F., *The Newer Spiritualism*, pp. 114-144.

more detailed criticism of the 1908 séances are advised to read Podmore's critical analysis referred to above.

The 1908 séances represent the zenith of Palladino's success. Thereafter her star fell rapidly. In 1909 she went to the United States with Hereward Carrington as her *entrepreneur*. The visit was disastrous. The American investigators were sceptical of her claims, and worse still, they could not be relied upon to behave like gentlemen at her séances—in point of fact they were downright deceitful. Yet they were cunning enough to keep their intentions from the Neapolitan. In a word they took her on at her own game.

On December 18th at a séance held at the instigation of Professor Münsterberg, a young man crept along the ground halfway into the cabinet behind Palladino. He put out his hand in the near darkness and grasped an unshod foot. Palladino screamed out that her foot had been touched. The ungentlemanly investigator had in fact caught hold of her left foot—the very same foot in fact that Professor Münsterberg had imagined to have been pressing on his own right foot all the while. Worse was to follow. On April 17th, the following year, Professors Lord and Jastrow arranged that two young men clad in black should crawl under the table, screened by the company of bystanders present at the séance. In Professor Jastrow's words : " From these favoured positions they observed the levitations, their eyes close to the left foot of Palladino, which proved to be the telekinetic instrument of uplift." One of the observers reported : " I was lying with my face on the floor within *eight inches* of the left leg of the table ; and each time that the table was lifted whether in a partial or a complete levitation, the medium's foot was used as a propelling force upward."[5]

At another séance the investigators deliberately exercised lax control and the " phenomena " occurred abundantly. Then at a pre-arranged signal the control was made fully effective. The " phenomena " ceased immediately. Palladino made every effort to throw the observers off their guard but to no avail—she no longer controlled

---

[5] Jastrow, J., *Wish and Wisdom*, p. 146, N.Y. 1935.

the conditions of the investigation. Her controllers, experienced conjurors, gently but firmly blocked all attempt at substitution of hand or foot.

Palladino's career of fraud was rapidly drawing to its predestined close. Her soft leather boots with the wide flanges on the soles, which she generally wore at her séances, soon ceased to mystify the scientific world. William James aptly summed up the verdict of the faithful but disillusioned devotees of psychical research : " Eusapia's type of performance is detestable—if it be not fraud simulating reality, it is reality simulating fraud." [6]

Hereward Carrington's faith in his protégè remained unshaken. His was a faith indeed ; more than ever are we in a position to estimate the psychological factors which aided Palladino at the eleven séances at Naples. Yet so effective was his work that today thousands regard Palladino as one of the great enigmas of the past. Such a belief is totally irrational. In the early days of the Palladino investigations Hodgson, Moll and Dessoir had described the tricks employed by Palladino to effect her " phenomena ". At the Cambridge investigation held under the aegis of the S.P.R. their forecasts were proved correct. Fourteen years later, in New York, Palladino was shown to have scarcely varied her methods in all that time. With the failure of the combined efforts of Palladino and her believers to justify her claims the whole case for the physical " phenomena " of spiritualism collapses—for hers was, undoubtedly, the test case.

---

[6] *Journ. Am. S.P.R.*, 29, 1935, p. 287.

Chapter Twenty-two

WATER DIVINING AND OTHER FORMS OF "DOWSING"

WATER DIVINING, or *dowsing* as it is generally called by those who practise it, still remains for many a fascinating enigma—savouring both of the occult and the practical. All over the world the dowsing fraternity are to be found. Their reputation is an odd one, for they themselves believe in occult or pseudo-scientific powers and forces which the scientific world rejects as naïve and absurd. But perhaps the question to which the average layman (and the scientist) would most like an answer is whether or not water divining is a possibility. The answer to such a question naturally depends on the interpretation given to the word "divining." If it is simply taken to mean the detection of underground water with the aid of a forked twig or similar apparatus, then indeed the claims of the water diviners are by no means to be scoffed at. But to impute anything occult or mystical to the process of detecting water by such means would be totally wrong. There is nothing about dowsing for water which cannot be accounted for in terms of present day psychology.

On the question of the abilities of water diviners in general we can do no better than to quote from the experience of a practical Australian farmer, Mr. N. A. Roddatz of Queensland, Australia. In the Queensland bush, he states, writing in *The Wide World* magazine, dowsers or water-diviners are almost as common as "cattle-ticks." The majority of them are amateurs whom the wise man avoids like the plague; but most districts also have a professional.

Can these dowsers really find water ?   Writes Mr. Roddatz :

" Without a doubt some of them can, but a great many more
can't.   Some fellows honestly believe they possess the gift, others
merely delude themselves, and a minority are just charlatans.   But
there remain a few star performers whose records prove incontestibly
that they are able to locate underground streams and even indicate
pretty accurately at what depth the spring will be reached."

This opinion excellently sums up the situation.   Relatively
few dowsers have acquired the gift of being able to locate
underground water by dowsing ; the great majority merely
delude themselves that they can.

The term " to dowse " most likely originated in the sea-
bound peninsula of Cornwall, whither the use of the forked
rod was introduced by German miners during the days
of Queen Elizabeth in order to prospect for tin.   The term
has a variety of meanings in Cornwall, but its connection
with ore and water divination probably derived from the
widespread colloquialism to " dowse a sail," meaning to
lower sail, the word being borrowed to describe the dipping
action of the divining rod.

It is interesting to note that there are relatively few
records of dowsing for *water* in Western Europe before the
eighteenth century.   It has, in fact, been suggested that
the use of the divining rod was transferred to water-finding
with the decline of tin mining in Cornwall.   Before this
period dowsing was used almost entirely for locating mineral
ores such as iron.

European dowsing probably reached its most efficient
use in the fifteenth century in the Harz Mountains of Germany, where prospectors employed dowsers to prospect
for metallic lodes.   Subterranean metallic ores, as is well
known, often show easily observable signs of their presence on the surface, such as discolouration and their effects
on vegetation.   This is only true, however, when the ores
are not far from the surface.   The medieval dowser of metallic ores undoubtedly found his services useful in the
location of subterranean ores which were sufficiently far
below the surface to reveal their presence only by slight
and scarcely perceptible traces ; for it is these that constitute the basis of the dowser's art.

The literature of dowsing is a vast one and to the un-initiated it offers a surprising wealth of technical and scientific terms. It should, however, be emphasised that the bulk of the theories, claims and observations in dowsing literature constitute some of the most portentous nonsense ever printed. Any investigation of the subject must therefore be undertaken in complete disregard of the views of the dowsers themselves, for very few have the remotest idea of the *modus operandi* of their art. In brief, the traditions and beliefs involving mysticism and pseudo-scientific theory must be distinguished from the ascertain-able facts. The fascination of dowsing for the layman lies in the intriguing mixture of the practical with the mystical ; so it is with a considerable sense of regret that we find the latter component to be without any valid foundations.

Water and mineral dowsing is usually accomplished by means of a forked twig of some suitable springy wood. Choice of wood is not confined to hazel or willow as tradition would have it ; metal springs, forked metal rods, in fact almost anything at all has, at one time or another, been used. The traditional belief in the special efficacy or hazel or willow twigs derives from their affinity with water and the mistaken assumption that some mysterious force eman-ating from the water acts directly upon the rod itself.

The belief that the water in some incomprehensible way " attracts " the rod is still largely prevalent among dowsers. This is not difficult to understand. The dowser generally holds the twin ends of the forked rod in such a way that they remain bent outwards at an angle ; with springy wood this bending imparts a very considerable torsion and a low degree of natural stability. A relatively slight movement of one of the hands in the right direction results in the apex of the twig twisting strongly downwards or upwards, often with considerable violence—the bark not infrequently peeling off in the palm of the hand. To any-one who tries dowsing for the first time the unexpected force of the rod's motion gives rise to a deceptively convinc-ing sensation of the rod being moved by an extraneous force. This illusion is not likely to be experienced, however, unless the expectation of such a force is already present in the dowser's mind.

The movement of the dowsing rod in the hands of a true dowser is but another instance of those subconsciously executed muscular movements upon which we have already touched in the chapter on automatic writing and which come under the general heading of *motor automatism.* Spelling out words and sentences by means of the pendulum, ouija-board and table-tilting are, in those cases where the movements are not faked, achieved by the same means. It is therefore not surprising to find that the dowsing rod can be satisfactorily employed for the same purposes. Barrett and Besterman quote an instance of this in *The Divining Rod.*[1] The method he adopted is as follows :

" The rod is held at forehead, almost vertical. Questions are asked in usual tone and pitch of voice. For ' Yes ' the rod moves forward and downward. For ' No ' the rod moves backward and downward." An interesting point is that the answers were sometimes given in morse-code, " a tremor representing a dot, a sharp downward stroke the dash !"

The forked rod of the dowser merely serves to register and magnify small automatic movements of the arm and wrist made independently of the conscious volition of the operator. The motion of the divining rod imparted by these automatic muscular movements serves to bring before the dowser's conscious mind the knowledge of the whereabouts of water which he acquires subconsciously. With this the majority of educated dowsers fully agree. The point of contention arises, however, over the way in which this subconscious cognition occurs ; it is this vexed question which has hitherto constituted the main mystery of dowsing phenomena. Before we go into this problem, however, it would perhaps be convenient at this point to review the problem of dowsing in some of its more general aspects

---

[1] p. 266.

PLATE X.   How the Divining Rod is Held (III)

Another commonly used method of water-divining.

PLATE XI. ZENER OR "ESP" CARDS

Used in telepathy and clairvoyant experiments.

(*See Chapter* 24)

THE AUTHENTICITY OF DOWSING

A great many people still believe all dowsing to be mere superstition inherited from a past age. This is far from the case. A great deal of confusion on the subject of dowsing is caused by the fact that almost everyone who discovers that he can obtain automatic or involuntary movements with a rod or pendulum imagines that he can " divine " water. In the great majority of cases there is no connection between the one thing and the other. The truth of the matter is that very few of those individuals who are able to acquire the gift of automatic movements of the divining rod are able to dowse successfully for water. Nevertheless, against the myriads who falsely believe themselves to possess the genuine gift of dowsing, there are a few exceptional individuals who have demonstrated beyond all doubt their ability to find water even under the most inauspicious circumstances.

There are many cases on record where the dowser has succeeded in locating water after expert geologists had failed to find any. Even today rural district councils still resort to the professional dowser on occasion, and hundreds of excellent and well-authenticated testimonials from private individuals and commercial firms bear witness to the value of the dowser's work. [1] The Italian army during the Abyssinian war even included among their water-supply companies an establishment of experienced dowsers.

The geologists as a whole decry, and with considerable justification, the employment of dowsers to find water. Yet although the dowser's art is uncertain and often inaccurate, a professional geologist has summed up his experience as follows :

> " When doubt exists as to whether sinking will yield water, or when great depths may have to be sunk, the services of a water diviner are very useful. Water divining is a gift ; and very few practise this art and some of these are not reliable. On the whole however, much reliance can be placed on a first-class man." [2]

---

[1] See Barrett and Besterman, *The Divining Rod*, 1926 ; also Besterman, T., *Water-Divining*, 1938.

[2] Taylor, F. N., *Small Water Supplies*, p. 23.

The opinion of the famous physicist, Sir J. J. Thompson, is well worth noting. He sets down the following interesting anecdote :

"There is no doubt of the reality of the dowsing effect. In fact, in many agricultural districts the dowser is the man they call in when they want to find the right place to dig a well, and he very often succeeds. We had an example of this at Trinity College. The water supply to one of our farms was very defective and a new well badly wanted. At first the Senior Bursar, who was a Fellow of the Royal Society, proceeded in the orthodox way and employed eminent geologists to report on where we ought to sink a well. Their advice, however, did not lead to the discovery of any water. Our land agent said, "If I were you, I would try old X, who has found a good many wells in this county and who will sink the well on the terms ' no water, no pay." As there seemed nothing else to be done, the Bursar employed him and he found water."[3]

Perhaps the most successful of all water-diviners has been Major C. A. Pogson, for whose services the Government of Bombay had petitioned the Secretary of State for India. As official Water-Diviner to the Government of Bombay, Major Pogson successfully passed the six months period of probation and remained in this post from October 1925 to the end of December 1928. His services were required in connection with famine relief and he was held responsible for the provision of water supplies to farms and villages in some of the most chronically drought-stricken areas in India. In such areas the usual method of well-boring, even by the most modern methods, generally failed.

Major Pogson's success amply confirms the reality of the dowsing faculty beyond any dispute, for he operated in "tracts where wells sunk haphazard have very little chance of striking water and where consequently nearly all such wells result in complete and absolute failure ". [4] His appointment was not made without opposition or criticism, but as *The Times* pointed out :

"When the Bombay Legislative Council was sitting recently there was much criticism of the Government's appointment of Major Pogson as a water diviner. The facts now published show how suc-

---

[3] Thompson, J. J., *Recollections and Reflections*, p. 159.
[4] *Report on the Work of the Water Diviner to the Government of Bombay for the Year* 1927, p. 1.

cessful Major Pogson has been and how fully he has justified his appointment at a high salary." [5]

The following day the *Indian Journal of Engineering* commented ruefully :

" It is a somewhat bitter pill to engineers to be told by an evening contemporary that a major is better than machines, yet there is more than a mickle of justification for this clever newspaper head. The point revolves around a review of the work accomplished by Major Pogson, the water diviner who was appointed by the Government of Bombay in the face of a deal of criticism. Major Pogson can find water, it appears, when the machines specially designed for the purpose have failed. It is an interesting situation. Out of 49 wells which have been sunk upon spots indicated by Major Pogson only two have failed to produce water. It is a notable achievement."

The wells referred to above were sunk in the districts of Ahmednagar, Sholapur and Bijapur where the water scarcity was most acute. In these districts the countryside is redundant with wells that have never yielded a drop of water. In view of this factor it is interesting to note that ten months after Major Pogson's appointment the Bombay " Government guaranteed the success of the water-diviner to the extent that if water was not struck in any of the sites pointed out by him a cultivator would be recompensed 50 per cent of his expenses up to a sum of Rs. 400 ". Within the next twelve months only one had to be made " and in this particular case water actually was tapped but dwindled down to a small quantity when further blasting was resorted to. [7]

The difficulties Major Pogson had to contend with were enhanced by the fact that the

" majority of the bores have been sunk in localities not where normal boring by chance methods prove successful, but in places where bores sunk at random have little or no chance of striking water owing to the fact that in these zones the underground supplies are flowing in defined currents, and unless the bore is sunk on these currents, the result is a failure." [8]

---

[5] *The Times*, April 30th, 1926.
[6] May 1st, 1926.
[7] *Report on the Work of the Water Diviner to the Government of Bombay for the Year* 1927.
[8] *Report the Work of the Water Diviner to the Government of Bombay for the Period October* 1925 *to January* 1927.

Major Pogson's spectacular success was not due to particular local knowledge, for previously his work had carried him far afield to other parts of India including the Nilgiris, Rajputana and the North-West Frontier. Nor, it seems, was he the only Government dowser known, for the 1927 Government report on his work makes reference to the methods of an officially appointed water diviner in Australia.

As noted before, individuals who find a dowsing-rod turning involuntarily in their hands immediately believe themselves to be capable of divining water. Nothing is further from the truth. Automatic movements of the dowsing rod may often be achieved with adequate practise and even their spontaneous occurrence seldom means that the person concerned is a potential dowser.

It cannot be emphasised too strongly that the majority of practising dowsers do *not* possess any exceptional gift of finding water—except in circumstances where the veriest beginner could scarcely fail. It is significant that the cult of dowsing, at least in Western Europe, flourishes at its brightest in those parts of the country where it is rather more likely than not that water will be found at random. In such districts " success " is virtually assured if the *soi-disant* dowser has some idea of the conditions under which water is usually found locally. Relatively few dowsers will be found in areas where water is scarce. Dowsing flourishes mainly in districts in which water exists in sheets of water-bearing strata, where almost any bore which is excavated below a certain depth will find water ; the water from the saturated strata surrounding the bore simply percolates into the bore.

Naturally the " successes " of the dowser under such conditions usually confirms his belief in himself. Furthermore, any failures he may meet are readily accounted for by any one of a number of stock excuses which satisfy him completely. Failures in any event are soon forgotten, while his successes are remembered.

The great fallacy of dowsing lies in the dowser's general tendency to think that almost all underground water is confined to running streams. Even in areas well-known to lie above a saturated and porous substratum, the dowser will trace the course of numerous imaginary streams, often for long distances. At a suitable spot, perhaps at the confluence of two or more of his " underground streams ", he will strike his marker into the ground. This indicates the point at which the well is to be sunk. When the well begins to fill, he regards it as proof positive that he has traced the courses of his " streams " correctly.

In such circumstances the only valid test for the demonstration of the genuine dowsing faculty is for the dowser to find water in areas where water is known to be extremely scarce. Such tests are impracticable for it will usually mean the sinking of a dozen or more wells and gauging the percentage of successes. The often tried water-pipe test, in which the dowser has to locate running water in underground pipes, is virtually useless since it is based on the dowser's own mistaken beliefs in regard to his own powers. As will be seen later, failure to pass such water-pipe tests does not constitute proof of the dowser's inability to find water under natural conditions.

THE MODUS OPERANDI OF DOWSING

We now return to the question of how the genuine dowsing expert locates the existence of underground water. He walks along holding a forked twig or rod in front of him. Suddenly it dips, indicating (to him) the likelihood of water below the surface. As explained, this movement of the rod is due merely to a subconsciously directed automatic movement of the dowser's arms or wrists. How does he gain his information about the presence of underground water, without which the dipping (or rising) of the rod would be totally ineffective? Put briefly, the art of dowsing may be said to consist mainly in the subconscious registration and interpretation of certain relevant *indicia* and their emergence into consciousness by means of a psychological automatism. The success of the true dowser lies in his subconscious powers of observation.

It is problematical whether there is any marked degree of mental dissociation involved in the operation of the genuine dowsing faculty. This would undoubtedly be the case if any evidence of hysteria were present. But the absence of hysterical symptoms does not preclude the existence of dissociation, since, as has been seen in the case of automatic writing, automatic actions involving marked dissociation can be acquired with practice. In view of the evidence the existence of at least some degree of dissociation must be assumed, for the registration and interpretation of various sensory stimuli appears to be carried out subconsciously while conscious thought-processes play merely a secondary rôle. The actual muscular automatism involved in the dipping action of the rod certainly implies some degree of dissociation.

With some dowsers the element of dissociation may be very considerable, analogous to certain hypnotic states. It is well-known that in the hypnotic state certain subjects experience a heightening of the sensory faculties—the senses of sight, hearing, touch and smell may become abnormally acute. This hyperacuity of the senses—mistakenly called hyperaesthesia—is not due to any increase in sensitiveness of the sensory nerve endings (as in the case of true hyperaesthesia). It results from purely psychological factors, and in hypnosis is due to an increase in powers of observation, discrimination, attentiveness and concentration with regard to that portion of the total situation exhibited to the senses and upon which the attention is focused—a process known as *hyperprosexia*.

Hyperprosexia may be developed to a great extent by practise and training. In certain instances virtually the maximum limits of human powers of observation may be reached, and this may be accompanied by a high degree of virtuosity in the interpretation of minute *indicia*. An excellent example of such a process is provided by the extraordinary skill of the aboriginal trackers of Australia. They can detect and interpret minute cues which are literally invisible to the untrained white man, with a speed and sureness that is truly amazing ; yet it has been established that the actual eye of the black tracker is no more sensitive or hyperaesthetic than that of the average white man. Indeed the comparison of the methods of the aboriginal tracker with those of the dowser is a good one, with the essential difference that a great part of the dowser's observation and interpretation of faint sensory cues is carried out subconsciously—the knowledge thus assimilated being brought before his conscious attention by means of automatic muscular movements magnified by the forked rod.

The dowser's subconscious observations and sensory awareness of relevant *indicia* can not be totally differentiated from those conscious processes of observation and calculation which all successful dowsers must employ to at least some degree. The subconscious mental functions of every one of us are normally geared to the needs and activities of the conscious personality. They are linked together to produce the maximum efficiency. It is the same with the dowser in action, except that his subconscious mental processes have a tendency to manifest themselves, not by what is generally called " intuition "—i.e. a spontaneous influx of ideas into his mind derived from what he has observed subconsciously ; but through the media of intelligible automatic movements. This transition can be attributed largely to the influence of suggestion, the basis of which lies in a combination of belief, tradition, expectation and example.

Probably some of the more experienced dowsers do not always rely on subconsciously registered indications and subconscious motor automatism for the detection of water or metal ores. With increasing attention paid consciously by the dowser to the topography and geology of the district, the reliance on subconscious observations must necessarily come to take a secondary place. One may suspect that the actions of the forked rod are not always involuntary and that its dipping or rising action is sometimes maintained for the sake of mystifying onlookers and for the prestige which always accompanies a successful demonstration of the occult.

What are the surface *indicia* denoting the presence of water which the true dowser's undoubted hyperprosexic faculty enables him to register and assess so accurately ? Since this side of dowsing has never been properly investigated, we can only deduce what these indications are : *viz.* slight modifications in the colour of the soil and vegetation ; scarcely perceptible changes in the health and the growth of grasses, plants, shrubs and trees, particular attention being paid to the spread and direction of their roots ; the type of vegetation ; texture and dampness of the soil, including the

" feel " of the ground underfoot ; differences of temperature in the atmosphere.

It is fairly certain that the senses of smell and hearing play a part in many instances of successful dowsing. Many animals are known to be able to sense water from long distances by means of their sense of smell, and there seems no reason why human beings who possess a highly developed olfactory sense should not be able to do the same at short distances. The view that this sense plays a considerable part in the dowser's detection of underground water which lies near the surface, or which has partial access to the surrounding air, receives some support from the fact that dowsing in many country districts, particularly in America, is known as " water-smelling ". Longstanding country traditions very often have some basis in fact.

The dowser's task is often rendered simpler when the substratum and sub-soil over which he is operating is naturally absorbent. The ground surface is then likely to be damp in the neighbourhood of a subterranean stream and the presence of the water may the more easily be detected by such factors as the growth and character of the vegetation, by the temperature of the surrounding air and by the characteristic smell of damp earth.

Many underground streams are audible to the normal ear, particularly when the stream is near the surface or descends through a fault in the rock substratum. To the dowser with a highly developed auditory sense the " hearing " of underground water would often be a very effective method of detecting its presence. It is also possible that some dowsers can detect the presence of large underground streams or falls near the surface by the vibration of the ground underfoot. In this connection the ability of many of the deaf-blind to detect ground vibrations is of considerable interest. With some dowsers the ability to detect water via the senses of small and hearing may possibly be linked with an element of true hyperaesthesia.

All the various surface *indicia* by which the dowser senses the presence of water may be so minute as to be impractical as guides to the average person. The ability to detect such *indicia* is—to use a term frequently applied in this instance— a " gift ". It is well known that sensory stimuli have to attain a certain intensity before they can enter the threshold of consciousness. Stimuli of insufficient intensity cannot do so, but there is a borderland region in which diffuse stimuli of low intensity may affect the individual subconsciously, and which are often responsible for intuitions, vague premonitions, " inspired " guesses and the like ; the sights, sounds and smells are not consciously registered as such but give rise to a vague feeling of awareness which cannot be specifically traced to any recognised cause. It is in this borderland region that the true dowser finds his metier. His subconscious impressions are conveniently brought to the light of consciousness by the unusual psychological device of a subconsciously operated muscular response—an automatic movement of his arms, wrists, hands or fingers which is magnified by means of his rod.

Many of the surface *indicia* may be quite large enough to be noticed by any normal person. The best dowsers consciously utilise these indications. But with other dowsers a mechanism of repression may operate which gives rise to an element of mental dissociation. The repression factor may, as noted before, result from the influence of suggestion. A few dowsers are liable to marked dissociation and may even walk around in a state of minor trance ; but they are not very proficient where large areas have to be surveyed. The trance state is almost certainly due to hysterical tendencies, and this factor alone renders such dowsers unreliable, since they are constitutionally incapable of attaining that degree of practical application without which the dowsing " gift " is uncertain and only sporadically successful.

The really expert dowser—necessarily one of long experience—does not rely only on his subconscious powers of observation. All his knowledge, experience and reasoning powers are brought to bear on the problem in hand. For this reason it is a mistake to believe that the ignorant uneducated " natural " dowser is the most successful. The fact is that the most consistently successful dowsers are men or women of good education, with a good capacity for reasoned calculation. Many have a working knowledge of geology ; and in all cases years of practical endeavour, with its inevitable sequence of successes and failures, constitute the background of their training.

Such high-class dowsers are extremely practical in their attitude to their work except in regard to one thing, namely the explanation of their faculty. Their explanations vary between clairvoyance and pseudo-scientific theories of electromagnetic radiations which are supposed to act on the body of the individual as if it were a mechanical robot! This latter theory is, of course, completely untenable. The former theory is nearer the mark if we substitute " subconscious observation" for the term clairvoyance. Plainly the dowser's fanciful theories must reduce his efficiency. Sometimes, however, the resultant metrical conventions to which they give rise may undoubtedly contribute in *some* respects to the dowser's accuracy.

The building up of a reliable dowsing technique is a long and difficult process. After a period of many years' experience the expert dowser will generally admit he has plenty to learn. The observations of Mrs. Norah Millen are of considerable interest here. Mrs. Millen, a dowser of many years' experience, carried out a considerable amount of work as official dowser to the Government of Ceylon during the last war, between 1941 and 1945. Like nearly all dowsers, her explanations of her faculty combine naïve mysticism with pseudo-scientific jargon. Her method of working, however, savours of the practise born of experience. She states that she possessed a working knowledge of Ceylon, its topography, weather and water supplies, gathered over a period of many years. Her equipment included compass, survey maps, surveyor's tape and notebooks. She claims that the requirements of a dowser should include " an almost microscopic memory for natural detail ", and refers to her own ability rapidly to " assess and differentiate " her impressions ; she emphasizes the necessity of constantly developing one's natural gifts on constructive lines. All this appears far removed from the outlook of the rustic dowser of tradition. Some dowsers even state that a working knowledge of geology is indispensible.

Mrs. Millen states that she works at high speed, finding it difficult to work slowly. The action of the rod occurs involuntarily. Meanwhile she notes and interprets its movements, registers " visually every detail of the land from a practical standpoint ", mentally makes her own assessments and, as the need arises, gives " verbal directions for marking, measurements and stakings to be done *en route* ". She also " dictates notes which are written down for . . . use in drafting the day's report later". The forked twig held in her two hands will, she adds, revolve at great speed when over large volumes of water. [1]

Enough has been written to show that to dowse with consistent success years of practice and training are necessary. Few reach this standard—although a great many individuals can obtain involuntary movements from their sensitively equilibriated rods and therefore imagine they are potential dowsers. Even then, and with the best of them, consistent success is not attainable. The " perfect dowser " does not exist and in the very nature of things is an impossibility.

It is not really surprising that dowsers are not cognizant of either the basic nature of their faculty or the limitations of their art. So far as the present writer is aware, this is the first time that a comprehensive review of the subject from the rational standpoint has been essayed, although at one time or another most of the principles expounded in these pages have been fragmentarily enunciated for nearly a century. The physicist Sir William Barrett, who spent a great deal of time investigating water-divining, clearly saw that the movements of the divinging rod were due to involuntary motor automatism " giving physical and visible expression to a mental and abstract cognition ". [2]

In a memorandum on the subject he explained how this cognition might be obtained :

" Underground water and metallic ores are often indicated by surface signs, imperceptible to the ordinary observer, but which become known to the experienced dowser. Such indications, even when not consciously perceived, may create a subconscious impression on the dowser that will excite the automatic motion of his rod."

Unfortunately, faulty procedure in his own experiments produced results which led him to accept Richet's theory of " cryptesthesia " or clairvoyance as the main operative factor in successful dowsing.

[1] Journ. B.S.D., March, 1946
[2] Barrett and Besterman, *The Divining Rod*, p. 268.

Professor J. Jastrow has pithily enunciated the *modus operandi* of dowsing as " involuntary movements founded on subconsciously registered indications ". Dr. Millais Culpin also pointed out that dowsing reactions are a form of psychological automatism produced unwittingly by the muscular action of the subject, and he indicated his belief that a number of dowsers are affected by a state of dissociation. The successes of dowsing he attributes to " a super-acuity of the senses, in the presence of a mental dissociation ". [b]

But since a great deal of the attraction of dowsing lies in its mystery such rational explanations as the above are anathema to most of the divining fraternity, and there is little doubt that many years will pass before the march of reason ousts the present naïve conceptions which brighten the lives of so many !

THE PROBLEM OF DOWSING TESTS

Despite the reasonably consistent success of some dowsers the gift of successful dowsing is not so widespread as those who practice the art would have us believe. It is an unfortunate fact that the majority of well-conducted experimental tests have produced negative or inconclusive results and in consequence the scientific world has turned its back on dowsing altogether. Part of the reason for this is that the geologists, physicists and hydrologists who have conducted these tests are not qualified for this type of investigation.

The individual best qualified to test the powers of the dowser is the psychologist, for the " mystery " of dowsing lies mainly in the sphere of psychological automatism, sensory perception, and, to a certain extent, subconscious ratiocination. When dowsers continually make reference to mysterious psychic powers or the action of electromagnetic fields and radiations, it is obvious nonsense. Nevertheless their tendency to think along those lines has had the result that almost invariably the wrong kind of experimental tests have been applied. The dowser's insistence that his faculty is due to something hitherto unknown to the world of science has led to his being tested for powers which it is quite certain

---

he does not possess. This undoubtedly accounts for a good many of the test failures. Again, through ignorance of what is involved the dowser has often succeeded in other types of experimental test, for the simple reason that the experimenters have remained unaware of the precautions necessary to render the tests valid.

An example of the kind of test which the dowser fails to pass is that in which he is asked to find the position and direction of a number of water pipes buried underground. Unless he has a hyperaesthetic sense of hearing and can hear the water running, he will not succeed in locating the pipes, for the usual slight surface indications upon which he relies will be lacking. Land drainage pipes whose segments are not joined together would offer a better proposition to the dowser ; similarly iron water pipes in the open country where the ground is more or less undisturbed might also offer him a chance, if not buried too far underground, through the effects of the metal on the vegetation or soil directly above it.

Pipes under road surfaces or concrete are useless for test purposes. If the pipes have been laid down after the concrete or asphalt, the signs will be there for all to see ; if the reverse, the dowser will inevitably fail if the tests are properly conducted.

An excellent series of dowsing experiments with water pipes were carried out by Professor G. Wertheimer in 1906. [1] His conclusion was that the " experiments do not answer definitely the question whether or not dowsers have the power to find water ". His subjects were all well-known dowsers. One of his experiments involved turning the water off and on at the main at times unknown to the dowser. The dowsers were supposed to be able to " divine " when the water was flowing through the pipe and when it was still. Naturally such a test as this, *although believed by the dowsers themselves to be completely in their powers*, bears little relation to the facts of dowsing. Only by auditory hyperaesthesia could the dowser gain the requisite sensory cues, while the evidence points to the fact that he relies mainly on his sense of vision to gain the information he requires.

---

[1] *Experiments with " Waterfinders,"* Water (supplement), Nov. 15th., 1906.

Another water-pipe test was organised by a special committee of scientists and specialists who investigated the subject of dowsing at the instigation of the journal *The Sanitary Record and Municipal Engineering*. [2] This committee came to much the same conclusions as Professor Wertheimer, i.e. that the experiments were inconclusive. The committee stated in its report that such evidence as was forthcoming for the ability to find water was " not sufficiently definite and trustworthy to be of much practical value ". While this verdict is fair enough in regard to the abilities of the majority of dowsers, it does not do justice to the expert dowser whose value has been proved often enough in all parts of the world.

The conclusion cannot be avoided that dowsing tests are impractical undertakings. The only genuine and convincing tests would be to put a dowser in a district where water is extremely scarce and tell him to find water. As Major Pogson has shown, this is the type of situation where the expert dowser has already been able to prove his worth.

Another aspect of dowsing tests is that the dowser may obtain his cues from unconscious movements of bystanders or the testers themselves. If those in charge of the experiments know the spot under which water lies, it would not require a dowser to find it ; any vaudeville " muscle-reader " would be able to do the same.

There is one type of " experiment " popular among dowsers themselves. A number of cups are laid on the floor, one of which is filled with water. Saucers are laid over each cup and one of the company attempts to " divine " which of the cups contains the water. Another variation is for a coin to be placed under one of a number of saucers or under a carpet. Since at least one, if not all of the company present, usually knows which saucer conceals the water or coin, or the position of the coin under the carpet, the dowser can often locate them, being guided by the unconscious reactions of those watching.

The same principle is used by the vaudeville telepathist who finds articles hidden upon the persons of those in the audience. It is dowsing " successes " such as these which

[2] *The Water Divining Demonstration*, ibid., April 11th., 1913, pp. 365-368 ; May 2nd. , pp. 462-466.

foster and perpetuate naïve beliefs in occult and " electro-magnetic " theories of dowsing—those concerned being unable to account for their success in any other way.

It is plainly a prime requisite of all dowsing experiments that no one present shall be aware of the location of the water or object to be " divined ". The saucer test is in any event quite useless—although it is remotely possible that by talking or singing the dowser could distinguish differences in tone provided by the reflection of the sound waves from the saucers or cups in much the same way as some of the blind locate the position of objects in the room. In the absence of *all* sensory cues the diviner is quite lost.

Tests devised to exclude all sensory cues are a waste of time. It follows from this that there must be numerous cases under field conditions where the dowser is helpless, as (for example) where a stratum of impermeable rock intervenes between the surface of the ground and the underlying water. Under certain conditions, of course, even this difficulty might be overcome, particularly if the dowser possesses a consider-able knowledge of geology. The modern geologist is quite capable of "divining" water on his own account, if by "divin-ing " one can mean using methods of observation and deduc-tion without the use of instruments. The trained expert geologist of long experience could certainly compete with all but the most practised and experienced of dowsers in most kinds of terrain—though not in all—solely by the use of observation and scientific methods of deduction. With a great many types of geological formation the expert geologist can easily find water without employing instruments or apparatus where the best dowser would be reduced to mere guesswork. On the other hand, it is equally true that the high-class dowser, through his exceptional powers of observing minute *indicia*, is perfectly capable of beating the geologist at his own game where the geological formations are un-favourable to the latter. And this is probably the case when it occurs that the dowser succeeds after the geologist has already tried and failed. A great deal, naturally, depends on the experience and skill of the geologist.

Where the geologist gains all round, however, is in the deducing of the existence of water at depths totally beyond the powers of the dowser. Using scientific techniques of observation based on sound technical knowledge, geologists have been known to make remarkably accurate estimates at depths of the order of a thousand feet. This is certainly beyond the ability of any dowser who is an untrained geologist.

There is no doubt at all that many of the dowser's successes can be attributed to local geological knowledge picked up at hazard through observation during the course of his work in his own locality or neighbouring districts. A dowser who has made hundreds of trials at locating underground water may gain a considerable working knowledge of local rock formations, types of soil and substrata and their relation to the finding of water. His successes and failures, combined with a good memory, would enable him to arrive at a fair geological knowledge of the terrain around his own locality. This factor should not be ignored when the dowser is under test.

ROD REACTIONS AND METRICAL CONVENTIONS

The dowser can quite often estimate the depth of an underground spring or pool with reasonable accuracy, particularly if the water lies within a comparatively short distance from the surface. Such estimations are never consistently successful and become even less so if the depth exceeds the neighbourhood of thirty or forty feet. Yet reasonably accurate estimations of depth have been made up to the hundred foot mark, though in such cases it is not possible to say how far an element of luck enters into the matter or to what degree the dowser is utilising his knowledge of geology.

In estimating depth the dowser will either make a consciously calculated estimate based on past experience, or else he may make use of a personal code or metrical convention based on the strength, speed and number of revolutions involved in the motions of the rod. So much nonsense has been written about these personal metrical codes that it is hard to estimate their value. The rod turns by the involuntary motor automatism of the dowser's arms and wrists. If he can subconsciously assess the depth of a subterranean stream with reasonable accuracy, there is no reason why a system of mental indexing should not be used to externalise this assessment by means of the rod's motion. If, for example, the rod turns in the dowser's hand three and a half times and, according to his code, a full turn equals ten feet, then it is evident that he has subconsciously assessed the depth of the stream to be about thirty-five feet. Similar conventions are used for externalising subconscious impressions re the volume of water and also direction of flow.

In most countries the conventional motion of the rod is forwards and down, but in a few it is up and back. Some dowsers, however, employ both these motions as a means of externalising their subconscious impressions concerning the direction of flow. Again, the strength or speed of the rod's movement is often taken to be an indication of the volume of water which the dowser has located. Yet again, the dowser may make shift to give the rate of flow in gallons per minute by using the same conventional codes.

The verdict on the use of these personal metrical devices must be that only the expert dowser of many years' standing could possibly use them to any degree of reliability, and then he must be able to assess whether or not the information which his rod imparts is to be trusted. There is nothing unacceptable in the idea that the subconscious mind can conform to a memorised system of metrical conventions with considerable accuracy ; nor is there anything particularly strange in its ability to use these mental scales of reference as channels of externalisation. No one need be surprised at such faculties of the subconscious mind for we are already acquainted with such phenomena as hypermnesia and the accurate estimation of time-intervals ; the subconscious " lightning calculation " of difficult mathematic problems by some child prodigies also helps to place the problem in correct perspective.

Some dowsers use a pendulum instead of a rod. The pendulum is a far more sensitive instrument than the forked divining-rod, but it has the disadvantage that it can only be used while the dowser is standing still. The pendulum will register the tiniest involuntary movements of the hand, and as is well-known, any simple idea in the mind can be reflected to some extent in the movements of the pendulum. Ideomotor movements should, properly speaking, be differentiated from the true motor-automatism ; they are, so to speak, motor-automatisms in embryo. Nevertheless, much the same types of metrical convention are used by pendulum-dowsers as with rod-dowsers. The various movements of the pendulum—to and fro, lateral, circular, elliptoid, clockwise and anti-clockwise, the extent of the arc described—all may be attributed a specific meaning, and by a process of autosuggestion become the channels whereby the subconsciously acquired impressions are objectified. The conscious mind of the dowser can then interpret without difficulty the movements of the pendulum, or the rod, held in front of him.

To acquire a suitable series of conventions whereby the reactions of rod or pendulum come to have a specific meaning may be a matter of training, invention or even chance, or it may be simply picked up through copying the personal metrical codes of other dowsers. It is a great drawback that all classes of dowser—those who merely delude themselves that they possess the gift, those who are charlatans or merely incompetent, even most of the experts—all write of their dowsing experiences as if the reactions of their rods and their metrical conventions were infallible. Nothing could be further from the truth ; the ideal robot dowser does not exist and the pretence of infallibility renders all such claims suspect.

The method of externalising subconscious impressions via an automatic code of conventional reactions is quite obviously an excellent one *provided it works*. To be able to give an indication of not only the location of the subterranean water but also its depth, volume, direction and rate of flow is most desirable. But to estimate these further factors is far harder than merely to locate the vertical position of water. Without the necessary clues upon which to base such an estimate— a good knowledge of geology would help enormously—no system of mental indexing or technique of externalisation will make up the lack. A few really good dowsers use systematised codes of rod-reactions regularly and to undoubted advantage ; but the majority of dowsers tend to think of all underground water in terms of *streams*, which makes one sceptical of the value of most such reaction-codes.

RADIESTHESIA

The claims of many of the dowsing fraternity brook no limits. With rod or pendulum they are able, as a perusal of their journals and literature will show, to forecast the future, dowse for water or minerals from plans and maps, sex eggs, diagnose and cure disease, detect thieves or missing persons, discover forces, fields, rays and beams galore, and explore the most intimate processes of the molecule and the atom with a degree of accuracy which must for long remain the envy of modern physical science. No literature in the world is so fantastic as the literature of dowsing, and all the books and articles have an air of earnestness and veracity which, were it not for the naïve blending of sympathetic magic with modern scientific ideas and terminology, would assuredly compel belief.

This jumble of science, dowsing, and the occult constitutes the modern cult of " Radiesthesia ". In this particular stretch of the country of the blind the rod and pendulum are kings. Their dippings, risings, swayings, wagglings and oscillations are infallible indications of some kind of force reacting upon the sensitive dowser. Science is regularly confuted ; yet at the same time all dowsers look to science for confirmation of their theories. To all those for whom the occult holds an irresistible appeal Radiesthesia is to be recommended ; for here is magic with a difference, combining in wondrous fashion the psychic with the energy of the atom.

The bulk of so-called dowsers, *i.e.* that vast crowd of individuals who delude themselves that automatic movements with rod or pendulum proves their ability as diviners, can make no practical use of a genuine reaction-code of metrical conventions. Even those experts who use such a device to good effect go astray when they attribute to their personal code of reactions an external objectivity. For the modern cult of radiesthesia has given a spurious scientific aura to the theories and beliefs of dowsers. They see in the systematised reactions of the rod or pendulum evidence of external emanations, radiations, rays, fields and forces of attraction and repulsion. To " explain " these various " forces " they have resorted largely to concepts derived from the physics of electro-magnetism. Other dowsing enthusiasts prefer " psychic " explanations, even searching for clues among ancient Yoga literature. The results in both cases are about the same.

The theorising of dowsers has done much to discredit dowsing generally. As Th. Besterman has observed, practical success does not always carry with it the ability to explain itself. " However," he adds, " no speculation is altogether wasted in a field where ignorance is practically complete." [1] And this caustic remark is very much to the point ; dowsers, with very few exceptions, show a naïvety in regard to the fundamentals of their subject which would be inexcusable in any other type of practical undertaking.

The *magnum opus* of dowsing theory is undoubtedly Maby and Franklin's *Physics of the Divining Rod*. This large volume was reviewed in the authoritative scientific weekly, *Nature*. The reviewer concluded his thoroughly justifiable criticism of the book thus : " The theoretical section, by the second author, postulates some form of cosmic radiation resulting in electro-magnetic waves of ten metres wavelength. There seems to be no direct evidence for such waves, and the author's discussion of their polarization cannot be justified on our present physical knowledge.

" In presenting facts and theories to the scientific world, there is a well-accepted and necessary procedure. It is to be regretted that the authors have not followed this procedure, thus making the position of the scientific reviewer impossible." [2]

Needless to say, in the years which have elapsed since the publication of this " treatise ", no further advances have been forthcoming to shake the scientific world. The only comment we need make on the scientific claims put forward by radiesthetists (as dowsers now call themselves) is that their " findings " invariably lack the support of the established sciences and if true would upset the whole structure of modern physics. There seems little likelihood of that eventuality. The best grounds of criticism against the radiesthetic theories are the extreme naïvety of their basic assumptions which possess no internal consistency, lack anything approaching a logical foundation, and are generally flatly contradictory

[1] Journ. S.P.R., 1933, p. 150.
[2] *Nature*, 1940, p. 150.

to each other ; each radiesthetist possesses his own interpretation of them and every dowser produces different
results trying to apply them. Radiesthesia is in fact no
more scientific than Mesmer's " explanation " of the phenomenon of hypnotism.

The electro-magnetic or " radiesthetic " theory of dowsing
is merely a modernised version of the long-since-discredited
theories of Mesmer, Riechenbach, Blondlot and Grimes.
The historical antecedents of radiesthesia are animal-
magnetism, od-rays, N-rays, electro-biology, and the " aes-
thesiogenic agents" of Charcot and Bernheim who used
magnets and metals of various kinds to cure hysterical
patients.   All these fallacious concepts have long been known
to be due to psychological suggestion in one form or another.
When, in 1850, Grimes came over from America to exhibit
the phenomenon of electro-biology it was soon realised that
it was nothing more than hypnotism despite the fanciful
though sincere theorising.

Electro-biology, like the theory of animal-magnetism
which preceded it, well demonstrates the extraordinary
facility with which suggestion and autosuggestion may
influence experimental results, making them appear to
accord fully with the theory held by the experimenter.   The
effects on human beings claimed by Charcot and Bernheim to
be due to metals and magnets were in fact due to suggestion
alone.   This was easily shown by the observation that *any*
kind of object or substance achieved precisely the same
effects, provided the patient had first been led to believe
that the object in question was in fact a magnet.   That
magnets and metals were efficacious in curing or relieving
the symptoms of hysterical patients is but another instance of the power of suggestion.   The main requisite
for such cures is that the patient should believe in the
efficacy of the method employed.

The complicated pattern of reactions obtained by some
proponents of the cult of radiesthesia are undoubtedly due
to the dowser's particular set of preconceptions concerning
the way in which he imagines his " radiations " to operate.
His mind has accepted the suggestion of electro-magnetic
waves, fields and rays together with a number of ideas
which he has culled or conceived concerning " reaction-

bands ", polarization, " phase reversals " and the rest.
Sometimes it may occur that the theorising has taken
place subconsciously, and his rod will then demonstrate
a new series of reactions ; the dowser will then claim to have
discovered new " phenomena " or " laws " of radiesthesia.
Or if his motor automatism spontaneously produces a new
type of reaction he will try to formulate a new radiesthetic
theory of radiations and " fields of force " to account for
it.

In *The Physics of the Divining Rod* we witness the fantastic results of such theorising. This lengthy " treatise "
represents an amazing mixture of dowsing, cosmic rays
and other types of electro-magnetic radiation, sub-atomic
physics, biophysics, geophysics, meteorology and geology.
By the end of the book one is left still wondering whether
the author's freely distributed scientific claims have much
substance. From the scientific standpoint *The Physics of
the Divining Rod* cannot be said to possess the slightest
validity.

The question of " phase-reversals " is of some interest—
if it is not, in fact, merely due to the effect of autosuggestion.
It may well find a parallel with the phenomenon of mirror-
writing or *Spiegelschrift*, which often occurs in cases where
mental dissociation is manifested.

There are several different " schools " of radiesthesia
on the Continent and the followers of each adhere to their
own particular brand of theory and practice. Despite
this the individual dowser seldom, if ever, appears able
to obtain the same pattern of measurement and figures
as that of his neighbour. Nor is this to be expected once
the facts of dowsing are properly understood. It is only
expected by the radiesthetists themselves who believe
that the dowser is largely a mechanical robot operated by
" radiations " emitted by water or metal ores.

Where a number of dowsers are trained by the same
master under the same conditions, nearly identical reactions
of the rod may be obtained—or so it is claimed. And if
a number of such dowsers, who accept the same radiation
theory, together with its complementary reaction-code,
arrive at approximately the same metrical results, it would
certainly confer a deceptive objectivity on the hypothecated

radiations for those who are ignorant of the real explanation of the facts.

All this leads us to ask whether the flood of literature on radiesthetic theories has any practical bearing on dowsing practice. With very few exceptions, those who have evolved a complicated theory of radiations to account for their rod reactions make highly exaggerated claims for their own successes ; for them the motion of their rod becomes an infallible indicator of rays or fields of one kind or another. And we may suspect that those who write with such uncritical *élan* of their own claims are not dowsers at all but have merely achieved a faculty of sporadic motor-automatism. Some of their " maps " of underground streams would, if accurate, confute most of the lessons of geology acquired over the past hundred years. With a few dowsers, however, it is quite probable that the adoption of a radiation hypothesis has been a main factor in the development of an accurate technique of externalisation.

A radiation theory, to be of any practical use, must possess a complementary set of conventional reactions of the rod. The " radiation-inspired " code of reactions *may*, quite obviously, be as good a channel of externalisation as any other. Yet on the whole the impression is gained that claims of dowsing successes by ardent radiesthetists are generally exaggerated and that in the great majority of cases are totally without foundation.

Several independent experiments have been carried out to test the validity of the dowser's theories concerning electro-magnetism as the operative factor. Many dowsers have asserted that if they are completely insulated from the ground all rod-reactions cease forthwith, even if the dowser knows himself to be standing over water. These tests have proved conclusively the autosuggestive origin of such ideas ; for it has been established that if the dowser is deceived into believing he is insulated when in fact he is not, his rod will still fail to move. Again, it has been found that insulation does not interfere with the rod's movements as long as the dowser is kept in ignorance of the fact of his insulation. The dowser's beliefs, not the fact of insulation, dictate the movements of the rod during such tests.

Little need be said concerning the higher flights of fancy in dowsing theory. In this faerie realm the pendulum holds sway both literally and figuratively. We find that diseases, drugs, microbes, blood, metals, plants, colours and objects of all kinds have a specific " colour ". Their radiations can be measured in degrees (Bovis) on the " Biometer ", which in turn can also indicate the wavelengths of sputum, fingernails, hair, signatures, photographs and paintings. The degrees (Bovis) are measured by holding the pendulum above a measuring tape; the length of the swing denotes the number of degrees (Bovis). An individual's " aura " also has a particular wavelength and colour which alter according to the person's state of health.

If wavelengths alone do not provide the necessary information, clairvoyance is not to be despised. Unaided thought can select electro-magnetic frequencies and reject others at will. If this does not work, the Cosmic Mind, Yoga or telepathy may be of some assistance. If your " serial numbers " appear hay-wire, then try another " test-substance ". If you wish to understand your wife's needs better, you can find out her psychological idiosyncracies by holding a pendulum over her cranium. In the Journal of the British Society of Dowsers [1] one " medical radiesthetist " was led to ask : " Does he (the dowser) detect psychical, chemical, electronic, etheric, mental and/or spiritual radiations, or their equivalent ?" Alas, no one knows.

The vogue in " map-dowsing " deserves mention. Unfortunately map-dowsing *tests* never succeed. In 1933 tests of dowsing from plans were carried out at Avignon under the auspices of the Congrés de Sourciers to decide once and for all if there was anything in these claims. They produced entirely negative results. In 1947, François Gramenia of Anrecy, France, was reported to have been awarded the sum of fifty thousand francs for locating by map-dowsing the body of a young man who had fallen to his death in the Alps. He had used a pendulum and

[1] *Radio-Perception*, Sept., 1947 p. 2 10.

a large scale map of the area. Since the area in which the young Frenchman was climbing must have been known and could not have been very extensive, a success such as this may be justifiably attributed to chance if not due to prior knowledge. Against thousands of map-dowsing failures, we must expect an occasional chance success. It will be surprising if the dowser of Anrecy is fortunate enough to hit the jackpot again.

Some dowsers use " samples " to aid them in their operations. A " sample " is generally a piece of iron, copper, gold or other metal held in the hand of the dowser, or, in the case of a pendulum-user, often suspended on the end of a piece of string ; it is used while prospecting for the respective ore of these metals, or for tracing underground metal pipes. When dowsing for oil or water, a vial of oil or pure water may be used. Some dowsers say that they cannot dowse without these aids and this may quite often be true. The dowser's beliefs may be sufficiently strong to inhibit his automatism if he dowses without such " samples ". With impressionable or suggestible dowsers the use of a sample of the element to be divined is undoubtedly a good psychological aid. From the anthropological standpoint the use of " samples " is, of course, merely another instance of sympathetic magic. We can see the same principle in what psychical researchers call " psychometry ".

Perhaps one of the most widespread beliefs of today is that pendulum users are able to detect the sex of unhatched eggs. The pendulum is held above the egg and ideo-motor movements cause it to swing to and fro, indicating male, or laterally, indicating female. No movement of the pendulum indicates that the egg is unfertilised.

There is no known method of detecting the sex of a chick until after it has hatched. Still less likely is the possibility of detecting the sex of a freshly-laid egg which many a pendulum-user claims he can do. Prophecy or clairvoyance would be the only explanation of such feats and the many successes claimed can only be due to delusion or fraud. On the radiesthetic hypothesis, of course, the male egg emits radiations of a different " wavelength " to that of a female egg which the human robot receiver picks up and registers on his pendulum. Competent tests of the dowser's ability to sex eggs have produced negative results. As with map-dowsing, however, individuals still continue to claim complete and consistent success. The parallel is instructive.

" Medical " Radiesthesia

In " medical " radiesthesia dowsing methods are adapted to the diagnosis—and even to the cure—of disease. There are some members of the medical profession who claim to use such methods to supplement normal clinical methods, with considerable success if one can judge from their published articles. Their claims, however, are somewhat suspect since they rarely, if ever, admit to a failure but write as if the pendulum were an infallible detector of diseases and their remedies. Most of these writers are obviously deluded, as Mesmer was deluded. But since the kind of people who frequent the waiting rooms of these medical radiesthetists are generally of a credulous and impressionable type, it may be assumed that the factor of suggestion may sometimes operate in bringing about cures or improvements in a good many cases, particularly when the patients' maladies are psychogenic origin.

Most of the medical radiesthetists' claims, however, constitute the most arrant nonsense. They are particularly keen on the supposed relation of colour to disease. In a volume entitled *La Radiesthésie* written by a well-known dowser, one is informed that a certain state of dark green is " in resonance with " b. koch, one of the bacteria associated with tuberculosis. If a culture of b. koch is covered with a cloth of this shade of green " all virulence ceases." More strange still, if a patient's " radiation " is found to be fifty-five centimetres and if " the pendulum stops in resonance also with black, the person examined is, without doubt, suffering from haemorrhoids." The English reviewer of this book submits this as an example of " a heterodyne effect ".[1]

---

[1] *Radio-Perception*, Sept. 1946 p 42.

The above example is perfectly typical. Colour-thera-pists have " perfected " a permanent table of up to a hundred diseases and ailments, each with its specific shade of colour and detectable with the aid of a pendulum. Diagnosis at a distance is also possible, say the radiesthetists. " All users of Radiesthetic methods ", it is claimed, " know that blood or serum or a letter will keep pace minute by minute with its owner. We know the fact but not the explanation."[1]

Diagnosing disease from thumb prints, a specimen of handwriting, photographs, sputum or a hair has an old familiar ring. It is a modern form of primitive sympathetic magic. In primitive societies today there are many groups who believe that if the medicine man obtains possession of anything belonging to a man, such as spittle, a drop of blood, hair or nail parings, he can inflict untold harm on the owner. The same principle was accepted in the concoction of medieval " love potions "; and even today, in the more primitive part of Europe, *menstrual* blood is considered by local witches as particularly effective for such purposes.

Diagnosis of disease by divination is widespread. Boas, for example, cites a curious instance of this form of divining used by the Central Eskimo *angakok* or shaman ; in this case the suggested response takes an unusual form :

" An individual with a thong placed around his head lies down beside a sick person. The thong is fastened to the end of a stick which is held in hand by the *angakok*. The *angakok* then makes interrogations as to the nature and issue of the disease. These questions are supposed to be answered by the soul of a dead person, in such a manner as to make it impossible for the head to be lifted if the answer is affirmative, while the head is raised easily if the answer is negative."[2]

It is not so big a step as it may seem from this divination method of the central Eskimoes to such modern radies-thetic " disease detectors " as " Abrams' Box " and the " Wigglesworth Pathoclast ". Underneath all the talk of radiations, wavelengths, heterodyning and the utilisation

[1] *Journal of the Medical Society for the Study of Radiesthesia*, 1942.
[2] Boas, *Central Eskimo*, Popular Science Monthly, LVII, p. 631.

of modern-looking apparatus there resides the old and well-tried magic-evoking formula of suggestion and autosuggestion, delusion and fraud.

The first big development in medical radiesthesia was due to Dr. Albert Abrams. Abrams, like Mesmer before him, was a brilliant eccentric. While Mesmer attributed the effect of suggestion to animal " magnetism ", Abrams postulated a theory of " Electronic Reactions ". The method of medical diagnosis employed by Abrams was founded upon his purported discovery that the presence of any disease could be detected by normal percussion of the stomach area. Each disease, Abrams claimed, has its own particular variations of pitch and resonance and its own particular location on the stomach area where these variations could be detected.

Abrams, after the " discovery " of the alleged percussion effect, adopted a scientifically untenable theory of electromagnetism—the so-called " electronic-reaction " theory—to account for it. Needless to say, modern physics and and modern medical science have failed to produce the slightest evidence for the validity of either the electronic reaction theory or the percussion effect; despite this, however, Abrams' theories, though naïve, might well have attracted attention from the world of orthodox science of his day, had not the character of the man's intellect been exposed by some of his more extreme claims, such as his professed ability to sex eggs and to diagnose disease from specimens of handwriting.

Once launched on the exhilarating road of medical discovery, Abrams soon discovered that every drug possesses the same " radiation " as that of the disease it cures. The radiations from mercury were identical with those of syphilis ; the radiations of quinine were similar to those of malaria, and so on. The simple association of ideas here is too evident for comment and reveals the essentially child-like quality of Abrams' intellect.

It seems clear, none the less, that Abrams was able to diagnose ailments and diseases with considerable success. This in itself is not really surprising, since he himself was a trained medical practitioner—a point usually ignored by his protagonists. During his " electronic " diagnoses, he may not have consciously analysed his patients' ailments ; but to the experienced eye of the trained medical practitioner a great many diseases are easily discernible at a glance. And even when this is not the case, a doctor may intuitively arrive at the right conclusion concerning the nature of the case by the patient's general appearance and the latter's general description of his symptoms. The only question that remains to be answered is how Abrams, and those other medical practitioners who have sincerely followed his lead, became subject to the auditory illusions involved in the complicated rigmarole of percussing for " electronic reactions ". The answer is that it is simply one more instance of the effects of autosuggestion originating from an *idée fixe*.

Abrams, following his preconceived notions concerning his " electronic reactions ", decided to construct an apparatus to simplify his procedure. This step resulted in what was popularly known as " Abrams' Box ", and was followed later by more complex pieces of apparatus, one of which he called a " reflexophone " and the other an " oscilloclast ". These cheap pieces of apparatus he sold for large sums—despite the fact that he was already a very wealthy man. He and his successors also founded a good many special clinics in the United States and their number has by no means diminished in the ensuing years.

Such " machines " as Abrams' reflexophone and oscilloclast, Wigglesworth's pathoclast and Boyd's emanometer are scientific absurdities. Wigglesworth's model, for example, is purportedly designed to pick up the patient's " high frequency radiations ", amplify them and transmit them back " in inverted phase " as a curative measure. " Radiations of disease " are thus claimed to be " damped out "! There is no need to comment on such facile theorising. Provision is also made on this apparatus for " colour therapists ". The instruction manual which is sold with this apparatus reads like an adolescent's dream of the future, and one can only suspect that these and other similar machines are constructed with the principle aim of fraudulently obtaining money from gullible or suggestible practitioners and patients. There is this to be said, however ; where suggestion-therapy is potentially of value to the patient, the use of such harmless machines as the pathoclast, with its impressive array of knobs, sockets, plugs, meters, plates and coils, may sometimes be beneficial to the patient. On the other hand, serious harm may result if credulous patients suffering from such diseases as cancer or tuberculosis—always great favourites with radiesthetists—interpret any subjective or temporary feeling of improved health as an indication that they are on the way to being cured.

Tuberculosis, as is well known, is often very responsive to the patient's psychological state, and there are clinics on the continent where suggestion-therapy is used in the treatment of this disease. With a particular type of patient it is quite possible that such machines as the pathoclast would be as effective a medium of beneficial suggestion-therapy as any. By and large, however, their use is to be deplored.

Such machines as the above mostly rely for their " operation " upon an alleged sensation of adhesion or friction felt by the palm of the hand in contact with a metal or vulcanised plate. In the case of convinced believers in the " electronic reaction theory " such sensations are undoubtedly subjective, being brought about through expectation and suggestion. Most professional users, however, can be properly classified as conscious frauds, and the fees charged by many of them in America and England leave no doubt of the motive behind their use. And as long as there are gullible and credulous people with real or imaginery complaints and with money to burn, the success of the " electronist " remains assured.

Chapter Twenty-Three

THE "SPONTANEOUS PHENOMENA"

TELEPATHY, CLAIRVOYANCE AND PRECOGNITION

MODERN EXPERIMENTS in telepathy, clairvoyance, precognition and psychokinesis derive directly and unashamedly from the "spontaneous phenomena" of psychical research, and what may euphemistically be termed the "induced phenomena" of spiritualistic mediumship.

The literature of the spontaneous phenomena of psychical research is fascinating and instructive.[1] Ghosts, hauntings, poltergeists, clairvoyant dreams, telepathic phantasms, prophetic visions, the supernatural movement of objects—all bear witness to the powers of human self-deception, wishful thinking and distorted recollection.

Modern psychical researchers and parapsychologists no longer consider "spontaneous phenomena" to be of any crucial value in their researches. They are considered as "suggestive" only.

Many of the psychological experiences which help perpetuate belief in these "spontaneous phenomena" are often puzzling. Everyone has had the experience of thinking about some thing, person or event, only to hear someone else mention it the very next instant. Or a tune may be going through one's head, and suddenly someone starts to sing or whistle it.

There is, of course, no need to postulate telepathy when

---

[1] The reader is here referred to Dr. D. J. West's interesting paper *The Investigation of Spontaneous Cases*, Proc.S.P.R., vol. 48, pp. 264-300 ; 1948.

this sort of thing occurs. There are several ways of explaining such coincidence. A remark, or casual incident, is quite likely to set off a similar train of association in two people's minds, particularly if they are well-acquainted or share a similar background. Pure coincidence is often the reason; people who are interested in the occult will always tend to read telepathy or clairvoyance into the simplest verbal coincidences. Unconscious vocal innervations, reflected in slight changes in the tone of breathing, can be quite sufficient to set off a similar train of mental activity in another person's mind.

People who are convinced of their own psychic powers are often fond of telling others that they " knew " of some future happening or distant event *before* they themselves were told about them. Such supernaturally acquired knowledge generally boils down to vague surmises, emotional intuitions, or mere guess-work ; those which prove incorrect are naturally forgotten, and those which prove to be right are remembered and become invested with an aura of certainty which the original " hunch " never possessed. Many a correct " hunch " of course, can be explained by subconscious inference, subconsciously perceived cues, or cryptomnesia.

DREAMS

Those who keep on the watch for clairvoyant, telepathic or prophetic dreams are seldom disappointed.

Everyone, at one time or another, has had dreams which appear to possess striking coincidences with external events not known to the dreamer at the time of dreaming. But when we consider the enormous multitude of dreams such coincidences are only to be expected from time to time. Most people recognize this fact. But to one who believes himself to be " psychic " such coincidences are convincing proof of supernatural powers.

When two people dream of the same thing, the " psychic " will not attribute it to coincidence or the influence of similar interests, occupations, background, hopes or fears ; he will attribute it to telepathy. Similarly, a dream of someone dying is sure to be connected with the subsequent news of an actual death, however irrelevant.

The believer in the supernatual will always be ready to interpret such dream experiences in the light most favourable to his beliefs. He deceives himself, and he often deceives others.

J. W. Dunne's book, *An Experiment with Time*, created a great interest in prophetic dreams. To account for such dreams the author built up an interesting and logical mathematical theory. But as Max Planck pointed out, while there was nothing wrong with Dunne's mathematics, the premises upon which they were based were unproved, and were incapable of proof.

Dunne's method was to note down upon awakening all that he could remember of his dreams, and look for coincidences during the next few days. Naturally, he found plenty. However, when the Society for Psychical Research later repeated Dunne's dream experiments, they failed to confirm his findings.

Dreams which appear to be prophetic can be accounted for in a number of ways. For the believer in the supernatural nothing is easier than transposing the dates of an event and a subsequent dream by a process of wishful thinking ; the dream is mistakenly recalled as having occurred *before* the actual occurrence which it resembled. Many honest people have deceived themselves in this way.

There are those " prophetic " dreams which bring about their fulfilment by subconsciously suggesting a particular course of action to the dreamer. Then again, dreams about another person may appear innocuous enough, until a death or accident occurs to the person dreamed of. The dream is then interpreted *and subsequently recalled* as a mysterious portent. For example, a wife dreams of her husband who is away at sea, as she is likely to do quite often. Then the news arrives that the husband has died. If she has dreamt of him recently the dream is instantly connected with the death. Within a week or two the good woman is going around saying that on the night her husband died she had " warning of it in a dream ".

Dreams which appear to be prophetic or clairvoyant may often be explained by subconscious inference on the part of the dreamer. And tales of lost objects having been found by dreams and crystal-gazing may easily be due to cryptomnesia or " hidden memory ".

Information which the dreamer has previously acquired from a chance remark or a glimpse of a newspaper heading, and subsequently forgotten, may emerge in dreams—to provide yet more " proof " of the clairvoyant powers of the mind.

Perhaps the most confusing cases of " psychic " dreaming are those in which an individual dreams *twice* about some person (or object)—once *before* and once *after* some particular event connected with the person dreamed of. The dreamer may subsequently confuse the two dreams and become convinced that he dreamed of *the event* before it actually occurred.

A " psychic " experience commonly reported is that of seeing a place, person or object never previously encountered, but which nevertheless seems familiar. Sometimes this is put down to having " seen it before in a dream " ; a frequent explanation is that of having encountered it " in a previous existence ". This type of memory delusion is generally referred to as *déja vu*, and the false recognition of sounds or words as *déja entendu*. It is usually associated with fatigue and is common in certain neurotic conditions.

THE PSYCHIC ANECDOTE

Every psychic anecdote has to have an originator. There are, broadly speaking, two types of people who set the ball rolling.

First, there are those who, faced with an experience or series of events which they cannot understand, fall back on the supernatural as the only possible explanation.

Second, there are those who, firmly believing in the occult (or in their own supernatural powers), are continually on the look-out for its occurrence ; these people may read telepathy or clairvoyance or the actions of discarnate spirits. into the most prosaic details of everyday life.

During the first stage of the development of the psychic anecdote, the narrator usually tells his story, not as something he cannot understand, but simply as another example of the supernatural in his own experience. To him telepathy, clairvoyance or the actions of discarnate spirits *are* the explanation of the event or experience in question. And so, when he narrates his story, the details become subordinated to the central theme of telepathy or some similar idea ; the story is no longer objective.

The first narration of the psychic story fixes the pattern of subsequent narrations. Since the point of telling such a story is to be believed, the narrator in his enthusiasm will tend to add embellishments, emphasizing favourable points, omitting unfavourable points. After two or three repetitions these additions and omissions will become part of his memory of the incident ; he will be prepared to swear to their truth with absolute sincerity. This process, in which the imagination becomes fused with the memory, is known to psychologists as *retrospective falsification.*

The final development of the psychic story is reached when the distorted version of the event becomes so completely part of his memory that no argument will avail to convince him of its falseness. This almost invariably occurs with those who believe strongly in the occult. Furthermore the whole cumulative process tends to make the original experiences seem a great deal more striking and distinctive than they really were ; and the story will often emerge with a trenchancy and simplicity which baffles the rational listener.

People of the highest intellect may deceive themselves in this way (witness Judge Hornby's story below). Well-educated and otherwise intelligent people will write the most ludicrous and impossible stories with transparent honesty and sincerity of purpose. The fact is that once a supernatural interpretation of an event has become *accepted,* the memory of that event will become inevitably and irrevocably distorted.

In a family of suggestible people subsequent conversation, speculation and retelling the story may result in the anecdote becoming objectified to a remarkable degree. When the psychicial researcher eventually gets a written account of

the occurrence, he is often presented with a coherent story
with numerous witnesses concerning the names, dates and so
forth.

The extent to which false corroborative detail can be
brought into the narrative of a personal " psychic " experience is really surprising. A perfect example of this form
of retrospective falsification is to be found in the well-known
book entitled *An Adventure*, [1] written by Miss Moberley
and Miss Jourdain, two ladies of the highest academic
standing. *An Adventure* is probably the world's greatest
ghost story, and when it first appeared it was regarded by
many as the culminating proofs of things supernatural.
It is, unfortunately, open to criticism at almost every point. [2]

HAUNTINGS, GHOSTS AND APPARITIONS

Most of the stories of hauntings and ghosts in the annals
of psychical research date from the pre-1914 era. Credulity
was stronger in those days, and belief in the supernatural
correspondingly more potent ; suggestion and autosuggestion had more fertile ground to take root in. People who
believed in ghosts and apparitions had only to have an odd
dream or hallucinatory experience in a strange room to think
it haunted. Or if a place had acquired the reputation of
being haunted the sight of an unrecognised figure in the
half-darkness would naturally become transformed into a
spectre or apparition ; any unusual or strange noises, too,
would add to the place's ghostly reputation ; temperatures
would begin to drop and rise ; odd smells would occur, and
perfectly ordinary minor occurrences would become charged
with mystery.

The similarity of form shared by most " true " ghost
stories often lends them a spurious air of objectivity. The
similarity of ghosts stories, however, is traceable to the

---

[1] First published in 1911 under the pseudonyms Elizabeth Morison and
Frances Lamont.

[2] See J. R. Sturge-Whiting's detailed criticism, *The Mystery of Versaille*,
1938. See also the following reviews : Proc.S.P.R., vol. 25,
p. 353 ; Journ.S.P.R., vol. 27, pp. 139-140 ; Journ.S.P.R., vol.
35. p. 178.

influence of Victorian romantic literature in which the ghost
or apparition was a familiar and stereotyped theme.

In all recorded cases of haunting there is never any need
to assume anything other than purely psychological causes
consonant with suggestion and autosuggestion.   Numbers
of " hauntings " may perhaps have their origin in ill-adjusted
individuals subject to dissociation " who can gain some relief
from inner conflict by means of a hysterical projection of
ghostly visions which serve to excuse their own failure ". [1]

It is in the field of optical illusion that the most striking
and convincing tales of ghosts and apparitions occur.   Optical illusions can be extremely complex and extraordinarily
deceptive.   Here are two good illustrations of an optical
illusion which have *no* occult significance :

1. A man riding a bicycle at night passed over a piece of
tin which clattered loudly.   His companion, who had been
riding ten or twenty yerds behind, overtook him in agitation,
swearing that he had seen him flung from his machine in
the gloom. [2]

2. A botanist student in Paris passes a restaurant and
sees the words " Verbascum thapsus " on the door.   After
proceeding a few paces he turns back, astonished that the
name of such a plant should appear on a restaurant door.
He reads the inscription again, which was simply " bouillon".
The cause of his illusion was clear, for the popular French
name for the plant Verbascum thapsus is *bouillon blanc.* [3]

In the above two examples we see how a simple association
of ideas can lead to the most complete and perfect illusions.
The mind deceives itself completely.   Many such an illusion
based on expectancy, has provided the basis for supposedly
telepathic or clairvoyant " phenomena ".

Two monumental works on ghosts and apparitions appeared about the end of the last century, which psychical
researchers still regard as classics.   In 1886 Gurney, Myers
and Podmore published their *Phantasms of the Living.*   And
in 1903 F. W. Myers produced his *Human Personality and
its Survival of Bodily Death.*   Both ran to two lengthy

[1] West, D. J., Journ.S.P.R., 36, 1948, p. 299.
[2] Parish, op.cit., p. 191.
[3] Parish, op. cit., p. 198.

volumes, and both had considerable influence owing to the high intellectual standard of the authors.

They were based on carefully recorded and sifted evidence of the appearance of apparitions to various people. And never was talent so wasted. The " evidence " they marshalled so assiduously was almost worthless. Gurney, Myers and Podmore even went so far as to admit that a small number of " fairly conclusive cases " was the best they had to offer, and that the vast majority were " confirmatory only and not crucial ". [4]

Even with the best authenticated stories of the supernatural there is always a lapse of time between the original event which fired the imagination, and its committment to paper. A purported telepathic, clairvoyant or prophetic experience must more or less correspond to some external event to render it veridical ; and the only admissable evidence in such cases, is an account of the experience written down, or otherwise recorded—*before* the external event takes place —in a diary, a letter, or other document.

But throughout both books there is a total lack of such contemporary written evidence ; and if the original experiences had really been as striking as they were later claimed to be, this is incredible. In *Phantasms of the Living*, for example, not one example of contemporary written evidence is to be found in 702 stories, including 350 at first hand. [*]

The authors introduced a theory of telepathic stimuli, of sufficient intensity to engender genuine sensory hallucinations. But as Parish pointed out, the great bulk of psychical research records concerning ghosts, phantoms, hauntings and apparitions are little more than records of optical illusion, delusion and dreams. Parish analysed the cases upon which the above two books were based, and concluded that a large percentage of them contained unmistakable evidence of a dream state of consciousness. [5]

The fact is that scholars (*and* scientists) make poor psychical researchers ; they are usually too used to breathing an atmosphere of trust and intellectual objectivity. They

---

[4] *Phantasms of the Living*, abridged edition, 1918, p. 127.
[5] Parish, E., *Hallucinations and Illusions*, p. 104.

are seldom equipped for a task which requires the training
of a psychologist, the flair of a detective, and the experience
of a conjuror.

Many an " apparition " has had its genesis in a simple
dream about a dead friend or relative ; with many people
it would not take them long to convince themselves that
they had received a " visitation " or warning of some kind.
The percipient will then keep on the watch for any outstanding event or dire happening which might be interpreted as
fulfilling the premonition. Inevitable he finds one. The
event itself is then imported into the memory of the original
dream, and is narrated accordingly.

Even for the most intelligent psychical investigator it is
often difficult to avoid putting leading questions ; many
a record of a purported supernatural experience has received
spurious coherence through this happening. The psychical
researcher, may, by his questions, give shape and form to
a story which only existed as a jumble of vague ideas at the
back of the narrator's mind. Gurney and Myers were only
too culpable in this respect. More than once they had to
retract what they had presented to the world as " well
authenticated evidence ". Their article on Sir Edmund
Hornby's apparition is an excellent case in point.

Sir Edmund Hornby was one-time Chief Judge of the
Supreme Court of China and Japan at Shanghai. His
story appeared in the *Nineteenth Century* in 1884, nine years
after the following events occurred :

On the night of January 19th 1875, the Judge records,
he heard a tap at his bedroom door, and a certain newspaper editor, with whom the Judge was well acquainted,
walked in. He ignored the Judge's requests to leave the
room and sat down on the foot of the bed. The time, Sir
Edmund noted, was twenty minutes past one. The purpose
of the visit was to obtain the Judge's statement concerning
the day's judgment for the morning paper. After refusing
twice, the request was granted for fear that further argument
would wake Mrs. Hornby. Finally the Judge angrily told
his visitor that it was the last time he would allow any reporter inside his house. The other replied : " This is the
last time I shall ever see you anywhere ". When he had
gone, the Judge looked at the clock ; it was exactly half

past one. Lady Hornby then awoke, and the Judge told her what had happened.

Next morning Judge Hornby repeated the story to his wife while dressing. When he went to court he was somewhat shocked to hear that his visitor had died during the night, at about one o'clock. In the dead man's notebook was the headline : " The Chief Judge gave judgment this morning in this case to the following effect " ; and then followed some lines of indecipherable shorthand. The result of the inquest showed that he had died of some form of heart disease. The coroner, at the Judge's previous request, ascertained that the dead man could not have left his house during the two hours before he died.

When he got home the Judge asked his wife to repeat what he had said to her during the night, and he " made a brief note of her replies and of the facts ".

The Judge records : " As I said then, so I say now—I was not asleep, but wide awake, After a lapse of nine years my memory is quite clear on the subject. I have not the least doubt I saw the man—have not the least doubt that the conversation took place between us."

The above is a resumé of the Sir Edmund Hornby's full and detailed account as Gurney and Myers took it down. Lady Hornby confirmed the facts, " as far as she was cognizant of them ".

Gurney, Myers and Sir Edmund, however, were due for something of a shock. A later issue of the *Nineteenth Century* revealed the following facts :

1. The editor in question was the Rev. Hugh Lang Nivens editor of the Shanghai Courier. The actual time of his death was nine o'clock in the morning.

2. At that time Judge Hornby was unmarried. His wife had died two years previously and he did not re-marry until three months after the events he described.

3. No inquest was held on the death of the Rev. Nivens.

4. There was no record of any such judgment as the Judge mentioned, and upon which the whole story turned.

Judge Hornby, when faced with these facts commented :
" If I had not believed, as I still believe, that every word of
it, the story, was accurate, and that my memory was to be
relied on, I should not have ever told it as a personal
experience."

There is no need at all to assume that the story was
consciously fabricated. It is sufficient to assume that a
good deal of it was the product of a vivid dream which was
later confused with reality, and rationalised and elaborated
during subsequent conversations. It is a fairly typical
case of retrospective falsification.

POLTERGEISTS

Once a person has come under the influence of supernatural beliefs his mind ceases to function at its normal
level of reasoning ; the simplest things may take on the
appearance of mystifying enigmas. Nowhere is this better
illustrated than in poltergeist hauntings. Once the belief
in the presence of a poltergeist exists, any odd noise or unusual accident will be attributed to the agency of the " play-
ful spirit ".

Poltergeist traditions occur in all parts of the world. And
the " phenomena " are surprisingly similar. In many
primitive societies it takes the form of " stone-throwing ".
In Europe and America it almost invariably manifests itself
in connection with one person in the household—usually
a young adolescent. Spiritualists say that such adolescents
are " psychic ", that they " attract " the poltergeist which
cannot " manifest " itself without their presence. The truth
of course, is that the adolescent girl or boy is solely responsible for the production of poltergeist phenomena ; in almost
every case which has been competently investigated, the
poltergeist activity has ended in the child being caught
red-handed in trickery. Such children are usually mal-
adjusted. Sometimes they have physical abnormalities ;
they find in poltergeist trickery an outlet for thwarted instinct. The skill with which, after a few weeks practice,
the child produces the " phenomena " are often extraordinary.

In the case of elderly people who complain of being pricked, poked or tickled by persecuting poltergeists the phenomena are usually attributable to neurotic delusions, or in some cases tactile hallucinations due to incipient psychosis.

It has also been suggested that certain poltergeist phenomena such as mysterious knocks, tappings, thumpings, tickings, buzzings, rumblings and hissings may sometimes have their origin in the not uncommon complaint called *tinnitis*—hallucinatory noises caused by inflammation of the middle ear. Such noises may appear to the percipient to reach him from outside sources.

Chapter Twenty-four

ESP[1] EXPERIMENTS AND THE PROBLEM OF SENSORY CUES

T HE PITFALLS which lie in the path of the experimenter in telepathy or clairvoyance are seldom appreciated by those who are conducting the experiments. In the past many experimenters with mediums and " psychics " have produced apparent evidence for the existence of super-natural faculties, simply because they have not taken into account such factors as sensory hyperacuity, the involuntary dissemination of sensory cues, and, equally important, the unconscious reception of those cues by the " telepathic " or " clairvoyant " percipient.

Involuntary articulation, from its most rudimentary forms to genuine unconscious whispering, plays a very large rôle in the " thought-reading " performances of many mediums. But the average medium relies mainly on her sitters' conscious or involuntary reactions to her verbal remarks, hesitations, hints, gestures and semi-articulated words. She fishes for reactions which will give her a clue to the circumstances, the names of relatives, and other personal details of her client's life.

It is not proposed, however, to enter here into the *modus operandi* of the successful professional medium. It is sufficient to observe at this point that the unconscious presentation of sensory cues, particularly auditory cues, may satisfactorily account for innumerable instances wherein the sitter has been puzzled by the supposed clairvoyant

[1] Extra-Sensory Perception : A general term which includes telepathy, clairvoyance, " precognition," etc.

power of the medium. Nowhere has the operation of this factor been more effectively displayed than in the experiments carried out by the worthy pioneer investigators of mediumistic   abilities.

The great bulk of experiments of Chowrin and Naum Kotik in Russia, of Abramowski in Poland, of Pagenstecher in Mexico, of Schmoll and Mabire in France, of Wassiliewski and Tischner in Germany, of the Sinclairs in America—to mention only a few of the more serious earlier experimenters —provided ideal situations for the involuntary presentation of auditory cues. Even Richet, who was very far from viewing such experiments without bias, observed that with Kotik's two mediums the " telepathic transmission " usually took a *forme phonetique*, and questioned the whole validity of Kotik's conclusions[2] mainly on that account. Yet to anyone unacquainted with the possibility of slight articulated cues being conveyed involuntarily to the percipient, Kotik's experiments must appear impressive.

In the earlier *clairvoyant* experiments it was usual for the percipient to try and guess words in sealed envelopes, objects in sealed boxes, or drawings in locked brief cases. In this type of experiment the medium often achieved a very high degree of success, but only in those cases when the experimenter or his assistant knew the nature of the item to be divined, which was usually the case. In *telepathy* experiments, when the "agent " is actually concentrating on or looking at the item to be transmitted, the scope afforded for the transmission of cues by involuntary articulation is obviously increased, and even in quite recent telepathy experiments allowance has seldom been made for this factor.

Dr. E. Abramowski's experiments[3] are of particular interest in this connection. In 1914, in his capacity as head of the Laboratory of the Polish Psychological Institute in Warsaw, he conducted a long series of purported telepathic experiments in which he, acting as agent, held the percipient's hand. In this manner up to fifty per cent. success in transmission was obtained ; but Abramowski

[2] Kotik, N., *Die Emanation der psycho-physischen Energie*, Grenzfragen des Nerven und Seelenlebens, 61, Wiesbaden, 1908.
[3] Abramowski, E., *Le Subconscient Normal*, Paris 1914.

admitted that this was due in part to the unconscious presentation and assimilation of sensory cues.   Nevertheless,
he believed that the unprecedented percentage of accurate
guesses could only be explained by means of telepathy.
In making this assumption he certainly erred ; not even
the most sanguine of modern ESP experimenters could
hope to rival his phenomenal results.

The main lesson to be learned from Abramowski's experiments in telepathy, which he included in his otherwise
excellent psychological treatise *Le Subconscient Normal*,
is the extraordinary extent to which certain individuals
may correctly perceive and interpret slight and unconsciously disseminated sensory cues.

In England and America criticism of experiments in psychical research has been sporadic and ineffectual.   In Germany,
however, many books have been published during the
present century attacking the shortcomings of such experiments and investigations.   The most effective counter-
blasts to the supernaturalism of earlier psychical research
have been written by Max Hopp[4] who conducted experiments of his own on traditional lines without the least
evidence of telepathy or clairvoyance forthcoming, and
by Moll and Baerwald, noted German psychologists.   Moll
possessed a wide knowledge of psychical research which
showed his fundamental interest in the subject, yet he had
no hesitation in rejecting the occult theories of the psychical
researcher.   In his book *Prophezeien und Hellsehen*[5] he
explained a great deal of the apparently supernatural powers
of telepathists, mediums and clairvoyants as due to sensory
hyperacuity.   Baerwald in his excellent book, *Die Intellektuellen Phänomene*,[6] also pointed out the large part
played by sensory hyperacuity and the unconscious dissemination of cues in psychical research experiments.

It is notable that the efforts of German savants to quash
the growing movement of " scientific occultism ", as psychical research was called for many years in Germany, largely
succeeded.   Other factors helped, and during the last

[4] *Uber Hellsehen*, Berlin 1916.
[5] Stuttgart, 1922.
[6] Berlin, 1925 ; second vol. in the series *Der Okkultismus in Urkunden*,
    edited by Max Dessoir.

twenty-five years no development in psychical research parallel to that which has grown up in Britain and the United States has occurred in Germany. Bonn University made a small effort to instigate scientific psychical research experiments under Dr. Hans Bender in 1933, but nothing of any importance materialised. The truth appears to be that the Germans have been far better acquainted with the fallacies involved in the type of investigation exemplified by ESP experiments than have the English or the Americans.

SENSORY HYPERACUITY

There are many ways in which the " telepathic " or " clairvoyant " percipient can gain information through normal sensory channels. The telepathic agent, for instance, may provide interpretable cues by involuntary muscular movements detectable by any of the three senses of sight, hearing or touch. Vaudeville telepathists who use such means as these are known as " muscle-readers ".· The telepathic percipient, also, may be aided by a highly trained or hyperacute sense of touch, hearing or vision, enabling him, in certain circumstances, to gain valuable sensory cues where the average person would perceive nothing.

People naturally vary from one another in the acuteness of their various senses. Sensory hyperacuity which owes its existence to an abnormally low threshold of sensation due to *physiological* causes, i.e. when the nerve receptors are themselves measurably more sensitive than the normal person's, is usually referred to as sensory *hyperaesthesia*. Genuine hyperaesthesia, however, is a relatively rare phenomenon and there is little evidence that it is responsible for extra-chance scoring rates in ESP experiments. The kind of sensory hyperacuity found among ESP percipients is often the result of training or practise. Even when this is not the case sensory hyperacuity is almost always due to psychological, not physiological, factors. A state of increased concentration and attention, for example, renders the senses more acute *in effect* than when the individual is bored or distracted.

Alternatively the person who possesses a natural mental

alertness, with a facility for fine discrimination, and has what is called a " good ear " or a " good eye " has, in general, far more subtlety of sense-perception than the naturally indolent whose mental equipment only enables him to deal with the more obvious sounds and sights which reach him. The former type can develop his already superior sensory faculties to an extent which often appears incredible. The Australian aboriginal tracker, for example, who rapidly and unerringly follows up a visual trail invisible to the white-man ; the proverbial North American Indian who possesses " the eye of an eagle " ; the musician who can distinguish simul-taneously a great variety of overtones when a bell is struck— overtones which to the majority of people constitute at most two or three separate sounds ; none of these is due in any way to hyperaesthesia but to training and practice plus a natural aptitude.

Genuine hyperaesthesia denotes an abnormal sensitivity of the physiological sense organs themselves. Although the eye can, with training, become a more perfect instrument, by enabling the percipient to use the muscles of his eye to better advantage, this does not of itself constitute hyper-aesthesia. Similarly, with some hysterical subjects extreme sensitivity to pain may occur without the least physical change in the sensory organs ; the sensitivity here is due to psychological causes alone. Under hypnosis some hysterical subjects can be made to see and hear far better than they can normally.

The term hyperaesthesia is commonly used in connection with psychical research experiments and investigations. It will be seen from the above, however, that its continued use would serve only to confuse the issue. Hyperaesthesia refers only to certain abnormal sensitiveness of the sensory nerve terminals themselves. The term *sensory hyperacuity*, which is altogether more appropriate, may denote either an unusual sensitivity in the percipient's *reactions* to given sensory stimuli due to psychological causes, or an increased efficiency of any of the senses brought about by training and practice. It depends largely on the psychological constitution of the percipient. Some people could never become tea-tasters while others could never become piano-tuners, even though their physical sensory equipment were perfect.

Some individuals possess naturally hyperacute sensory faculties, although pronounced hyperacuity is comparatively rare without training. It is, however, these rare individuals with abnormally developed sensory faculties to whom we must turn our attention if we are to explain some of the apparently inexplicable results produced in numbers of ESP experiments.

William James rightly observed that the limits of the powers of the human mind are unknown; the range of its potential abilities is virtually unexplored territory. Such phenomena as lightning mathematical calculators, infant musical prodigies, accurate estimation of time intervals whilst asleep, increased muscular strength and powers of concentration under hypnosis—all these hint at the existence of mental potentialities about which we know comparatively little.

Hypnotised subjects not infrequently use their normal faculties with considerably greater efficiency than when they are fully conscious. They may lift greater weights, exhibit greater acuteness of sight or hearing and, in general, exercise their talents with increased success. This is because suggestible subjects can usually be brought to a state in which they are entirely concentrated upon one task in hand to the exclusion of everything else. Some individuals achieve such an extention of their normal powers spontaneously without the use of hypnosis, and this applies particularly to the sphere of auditory perception. With the hypnotised subject the sensory faculties may sometimes be heightened to a degree reaching genuine hyperacuity.

Such a heightening of the senses, whether self-induced or brought about by hypnosis, comes from concentrating every mental faculty to the limit of its efficiency. Such concentration may be a subconscious process, the subject remaining, to all intents and purposes, quite relaxed. The great value of hypnosis is that it frees the subject from those inhibitions and self-consciousness which otherwise stop him reaching that peculiar pitch of concentration where his mental faculties achieve the maximum efficiency.

Experiments in increased sensory acuity by means of

hypnosis have, in the main, been confined to subjects with hysterical tendencies. The relationship between hysteria and hypnosis is a close one, and many hysterical patients in the past have shown a high degree of spontaneous sensory acuity. Many mediums show well-developed hysterical symptoms, and in trance states of hysterical origin the medium is probably helped a great deal by an accentuated sensory acuity or heightened powers of observation due to this factor.

To some extent the normal individual also can achieve heightened states of concentration conducive to the increase of his sensory acuity. If he relaxes his muscles, forgets the world around him and fixes his mind on one task—for example the task of picking up slight informative cues disseminated involuntarily by an ESP experimenter or a " telepathic " agent—he will often be able greatly to augment those powers of attention, discrimination, concentration and subtle rationalisation upon which the increased efficiency of his sensory faculties depend. Such methods bring into operation the full powers of the subconscious mind undistracted by events in the immediate environment.

SENSORY CUES

In telepathic and clairvoyant exhibitions by mediums, vaudeville telepathists or ESP subjects, it is surprising how much can be inferred from slight cues provided by involuntary movements and sounds, barely perceptible differentiations of light and shade, changes of facial expression, innervations of the vocal muscles, tensions of the facial and cervical muscles, alterations in rate, rhythm, time and evenness of the breathing, *apart* from any question of sensory hyperacuity on the part of the percipient. With gifted subjects who can use to the full their powers of subconscious assimilation and ratiocination, the chances of correctly interpreting such faint cues are greatly increased. The ability of the subconscious mental processes to utilise the slightest cue has been shown time and again in experiments with hysterics. The powers of lightning calculation possessed by some infant prodigies well exemplify the potentialities of subconscious mental operations.

The psychical researcher and ESP experimenter must be fully cognizant of the difficulties of excluding sensory cues before he undertakes any investigations in his chosen sphere. Very seldom, however, have such investigators shown, judging from their books and reports, that they possess the requisite knowledge ; and it is hard to avoid the conclusion that the great bulk of the " successful " experimental results reported are directly attributable to ignorance of the difficulties involved.

It is evident from this brief introduction that all telepathy and clairvoyant investigations should be carried out under such conditions as to leave not the slightest doubt as to the complete *physical impossibility* of sensory cues being gained by the percipient. The vast majority of ESP tests do not observe this condition. If the possibility of subconsciously-motivated scoring errors, fraud and the like are excluded, the relatively small amount of extra-chance successes achieved by the averagely successful ESP percipient in reasonably well controlled zener-card experiments may well represent the degree to which the occasional sensory cue has been unconsciously disseminated, observed and interpreted—perhaps once or twice in every hundred or so guesses.

Where constant and slight *enneurosis* (innervation) of the vocal muscles on the part of a telepathic agent is the only source of the sensory cues, the average percipient will be lucky—if the distance is over a yard or two—to catch more than an occasional indication of the nature of the card the agent is looking at ; and only a percipient with very acute hearing will be able to register them to any marked extent. This is undoubtedly the main explanation of Dr. S. G. Soal's amazing experiments. although one curious feature of these experiments demands something more than simple explanation on these lines. Yet Dr. Soal's experiments, it may be noted in passing, do *not* exclude an explanation in terms of the operation of sensory cues, as will be seen in a later chapter.

To render the operation of sensory cues totally out of the question in ESP experiments, recourse should be had to a lightproof and soundproof cabinet in which to seat the percipient ; or alternatively he must be placed at such a distance from the agent that all physical means of communication between them would be a literal impossibility. Such a cabinet has not been used by ESP experimenters, and although a fair number of distance experiments have been carried out few will claim that such experiments present cogent evidence for the operation of telepathy or clairvoyance.

Even in clairvoyance (as opposed to telepathy) experiments the situation is not so simple as might at first appear. For example, the percipient may be required to guess the order of a pack of cards enclosed in a *locked metal box*. Yet the precaution of a locked metal box would not in itself be enough. The person who places the pack in the box must also be prevented from either seeing or conversing with any person who is going to make contact with the percipient (after the cards are in the box) either before or during the experiment. In other words the person who places the cards in the box must be allowed no subsequent contact with *any-one* who is involved in the experiment until after the cards have been checked. This precaution has seldom been taken. Chowrin's experiments in hysterical hyperacuity of the senses suggest only too clearly the possibility that the *super-visor* of the experiment may unconsciously gain cues at second or third hand through the medium of involuntary articulation and convey them to the percipient by the same means.

The well-publicised experiments of Rhine and other American ESP experimenters must be rejected on collateral evidence of bias and tendentiousness as judged from the presentation of their reports. Even so, the great majority of their clairvoyant experiments are indictable on grounds of insufficient precautions against the sensory cues. For example, an apparently excellent series of clairvoyant experiments carried out by Pratt and Woodruff at Duke University [1] were designed to demonstrate the influence of novelty in the target material. The actual report of the experiments is of a high standard and triple score-records were made. In these experiments a total of 66 subjects were tested. The number of card guesses involved was 97,000. The technique generally used was *screened touch-matching* with modifications.

---

[1] *Size of Stimulus Symbols in Extra-Sensory Perception*, J. Parapsychol., III, 1939, pp. 121-157.

There were two main series of experiments. In the larger B series the results of over 60,000 guesses produced a relatively low critical ratio of 4.99. Series A, which were conducted under less well controlled conditions, showed a correspondingly higher critical ratio of 6.28, which is precisely what might be expected if the scoring successes were due solely to the intervention of sensory cues. Alternative theories to explain the greater success of the less well controlled series can be considered only when it has been proved that the intervention of sensory cues was not only improbable but *impossible*. Analysis of the screened touch-matching method, however, renders this out of the question.

That 66 subjects should show, *en masse*, strong evidence of " extra-sensory " perception is so contrary to what other ESP experimenters have found, particularly Soal, that the results are in themselves automatically suspect. When we hear that the screened touch-matching technique involves the personal handling of a face-down pack of cards by the experimenter who is sitting only a couple of feet away from the percipient, the claim to have imposed the strictest experimental controls must raise a smile.

The only value of a screen between the percipient and the experimenter is that it probably prevents direct visual cues from reaching the percipient. If, in the absence of a screen, the possibility of direct visual cues reaching the *percipient* is admitted, then plainly the same possibility exists in regard to the experimenter ; for he can not only see the backs of the cards but he can also touch the backs of the cards and probably the faces as well. Any information he may get from the cards, perhaps subconsciously, may be readily transmitted by unconscious articulation or *endophasic enneurosis*, by an auditory code of ideomotor movements, by intonations and variations in the breathing, or by involuntary reactions to any tentative movements of the percipient's pointer over the exposed " key-cards ". Both series of the Pratt-Woodruff experiments are potentially open to an interpretation on these lines.

In the conscious or unconscious detection of slight sensory cues a certain degree of mental alertness is essential. Where boredom intervenes, the subject's alertness drops. Novelty or other aids to re-engage the interest will naturally revive the *qui-vive* of the subject and prevent staleness. This is all that Pratt and Woodruff appear to have established—not, as Dr. J. B. Rhine hints, something bearing on the " laws " of extra-sensory perception.

The shortcomings of the screened touch-matching technique are quite obvious. Yet of these Pratt-Woodruff experiments Rhine has written : " For sheer top-heaviness of safeguarding measures, probably no comparable experiment has ever been conducted." [2]

The claim to have established by such experiments the existence of a new causal principle unknown to modern science is, of course, ludicrous. To prove such claims the criteria of the *exact sciences* must be rigidly adhered to ; they are the only ones which could satisfy the scientific world, and this is what all psychical researchers and ESP experimenters fail to recognise. Rhine's comment on the Pratt-Woodruff experiments is a good illustration of the occult researcher's fallacious outlook.

There are several different ways in which the percipient may gain the requisite sensory cues during clairvoyance or telepathy experiments. First, there is the straightforward possibility of direct vision—the percipient being able to see the card or object to be guessed or to infer their nature by slight visual cues. Another possible source of information is through the sense of touch. Allied to this is the faculty we possess of detecting differences in the weights of objects ; this, and the use of the sense of smell, may be of some value to the medium or clairvoyant, although in the average zener-card experiment they can be discounted.

The sense of hearing is the chief means by which informative cues are conveyed to the ESP percipient; and directly connected with this is the whole problem of unconscious movements and endophasic enneurosis on the part of the agent or experimenter, and the conscious or *unconscious* detection and interpretation of the resultant sounds by the percipient. Obviously, both the dissemination and reception of such sensory cues can be a conscious, and even a deliberate business ; but in the following pages we shall concern ourselves mainly with the more interesting unconscious variety.

[2] *The Reach of the Mind*, 1947, p. 37.

Unconscious movements by the telepathic agent may not only be seen—they may be *heard* by the percipient; or, if they are in contact, they may be felt. In modern ESP experiments, however, the latter possibility seldom occurs, although in Abramowski's long series of telepathic experiments already referred to, detection of the agent's unconscious movements occurred mainly through the sense of touch— the percipient holding the agent's hand.

It would seem a very simple matter in ESP experiments to exclude the possibility of the percipient obtaining information by the direct use of the sense of sight. Yet in Rhine's early zener-card experiments, as was subsequently shown, it was often quite easy to detect the symbol on the card-face from the back when viewed from certain angles. The symbols printed on the front of the cards had been impressed too hard, rendering their outlines discernible on the reverse sides. That Dr. Rhine should have published the results of such experiments in the first instance as evidence of *telepathy* or *clairvoyance* is almost incredible. Nothing can dispel the impression of carelessness thus created, which the partisan tendentiousness of subsequent reports and books has done little to dispel. Yet it is Dr. Rhine himself who, more than any other ESP experimenter, upbraids the world of science for not having the breadth of outlook to admit the " fact " of extra-sensory perception !

In these early card-guessing trials the percipient was generally allowed to see the backs of the cards, and even to handle them. The possibility of obtaining visual and tactile cues by such means—apart from the question of the symbols showing through the backs—is evident. Any card can be identified visually from its back once the percipient has had a chance to see the front. It is similarly possible to identify a card by touch through noting small irregularities on the back or edges.

Reflections, of course, are easily guarded against if the proper precautions are taken. But the test-table is not the only possible source of reflections. Slight variations in reflected light and shade, even on relatively poor reflecting surfaces, may be sufficient to provide the necessary cue when the percipient has only a limited number of symbols to guess from, each with its characteristic shape. There is always the very important possibility, too, that the test supervisor or one of his assistants may catch some visual cue and pass it on unconsciously to the percipient.

The question of the unconscious dissemination of sensory cues by telepathic agents will be dealt with at length later. Meanwhile we may note that in *clairvoyance* tests, where there is no ostensible agent, the supervisor, his assistant, or an observer may unconsciously provide cues to the percipient when the conditions of the experiment allow the cards to be seen or touched by them, as has been the case in a great many of the American clairvoyance experiments.

The sense of touch is capable of great development beyond the normal degree of sensitiveness. It is in fact possible for some people to designate correctly, by touch alone, the name of most cards in the pack, using the average commercial brand of playing-cards. Among the blind tactile sensitivity is sometimes remarkably developed. For example, Professor Villey records that the *hyperaphia*, or extreme tactile sensitivity, of some blind women enables them to distinguish the different colours of the wool they are using through the effect produced on the wool by the dye ; while Professor Fontan once reported a case of hystero-epilepsy in which the patient could discriminate between variously coloured wools in complete darkness by virtue of her increased tactile responsiveness. Hyperacuity of the senses, as we have already seen, may be occasioned by hysteria or hypnosis.

Despite some extraordinary feats of the tactile sense by a few individuals, there is no basis whatever in the claims once made by the renowned French writer, Jules Romains, that there exists any such faculty as " Extra-Retinal Vision " or the " Paroptic Sense ". Romains, in his book *Eyeless Sight*, describes how he made numerous experiments early on in his career regarding a hypothetical sensory function analogous to sight but operating via the medium of the subject's skin. Colours and letters could thus, according to Romains, be identified at a distance. Furthermore, he claimed that the " paroptic perception of colours continues noticeably beyond the lowest illumination with which visual perception of colours can occur ". This, oddly enough, is precisely what Chowrin claimed to have found years previously in his experiments with a hysterical subject. [1] But these fantastic results of Romains and Chowrin were quite certainly due to unconsciously articulated cues against which neither experimenter seems to have taken any precautions at all.

The whole of Romain's book *Eyeless Sight* is an excellent illustration of the degree to which self-deception may occur when there is complete ignorance of such psychological principles as the involuntary and unconscious dissemination of sensory cues. The detailed telepathic experiments of the Polish psychologist Abramowski is another case in point. [2]

Dr. Soal's investigation of the vaudeville telepathist " Marion " was a good demonstration of how the practised individual can detect a playing-card blindfold or in the dark once he has had an opportunity to touch it beforehand : " Marion displayed great aptitude for recognising a playing card that he had once touched when this card was mixed with several other cards of similar make and pattern." [3] Marion usually did this by imparting a slight bend to the card in question ,which he was able to detect when he later went through the pack to locate it. He could also identify in the dark. stiff millboard cards, which he had previously been allowed to hold, by means of his sensitive touch alone. But, reported Dr. Soal, " when tactual and visual cues are completely ruled out Marion succeeds no more often than chance would predict ". The skill needed to memorise and detect slight irregularities in a stiff card is, in Marion's case, acquired through years of practise. It can not, however, be ruled out that specially gifted individuals are able to do this spontaneously and even unconsciously.

The means used by Marion to detect cards cannot be directly applied to the usual type of ESP experiment, except perhaps where the percipient—or any other person present during the experiment who remains within visual and auditory range of the percipient—has had an opportunity of seeing or holding the pack of cards used during, *or previous to,* the experiment. This, however, has very often happened :

[1] Chowrin, A. N., *A Rare Form of Hyperaesthesia of the Higher Sense-Organs*, Contributions to Neuropsychic Medicine, Moscow, 1898.
[2] See *Le Subconscient Normal.*
[3] Soal, S. G., *Preliminary Studies of a Vaudeville Telepathist*, University of London Council for Psychical Investigation, Bulletin III, 1937.

the contingency is aggravated when a particular pack has been used in more than one experiment. Dr. Soal, himself a firm believer in telepathy, points out in his report that these experiments with Marion " suggest a most serious source of error in a great many of the card-guessing tests described by Miss Ina Jephson and Dr. J. B. Rhine."

Another source of sensory cues in Rhine's earlier experiments has already been referred to : namely, that the impress of the symbol on the face of the card was often visible from the back when held at certain angles. In these experiments the identity of such cards could clearly have been revealed by the sense of touch alone, if the percipient was allowed to handle them, which in many cases he was.

In view of the great uncertainty involved in allowing the percipient to handle the cards, it must be accepted as a cardinal principle in all ESP experiments that the percipient be allowed no possible chance of touching them. Yet even if the percipient is effectively prevented from receiving any *direct* visual or tactile clues, the possible sources of sensory cues, apart from those already mentioned, are still numerous —a fact seldom appreciated by ESP experimenters.

Telepathy and Ideomotor Movements

We now come to a range of psychological phenomena which, following Tarchanow, we shall classify under the single heading of *ideomotor movements*. These may be loosely defined (in this context) as slight *involuntary* muscular actions which are directly attributable to the existence of a prevailing idea in the mind. *Ideomotor action* was a term originally introduced by Carpenter in 1874 and the concept was developed by William James as a theory of conation. Although the term has since been largely discarded by psychologists, we shall retain it here, confining it to the sense in which Tarchanow employed it in his study of involuntary movements in relation to " thought-reading " [5].

---

[4] op. cit., p. 94.
[5] Tarchanow, J., *Hypnotisme, Suggestion et Lecture des Pensées*, Paris, 1891.

Ideomotor actions may result either from conscious ideas, or from ideas of which the subject is not immediately aware and which may be called subconscious. A distinction must be made, however, between ideomotor action and psychological automatism. For in the latter the idea which produces the movement is said to be dissociated from the main stream of consciousness of the individual; this is not necessarily the case with ideomotor movements, which are in fact a natural and constant accompaniment, in one form or another, of all our mental activity, particularly when the emotions are in any way aroused.

The two chief investigators of ideomotor actions in relation to the occult were the Russian psychologist Tarchanow, and the well known American psychologist Jastrow. It is doubtful whether either had studied the reports of the other on the relation of ideomotor movements to telepathy and muscle-reading. But they both came to the same conclusions and arrived at them by using much the same methods —though the Russian psychologist used a rather more elaborate equipment and technique than his American confrère.

To give an illustration of the operation of ideomotor movements, we can do no better than to describe the main features of Jastrow's apparatus and one of the techniques which he used for studying them.

Since ordinary ide motor movements are often very slight' Jastrow and Tarchanow required apparatus of considerable delicacy for registering them. Jastrow's apparatus was simple : a square wooden frame contained a plate of glass upon which were placed three polished steel balls. These balls supported another framed plate of glass. Attached to the upper frame was a rigid rod which terminated in a recording apparatus. A complete record of every movement of the upper glass frame could thus be traced upon sheets of glazed paper by this means.

To use this automatograph, or tremograph, the subject places the tips of his fingers upon the glass plate which is supported by the three ball-bearings. It is virtually impossible to hold the plate still for more than a few seconds, particularly if a screen renders the subject's hand invisible to its owner. Under these conditions the subject is instructed to think as little as possible of his hand, and at the same time to make a reasonable effort to prevent it from moving. As long as the subject's attention is not fixed upon anything in particular, the resulting involuntary shaky movements of his hand produce a random meaningless pattern on the recording apparatus. But if the subject's attention is fixed on some object in the room, the pattern produced is that of an irregular line whose general direction lies towards the focus of attention. Again, if the subject is directed to count silently the ticks of a metronome, or even merely to watch its movements, the record shows that his hand moves to and fro—not accurately but in a general way—in time with the instrument. Tarchanow's experiments showed that if his subjects concentrated for any length of time upon an object, the resultant pattern showed " sometimes the figure of a square, sometimes the figure of a triangle or a circle, according to the dominant form of the object ". With geometric figures this tendency was even more marked.

In one of Jastrow's experiments the subject was asked to concentrate his attention for thirty-five seconds upon some patches of colour on the wall opposite. Without warning, the subject was then directed to count the strokes of a metronome for the same length of time. The sudden change completely altered the style of the ideomotor movements as revealed by the automatograph.

Jastrow and Tarchanow both found that unconscious ideomotor actions manifested themselves in slight movements of the whole body, generally in the form of an irregular swaying. By fixing the apparatus to the subject's head the movements could be recorded. It was found that in regard to these slight swaying movements there was a general movement towards any object of attention.

Not everybody shows the same degree of style of ideomotor activity ; some people show very little, while others can be extraordinarily responsive. The latter are potentially ex- cellent agents in certain types of vaudeville " telepathy " exhibitions.

Towards the end of the last century in Europe and America, great interest was aroused by the seemingly inexplicable feats of telepathy performed by professional " telepathists ", both on the public stage and at private exhibitions. Some of the exhibitions were extremely impressive, but in time the secret leaked out, and those who knew what was involved no longer talked about " thought-reading " but of " muscle-reading " instead. Thought-readers, it was noted, preferred to take hold of the hand, or place their palm on the forehead of the person whose thoughts they wished to " read ". Alternatively they kept them well within sight. When either of these conditions was absent—unless the thought-reader attached himself to his subject, as for example, by means of a rod or piece of string—nothing very much occurred.

Now " muscle-reading " is usually a highly skilful business. It is not limited only to the correct interpretation of slight ideomotor movements. Changes in breathing, slight flushing and tremors, changes of tension and relaxation, changes of expression—these factors and many others all help the muscle-reader in his act.

The traditional muscle-reading act is very different from, and relatively far simpler than, the modern ESP type of experiment. The former, in point of fact, is confined to a very limited kind of performance and depends almost entirely upon the muscle-reader playing a kind of "hot or cold " game with his subject or with his audience.

The older brand of muscle-reader excelled in such problems as finding objects hidden about the room or on one among a number of persons, finding a letter or a word on a certain page of a book, writing down words or ciphers thought of by another person, finding on a piano the notes of well-known melodies, identifying playing-cards chosen from a pack by members of the audience, or finding an object hidden in one of a number of identical boxes. Some of the tricks require greater skill and practice than others. The finding of hidden objects in the auditorium of a theatre is relatively simple ; for the unconscious reaction and the involuntary movements of the audience often enable the experienced muscle-reader to go straight to the place where the object is hidden with the minimum of hesitation.

On the other hand, such tricks as finding a melody on the piano take the muscle-reader a longer time and depend on the skilful use of tentative trials of notes and observing the reactions of the audience, or on noting their reactions as his fingers hover tentatively over the keys. To find a word in a book the same tentative and exploratory method is used. In both these types of performance, which naturally depend on a limited number of witnesses, the spectators must, of course, be able to watch what the muscle-reader is doing. All such performances of muscle-reading are much facilitated if the muscle-reader holds the hand of the subject whose thoughts he is trying to " read ", or touches some part of him ; with this aid most of the muscle-reader's tricks can even be carried out blind-folded. With very acute hearing he could undoubtedly solve the problems by hearing alone. Again, some of Tarchanow's experiments in muscle-reading were effected successfully through the muscle-reader being connected to his agent by a chain or a wire after having been blindfolded and having had his ears plugged !

Jastrow sums up thus the means whereby the vaudeville telepathist solves his problems : " In the exhibitions of muscle-reading, the changes in breathing, the flushing, the tremor of the subject when the reader approaches the hiding place, and the relative relaxation when he is on the wrong scent, serve as valuable clues ; to borrow the apt expression of " hide and seek ", the performer grows " hot " and " cold " with his subject. Then, too, the tentative excursions in one direction and another, to determine in which the subject follows with least resistance, present another variation of the same process. The hushed calm of the audience when success is near, the restlessness and whispering during a false scent, are equally welcome suggestions which a clever performer utilizes, thereby adding to the éclat of his exhibition. . . . When a combination of numbers or of letters in a word is to be guessed, the operator passes over with the subject the several digits or the alphabet, and notes at which the tell-tale tremor or mark of excitement occurs, and so again performs the feat on the basis of the involuntary contractions that express the slightest changes of attention or interest when the correct number or letter is indicated."[1]

Many spiritualistic mediums use the method of " muscle-reading " to gain their information. They talk, often at random, throwing out tentative suggestions, words, places,

---

[1] *Fact and Fable in Psychology*, p. 334.

names and the rest and noting the reactions of their " sitters". With an ouija-board some American mediums have, in the past, acquired an uncanny skill in interpreting the slight hesitations and ideomotor movements of their clients. Jung himself has investigated this aspect of the subject. [2]

One trick reported in connection with muscle-readers is that of reproducing a line drawing of some object or figure held in the hand of the agent. The tentative strokes of the pencil and the presence or absence of incipient success in what is being drawn produce slight but perceptible involuntary reactions in the agent; whereby the percipient may gauge the failure or success of his drawing as it develops before the agent's eyes.

In most cases muscle-readers detect their agents' involuntary reactions by watching them, i.e. by the sense of sight. The main exception to this is when the muscle-reader is touching the person of the agent or is connected to him in some way—such as by a rod or piece of string. In Soal's investigation of the vaudeville-telepathist Marion it became clear that Marion confined his observations in the main to watching the agent's face and head. When the agent's body was hidden by a screen, Marion was still able to locate hidden objects, to identify playing cards chosen by the agent from among a number of others, and to carry out other exhibitions of " psychometry " and " telepathy ". Once the agent's face was covered, however, Marion was helpless.

An important question arises as to whether muscle-readers are always aware of the method they themselves use to carry out their feats of "telepathy". In Marion's case Dr. Soal reports that he quite genuinely believes that he does it by telepathy. It is probable, writes Soal " that after years of practice, the reading of *indicia* has become a subconscious mental process which Marion is entirely unable to analyse ". [3]

Unconscious observation and interpretation of sensory cues can be a very deceptive phenomenon, and there is no longer the least shadow of doubt that it occurs with many ESP percipients. It is deceptive in that *the percipient him-*

[2] See *Collected Papers on Analytical Psychology*, 1920.
[3] *Preliminary Studies of a Vaudeville Telepathist*, p. 36.

self, with his mind impregnated by notions of telepathy and other occult ideas, cannot recognise the true cause of his success in such experiments, and finds in these successes false confirmation of his own irrational beliefs.   That cues can be gained and utilised without the conscious awareness of the individual is well exemplified by the unexpected results of Jastrow's experiments with an electro-magnet.[4]

IDEOMOTOR MOVEMENTS AND ESP TESTS

While the traditional muscle-reader probably shares to some extent with the ESP percipient the faculty of noting and interpreting involuntarily-given clues without conscious awareness, the traditional muscle-reading act has little connection with the modern type of ESP experiment.   The methods of muscle-readers have been mentioned in some detail because by no means all ESP experimenters appear to be aware of them, and they indicate very clearly the type of experiment which any believer in extra-sensory perception must avoid if he wishes to have his results taken at all seriously.

The modern type of ESP experiment generally consists in the percipient guessing the order of a pack of 25 cards containing five symbols—star, waves, circle, cross and rectangle.   He cannot make tentative calls to test out the involuntary reactions of the agent, the superviser, or any one else who is cognizant by accident or design of the order of the cards, although in some types of ESP experiment exploratory movements of a pointer could bring about the same result.   This would therefore appear almost to rule out the possibility of any form of muscle-reading in the majority of ESP tests, for even if the percipient were able to see or hear any involuntary movements he would have difficulty in identifying them with any particular symbol. Yet there is one possibility, which we shall now proceed to discuss.

As will be seen in the next chapter, the Danish experimenters Lehmann and Hansen noted that the concentration for any length of time on a word tends to produce an innerva-

⁴ See p. 418–420.

tion or *enneurosis* of the vocal muscles, corresponding to a rudimentary or incipient form of articulation. They concluded that alterations in the tone of breathing brought about by such a muscular innervation was sufficient to provide the percipient with requisite clues as to the nature of the word in question—provided that the percipient had a limited number of words from which to guess.

Such ideomotor reactions more properly pertain to the subject of involuntary articulation, but they are mentioned here because they form a helpful link between involuntary articulation proper and simple ideomotor reactions. They further point to the possibility of a code being developed from spontaneous ideomotor movements of the lips, tongue and throat muscles. In this connection it is interesting to note a conclusion of Tarchanow's : that after constant repetition—as, for example, in a situation provided by ESP types of experiment—a particular pattern of ideomotor movements of the lips and tongue tends to become associated with particular words *or their corresponding mental images,* unless the attention is directed towards their suppression.

That a particular pattern of ideomotor movements of the lips and tongue, may, after constant repetition, become associated with a particular word, appears to be of great relevance to the standard ESP type of experiment; for here the telepathic agent is trying to " transmit " mentally a continual and random succession of only five symbols. Clearly the constant repetition of the five symbols by the agent ideally fulfils Tarchanow's condition. In many ESP experiments the agent does not " concentrate " on each symbol as it appears but merely gives it a glance without involving the least conscious effort. It is perhaps significant that Tarchanow did not merely confine the pattern of ideo-motor movements to *words* only, but also to their corresponding mental images : i.e. the mere sight of an object or its mere mental representation may lead after constant repetition to a consistent pattern of slight ideomotor movements of the lips and tongue. Such a pattern can be regarded as something in the nature of a code—each symbol possessing its own particular pattern of movements.

Soal himself appears to have envisaged approximately

the same idea ; in regard to Rhine's ESP experiments he comments :

> " No such experiments can be considered of any crucial importance if the percipient is able to see any part of the agent's body. Where the percipient has only a small number (5 or 6) figures from which to make his choice, the possibility of visual codes *elaborated unconsciously* when the same agent and percipient work together over any considerable period of time is too patent to be overlooked." [1]

Unfortunately Soal throughout most of his own experiments has almost invariably overlooked the possibility of such a code being transmitted auditorily to the percipient by means of sounds which the supervising experimenters fail to perceive *or recognise* ; the case of Ilga K., which will be discussed in detail further on, lends further emphasis to this possibility. Variations in the tone or evenness of the breathing are all that would be required. Soal's precautions would serve only to obviate *visual* cues afforded by a code derived from ideomotor hand-movements, limb or body movements, movements or expressions of the face, and ideomotor movements of the larynx, lips and tongue other than actual involuntary articulation.

It may be objected that any such visual or auditory codes, whether " elaborated unconsciously " or arrived at fortuitously (as Tarchanow has suggested) through the more primitive means of involuntary ideomotor movements, can only operate in ESP tests provided that one condition is fulfilled : viz. provided that the percipient has at some time gained the chance of seeing each type of card at the same time as the agent made the particular pattern of movements or sounds connected with it, so that the percipient can identify the different code movements or sounds which pertain to each card–symbol.

There are several ways by which the percipient might learn the correspondence of the cards with the ideomotor code. Occasional *endophasic* articulation might provide him with the necessary cues. An alternative has been pointed out by the Polish experimenter Abramowski. Abramowski, although convinced of the " fact " of telepathy, did not deny that unconsciously given cues played a con-

---

[1] *Preliminary Studies of a Vaudeville Telepathist*, p. 33.

siderable part in his experiments, notably through the
sense of touch. Unconscious muscular movements by the
agent, he explained, can provide the percipient with good
clues as to the identity of the words to be guessed, by indicating either the number of syllables in the word, the
rhythm of the word, or the accent on the syllables. But
such movements also offer the possibility of being seen or
as well as being felt, and if ideomotor movements are to be
" unconsciously elaborated " into some kind of a code then
it is extremely likely that this code would arise spontaneously
through the natural rhythms and accentuations associated
with normal articulation. Any such code would stand a
very good chance of being interpreted very rapidly by the
conditions of the ESP tests where only five symbols are
used. This is only possible in cases where the percipient has
to guess a word from among a limited number, as was actually the case in Abramowski's experiments.

There are, naturally, many limitations to any theory of
the transmission of sensory cues solely by this method
under the conditions of modern ESP experiments. But
sometimes, certainly, it may play a big rôle in helping the
percipient to interpret any code based on an individual
pattern of ideomotor movements for each particular word,
symbol, object or picture in constant use during an experiment.

ESP experimenters should not forget that where the
experimental conditions permit the possibility of a person
other than the agent touching or seeing the cards—as often
occurs, for example, in clairvoyant experiments—it is also
possible, apart from any question of unconscious articulation
that information concerning their order may be conveyed to
the percipient, through hearing or sight, by involuntary
movements or a rough ideomotor code.

It is interesting to note that over forty years ago, Northcote Thomas, suggested another source of sensory cues. He
attributed many of his own successful results in telepathy
tests to the percipient's keen hearing and his ability to
interpret the noise of the scorer's pencil on the score-sheet,
as the latter wrote down the initial letter of each card for
the purpose of subsequent checking. " It is clearly no far-

fetched hypothesis that the ear could detect and interpret the difference of the sound of the pencil according to the name of the suit that was being written." [1]

Where the percipient gains his cues through variations in the agent's breathing, we are not, properly speaking, justified in differentiating the process from what we have called " unconscious articulation ", a subject which will be discussed in considerable detail in the next chapter.

---

[1] *Thought Transference*, 1905.

Chapter Twenty-five

" INVOLUNTARY WHISPERING " AND AUDITORY HYPERACUITY

W̲E̲ ̲H̲A̲V̲E̲ ̲J̲U̲S̲T̲ seen that one of Tarchanow's conclusions was that after constant repetition a particular pattern of ideomotor movements of the lips and tongue may become associated with a particular word or its corresponding mental image. We now come to another form of involuntary activity on the part of the " telepathic " agent—that of rudimentary or incipient articulation—sometimes referred to as " involuntary whispering ". Muscle reading provides an excellent illustration of the view that all thought is, in Jastrow's words, " more or less successfully suppressed action " ; that " the tendency of thought to find an outlet in the muscles is inherent in the action of the nervous system". This principle applies no less to the muscles connected with the mechanism of speech than to other parts of the body.

The subject of " involuntary whispering " has been almost entirely neglected by psychical researchers since the beginning of the century. Yet it is undoubtedly a fact that unconscious articulation plays a very large rôle in the communication of cues during ESP tests.

The first serious experiments in connection with unconscious articulation were carried out by Lehmann and Hansen. These were instigated in the first instance as a result of the experiments of Professor H. Sidgwick of Cambridge University which, he claimed, conclusively established the existence of telepathy. The Danish experimenters desired to find out whether or not the apparent telepathic effect could be magnified by artificial means. Accordingly, they placed two concave spherical mirrors opposite each other, the distance between their respective foci being two metres. The experimenters sat down back to back with their heads opposite the focal point of each mirror. They tried to transmit, telepathically, numbers ranging from 10 to 99, which were written on counters and taken out of a bag haphazardly by the agent.

During the experiments it was soon observed that there existed a strong tendency to enneurosis of the vocal muscles after a particular number had been thought of for some time. In order, therefore, to convince themselves that the hearing of semi-articulated words had not been responsible for the results, the agent placed his mouth, and the percipient his ear, at the respective focus of each mirror, while the former allowed free play to the hitherto restrained vocal movements. At the same time he took care to keep his mouth closed and his lips from moving. Under these conditions the experimenters soon became convinced that rudimentary vocalisation had been responsible for Professor Sidgwick's " telepathic " effect. Out of 500 such tests, in the course of which each of the experimenters took his turn acting as agent and percipient, 33.2 per cent of the numbers were transmitted correctly, 41.2 per cent were so far correct that one of the figures was right, while only 25.6 per cent were totally incorrect.

Some of the experimenters' findings were open to criticism, but even Professor Sidgwick held that they had proved their main contention :

" That is, they have certainly proved experimentally—what, in our discussion we could only surmise as possible—that a number of two digits may be communicated from agent to percipient, by faint whispering with closed lips, so that a bystander in a slightly less favourable position for hearing than the percipient would hear no sound and probably observe no external signs of movement of the organs of speech." [1]

In Professor Sidgwick's original telepathy experiments the percipients had been hypnotised. We have already seen that an increase in the acuity of one or more of the senses often accompanies certain hysterical and hypnotic states.

[1] Sidgwick, H., *Involuntary Whispering*, Proc. S.P.R., 1897, p. 298.

The concave mirrors in the experiments of Lehmann and Hansen were reasonably held to act as an artificial substitute for any such auditory hyperacuity or *hyperacusia*, and provided they could establish the fact that numbers may be communicated with a fair degree of success by means imperceptible to a bystander, the experimenters were well on their way to establishing their theory of involuntary articulation as an explanation of Professor Sidgwick's experiments.

They had stated, in their report, that " no movements of the lips were visible, and a bystander could not hear any sounds ". Accordingly, Professor Sidgwick, omitting the concave mirrors but with the distance between agent and percipient considerably reduced, carried out some experiments of his own to establish these points. He reports :

> " I found that it was quite possible for an observer, fixing his gaze on the agent's mouth, neither to hear nor see any sign of a whisper at a distance of two feet from the agent, while the percipient, at a distance which varied, but was ultimately extended to 18 inches—measured from the agent's mouth to the percipient's ear—heard with sufficient distinctness to attain a considerable amount of success in guessing." [2]

The only criticism against the theory of involuntary whispering so far as these experiments were concerned was that the whispering was not involuntary. But this criticism is of little importance. One of the main points of the experiments was that the Danish experimenters had found in their earlier tests a strong tendency to innervation of the vocal muscles when a particular number was thought of for any length of time. Such movements of the vocal apparatus are a perpetual accompaniment to our thinking, a fact which has led many Behaviourists to postulate all thinking as " silent speech ". They may easily be detected by the use of a laryngograph, an instrument which records movements of the larynx and which is often used in empirical investigation of behaviourist theories of consciousness. The Behaviourists base the use of this and similar instruments on the assumption that thinking is merely implicit speech behaviour. They also make considerable use of the labio-

---

[2] Sidgwick, H., ibid., p. 299.

graph, an instrument which records slight lip movements. ESP investigators might well take a tip from the Behaviourists by using such instruments in their own experiments.

In weighing the results of the Lehmann and Hansen experiments, we must naturally take into account the fact that free play was given to the natural tendency to innervate the vocal muscles. The result of the consequent exaggeration of this tendency is precisely what one might have expected, namely a very large percentage of successful " transmissions "—over 74 per cent being successful or half successful. When all allowances are made for the reflecting mirrors which were used, the degree of success in these experiments is enormously higher than that found in modern ESP tests. Not only were the lips firmly closed, but the percipient had a total of ninety numbers from which to guess instead of only five. If Lehmann and Hansen had carried out their experiments with only five numbers, each easily distinguishable in sound from the others, then we might have expected as many as ninety per cent of the transmissions to be successful. In the modern type of ESP experiment only five types of symbol are used; such a small number is ideal for aiding the successful reception of sensory cues due to incipient articulation or other involuntary reactions.

Such terms as " involuntary whispering " or " unconscious articulation " are highly inappropriate, unless, of course, they refer to actual whispering or genuine articulation. The slight movements of the vocal apparatus which are known to accompany, in varying degree, the processes of conscious thinking, are better represented by the term *endophasic innervations*. Properly speaking, endophasia refers to the silent reproduction of words or sentences " in one's head " without overt movements of the apparatus of speech. Generally, however, endophasia is accompanied by a slight but detectable activity of the vocal organs; and if, as may happen, the individual starts " furiously to think " the endophasic innervations of the articulatory apparatus may blossom out into full-fledged involuntary whispering or even loud vociferation of which the individual himself remains unaware. There is, naturally, a large series of gradations between simple endophasic innervations and the action of unconsciously talking aloud.

The speed with which modern ESP tests are carried out and the lack of any artificial hearing aids must naturally tend to reduce very greatly the successful transmission of informative cues by endophasic innervation. It is noticeable, however, that very few ESP reports state whether the mouth of the agent, or any other person to whom the cards are visible, remained firmly closed during the experiments. Yet the experiments of Lehmann and Hansen are obviously very important in relation to all ESP experiments where the percipient is within hearing range of the agent. Admittedly in these experiments, and in Professor Sidgwick's subsequent confirmatory experiments, the articulation with closed lips was not carried out unconsciously. Nevertheless, they do prove that intelligible articulation with closed lips is not only a possibility but that by such means information can be conveyed to another person with sufficiently keen hearing, and that a bystander may have the greatest difficulty in detecting the process.

Unconscious articulation is a common enough phenomenon, and the above experiments prove that intelligible auditory cues may be unconsciously provided with closed lips during many types of ESP experiment. When the symbols to be conveyed " telepathically " are few in number, this is still more likely to occur. Mere differences in the tone of breathing may very well become associated in the percipient's mind with a specific symbol. But apart from this it seems probable that the *actual sound of the words* can be transmitted through closed lips. With the lips slightly apart, transmis ion of verbal clues to a hyperacusic percipient presents no difficulty at all ; and all ESP experimenters should note that it is very easy to allow the passage of air through the lips while the lips themselves are, to all appearances, firmly closed.

We need not discuss further the conveyance of auditory cues by means of articulation with closed lips. The fact has been sufficiently well established experimentally, and anyone can try the experiment out for himself. The experimenter in telepathy has almost always ignored this possibility. *Yet it is perfectly obvious from the above that all experiments in telepathy must be deemed totally invalid where the percipient is within possible auditory range of the agent.* In the case of a hyperacusic subject the maximum extent of the auditory range, when the agent's lips are closed, is difficult to fix, and may well extend to a *score of yards or even more under favourable acoustic conditions.*

The high percentage of successes of the Danish experimenters was entirely due to the fact that the experiments were carried out under ideal conditions. These conditions do not usually pertain to the modern ESP experiment. In such experiments the speed of guessing the cards is high. One is not surprised, therefore, to find that articulated (and other auditory) cues " get across " to the percipient relatively infrequently. Even with a hyperacusic percipient the degree of success would only be detected by methods of statistical analysis.

The great majority of telepathy experiments carried out hitherto have been arranged so that the percipient is within easy auditory range of the agent. Many of the clairvoyant experiments are open to the same criticism, because the experimenter or his assistant have had the opportunity to touch or see the cards before or during the experiment, thereby laying the experiment open to the same objection as one in which a " telepathic " agent is taking part. However capably the ESP experimenter may defend such experiments, the fact remains that once the smallest flaw in the experimental situation is admitted, the need for a supernatural or " paranormal " explanation of the result becomes totally redundant.

It seems an almost inevitable conclusion that the good telepathic agent is nothing more than a responsive " endophasic innervator " or " involuntary whisperer "; and that the success of the good " telepathic " percipient and the successful clairvoyant depends mainly on his or her keenness of hearing.

THE CASE OF ILGA K

The case of Ilga K provides an extremely good example of the type of situation which may arise in telepathy investigations. We have here a series of investigations where the telepathy hypothesis appeared at first to be well and truly established, but where it was later found that the words conveyed " telepathically " were due to actul articulation by the " telepathic " agent and to a highly developed auditory sense on the part of the percipient. Typical of telepathy investigators, too, was the dogmatic certainty with which the telepathy hypothesis was enunciated by Professor von Neureiter, Professor of Forensic Medicine at the University of Riga ;[1] Neureiter, incidentally, had originally shown himself extremely sceptical when it was suggested that he undertake an investigation of Ilga K. Both he and his colleague, Professor Amsler, were both professional men of high academic standing and it is an object lesson to observe how they, as thousands of other less gifted individuals have done in the past, fell back on supernaturalism as the explanation of Ilga's extraordinary faculty.

Ilga K was a nine year old Lithuanian peasant girl of inferior mental capacity born of normal parents. She was exceptionally backward at speaking, and only at the age of eight had she eventually managed to speak so far as to be enabled to attend an elementary school. After a while she was able to read individual letters but showed no capacity for reading words or even single syllables. The teacher found, however, to his amazement, that if he stood by her with his eyes on the book she was trying to read, Ilga was able to " read ", without error, any text he put before her, even one in a foreign language ! Similarly, with arithmetical problems which the child was totally incapable of solving by herself, if the teacher or the mother worked out the answers mentally, Ilga gave them the solution without hesitation. The child's mother also complained that she could not hide anything from the child, for Ilga immediately knew where the object was hidden without being told. Was this extraordinary faculty of Ilga's attributable to telepathy ?

---

[1] *Wissen um Fremdes Wissen*, Gotha, 1935.

This is what Professor Neureiter and his collaborators wished to find out.

In these tests the mother acted mainly as the agent. All that the teacher and the mother had told the learned investigators about the child's faculty was fully borne out during these tests. Ilga " solved " arithmetical problems and " read " not only in Lithuanian but also in German, French, English and Latin. It was noted that mistakes of pronunciation were precisely those appropriate to her mother's education. Ilga had no need to look at a book. Thoughts could, apparently, be " transmitted " merely by the act of thinking. Lists of words and figures could be repeated accurately by the child without, it appeared, the slightest intervention of sensory cues. Neureiter became convinced that telepathy was the only explanation, and the authenticity of his experiments were vouched for by several members of Riga University. The press hailed his report as something for which the world had long been waiting—positive proof of the existence of telepathy.

This verdict did not, alas, remain unchallenged. In 1936 and 1937 other tests were carried out by a Latvian Ministry of Education commission led by Professor Dahle, Director of the Institute of Psychology of Riga University. The verdict of this Latvian Commission was that Ilga's faculty was based upon auditory hyperacuity and that the mother and teacher provided her (consciously or unconsciously) with definite auditory and possibly optical aids.

This conclusion was not reached without extended experiments and the use of modern technical equipment. Yet Neureiter could very well have guessed the ultimate cause of Ilga's reputed " telepathic " function. For when the mother concentrated on written words and sentences Ilga repeated them in an odd monotonous tone, dividing each word up into separate syllables, which would certainly have caused most investigators to suspect that she was receiving auditory cues syllable by syllable. As the later Commission subsequently found out, this was precisely the case.

But Neureiter was so certain that the mother, acting as the agent, did not provide any auditory cues—at least none so far as he was able to detect—that he committed himself to what appeared the only other alternative, namely the theory of telepathy.   He reported : " Every possibility of transmission of the conceptual contents by the way of the normally known sensory channels—whether optic, acoustic or otherwise—has been excluded. We have to deal with a ' paranormal ' relation of person to person."   This type of statement has a familiar ring. All psychical researchers or parapsychologists have repeated it in one form or another.   The dogmatic *certainty* of such pronouncements in regard to the exclusion of sensory cues is completely typical.   Yet the later Commission proved Professor Neureiter's claims to be nonsense.   One cannot help wondering whether all such claims made by ESP experimenters are as groundless as Neureiter's.   In any event the case of Ilga K. provides an excellent object lesson and for that reason alone is well worth going into at some length.

The whole history of the Ilga K case demonstrates the extraordinary care necessary in " telepathic " or similar types of experiment.   Above all, it shows that the untrained or self-trained person is very easily mislead into faulty conclusions ; and under the heading of self-trained in this particular connection may be reckoned almost every one of those psychologists and ESP experimenters who have published results confirming telepathy or clairvoyance.   The psychical researcher is seldom fitted by outlook or by training to study problems involving sensory hyperacuity and the unconscious presentation of sensory cues.   And it must be added that he does not in general wish his investigations into the supernatural to be explained away by any such unexciting means.

The Latvian Commission possessed both the equipment and the trained personnel for tackling the problem presented by Ilga, including a dictaphone, electric amplifiers, a phoneticist and an expert in lip-reading.   The secret of her performance was traced, in the main, to the auditory cues contained in the mother's continual words and cries of encouragement.   The phoneticist in the report on the case stated that the opening sound of the next syllable to be conveyed to Ilga was tacked on to the end of each word of encouragement or admonishment offered by the mother. In this way Ilga was unable to pronounce a whole word but repeated the syllables of the word separately. Proof of this was forthcoming when the deaf-mute specialist found he could read each of the words from the movements of the mother's lips while watching her through the window of a sound-proof chamber; while Ilga herself, being unable to hear, was unable to " read " the words being transmitted !

This quiet articulation of the opening sound or separate syllables of the words being transmitted was not noticed in the early part of the Latvian Commission's experiments with Ilga. The fact is important, for it supports what Lehmann and Hansen demonstrated in principle—that articulated sounds can be picked up by practised or hyperacusic individuals, while other less gifted or inexperienced persons present at the time may be unable to hear them. This is a fact which the ESP experimenter seldom appears to appreciate.

It was usually found that the greater the distance between Ilga and her mother the louder became the articulated sounds. In one series of tests, says the report, the mother gave so many aids over a distance of thirty-three feet that several of the observers were able to hear the correct syllables before Ilga herself uttered them.

Nevertheless, the acuity of Ilga's hearing was phenomenal. The child's governess had trained herself to breathe softly the opening sound of the next syllable to be transmitted. She succeeded by this method in transmitting words to Ilga with as great a success as the mother. It was only with difficulty, especially at some distance, that observers standing by could detect the sounds being breathed which Ilga picked up so rapidly.

It was Ilga's schoolmaster who had been largely instrumental in bringing the amazing faculty of the mentally retarded child before the attention of the world of science. But repetitions of his book-reading with Ilga showed that the teacher whispered audibly ! Presumably he was unaware of this fact, otherwise he would not have been so puzzled over the strange reaction it produced in his young charge. This was almost certainly a genuine case of unconscious whispering. The mother's vocal hints might also very easily have been an unconscious reaction. Such whispering, however, is controllable once the agent has had his or her attention drawn to the fact. Professor Neureiter, too, provides an excellent example of unconscious whisperings in his original investigations of Ilga. Needless to say, he attributed Ilga's response to telepathy.

Neureiter, acting as agent, was attempting to transmit a sentence in a child's Lithuanian primer—*mate gaja uz kleti*. He states that he concentrated hard on his task, mentally accentuating every syllable but without the least response from Ilga. He was just about to finish the experiment when his eye was caught by an archaic Lithuanian word *Bruhte*, which he was surprised to see in a modern school primer. Immediately Ilga, next door, uttered this very same word. What Neureiter had believed to be an instance of telepathy was quite obviously an instance of unconscious articulation brought about by the sudden relaxing of his attention from the task in hand.

The part played by auditory cues in the case of Ilga K has been thoroughly established. But how could Ilga without training and conscious practice, acquire such an astonishing faculty ? She had in fact acquired a spontaneous habit of picking up scarcely perceptible semi-articulated sounds and uttering them almost simultaneously —a habit which would take a normal person months of practise. As often as not, she achieved verbal repetition of syllables and words which she had heard but which were inaudible to observers present.

One series of experiments brings out the singularity of Ilga's powers of auditory discernment. While the mother was acting as agent, dictaphone records were made of her incessant verbal encouragements, which, of course, included the softly articulated sounds and syllables enabling Ilga to " read " her mother's " thoughts ". The records were subsequently played back to Ilga, who reproduced successfully a good proportion of the words or separate syllables contained in the mother's continual encouragements. The remarkable thing was that no one else was able to detect any other sounds apart from the encouragements of the mother, even with the highest degree of amplification.

Evidently Ilga's gift did not depend so much on auditory hyperacuity as a practised ability to discern and differentiate those particular sounds constituting the cues from those which constituted the mother's encouragements. She possessed, in fact, the same kind of practised gift whereby the expert piano-tuner can hear dissonant overtones quite indiscernible to the average person. *The fact that some individuals can differentiate and interpret auditory cues which are indiscernible or meaningless to the average observer is probably the main factor contributing to the misinterpretation of all types of " successful " ESP experiments.*

In the Lehmann and Hansen experiments the articulation with closed lips was deliberate, while the convex mirror amplified and caught the sounds thus made. In the case of Ilga K. the agent's lips were open and moving but there was no artificial aids to facilitate hearing. We cannot but accept the fact that this mentally retarded child demonstrated much the same phenomena as that which the Danish scientists demonstrated with the aid of convex mirrors— Ilga's hyperacusia largely fulfilling the function of the latter's mechanical device.

It would be natural to ask at this stage whether modern ESP experimenters have conducted any research into hyperacusia and allied subjects. So far is this from being the case that the subject appears to be virtually taboo in all the leading psychical research journals today. There is apparently a real fear that once the floodgates of rational explanation are opened the hosts of experiments which are claimed to have " proved " telepathy and clairvoyance will be washed away by the tide. A myth has been built up which must be preserved at all costs—a myth which states that telepathy and clairvoyance have been empirically established as scientific phenomena and that there is no more any need to question the fact. Such myths can only be preserved by ignoring all those factors which would otherwise destroy them.

The following is a good example of the uncritical attitude adopted by both experimenter and editorial staffs in the conduct and reporting of ESP experiments.

In the *Journal of Parapsychology* for 1938, Dr. R. Drake published a report of a case very similar to that of Ilga K. He presented this case as an example of " extra-sensory perception ". His report is remarkable for the fact that it ignores all the findings of the Latvian Commission concerning their tests with Ilga, which had appeared only six months earlier in the same Journal. Even more surprising was the fact that the editorial abstract preceding Drake's report made no reference to the Ilga K case. Yet, as will be seen, the two reports, following so closely one upon the other, admit of such a close resemblance that their similarity could not have been ignored by a mere oversight, but must be attributed mainly to the policy pursued by the editors of the above-mentioned Journal. Comparison between the two cases will show how little the title of Dr. Drake's report—" An Unusual Case of Extra-Sensory Perception "—was justified.

Drake's subject, a mentally deficient boy referred to as " Bo ", had received a cerebral injury at birth. At the age of eleven he was unable to run properly, could not concentrate except over short periods, possessed an extremely poor memory and was generally mentally backward to a marked degree.

Like Ilga, he could only read when his mother was looking at the book by his side, and he too possessed a marked facility for " reading " his mother's thoughts. In the above respects Bo's case was almost identical with that of Ilga's. He was not subjected, however, to the same intensive study as Ilga. Her investigators pronounced, on excellent grounds, against the hypothesis of telepathy. If Bo had been subjected to the same type of experiments as Ilga, it may be fairly assumed that the same conclusions would have been reached.

With few exceptions both Ilga and Bo gave evidence of their unusual abilities only when their respective mothers were acting as agents. Dr. Drake undertook a considerable number of tests with zener cards, often with phenomenal success—one series of 14 runs, each of 25 card-calls, producing the unparalleled average of 21 successful guesses per run. Like Ilga again, this successful reproduction of whichever word or symbol his mother was concentrating on was invariably preceded by a verbal direction or some form of verbal utterance by the mother.

In those cases where Bo's mother did not give a verbal signal, such as the words " ready " or " go ", a toy clicker was substituted; in these " clicker trials " his scoring dropped immediately. That it did not drop to chance level was probably due, we may assume, to the fact that the boy's mother was still acting as agent and that she was still quietly breathing the symbol upon which she was concentrating. When someone other than his mother acted as agent, Bo failed to score above chance expectation.

The great similarity between this " unusual case of extra-sensory perception " and that of Ilga K can leave us in no doubt of the explanation of Dr. Drake's card scores. It is certainly curious that such evident hyperacuity of hearing and quick verbal reactions should be found to occur in two mentally retarded children. A useful analogy may, perhaps, be found in those children who possess a faculty of extremely rapid mental calculation of mathematical problems—many of these children being mentally deficient to a high degree in most other respects.

Hyperacusia and the Unconscious Perception of Sensory Cues

In the annals of psychical research frequent reference has been made to the " telepathy " experiments of Professor Gilbert Murray, the famous classical scholar. These experiments were even quoted by Professor Jaensch as instances of the occurrence of telepathy in the grave pages of *Zeitschrift für Psychologie* in 1931. It is curious, and very typical, that psychical researchers have been content to ignore the opinion of Gilbert Murray himself in regard to these experiments.

" Professor Murray himself does not believe that the results he gets are due to telepathy, if by that is meant the transmission of thought without aid from the ordinary senses, hearing, sight, touch, etc. As I understand him, he believes he gets into a state when he is peculiarly sensitive to noise, and his hearing becomes so acute that he hears something of the conversation between the thinkers when they are settling the subject they are to think about. It is not so acute, however, that he can distinguish the words they say, but he hears enough to suggest something to him . . . . It is clear that if this were the process the percipient would have a much better chance of success if, as in this case, the thinkers were either members of his family or intimate friends with whose special interests in literature, history or politics, as well as incidents in their lives, he was well acquainted." [1]

These experiments of Gilbert Murray are instructive, for they bear out once again the fact that some individuals are capable of auditory acuity far beyond the normal range. In this particular case also there is little doubt that the reception and interpretation of the auditory cues took place mainly subconsciously. This factor throws a good deal of light on the delusionary beliefs of many " telepathic " percipients. Their belief in a supernatural causation of their successes may be largely attributed to the fact that they do not consciously hear the auditory cues.

We can do no better than to quote Lloyd Tuckett in this connection :

" Another most important possibility must always be borne in mind in telepathic experiments, namely that sensory impressions may affect consciousness without being consciously perceived—in other words, a subconscious impression may subsequently effect consciousness." [2]

In Professor Murray's case the subconscious impression registered in his conscious mind a tentative idea which, on being checked, was generally found to correspond with what his agents had been quietly discussing at the other end of the house.

In 1886 Professors Jastrow and Nuttall conducted some experiments to ascertain whether the human organism could in fact be sufficiently affected by magnetism for a person to become aware of it in some slight degree. Naturally enough, the results were negative, but these experiments were of value in showing how the operation of sensory

---

[1] Sir J. J. Thompson, *Recollections and Reflections*, p. 157.
[2] *The Evidence for the Supernatural*, p. 305.

cues might affect the individual's mental activity without his being aware of them ; if such a situation as this arose where a *telepathic agent* was unconsciously providing the sensory cues in question, the illusion of telepathy operating would be complete. And precisely this type of situation is likely to occur in a great many telepathic and clairvoyant experiments. It is therefore worth while here to give Lloyd Tuckett's summary of Jastrow's experiment with electro-magnetism :

" One observer (the percipient) sat on a chair in a room on the third floor of a tall building with his head between the two poles of the magnet, which was supported on two adjoining tables. The other observer (the agent) was in a room on the ground floor, turning by hand a gramme-dynamo machine, and so generating the current which was conducted to the electro-magnet by heavy insulated wires running out of the windows along the wall of the building and in through a window on the third floor. The agent communicated with the percipient by a system of electric signals ; otherwise they were *completely isolated* from one another, with over thirty feet and two heavy floors between them. The experiment consisted in the percipient trying to say when the coil was magnetised. They made eight hundred observations during a week, and on one of the last days, a quiet Sunday when the trams had stopped running, they came to the conclusion that at times they were able to detect the noise resulting from the turning of the dynamo, and that it was conducted along the wires. There was also another fallacy. For they found that on magnetising and demagnetising the magnet, a faint but yet audible molecular crepitation occurred, the sound produced being a very dull, rather sudden, click. The click accompanying demagnetisation was much more distinct than that accompanying magnetisation.

" During the first eight hundred experiments, the proportion of correct guesses indicated that there was some factor at work other than that of pure chance, and if they had not discovered the two fallacies, above-mentioned, their experiments would have been supposed to prove the existence of a magnetic sense for the detection of magnetic waves, the ' odyllic fluid ' of the old mesmerists. However, they were able to exclude these two fallacies, and then made 1,950 more observations on themselves and various students ; whereupon the proportion of correct guesses showed that there was no other factor present than that of pure chance.

" Thus auditory indications of which the percipient was utterly unconscious were used as a basis for forming the judgment during their first series of 800 experiments." [3]

The lesson to be learned from the above experiments should be noted by all psychical researchers. The fallacious conclusions drawn in the first 800 observations by such a cautious investigator as Jastrow indicates the extent to which self-deception may occur in ESP experiments.

The failure fully to appreciate the issues involved in the unconscious perception of sensory cues is not the only shortcoming which may be laid at the door of the psychical researcher. His complete indifference to the whole problem of the involuntary communication and unconscious reception of sensory cues is apparent from the entire lack of serious investigation into the problem. One may say without exaggeration that nearly all the deductions of the ESP experimenters are reached by virtue of their ignorance of such factors.

The most deceptive of all experimental situations in ESP research is that in which sensory cues are provided involuntarily by the agent and picked up unconsciously by a hyperacusic percipient. That such situations may occur is reasonably well substantiated by the case of Ilga K. With a hyperacusic percipient the danger of misinterpreting the experimental results is increased by the possibility that observers possessing normal hearing are unlikely to detect the process of transmission between agent and percipient.

It was pointed out near the beginning of the previous chapter that sensory hyperacuity is generally the result of psychological, as opposed to physiological, factors. The psychology of sensory hyperacuity is still not fully understood; so many imponderable factors enter into the problem. There are instruments for measuring auditory acuity, such as the *phonometer*; similarly there is the *acoumeter*, an instrument for determining auditory thresholds.

While such instruments as these would be a great asset

---

[3] *The Evidence for the Supernatural*, appendix J, p. 305.

to the psychical researcher, they cannot measure such factors as the subject's powers of subtle discrimination or differentiation of sounds. Nor do they make adequate allowance for the emotional state of the subject or his mental state at the time. *Hyperprosexia*, definable as extreme fixity of attention, is often a major element in sensory hyperacuity, together with a faculty for selective perception which can be acquired with practice or which may be a natural gift.

Such instruments as the phonometer and the acoumeter are designed to measure the point at which sensory stimuli attain sufficient magnitude to elicit a conscious response. Where unconscious responses are the main focus of interest, their use is obviously limited. In the ESP experimental situation the problem is to determine not merely the auditory threshold of the percipient, but the dominant psychological factors responsible for the hyperacusic effect—the extent to which the percipient can discriminate or differentiate between the dozens of minute noises which are reaching his ear simultaneously, the facility with which he recognises a particular noise as the one useful to him and whether he can correctly interpret that noise once he has recognised it. All these factors depend upon the make-up of the individual concerned and they are only measureable indirectly.

Auditory hyperacuity in the ESP experimental situation may be said to depend upon four variable factors : perception, discrimination, recognition, and interpretation ; any or all of which may take place at the unconscious level. These factors are in their turn influenced by the degree of natural alertness, the degree of concentration attained, and the extent to which the individual concerned can exclude irrelevant sensory stimuli ; it is the variations in these psychological factors which are almost certainly responsible for many of the various " decline " and " position " effects found by Rhine and his collaborators.

It may be seen, from the above, that the successes of the successful ESP percipient may be due not to any actual keenness of hearing, but to a natural or a trained faculty for discriminating and interpreting minimal sounds and movements from among the total number of sensory stimuli presenting themselves to the percipient's senses.

THE " SIXTH SENSE " OF THE BLIND

The extent to which the sense of hearing can be developed and the uses to which the resulting hyperacuity can be put is well exemplified by the way in which blind people may gain information from slight noises and echoes, which are imperceptible to the ear of those who possess the sense of sight. The subject is one of extraordinary interest and is well worth discussing briefly even though it is something of a diversion from the main subject.

The amazing faculty, which the blind often possess, of sensing obstacles in their path, has long been a source of controversy among psychologists. During the last thirty years, however, a great deal has been done to clarify the position, and it is now possible to state with accuracy the main principles whereby the blind achieve their skilful sensing of obstacles and the objects which surround them.

Their faculty for sensing objects, although explicable by normal psychological principles, has nevertheless given rise to the myth of a " sixth sense ". This was perhaps inevitable, for the mass of mankind almost invariably reverts to mystical explanations when faced with problems beyond its immediate comprehension. The blind have themselves, until fairly recently, believed in and contributed to this theory of a sixth sense. Indeed, in many countries, ancient and modern, the blind have received considerable advantages and have been highly respected through the mystic qualities ascribed to them. Throughout the ages they have been credited with the gift of being able to " see " or " sense " not only those things in immediate proximity to them, but also *distant* objects and events, whether in the past, the present or the future in point of time.

The fact remains, however, that the normal blind person uses the senses still remaining to him to facilitate his activities, particularly the senses of touch and hearing. It is his skill, and the use to which he puts his *auditory* sense,

which seems so uncanny at the time, and which has given
rise to the belief in the blind man's supernatural powers
of vision.

Many blind people can sense, at some distance away,
the presence of objects in or near their line of advance.

" They generally localise these sensations on their forehead, or on
their temples, and only those objects which are high as the face are,
as a general rule, perceived by them in this way . . . . The blind
perceive by the ear what they believe they perceive by the skin." [1]

Those who wish to go a little deeper into this problem
would do well to read the chapter on " The Substitution
of the Senses " in Villey's excellent monograph, *The World
of the Blind* ; M. Villey, although a professor of literature
at Caen University, has himself been totally blind from
a very early age.

By no means all the blind possess this faculty of sensing
obstacles ahead of them, and with those who do possess it
there are great variations in its efficacy.   Those who have
it in a highly developed degree will amaze those who observe it in operation for the first time ; objects may be
sensed at surprising distances.   However, " it is generally
those who become blind when young who avoid obstacles
with the greatest success, and who have the presentiment
of them at the greatest distances." [2]

The auditory sense is the main factor in blind people's
sensing at a distance.   Other contributory factors, however,
are skilful interpretation of variations in temperature,
variations in direction and strength of breezes and draughts,
and in the case of the deaf-blind, the sense of smell and the
detection and interpretation of vibrations through their
feet or those parts of their bodies in contact with the vi-
brating medium.   These subsidiary methods, however,
are used more or less consciously and supplement the auditory sense, which Villey compares to the subtle faculty
of the bat, an animal which guides itself in the dark by
hearing alone.   Like the bat, too, the sensing of objects
practically vanishes when the ears are hermetically sealed,

[1] Villey, ibid., pp. 101 and 104.
[2] Villey, ibid.

or, in the case of the deaf-blind, with the sealing of the nostrils.

It is the little continuous noises which help the blind most—the crackling of a fire, a fountain heard in the distance, or the rumble of traffic. These noises are continuously being deflected from every object surrounding the blind man, and it aids both his sensing of these objects and his orientation in regard to them.

One of the chief factors giving rise to the belief in a sixth sense lies in the remarkable fact that the blind, generally speaking, localise their auditory impressions on the forehead. This is a most interesting phenomenon. As Kunz pointed out, most of the blind tend to present their forehead towards the object they wish to locate, a spontaneous gesture explicable by the fact that the forehead lies more or less centrally between the two ears which are the real sensory organs, although the vague and fleeting sensations are not recognised as auditory impressions. In this connection Villey, himself blind, writes :

"The localisation is, however, so decided, that many blind persons refuse to admit the hypothesis of an illusion. And yet the illusion appears clearly in an experiment like the following : I place the plank, of which we have already spoken, at 70 centimetres from my forehead. I have no sensation of it at all. It is all in vain that I concentrate my attention. I do not perceive anything. I let my first finger slide over my thumb so that my fingers make a slight noise. Immediately the obstacle sensation invades the whole surface of my forehead. The auditive surroundings alone have been changed; the cause of the sensation appears exclusively tactile. If, on the contrary, I move my fingers without making any noise, no sensation is perceived." [3]

Villey has not recognised the autosuggestive nature of this sensory hallucination. It is produced by a combination of suggestive influences, which are composed of several factors : the fear of hitting or bumping the face, the traditional belief among the blind that the forehead is the centre of a sixth sense, the forehead's flat expanse which to the imagination appears naturally suitable for

---

[*] ibid., p. 115.

the " imprint " of impressions, and the central position in regard to the real organs of sense, in this case the ears. For the blind the forehead acts as a direction-finder to synchronise the auditory impressions reaching the two ears.

There is no doubt that if a blind child knew the true state of affairs from earliest infancy and were kept insulated from the ideas possessed by other blind individuals, the forehead sensation would usually be lacking. One may note in passing that many normal individuals can feel a similar sensation if they bring a sharp object, such as a needle, within a fraction of an inch of the nose or forehead without actually touching the skin. The expectancy evoked, with a probable component of apprehension, combines to produce a mild but distinct sensation in that part of the skin which appears most likely to be touched by the object.

Chapter Twenty-Six

CRITICISM OF THE AMERICAN ESP EXPERIMENTERS

For OVER HALF A CENTURY enthusiasts of psychical research, scientific occultism, or *parapsychology* as it is now frequently called, have been trying to demonstrate the existence of telepathy and clairvoyance by statistically assessable experiments. Each experimenter in turn has claimed to have proved the existence of one or the other, apparently impelled to do so by the short-comings in the experiments of his predecessors. Today universities in England, Holland and the United States have given official recognition to the work of such experiments, and have on at least eight occasions granted bachelors' and even doctors' degrees for experimental work or written theses on parapsychology. The man in the street cannot therefore be blamed if he has come to believe that telepathy and clairvoyance are now scientifically established facts. Yet scientific recognition of these experiments has not, in fact, been forthcoming and only a very small minority of psychologists and scientists give them credence.

The evidence for telepathy and clairvoyance is demonstrably of a very poor quality, despite the great mass of experiments that have been carried out. The grounds of criticism are numerous, the chief ones being the bias and unreliability of the experimenters, the vagueness of such terms as telepathy and clairvoyance which have never been given a definition in any scientific sense of the word, and the fact that parapsychologists in general tend to ignore such factors as hyperacuity of the senses and the unconscious dissemination and assimilation of sensory cues during their experiments.

Today the main proponent of extra-sensory perception —a term which subsumes both telepathy and clairvoyance —is Dr. Joseph Rhine of Duke University in the United States. Dr. Rhine has published several books on his experiments and those of his followers, and he also edits the *Journal of Parapsychology*, now in its sixteenth or seventeenth year. The volume of experimental work reported under his auspices is considerable, and if the claims of the American ESP experimenters were to be judged by the number of experiments they have carried out, the case for ESP or extra-sensory perception would have been accepted long ago. Such, however, has not been the case, and for several very good reasons.

In England the main focus of interest in ESP research has been the telepathy experiments of Dr. S. G. Soal of London University. Though relatively few in number compared with the large numbers of experiments reported by his transatlantic confrères, Soal's experiments are of a far higher quality and present a feature which until now has defied rational explanation. In view of the fact that many people regard Soal's experiments as the test case for extra-sensory perception, special attention has been given to them and a full critical analysis is given in the next chapter.

American ESP experimenters use a variety of procedures based on the use of " zener " cards. A pack or deck of zener cards consists of twenty-five cards, the face of each being marked with one or another of the following symbols—cross, waves, rectangle, star and circle. There are five of each symbol in each pack or deck. The aim of the experiment is for the *percipient* to guess the order of the cards without looking at them. Theoretically sensory cues of any kind are excluded from reaching the percipient. In practice this is a relatively rare occurrence owing to the experimenter's ignorance of the modes in which minute sensory cues may be disseminated.

The first and most obvious criticism of ESP experiments in general is that in few experiments have scientific methods of experimental control been employed. Unless considerations of distance have forced it on them ESP experimenters seldom take the trouble to isolate the percipient completely from all possible sources of information or informatory cues ; nor have they used automatic recording devices —devices which should record automatically both the order of the cards to be guessed if there is no previously prepared list, as well as the order of the percipient's guesses.

If ESP experiments are to become conclusive, then the procedure used must be such as to render both recording errors and the operation of sensory cues a physical impossibility. Most scientists would regard these precautions as the absolute minimum required. When rigid controls are consistently avoided, scientists smell a rat and usually with good cause. And the proponents of extra-sensory perception and psychokinesis must face the fact that in not a single " successful " parapsychological experiment has this minimum degree of experimental control been applied. The " down through " technique, in which the percipient has to guess the order of a pack of zener cards as they stand, could well be rendered foolproof if used in conjunction with an automatic recorder. Even then, experience has shown that the pack would have to be placed in a box with a locked lid by an assistant who had no contact with any one present at the card-guessing, neither immediately before nor during the experiment, if all possibility of sensory cues is to be ruled out. Genuine random distribution of the cards through effective shuffling or other means would also be required.

The fact is that card-guessing is the least practical way of testing subjects for extra-sensory perception. The method is too clumsy altogether and the exclusion of sensory cues is a far more difficult problem than one might naturally expect. Only experiments involving the complete isolation of the percipient and the use of automatic recording devices can ever be regarded as crucial in any except long-distance experiments.

One of the possible reasons why Rhine and his brother ESP experimenters have never taken the maximum safeguards against the possibility of sensory aids is that on Rhine's own admission such experiments have almost invariably proved failures. In introducing a percipient new to ESP test-procedure, he advises the ESP experimenter to start under more or less informal conditions and not to trouble very much about the actual experimental controls—the latter, he says, can become stricter once the new percipient has demonstrated his capacity under the more informal conditions.

To lead the new percipient straight into the conditions of a rigid test-procedure, it is claimed, must subject him inevitably to a sense of strain and produces a lack of confidence in himself; inhibitions are developed. This argument is valid as far as it goes, but the results of such informal experiments are far more likely to be due to the operation of the percipient's sensory faculties than to extra-sensory perception ; certainly there is no means of ascertaining— if we accept for the sake of argument the validity of the ESP hypothesis—which of the two modes of perception is likely to be operating. It almost invariably happens that if a percipient is subjected to increasingly stricter experimental controls, his score averages become correspondingly lower, if not petering out altogether. The significance of this fact needs little comment.

Out of the dozen or more experimental procedures used at one time or another by American parapsychologists, only the " down through " technique is capable of totally excluding sensory aids and even in this case much depends on the experimenters' care and the manner in which the procedure is used. As it is, the packs are seldom put in closed containers and there is usually someone in the room who has the pack in full view.

The obvious solution to all such difficulties would be to place the percipient half a mile away and arm him with a stop watch to synchronise his guesses with the cards of the agent or experimenter. Yet apart from a number of badly supervised early experiments at Duke University most long distance experiments have provided results varying little from chance-expectation ; the vast majority of ESP experiments have been carried out with the percipient in the same room as the cards. It never seems to have occurred to the experimenters that *anyone* who has a chance of seeing or touching the cards is capable of passing information to the percipient by involuntary signs or sounds, including involuntary articulation.

Professor Wm. McDougall, a keen supporter of parapsychology, once wrote : " I need not set forth again here the reasons why in this field the observer and reporter must have more than common honesty and competence, more than the observer and reporter in any other branch of science." [1] Can Rhine and his associates be said to have maintained this high standard ? A perusal of Rhine's own books and the contributions and reports in the *Journal of Parapsychology* reveal a standard quite unacceptable to orthodox science, even taking into consideration that many such reports are intended for the general public (which is far from being always the case).

The validity of the American experiments in telepathy and clairvoyance ultimately boils down to the competence and the good faith of the experimenters. Most of the " successful " American ESP experiments can be accounted for by a patent laxity in guarding against sensory cues of one kind or another, and from this fact we may reasonably infer that ESP experimenters as a whole lack technical insight and efficiency. From collateral evidence we further infer that they are lacking also in scientific detachment and critical ability ; the nature of this collateral evidence will be discussed further on. It is not surprising to find, therefore, that much of Rhine's defence of ESP experiments has had to be devoted to the question of the good faith of the experimenters concerned—which, as Dr. McKeen Cattell pointed out in 1938, is not of the least scientific interest to anyone.

This lack of insight and critical ability is nowhere better illustrated than by the fact that in the *Journal of Parapsychology* and other journals of psychical research the explanation of telepathic and clairvoyant experiments in terms of sensory cues is never even attempted. Invariably the interpretation given is the one most favourable to the " theory " of supernatural agencies or faculties.

Many of Rhine's earlier telepathy experiments were conducted with only the most naïve precautions against sensory aids. The subject was generally allowed to see

---

[1] Foreword to *Beyond Normal Cognition*, p. 5.

the backs of the cards, and was often allowed to touch them, while no precautions were taken to exclude the possibility of the involuntary dissemination of sensory cues by the agent, or by the controlling experimenter himself when the latter was looking at the card-faces. Even the card-symbols themselves were subsequently found to be observable from the back if held at a certain angle, while the irregular patterns on the backs were an obvious source of information to anyone who had previously inspected the pack.

As an example of Rhine's attitude to his early experiments, we may quote the instance in which one of his best subjects, Linzmayer, guessed correctly a total of 21 cards out of 25, the first fifteen being guessed without a single error. If we enquire as to the conditions of this test of extra-sensory perception, we find that it took place in an automobile with Rhine and Linzmayer sitting in the front seat. Yet Rhine could still write : " With all the scepticism I can muster, though, I still do not see how any sensory cue could have revealed to Linzmayer the symbols of those 21 cards he called correctly." [1] That Rhine himself could have provided the necessary cues does not appear to have occurred to him. Such a baffling demonstration of ignorance, is instructive, however, for it shows perfectly clearly that Rhine's preoccupation in things occult has from the start been perpetuated by badly controlled " experiments " and a concomitant misinterpretation of the results.

An even more extreme example of Rhine's early attitude is provided by his experiments with a horse. The conclusion he arrived at was that there was strong evidence for the possibility of telepathy operating between man and the equine species. These " experiments " are reminiscent of Clever Hans, one of the notorious Elberfeld horses. Clever Hans, by his genuine mathematical calculations, aroused such public interest that the German psychologist Stumpf was asked by the authorities to investigate. Stumpf reported that Clever Hans, who gave his answers by head-nodding and hoof-tapping, responded to small involuntary signs (" sensory cues ") given by his trainer. Dr. Rhine

---

[1] *New Frontiers of the Mind*, p. 92.

was presumably acquainted with this case at the time of his own " investigation ".

A typical example of Dr. Rhine's facile approach to his subject is provided by his comments on Professor B. Riess' experiments. This is a case where the experimental results were almost certainly obtained by fraud on the part of the percipient; where the experimental controls were so poor as to be non-existent; where even the experimenter, Professor Riess himself, attached little importance to the results; and where the enormous proportion of success obtained was itself a serious ground for suspicion of fraud. Yet in the *Journal of Parapsychology* Rhine included this very series of experiments among those which, in his own words " have hardly been surpassed on safeguards, if indeed they can be."[3] Nine years later Rhine reaffirmed his belief in the validity of these experiments in his book *The Reach of the Mind*, where he referred to Professor Riess' percipient as a " very able subject."[4]

" Dr. Riess' famous, though anonymous, subject "— to quote Dr. Rhine again, was a young woman of twenty-six who at a distance of approximately a quarter of a mile guessed correctly 1,349 cards out of a total of 1,850. This feat is without any parallel in the entire history of psychical research experiment. The extremely high scores of the subject are so exceptional as to demand the most rigorous and detailed examination of the conditions under which the experiments were carried out before the results may be accepted as due to telepathy even by those who regard telepathy as proved. Yet Rhine unhesitatingly committed himself to the genuineness of the experiments to the extent of hailing the results " as the highest rate of scoring thus far reported in the entire history of parapsychology."[5] " This marvellous series ", says Rhine, was conducted " under good conditions "[6]—all this despite the fact that Professor Riess himself reported that " In view of the *many uncontrolled factors*,[7] the data as presented are to be

[3] 1938, p. 242.
[4] p. 135.
[5] *The Reach of the Mind*, p. 48.
[6] ibid., pp. 49 and 48.
[7] author's italics.

thought of as suggestive only."[8]   It is also worth noting Professor Riess' own admission that subsequent control groups with 67 college girls " *under much better conditions* " yielded no significant results.[9]

In view of the suspicion naturally aroused by the production of such an extremely high rate of scoring, together with Professor Riess' own observations concerning the paucity of experimental controls, it may be wondered whether Rhine's motives are purely to serve the cause of science. What were the actual conditions of the experiment which Rhine claims to be of such excellence ?

The subject, Miss S., had a reputation of being an amateur " psychic ". She had come to the notice of Professor Riess in the following manner.   Professor Riess had proclaimed his disbelief in telepathy and clairvoyance to his students and decided to undertake experiments to establish his contention.   During a discussion on ESP at one of Professor Riess' general psychology classes one of the students stated that he had a friend who possessed " high ESP " and who would act as a test subject.   With his anonymous subject Professor Riess carried out two thousand card-guessing trials using synchronised watches and proceeding at the rate of a trial a minute.   Professor Riess and Miss S. remained in their own homes, which were about 500 yards apart, during the tests.

So far all seems well.   But the question must be asked : did the conditions of the experiment allow the possibility of the amateur " psychic " or one of the students—not forgetting the student who had suggested Miss S. in the first instance—to alter the percipient's records during the course of the tests ?   Or alternatively, did they permit the possible inspection of Professor Riess' own records before the percipient's records had been inspected by Professor Riess himself ?   The answer is emphatically in the affirmative ;   the conditions were exceedingly favourable to such practices.   For note the following points which Professor Riess quite openly and candidly gives us for our perusal.

---

[8] *J. Parapsychol.*, 1937, p. 263.
[9] ibid., p. 261.

(1) the card-records were kept in a desk drawer—in Professor Riess' home presumably.

(2) the card-records were not locked up during the day.

(3) "*during the day following the session*, the subject's records were mailed or *delivered* to the experimenter." [1]

(4) " as a rule the sheets were compared during the week-end." [2]

(5) the subject's home was only a few hundred yards from that of Professor Riess.

It may be seen that the records were easily accessible to anyone reasonably well known to Professor Riess, and that there was plenty of time available for any such person to inspect them before the records were checked—in some cases an entire week and possibly longer. One is bound to ask whether, if Miss S. delivered her score sheets in person, Professor Riess was always at home ; presumably he was usually absent during most of the day attending to his duties as a college professor. It is also to be presumed, in absence of evidence to the contrary, that discussion of the experiments meant that the percipient was fairly often in Professor Riess' home. If all these factors are taken into consideration, the unlocked desk and the weekly check-up begin to appear somewhat questionable ; it seems an almost foregone conclusion that the percipient obtained her high scores by the simple process of inspecting Professor Riess' records and copying them out.

This was the experiment which Rhine included as among those which " have hardly been surpassed on safeguards." In view of the exceptional score obtained by the subject, fraud as an explanation was the first hypothesis to be investigated. It is typical that this most obvious line of approach was totally ignored by Rhine, though it appears to have been entertained by Professor Riess himself, who offers in his report the opinion that the experiments were nothing more than " suggestive " in view of the laxness of the controls.

This glossing over the unfavourable features of experiments in ESP is noticeable in nearly all the written reports of Rhine and his associates. His treatment of the Riess case is not

---

[1] author's italics.

[2] *J. Parapsychol.*, 1939, p. 79.

exceptional ; " experiments " with an even less degree of scientific control are reported in the *Journal of Parapsychology* as contributing to the evidence for telepathy and clairvoyance. That the results of the Riess experiments were fraudently obtained there is scarcely a shadow of doubt, and Professor Riess himself was the unwitting victim. Professor Riess need not have been placed in the awkward situation of having to uphold a badly controlled series of experiments which he himself clearly points out as poor, and it was certainly never his intention to have these tests ballyhooed as the highest scores ever achieved in ESP tests. Rhine's enthusiasm undoubtedly placed him in a false position.

Concerning the anonymous subject with " high ESP " we will quote for the last time from Professor Riess and leave it at that. " She has since unfortunately, disappeared into the Middle West and at present is not available for further work."[3] Was that the final " safeguard "?

It is quite evident that Dr. Rhine's judgment is persistently dominated by a wholehearted and uncritical enthusiasm for the cause of ESP. To convince the scientific world of the existence of ESP has long been his unremitting aim. Did Rhine *know* that the Riess experiments were poorly controlled ? It seems impossible that he did not, when Professor Riess had specifically pointed it out in considerable detail. Either Rhine was prepared to ignore the facts in the interests of his campaign to foster interest in ESP in the United States, or else a charge of gross carelessness must be inferred. The latter hypothesis seems too incredible to believe. Yet the fact remains that Rhine has naïvely accepted these tests as authentic, and unconcernedly accepts the results as due to extra-sensory perception without apparent thought for the weakness of the entire case.

The deliberate glossing over of the weak spots in ESP experiments, of which the above example is but one out of many, is not only extremely damaging to Rhine's reputation as a scientific psychologist, but puts into disrepute the whole parapsychological field of study of which he is, in the United States, the acknowledged leader. The conclusion cannot be avoided that all ESP experiments in the United States which

---

[3] *J. Parapsychol.*, 1938, p. 270.

have been conducted on the basis of the criteria accepted by Rhine are open to suspicion.   Such an uncritical attitude of mind, which is in evidence in almost every report, paper and article on ESP in the United States, cannot, in the opinion of the orthodox scientist, be productive of experimental accuracy—much less so when operative principles new to science are deduced from such experiments !

Before a piece of scientific research is accepted, we must either be able to verify the results by a repeatable experiment or else we must be convinced of the competence and perspicacity of the experimenter.   In the case of ESP experiments neither of these conditions are fulfilled.   It is claimed that ESP experiments have been repeated, but they are not repeatable in the technical sense of the term.   Moreover, as we have seen, the experimenters themselves tend always to gloss over unfavourable facts while accentuating those findings favourable to preconceived notions of a supernatural faculty.   Such bias as this must certainly reflect on their ability as *scientific* experimenters.

The charge of deliberate fraud against the American ESP experimenters is not one to be considered very seriously, with, perhaps, a few exceptions.   The reported results in the main are due to faulty methods of observation and to erroneous interpretations.   Yet wishful-thinking is so evident in parapsychological literature that it is surprising the parapsychologists themselves appear ignorant of it.

Another factor of great importance in illustrating Rhine's unscientific approach to his subject is the way in which he has extensively popularised his findings before the scientific world has accepted them—without, in fact, waiting for adequate confirmation of his results.   This " plugging " of ESP savours more of trade-advertising than of scientific enlightenment.

Rhine's three books, *Extra-Sensory Perception*—1934, *New Frontiers of the Mind*—1937, *The Reach of the Mind*—1947, all written for the general public, have this major fault—a fault which robs them virtually of all serious value.   For Rhine, concerned, it seems, more with the idea of selling " ESP " and " PK "[1] to the lay public, casts all scientific

---

[1] *Psychokinesis* :   the alleged ability of some individuals to influence the motion of solid objects at a distance merely by " willing."

caution to the winds and throws " facts " and figures around in happy abandon, making little or no discrimination between those experiments which are highly suspect and those worthy of respect even judging by the low standards of parapsychology. Whether the experimental conditions are downright bad or of an altogether higher standard, the results of both are accorded virtually equal validity. This same approach is to be seen throughout the *Journal of Parapsychology*, and one begins to wonder *whether or not this kind of bias is accorded to the actual experiments themselves.* The ballyhoo which surrounds parapsychology in the United States may well be regarded as symptomatic of the internal state of the subject.

To view the modern ESP movement in true perspective, one must realise that it is basically a cult—a cult of the supernatural in technical dress. The perpetuation of all such cults depends ultimately on irrational beliefs and the ignoring or " explaining away " of rational criticism. The focus of interest must, in such cases, remain directed away from the rational elucidation of mysterious phenomena by orthodox scientific methods ; where the scientist seeks the solution of unexplained causal sequences by rational principles, the occultist or the parapsychologist falls back on irrational supernatural agencies. Such an attitude, if the rational scruples of the individual are to remain lulled, can only be maintained by continued ignorance and wishful thinking which, incidentally, is often evidenced in the strong desire to convert others to the beliefs so ardently held.

All evidence, no matter how unreasonable to the careful mind, is worthy of consideration to the occultist. This attitude is clearly reflected in the journals of psychical research, and especially in the volumes of the *Journal of Parapsychology*—where experiments carried out privately in individuals' homes are accorded the same degree of importance and validity as those carried out in the laboratory.

Through the façade of scientific jargon there peep through the pages of this journal hints of the informality of experimental conditions which belie the grave and technical presentation of so many of the reports, and make us wonder what precisely were the actual conditions of ESP and PK experiments. More often than not there is a complete failure

to specify the exact conditions during each particular experiment which would enable us to gauge its validity.   Much of
this failure is due to ignorance of the many ways in which the
dissemination of sensory cues can operate and a consequent
failure to perceive the type of safeguard necessary to exclude
them.

There is no evidence that a single ESP experimenter has
made a genuine study of such factors as involuntary articulation, endophasic reactions, the unconscious dissemination
and reception of sensory cues, hyperacuity of the senses and
ideomotor reactions.   Most ESP experimenters seem to be
largely ignorant of the very existence of such pitfalls.   The
Journal of Parapsychology has not devoted a full article to
them since it was first published, if one excludes the report on
Ilga K by a German psychologist, Hans Bender.

Many of the American ESP experiments—particularly
Dr. Rhine's earlier ones—have been undertaken in total
disregard of the most obvious precautions against the operation of sensory cues.   So much is this the case that one
wonders why Rhine has never retracted his original claims
in regard to their validity.   Is it possible, we ask, that Rhine,
and all ESP experimenters who accept his standards as valid,
are *still* ignorant of the possible ways in which sensory cues
may be conveyed to the percipient?   The author's personal
opinion is, that no ESP experimenter is fully aware of the
difficulties inherent in ESP experiments, where neither
distance nor lightproof and soundproof cabinets form part
of the experimental situation, and where no automatic
recording apparatus is used.   These conditions are almost
invariably absent from such experiments.

Where there exists ignorance of the difficulties involved,
no measures, of course, will be taken to deal with them except
incidentally.   This is revealed only too clearly by reading
some of the most impressive ESP experimental reports.
One of the most serious consequences is that information
whereby we could assess correctly the validity of such experiments is excluded from the published reports of the experiments—a factor which virtually destroys their scientific
interest.

But perhaps the most damning factor present in the pages
of the *Journal of Parapsychology* is the all-pervading tendency

to regard as conclusive experimental results which are, in fact, far from established, and whose theoretical premises still remain blatantly metaphysical. *Again one wonders how much of this uncritical and complacent attitude of easy acceptance is carried into the experimental situation.* Perhaps some clue is provided by the almost complete lack of any evidence of progressive planning over the last fifteen years.

Throughout the *Journal of Parapsychology* there is to be seen a tendency to stress the points favourable to telepathy and clairvoyance, and a corresponding tendency to gloss over those more debatable points. Seldom is fair emphasis given to the conditions of experiment or the many other secondary factors needed for a sound judgment on what has actually been proved or disproved. Yet again it must be asked whether this lack of scientific detachment is present during the conduct of the actual experiments.

The scientific world can never accept the claims of parapsychology until it has been convinced of the genuine scientific ability of the parapsychologists themselves, and until it is sure that the very highest scientific standards have been consistently applied. Even in those very few experiments where the experimental conditions seem to reach the requisite standard, the reports will almost always provide collateral evidence of bias, which throws doubt on the reliability or the intellectual integrity of the experimenter. In the reports of all the chief proponents of parapsychology in the United States such evidence is abundant, nor can any deceptive technological façade disguise the fact.

Rhine's later experiments must be judged against the background of those earlier ones whose validity is entirely vitiated by glaring faults in the experimental set-up and by the easy-going supervision of those who were mainly instrumental in carrying them out. Why has he never retracted his claims regarding the validity of those experiments, especially in view of the exceptionally high scores so often produced? Scores of twenty-five correct card guesses in a row have been recorded under the most absurd conditions and later reported as evidence of extra-sensory perception. But we should perhaps remember that leaders of pseudo-scientific cults are never anxious to retract previous claims, for admissions of fallibility spell the ultimate doom of the basic conceptions upon which the cult is based.

The facility with which the American ESP experimenters have obtained evidence of extra-sensory perception leaves us wondering why more orthodox scientists do not settle the issue once and for all by repeating the experiments with the same results. But experimenters who do *not* accept the uncritical standards adopted by Rhine and his co-workers do not obtain such prolific evidence of telepathy and clairvoyance. Within the narrow compass of Duke University Rhine claims that a large proportion of individuals were found to possess telepathic or clairvoyant ability. This has led him to state that the faculty of extra-sensory perception is widely distributed, and that effective ESP and PK subjects may be obtained without difficulty from among a typical crowd of men, women and children.

In some ESP experiments published in the *Journal of Parapsychology* it was reported that over forty per cent of the persons tested demonstrated extra-sensory perception ! Yet among the more critical parapsychological experimenters in England the distribution of the extra-sensory perception faculty is believed to be extremely rare, nor have they detected the least evidence of psychokinesis—the alleged movement of objects by supernatural or " paranormal " means. The ease with which the American experimenters find individuals with supernatural powers is in direct contrast to the findings of the English experimenters whose experimental controls and supervision, to judge from their reports, appear to be far stricter than those of the Americans.

Rhine attributes the English experimenters' lack of success to the lack of a sympathetic or congenial atmosphere for the ESP percipient or PK agent ; but considering that failure often follows the tightening up of experimental controls in America, we may regard this explanation as a piece of convenient rationalisation. Rhine and his co-workers attribute almost *all* failure in once-successful subjects to psychological inhibitions of one kind or another and seldom to the direct effects of stricter controls and supervision; the reader must draw his own conclusions.

The abundance of extra-sensory perception in the United States and its extreme scarcity in Great Britain is undoubtedly due to the more efficient experimental controls and supervision of the latter. The claim has not yet been made that the Americans are a nation of natural " psychics ", but this might be a way out for the American parapsychologists and is a claim which would doubtless have interesting repercussions !

A very great deal of the criticism levelled against Rhine and his confrères has been directed towards their methods of statistical evaluation. Rhine took up this challenge with complete success and has fully vindicated his claim that the results of his experiments cannot be attributed to the operation of chance alone. His methods of statistical analysis are essentially valid, but the arguments over the mathematical aspects of ESP research were for a long time successful in focussing attention away from the shortcomings of the experimental procedures themselves. Rhine hailed the official acceptance of his method of statistical analysis as a triumph for the cause of ESP. Yet in fact the fundamental position was unchanged. For unless the actual experiments were properly carried out, no mathematical skill could provide them with even the smallest degree of validity. The arguments over ESP mathematics were, in fact, something of a red herring, for there never had been much doubt that the results attained by Rhine and other ESP experimenters were due to causes other than mere chance.

The same red herring is frequently seen in the *Journal of Parapsychology* wherein reports of experiments are often accompanied by pages of probability mathematics and statistical calculations designed to show that the results attained could not be attributable to the operation of chance. It almost appears as if the ESP experimenters were trying to persuade us of the scientific character of their pseudo-scientific experiments through an impressive exhibition of mathematical virtuosity ! And certainly they have been quite successful in this attempt.

Many people have undoubtedly been impressed by the *prima facie* scientific character of many of the reports in the *Journal of Parapsychology*, with their tables of statistics and the profusion of symbols pertaining to probability mathematics. Probably few of its readers have realised that these erudite mathematical peregrinations are totally irrelevant to the main question at issue—whether or not the experiments themselves have been efficiently carried out. In view of the many reasons adduced for believing in the unreliability of the American ESP experimenters *qua* experimenters, we can only regard their excellent mathematical superstructure as largely wasted effort so far as establishing the existence of extra-sensory perception is concerned.

The unreliability of the American parapsychologists in regard to ESP experiments, and the general excellence of much of their statistical evaluations, might seem a paradox. But the crusading ardour which the genuine believer in extra-sensory perception brings to his experiments and which, psychologically, springs from the lure of the mysterious and the unknown, is also responsible for his attempts to convince the scientific world of their validity. Here it is in his interest to meet the scientist on his own ground and accept the rulings of the exact sciences—rulings which were glaringly and ignorantly transgressed during the conduct of the actual experiments. In consequence, the mathematical evaluation of ESP experiments has reached a level far beyond what the standard of the experiments themselves warrant.

Since 1945 the experiments of Dr. Gertrude Schmeidler of New York have attracted the attention of parapsychologists. She claims to have found that extra-sensory perception is statistically demonstrable with numbers of subjects chosen at random. By means of the Rorschach Test she divided her subjects into two groups—persons who were well-adjusted and those who were mal-adjusted to life and their environment. She found that the *difference* between the scores of the two groups was statistically significant. But as Soal has pointed out, the odds against probability expectation do not reach the figure she has claimed for them, since she selected her associated pair of figures as being the one which shows the *maximum* difference out of six possible pairs [1]. Such a piece of evident axe-grinding does not give

---

[1] Soal, S. G., *The Experimental Situation in Psychical Research*, 1947, p. 33.

confidence in the objectivity of the experiments themselves. A point like this may reveal a good deal concerning the attitude of the experimenter, for it is doubtful whether such a fortuitous selection could have been due to mere inadvertence.[2]

VARIATIONS AND DECLINES IN ESP SCORING RATES

Many ESP experiments have been carried out with the claimed intention of discovering the effects of such stimuli as rewards or incentives upon the percipients' " paranormal " faculty. It generally appeared that with successful percipients incentives and a congenial atmosphere improved the scoring rate, whilst boredom, fatigue and distracting influences lowered them. If perception and correct interpretation of sensory cues are responsible for the successful scores, there is, of course, nothing surprising about such findings. Where Rhine makes his most pernicious error, however, is in the way he interprets the subsequent failure of successful percipients

Lack of a congenial atmosphere, boredom, fatigue, distraction, indisposition, lack of confidence and " inhibitions " are held to account for such failures (or for drops in the scoring rate) even when it is perfectly obvious that more rigid experimental conditions are the main cause. Extrasensory perception, we are told, ignores mere physical barriers ; it cannot therefore be affected by extra precautions against sensory cues. When, therefore, the scoring rate drops or vanishes in consequence of such precautions, this must be due to one of the factors enumerated above ; Q.E.D.

In any monotonous skilled task, such as type-setting or operating a telegraphic morse-key, such stimuli as rewards, change of subject matter, the approach of the dinner hour, new motivations of almost any kind, will increase the efficiency of the operator. Aschoffenburg's well-known method of measuring such improvements in tasks has been used in one form or another for over fifty years. Again,

---

[2] A critic has claimed, after going to press, that she was entitled to select her pair, as she had decided in advance on the basis of preliminary work which figure to take.

boredom, fatigue and similar factors all tend to decrease the operator's efficiency.

During "successful" ESP experiments when the percipient is perceiving and interpreting, perhaps unconsciously, minute sensory cues, variations in scoring successes are easily accounted for by orthodox psychological principles. We have noted that the hyperacusic auditory sense of the blind which is responsible for detecting objects in their path produces sensations which are located on the forehead. Such sensations vary greatly in scope and intensity in the same individual. Villey writes :

> "They change with the slightest variations of external conditions, or of the physical condition of the subject. The atmospheric state suffices for modifying them considerably. Fatigue, a headache or any pre-occupation will reduce them sometimes in incredible proportions. Within two minutes of interval, I have seen the same subject perceive a plank that was being held out for him at 90 centimetres, and then not perceive it at a distance of more than 35 or 40 centimetres, without anything being changed, apparently, in the conditions of the experiment." [1]

The parallel of Villey's experiment with those of the ESP fraternity is too close to be missed.

The experiments in muscle-reading by Tarchanow are also of great interest in this connection. Tarchanow, who, with Féré, is credited with the discovery of the psychogalvanic reflex, carried out experiments in the detection and interpretation of ideomotor movements, mainly by percipients who were permitted contact with the agent only through the sense of touch.

Sometimes contact was direct, at other times they were connected by a wire or chain. The eyes were usually bandaged in order to allow the percipient maximum concentration on the minimal variations in cutaneous and muscular sensations due to barely perceptible pressures, tappings, strokings and resistances. The only way to bring about this maximum concentration, writes Tarchanow,[2] is to divorce the attention from all other impressions which fall

[1] *The World of the Blind*, p. 104.
[2] op. cit.

on the other senses—above all from the distracting visual impressions, which stop the attention being concentrated on the desired sense impressions. The thought-reader tries, during the experiment, not to think of anything at all and abstains from all supposition, all conjecture.

This type of concentration is often only achieved at the expense of a great deal of effort and may lead to subsequent fatigue and headaches. Sometimes, says Tarchanow, this uniform and continuous concentration results in a great increase in sensitivity of the mind and of the muscular sense, and throws some muscle-readers into a state " very reminiscent of the first stages of hypnosis in which consciousness still remains but the acuteness of the senses is sensibly increased ".

Tarchanow's observations are applicable to the detection of sensory cues by sight and hearing. If, as seems probable, some ESP percipients attain to this type of concentration, it is easy to see that the least distraction, boredom or unease would upset the delicate psychological balance, which in turn would produce variations in the percipient's scoring. Apart from this, however, Tarchanow's observations throw real light on the way in which ESP percipients may reach a state of hypersensitivity to sensory impressions. The minor trance state of many mediums appear analogous to Tarchanow's method of achieving concentration through banishing all irrelevant sensory stimuli.

In hypnosis too, some subjects may possess abnormal powers of attention, discrimination and subtle ratiocination far beyond that which their conscious minds can normally evoke. It seems likely that many a successful ESP percipient is simply an individual who can attain, either naturally or with practice, to this method of concentration.

According to Rhine, loss of favourable " mental atmosphere " during ESP experiments results in diminution or disappearance of the " paranormal " faculties. At all costs, therefore, the correct atmosphere must be preserved. Isolation of the percipient or the introduction of mechanical devices are consequently forbidden because of the resulting loss of " atmosphere ". Hence the need, says Rhine, to preserve a large degree of informality in ESP and PK experiments.

This insistence on informality, and the refusal to " mechanise " ESP and PK experiments, inevitably results in the experiments remaining badly controlled. As long as these conditions exist, it is only to be expected that ESP experimenters will continue to find traces of supernatural power in their subjects.

It would appear, according to Rhine, that if the correct " mental atmosphere " were maintained or even improved *despite* increasing rigidity of experimental controls, no loss of supernatural vision—for this is what the term extrasensory perception amounts to—would supervene. But the following investigation by Soal of a well-known medium's telepathic and clairvoyant powers is a case in point where precisely the opposite effect occurred.

In regard to the ESP experiments of Dr. Rhine there is only one instance where a " successful " subject of his has been re-tested by a totally independent investigator. Dr. S. G. Soal has a not undeserved reputation, both in England and America, as a competent and careful ESP experimenter. Soal's investigation of one of Rhine's high-scoring percipients is worth attention, if only because he has never accepted the relatively lax standards of the American ESP experimenters.

The subject in question was a professional medium, Eileen Garrett, whom Rhine had tested for telepathy and clairvoyance, employing zener cards for the purpose. Rhine reported that she averaged a total of approximately 9.5 correct card-calls per run of 25 in telepathy tests, while in clairvoyance tests her average totalled 5.6 per run of 25. During one three-day period her telepathy scores reached the relatively enormous average of 13.4. However, when Soal subsequently tested her for evidence of telepathy, her scores showed an average attributable to chance alone.

Rhine himself tried to explain this anomalous situation by using a stock rationalisation of the ESP experimenter, namely, that in Soal's tests with Mrs. Garrett the right " atmosphere " was lacking, in which case all telepathic and clairvoyant subjects invariably fail to give of their best. Yet until she knew of the results of Dr. Soal's tests, Mrs.

Garrett herself believed the tests to have been highly successful. Her work with Soal, she felt, was more likely—to use
her own words—" to bring out her mediumistic capabilities
than would the Duke conditions ", while Soal recorded in
the spiritualist journal *Light*[1] : " Mrs. Eileen Garrett actually preferred my mental atmosphere of passive expectation
to the emotional tension which she states exists when
working with Dr. Rhine."

Evidently it was not the question of an " unfavourable
atmosphere " which precluded the medium from obtaining
high scores but the known precautions which Soal takes to
obviate sensory cues, even though these are by no means
all that they should be—a point which will be dealt with at
length in the next chapter. Rhine has never retracted the
findings of such high " telepathic " capacity over the three-
day period just referred to, even though it must be obvious
to all who care to go into the question that the results he
obtained do not require the existence of any weird supernatural faculty to account for them. As with Ilga K. the
exclusion of sensory cues had, in Mrs. Garrett's case also,
resulted in a failure to demonstrate any telepathic capacity
whatsoever.

One may hazard a guess as to the primary reason why
parapsychologists deliberately avoid the study of sensory
hyperacuity, and the unconscious presentation and reception
of sensory cues : such study would inevitably jeopardise the
great majority of those ESP experiments which have in the
past been reported as evidence of extra-sensory perception
and which still form the basis for contemporary ESP research.

It may be noted, in passing, that whereas the American
ESP experimenters have found an abundance of clairvoyance
without the least difficulty, the far more meticulous Dr. Soal
states that *he has found no evidence at all of clairvoyance*
after testing over one hundred and sixty subjects ! His
two ace " telepathy " performers failed completely to score
when no one was looking at the target cards.

---

[1] 1938, p. 391.

RECORDING-ERRORS IN PK AND ESP EXPERIMENTS

Apart from the problems posed by the possibilities of hyperacuity of the senses and the conscious or unconscious dissemination of sensory cues there is a very important point to be considered. This is the question of the recording of the scores obtained by the experimental subjects. It has been argued that, although sensory cues might have been largely responsible for the success of the ESP experiments, the case for the results being due to the exercise of a supernatural or " paranormal " faculty is greatly reinforced by the results of the PK experiments, *for in the latter the objections which pertain to the ESP experiments have seldom any relevance.* This argument is certainly valid so far as it goes. It is, however, easily dealt with.

Clearly the only *common* source of error between ESP and PK experiments lies in the possibility of recording-errors. Furthermore, taking the PK experiments by themselves— including the machine-thrown series—recording-errors are the most likely source of error which embraces all types. The question of recording-errors is therefore very important. If they are found to be indicated in the PK experiments, it will at once dispose of the formidable claim that PK experiments reinforce the case for the existence of a paranormal faculty as adduced from ESP experiments, and *vice versa.*

It has been reasonably well established that subconsciously motivated scoring errors may, in simple experimental situations, influence the experimental results according to the attitude of the recorder towards ESP[1]. Yet the competent Sells Committee came to the conclusion that the experiments of Kennedy on motivational-scoring could not be held to apply to the more advanced of the Duke University and other American ESP experiments[2].

But the Kennedy experiments in motivational-scoring are extremely relevant to PK tests, for here is an inherently simple test-situation highly favourable to subconsciously

---

[1] Kennedy and Uphoff, *Experiments on the Nature of Extra-Sensory Perception*, III; *The Recording Error Criticism of Extra-Chance Scores*, J. Parapsych 1 3, 1939, pp. 226-245. Stanford University Psychical Research Laboratory, Communication No. 5.
[2] *J. Parapsychol.*, 3, 1939, pp. 349-350.

motivated scoring. That some such errors have at times occurred in PK tests is patent. The published records of Rhine's own earliest PK experiments show the huge average of over 5.5 per run against an expectation of 4^{*}. This is extremely reminiscent of the equally huge successes in some of the early Duke ESP tests—successes which diminished as time went on and as experimental procedure became relatively stricter. It still remains a matter for speculation whether the slack conditions which inspired the " successes " of these early ESP and PK experiments have ever been entirely obviated in " successful " experiments carried out at Duke University Parapsychology Laboratory in later years.

The existence of ESP recording errors is not only to be inferred from Dr. Kennedy's experiments. They have been detected and reported in all honesty by Martin and Stribic in their experiments at Colorado University, and also by Macfarland.

In the Sharp-Clark ESP experiments the students were permitted to do their own checking with their guesses in one column and the correct card-order in another, both columns being on the same sheet. Such experiments of course, lend themselves to recording-errors and should never have been reported—a fact which should be more than apparent to the experimenters themselves. It is truly surprising how individuals of considerable academic distinction, members of university faculties, appear unable to observe the most elementary precautions in the conduct of experiments.

In another series of 10,000 ESP trials carried out by Dr. C. R. Carpenter, Fellow in Psychology, and Dr. H. R. Phalen, Professor of Mathematics at Bard College, Columbia University, " confirmatory " results of ESP were obtained, but here again the scoring method was at fault—a fact which they quite correctly pointed out. In this case the percipient himself read back to the experimenter the correct order of the cards for checking purposes. He had in full view his own guesses on the record-sheet and he was eventually detected making " an error " favourable to his own score.

Whilst a number of experimenters have been honest enough to point out the occurrence of recording-errors, we

* J. Parapsychol., 7, 1943, pp. 20-43.

have no means of learning whether all ESP crusaders, most of whom are amateurs, are likely to be so scrupulous; nor can we ascertain whether they always succeed in discovering that such errors have in fact occurred at all. After weeks, perhaps months, of sincere work, the discovery of a few scoring errors may be wishfully disposed of as irrelevant. The greater the crusader's ardour in the cause of ESP and PK, the more may we expect this tendency to be exaggerated.

The question of scoring-errors in many of the better-controlled ESP experiments is, according to the Sells Committee, largely irrelevant. It is significant, however, that they have been observed and reported by ESP experimenters themselves. Even though motivational-scoring may be regarded as an impossibility in some of the more complex ESP experimental situations, the simple PK experimental situation allows full scope for such tendencies. *It is in relation to the PK experiments* that the Kennedy experiments in subconsciously motivated recording-errors have most significance. The scorer usually knows which face of the dice the subject is " willing " uppermost and it would be the simplest thing in the world for him involuntarily to make slips favourable to the score of the PK subject.

In the average PK experiment there is no effective way of checking the scorer's figures unless a second independent scorer keeps a record at the same time, and even this arrangement has its own objections if the scorers are within sight or hearing of each other.

Much of the " evidence " for PK, or psychokinesis, rests upon the widely trumpeted " position effects "—" declines ", " salience ", and the rest. Such statistical configurations are unlikely to be due to the vagaries of chance. But this fact alone scarcely justifies their being attributed to the ebb and flow of the PK agent's supernatural or paranormal powers, or to the alleged " laws " governing these powers. They are far more likely to be due to spontaneous variations in the degree to which unconscious motivational scoring-errors are operating. During control-tests, of course, the motive responsible for the tendency to error-bias would naturally be absent.

Yet even if it were supposed that the results of the American PK experiments were not due to scoring errors, these experiments, taken as a whole, are far from convincing. More often than not they are carried out by amateurs in private houses instead of in the laboratory; obviously no adequate supervision is to be expected.

Very frequently it is reported that the PK subject is allowed to choose which die-face he wishes to " will " upper-most. It might be expected that enthusiastic amateurs dabbling (unknown to themselves) in the occult occasionally see which die-face turns up most frequently before "choosing" it. The six-face has generally been the favourite choice; and it frequently obliges the amateur sorcerer by providing evidence of " psychokinesis " ! Scoring errors are likely to increase this " psychokinetic effect ".

It is remarkable that scarcely any PK experiments have been reported where all six faces of the die have been nomin-ated as the " target-face " an equal number of times. Al-most invariably the subject's choice of target-face has been the over-riding factor, ostensibly on the grounds that if he is allowed to choose the face about which he felt most confident of success, the less would his natural inhibitions retard the effectiveness of his psychokinetic powers. The six-face, having six cavities, is the lightest, and would normally turn up more often than the others; this may be the dominant factor in the choice of most PK subjects. The relative lightness of the six-face would naturally accentu-ate any tendency to recording error-bias, while comparison with control experiments (without the error-bias motive operating) could still reveal a statistically significant dif-ference between the two types of experiment.

The overall picture of American PK experiments gives an impression of amateurishness and haphazardness which belies their grave technical presentation in the published reports. Another factor which compels us to dismiss them is the fact that outside America PK experiments with dice have failed entirely to corroborate the findings of Rhine and his confrères. The findings of the English PK experi-menters are particularly relevant in this respect.

Brief though this reference to PK has been, it has been enough to show that the " paranormal " interpretation of ESP experiments receives little support from PK experi-ments. The argument that only the hypothesis of a " paranormal " faculty could account for both the alleged ESP and PK effects, on the grounds that the objections which might be held to operate against it in the one case are inapplicable as regards the other, is seen to be invalid. Such an argument could only be regarded as valid if the PK experiments themselves were conclusive.

It is highly unlikely that the scientific world will regard the American PK experiments as conclusive proof of supernatural or " paranormal " faculties, until automatic recording devices are used during the experiments.

As long ago as 1917 Professor L. T. Troland realised the necessity of a mechanically operated recorder as a minimal condition in ESP experiments, and actually constructed one. His aim was to eliminate the personal equation of the researcher so far as it could reflect adversely on the validity of the experiment. Rhine's argument for not following Troland's excellent example is that under such impersonal conditions the telepathic or clairvoyant subject becomes inhibited. The speciousness of such an argument is not difficult to appreciate. Even if " inhibition " were a cogent reason why foolproof experimental conditions are not permissible, it would be utterly useless on such grounds to expect the scientific world to accept as valid the experimental results thus gained, still less any speculative theories based upon them. It would always be reasonable to attribute the results to faulty experimental conditions in preference to speculative metaphysical theories which, in the eyes of many, amount to nothing less than a recrudescense of primitive supernatural belief.

The automatic recording of ESP tests is simply enough arranged, yet in not one of the " successful " experiments of Rhine or his colleagues at Duke University Parapsychological Laboratory has such a device been used. With the dice-throwing experiments more expensive recording-apparatus would be required, involving the use either of an automatically operated camera or else a specially constructed device, as for example, radioactive paint on the " spots " on the dice used in conjunction with a photo-electric cell.

The neglect to provide the most accurate experimental conditions reflects on the scientific ability of the workers in Duke University Parapsychology Laboratory. It may even be asked whether this neglect has been deliberate. Were automatic recording machines ever used in PK experiments and the results found deleterious to the production of positive scores ? Has the effect of complete isolation upon ESP percipients in fact been tried out and the experimental results withheld from publication because of the negative scores obtained—on the specious grounds that the experiments furnished no further light on extra-sensory perception and were therefore not worth reporting ?

The perpetuation of casual experimental conditions appears to be the *sine qua non* of " successful " ESP and PK experiments ; many might interpret the persistent avoidance of foolproof experimental techniques as an indication that at least some of the staff of the Duke University Parapsychology Laboratory are not altogether unaware of this. Whether or not this is so, it is at least certain that in normal scientific research the continuance of such an anomalous situation could never have been tolerated without the strongest censure being directed upon both the experimenters themselves and upon any University which had sanctioned for so long the continuance of such dubious experiments.

Conclusion

The American experiments in extra-sensory perception and psychokinesis cannot be regarded as of any serious scientific interest. This is mainly because the experimenters themselves cast such doubt upon their own fitness to carry out the experiments, through the patent lack of objectivity which is everywhere observable in their published reports and papers. In this respect Dr. Rhine himself is the chief offender.

The continual stream of propaganda and special pleading conducted by Rhine with all the zest of a self-discovered prophet do not supply the best conditions for scientific calm and judgment. Nor do such methods inspire much confidence in the intellectual integrity of those responsible. In the bias of the reports and articles, in the glossing-over of unfavourable and debatable points, in the facile conclusions and naïve theorising, in the vague metaphysical

speculations, in the casting of results into a mould of preconceived ideas, in the acceptance of results as conclusive
which fail to find confirmation elsewhere, in the placid
acceptance of badly controlled or even uncontrollable experiments, in the deliberate ignoring of the possibilities
contingent upon sensory hyperacuity and the involuntary
dissemination of sensory cues, in the basic acceptance of
supernatural causation—in all these we see overwhelming
signs of self-deception and wishful thinking and an inability
to exercise critical judgment.

All these factors throw the gravest doubts on the reliability
of Rhine's parapsychological experiments and of those who
accept his standards ; *for these same factors reflect an attitude
of mind which we have no reason to assume would have been
absent in the actual conduct of the experiments themselves.* If
this is so, no amount of technological argument will avail to
persuade us of the validity of either the ESP or the PK
experiments.

In one volume[1] thirty-five separate arguments against
the validity of ESP experiments were stated and answered
with varying degrees of success. The one criticism which
the authors neglected to answer fully was the question of
the reliability of the experimenters themselves, for in the
final analysis the acceptance or non-acceptance of the
experimental results revolve on this very point.

Another vital question which was far from satisfactorily
dealt with was the question of sensory hyperacuity and the
unconscious presentation of sensory cues by the telepathic
agent, the experimental supervisor, or his assistants. The
obvious ignorance of the possibilities afforded by such means
undoubtedly accounts for a very large part of the " positive "
experimental results achieved and is one reason why the
authors of *Extra-Sensory Perception after Sixty Years* were
unable to deal with the question. The maintenance of
adequate safeguards presupposes a prior knowledge of the
contingencies to be guarded against.

There is only one paper in all the volumes of the *Journal
of Parapsychologoy* which deals objectively with the problems
of hyperacusia and the unconscious dissemination of sensory

---

[1] *Extra-Sensory Perception after Sixty Years.*

cues. This report[2] was not written by an American parapsychologist but by a German, Dr. Hans Bender, and although it appeared as long as eleven years ago its lessons were lost upon Rhine and his co-workers. Yet the paramount importance of these problems to experimental research in extra-sensory perception is glaringly obvious. Research into such questions is the logical first step of *any* investigation into extra-sensory perception. The neglect of so vital a piece of research represents a first-class indictment of the outlook and abilities of parapsychologists the world over.

Others have criticised individual ESP experiments on grounds of motivated scoring errors, faulty shuffling of the cards, correspondence of mental habits, rational inference, optional stopping, invalid methods of statistical evaluation, and on many other grounds. In the main, however, the " successful " results of ESP experiments cannot be attributed solely to such types of error as these. Faulty shuffling, admittedly, may sometimes be a source of the " position effect ", just as irregularities in the dice and in the manner of throwing may be the cause of " position effects " in PK tests.

Yet it is on the question of safeguards against sensory cues that all ESP experimenters are shown to be at fault. *None* of them appear to have studied this problem seriously and their claims to have " obviated " all sensory cues is often pathetic in its naïvety and evident sincerity. Pathetic too is their much advertised confidence that only parapsychologists can fully appreciate the problems raised by the exclusion of sensory cues in the ESP experimental situation. It is perhaps significant that nearly all the competent work on this important question has been carried out by individuals who were not parapsychologists at all.

---

[2] *The Case of Ilga K : Report of a Phenomenon of Unusual Perception,* J. Parapsychol, 1938.

Chapter Twenty-Seven

THE TELEPATHY EXPERIMENTS OF DR. S. G. SOAL

AT THIS STAGE it is desirable that we should enter into a detailed critical analysis of an important series of ESP experiments. This honour, for several good reasons, has been reserved for the well-known investigations into " precognitive telepathy " conducted by Dr. S. G. Soal.[1] This series of experiments is generally conceded to be the most cogent of all the evidence brought forth to substantiate the theory of transcendental mental processes in mankind. In view of Dr. Soal's reputation for painstaking patience and the elaborate lengths to which he has gone to obviate sensory cues, many people interested in psychical research believe that the proof of a transcendental faculty in man stands or falls by these experiments (which are by far and away the most interesting and convincing of all ESP experiments carried out in America or England). As has already been noted, these same experiments gained for their instigator from London University the degree of Doctor of Science.

Since the Soal experiments represent a veritable bastion perpetuating belief in transcendental or supernatural faculties of the mind, it is fitting that the main critical analysis should be reserved for them. The reason why Soal's experiments appear so impressive *prima facie* is contained in the apparently ine plicable element of precognition which characterises them throughout.

A hypothesis of genuine prophetic faculty has hitherto seemed the only way of explaining the curious experimental results obtained. The apparent prophetic faculty of Soal's

[1] Soal and Goldney, *Experiments in Precognitive Telepathy*, Proceedings of the S.P.R., December, 1943, pp. 21-150.

456

percipient appeared quite unexpectedly, and was hailed, not only as an excellent demonstration of the transcendental powers of the mind, but as a final safeguard against the possibility of the experimental results being brought about by the operation of sensory cues.

What, it was asked, can rationally account for the fact that one man can cognize what is *about to* enter the mind of another throughout thousands of tests, when all sensory cues are excluded ? This is the situation which has hitherto faced the sceptics. Fraud or collusion may be an answer, but this hypothesis is extremely unlikely. The records of the experiments together with their statistical analysis may confidently be accepted as valid. The only question involved is what interpretation should be given to the experimental results ? It is this question which will be dealt with at length in the following pages.

We may say here and now that Soal has overlooked certain possibilities in regard to the transmission of sensory cues from agent to percipient ; while guarding effectively against sensory cues occurring between *two* individuals, he over-looked the fact that what may appear to be impossible between two persons may well be possible when three are involved.

One reason has already been given why Soal's experiments have been chosen for a detailed critical analysis. Another very important reason for the choice is that we have felt obliged to dismiss the experiments of Dr. Rhine and his American confréres as unacceptable on collateral evidence of bias and tendentiousness. The evidence of partisan prejudice in the selection, presentation and interpretation of experimental results is so overwhelming, that we cannot help believing such a bias to have been present in the ex-periments themselves. In the ESP experiments of Dr. S. G. Soal, a mathematics teacher in London University, this presentational bias largely disappears, although it can-not be said to be altogether absent. Soal's reports do offer grounds for confidence in their objectivity and therein lies their importance ; for even though the " theory " of tele-pathy is shown to be unnecessary, these investigations undoubtedly represent an interesting addition to the body of knowledge acquired by experimental psychology, and as such they are perhaps worthy of the recognition which Soal's own university has bestowed on him.

Soal's experiments were experiments in telepathy. That is to say, they were carried out to test a theory that one human mind could interact directly with another in some kind of way other than through the senses. The term " mind ", as is so often found in psychical research and metaphysical speculation, remains undefined. The mind, furthermore, is a hypothetical assumption in its own right ; so that in telepathic theories generally we find we are using *two* speculative hypotheses, each of which remains indefinable in any scientific sense, for the simple reason that they are basically metaphysical concepts.

In Soal's experiments, as in the usual run of telepathic experiments, the " sensitive " or " percipient " had to guess the symbols or pictures in a pack of cards upon which another person known as the " agent " was fixing his gaze. This type of experiment is very different from most of those undertaken by Dr. Rhine and the American ESP experimenters, who concentrated mainly on a " clairvoyance " type of test where the percipient's supposed supernatural faculty is expected to help him identify the cards in question without the aid of another " mind ". Soal himself has found no evidence of clairvoyance in his own experiments.

As has already been mentioned, Soal was granted a Doctor of Science degree by London University for his investigations in telepathy. Further, in 1947 the Central Research Fund of London University awarded him a money grant for the continuation of this work and for the purchase of apparatus. To many, including the present writer, it would appear as if one of our greatest universities is not only condoning but actively assisting in the furtherance of occult beliefs and practices. It is useless to urge in reply that even if the telepathic " theory " is of no material consequence, the experiments and the results achieved may very easily stand by themselves ; for the fact remains that if a purely rational approach had been tried from the beginning, the course of the experiments would inevitably have been very different from the one that they actually took.

The Soal experiments were first and foremost designed to establish *scientifically* the validity of a purely *metaphysical*

concept.   Such a thing is, of course, a total impossibility.
And yet this was in fact the *animus* which motivated the
experiments.   It is quite remarkable that certain universities
in England and America should be dealing out degrees and
doctorates on the basis of what are no more than excursions
into the occult.

By 1939 Soal had been experimenting in card-guessing
experiments for over four years in an attempt to find confirmation of the prolific successes in " extra-sensory perception " published by Rhine and others at Duke University
in America.   He had tested 160 different subjects and had
recorded 128,000 guesses without the least indication of
anything that could even be hypothetically attributed to
extra-sensory perception, and was beginning to arrive at
the conclusion that the quest was a dead-end.   The great
significance of these four years of negative ESP tests is that
it establishes Soal's *bone fides* as nothing else could.   It
bears witness to his patience, integrity, and a high standard
of experimental control which is unusual in the general run
of ESP experimentation.

Soals' patience, however, had its reward.   Another ESP
experimenter, Whately Carington, mentioned that he had
found evidence of " displacement ", and pressed Soal to
undertake the task of checking through his own records for
this same effect.   " Displacement " merely means that the
records of the ESP subject show a tendency for the latter to
guess correctly, not the card that he was supposed to be
guessing, but either the one before it or the one following it.
Out of 160 subjects which Soal had tested, the records of
two of them showed marked evidence of the percipients
having scored above chance on the cards which either preceded or followed the target card during each run of guesses.
Some of these displacement effects are really puzzling ; for
while the " backward displacement " can be readily attributed to a delay of two of three seconds in uttering the name
of the card (the identity of which has been conveyed unconsciously by some form of articulation), the " forward
displacement " is not so easily accounted for.   This forward
displacement, i.e. the correct guessing of the card *about to
become the target-card*—as revealed by subsequent analysis,
has until recently defied explanation.

When Soal had arduously checked through the score sheets of his 160 subjects and found two who appeared to reveal the displacement effect in their records, he instituted a further series of telepathy experiments with one of them, a Mr. Basil Shackleton, to see whether he would continue to demonstrate the same mysterious phenomenon of forward displacement. Over a period of two years, in tests involving thousands of card guesses, it was found that Shackleton maintained consistently his ability to guess the card which was about to become the target-card. Soal took precautions to guard against anyone present becoming aware of what the card ahead was going to be, and (to illustrate the effectiveness of his safeguards) here is a brief account of the method used in one of the principal types of experiment.

The so-called " telepathic agent " was seated in a room behind a box-like screen. In front of him lay five different cards in a row face downward. We may call them A, B, C, D and E. An assistant experimenter on the *other* side of the screen held a bag containing 200 counters of five different colours in equal amounts. Every two seconds or so he thrust his hand into the bag, took hold of a coloured counter, and held it up at a small aperture cut in the screen. The agent, observing the colour of the disc, immediately turned up the corresponding card from his row of five different cards, giving it a brief glance as he did so. This was the " target-card ", the identity of which Shackleton, out of sight in the next room, was to try and guess. It will be seen that by this arrangement a random order of target-cards was produced by the assistant experimenter for the agent to transmit.

The agent's five cards were shuffled at the beginning of each series of tests in order to preclude the assistant experimenter, who held the counters, from gaining knowledge of their order. So that, although the assistant experimenter was responsible for giving the verbal signal to Shackleton next door whenever he blindly produced a counter out of the bag, he never knew which card was the target card. The arrangement also provided an excellent method of producing a random distribution of target-cards without anyone present having any idea concerning which card was to be turned up next. An " observer " took down the order of the target cards as the experiment progressed, while a second observer watched Shackleton as he recorded his guesses.

These arrangements, as may be seen, were well thought out. Even so, further controlling conditions were imposed by the results of the experiments which showed the mysterious precognitive trend. For what Shackleton in fact appeared to be doing was to show a marked and consistent tendency to guess correctly the card which was about to be turned up and which neither the agent nor the assistant experimenter were apparently in the slightest degree capable of forecasting. The majority of these and similar experiments demonstrated this precognitive effect to such an extent that evaluation by the calculus of probability showed that the odds against chance alone producing such a result lies in the amazing order of 10^{35} to 1.

Yet most scientists are unlikely to fall back on an ancient tradition of supernatural causation to account for such precognitive results. Several alternatives are open to consideration if we take the rational standpoint. One, that Shackleton was able in some manner to identify the target cards by auditory cues and made some kind of lightning calculations as to the possible identity of the next card ; this, however, can be dismissed on several grounds. Two, that by accident or design Shackleton or the observer who was keeping the target-card record shifted their scores one or two places in the score-column, thereby giving an apparent precognitive effect to those of Shackleton's successful guesses which were due to the transmission of auditory cues. This again appears highly unlikely unless the experimenters and witnesses were party to open fraud. Three, that Soal's list of random figures, or the assistant experimenter's selection of counters, according to the method in use at the time, were not strictly random at all but were harmonised in some way with Shackleton's unconscious number habits. Four, that during the experiments with the counters, the target-card recorder heard Shackleton's guess by involuntary articulation *or from the sound of his pencil,* and that it unconsciously biased the accuracy of his scoring. Unconscious motivational scoring occurs only too easily with some individuals.

This last possibility seems, on collateral evidence, the only one out of the alternatives enumerated above to be worthy of consideration, and this could only be regarded as pertinent to the experiments in which the random distribution of target cards was obtained by the use of coloured counters. On the whole, therefore, we can dismiss these suggested explanations as unsatisfactory. We must search for another theory to account for Soal's extraordinary results—one, moreover, which will cover all the variations in experimental technique with equal efficiency. Such a theory is, in fact, forthcoming.

Before we tackle this question, however, the possibility of fraud must be briefly discussed. Collusion during the actual experiments seems out of the question even if one doubts the integrity of one or more of the experimenters or the critical ability of the independent witnesses. Moreover, Soal's own statistical analysis of the experiments is fundamentally sound. The charge may be made that Soal or someone else faked the records, including the copies which were posted to Cambridge for safe-keeping. To anyone who has full knowledge of the facts, however, this would appear scarcely feasible.

In the opinion of the present writer we are bound to accept the results of Soal's " precognitive telepathy " experiments as authentic. In support of this statement it may be observed that four years of negative tests in telepathic research put Soal in a very strong position, both in regard to any charge of his having faked the record sheets and in regard to his efficiency in excluding sensory cues from the percipients. But it should be emphasised that the acceptance of Soal's experimental results does not involve the acceptance of his interpretation of them. His failure to find a rational solution to explain his results cannot by itself justify the adoption of a supernatural explanation or the hypothesis of " an operative principle unknown to science " —in whichever category telepathy may be placed ; such an attitude merely shows the intuitive bias of the experimenter.

A RATIONAL EXPLANATION OF SOAL'S EXPERIMENTS IN " PRECOGNITIVE TELEPATHY "

The first thing to note, in studying the report of Soal's experiments with Shackleton,[1] is that Shackleton scored above chance only when sensory cues of one kind or another appeared at least to be a possibility. While the telepathic agent was in a position to know the identity of the target-card—and was thus in a position to transmit auditory cues of some kind—Shackleton was generally successful in scoring above chance. But in tests designed to exclude the possibility of telepathy, as, for example, in clairvoyance tests, Shackleton's score was negative and agreed with mean probability expectation, both on the target-card and on the forward and backward displacement. These clairvoyance tests without an agent were interspersed with telepathy tests, but Shackleton continued to score only during the latter, even when he was not informed of the changes from " telepathy " to " clairvoyance " conditions.

The exposure of the target-cards during the telepathy experiments produced results, therefore, which were not in evidence during experiments where the target-cards were concealed from view. This is the logical starting point of any investigation into Soal's results. The question which has to be answered is whether or not the exposure of the target-cards could involve the transmission of auditory cues from agent to percipient under the conditions allowed by the experimental situation and in accordance with the results obtained.

For a clear presentation of the problems involved, it is proposed to deal first with those experiments where a random distribution of target-cards was achieved by means of prepared lists of random figures. The experiments where random distribution was obtained by the use of counters of five different colours will be dealt with at a later stage.

In the prepared-list experiments the assistant experimenter presented to the agent's view through the aperture

---

[1] Soal and Goldney, *Experiments in Precognitive Telepathy*, Proc. S.P.R., vol. 47, 1942-5, pp. 21-150. See also :
Soal, S.G., *Fresh Lights on Card Guessing—Some New Effects*, Proc. S.P.R., 1940-41, pp. 152-198.

in the screen a random sequence of numbers, ranging from one to five, corresponding to those in his prepared list. The agent, whose five different cards lay in front of him under cover of the box-like screen, merely had to glance at the card corresponding to the number presented to him at the aperture in the screen ; the card he glanced at was then the target-card. Each time the assistant-experimenter presented his number at the aperture, he gave a verbal signal to Shackleton next door, by this means notifying him that the identity of another card was to be guessed. The agent glanced at each target-card every two or three seconds.

In these circumstances it is not surprising that all attempted explanations along rational lines of the results of these experiments have hitherto failed. For statistical analysis of the percipient's records showed conclusively not only that Shackleton consistently and successfully guessed the identity of the card ahead of the target card, but that when the speed of guessing was doubled, he successfully "prophesied" the identity of cards *two ahead of the target-card* ! i.e. he achieved a forward displacement of two places instead of the usual one. This on the face of it appears incredible. Yet with the case of Ilga K before us, both as an example and a warning, the possibilities of the operation of sensory cues via the medium of involuntary articulation or some other form of vocal innervation must be probed to the utmost.

Out of eleven *agents* whom Soal tested, only two were successful, although a third was discovered later. This evident scarcity of good " telepathic " agents is significant, for on several grounds it seems probable that most successful " telepathic " agents are nothing more than good " involuntary articulators "; some of them no doubt consciously " give free play ", to use Sidgwick's expression, to the natural tendency to innervate the vocal muscles during ESP tests. It is also certain that good " involuntary articulators " are comparatively rare.

The Ilga K case has shown us that it is not so difficult as might be expected to transmit vocal cues to a keen-eared person in another room without revealing the fact to others present. Further, the experiments of Lehmann and Hansen produced evidence that articulation *with closed and immobile lips* can be heard and correctly interpreted at a considerable distance if the percipient possesses hyperacute hearing ; Professor Sidgwick subsequently confirmed this, using an ordinary subject at a distance of four feet from the agent.

In Soal's experiments only five symbols have to be transmitted. In Sidgwick's and the Danish experiments, on the other hand, ninety—from 10 to 99—were employed. Furthermore, in the case of Ilga K, whole words were transmitted syllable by syllable—words which were entirely unexpected by Ilga—each syllable being imperceptibly tacked on to the end of the verbal admonishments and encouragements of the child's mother who acted as " agent". Obviously the ESP experiment in which only five symbols are to be guessed presents a situation far more favourable to the correct interpretation of slight vocal sounds than when a greater or idefinite number of symbols, figures or words are to be transmitted. Mere changes in the tone of the agent's breathing could suffice for successful identification.

If the case of Ilga K is any criterion, then one may reasonably infer that the chief requirements of a good " telepathic " percipient are little more than the possession of a sense of hearing considerably above average. This does not require any assumption of actual hyperaesthesia, i.e. extra-acute sensitiveness of the physiological sensory organs of the ear and afferent nervous system. As has been observed in an earlier chapter, hyperacuity of the senses may be entirely dependent upon psychological factors or upon the results of training and practice. Apart from physiological hyperaesthesia, among the factors which may be said to contribute to sensory hyperacuity, that of *discrimination* is the most important, i.e. the faculty of being able to discriminate between the scarcely perceptible sounds which convey the actual sensory cues and the myriad slight sounds which unceasingly fill the air. In another context it is this same ability to discern the relevant cues from among the thousand and one other surface disturbances which enables the aboriginee tracker of Australia to pursue the trail of his enemy with such amazing accuracy.

The ability of the percipient to *interpret* correctly what his discriminating ear picks out is also a major factor in auditory hyperacuity. This depends a great deal on the ability of the individual to concentrate all his mental resources on the task, and apparently this particular type of mental concentration and alertness often operates at a subconscious level, with the percipient making only a minimal conscious effort.

Without recapitulating further the discussions of a previous chapter, we can assume that auditory cues of one kind or another did in fact form the basis of Shackleton's astonishing performance, and that these cues were transmitted by the vocal apparatus of one *or more* of those present during the experiments. It appears utterly out of the question that simple involuntary articulation or vocal innervation on the part of the *agent alone* could have produced the precognitive effect found by Soal. We must therefore consider whether involuntary articulation by the agent and another person *together* could have produced the same result.

The suggestion of involuntary articulation à *trois* was first considered by Chowrin and was upheld by Baerwald[1] to account for certain of the former's experiments in hyperaesthesia with an advanced hysterical subject. In the case of Soal's experiments the two people most likely to be concerned in the transmission of auditory cues, if such was the case, would be the assistant-experimenter responsible for presenting the random numbers or coloured counters at the screen-aperture, and the agent.

We will take first those experiments where the assistant-experimenter shows a number at the aperture in the screen— a number chosen from a prepared list of random numbers. This type of experiment comprised over half the total number of guesses in Shackleton's " precognitive " series. If our assumption is correct, the most likely sequence of events is as follows :

It was the duty of the assistant-experimenter to hold up a random number before the screen-aperture and to give a verbal signal to Shackleton next door at the same time as he did so. With this arrangement it is easy to believe that he sometimes, perhaps often, involuntary articulated the *following* listed number on his prepared list and that the agent heard him.

Taking the precept of Ilga K, we may suppose that the involuntary articulation of the next listed number took the

---

[1] *Die Intellektuellen Phanomene*, Berlin, 1925.

form of an isolated syllable tacked on to the end of the verbal signal which the assistant-experimenter gave each time he presented a card at the aperture. In any event, whatever mode was unconsciously (or even consciously) adopted, the fact remains that under the experimental conditions then in force, the assistant-experimenter could very easily have informed the agent, a foot or two away, of the number which was to follow the one being presented at the aperture. Moreover, it seems only too likely—remembering Ilga K— that this process could have escaped the eye or the ear of the observer present.

The agent was generally given the opportunity of learning the order of the five target-cards in front of him. In those cases when he did not have a chance to glance at their order before Shackleton began guessing, the first few guesses would reveal their order as he turned them up. Thus the agent was almost always aware of the correspondence between each of the assistant-experimenter's random numbers and his own five picture cards. As mentioned before, when the agent had no chance of seeing the actual card faces, as in clairvoyance tests, Shackleton failed to score above probability expectation.

We may suppose that when the assistant-experimenter articulated the listed random number which was to follow the one he was then showing at the aperture, the agent unconsciously (or consciously) " echoed " it, spontaneously transposing it, however, into the name of its corresponding card-symbol, the identity of which he already knows.

To recapitulate briefly the outline of the hypothesis : the assistant-experimenter articulates involuntarily the number which is next on his list at the same time as he presents the target-card number to the agent at the aperture in the screen. The agent hears the number articulated and in turn articulates the corresponding card-symbol at the same time as he glances at the actual target-card. This is heard by Shackleton and recorded, thereby producing the impression that he had actually foreseen the card which is to follow the target-card. Whether the entire process was conducted at the unconscious level or whether the three persons concerned were in some degree aware of their vocal innervations and their reception of the auditory cues is open to question. The former possibility is perfectly feasible ; the unconscious reception and dissemination of sensory cues is, as we have seen earlier, more common than might be supposed.

The above general description of how Shackleton *may* have produced a precognitive trend on his score sheets is, of course, considerably over-simplified. The apparent precognitive trend was only revealed by a statistical analysis of his scores, and a number of factors probably enter into the picture which we could not discover without repeating the experimental situation as it actually was. The above theory as to how Soal arrived at his experimental results remains a possibility only. But that possibility destroys all necessity for postulating a theory of telepathy or the need for any other supernatural explanation.

With the " random-numbers " experiments the " chain of articulation " theory is relatively simple. It also has the advantage that it offers an equally simple solution to Shackleton's success in " guessing " *two* cards ahead of the target-card when the speed of card-calling was doubled. For it is then seen that the assistant-experimenter is merely articulating unconsciously the numbers which lie two ahead on his list instead of only one ahead as previously—a change presumably brought about by the doubling of the speed of presentation.

THE EXPERIMENTS WITH COUNTERS

When the assistant-experimenter used counters of five different colours to obtain a random selection of target cards, the situation is complicated by the fact that he no longer had before him a list of random-numbers from which to ascertain the subsequent sequence. Nevertheless, there does not seem any strong reason why the theory of unconscious articulation à *trois* should not hold good.

In the case of the counters-series at the normal rate of guessing, the assistant-experimenter drew the counters *out of a bag*. While he was showing one counter at the screen aperture with one hand, he was delving into the bag with the other. In these circumstances we may suppose that the assistant-experimenter frequently caught a glimpse of the colour of the counter which was to follow the one he was presenting at the aperture, and that (as with Ilga K) he could pass the information on to the *agent* by tacking the requisite syllable on to the end of his verbal signal to Shackleton. Alternatively, he may have articulated the colour of the counter before he gave the verbal signal, thereby giving the agent more time in which to transmit the corresponding card-symbol to Shackleton.

With the introduction of the double rate of calling (still using counters) the above explanation of the results would be out of the question if the use of the bag had been continued. So it is of interest to note that in these rapid-guessing experiments *an open bowl* was substituted for the bag. In order to articulate information concerning the colour of the counter which was to follow *two* ahead, the assistant-experimenter would need to be able to see at least some of the counters which he was likely to choose from the bowl. This, according to the conditions of the experiment, appears perfectly feasible. For owing to the speed at which the counters had to be presented at the screen-aperture, the assistant-experimenter had no time to delve deeply into the bowl and was obliged to pick the counters off the *top* of the heap. It may even be that he had unconsciously selected the particular counter before he had picked it up. But even omitting this possibility, if a preponderance of counters of any one colour lay on the top of the heap, the chances of the assistant-experimenter seeing them and picking one of them up were very considerable, as Soal himself pointed out[1].

To guard against this possibility and the possibility of conscious or unconscious selection, the assistant-experimenter stood up (thereby improving conditions for the effective transmission of cues by involuntary articulation) and looked, in the words of Soal's report, " straight over the top of the screen ". Anyone familiar with the subject of peripheral vision will at once see the inadequacy of this measure. It could not by itself have prevented unconscious (or conscious) selection of counters at the top of the bowl.

---

[1] ibid., p. 52.

Even if the assistant-experimenter could not use his powers
of peripheral vision, a good case could be made out for a
prior knowledge of a considerable percentage of the counters
to come. For after showing the counters at the screen-
aperture he dropped them back into the bowl, and we must
assume that during the course of fifty guesses a great many
of the counters which had previously been used were in fact
used again, perhaps several times over. By the end of the
experiment the assistant-experimenter would have had a
fairly clear idea of the percentage of each colour which lay
in the top of the bowl.

Using his powers of peripheral vision, together with the
occasional downward glances which must have occurred from
time to time, the assistant-experimenter was in very favourable position for being able to ascertain or select the colour
of the counter which was to be presented two places after the
target-counter. For to facilitate speed of presentation the
assistant-experimenter was obliged to use both hands; presumably, as one counter was being presented at the aperture,
his other hand was usually engaged in lifting out a second
counter, giving him the chance to see or even *to pre-select* the
third counter. If the colour of this third counter were
articulated each time by the assistant-experimenter as he
presented the first counter at the screen-aperture, it would
follow that, if the agent heard it, he would be able, by
articulating the corresponding card-symbol, to convey to
Shackleton the identity of the card-symbol which was to
follow *two* places after the actual target-card.

This explanation of the rapid-guessing series with counters
may appear at first sight more complicated than it is.   Really
it is no more complex than the slower series ; the main
difficulty being that the increased speed of guessing provided
less time for the process of involuntary articulation *à trois*
to operate.   To offset this disadvantage, the open bowl may
have actually given the assistant-experimenter a better
chance to cognize the third counter each time than did the
bag (in regard to the one-ahead counters-experiments).

It has been shown that a rational explanation is forthcoming for all of Soal's experiments with Shackleton, both
for those series where the random distribution was achieved
by prepared lists of random numbers and those where

counters were employed. Moreover, virtually the same process is seen to account for both Shackleton's successes at the normal rate of guessing when he guessed correctly the card one ahead of the target-card, and his rapid-guessing successes when he guessed correctly the card two ahead of the target-card.

If, as many of the leading psychical researchers in England believe, the main case for telepathy or any other form of supernatural acquisition of knowledge stands or falls by Soal's experiments in " precognitive telepathy ", the reed upon which that case leans is a weak one. For, apart from the considerations just enumerated, these much-vaunted experiments in " precognitive telepathy " involve a total of only 6,690 guesses, a very small number compared to the experiments of the American experimenters. Of these, 3,789 constituted the random-numbers series at the normal rate of guessing. Only 529 guesses were devoted to the random-numbers series at the double rate of guessing. These seem open to the charge of optional stopping. This last criticism can also be directed to the double-rate counters-series. In any event the low number of guesses, 529 in the former and 794 in the latter case, is not impressive, particularly if the charge of optional stopping of these series cannot be shown to be false.

It was Soal's contention that the changes from forward displacement to backward displacement and forward again were mainly due to the effect of suggestion. On reading the report, one does indeed obtain this impression. But whereas Soal believed that Shackleton was being affected by suggestion, it appears more likely that the assistant-experimenter was the one thus affected.

SOAL'S TELEPATHY EXPERIMENTS WITH MRS. STEWART

Since his experiments with Shackleton, Soal has carried out another series with Mrs. G. Stewart, involving a total of approximately 17,000 card-guessing trials. The same cautious and elaborate steps to provide independent witnesses at every stage were not followed in these experiments as they were with Shackleton. In fact, in certain well-informed quarters, complaint has been made that the conditions of the experiments with Mrs. Stewart have not been independently witnessed, and there seems good reason to believe that the conditions of the Stewart experiments were considerably less rigorous than those with Shackleton. Certainly there is an unwarrantable atmosphere of secrecy surrounding these latter experiments.

Mrs. Stewart did not succeed in achieving scores with a precognitive trend. Her records showed only a consistent success in scoring on the actual target-card—a situation which is very simply explained by unconscious (or intentional) articulation of the target-card symbol by the agent.

We can afford to ignore those experiments where major variations in experimental technique were tried out, with varying degrees of success, on account of the small number of trials in each type of experiment. The one exception we must make is the series of 1,000 guesses in a " pure telepathy " experiment where the agent, referred to as Z, concentrated on cards which provided only indirect reference to the usual symbols.

Without going into the complicated details of the experiment, which were designed to exclude all possibility of clairvoyance as opposed to telepathy, we may note that this experiment is so easily explainable by unconscious articulation that it is surprising Dr. Soal and his colleague went to such enormous trouble in planning it. The score achieved by the percipient was certainly impressive ; she obtained a total of 293 correct guesses as against a chance expectation of 200. providing " odds of many millions to one against chance ".

In regard to a further 1,000 trials over the telephone, the most striking thing about these is their naïvety. Sensory cues can be conveyed through the phone as easily as by any other means. Only the last series of 200[1] are surprising, for in these the agent sat ten feet away from the phone at the transmitting end while the percipient sat ten feet away from the receiver. But 200 trials is too small a number to be of any significance.

The only point of real interest in the experiments with Mrs. Stewart is that she succeeded in attaining positive

[1] Soal, S.G., *The Experimental Situation in Psychical Research*, 1948, p.54.

scores with eight different agents out of a total of twelve who
were tried.   With Shackleton only three successful agents
out of twelve were successful.   But as has been mentioned
before, the conditions of the Stewart experiments seem to
have been far below the meticulous standards of the other,
while the secrecy attached to them inevitably lays them
open to a certain amount of scepticism.

Dr. Soal on " Involuntary Whispering "

We saw in the last chapter that most ESP experimenters
seem completely unaware of the danger of sensory cues via
the medium of involuntary articulation.   But Dr. Soal
certainly knew this danger better than most, and has at
various times referred to " unconscious whispering ", " involuntary whispering ", and " incipient vocalisation ".   It
seems curious that if Soal did recognise the dangers from
this source, he should have largely disregarded them in his
experiments—particularly those with Mrs. Stewart.

Rhine too has shown evidence of his belief in the possibility
of transmitting auditory cues by involuntary articulation.
Not only was he editor of the *Journal of Parapsychology* when
the case of Ilga K was published, but in 1938 in his book
New Frontiers of the Mind, he wrote the following :

> " When Professor A. Lehmann, a Danish psychologist, raised the
> question as to whether ' involuntary whispering ' (with closed lips)
> could explain the English Society's result in thought-transference he
> showed that involuntary whispering did occur with some people when
> they were thinking intently and that under certain circumstances
> which he devised in his laboratory others could be guided by it."

This is not a very clear summary of the Lehmann and
Hansen experiments, and possibly Rhine missed the main
significance of these experiments—namely, as Professor
Sidgwick himself confirmed subsequently, that articulation
with closed and immobile lips could convey information
across a distance of several feet with people of perfectly
ordinary powers of hearing.   It is strange that, having read
the Lehmann and Hansen report, Rhine himself should have
conducted many experiments which, while fully permitting
the operation of " unconscious whispering ", he attributed
to the operation of *extra-sensory perception* !

Soal, like Rhine, had become interested in telepathy and clairvoyance experiments through a general interest in psychical research. Both Rhine and Soal had investigated spiritualistic mediums, the former with alleged reservations, the latter with keen interest. Both deemed there was evidence of " psychic " faculties amongst the large amount of nonsense which characterised spiritualistic utterances. In one detailed investigation of the spiritualist medium Blanche Cooper, Soal came strongly out in favour of her " paranormal " faculties. Later, however, he almost entirely retracted his findings mainly on grounds of " involuntary whispering ". Wrote Soal :

> " Were it not for certain episodes in the case of ' Gordon Davis,' I should not be afraid to face the possibility of the hypothesis of a mixture of involuntary whispering on my own part and the occasional reading into vague sounds words that were not really articulated by the Medium."[1]

The spiritualistic press did not receive this announcement too kindly, and Soal apparently found himself obliged to defend his theory :

> " There is nothing inherently absurd in the hypothesis of unconscious whispering. Incipient vocalization is known to be an accompaniment of conscious thinking in many persons ; it certainly occurs in much of my own. Why then, should it not frequently take place during unconscious cerebration. The question whether there are certain hyperaesthetic subjects in whose minds involuntary whispering is able to start trains of thought, is a matter for experiment and not for dogmatism."

He went on to add :

> " At this date I do not attach much scientific value to my Cooper records ; they were obtained under conditions that were far from ideal. In fact, had I obtained such results today under the same defective conditions I should never dream of allowing such records to be published."[2]

That Soal should publicly retract the validity of past experiments is a tribute to his honesty. Rhine has never, to the author's knowledge, retracted his original claims in regard to experiments often far more questionable than any

---

[1] *Psychic Science*, April 1938.
[2] *Light*, 1938, p.262.

of Soal's. The most likely reason why Rhine has not retracted his past claims is probably due to his many *ex cathedra*
pronouncements. Pontificating depends for its success on its
continuing as a one-way process, and retraction can only
result in a serious weakening of prestige and eventual eclipse,
unless there is a solid basis of fact upon which to fall back.
The ESP experimental situation has no such solid basis.

Highly pertinent was Soal's comment in the same letter
to *Light* in 1938 : "*I suggest that a laboratory examination
into the possibility of unconscious vocalisation in connection
with subjects showing auditory hyperaesthesia should be
carried out.*" It is curious that never in the annals of psychical research or parapsychology has any such investigation
been undertaken—the case of Ilga K was an incidental one,
and its lessons were almost entirely ignored.

Soal certainly envisaged the possibility of the transmission
of the sensory cues during his experiments with Mrs.
Stewart. In his *Experimental Situation in Psychical
Research*[3] he includes several paragraphs under the sub-
title *Unconscious Whispering*. Here Soal puts the case of
Ilga K as an example of both auditory hyperacuity and involuntary articulation. He even went so far as to admit
the possibility of the percipient receiving vocal cues without being consciously aware of them. As he himself wrote:

> " Now though these sounds emitted by the agent might be far too
> faint for Mr. P. [the percipient] to be consciously aware of them
> in the next room, they might yet be of sufficient intensity to set a
> train of thought moving in his mind. That is to say that some part
> of his mind might register them and thus Mr. P. might get a clue to
> the initial sound of the name of the animal [card-symbol]. That
> the above possibility is more than a mere hypothetical conjecture
> is confirmed by the case of the Latvian peasant child Ilga K."[4]

The really surprising thing is that Dr. Soal, after having
written this, concluded that Mrs. Stewart's successes were
not in fact achieved by " unconscious whispering." He
buttressed this conclusion by referring us to a successful
series of a mere 600 guesses conducted over the telephone,

---

[3] 1947.

[4] op. cit, p.12.

with the last 200 involving a distance of some ten feet between the agent and his telephone and same distance between Mrs. Stewart and her receiver.   After that, to judge
from the record, she failed to continue to score successfully.

These telephone experiments cannot, it is clear, be held
to confute the theory of involuntary articulation for any one
of three reasons, *viz.* their small number, the possibility of
optional stopping, and the fact that sensory cues can be
conveyed over a telephone.   The charge of optional stopping
appears to be more of a fact than a possibility in these telephone experiments.

If any doubt remains as to Soal's belief that sensory cues
may be conveyed by involuntary articulation, the following
quotation should dispel it :

> " Our card-guessing experiments of 1934-1939 failed to produce
> any evidence whatever that ordinary persons sitting at a distance of
> about three feet from an agent were able to score by picking up
> whispers or faint articulations.   But though I am quite certain that
> ordinary people are incapable of such a feat at the distance of 6-8
> yards which obtained in the Shackleton and Stewart experiments,
> even if there were any whispers to pick up, it is still conceivable that
> exceptional persons like Ilga K are able to manage it, and Mrs.
> Stewart might be one of these exceptions." [5]

In his investigations into the vaudeville telepathist,
" Marion ", Soal arrived at the positive conclusion that his
subject gained a great deal of information from the behaviour
of his agent.   From his experience in one type of experiment
with Marion, Soal was led to criticise some of Rhine's ESP
experiments on the ground of visual cues.   He states :

> " . . . the experiment has an important lesson in connection with the
> telepathic experiments of Dr. Rhine.   *No such experiments can be
> considered of any crucial importance if the percipient is able to see any
> part of the agent's body.*   Where the percipient has only a small
> number (5 or 6) of figures from which to make his choice, the possibil-
> ity of visual codes *elaborated unconsciously* when the same agent and
> percipient work together over any considerable period of time is too
> patent to be overlooked.   In my repetition of the experiments in
> *telepathy*, I have used a screen from the very beginning and consider

[5] op. cit, p. 53.

that experiments conducted without the use of a screen are valueless so far as the demonstration of telepathy is concerned." [1]

Elsewhere Soal records : " Personally, I have never exposed a naked card to a subject in the course of over 100,000 trials."

Why did not Soal show the same care in preventing the transmission of auditory cues, as in excluding visual cues, when on his admission he was aware of the dangers from such a source ? A sentence from his pamphlet *Advice to Experimenters and Instructors* (1948) makes his attitude even more inexplicable : " From the very start let the cards and the percipient be in separate but adjoining rooms with a door between them." Yet it was under precisely such conditions as these that Ilga K achieved her phenomenal successes in detecting syllables and words through her abnormally developed sense of hearing. For an instructor of would-be ESP experimenters, his advice appears to fall far short of the requisite standards. The door in his Shackleton experiments was purposely " left an inch or two ajar in order to facilitate hearing " the verbal signals of the assistant-experimenter—an unwise precaution at best !

Soal never imagined, apparently, that the assistant-experimenter might give cues to the agent concerning the order of the listed random-numbers or counters. He remarks[2] that the assistant-experimenter could have given nothing away to the *percipient* " by any inflection of the voice " each time he gave verbally the synchronisation signal, since he did not know the order of the agent's cards. He completely overlooked the point that the *agent* could easily have acquired vital information by such means.

The best test of the practicability of involuntary articulation à *trois* would be to try it out. With a little practice the precognitive effect could very easily be achieved if the participants used their normal manner of speaking. One may say, with certain reservations, that what is practicable at the conscious level using normal modes of vocalisation may also, with certain people, be practicable at the unconscious level through the medium of involuntary articulation.

---

[1] *Preliminary Studies of a Vaudeville Telepathist*, p. 33.
[2] *Experiments in Precognitive Telepathy*, Proc. S.P.R., vol. 47, p. 39.

To sum up : little confidence can be placed in the ability of experimenters who fail to see the necessity of maintaining the very highest scientific standards ; compared to the rigid experimental standards of the physics laboratory the experiments of Soal and Rhine and the rest must inevitably meet with scepticism. We can, perhaps, with tongue in cheek, agree with Soal that " with our present rough methods it is impossible to do more than to suggest lines for future research." [3]   As a final word on ESP experiments generally, we can again refer to Soal : " The number of experiments carried out and the number of good subjects discovered are both so ludicrously small that there is hardly a finding reported that has been adequately confirmed." [4]   This is a healthy admission of the state of ESP research and one which reflects great credit on the sincerity and forthrightness of its author.   It is to be hoped that Dr. Joseph Rhine and his colleagues would agree with this opinion.

---

[3] op. cit., p. 57.
[4] *The Experimental Situation in Psychical Research*, 1947, p. 14.

Chapter Twenty-eight

THE LOGICAL STATUS OF TELEPATHY AND ANALOGOUS CONCEPTS

THE experiments conducted by " parapsychologists " in the United States and England are, as we have seen, open to criticism on grounds of the failure to guard against the operation of sensory cues, or, where this is not directly observable, on grounds of the bias or incompetence of the experimenters concerned as evidenced in their written reports and papers. There are, however, other grounds for rejecting such experiments, namely the *metaphysical*, as opposed to scientific, nature of the hypotheses upon which they are based. Metaphysical hypotheses, such as those founded on the idea of a transcendental mental faculty, can never possess any *scientific* significance, a fundamental fact which ESP experimenters have apparently never appreciated. Nor do parapsychologists seem aware that can never be empirically proved.

The first thing to consider, in entering upon the question of the logical and epistemological status of telepathy and similar ideas, is whether such terms denote a fact, or a *theory* (or hypothesis). Usually they are treated without any distinction being made and are spoken of indiscriminately both as facts *and* theories.

Both the exact and the comparative sciences insist upon facts which are, in principle at least, observable by means of our sensory apparatus. In applying this principle to the situation found in, say, telepathy experiments, we note that the outstanding *fact* which requires an explanation is—to generalise briefly—an observed temporal simultaneity or an

479

objective correspondence between certain related written or spoken symbols involving two or more people. In other words, observable *coincidences* are found, and in the case of the " successful " ESP experiment a certain type of coincidence is observed which happens far more often than mere chance would account for.

Behind the objective expression of written or verbal symbols, however, lie the mental functions of the two people concerned ; without mental activity involving some degree of consciousness, the symbols in question would neither have been written nor spoken. We can therefore take little exception, apart from its vagueness, to Soal's definitive statement that " the term Telepathy is merely a name attached to ce tain unexplained types of mental coincidence."[1]

Parapsychologists claim that the existence of telepathy has been scientifically proved. What do they mean by this? Do they mean that certain unexplainable coincidences have been discovered which have been termed telepathy ? Or do they mean that the theory of transcendental mental faculties has been demonstrated beyond all shadow of doubt ? It is quite evident from their journals and papers that parapsychologists mean neither of these things ; they confuse the fact of certain " mental coincidences " with the hypothesis of extra-sensory perception, and lump them all into one.

Naturally, what the parapsychologist observes, i.e. certain coincidences, require a theory to explain them. If he postulates a theory of cognition acting independantly of the human senses and calls it telepathy or ESP, then it is quite clear that telepathy and ESP are not the " scientifically demonstrated facts " he claims them to be. Neither are they theories in the scientific sense of the word ; furthermore, it is abundantly clear that the parapsychologist has not yet produced a logical and internally consistent theory.

In answer to these arguments the parapsychologist may say that telepathy and ESP are preliminary hypotheses only. He might even go so far as to admit that they are metaphysical, as opposed to scientific, hypotheses. He might even go further and say that the facts warrant a metaphysical hypothesis. And if he had a repeatable

[1] *Light*, 1938, p. 262.

experiment, who could gainsay him ? But he has no repeatable experiment to offer us. Nor does he give us any hope that he will some day produce one. And his own experiments, as has been seen, are open to criticism on many counts. In view of the extraordinary ambiguity of his terminology, the gross incompetence of many of his published experiments, and his confusion of metaphysical hypotheses with scientific theory, it is clear the parapsychologist seldom thinks as scientist. His approach to his subject is fundamentally that of the amateur. It is little wonder that the scientific world remains sceptical.

" Mental coincidences " do not by themselves, it is clear, demand a theory of telepathy to explain them. Chance may account for much, while inference, sensory stimuli or convergent lines of thought might account for the rest. But, let us suppose that, taking into account all possible factors, Soal's experimental results defied any kind of rational explanation ; would it then be justifiable to assume that these results were due to the operation of a causal principle at present unknown to modern science ? It would. But in actual fact Soal used admittedly " rough methods " in his experiments and, as has already been seen, one formidable loophole was left for the possible transmission of sensory cues. So in this particular instance the question of an operative principle new to science scarcely arises.

Even so, if such an assumption were in fact justified, does the concept of telepathy, or any similar concept, warrant serious scientific consideration ? Here the answer must be firmly in the negative, for the reason that such concepts possess no logical status either as logical deductions or as scientific inductions. We can, in fact, reject them for three good reasons : One, that they are purely metaphysical in outlook. Two, that their historical antecedents lie entirely in the sphere of magic, superstition and mysticism. Three, that as scientific inductions *they fail completely, since no deductions can be made from them by which to test their validity.*

The first point explains itself, i.e. metaphysical speculation is totally incompatible with scientific induction. In the philosophical systems of Leibnitz, or even of Kant, " mind-to-mind " or " extra-sensory perception " theories might not appear unduly out of order. But it must be emphasised that such ideas are, even in the most favourable light, mere metaphysical concepts which can have no possible application to empirical experiment, either as preliminary hypotheses or as developed theories. Science and metaphysics are two things totally apart.

In regard to the second point, namely the historical background of supernatural belief which pertains to telepathy and allied concepts ; it must be observed that, while this factor does not of itself invalidate these concepts, it does throw them into a highly dubious perspective and on that account they will be regarded with more than average suspicion by the scientific mind. The commonsense view of such theories, bearing this historical background in mind, is that telepathy and extra-sensory perception are nothing more than thinly disguised attempts to rationalise the occult, or else merely pretentious abstractions from primitive witch-lore.

Historically speaking, such ideas stem from ancient beliefs in magic and sorcery. The historical traditions can be traced in an unbroken line from the earliest supernatural beliefs to the latest metaphysical theories of the modern ESP experimenter. This is a point which modern occultists, such as Rhine and Soal, do their utmost to ignore ; for them the " supernatural " becomes the more euphemistic but equally question-begging " paranormal "—a device which may deceive many.

The long unbroken tradition of occultism and belief in the supernatural which forms the historical background to modern ESP experimentation is a factor which the impartial investigator cannot afford to ignore. From the point of view of the scientist the position of Soal or Rhine may be said to amount to this : granted the necessity for postulating the existence of a causal connection in order to account for the experimental results achieved ; but why not, asks the scientist, actively *seek* the causal connection instead of passively falling back on a tradition of occultism to explain these experimental results ? In any event, he might well add, ignorance is not dispelled by reversions to the supernatural, to streamlined soul-theories, to mysticism or to metaphysics, however technological the jargon in which they are expressed.

Soal's experiments in telepathy come at the end of a long series of investigations into the various phenomena of spiritualism. Soal was once himself a very competent automatic writer. His considerable automatic output has largely been published in the *Proceedings* of the Society for Psychical Research. His script personalities usually purported to be spirits on the other side of the grave—a piece of fiction which did not appear to impress Soal himself but which led him to undertake investigations in an effort to ascertain whether or not the scripts contained evidence of knowledge supernaturally or " paranormally " acquired.

With this background to his own ESP experiments it is not surprising that even Soal confuses occult and meta-physical speculation with scientific theory. Rhine is even worse situated in this respect. His theories, largely bor-rowed from Myers via the writings of G. N. M. Tyrrell, expound a metaphysics of " anthropocentrism ", which is very similar in many respects to the oriental doctrines of *Sankhya-Yoga*.

In regard to the third point, that telepathy *et alia* are not true scientific hypotheses or inductions, this naturally follows from the first one. But the futility of such theorising will be brought out clearly by a brief discussion of scientific theories in general. While the search for a new operative principle hitherto unknown to science is not of itself open to any logical objection, the assumption that metaphysical " mind-to-mind " or " extra-sensory perception " theories might fit the bill is naïve in the extreme.

Such theories are, from any scientific criterion, not only useless but literally meaningless. For consider the nature and purpose of any scientific hypothesis : it is little more than an arbitrary assumption made for the purpose of further reasoning and chosen, for one reason or another, in preference to other arbitrary assumptions. It serves as a starting point for further empirical or theoretical investigation. If it leads to useful practical results its validity is assured. For there is only *one* test of the validity of a scientific hypo-thesis, and that test is the pragmatic one, i.e. does it lead to further practical results ? By this criterion telepathy and similar concepts are obviously quite redundant.

Again, the prime necessity of any exploratory hypothesis is that it should be unambiguously formulated so that no one shall remain in doubt as to what it means, i.e. all its terms must be strictly definable ones. No one, for example, was in any doubt when Copernicus put forward his hypothesis that the planets went round the sun instead of the earth. In such " hypotheses " as telepathy and clairvoyance we find an abundance of highly ambiguous terms such as " mind ", the " action " of one " mind " on another, and the *scientifically* incomprehensible terms " extrasensory " perception or cognition.

There must be at least a score of markedly divergent views as to what is meant by " mind ", varying from metaphysical soul-theories to the semi-mechanical theories of Freud. " Mind " has *never* been properly defined in any scientific sense, and it remains a metaphysical concept only. The Concise Oxford Dictionary defines mind as " the seat of consciousness ". If we ask for a precise definition of " seat " all we are given is further figurative or analogical synonyms—nothing concrete or verifiable, nothing that could even be termed a logical abstraction ; nothing, in fact, beyond a vague metaphor or the addition of yet another " indefinable definition " such as " that which causes our thoughts " (which is to be found in Webster's excellent International Dictionary).

We can, of course, substitute the term " mental activity " for mind, for mental activity is a fact of direct subjective experience. But to hypothecate that mental activity itself possesses *transcendental* aspects of its own immediately involves us in even further metaphysical—some would say mystical—ambiguities of a highly speculative order. Lacking any internal logical structure of their own, the concepts of telepathy and extra-sensory perception are, and must remain, quite meaningless from the scientific standpoint.

Whither does all this argument lead, as far as the psychical researcher is concerned ? We can summarise the situation thus : One, certain coincidences occur which are thought to be unexplainable by normal means. Two, a hypothesis is required, but since telepathy and extra-sensory perception are metaphysical concepts, meaningless from the scientific standpoint, another approach, a strictly *scientific* one, must be tried—assuming, for the sake of argument only, that sensory cues are out of the question as an explanation of ESP experiments. Three, the final aim of any exploratory hypothesis put forward must be the development of a comprehensive scientific theory. Before this can be done, however, it is first necessary to understand both the purpose, the scope and the limits of scientific theories in general. This is precisely what parapsychologists have conspicuously failed to do.

In considering the possibility of a new scientific theory to explain the experimental results of Soal and Rhine, all such mystical notions as transcendental powers of the mind must be firmly relegated to the spheres of occultism, metaphysics or theology, and kept there. A scientific theory in the modern sense is first and foremost a product of inductive reasoning. Moreover, the sole test of its validity is whether *all* of its verifiable logical consequences are realisable in fact. If a single one is not realised in fact when put to experimental test, then that theory is automatically invalidated.

As may be seen, this is no happy hunting ground for the amateur who wishes to formulate theoretical principles new to science ; and few of us possess the intellect of a Newton or an Einstein.

Since the purpose and value—or, as some would even say, the relative truth—of a scientific theory depends on the possibility of deducing logically its consequences, the need for an accurate and clearly defined formulation of any such theory is immediately obvious. This is invariably true in all the exact sciences. The comparative sciences neither require mathematical exactness of theoretical formulation nor (since they deal with relatively inexact data) can they attain to it.

But the methods of the comparative sciences will not do for the ESP experimenter. If he is to formulate an operative principle new to science, he is bound to accept the criteria of the exact sciences, in the same way that his actual experiments are bound to conform to them before anyone will believe in their accuracy.

But the insoluble difficulty of the ESP experimenter, assuming his views to be somewhere in the right direction, is to produce experiments which will provide the needed basis upon which to erect an exact inductive theory. Only with the employment of mathematics is exact theoretical formulation possible. But the application of mathematical theory presupposes exactness of observation—just the very thing that can *never* be attained in ESP experiments, or, for that matter, in any type of psychological experiment.

The conclusion to be drawn is that, even if the ESP experimenter is correct about the need for a new scientific operative principle to explain his experimental results, the search for such a principle is doomed to failure. But, as has been seen in earlier chapters, the parapsychologist's experimental results are open to criticism on grounds of the experimenter's bias and incompetence, or else are open to a rational explanation; so far as he is concerned the need for an operative principle new to science has not in fact arisen.

Apparently the parapsychologist or psychical researcher does not realise that a scientific theory is nothing more than a tool—a *device for calculation and prediction*—and that in the exact sciences abstract mathematical theory has almost entirely taken the place of verbal theorising.

The position of the psychical researcher is not enviable. He seeks a logical explanation for anomalies which apparently cannot be explained by contemporary scientific principles. He wishes to explain the anomaly of certain " mental coincidences " which allegedly occur without the operation of sensory cues, in much the same way as Einstein wished to find a logical reason to explain the anomaly of the observed constant velocity light. Now it is quite true that a few unexplained scientific anomalies have, in the past, led to older scientific ideas being superseded by totally new and revolutionary principles.

Einstein's new ideas meant that the old Aristotelian logic and the old Newtonian " laws " were overthrown from their hitherto invincible supremacy. This, apparently, is what the ESP experimenter seeks to do. His task is formidable indeed. For he must be prepared not only to try his hand at the three-valued mathematical logic of modern science but to institute yet *another* revolution in scientific thinking which will contain the modern scientific theories as Einstein's contained those of his predecessor ! Certain it is that to evoke principles not yet known to modern science will require at least a two-valued logic. And this will inevitably mean that any such theory as the parapsychologist may evolve will be incapable of formulation in terms of verbal logic.

When the convenient Newtonian fiction of " the law of gravity " was superseded by the modern mathematical theory of relativity, no one was certain how to describe the new concept in words. Minkowski and Eddington, amongst others, tried to give it verbalised expression by describing the behaviour observed when two bodies approach one another as due to the effects of the "curvature in the space-time continuum "—the bodies following the line of least resistance. This verbal description is largely analogical, for there exist no verbal concepts to express abstract mathematical ideas once we leave Euclidean logic behind. The reason why this is so is that mathematics is itself *an extension* of verbal logic and is therefore able to penetrate where verbal logic alone can never reach.

It may be worth noting at this point that the operative principles which underlie the parapsychologist's own metaphysical hypotheses are mainly drawn from nineteenth century physics—principles which have since been replaced by others in present-day physics.

The impossibility of describing modern physical theories in terms of verbal logic is mainly due to the fact that verbal logic has never gone very far beyond the Aristotelian or Euclidean kind with its single set of rules; while modern physics uses a three-valued logic each with its own entirely different set of rules. Minkowski's " four dimensional space-time continuum " just mentioned is merely a piece of verbal symbolism expressing, somewhat picturesquely, the underlying mathematical concepts ; it provides analogical expression for the fact that relativity physicists have, for purely practical reasons, arbitrarily chosen to measure time in terms of the measurements of space.

The scientist today cannot give a true representation of abstract physical theories in words; all he can do is to draw analogies.   Yet our psychical researcher apparently believes that his simple verbal " theories " are potential rivals to the three-valued mathematical logic which underlies modern scientific concepts.   It is the wishful naïvety of such ideas as telepathy and " extra-sensory perception " which lends to them the folk-lore charm of one of Grimm's or Afanas'ef's fairy tales.

Whereas the scientist is concerned only with *practical* results and applications of his theories, the ESP experimenter believes that *his* theories possess an ulterior significance apart from the question of any practical value they might have.   That is to say, he believes wholeheartedly that his experiments prove the transcendence of " mind " over matter, that human knowledge can free itself from the bonds imposed by the phenomenal universe, that the philosphy of idealism may be yet proved by empirical experiments, that " mind " may react on " mind " by means of an operative principle as yet unsuspected by the scientific world ; he believes, in fact, what mystics of all climes and all lands have believed for thousands of years—it is surprising how little this " perennial philosophy " changes after it enters the laboratory !

Scientific theory being essentially pragmatic, possesses no metaphysical significance whatsoever. So that even if parapsychologists did succeed in formulating a genuinely scientific theory of extra-sensory perception, they could draw from it nothing of any metaphysical import.   Rhine, following Myers and Tyrrell, ignores this factor completely, and continues to insist that extra-sensory perception (now taken as a fact, not a theory) proves the essential correctness of Kantian idealism. Such philosophising is perfectly permiss ble up to a point : but even where scientists are prone to metaphysical or even mystical speculation, as in the case of Eddington and Jeans, they do not allow such speculation to enter into their work or practical research.

Some philosophers have attempted to base their metaphysical systems upon purely scientific concepts, the folly of what was brilliantly exemplified by S. Alexander's monumental failure to adopt the space-time continuum of relativity theory as the basic conception of his metaphysical theorising. Psychical researchers have often referred optimistically to Eddington's version of Kantian idealism in connection with their own viewpoint; Alexander's *Space, Time and Deity* might have suited their purpose still better!

In the philosophical pseudo-controversy between idealism and materialism Rhine comes down heavily yet superficially on the side of idealism, which he illogically believes his ESP experiments to have fully substantiated as the only correct viewpoint. He even advocates a revision of the basic principles of contempoary science on this account! His experiments, and the theories based upon them can, of course, throw no more light on the idealism-materialism controversy than Minkowski's concept of space-time which Alexander so misused.

The parapsychologist's delusions have sometimes led him to claim that his experiments have uprooted the traditional concepts of science. This finds expression in two ways: his belief that new " laws of nature " are awaiting discovery just around the corner; and his belief that these new laws will, when discovered, throw revolutionary light on the cosmos and the nature of man's relation to it. Herein he makes two fallacious assumptions: namely that " a law of nature " is something objective and external, existing in its own right; and that the " discovery " of any such law would possess a metaphysical significance. These errors stem naturally from his ignorance of what constitutes a "law of nature". Briefly, a scientific or natural "law" is basically nothing more than a highly generalised description of what is observed. The idea of a " a law of nature " is now scientifically obsolete, its place having been taken by the more practical functional and differential equations of modern physics.

The ESP researcher must bear in mind that any laws he may "discover " can only be laws of his own devising; he must recognise that no "fundamental truths " revealing the nature of man or the universe can ever be found this way; that no union between transcendental metaphysics and science is even remotely possible; that the sole purpose of all scientific theory is to predict the most likely course of events or to control in some measure the events themselves; that the fundamental nature of the universe and of man are problems not even touched upon by science because science deals only with the internal or external relations of observed phenomena.

In conclusion it may be said that as long as the ESP experimenter is more interested in trying to prove such preconceived metaphysical " theories " as telepathy, clairvoyance and non-sensory perception, instead of trying to find a rational explanation of his experiments, his efforts, sincere though they may be, are doomed to frustration and failure.

Experiments in telepathy and clairvoyance, indeed all " psi-phenomena ", as we have seen, can be explained away on rational grounds. Even if this were not so, the telepathic or clairvoyant interpretation given to any such experiments is seen to be quite meaningless from the scientific standpoint. It has also been seen that the *animus* of such experiments is derived historically from beliefs in magic and the supernatural.

In view of these conclusions one might naturally ask whether English and American Universities are to continue their active support of such experiments. It is to be sincerely hoped not. For the resurgence of supernatural beliefs within the precincts of modern universities cannot be regarded otherwise than as a retrograde step of the first magnitude. It is virtually a reversion to the irrational beliefs of the Middle Ages.

When the state of the world demands the ever-increasing development of human powers of reason, it is somewhat ominous to find that occultism still rears its head in many of our seats of learning and culture. It is, perhaps, a fitting commentary on the times in which we live.

APPENDIX

Further Experiments in Long-Distance Telepathy

Since going to press my attention has been drawn to a series of long-distance experiments carried out by Dr. S. G. Soal during his tenure of the Cambridge University Perrott Studentship in Psychical Research in 1949, and which were reported in the Journal of the Society for Psychical Research (**XXXV**, 1950, pp.257-272). These experiments deserve some comment :

There were two series of experiments ; in each Mrs. G. Stewart was the percipient. In the first, the telepathic agent was situated in Cambridge and the percipient in Richmond, a distance of some fifty miles.

The scores were not significant, though in " control experiments " in which Mrs. Stewart and another agent sat in adjoining rooms (and which were held a few minutes after each long-distance session) highly successful scores were obtained. All score sheets were kept in triplicate and effective precautions taken to obviate any possible charge of fraud or collusion. Had this series of long-distance experiments yielded significant results, Soal's position would have been unassailable.

In the second series of experiments the percipient, Mrs. Stewart, was situated in Antwerp, Belgium, and the two agents in London. The check-up indicated that this series involving a total of 1,200 card-guesses, was highly successful. Nevertheless it is only fair to point out that Soal neglected to take the same precautions which characterised the Cambridge-Richmond series with Mrs. Stewart and his previous experiments with Shackleton. These precautions, as just noted, obviated the slightest possibility of fraud. But in the Antwerp-London experiments such precautions were not taken : Soal himself had access to both Mrs. Stewart's score sheets and his own list of random numbers before he handed them over to a colleague for checking.

Soal could so easily have avoided this situation, that it raises the question why he favoured such a procedure. He well knew that such a procedure would lay this important series of experiments open to criticism on grounds that either his own figures or those of his percipient could have been altered to produce the desired result. In view of his previous precautions to obviate such charges it seems curious that he should have neglected the one obvious step which would have rendered these Antwerp-London experiments completely foolproof.

The experimental proof of such metaphysical hypotheses as telepathy and clairvoyance (if such a thing is indeed possible) requires that the experiments be not only convincing in themselves but totally foolproof, and that they shall be *proved* foolproof. Only then can the scientist be certain that the experiments contained no flaw or fraud and that they will stand the test of time. In point of fact no such experimental proof has ever been produced by parapsychologists, and the experiments of Dr. Soal are no exception.

GLOSSARY OF TERMS

The following list of words has been specially compiled to help the reader whose knowledge of psychology and psychical research is limited. Technical terms mentioned only once in the book have not necessarily been included.

ACENESTHESIA. An intense feeling of depersonalisation. An acute sensation of having no material existence. *See* DEPERSONALISATION.

ACOUMETER. *See* AUDIOMETER.

AESTIVATION. " Summer sleep ". The habit of some members of the animal kingdom to pass the summer months in a state of catalepsy or " suspended animation " to avoid the rigours of great heat and drought. *Cf.* HIBERNATION.

AFTER-IMAGE. The temporary continuation of a sensory experience after the original stimulus has gone.

AGENT. Means telepathic agent. The person who does the " transmitting " in telepathic experiments. *Cf.* PERCIPIENT.

ALTERNATING PERSONALITY. *See* DUAL PERSONALITY.

AMNESIA. Loss of memory. A partial or complete inability to recall or identify past experiences.

ANAESTHESIA. Partial or complete absence of the sense of touch.

ANALGESIA. Loss of sensitivity to pain.

ANIMAL MAGNETISM.   Mesmer's term for hypnotism, based on the incorrect notion that the phenomena observed were due to the emanation of a magnetic fluid or force.

ANOPSIA.   Blindness.

ANTHROPOLOGY.   The scientific study of the human race in all its aspects, particularly the study of behaviour, beliefs, traits and customs in primitive races.

APHONIA.   An inability to utter vocal sounds.

AURA.   A term common in spiritualism and similar cults denoting anything from a halo to a coloured irridescence emanating from persons, animals, and inanimate objects, especially magnets.

ASTROLOGY.   Divination by studying the conformations of the heavenly bodies. No connection with scientific astronomy.

AUDIOMETER.   A device for determining the smallest sounds which a person can hear.

AUTISTIC THINKING.   The gratification of unfulfilled longings by imaginary phantasy.

AUTOMATIC WRITING.   *See* AUTONOGRAPHY.

AUTOMATISM ;   *Adj.* AUTOMATIC.   Any activity performed without the conscious awareness of the individual concerned, or in which the normal exercise of the will is in abeyance.

AUTONOGRAPHY.   Automatic writing. There are several distinct forms of autonography, ranging from purely automatic activity of the hand while the subject's attention is directed elsewhere, to consciously writing down words which appear to the writer to enter his mind from an external source.

AUTONOMIC NERVOUS SYSTEM.   That part of the nervous system which regulates many of the internal organs of the body whose functions are not subject to the control of the will.

AUTOSCOPIC HALLUCINATION. An hallucination which depicts one's own body or self. If this phenomenon is accompanied by delusion the percipient may believe that he is actually seeing himself from a detached viewpoint.

AUTOSUGGESTION. Suggestion which emanates from the individual himself. *Cf.* HETEROSUGGESTION.

AWAKEN FROM HYPNOSIS. The traditional term used to denote the resumption of the normal state (usually at the command of the operator) by a person who has been rendered abnormally suggestible by hypnotic methods.

CAPILLARIES. The minute blood vessels which carry the blood through the tissues of the body.

CATALEPSY. Generally speaking, a condition of muscular rigidity sometimes accompanied by unconsciousness. Plastic catalepsy (especially found in schizophrenics) denotes that the limbs are moveable and retain the position in which they are placed. Often a hysterical syndrome. It may be produced by great emotional shock or artificially in hypnosis.

CATAPLEXY. May be taken as synonymous with CATALEPSY. The term is used most often, however, in connection with animals.

CEREBRAL. Pertaining to the brain.

CEREBRAL CORTEX. The " grey matter " of the brain. The neopallium. It is responsible for all the higher mental activities.

CHOREA. The disease known as St. Vitus's Dance. Sometimes imitated by hysterical persons. Involves spasmodic twitchings of the face, shoulder or arm muscles.

CLAIRVOYANCE. Purportedly the cognition of objects or events by means other than through the five senses.

COENESTHESIA. The diffuse mass of bodily sensations which go to make up one's feeling of tiredness, well-being, discomfort, etc. The general body-sense.

COMPLEX. Associations of emotionally charged ideas which are repressed and of which the individual is unaware. They are usually linked to some instinctive urge whose expression is undesired by the person concerned. *See* REPRESSION.

CONSCIOUSNESS. The subjective aspect of brain activity. The unexplained phenomenon which converts electro-physiological changes in the brain into awareness, feeling, experiencing, remembering, knowing, seeing, hearing, etc.

CRITICAL RATIO. A technical term used in statistical analysis and probability mathematics. As applied to telepathy and clairvoyance card-guessing experiments it is a measure of whether or not the number of correct guesses is significantly greater than chance or luck would account for.

CRYPTOMNESIA. Literally " hidden memory ". The spontaneous recalling of events or items of knowledge without being able to recall the circumstances or time when the knowledge was originally gained.

CRYSTAL GAZING. *See* SCRYING.

CUE. An obscure identifying mark. A scarcely perceptible sensory stimulus. A sensory stimulus not perceived consciously, but which is nevertheless registered and is responsible for many correct " intuitions ".

CUTANEOUS. Pertaining to the skin.

DÉJA-VU. An illusion of memory in which a person believes he has seen a thing, person or scene never previously encountered in actual fact. A particular form of PARAMNESIA (*q.v.*).

DELUSION. A mistaken belief ; a false conviction. A delusion may be permanent or transitory.

DEPERSONALISATION. A feeling of unreality. Loss of the sense of personal identity, or a sensation of having no material existence.

DERVISH. A member of one of the Moslem orders or fraternities practising austerity or asceticism. Most notorious are the Mawlawis or " whirling dervishes ", and the Rifa'is, or " howling dervishes ".

DISSOCIATION. No single sentence definition available. Denotes amongst other things that coherent mental activity may, in certain circumstances, operate more or less independently of the main mental system which constitutes the normal conscious personality. *See* Chap. 3.

DIVINATION. Discovery of the unknown or future by supernatural means.

DIVINING ROD. A forked twig or stick of springy wood, which, when held in a certain position of tension, will greatly magnify small movements of the arms and wrists. It can also be made of metal. *See* WATER DIVINING.

DOPPELGANGER. A " double ". A ghost- or spirit-counterpart of one-self. The doppelgänger was a familiar theme in Victorian literature.

DOWSING. The divination of water, metallic ores, missing persons, etc., through the use of a forked rod, pendulum or similar instrument.

DUAL PERSONALITY. A hysterical syndrome in which two distinct personalities appear to exist alternately (and sometimes simultaneously) in the same individual. Often each personality appears to have no direct knowledge of the existence of the other.

ECTOPLASM. A visible " emanation " from the body of a spiritualistic medium ; invariably faked.

EIDETIC IMAGERY. Mental images of unusual vividness which many children can project (on to a screen provided for the purpose) with the clarity approaching that of a visual hallucination. It is connected with the imagery of memory and imagination. With some subjects the projected imagery is changeable, following the flow of ideas. Comparatively rare in adults.

EMPIRICAL. Based upon experiment, observation or experience, as opposed to *theoretical*.

ENDOPHASIA. " Silent speech ". The silent reproduction of words or phrases without observable activity of the organs of speech. " Mentally " articulating words or sentences. *See* UNCONSCIOUS WHISPERING

ENDOPHASIC ENNEUROSIS. This term denotes that mentally articulating a word, or thinking of a word, or merely visualising it mentally, may produce slight articulatory movements of the vocal apparatus. It is often the explanation of purported cases of telepathy, clairvoyance, etc.

ENNEUROSIS. *See* INNERVATION.

EPISTEMOLOGY. The branch of philosophy which deals with the nature of knowledge and knowing, i.e. how we know and what we mean by " knowing ", with reference to the limitations of knowledge and the different modes of knowledge such as deduction, induction, direct experience, practical knowledge, memorised knowledge, etc.

ERYTHEMA. Congestion of the capillaries below the skin, producing redness and swelling.

ESP. Extra-sensory perception.

EUPHORIA. An abnormal degree of elation, optimism and feeling of well-being, often symptomatic of neurosis or insanity. In its non-technical sense it also connotes contentment or happiness.

EXTRA-SENSORY PERCEPTION. Defined in the *Journal of Parapsychology* as " response to an external event not presented to any known sense ". It is a somewhat question-begging term which embraces telepathy, clairvoyance and precognition.

FAKIR. A Hindu religious mendicant, especially one who claims supernatural powers.

FLAGELLANTISM. Self-whipping under the influence of ecstacy, drugs, eroticism or hysterical compulsion.

FUGUE. A temporary forgetfulness of personal identity and the past, with a tendency to wander from home.

FUNCTIONAL DISORDER. An impairment to one or more of the body's normal functions which can not be traced to any organic or structural defect. Functional disorders and diseases are therefore usually attributable to psychological causes. They are commonly the product of hysteria, e.g. functional paralysis, deafness, local analgesia, etc.

GLOSSOLALIA. Speaking in a language fabricated by the individual himself. Sometimes occurs in hysterical persons or in mediumistic trance, though it is rare. *Cf.* XENOGLOSSIA.

GLOVE-ANAESTHESIA. Glove-anaesthesia, stocking-anaesthesia and hemianalgesia were terms first used by Janet to describe hysterical anaesthesia of the hand, feet and one side of the body respectively. The areas affected conform to the patient's naïve ideas and do not correspond with the correct neurological patterns.

HALLUCINATION. A sensory perception which occurs without a corresponding sensory stimulus, due to faulty functioning of the perception-mechanism in the brain. The percipient may see or hear, with perfect clarity, objects or sounds which have no objective existence. *See* Chap. 7. *Cf.* ILLUSION and PSEUDO-HALLUCINATION.

HARUSPICATION. Divination by inspecting the entrails of sacrificed animals and birds.

HEMIANOPSIA. Being able to see in one half of the visual field only.

HEMIPLEGIA. Paralysis of one side of the body only.

HETEROSUGGESTION. Suggestion which is given by another person as distinct from suggestion which springs from the individual's own mental processes.

HIBERNATION. " Winter sleep ". The habit of many animals to pass the winter in a state of coma or torpidity, as a protective measure against cold and lack of food. *Cf.* AESTIVATION.

HISTRIONIC. Pertaining to acting, or dramatic representation.

HYPERACUITY. Or, more strictly speaking, sensory hyperacuity. An unusual degree of sensitiveness of sight, hearing, touch, smell or taste. Due to psychological causes alone. *Cf.* HYPERAESTHESIA.

HYPERACUSIA. Abnormal keenness of hearing.

HYPERAESTHESIA. An unusual degree of sensitivity of the actual sense organs. *Cf.* HYPERACUITY.

HYPERAPHIA. Abnormal sensitivity of the sense of touch.

HYPERMNESIA. Unusual or extraordinary ability to recall or remember past experiences.

HYPERPNEA. Or Polypnea. Very rapid breathing. Sometimes a hysterical symptom.

HYPERPROSEXIA. Extreme concentration of the attention on a part of the field of observation to the exclusion of everything else.

HYPNAGOGIC. Pertaining to the transitory stage between waking and sleeping. Half asleep.

HYPNOGENIC. Sleep-producing. Inducing hypnosis or trance states by methods which first bring about drowsiness or sleep.

HYPNOSIS. A state of trance or increased suggestibility brought about by first inducing drowsiness, sleep or a state resembling sleep, through the use of any of a number of methods.

HYPNOTHERAPY. The use of hypnosis in the cure or alleviation of disorders, particularly those of hysterical origin.

HYPNOTISM. The study of hypnosis. The practice or art of inducing hypnosis.

HYPOCHONDRIASIS. Or hypochondria. A morbid concern with one's health and an exaggerated anxiety over trifling ailments. May become so severe as seriously to affect the health of the patient and even lead to death.

HYSTERIA. No generally accepted single-sentence definition available. The term denotes a form of mental disorder producing syndromes ranging from mild mental instability to functional paralysis, somnambulism, trance states, or loss of memory, etc. *See* Chap. 5.

HYSTERO-EPILEPSY. The onslaught of violent convulsions similar to an attack of epilepsy but hysterical in origin.

IDEOMOTOR MOVEMENTS. Slight involuntary muscular movements which are an indirect expression of a prevailing idea in the mind.

ILLUSION. A faulty sensory perception ; e.g., a cow is seen in the dusk which on closer approach is recognised to be nothing more than a bush. There are many different types of illusion. *Cf.* HALLUCINATION.

IMAGERY. Collective term for mental images. What one can " see in the mind's eye "; as for example when recalling a well remembered scene, or mentally visualising an imaginary one. Imagery may pertain to any of the five senses, though it usually refers to those of vision or hearing.

INDICIUM. Pl. INDICIA. Sign, mark, indication, pointer, clue or cue.

INNERVATION. Nervous excitation or stimulation of a muscle or other organ.

JU-JU. Native magic, charm, spell, idol or fetish in West Africa.

KINESTHESIA. Or kinesthesis. The " muscle sense ". The sensations which attend the movement of the muscles, tendons and joints.

LABIOGRAPH. A device for recording lip movements while either speaking or thinking.

LAMA. A Tibetan monk or priest belonging to the sect of Buddhism known as Lamaism. Many of them claim occult powers and practise asceticism.

LARYNGOGRAPH. A device for recording and measuring the movements of the larynx, while either speaking or thinking.

LEVITATION. The claim made by mediums and other occultists that they can make their bodies leave the ground by supernatural means.

LYCANTHROPY. Beliefs and practices based upon the purported ability of certain persons to transform themselves into animals, especially wolves. In psychiatry it denotes obsessions and delusions of a similar character. *Cf.* ZOANTHROPY. *See* Chap. 15.

MEDIUM. *Adj.* MEDIUMISTIC. A person who claims or believes in his or her ability to contact the spirits of the dead. In psychical research they are often divided into two categories; i.e. "mental" mediums who act as the mouth-piece of discarnate spirits; and "physical" mediums who specialise in the production of visible spirit forms, ectoplasm, moving lights, movement of objects at a distance, raps, knocks, etc. *See* Chap. 11.

MEDIUMISTIC TRANCE. The faculty which some mediums have of being able to induce at will states of consciousness involving varying degrees of mental dissociation and subsequent amnesia. Such trance states are often simulated.

MENORRHAGIA. Excessive menstrual discharge.

MESMERISM. An obsolete term for HYPNOTISM which was abandoned because of its association with superstition and incorrect theorising.

METAPHYSICS. That branch of philosophy which deals with the ultimate nature of the universe, mind and man.

METAPSYCHICS. *See* PARAPSYCHOLOGY.

MIMETIC. Imitative.

MIND, the. A vague term derived from philosophy defined variously as "the seat of consciousness", "that which causes our thoughts" etc.

MIRROR-WRITING. *See* STREPHOGRAPHIA.

MODUS OPERANDI. The method or system of operation. The actual manner in which a thing works. The explanation of how a thing is done.

MONOIDEIC SOMNAMBULISM. A hysterical malady in which the patient carries out the same ritual or pantomime each time a somnambulic attack occurs.

MONOPLEGIA. Paralysis of a single group of muscles, especially a limb.

MULTIPLE PERSONALITY. The apparent existence of two *or more* alternating personalities in the same person; each personality may have no conscious knowledge of the existence of the others. It is a hysterical syndrome. *See* DUAL PERSONALITY.

MUSCLE-READING. The art of inferring the thoughts of a person in simple situations (*e.g.*, finding out the nature or location of hidden objects) through his involuntary muscular movements.

NECROPHILIA. Sexual assaults on corpses.

NEGATIVE HALLUCINATION. This is said to occur when a hypnotised subject appears no longer to see certain persons or objects which the operator has told him are no longer there. It is, at most, a temporary delusion.

NEURASTHENIA. A condition characterised by such symptoms as lack of mental and physical vigour, heightened fatigability, insomnia, headaches, upset digestion and other minor ailments. Many neurasthenics have phobias of one sort or another.

NEUROSIS. A group of disorders, psychological in origin, which do not normally warrant the individual being sent to an institution. Well known examples are anxiety neurosis and hypochondriasis. A distinction is usually made between neurosis and hysteria. *Cf.* PSYCHOSIS.

NYMPHOLOEPSY. A state of virtual trance brought about by erotic day-dreaming.

OBEAH. A species of magic or sorcery practised in the West Indies.

OCCULT. Pertaining to the supernatural, magical, or esoteric.

OPERATOR. The person who does the hypnotising in hypnotic experiments.

OUIJA-BOARD. A board on which the letters of the alphabet are arranged in a circle, together with any other signs required. A pointer, moved automatically by the hands of two or more persons, spells out messages ; often used by spiritualists.

PARAMNESIA. " False memory ". Distorted recollection or memory of some past event. It may refer to the inclusion of false details, the omission of details, or the distortion of the time-references.

PARANOIA. A form of insanity characterised by fixed and systematised delusions.

PARANORMAL. The parapsychologist's term for what the scientist would call the supernatural.

PARAPLEGIA. Paralysis of the lower limbs or the lower half of the body.

PARAPSYCHOLOGY. In principle, the application of psychological techniques in studying such purported phenomena as telepathy, precognition, clairvoyance, psychokinesis, and the occult powers of mediums, etc. Also known as metapsychics, scientific occultism, and psychical research.

PERCIPIENT. 1. The person who endeavours to receive the thoughts, messages, words or symbols which another person is trying to transmit telepathically.
2. The person who endeavours to apprehend the nature of concealed objects or symbols in clairvoyant experiments. *Cf.* AGENT.

PHILOSOPHY. The non-empirical study of a wide group of intellectual subjects such as the nature of knowledge ; the nature of man, mind and the universe theory of logic ; ethics, aesthetics and semantics. *See* EPISTEMOLOGY and METAPHYSICS.

PHOBIA. An exaggerated or unjustifiable fear. Typical examples : fear of confined spaces, dread of meeting strangers.

PHYSIOLOGICAL. Pertaining to the functions, activities and structure of the organs, tissues and cells of the living body.

PK. SEE PSYCHOKINESIS.

PLANCHETTE. A heart-shaped board supported by two legs and a pencil used for obtaining automatic writing through contact with the hands of one or more persons. It is often used by spiritualists and is one of the devices of the professional medium. *Cf.* OUIJA-BOARD.

POINTS DE RÉPÈRE. Points of light or specks of dust, etc., on the surface of a crystal or other scrying-speculum, to which some scryers trace the genesis of their hallucinatory images.

POLTERGEIST. A mischievous spirit.

POLYIDEIC SOMNAMBULISM. The average sleep-walking performance ; varied behaviour results in contrast to that observed in MONOIDEIC SOMNAMBULISM.

POST-HYPNOTIC SUGGESTION. An order given during hypnosis which the subject later carries out in the waking state, usually without recalling the order originally given him.

PRECOGNITION. The parapsychologist's term for prophecy. The purported cognition of future events by means other than through the five senses, guessing, coincidence or inference.

PRESTIDIGITATION. Conjuring. Sleight of hand.

PRODROMAL. Pertaining to the first indications of an impending disease. That which gives warning of incipient illness.

PSEUDO-HALLUCINATION. Any subjective experience which is remembered as having all the vividness usually associated with a genuine sensory hallucination, but which is attributable to delusion, illusion, dreams, dreamlike states, prolonged after-images, suggestion, hypnosis, trance states of consciousness, or quirks of memory. Pseudo-hallucinations play a large part in the perpetuation of certain occult beliefs.

PSI-PHENOMENA. A modern term which can be regarded as synonymous with " psychic phenomena ". It embraces all such purported phenomena as telepathy, clairvoyance, precognition, telekinesis, etc.

PSYCHASTHENIA. A form of neurosis characterised by lack of energy, decision, and concentration, and by doubts, fears, phobias and feelings of depersonalisation and unreality.

PSYCHIATRY. The branch of medicine which deals with the treatment of all types of mental disorders.

PSYCHIC. A term common in spiritualistic circles denoting a limited supernatural faculty. A medium or clairvoyant. (It is also a normal synonym for " psychological ").

PSYCHICAL RESEARCH. *See* PARAPSYCHOLOGY.

PSYCHIC HEALING. Healing by supernatural means, based on the belief that some individuals are able to cure disease through virtue of some mysterious occult power or through the media of unknown rays and emanations.

PSYCHOANALYSIS. A special form of psychotherapy, originated by Freud, which emphasises the importance of unconscious mental processes in causing nervous disorders.

PSYCHOKINESIS. The purported movement of objects by merely " willing " or otherwise without physical means.

PSYCHOLOGY. No comprehensive single-sentence definition available. Roughly, the scientific study of the mind and mental processes.

PSYCHOMETRY. Hylomancy. The purported supernatural acquisition of knowledge by mediums or " sensitives " through handling inanimate objects. The knowledge obtained usually pertains to the history of the object or to people connected with it. *See* SYMPATHETIC MAGIC.

PSYCHONEUROSIS. Generally used as a synonym for NEUROSIS. (*q.v.*)

PSYCHOPATHOLOGY. The scientific study of mental disorders and mental factors in disease generally. As compared with PSYCHIATRY which involves *treatment* of mental disorders.

PSYCHOSIS. *Adj.* PSYCHOTIC. Any severe mental disorder, whether brought about by psychological or physical causes. More or less synonymous with insanity.

PSYCHOSOMATIC. Pertaining to both mind and body; especially bodily disorders and physical symptoms brought about by psychological causes, and the cure of bodily disorders by psychotherapy.

PSYCHOTHERAPY. *Adj.* PSYCHOTHERAPEUTIC. The treatment of disorders by psychological methods, such as suggestion, hypnosis, persuasion, re-education and psychoanalysis.

R

ADIESTHESIA. 1. Now often used as a synonym for DOWSING. (*q.v.*) 2. A cult whose exponents attribute water divining, psychic healing, etc., to the operation of unknown rays, emanations or electronic forces.

RAPPORT. A special relationship between a hypnotised subject and the operator, in which the subject apparently hears the commands of the operator only and remains deaf to the commands of others. At one time believed to be an inevitable accompaniment of hypnosis, it is now recognised to be nothing more than the product of suggestion or expectation and is easily countered.

RATIONALISATION. Producing apparently logical or sensible reasons to justify impulsive or irrational actions.

REPRESSION. The tendency to exclude from conscious awareness unpleasant or painful ideas or memories. It is a normal psychological mechanism, but when over-worked it may lead to hysterical syndromes.

RESPAS. A Tibetan ascetic.

Schizophrenia. Formerly known as dementia praecox. A type of insanity characterised by delusions and loss of contact with the world of reality. The patient lives in a world of his own imagination. *Cf.* Dual Personality.

Scrying. The art of producing visual hallucinations or projected visual imagery through staring at clear, translucent or bright objects. Crystal gazing is a form of scrying in which the object stared at is a solid glass ball. *See* Chap. 8.

Séance. A " sitting ". A term common to spiritualism and psychical research denoting a gathering of persons for the purpose of witnessing or obtaining spiritualistic phenomena. The modern séance stems directly from the spirit-evoking practices of the North American Indians, and was introduced into civilised society during the middle of the nineteenth century.

Sensory. Pertaining to the five senses of sight, hearing, touch; taste and smell.

Shaman. A medicine-man. A priest-magician. The term was originally confined to the medicine-men of northern Asia. Now it is used by anthropologists to denote a priest, medicine-man or witch-doctor in any primitive religion. *See* below.

Shamanism. 1. Practices designed to control, placate, communicate with or influence the spirits of nature or the dead. 2. The practice of magic or the acquiring of supernatural powers by these means.

Somnambulism. Ordinarily means sleep-walking. In psychology the term covers a variety of hysterical and hypnotic behaviour in which the individual's normal waking consciousness is more or less in abeyance.

Speculum. In reference to scrying and crystal gazing this term denotes any object used for the purpose of obtaining projected visual imagery. *See* Scrying.

SPIRITUALISM.   1.   A branch of the Christian religion whose chief tenet is a belief in the ability of certain persons to contact the spirits of the dead.   2.   A modern development of primitive shamanism which might be defined as the cult of the spiritualistic medium. *See* SHAMAN, MEDIUM, and SEANCE.

S.P.R.   Society for Psychical Research. Headquarters in London.

STIGMATA.   *Adj*. STIGMATIC.   The supernatural appearance of the wounds or marks of the Crucifixion on the bodies of saints and mystics.   Wounds or lesions brought about by non-physical means. *See* Chap. 14.

STIGMATIST.   One who claims to have experienced the stigmata.

STREPHOGRAPHIA.   Mirror-writing; *spiegelschrift*.   Writing in which the characters are reversed so that it appears in normal form when held before a mirror.

SUBCONSCIOUS MIND.   A confusing term.   It denotes the fact that most of a person's mental activity takes place without any conscious awareness.   *See* Chap. 2.

SUBCUTANEOUS.   Beneath the skin.

SUBJECT.   1.   A person who is used in psychological experiments.   2.   A hypnotised person.

SUBLIMATION.   The deflection of primitive impulses into useful or socially acceptable activities.

SUGGESTIBLE.   Unusual susceptibility to the suggestions, authority or influence of others.   Easily influenced by suggestion (*q.v.*).

SUGGESTION.   The inculcation of ideas and beliefs in a person's mind while his critical faculties are more or less dormant.   The orders given by an operator to a hypnotised subject. *See* Chap. 4.

SUGGESTION THERAPY.   The use of waking or hypnotic suggestion in the cure or alleviation of disorders, particularly those of psychological origin.

SUPERSTITION. Credulity regarding the supernatural.

SYMPATHETIC MAGIC. Magical and divinatory practices and beliefs which are based on the notion that things similar in form or quality have an occult affinity. The notion extends to objects, people or events which are in any way connected (in fact, or in the imag nation). Examples : the sprinkling of water on the ground in rain-making rituals ; personal belongings used for the casting of harmful spells against their owners, or used as psychometric objects.

SYMPTOMATIC CURE. Removal of the overt symptoms of a disease without curing the disease itself. It is often the only way of alleviating incurable maladies.

SYNDROME. A number of symptoms which together indicate the nature of a disease or mental disorder.

TABLE-TURNING, -TAPPING OR -TILTING. The use of a light table for converting automatic or involuntary muscular movements into audible sounds or visible (or otherwise significant) movements. A device commonly used by spiritualists with the aim of obtaining answers to questions addressed to the spirits of the dead.

TARGET CARD. The particular card or symbol (in a series) on which the agent or percipient is concentrating his attention in telepathy or clairvoyant experiments. *See* ZENER CARDS.

TELEKINESIS. The equivalent of psychokinesis in spiritualistic circles.

TELEOLOGICAL. That which serves an end or purpose.

TELEPATHY. Purportedly the communication between one mind and another by means other than through the five senses. " Thought-transference."

THANATOMANIA. Originally a psychiatric term ; now also used by some anthropologists to denote that suggestion, intense expectation, fear, or belief in magic, may, among primitive communities, produce a coma resulting in death.

THAUMATURGIST. A wonder worker.

THERAPEUTIC. Healing ; curative.

TOPOALGIA. A localised sensation of pain without any corresponding organic cause. An hallucinatory sensation of pain.

TRANCE. A popular term loosely used to denote a number of differing psychological states characterised by temporary unawareness of the immediate environment or the suspension of normal voluntary activity. It may denote total unconsciousness as in extreme cataleptic " trance ". Other prefixes are hypnotic-, ecstatic-, mediumistic-, somnambulic-, yoga-.

TUMO. The mystical force by which Tibetan ascetics claim to keep themselves warm in severe cold.

UNCONSCIOUS WHISPERING. The whispered utterance of intelligible vocal sounds without the person concerned being aware of it. *See* ENDOPHASIA.

URTICAREA. Nettle rash. A disorder affecting the skin characterised by raised blotches, weals or patches resembling those produced by the sting of a nettle.

VASOMOTOR SYSTEM. The mechanism which controls the normal dilation and constriction of the blood vessels.

VOODOO. Witchcraft or black magic practised by negroes in the West Indies and the United States.

WAKING SUGGESTION. Suggestion given while the subject is in the waking, as opposed to the *hypnotic*, state.

WATER-DIVINING. 1. The purported divination of water by occult means, usually with the aid of a forked twig or rod. 2. The detection of water by subconsciously registering minute surface indications, which produce an automatic reflex of arms and wrists thereby causing a dipping or rising action of a divining rod held in the hands.

WERE-WOLF (*Folklore*). A " wolf-man "; one who can transform himself, or is periodically transformed, into a wolf. *See* chap. 15.

XENOGLOSSIA. Or xenoglossis. The uncontrollable utterance of gibberish or unintelligible sounds under hysterical compulsion. " Speaking in tongues ". *Cf.* GLOSSOLALIA.

YOGA. A collective term for the various systems of mental and physical training (in India) designed to make the mind function at higher levels than normal. These systems are often subsumed by advanced metaphysical and mystical theory. Best known are Rajah Yoga, Hatha Yoga and Bhakti Yoga, which lay the chief emphasis on Will, Courage and Love respectively. *See* chap. 16.

YOGI. One who practices yoga.

ZENER CARDS. Or " ESP " cards. Cards bearing one of the five symbols, star, circle, wavy lines, cross and rectangle, which the percipient has to try and guess in telepathy and clairvoyant experiments. A pack or deck contains twenty-five cards, five cards bearing a star, five a circle, etc.

ZOANTHROPY. A form of paranoiac insanity in which the patient has delusions of being an animal.

ZOERASTY. Sexual relations with animals.

ZOMBIE. A corpse reanimated with a mechanical resemblance to life by sorcery ; especially in Haiti.

BIBLIOGRAPHY

Among the chief sources of reference for the present volume are the Proceedings and Journals of the Society for Psychical Research (London), 1882-1949 ; the Journal of Parapsychology (Duke University Press, U.S.A.), 1937-1949 ; and the Journal of the American Society for Psychical Research, 1940-1949.

The following periodicals were also consulted :

Journal of the American Society for Psychical Research (1907-1939) ; Bulletins of the Boston Society for Psychical Research ; Proceedings of the American Society for Psychical Research ; Revue Métapsychique (Paris) ; Tidschrift voor Parapsychologie (Amsterdam) ; Zeitschrift für Parapsychologie (Leipzig) ; Psychischen Studien (Leipzig) ; Radio-Perception—Journ. B.S.D. (London) ; Revue Internationale de Radiesthésie (Brussels).

Use was made of the following :

Encylcopaedia Britannica. 1947.
Encyclopaedia of Religion and Ethics (ed. J. Hastings). 13 vols. Edinburgh and New York 1925-1940.
Hartmann's International Directory of Psychic Science and Spiritualism. New York 1930.
Collin de Plancy. Dictionnaire Infernal. Paris 1863.
Caillet, A. L. Manuel Bibliographique des Sciences Psychiques. 3 vols. Paris 1912.
Fodor, N. Encyclopaedia of Psychic Science. London 1934.
Spence, L. An Encyclopaedia of Occultism. London 1920.

The following bibliography is supplementary to the publications listed above ; for this reason few references to
psychical-research and parapsychological periodicals have
been included. A valuable aid to the study of such
periodical literature is provided by these four publications
of the Society for Psychical Research :

Combined Index to " Phantasms of the Living " vols.
I and II, Proceedings S.P.R. vols. I-XV, Journal
S.P.R. vols. I-IX, and the Proceedings of the American
S.P.R.   London 1904.
Combined Index to Proceedings S.P.R. vols. XVI-XXVI,
Journal S.P.R. vols. X-XV.   London 1914.
Combined Index to Proceedings S.P.R. vols. XXVII-
XLVII, Journal S.P.R. vols. XVI-XXXIII.   London
1949.
Principal Contents of the Proceedings of the Society
for Psychical Research 1882-1945.   London 1946.

ABRAMOWSKI, E.   " The Phenomena of Cryptomnesia in
  Telepathy ", chapter in Le Subconscient Normal, pp.364-407.   Paris
  1914.

ANSPACHER, L. K.   Challenge to the Unknown. N.Y.
  1947.

ANSTIE, F. E.   Lecture on Disorders of the Nervous
  System—IV, Lancet, 1873, 1, pp.39-41.

BAERWALD, R.   Die Intellektuellen Phänomene.   Der
  Okkultismus in Urkunden vol. 2, ed.
  M. Dessoir.   Berlin 1925.
  Okkultismus und Spiritismus.   Berlin
  1926.

BAKER, K. H.   Report of a Minor Investigation of
  Extra-Sensory Perception, J. Exp. Psychol., 21, 1937, pp.120-125.

BARRETT, W. F.   Psychical Research.   London 1911.
BARRETT, W. F. and   The Divining Rod : an experimental
  BESTERMAN, T.   and psychological investigation.   Lon-
  don 1926.

BASS, M. J. *Differentiation of the Hypnotic Trance from Normal Sleep*, J. Exp. Psychol., 14, 1931, pp.382-399.

BATEMAN, F. and SOAL, S. G. *Long-D'stance Experiments in Telepathy*, J.S.P.R., 35, 1950, pp.257-272.

BAVINK, B. The Anatomy of Modern Science. London 1932.

BECKNELL, E. A. *The Function of Dependent Probability in ESP Data*, J. Gen. Psychol., 19, 1938, pp.373-381.

B E C H H O F E R ROBERTS, C.E. (ed.) The Trial of Mrs. Duncan. London 1945.

BEHANAN, K. T. Yoga : a Scientific Evaluation. N.Y. 1937.

BELL, H. J. Obeah. Witchcraft in the West Indies. London 1893.

BENDER, H. *Zum Problem der aussersinnlichen Wahrnehmung*, Zeitschrift für Psychologie, Bd. 135, 1935, pp.20-130.

———————— Psychische Automatismen. Leipzig 1936.

BENDIT, L. J. Paranormal Cognition. London 1944.

BESTERMAN, T. Crystal-Gazing : a study in the history, distribution, theory and practice of scrying. London 1924.

———————— Some Modern Mediums. London 1930.

———————— *A Critical Estimate of the Present Status of Psychical Research*, Transactions of the Fourth International Congress for Psychical Research, p.119. London 1930.

——————————, (ed.) Inquiry into the Unknown. London 1934.

———————— Water-Divining. London 1938.

BLACKMORE, S. A. Spiritism, Facts and Frauds. London 1924.

BOESTROEM, A. *Methodik der Erzielung des hypnotischen Schlafes beim Menschen*. Abderhalden's Handbuch der biologischen Arbeitsmethoden, Abt. 6, Teil C, Heft 5, pp.308-318.

BOMBAY, GOVERN-
MENT OF.
Report on the Work of the Water Diviner for the Period October 1925 *to January* 1927. Bombay 1927.
Report on the Work of the Water Diviner to the Government of Bombay for the Year 1927. Bombay 1928.
Report on the Work of the Water Diviner for the Year 1928. Bombay 1929.

BOUSFIELD, P. and
BOUSFIELD, W. R.
The Mind and its Mechanism. London 1927.

BRENMAN, M.
Experiments in the Hypnotic Production of Anti-Social and Self-Injurious Behaviour, Psychiatry, V, 1942, pp.49-61.

BROAD, C. D.
" Summing Up ", chapter in Inquiry into the Unknown, ed. T. Besterman, London 1934.
The Mind and its Place in Nature. London 1937
The Philosophical Implications of Foreknowledge, Aristotelian Society Supp. vol. 16, pp.177-209, and pp.229-245. London 1937.
Science and Psychical Phenomena (a discussion of the book of the same name by G. N. M. Tyrrell), Philosophy, 52, 1938, pp.466-475.
The Experimental Establishment of Telepathic Precognition, Philosophy, 74, 1944, pp.261-275.
Philosophical Implications of Precognition, Listener, May 8th, 1947, pp. 709-710.
The Relevance of Psychical Research to Philosophy, Philosophy, 91, 1949, pp. 291-309.

BROWN, G. B.
A Report on Three Experimental Fire-Walks. University of London Council for Psychical Investigation, Bulletin 4, 1938.

BROWN, WM. (ed.)   Psychology and the Sciences. London, 1924.

——————————   Sleep, Hypnosis and Mediumistic Trance, Character and Personality, 3, 1934, pp.112-126.

——————————   Mind, Medicine and Metaphysics. London 1936.

——————————   Psychology and Psychopatholgy. London 1940.

BRUCK, C.   Experimentelle Telepathie. Stuttgart 1925.

BRUGMANS,   Une communication sur des expériences
H. J. F. W.   télépathiques au laboratoire de psychologie à Groningue. Compte Rendu du Premier Congrès International des Recherches Psychiques. Copenhagen 1922.

——————————   "L'état passif" d'un télépathe contrôlé par le phénomène psychogalvanique. Compte Rendu du 2e Congrès International de Metapsychie. Warsaw 1924.

BURLINGHAM, D. T.   Child Analysis and the Mother, Psychoanalytic Quarterly, 4, 1935, pp.69-92.

CARINGTON, W.   Experiments on the Paranormal Cogni-
WHATELY   tion of Drawings, Proc. S.P.R., 46, 1940, pp.34-157.

——————————   Telepathy. An Outline of its Facts, Theory and Implications. London 1945.

——————————   Matter, Mind and Meaning. London 1949.

CARINGTON, W.   Experiments in Non-Sensory Cognition,
WHATELY and SOAL,   Nature, 145, 1940, p.389.
S. G.

CARRINGTON, H.   Laboratory Investigations into Psychic Phenomena. London n.d.

——————————   Psychology in the Light of Psychic Phenomena. Philadelphia 1940.

CASSIRER, K. T. Determinismus und Indeterminismus in der Modernen Physik. Göteborg 1937.

CASTIGLIONI, A. Adventures of the Mind. London 1947.

CHOWRIN, A. N. *A Rare Form of Hyperaesthesia of the Higher Sense Organs* (orig. in Russian), Contributions to Neuropsychic Medicine, Moscow 1889. Translated by Schrenck-Notzing under the title : Experimentelle Untersuchungen auf dem Gebiete des raumlichen Hellsehens. Munich 1919.

COMAR, G. *L'Autoréprésentation de l'organisme chez quelques Hysteriques*, Revue Neurologique, 9, 1901, pp.490-495.

COOVER, J. E. Experiments in Psychical Research at Leland Stanford Junior University. Stanford University, California 1917.

———————— " Metapsychics and the Incredulity of Psychologists ", chapter in The Case for and against Psychical Belief, ed. C. Murchison. Mass. 1927.

COX, W. S. *An Experiment on Extra-Sensory Perception*, J. Exp. Psychol., 19, 1936, pp.429-436.

CRITCHLEY, M. Mirror-Writing. London 1928.

CUDDON, E. Hypnosis : its Meaning and Practise. London 1938.

CONSTABLE, F. C. Personality and Telepathy. London 1911.

COSTER, G. Yoga and Western Psychology. London 1935.

CULPIN, M. *Behind the Divining Rod*, Nature, 119, 1927, p.783.

———————— Spiritualism and the New Psychology. London 1920.

CURRAN, D. and Psychological Medicine. Edinburgh
  GUTTMAN, E. 1946.

CUTTEN, G. B. Mind, its Origin and Goal. N.Y. 1925.

———————— Speaking with Tongues. N.Y. 1926.

DAVID-NEEL, A.   With Mystics and Magicians in Tibet. London 1931

DEONNA, W.   De la Planète Mars en Terre Sainte. Paris 1932.

DESSOIR, M. (ed.)   Der Okkultismus in Urkunden.   2 vols. Berlin 1925.   *See* Baerwald, R., and Gulat-Wellenburg.

——————   Vom Jenseits der Secle.   Stuttgart 1931.

DEUTSCH, H.   *Okkulte Vorgänge während der Psycho-analyse*, Imago, 12, 1926, pp.418-433.

DIETZ, P. A.   Telepathie en Psychologie der Menigte. Amsterdam 1931.

DINGWALL, E. J.   Ghosts and Spirits of the Ancient World.   London 1930.

——————   *Recent Trends in Psychical Research,* Nature, 147, 1941, p.217.

——————   *A Theory of Telepathy,* (Review), Nature, 155, 1945, pp.619-620.

DINGWALL, E. J. and PARSONS, D.   *Telepathy* ;   Science News No. 9, Pen-guin Books, Ltd., London 1948.

DRIESCH, H.   The Crisis in Psychology.   Princeton 1925.

——————   " Psychical Research and Philosophy", chapter in The Case for and against Psychical Belief, ed. C. Murchison. Mass. 1927.

——————   *Parapsychologische Hypothesen,* Der Morgen, 6, 1930, pp.11-35.

——————   Parapsychologie.   Munich 1932.   (Eng-lish edition :   Psychical Research. London 1933).

DUNNE, J. W.   An Experiment with Time.   London 1927.

——————   The Serial Universe.   London 1934.

——————   The New Immortality.   London 1938.

EASTABROOKS. G. H.   A Contribution to Experimental Tele-pathy.   Boston S.P.R., Bulletin 5, 1927.

EHRENWALD, H. J.   *Telepathy in Dreams*, Brit. J. Med. Psychol., 19, 2, 1942, pp.313-323.

——————— *Telepathy in the Psychoanalytic Situation*, Brit. J. Med. Psychol., 20, 1, 1944, pp.51-62.

——————— Telepathy and Medical Psychology. London 1947.

EISENBUD, J.   *Telepathy and Problems of Psychoanalysis*, Psychoanalytic Quarterly, 15, 1, 1946, pp.82-87.

——————— *The Dream of Two Patients in Analysis Interpreted as a Telepathic Rêve à Deux*, Psychoanalytic Quarterly, 1, 1947.

EMMETT, D. M.   The Nature of Metaphysical Thinking London 1946.

ERMACORA, G. B.   La Telepatia. Padova 1898.

ESDAILE, J.   Record of Cases Treated in the Mesmeric Hospital from November 1846 to May 1847. Calcutta 1847.

——————— The Introduction of Mesmerism into the Public Hospitals of India. London 1856.

EVANS-PRITCHARD, E. E.   Witchcraft, Oracles and Magic Among the Azande. Oxford 1937.

EYSENCK, J.   Dimensions of Personality. London 1947.

F ARIGOULE, L.   Eyeless Sight. A Study of Extra-Retinal Vision and the Paroptic Sense. London and N.Y. 1924.

FERNBERGER, S. W.   '*Extra-Sensory Perceptions*' *or Instructions*? J. Exp. Psychol., 22, 1938, pp.602-607.

FICHTE. I. H., von.   Der neuere Spiritualismus, sein Werth und sein Tauschungen. Ein anthropologische Studie. Leipzig 1878.

FISCHER, O.   Illustrated Magic. N.Y. 1931.

FISHER. V. E.   Introduction to Abnormal Psychology. N.Y. 1932.

FLOURNOY, T.

From India to the Planet Mars : a Study of a case of Somnambulism with Glossolalia. N.Y. and London 1900.

Nouvelles Observations sur un Cas de Somnambulisme avec Glossolalie. Offprint from Archives de Psychologie (pp.101-255). Geneva 1901.

Spiritism and Psychology. N.Y. and London 1911.

FODOR, N.

Telepathic Dreams, American Imago, 3, 1942, pp.61-87.

Lycanthropy as a Psychic Mechanism, J. Am. Folklore, Dec. 1945, pp.310-316.

Telepathy in Analysis, Psychiatric Quarterly, 21, 1947, pp.171-189.

FOREL, A.

Ein Gutachten über einem Fall von spontanem Somnambulismus mit angeblicher Wahrsagerei und Hellseherei. Schriften der Gesellschaft für psychologische Forschung 1891, 1, pp.77-90. Leipzig

FRAZER, J. G.

The Golden Bough ; a Study in Magic and Religion. 12 vols. London 1911-1927

FREIMARK, H.

Die Okkultistische Bewegung. Leipzig 1912.

Das erotische Element im Okkultismus. (Die Okkulte Welt No. 90/93).; Pfullingen 1922.

Okkultismus und Sexualität. Leipzig n.d.

FREUD, S.

Dreams and Telepathy, Int. J. Psa., 3, 1922, pp.283-305.

" Dreams and the Occult ", chapter in New Introductory Lectures in Psychoanalysis. London 1933.

Psychoanalyse und Telepathie ; Schriften aus dem Nachlass. Imago Pub. Co., London 1941.

Some Additional Notes upon Dream-Interpretation as a Whole (1925). Int. J. Psa., 24, 1943, pp.71-75.

FÜNFGELD, E.   *Über die seelische Struktur einer "Hellseherin "*, Zeitschrift für die gesamte Neurologie und Psychiatrie, 119, 1929, pp.547-560.

GLYNN, T. R.   *Hysteria in Some of its Aspects*, Brit. Med. J., 1913, 2, pp.1193-1198.

GOODFELLOW, L. D.   *A Psychological Interpretation of the Results of the Zenith Radio Experiment in Telepathy*, J. Exp. Psychol., 23, 1938, pp.601-632.

GRASSET, J.   Le Spiritisme devant la Science. Foreword by Pierre Janet. Paris 1904.

————   L'Occultisme. Paris 1907.

GREEN, G. H.   The Daydream : a Study in Development. London 1923.

GREENWOOD, J. A.   *Variance of a General Matching Problem*, Ann. Math. Stat., 9, No. 1, 1938, pp. 56-59.

GREENWOOD, J. A. and GREVILLE, T. N. E.   *On the Probability of Attaining a Given Standard Deviation Ratio in an Infinite Series of Trials*, Ann. Math. Stat., 10, 1939, pp.297-298.

GRUBER, M.   Parapsychologische Erkentnisse. Munich 1925.

GULAT-WELLENBURG,W., KLINCKOWSTROEM, C. and ROSENBUSCH, H.   Der Physikalische Mediumismus. Der Okkultismus in Urkunden, ed. M. Dessoir vol. 1. Berlin 1925.

GULLIKSEN, H. O.   *Extra-Sensory Perception : What is it?* Am. J. Sociol., 43, 1938 pp.623-631.

GURNEY, E., MYERS, F. W. H. and PODMORE, F.   Phantasms of the Living. 2 vols. London 1886. (Abridged edition 1918)

HADFIELD, J. A.   *The Influence of Hypnotic Suggestion on Inflammatory Conditions*, Lancet 1917, 2, pp.678-679.

————   *The Influence of Suggestion on Body Temperature*, Lancet, 1920, 1, p.68.

HALDANE, J. S.   Mechanism, Life and Personality. London 1921.

HALLOWELL, A. I.   The Role of Conjuring in Salteaux Society. Philadelphia 1942.

HAPPICH, C.   " Psychoanalyse und Parapsychologie" chapter in Auswirkung der Psychoanalyse, ed. H. Prinzhorn. Leipzig 1928.

HEILIG, R. and   *Beiträge zur hypnotischen Beeinflussung*
HOFF, H.   *der Magenfunction*, Medizinische Klinik, 21, 1925, pp.162-163.

————————   *Uber hypnotische Beeinflussung der Nierenfunction*, Deutsche Medizinische Wochenschrift, 51, 1925, pp.1615-6.

HEINLEIN, C. P. and   *Critique of the Premises and Statistical*
HEINLEIN, J. H.   *Methodology of Parapsychology*, J. Psychol., 5, 1938, pp.135-148.

HELLWIG, A.   Okkultismus und Verbrechen. Berlin 1929.

————————   *Betrugsverfahren gegen Kriminaltelepathen*, Archiv für Kriminalogie, 84, pp.15-48. Leipzig 1929.

HERR, D. L.   *A Mathematical Analysis of the Experiments in Extra-Sensory Perception*, J. Exp. Psychol., 22, 1938, pp.491-495.

HESSE, E.   Narcotics and Drug Addiction. N.Y. 1946.

HETTINGER, J.   The Ultra - Perceptive Faculty. London 1940.

————————   Exploring the Ultra - Perceptive Faculty. London 1941.

HEUZÉ, P.   Fakirs, fumistes et Cie. Paris 1926.

————————   La Plaisanterie des Animaux Calculateurs. Paris 1928.

HEYER, G.   Hypnosis and Hypnotherapy, and Jolowicz, E., Suggestion Therapy. London 1931.

HEYWOOD, R.   Telepathy and Allied Phenomena. S.P.R. publication, London 1948.

HITSCHMANN, E.   *Telepathie und Psychoanalyse*, Imago, 9, 1923, pp.368-382.

HOBLEY, C. W. — Bantu Beliefs and Magic. London 1922.

HOLLÓS, I. — *Psychopathologie alltäglicher telepathischer Erscheinungen*, Imago, 19, 1933, pp.529-546.

HOLMES, T. V. — *On the Evidence for the Efficiency of the Diviner and his Rod in Search for Water*, J. Anthropological Institute, Nov. 1897, pp.233-259. (London).

HOOPER, S. E. — *Telepathy in the Light of Whitehead's Philosophy*, Hibbert Journal, 42, 1944, pp.248-253.

HOPP, M. — Uber Hellsehen. Berlin 1916.

HULL, C. L. — Hypnosis and Suggestibility. N.Y. 1933.

HUMPHREY, B. M. — Handbook of Tests in Parapsychology. Duke University, Durham, N.C. 1948.

HUNTINGTON, E. V. — *Is it Chance or ESP?*, Am. Scholar, 1938, 7, pp.201-210.

HUXLEY, J. — *Science and Psychical Research*, Weekend Review, 6, 1932, pp.278-279. (London).

IMBERT - GOURBEYRE, A. — La Stigmatisation. Paris 1894.

JACOBI, W. — Die Stigmatisierten. Grenzfragen des Nerven- und Seelenlebens No. 114. Munich 1923.

JACOBSEN, E. — Progressive Relaxation. Chicago 1938.

JAENSCH, E. R. — Eidetic Imagery. London 1930.

——— *Uber einige auffällige psychische Phänomene und die Wahrscheinlichkeit ihrer Bedeutung für das Kategorienproblem*, Zeitschrift für Psychologie, 120, 1931, pp.113-125.

JAMES, WM. — Varieties of Religious Experience. London 1902.

JANET, P.   Divination par les Mirroirs, Bulletin
                            de L'Universite de Lyons, July, 1897.
——————   L'Automatisme psychologique. Paris
                            1889.
——————   The Major Symptoms of Hysteria.
                            N.Y. 1907.
——————   Psychological Healing. 2 vols. Lon-
                            don 1925.
JASTROW, J.   Fact and Fable in Psychology. N.Y.
                            1901.
——————   The Psychology of Conviction. N.Y.
                            1918.
——————   " The Animus of Psychical Research",
                            chapter in The Case for and against
                            Psychical Belief, ed. C. Murchison.
                            Clark University Press, Mass. 1927.
——————   Wish and Wisdom. N.Y. 1935.
JOLOWICZ, E.   Suggestion Therapy ; and Heyer, G.,
                            Hypnosis and Hypnotherapy. Lon-
                            don 1931.
JONES, E. H.   The Road to Endor. London 1919.
JUNG, C. G.   Collected Papers on Analytical Psycho-
                            logy. London 1920.

KELLOG, C. E.   New Evidence (?) for Extra-Sensory
                            Perception, Science Monthly, 45, 1937,
                            pp.331-341.
——————   The Problems of Matching and Sampling
                            in the Study of Eatra-Sensory Percep-
                            tion, J. Abn. and Soc. Psychol., 32,
                            1937, pp.462-479.
——————   The Statistical Techniques of ESP, J.
                            Gen. Psychol., 19, 1938, pp.383-390.
KENNEDY, J. L.   The Visual Cues from the Backs of the
                            ESP Cards, J. Psychol., 6, 1938, pp.
                            149-153.
——————   A Methodological Review of Extra-
                            Sensory Perception, Psychol., Bull. 36,
                            1939, pp.59-103.

KEYSERLING, H.,   Das Okkulte. Darmstadt 1923.
HARDENBERG, K.
and HAPPICH, C.

KITTREDGE, G. L.   Witchcraft in Old and New England.
Cambridge, Mass. 1929.

KLINCKOWSTROEM,   Handbuch der Wünchelruthe. Mun-
C. von, and MALT-   ich and Berlin 1931.
ZAHN, R. V.

KOTIK, N.   Die Emanation der psycho-physischen
Energie. Grenzfragen des Nerven-
und Seelenlebens (No. 61). Wiesbaden
1908.

KRALL, K.   Denkende Tiere. Leipzig 1912.

KRÖNER, W.   Befunderhebung durch Fernfühlen.
Leipzig 1924.
Parapsychologie und Psychoanalyse,
Zeitschrift für Parapsychologie, 1926,
2, pp.99-104.

LEHMANN, A.   Aberglaube und Zauberei. Stuttgart
1925.

LEHMANN, A. and   *Über unwillkürliches Flüstern*, Phil.
HANSEN, F. C. C.   Stud. 11, 1895, pp.471-530. (Leipzig).

LEMMON, V. W.   *Extra-Sensory Perception*, J. Psychol.,
1937, 4, pp.227-238.

LEROY, E. B.   Les Visions du Demi-Sommeil (Hallucinations Hypnagogiques). Paris
1926.

LEUBA, C.   *Has Recent Research Undermined the
Evidence for Extra-Sensory Perception?*
J. Appl. Psychol., 22, 1938, pp.549-553.
The Psychology of Religious Mysticism.
N.Y. 1925.

LEVINE, M.   *Psychogalvanic Reaction to Painful
Stimuli in Hypnotic and Hysterical
Anaesthesia*, Bulletin of the John
Hopkins Hospital, 1930, pp.331-339.

LIÉBAULT, A. A.   Du Sommeil et des États analogues.
Paris 1886.

LOEWENFELD, L.   Somnambulismus und Spiritusmus.
                        Wiesbaden 1907.
LUND, F. H.   *Extra-Sensory Perception Another Name
                        for Free Association*, J. Gen. Psychol.,
                        20, 1939, pp.235-238.
LUNN,   A.,   and   Science and the Supernatural. London,
   HALDANE, J. B. S.   1935.

MABY, J. C. and   The Physics of the Divining Rod.
   FRANKLIN, T. B.   London 1939.
McCABE, J.   The Lourdes Miracles. London 1925.
MACDOUGALL, WM.   Body and Mind. London 1911.
─────────────────   An Outline of Abnormal Psychology.
                        London 1926.
─────────────────   " Psychical Research as a University
                        Study ", chapter in The Case for and
                        against Psychical Belief, ed. C. Murchi-
                        son. Mass. 1927.
─────────────────   The Frontiers of Psychology. London
                        1934.
MACE, C. A.   The Psychology of Study. London
                        1932.
─────────────────   Supernormal Faculty and the Structure
                        of the Mind. S.P.R. Myers Memorial
                        Lecture, London 1937.
MACEY, A.   Hypnotism Explained. London 1933.
MADDOX, J. L.   The Medicine Man. N.Y. 1923.
MAGER, H.   Water Diviners and their Methods.
                        London 1931.
MARX, H.   *Untersuchungen über den Wasserhaus-
                        halt die psychische Beeinflussung des
                        Wasserhaushaltes*, Klinische Wochens-
                        chrift, 5, 1926, pp.92-94.
MAXWELL, J.   La Divination. Paris 1927.
MESSER, A.   Wissenschaftlicher Okkultismus. Leip-
                        zig 1927.
MILL, H. R.   *Behind the Divining Rod*, Nature. 119,
                        1927, p.311.

MITCHELL. T. W. Medical Psychyology and Psychical Research. London 1922
———————— "Psychology and Psychical Research", chapter in Psychology and the Sciences, ed. Wm. Brown. London 1924.
———————— Beneath the Threshold. S.P.R. Myers Memorial Lecture, London 1931.

MOBERLEY. C. A. E. and JOURDAIN. E. F. An Adventure. London 1931.

MOLL, A. Hypnotism. London 1906.
———————— Prophezeien und Hellsehen. Stuttgart 1922.
———————— Psychologie und Charakterologie der Okkultisten, Abhandlungen aus dem Gebiete der Psychotherapie und medizinischen Psychologie. Heft 11. 1929. (Stuttgart)

MONCRIEFF, M. M. The Clairvoyant Theory of Perception. London 1951.

MOODY, R. L. Bodily Changes during Abreaction. (Letter), Lancet. 1948. 1, p.964.

MOORE E. H. Elements of Error in Testimony. J. Appl. Psychol.. 19. 1935. pp.447-462.

MOTTRAM, V. H The Physical Basis of Personality. London 1946.

MÜHL. A. M. Automatic Writing. Dresden and Leipzig 1930.

MULHALL, E. F. Experimental Studies in Recall and Recognition. Am. J. Psychol., 26, 1915, pp.217-228.

MULLER, R. Naturwissenschaftliche Seelenforschung Leipzig 1897.

MULLHOLLAND, J. The Art of Illusion. N.Y. 1944.

MURCHISON, C. (ed.) The Case for and against Psychical Belief. Clark University Press, Mass. 1927.

MURPHY, GARDNER   " Telepathy as an Experimental Problem ", chapter in The Case for and
against Psychical Belief, ed. C. Murchison. Mass. 1927.

———————————   *Dr. Rhine and the Mind's Eye*, Am.
Schol.. 7, 1938, pp.189-200.

———————————   Parapsychology. In Encyclopaedia of
Psychology, ed. P. L. Harriman. N.Y.
1946.

MYERS, F. W. H.   Human Personality and its Survival
of Bodily Death. 2 vols. London
1903. (Abridged edition, 1919.)

N EUREITER, F.
VON   Wissen um Fremdes Wissen. Gotha.
1935.

NEVIUS, J. L.   Demon Possession and Allied Themes.
Chicago. N.Y. and Toronto 1894.

O ESTERREICH, T.
K.   Grundbegriffe der Parapsychologie.
(Die Okkulte Welt No. 25) ; Pfullingen
1921.

———————————   *Das Problem der Ich-Spaltung*, Compte
Rendu du IIIéme Congrès Internation-
ale de Recnerches Psychiques, 1927,
pp.139-148. Paris 1928.

———————————   Das Mädchen aus der Fremde. Ein
Fall von Störung der Persönlichkeit.
Stuttgart 1929.

———————————   Psychologisches Gutachten in einem
Hellseherprozess. Stuttgart 1930.

———————————   Possession. London 1930.

———————————   " Parapsychologie ", chapter in Ein-
führung in die neuere Psychologie,
ed. E. Saupe. Berlin 1931.

OSTY, E.   Supernormal Faculties in Man. London 1923.

Le Diagnostic des Maladies par les Sujets doués de Connaissance paranormale. Offprint from *Revue Metapsychique*, Paris 1929-30.

Supernormal Aspects of Energy and Matter. S.P.R. Myers Memorial Lecture, London 1933.

OSTY, E. and OSTY, M.   Les Pouvoirs Inconnus de l'Esprit sur la Matière. Paris 1932.

PAGENSTECHER. G.   Aussersinnliche Wahrnehmung. Halle a.S. 1924.

PARISH, E.   Über die Trugwahrnehmung (Hallucination und Illusion) mit besonderer Berucksichtigung der internationalen Enquete über Wachhallucinationen bei Gesunden. Schriften der Gesellschaft für Psychologische Forschung (Heft 7-8) ; Leipzig 1894.

Zur Kritik des Telepatheschen Beweismaterials. Leipzig 1897.

Hallucinations and Illusions. London 1897.

PEDERSON-KRAG, G.   *Telepathy and Repression*, Psychoanalytic Quarterly, 16, 1947, pp.61-68.

PLATZ, W.   Das Forschungsgebiet des Okkultismus. Stuttgart 1924.

PODMORE, F.   The Naturalisation of the Supernatural. N.Y. and London 1908.

Modern Spiritualism, a History and a Criticism. 2 vols. London 1909.

Telepathic Hallucinations. London 1909.

The Newer Spiritualism. London 1910.

PRATT. J. G.   Towards a Method of Evaluating
                      Mediumistic Material. Boston S.P.R.,
                      Bulletin 23. Foreword by Gardner
                      Murphy and an Analysis by J. B.
                      Rhine. Boston 1936.

PRICE. H.   Rudi Schneider : a Scientific Exam-
                      ination of his Mediumship. London
                      1930.

—————————   Regurgitation and the Duncan Medium-
                      ship. Bulletin of the National Labor-
                      atory of Psychical Research, London
                      1931.

—————————   Further Experiments with Rudi
                      Schneider. Bulletin of the National
                      Laboratory of Psychical Research.
                      London 1933.

—————————   A Report on Two Experimental Fire-
                      walks. University of London Council
                      for Psychical Investigation, Bulletin 2.
                      1936.

PRICE. H. H.   Perception. London 1932.

—————————   *The Philosophical Implications of Pre-
                      cognition*, Aristotelian Society Supp.
                      Vol. 16, 1937, pp.211-228 (London)

—————————   *Some Philosophical Questions about Tele-
                      pathy and Clairvoyance*, Philosophy,
                      60, 1940, pp.363-385.

—————————   *Philosophical Implications of Telepathy*,
                      Listener, Feb. 13th, 1947, pp.277-278.

—————————   *Mind over Mind and Mind over Matter*,
                      Enquiry, July, 1949, pp. 20-27, and
                      September, 1949, pp. 5-14.

—————————   *Psychical Research and Human Person-
                      ality*, Hibbert Journal. 47. 2. 1949.
                      pp.105-113.

PRINCE, MORETON — *An Experimental Study of Visions*, Brain, 1898, pp.528-546.
—— The Dissociation of a Personality : a Biographical Study in Abnormal Psychology. N.Y. 1906.
—— *An Experimental Study of the Mechanism of Hallucinations*, Brit. J. Psychol., Med. Sect., 2, 1922, pp.165-208.

QUACKENBOS. J. D. — Hypnotic Therapeutics. London 1908.

RELE, V. G. — The Mysterious Kundalini. Bombay 1927.

RHINE, J. B. — Extra-Sensory Perception. Boston 1934.
—— *Telepathy and Clairvoyance in the Normal and Trance States of a " Medium "*, Character and Personality, 3, 1934, pp.92-111.
—— New Frontiers of the Mind. London 1938.
—— The Psychokinetic Effect : A Review. Reprint from the Journal of Parapsychology, vol. 10, 1946.
—— The Reach of the Mind. N.Y. 1947.
—— Telepathy and Human Personality S. P. R. Myers Memorial Lecture, London 1950.

RHINE, J. B. and others — Extra-Sensory Perception after Sixty Years. N.Y. 1940.

RICHET, C. — Thirty Years of Psychical Research : a Treatise on Metapsychics. London 1923.
—— L'Avenir et la Prémonition. Paris 1931.

RICHMOND, K. — Evidence of Identity. London 1939.
RICHMOND, Z. — Evidence of Purpose. London 1938.
RIGGALL, R. M. — *A Case of Multiple Personality*. Lancet. 221. 1931. pp.846-848.

ROGOSIN, H.   *Some Implications of Extra-Sensory Perception*, Psychol. League J., 1938, 2, pp.47-49.

————————   *Telepathy, Psychical Research and Modern Psychology*, Philosophy of Science, 5, 1938, pp.472-483.

————————   *Probability Theory and Extra-Sensory Perception*, J. Psychol., 1938, 5, pp. 265-270.

————————   *An Evaluation of Extra-Sensory Perception*, J. Gen. Psychol., 21, 1939, pp.203-217.

RÓHEIM, G.   Animism, Magic, and the Divine King. London 1930.

————————   *Telepathy in a Dream*, Psychoanalytic Quarterly, 1, 1932, pp.277-291.

ROMAINS, JULES   See Farigoule, L.

ROSENBUSCH, H.   *Parapsychologie*, Handwörterbuch der medizinischen Psychologie, 1930, pp. 379-388.   (Leipzig)

ROSETT, J.   The Mechanism of Thought, Imagery and Hallucination. N.Y. 1939.

ROTH. W. E.   Ethnological Studies among the North-West-Central Queensland Aborigines. Brisbane 1897.

————————   North Queensland Ethnography, Bulletin No. 5, 1903, (pp.27-31).   (Brisbane)

SADLER, W. S.   The Mind at Mischief. N.Y. and London 1929.

————————   The Truth about Mind Cure.   London 1929.

SALTER, W. H.   Ghosts and Apparitions.   London 1938

————————   Trance Mediumship. S.P.R. publication, London 1950.

SALTMARSH, H. F.   Evidence of Personal Survival from Cross Correspondence. London 1938.

————————   Foreknowledge.   London 1938.

SAUL. L. J.   *Telepathic Sensitiveness as a Neurotic Symptom*, Psychoanalytic Quarterly. 7, 1938, pp.329-335.

SCARNE, J. and
RAWSON, C.
SCHILDER, P.

SCHILLER, F. C. S.

SCHMEIDLER, G. R.
and MURPHY,
GARDNER
SCHOLE, H.

SCHRENCK-NOTZING,
A. von
SCHROEDER, C.

SCHULHOF, F.

SEABROOKE, W. B.
SEITZ, A.

SELIGMAN, C. G.

SERVADIO, E.

SINCLAIR, U.

Scarne on Dice. Harrisburg, Pensylvania 1946.
Psychopathologie alltäglicher telepathischer Erscheinungen, Imago, 20, 1934, pp.219-224.
" The Progress of Psychical Research ", chapter in Studies in Humanism. London 1912.
" Some Logical Aspects of Psychical Research ", chapter in The Case for and against Psychical Belief, ed. C. Murchison. Mass. 1927.
Psychology and Psychical Research, Monist, 40, 1930, pp.439-452.
The Influence of Belief and Disbelief in ESP upon Individual Scoring Levels, J. Exp. Psychol., 36, 1946, pp.271-276.
Okkultismus und Wissenschaft. Göttingen 1929.
Die Traumtänzerin Madeleine. Stuttgart 1904.
Grundversuche auf dem Gebiete der psychischen Grenzwissenschaften. Berlin 1924.
Sind Sensitive und Medien Hysteriker ? (Die Okkulte Welt No. 132.) ; Pfullingen 1925.
The Magic Island. London 1929.
Okkultismus, Wissenschaft und Religion. 3 vols. Zur religiösen Lage der Gegenwart (Heft 11, 17, 18). Munich 1926-1929.
" Ritual and Medicine ", chapter in Enquiry into the Unknown, ed. T. Besterman. London 1934.
La Ricerca Psichica. Rome 1930. Psychoanalyse und Telepathie, Imago, 21, 1935, pp.489-497.
Mental Radio : Does it Work, and How ? Introduction by Wm. MacDougall. London 1930.

SOAL, S. G.   *Experiments in Supernormal Perception at a Distance*, Proc. S.P.R., 40, 1932, pp.165-362.

Preliminary Studies of a Vaudeville Telepathist. University of London Council for Psychical Investigation. Bulletin 3. London 1937.

Fresh Lights on Card Guessing—Some New Effects, Proc. S.P.R., 46, 1940, pp. 152-198.

The Experimental Situation in Psychical Research. S.P.R. Myers Memorial Lecture, London 1947.

Advice to Experimenters and Instructors. (Pamphlet). London 1948

Some Aspects of Extra-Sensorp Perception, Proc. S.P.R., 49, 1951, pp.131-153.

SOAL, S. G. and   *Experiments in Precognitive Telepathy*,
GOLDNEY, K. M.   Proc. S.P.R. 47. 1943, pp.21-150.

SPECHT, G.   Die Mystik im Irrsinn. Wiesbaden 1891.

STEKEL, W.   Der Telepathische Traum. (Die Okkulte Welt No. 2) ; Berlin 1920.

STEVENS, W. L.   *Tests of Significance for Extra-Sensory Perception Data.* Psychol. Rev., 46, 1939, pp.142-150.

STUART, C. E.   *The Willoughby Test of Clairvoyant Perception*, J. Appl. Psychol., 19, 1935, pp.551-554.

In Reply to the Willoughby Critique, J. Abn. & Soc. Psychol., 30, 3, 1935, pp.384-388.

A Review of Certain Proposed Hypotheses Alternative to Extra-Sensory Perception, J. Abn. and Soc. Psychol., 33, 1938, pp.57-70.

STUART, C. E. and   A Handbook for Testing Extra-Sensory
PRATT, J. G.   Perception. N.Y. and Toronto 1937.

STURGE-WHITING,   The Mystery of Versailles. London
J. R.   1938.

SUDRE, R.　　　　　Introduction a la Metapsychique Humaine. Paris 1926.

TARCHANOW, J.　　　Hypnotisme, Suggestion et Lectures des Pensées. Paris 1891.

TAYLOR, F. N.　　　Small Water Supplies. London 1912.

TELLING, W. H.　　*The Value of Psychical Research to*
MAXWELL　　　　　*a Physician.* Journal of Mental Science, Oct. 1928 ; (offprint).

THOMAS, J. F.　　　Beyond Normal Cognition. Boston 1937.

THOMAS, N. W.　　　Thought Transference. London 1905.

THOMPSON, B.　　　*Water Divining and Radioactivity.*
Some Experiments with Reputed " Water Diviners ". J. Northants Nat. Hist. Soc., 16, 1911, pp.92-100.

Thompson, J. J.　　Recollections and Reflections. London 1936.

THOULESS, R. H.　　An introduction to the Psychology of Religion. Cambridge 1928.
　　　　　　　　　Experiments on Paranormal Guessing, Brit. J. Psychol., (General Section), 33, 1, 1942, pp.15-27.
　　　　　　　　　Psychical Research—the Next Step, The Listener, May 15th, 1947, pp.754-755.

TICHY, H.　　　　　Tibetan Adventure. London 1938.

TILLYARD, R. J.　　*Science and Psychical Research,* Nature, 118, 1926, p.147.

TISCHNER, R.　　　Telepathy and Clairvoyance. London 1925.

TROLAND, L. T.　　A Technique for the Experimental Study of Telepathy and other Alleged Clairvoyant Processes. Cambridge, Mass. 1917.
　　　　　　　　　The Fundamentals of Human Motivation. London 1928.

TROWBRIDGE, W.　　Cagliostro. London 1936.
R. H.

TUCKETT, I. LLOYD　The Evidence for the Supernatural. London 1911.

TYRRELL, G. N. M.   Science and Psychical Phenomena. London 1938.
————   Apparitions. S.P.R. Myers Memorial Lecture, London 1942.
————   The Personality of Man. London 1946
————   *The Implications of Psychical Research,* Listener, May 22nd, 1947, pp.790-791.

USHER, F. L. and BURT, F. P.   *Thought Transference,* Annals of Psychical Science, 8, 1909, pp.561-600.

VAKIL, J.   *Remarkable Feat of Endurance by a Yogi Priest,* Lancet, 1950, 2, p.871.
VASCHIDE, N.   *Experimental Investigations of Telepathic Hallucinations,* Monist, 1902, pp.273-307.
————   Les Hallucinations Télépathiques. Paris 1908.
VERWEYEN, J. M.   Die Probleme des Mediumismus. Stutgart 1928.
VESME, C. de   A History of Experimental Spiritualism 2 vols. London 1931.
————   Merveilleux dans les Jeux de Hazard. Paris 1929.
VILLEY, P.   The World of the Blind. London 1930.
VIOLLET, M.   Spiritism and Insanity. London 1910.
VIVEKANANDA (SWAMI)   Raja-Yoga. Calcutta 1944.

WARCOLLIER, R.   Experimental Telepathy. Boston S.P.R. 1938.
————   Mind to Mind. N.Y. 1948.
WASIELIEWSKI, W. VON   Telepathie und Hellsehen. Halle a.S. 1922.
Water Divining Demonstration, The.   Sanitary Record and Municipal Engineering, April 13th, 1913, pp.365-368; May 2nd, 1913, pp.462-466.

WELLS, H. G., HUX-   The Science of Life.   London 1938.
LEY, J., & WELLS.
G. P.

WELLS, W. R.   *Experiments in the Hypnotic Production of Crime*, J. Psychol., 2, 1941, pp.63-102

WERTHEIMER, G.   *Experiments with "Waterfinders"*, Water (Supplement), Nov. 15th, 1906.

WEST, D. J.   *The Investigation of Spontaneous Cases*, Proc. S.P.R., 48, 1948, pp.264-300.

WILLIAMS, J. J.   Psychic Phenomena of Jamaica.   N.Y. 1934.

WILLOUGHBY, R. R.   *Critical Comment : The Use of the Probable Error in Evaluating Clairvoyance*, Char. and Personality, 4, 1935, pp.79-80.

————————   *A Critique of Rhine's 'Extra-Sensory Perception '*, J. Abn. & Soc. Psychol., 30, 1935, pp.199-207.

————————   *Prerequisites for a Clairvoyance Hypothesis*, J. Appl. Psychol., 19, 1935, pp.543-550.

————————   *Further Card-Guessing Experiments*, J. Gen. Psychol., 17, 1937, pp.3-13.

WINTERSTEIN, A.   Telepathie und Hellsehen.   Berlin 1937.

WOLFLE, D. L.   *A Review of the Work on Extra-Sensory Perception*, Am. J. Psychiat., 94, 1938, pp.943-955.

WOLTERS, A. W. P.   The Evidence of our Senses.   London 1933.

WOOD, E.   The Occult Training of the Hindus London 1931.

INDEX

550

A CATALOGUE OF SELECTED DOVER BOOKS
IN ALL FIELDS OF INTEREST

A CATALOGUE OF SELECTED DOVER BOOKS
IN ALL FIELDS OF INTEREST

AMERICA'S OLD MASTERS, James T. Flexner. Four men emerged unexpectedly from provincial 18th century America to leadership in European art: Benjamin West, J. S. Copley, C. R. Peale, Gilbert Stuart. Brilliant coverage of lives and contributions. Revised, 1967 edition. 69 plates. 365pp. of text.

21806-6 Paperbound $3.00

FIRST FLOWERS OF OUR WILDERNESS: AMERICAN PAINTING, THE COLONIAL PERIOD, James T. Flexner. Painters, and regional painting traditions from earliest Colonial times up to the emergence of Copley, West and Peale Sr., Foster, Gustavus Hesselius, Feke, John Smibert and many anonymous painters in the primitive manner. Engaging presentation, with 162 illustrations. xxii + 368pp.

22180-6 Paperbound $3.50

THE LIGHT OF DISTANT SKIES: AMERICAN PAINTING, 1760-1835, James T. Flexner. The great generation of early American painters goes to Europe to learn and to teach: West, Copley, Gilbert Stuart and others. Allston, Trumbull, Morse; also contemporary American painters—primitives, derivatives, academics—who remained in America. 102 illustrations. xiii + 306pp.

22179-2 Paperbound $3.00

A HISTORY OF THE RISE AND PROGRESS OF THE ARTS OF DESIGN IN THE UNITED STATES, William Dunlap. Much the richest mine of information on early American painters, sculptors, architects, engravers, miniaturists, etc. The only source of information for scores of artists, the major primary source for many others. Unabridged reprint of rare original 1834 edition, with new introduction by James T. Flexner, and 394 new illustrations. Edited by Rita Weiss. 6⅝ x 9⅝.

21695-0, 21696-9, 21697-7 Three volumes, Paperbound $13.50

EPOCHS OF CHINESE AND JAPANESE ART, Ernest F. Fenollosa. From primitive Chinese art to the 20th century, thorough history, explanation of every important art period and form, including Japanese woodcuts; main stress on China and Japan, but Tibet, Korea also included. Still unexcelled for its detailed, rich coverage of cultural background, aesthetic elements, diffusion studies, particularly of the historical period. 2nd, 1913 edition. 242 illustrations. lii + 439pp. of text.

20364-6, 20365-4 Two volumes, Paperbound $6.00

THE GENTLE ART OF MAKING ENEMIES, James A. M. Whistler. Greatest wit of his day deflates Oscar Wilde, Ruskin, Swinburne; strikes back at inane critics, exhibitions, art journalism; aesthetics of impressionist revolution in most striking form. Highly readable classic by great painter. Reproduction of edition designed by Whistler. Introduction by Alfred Werner. xxxvi + 334pp.

21875-9 Paperbound $2.50

ALPHABETS AND ORNAMENTS, Ernst Lehner. Well-known pictorial source for decorative alphabets, script examples, cartouches, frames, decorative title pages, calligraphic initials, borders, similar material. 14th to 19th century, mostly European. Useful in almost any graphic arts designing, varied styles. 750 illustrations. 256pp. 7 x 10.
21905-4 Paperbound $4.00

PAINTING: A CREATIVE APPROACH, Norman Colquhoun. For the beginner simple guide provides an instructive approach to painting: major stumbling blocks for beginner; overcoming them, technical points; paints and pigments; oil painting; watercolor and other media and color. New section on "plastic" paints. Glossary. Formerly *Paint Your Own Pictures.* 221pp.
22000-1 Paperbound $1.75

THE ENJOYMENT AND USE OF COLOR, Walter Sargent. Explanation of the relations between colors themselves and between colors in nature and art, including hundreds of little-known facts about color values, intensities, effects of high and low illumination, complementary colors. Many practical hints for painters, references to great masters. 7 color plates, 29 illustrations. x + 274pp.
20944-X Paperbound $2.75

THE NOTEBOOKS OF LEONARDO DA VINCI, compiled and edited by Jean Paul Richter. 1566 extracts from original manuscripts reveal the full range of Leonardo's versatile genius: all his writings on painting, sculpture, architecture, anatomy, astronomy, geography, topography, physiology, mining, music, etc., in both Italian and English, with 186 plates of manuscript pages and more than 500 additional drawings. Includes studies for the Last Supper, the lost Sforza monument, and other works. Total of xlvii + 866pp. $7\frac{7}{8}$ x $10\frac{3}{4}$.
22572-0, 22573-9 Two volumes, Paperbound $10.00

MONTGOMERY WARD CATALOGUE OF 1895. Tea gowns, yards of flannel and pillow-case lace, stereoscopes, books of gospel hymns, the New Improved Singer Sewing Machine, side saddles, milk skimmers, straight-edged razors, high-button shoes, spittoons, and on and on . . . listing some 25,000 items, practically all illustrated. Essential to the shoppers of the 1890's, it is our truest record of the spirit of the period. Unaltered reprint of Issue No. 57, Spring and Summer 1895. Introduction by Boris Emmet. Innumerable illustrations. xiii + 624pp. $8\frac{1}{2}$ x $11\frac{5}{8}$.
22377-9 Paperbound $6.95

THE CRYSTAL PALACE EXHIBITION ILLUSTRATED CATALOGUE (LONDON, 1851). One of the wonders of the modern world—the Crystal Palace Exhibition in which all the nations of the civilized world exhibited their achievements in the arts and sciences—presented in an equally important illustrated catalogue. More than 1700 items pictured with accompanying text—ceramics, textiles, cast-iron work, carpets, pianos, sleds, razors, wall-papers, billiard tables, beehives, silverware and hundreds of other artifacts—represent the focal point of Victorian culture in the Western World. Probably the largest collection of Victorian decorative art ever assembled—indispensable for antiquarians and designers. Unabridged republication of the Art-Journal Catalogue of the Great Exhibition of 1851, with all terminal essays. New introduction by John Gloag, F.S.A. xxxiv + 426pp. 9 x 12.
22503-8 Paperbound $4.50

THE ARCHITECTURE OF COUNTRY HOUSES, Andrew J. Downing. Together with Vaux's *Villas and Cottages* this is the basic book for Hudson River Gothic architecture of the middle Victorian period. Full, sound discussions of general aspects of housing, architecture, style, decoration, furnishing, together with scores of detailed house plans, illustrations of specific buildings, accompanied by full text. Perhaps the most influential single American architectural book. 1850 edition. Introduction by J. Stewart Johnson. 321 figures, 34 architectural designs. xvi + 560pp.
22003-6 Paperbound $4.00

LOST EXAMPLES OF COLONIAL ARCHITECTURE, John Mead Howells. Full-page photographs of buildings that have disappeared or been so altered as to be denatured, including many designed by major early American architects. 245 plates. xvii + 248pp. 7⅞ x 10¾. 21143-6 Paperbound $3.00

DOMESTIC ARCHITECTURE OF THE AMERICAN COLONIES AND OF THE EARLY REPUBLIC, Fiske Kimball. Foremost architect and restorer of Williamsburg and Monticello covers nearly 200 homes between 1620-1825. Architectural details, construction, style features, special fixtures, floor plans, etc. Generally considered finest work in its area. 219 illustrations of houses, doorways, windows, capital mantels. xx + 314pp. 7⅞ x 10¾. 21743-4 Paperbound $3.50

EARLY AMERICAN ROOMS: 1650-1858, edited by Russell Hawes Kettell. Tour of 12 rooms, each representative of a different era in American history and each furnished, decorated, designed and occupied in the style of the era. 72 plans and elevations, 8-page color section, etc., show fabrics, wall papers, arrangements, etc. Full descriptive text. xvii + 200pp. of text. 8⅜ x 11¼. 21633-0 Paperbound $5.00

THE FITZWILLIAM VIRGINAL BOOK, edited by J. Fuller Maitland and W. B. Squire. Full modern printing of famous early 17th-century ms. volume of 300 works by Morley, Byrd, Bull, Gibbons, etc. For piano or other modern keyboard instrument; easy to read format. xxxvi + 938pp. 8⅜ x 11. 21068-5, 21069-3 Two volumes, Paperbound $8.00

HARPSICHORD MUSIC, Johann Sebastian Bach. Bach Gesellschaft edition. A rich selection of Bach's masterpieces for the harpsichord: the six English Suites, six French Suites, the six Partitas (Clavierübung part I), the Goldberg Variations (Clavierübung part IV), the fifteen Two-Part Inventions and the fifteen Three-Part Sinfonias. Clearly reproduced on large sheets with ample margins; eminently playable. vi + 312pp. 8⅛ x 11. 22360-4 Paperbound $5.00

THE MUSIC OF BACH: AN INTRODUCTION, Charles Sanford Terry. A fine, non-technical introduction to Bach's music, both instrumental and vocal. Covers organ music, chamber music, passion music, other types. Analyzes themes, developments, innovations. x + 114pp. 21075-8 Paperbound $1.25

BEETHOVEN AND HIS NINE SYMPHONIES, Sir George Grove. Noted British musicologist provides best history, analysis, commentary on symphonies. Very thorough, rigorously accurate; necessary to both advanced student and amateur music lover. 436 musical passages. vii + 407 pp. 20334-4 Paperbound $2.25

POEMS OF ANNE BRADSTREET, edited with an introduction by Robert Hutchinson. A new selection of poems by America's first poet and perhaps the first significant woman poet in the English language. 48 poems display her development in works of considerable variety—love poems, domestic poems, religious meditations, formal elegies, "quaternions," etc. Notes, bibliography. viii + 222pp.

22160-1 Paperbound $2.00

THREE GOTHIC NOVELS: THE CASTLE OF OTRANTO BY HORACE WALPOLE; VATHEK BY WILLIAM BECKFORD; THE VAMPYRE BY JOHN POLIDORI, WITH FRAGMENT OF A NOVEL BY LORD BYRON, edited by E. F. Bleiler. The first Gothic novel, by Walpole; the finest Oriental tale in English, by Beckford; powerful Romantic supernatural story in versions by Polidori and Byron. All extremely important in history of literature; all still exciting, packed with supernatural thrills, ghosts, haunted castles, magic, etc. xl + 291pp.

21232-7 Paperbound $2.00

THE BEST TALES OF HOFFMANN, E. T. A. Hoffmann. 10 of Hoffmann's most important stories, in modern re-editings of standard translations: Nutcracker and the King of Mice, Signor Formica, Automata, The Sandman, Rath Krespel, The Golden Flowerpot, Master Martin the Cooper, The Mines of Falun, The King's Betrothed, A New Year's Eve Adventure. 7 illustrations by Hoffmann. Edited by E. F. Bleiler. xxxix + 419pp. 21793-0 Paperbound $2.50

GHOST AND HORROR STORIES OF AMBROSE BIERCE, Ambrose Bierce. 23 strikingly modern stories of the horrors latent in the human mind: The Eyes of the Panther, The Damned Thing, An Occurrence at Owl Creek Bridge, An Inhabitant of Carcosa, etc., plus the dream-essay, Visions of the Night. Edited by E. F. Bleiler. xxii + 199pp. 20767-6 Paperbound $1.50

BEST GHOST STORIES OF J. S. LEFANU, J. Sheridan LeFanu. Finest stories by Victorian master often considered greatest supernatural writer of all. Carmilla, Green Tea, The Haunted Baronet, The Familiar, and 12 others. Most never before available in the U. S. A. Edited by E. F. Bleiler. 8 illustrations from Victorian publications. xvii + 467pp. 20415-4 Paperbound $3.00

THE TIME STREAM, THE GREATEST ADVENTURE, AND THE PURPLE SAPPHIRE—THREE SCIENCE FICTION NOVELS, John Taine (Eric Temple Bell). Great American mathematician was also foremost science fiction novelist of the 1920's. *The Time Stream,* one of all-time classics, uses concepts of circular time; *The Greatest Adventure,* incredibly ancient biological experiments from Antarctica threaten to escape; The *Purple Sapphire,* superscience, lost races in Central Tibet, survivors of the Great Race. 4 illustrations by Frank R. Paul. v + 532pp.

21180-0 Paperbound $3.00

SEVEN SCIENCE FICTION NOVELS, H. G. Wells. The standard collection of the great novels. Complete, unabridged. *First Men in the Moon, Island of Dr. Moreau, War of the Worlds, Food of the Gods, Invisible Man, Time Machine, In the Days of the Comet.* Not only science fiction fans, but every educated person owes it to himself to read these novels. 1015pp. 20264-X Clothbound $5.00

LAST AND FIRST MEN AND STAR MAKER, TWO SCIENCE FICTION NOVELS, Olaf Stapledon. Greatest future histories in science fiction. In the first, human intelligence is the "hero," through strange paths of evolution, interplanetary invasions, incredible technologies, near extinctions and reemergences. Star Maker describes the quest of a band of star rovers for intelligence itself, through time and space: weird inhuman civilizations, crustacean minds, symbiotic worlds, etc. Complete, unabridged. v + 438pp. 21962-3 Paperbound $2.50

THREE PROPHETIC NOVELS, H. G. WELLS. Stages of a consistently planned future for mankind. *When the Sleeper Wakes,* and *A Story of the Days to Come,* anticipate *Brave New World* and *1984,* in the 21st Century; *The Time Machine,* only complete version in print, shows farther future and the end of mankind. All show Wells's greatest gifts as storyteller and novelist. Edited by E. F. Bleiler. x + 335pp. (USO) 20605-X Paperbound $2.25

THE DEVIL'S DICTIONARY, Ambrose Bierce. America's own Oscar Wilde— Ambrose Bierce—offers his barbed iconoclastic wisdom in over 1,000 definitions hailed by H. L. Mencken as "some of the most gorgeous witticisms in the English language." 145pp. 20487-1 Paperbound $1.25

MAX AND MORITZ, Wilhelm Busch. Great children's classic, father of comic strip, of two bad boys, Max and Moritz. Also Ker and Plunk (Plisch und Plumm), Cat and Mouse, Deceitful Henry, Ice-Peter, The Boy and the Pipe, and five other pieces. Original German, with English translation. Edited by H. Arthur Klein; translations by various hands and H. Arthur Klein. vi + 216pp.
20181-3 Paperbound $2.00

PIGS IS PIGS AND OTHER FAVORITES, Ellis Parker Butler. The title story is one of the best humor short stories, as Mike Flannery obfuscates biology and English. Also included, That Pup of Murchison's, The Great American Pie Company, and Perkins of Portland. 14 illustrations. v + 109pp. 21532-6 Paperbound $1.00

THE PETERKIN PAPERS, Lucretia P. Hale. It takes genius to be as stupidly mad as the Peterkins, as they decide to become wise, celebrate the "Fourth," keep a cow, and otherwise strain the resources of the Lady from Philadelphia. Basic book of American humor. 153 illustrations. 219pp. 20794-3 Paperbound $1.50

PERRAULT'S FAIRY TALES, translated by A. E. Johnson and S. R. Littlewood, with 34 full-page illustrations by Gustave Doré. All the original Perrault stories— Cinderella, Sleeping Beauty, Bluebeard, Little Red Riding Hood, Puss in Boots, Tom Thumb, etc.—with their witty verse morals and the magnificent illustrations of Doré. One of the five or six great books of European fairy tales. viii + 117pp. 8⅛ x 11. 22311-6 Paperbound $2.00

OLD HUNGARIAN FAIRY TALES, Baroness Orczy. Favorites translated and adapted by author of the *Scarlet Pimpernel.* Eight fairy tales include "The Suitors of Princess Fire-Fly," "The Twin Hunchbacks," "Mr. Cuttlefish's Love Story," and "The Enchanted Cat." This little volume of magic and adventure will captivate children as it has for generations. 90 drawings by Montagu Barstow. 96pp.
(USO) 22293-4 Paperbound $1.95

THE RED FAIRY BOOK, Andrew Lang. Lang's color fairy books have long been children's favorites. This volume includes Rapunzel, Jack and the Bean-stalk and 35 other stories, familiar and unfamiliar. 4 plates, 93 illustrations x + 367pp.
21673-X Paperbound $2.50

THE BLUE FAIRY BOOK, Andrew Lang. Lang's tales come from all countries and all times. Here are 37 tales from Grimm, the Arabian Nights, Greek Mythology, and other fascinating sources. 8 plates, 130 illustrations. xi + 390pp.
21437-0 Paperbound $2.50

HOUSEHOLD STORIES BY THE BROTHERS GRIMM. Classic English-language edition of the well-known tales — Rumpelstiltskin, Snow White, Hansel and Gretel, The Twelve Brothers, Faithful John, Rapunzel, Tom Thumb (52 stories in all). Translated into simple, straightforward English by Lucy Crane. Ornamented with headpieces, vignettes, elaborate decorative initials and a dozen full-page illustrations by Walter Crane. x + 269pp.
21080-4 Paperbound $2.50

THE MERRY ADVENTURES OF ROBIN HOOD, Howard Pyle. The finest modern versions of the traditional ballads and tales about the great English outlaw. Howard Pyle's complete prose version, with every word, every illustration of the first edition. Do not confuse this facsimile of the original (1883) with modern editions that change text or illustrations. 23 plates plus many page decorations. xxii + 296pp.
22043-5 Paperbound $2.50

THE STORY OF KING ARTHUR AND HIS KNIGHTS, Howard Pyle. The finest children's version of the life of King Arthur; brilliantly retold by Pyle, with 48 of his most imaginative illustrations. xviii + 313pp. 6⅛ x 9¼.
21445-1 Paperbound $2.50

THE WONDERFUL WIZARD OF OZ, L. Frank Baum. America's finest children's book in facsimile of first edition with all Denslow illustrations in full color. The edition a child should have. Introduction by Martin Gardner. 23 color plates, scores of drawings. iv + 267pp.
20691-2 Paperbound $2.25

THE MARVELOUS LAND OF OZ, L. Frank Baum. The second Oz book, every bit as imaginative as the Wizard. The hero is a boy named Tip, but the Scarecrow and the Tin Woodman are back, as is the Oz magic. 16 color plates, 120 drawings by John R. Neill. 287pp.
20692-0 Paperbound $2.50

THE MAGICAL MONARCH OF MO, L. Frank Baum. Remarkable adventures in a land even stranger than Oz. The best of Baum's books not in the Oz series. 15 color plates and dozens of drawings by Frank Verbeck. xviii + 237pp.
21892-9 Paperbound $2.00

THE BAD CHILD'S BOOK OF BEASTS, MORE BEASTS FOR WORSE CHILDREN, A MORAL ALPHABET, Hilaire Belloc. Three complete humor classics in one volume. Be kind to the frog, and do not call him names . . . and 28 other whimsical animals. Familiar favorites and some not so well known. Illustrated by Basil Blackwell. 156pp.
(USO) 20749-8 Paperbound $1.25

THE PHILOSOPHY OF THE UPANISHADS, Paul Deussen. Clear, detailed statement of upanishadic system of thought, generally considered among best available. History of these works, full exposition of system emergent from them, parallel concepts in the West. Translated by A. S. Geden. xiv + 429pp.
21616-0 Paperbound $3.00

LANGUAGE, TRUTH AND LOGIC, Alfred J. Ayer. Famous, remarkably clear introduction to the Vienna and Cambridge schools of Logical Positivism; function of philosophy, elimination of metaphysical thought, nature of analysis, similar topics. "Wish I had written it myself," Bertrand Russell. 2nd, 1946 edition. 160pp.
20010-8 Paperbound $1.35

THE GUIDE FOR THE PERPLEXED, Moses Maimonides. Great classic of medieval Judaism, major attempt to reconcile revealed religion (Pentateuch, commentaries) and Aristotelian philosophy. Enormously important in all Western thought. Unabridged Friedländer translation. 50-page introduction. lix + 414pp.
(USO) 20351-4 Paperbound $2.50

OCCULT AND SUPERNATURAL PHENOMENA, D. H. Rawcliffe. Full, serious study of the most persistent delusions of mankind: crystal gazing, mediumistic trance, stigmata, lycanthropy, fire walking, dowsing, telepathy, ghosts, ESP, etc., and their relation to common forms of abnormal psychology. Formerly *Illusions and Delusions of the Supernatural and the Occult.* iii + 551pp.   20503-7 Paperbound $3.50

THE EGYPTIAN BOOK OF THE DEAD: THE PAPYRUS OF ANI, E. A. Wallis Budge. Full hieroglyphic text, interlinear transliteration of sounds, word for word translation, then smooth, connected translation; Theban recension. Basic work in Ancient Egyptian civilization; now even more significant than ever for historical importance, dilation of consciousness, etc. clvi + 377pp. 6½ x 9¼.
21866-X Paperbound $3.95

PSYCHOLOGY OF MUSIC, Carl E. Seashore. Basic, thorough survey of everything known about psychology of music up to 1940's; essential reading for psychologists, musicologists. Physical acoustics; auditory apparatus; relationship of physical sound to perceived sound; role of the mind in sorting, altering, suppressing, creating sound sensations; musical learning, testing for ability, absolute pitch, other topics. Records of Caruso, Menuhin analyzed. 88 figures. xix + 408pp.
21851-1 Paperbound $2.75

THE I CHING (THE BOOK OF CHANGES), translated by James Legge. Complete translated text plus appendices by Confucius, of perhaps the most penetrating divination book ever compiled. Indispensable to all study of early Oriental civilizations. 3 plates. xxiii + 448pp.   21062-6 Paperbound $3.00

THE UPANISHADS, translated by Max Müller. Twelve classical upanishads: Chandogya, Kena, Aitareya, Kaushitaki, Isa, Katha, Mundaka, Taittiriyaka, Brhadaranyaka, Svetasvatara, Prasna, Maitriyana. 160-page introduction, analysis by Prof. Müller. Total of 826pp.   20398-0, 20399-9 Two volumes, Paperbound $5.00

MATHEMATICAL PUZZLES FOR BEGINNERS AND ENTHUSIASTS, Geoffrey Mott-Smith. 189 puzzles from easy to difficult—involving arithmetic, logic, algebra, properties of digits, probability, etc.—for enjoyment and mental stimulus. Explanation of mathematical principles behind the puzzles. 135 illustrations. viii + 248pp.

20198-8 Paperbound $1.75

PAPER FOLDING FOR BEGINNERS, William D. Murray and Francis J. Rigney. Easiest book on the market, clearest instructions on making interesting, beautiful origami. Sail boats, cups, roosters, frogs that move legs, bonbon boxes, standing birds, etc. 40 projects; more than 275 diagrams and photographs. 94pp.

20713-7 Paperbound $1.00

TRICKS AND GAMES ON THE POOL TABLE, Fred Herrmann. 79 tricks and games— some solitaires, some for two or more players, some competitive games—to entertain you between formal games. Mystifying shots and throws, unusual caroms, tricks involving such props as cork, coins, a hat, etc. Formerly *Fun on the Pool Table*. 77 figures. 95pp.

21814-7 Paperbound $1.00

HAND SHADOWS TO BE THROWN UPON THE WALL: A SERIES OF NOVEL AND AMUSING FIGURES FORMED BY THE HAND, Henry Bursill. Delightful picturebook from great-grandfather's day shows how to make 18 different hand shadows: a bird that flies, duck that quacks, dog that wags his tail, camel, goose, deer, boy, turtle, etc. Only book of its sort. vi + 33pp. 6½ x 9¼.

21779-5 Paperbound $1.00

WHITTLING AND WOODCARVING, E. J. Tangerman. 18th printing of best book on market. "If you can cut a potato you can carve" toys and puzzles, chains, chessmen, caricatures, masks, frames, woodcut blocks, surface patterns, much more. Information on tools, woods, techniques. Also goes into serious wood sculpture from Middle Ages to present, East and West. 464 photos, figures. x + 293pp.

20965-2 Paperbound $2.00

HISTORY OF PHILOSOPHY, Julián Marias. Possibly the clearest, most easily followed, best planned, most useful one-volume history of philosophy on the market; neither skimpy nor overfull. Full details on system of every major philosopher and dozens of less important thinkers from pre-Socratics up to Existentialism and later. Strong on many European figures usually omitted. Has gone through dozens of editions in Europe. 1966 edition, translated by Stanley Appelbaum and Clarence Strowbridge. xviii + 505pp.

21739-6 Paperbound $3.00

YOGA: A SCIENTIFIC EVALUATION, Kovoor T. Behanan. Scientific but non-technical study of physiological results of yoga exercises; done under auspices of Yale U. Relations to Indian thought, to psychoanalysis, etc. 16 photos. xxiii + 270pp.

20505-3 Paperbound $2.50

Prices subject to change without notice.
Available at your book dealer or write for free catalogue to Dept. GI, Dover Publications, Inc., 180 Varick St., N. Y., N. Y. 10014. Dover publishes more than 150 books each year on science, elementary and advanced mathematics, biology, music, art, literary history, social sciences and other areas.